CULINA MEDITERRANEA

CULINA
MEDITERRANEA

h.f.ullmann

Acknowledgment

We wish to thank all the restaurants, people, and organizations whose gracious collaboration has made it possible for us to bring this project to fruition.

Degree of difficulty

★	easy
★★	medium
★★★	difficult

Abbreviations and quantities

1 oz	=	1 ounce	=	28 grams		
1 lb	=	1 pound	=	16 ounces		
1 cup	=	8 ounces* (see below)				
1 cup	=	8 fluid ounces	=	250 ml (liquids)		
2 cups	=	1 pint (liquids)				
1 glass	=	4–6 fluid ounces	=	125–150 ml (liquids)		
1 tbsp	=	1 level tablespoon	=	15–20 g* (see below)	=	15 ml (liquids)
1 tsp	=	1 level teaspoon	=	3–5 g* (see below)	=	5 ml (liquids)
1 kg	=	1 kilogram	=	1000 grams		
1 g	=	1 gram	=	1/1000 kilogram		
1 l	=	1 liter	=	1000 milliliters	=	approx. 34 fluid ounces
1 ml	=	1 milliliter	=	1/1000 liter		

*The weight of dry ingredients varies significantly depending on the density factor, e.g. 1 cup flour weighs less than 1 cup butter.
Quantities in ingredients have been rounded up or down for convenience, where appropriate. Metric conversions may therefore not correspond exactly. It is important to use either American or metric measurements within a recipe.

© for the original editions:
Fabien Bellahsen and Daniel Rouche

Photographs and technical direction: Didier Bizos
Photographic assistants: Gersende Petit-Jouvet, Morgane Favennec, Hasni Alamat
Editors: Élodie Bonnet, Nathalie Talhouas
Assistant editor: Fabienne Ripon

© for this English edition:
h.f.ullmann publishing GmbH

Translation:
Spain: Mo Croasdale for Cambridge Publishing Management Ltd
Italy: Judith Phillips for First Edition Translations Ltd
France: Karen Green for First Edition Translations Ltd
Greece: Marilyn Myerscough for First Edition Translations Ltd
Turkey: Mo Croasdale for First Edition Translations Ltd
Tunisia: Vivien Groves for Cambridge Publishing Management Ltd
Morocco: Susan James for Cambridge Publishing Management Ltd
Islands of the Mediterranean: Caroline Higgitt for Cambridge Publishing Management Ltd

Assembly of the recipes: Kirsten E. Lehmann
Cover design: Simone Sticker
Cover photograph: Karl Newedel

Overall responsibility for production: h.f.ullmann publishing GmbH, Potsdam, Germany

Printed in China

ISBN 978-3-8480-0004-3

10 9 8 7 6 5 4 3 2 1
X IX VIII VII VI V IV III II 1

www.ullmann-publishing.com
newsletter@ullmann-publishing.com

Contents

7   Preface

8   Cold Appetizers

Fish & Seafood   362

88   Hot Appetizers

Meat & Poultry   496

186   Soups & Tagines

Desserts & Pastry   636

284   Pasta, Rice, Couscous & Co.

The Chefs & Pastry Cooks   782

Recipe Index   800

British Cookery Terms   792

Preface

CULINA MEDITERRANEA combines a rich and inspiring collection of culinary delicacies from the entire Mediterranean region: 380 recipes by 92 experienced chefs from Spain, France, Italy, Greece, Malta, Turkey, Tunisia, and Morocco offer a unique insight into the multifaceted Mediterranean cuisine, whose spectrum by far surpasses favorite classics such as pizza, pasta, and paella. Indeed, it is enriched by various influences. This volume joins traditional and extravagant dishes, simple and opulent ones, characteristic western and oriental food to create an exceptional panorama of exquisite delights of the table which even offers exciting unknown territory for experienced chefs.

The chefs and pastry cooks that have contributed to this volume are all accounted experts of the culinary tradition of their country and connoisseurs of its mysteries and refinement. In seven chapters, oriented on the various parts that make up the Mediterranean menu, they give an insight into their art, disclosing their best recipes and offering precious tips for a successful preparation of each dish. The choice on offer has delicacies in store for every occasion and every taste, be it the fast in-between snack, the refined party nibble, or the exquisite menu consisting of several courses.

The chapters "Cold Appetizers" and "Hot Appetizers" present a wealth of recipes for starters and salads, including those little nibbles that are so typical of the Mediterranean: Spanish tapas, Turkish meze and kebab, which are also ideally suited for a quickly prepared snack or for parties and buffets.

The chapter "Soups & Tagines" includes a large variety of international soup specialties ranging from the traditional Spanish cold soups via French Bouillabaisse to the Greek Trachanosoupa. It also covers recipes for tagines, typical North African dishes that are prepared in a special clay pot, the tagine, hence their name. Long cooking times and low temperatures make the meat cooked in a tagine exceedingly tender as well as lending vegetables and sauces an incomparable aroma.

The chapter "Pasta, Rice, Couscous & Co." brings together international specialties based on grains, many of which are vegetarian main dishes. It offers a large variety of Italian pasta and risotto dishes, Spanish paellas and Turkish pilafs (rice dishes) as well as appetizing recipes with Bulgur (wheatmeal) plus Moroccan and Tunisian couscous specialties.

In the chapter "Fish & Seafood", the original recipes by Spanish, French, and Greek master chefs dominate. Oriental fish specialties as well as exquisite recipes from the Mediterranean islands of the Balearics, from Corsica, Sicily, Crete, and Malta, round off the culinary foray through Neptune's Mediterranean realm.

The chapter "Meat & Poultry" unites the epitome of Mediterranean festive menus and culinary landmarks of the countryside of the Mediterranean region. Be it veal or beef, lamb, pork, or rabbit: the wealth of tastes and preparation methods—from broiling to slow stewing in the tagine—seems to be unending. The meat dishes are complimented by a variety of equally exceptional and traditional poultry dishes.

Finally, "Desserts & Pastry" presents a choice of irresistible desserts, sweets, and pastries from Orient and Occident. All of them are characterized by the use of fruits that have ripened in the warm sun. This chapter gives enticing proof of the fact that the pastry cooks of Tunisia, Morocco, and Turkey are true masters in the art of sweet seductions.

More than 3000 color photographs and reliable step-by-step instructions will make you want to start preparing these dishes yourself and guarantee a success even for the less skilled cook. Bring the tastes, smells, and delicacies of the Mediterranean to your home!

Cold Appetizers

Tapas

Preparation time:	45 minutes
Marinating time:	1 hour
Soaking time:	overnight
Cooking time:	1 hour 15 minutes
Difficulty:	★

Serves 4

For the anchovies in sherry vinegar:

6	large fresh anchovies
3 tbsp/45 ml	sherry vinegar
3 tbsp/45 ml	water
1 clove	garlic, chopped
2 tbsp/30 ml	olive oil
1 sprig	rosemary
	salt and pepper

For the bell pepper escalivada:

2	green bell peppers, halved
2	red bell peppers, halved
4	silver onions
2	tomatoes

2 tbsp/30 ml	olive oil
	chives
	salt and pepper

For the garbanzo beans with ham:

4 tsp/20 g	dried garbanzo beans (chickpeas)
4 tsp/20 g	dried cannellini beans
1	red bell pepper
1	green bell pepper
2	silver onions
1	carrot
3	parsley stalks
1 clove	garlic
	olive oil
2 slices	Serrano ham
2 slices	white bread
	salt and pepper

Javier Valero suggests three classic yet very simple tapas. These tapas are typical of the region, and are served with aperitifs in Málaga's bars.

The anchovies are marinated in a spicy combination of olive oil, sherry vinegar, garlic, and rosemary. The marinating time depends on the size of the fish, but an hour is usually ideal. The color and aroma of the anchovies are enhanced by the addition of a pinch of ground paprika. The anchovies are garnished with aromatic rosemary leaves.

The salad of red and green bell peppers is a typically Spanish *escalivada*, which is to say the vegetables are roasted in the oven or under the broiler until they are almost black. Other suitable vegetables are silver onions, tomatoes, and eggplants. The skin is then lifted away with a sharp knife.

The vegetables are arranged in a bowl, a little olive oil drizzled over the top, and a garnish of chives added.

The salad of garbanzo beans and Serrano ham is spicy, and the combination of flavors and textures make it a delicious treat. The aroma is further intensified if the pulses are cooked in chicken stock with a little thyme and bay leaf. Remember that dried garbanzo beans and cannellini beans are as hard as stone, and need to be soaked overnight in cold water. Garnished with blanched julienne vegetables, fried ham, and croutons, the only thing still missing is perhaps a little parsley. If you like, a touch of cinnamon will round off this salad perfectly.

Anyone who likes high-quality, aromatic olive oil will not be disappointed by these tapas!

Wash the anchovies, clean inside and remove the bones. Combine the vinegar and water, and marinate the anchovies in this for about 1 hour.

To make the dressing, combine the chopped garlic with the olive oil, rosemary, salt, and pepper in a bowl. Cut the marinated anchovies in half, arrange on a plate, and pour over the dressing. Garnish with rosemary leaves.

To make the escalivada, cover a baking sheet with aluminum foil, and roast the halved bell peppers and whole onions for about 10 minutes. Then remove the skins.

from Málaga

Cut the broiled bell peppers into strips. Dip the tomatoes in boiling water, then into cold, and remove the skins. Arrange the red and green bell peppers on a plate, and season with salt and pepper. Garnish with sliced tomatoes, onions, olive oil, and chives.

Boil the soaked garbanzo beans and cannellini beans for about 1 hour. Roast the bell peppers, onions, and garlic. Blanch the carrot and cut into julienne strips. Combine everything with chopped parsley, oil, salt, and pepper.

Sauté the ham and diced bread in olive oil in a skillet. Arrange the salad on a plate with ham and bread. Garnish with a little parsley.

Anchovies with

Preparation time:	*10 minutes*
Marinating time:	*10 hours*
Chilling time:	*3 hours*
Difficulty:	★ ★

Serves 4

For the raspberry oil:
6½ tbsp/100 g raspberries
1¼ cups/300 ml olive oil

For the anchovies:
2 cups/500 g   fresh anchovies
1 cup/250 ml   wine vinegar
³/₄ cup/200 ml   native olive oil
                 salt and pepper

For the garnish:
                 cherry tomatoes
                 chives
                 lettuce leaves

The secret of this very popular dish of marinated anchovies is the quality of the olive oil. Back in Roman times, olive oil was an important commodity; indeed, it is still produced all over the country today. The oil is usually so pure and delicious that it can be drizzled generously over fish and salads without impairing the flavor. And, above all, it can be used to preserve foods such as sardines and anchovies.

Oil from the Ceuta region is particularly good. It is made from small, round olives with a thin skin. Half a spoonful is all that is needed to add a slightly fruit-acidic aroma to the marinade. Cherries or strawberries can be used instead of raspberries.

Anchovies are a firm fixture on menus all over Spain. These tiny herring are sold, preserved in salt or oil, in glass jars. Fresh anchovies have a silvery, shimmering skin and shiny eyes. They need to be filleted before marinating so they are covered entirely by the marinade. With a little practice, you will soon be able to remove the head and main bones in one move. The fillets are rinsed, patted dry, and placed skin side down in a mold. They are then marinated in a mixture of water and vinegar, which ensures the flesh stays nice and firm. This marinade is poured away after 10 hours, and then the anchovy fillets are covered in olive oil and left for a further 3 hours. The small fish survive this marinating with no ill effects. Directly before serving they can be sprinkled with a little raspberry-flavored olive oil.

Stored in an airtight jar in the refrigerator, the raspberry oil will keep for about two weeks. It goes extremely well with salads, cold roast meats, and cold cuts.

Purée the raspberries and pass them through a sieve. Put 3 tbsp of this raspberry coulis into the olive oil, then pour into a small bottle.

Cut into the anchovies behind the head, and remove the head and main bone in one move. Carefully open out the fish and remove the insides. Rinse briefly under running cold water.

Put the anchovy fillets skin side down in a flat dish. Cover with water and the wine vinegar, and leave to marinate for 10 hours.

Raspberry Oil

Remove the anchovies from the marinade and pat dry. Place in a dish, then season with salt and pepper, and pour over the olive oil. Chill for 3 hours.

Place the anchovies skin side down on paper towels, then leave for 10 minutes until some of the oil has been absorbed.

Now place the anchovies skin side up on plates. Garnish with cherry tomatoes, chives, and lettuce leaves. Drizzle generously with raspberry oil.

Diced Bread

Preparation time:	15 minutes
Standing time for the bread:	12 hours
Cooking time:	15 minutes
Difficulty:	★

Serves 4

3 lb 5 oz/1.5 kg	white bread
3	chorizo sausages

12 oz/300 g	bacon slab
2¼ lb/1 kg	grapes
	a little olive oil
6 cloves	garlic
2 tsp	ground paprika (pimentón)
	salt

This very simple dish is typical of Castile and the Estremadura. Grape pickers meet in September to enjoy this traditional specialty. The olive oil, chorizo, bacon, garlic, ground paprika, and salt are what give the bread its special flavor. Juicy grapes are the perfect complement. *Migas*—which translates as breadcrumbs—has been prepared in many different ways for thousands of years. The original inhabitants of the Iberian Peninsula prepared a dish of stale bread and fat. Shepherds and muleteers did not need to be near a town or village to enjoy this simple, rustic dish. Over the course of time the dish was incorporated in Spanish cuisine, and each region has developed its own variation.

According to purists, the bread for *migas* needs to be very dry and ideally four days old. The chef recommends soaking it in a little water and leaving it to stand for at least twelve hours before preparing the dish. This prevents the bread from absorbing too much fat. The extremely popular *migas ruleras* are served with grapes. The texture of the grape skin and sweetness or acidity of the flesh are determined by the quality and origin. The season for red grapes is from August to November.

Make sure that the grapes are fresh and ripe. Use them at room temperature so the full flavor and aroma can develop, and remember to wash them thoroughly. Alberto Herráiz recommends using sweet melon instead of grapes in summer. Some families serve dried sardines or fried eggs with their *migas*.

The evening before, cut the bread into slices, remove the crusts, and dice the bread. Place the bread cubes in a bowl and sprinkle with a little water. Cover with a clean cloth and leave to stand for 12 hours.

Slice the chorizo and dice the bacon. Remove the grapes from the stalks and wash them thoroughly.

Heat a little olive oil in a skillet and fry the bread cubes. Then add the sliced garlic and the diced bacon. Combine well and cook, then remove from the skillet and set aside.

with Grapes

Sprinkle the ground paprika into the skillet and stir with a spatula.

Add the softened bread cubes. Sauté, stirring continuously, until golden and crispy. Season with salt.

Add the sliced sausage and diced bacon, and reheat gently over a low heat. Arrange the migas on a plate, and garnish with the grapes.

Salmorejo

Preparation time:	*15 minutes*
Cooking time for	
the eggs:	*10 minutes*
Difficulty:	*★*

Serves 4

2	eggs
2¼ lb/1 kg	ripe tomatoes
6 cloves	garlic

12 oz/300 g	bread
¾ cup/200 ml	native olive oil
7 tbsp/100 ml	sherry vinegar
6 oz/150 g	smoked ham
	salt

Salmorejo de Córdoba is basically a cold purée of fresh tomatoes and garlic. The difference between it and gazpacho is that the latter is made of various vegetables flavored with cumin and paprika, and is thinner in texture. In Andalusia, *salmorejo* is often served as a topping for bread rather than as a meal in itself. It is particularly refreshing on a hot summer's day. During the traditional parades, the *Romerías* (the village dwellers) prepare *salmorejo* at home, then share it at the festivities.

It is essential that the tomatoes for this dish are red and soft. Strictly speaking, they should be crushed in a mortar and pestle with the garlic, but a kitchen blender is used in Córdoba today. The dish contains plenty of garlic, but you can use less if you prefer. However, the indigestible green core should be removed. If you add a little coarse salt, you will find it easier to crush the garlic; the salt helps the garlic to adhere to the bottom of the mortar and prevents it from escaping as you crush it.

The chef recommends a high quality, finely grained white bread, ideally baked the day before. The quality of the bread is essential, because it adds its velvety consistency to the dish. In Spain there is a rustic, round variety of bread called *candeal*, which is ideal.

The final step in the preparation is to add oil and vinegar to the *salmorejo*. The vinegar should only be added just before it is served; otherwise it will become too acid. José-Ignacio Herráiz garnishes the dish with hard-boiled eggs and smoked ham, but you could also use tuna, slices of sour gherkin, mint leaves, or grated cheese.

Boil the eggs for 10 minutes, then plunge them into cold water and peel. Wash and dry the tomatoes, cut out the stalks, and cut the tomatoes into quarters.

Peel the garlic and crush with a pinch of salt in a mortar and pestle.

Put the garlic in the mixing bowl of the blender. Add the tomatoes and process.

de Córdoba

Cut the crust off the bread and chop the bread roughly. Moisten with water in a bowl, then crush with a fork. Put the bowl in the blender with the tomatoes.

Run the appliance until the mixture becomes a smooth pink purée.

Add the oil and vinegar, and season to taste. Garnish the salmorejo with quartered eggs and strips of ham.

Xatonada

Preparation time: 30 minutes
Soaking time
    stockfish: 48 hours
Soaking time
    pimiento ñora: 2 hours
Chilling time: 1 hour
Cooking time: 25 minutes
Difficulty: ★

Serves 4

8 oz/200 g   stockfish
1 head   curly endive
12   anchovy fillets (glass)
³/₄ cup/200 g   tuna (canned)
30   black olives

For the romesco sauce:

1	dried red paprika (pimiento ñora)
3 cloves	garlic
1¼ cups/300 ml	olive oil
4 tsp/20 g	skinned almonds
4 tsp/20 g	skinned hazelnuts
3	ripe tomatoes
2 slices	bread
6½ tbsp/100 ml	red wine vinegar
	salt

Xatonada is from Catalonia—from the region around Tarragona, to be precise. Whether this popular salad actually originates from Sitges or Vilanova is hotly contested between the two rival towns. Competitions take place regularly at public festivals to see whose is the best *Xatonada*. Pep Masiques' version is more of a winter dish, because that is when curly endive is widely available.

Soak the stockfish (dried salted cod) in water for 24 to 48 hours. The water should be changed frequently to rinse away the salt. Then pull off the skin and carefully remove all the bones. Finally, break the stockfish into small pieces.

The romesco sauce is bound with almonds, bread, and hazelnuts, and is an ancient dish from the mountain country

of Catalonia. It is particularly tasty with stockfish and seafood. It is named after the romesco pepper. This vegetable, which was brought from America to Europe in the 16th century, is often called *pimiento ñora*. The small, round pod develops an exceptionally spicy aroma without bite. It is garnet red when dried. Remove the stalk and seeds before soaking.

Blanch the almonds before using them. Put them in a pot of boiling water and boil them until the skins come off. Then drain them, place on a cloth, and rub thoroughly. If necessary, remove the skin with a sharp knife. Rinse the anchovies and remove the bones if necessary. Sauté the tomatoes for the sauce last, as they create lots of juice that blends with the oil.

Soak the stockfish for 48 hours. Remove the skin and bones, and break the fish into pieces using your fingers.

Soak the dried paprika in a bowl of cold water for 2 hours. Then cut the pod open and scoop out the pulp with a teaspoon. Peel and slice the garlic.

Fry the garlic in ³/₄ cup/200 ml of very hot olive oil for 5 minutes until golden. Remove and set aside. Fry the almonds in the same skillet for 5 minutes. Set aside. Repeat the process with the hazelnuts, quartered tomatoes, and bread.

Place the ingredients in the mixing bowl of your blender and add the paprika pulp. Blend until smooth.

Add the remainder of the olive oil and the vinegar to the sauce and stir again. Pour the romesco sauce into a bowl, then chill for 1 hour. Season if required.

To prepare the salad, wash and spin dry the endive. Cut out the core with a sharp knife so the leaves come loose. Put the salad leaves in a bowl and arrange the stockfish, tuna, anchovies, olives, and romesco sauce on top.

Langoustine Carpaccio

Preparation time: 40 minutes
Chilling time: 20 minutes
Cooking time: 20 minutes
Difficulty: ★

Serves 4

12	fresh langoustines
2 bundles	asparagus spears
6 tbsp	olive oil
4	oranges

1	lemon
1 bunch	fresh tarragon
1 tsp	coarse grain mustard
	salt
	pepper
few sprigs	fresh dill

This recipe is summer on a plate! We owe a big thank-you to Italian artist Vittore Carpaccio, who gave his name to this refreshing appetizer. This low-calorie appetizer is easy to prepare.

Alain Carro prefers langoustines because the flesh soaks up the flavors of the other ingredients wonderfully well, but these shellfish have been chosen for their attractive color too. The langoustines must be absolutely fresh, with shining, black eyes and a pleasant, unobtrusive smell. If langoustines are not available, our chef advises using mackerel fillets. They are equally suitable for this recipe and are much cheaper! If you ask your fishmonger to slice the fillets, you will get the very thin slices you want. Where freshness is concerned, the same applies to mackerel, with its rainbow scales, as to the langoustines. Remove all the little bones with tweezers.

Asparagus, which heralds the warmer time of year, is widely grown in the south of France. The spears should be straight. Bear in mind that asparagus keeps for up to three days only but, depending on the time of year, you can, of course, use white asparagus. Before peeling, rinse the spears in hot water. Generally, asparagus is cooked in boiling, salted water for 5–10 minutes, depending on the spears' thickness. After cooking, the asparagus can be placed in a bowl of ice water so that it cools down quickly.

The tarragon used to flavor the olive oil is chopped finely. You should always use this herb fresh; if you can't find fresh tarragon you could use fresh chervil. If you want to use the langoustine heads as a garnish for this appetizer you must blanch them first.

Peel the langoustines and slice them open lengthwise. Spread them out and remove the black intestines. Meanwhile, bring a pan of salted water to the boil, add the asparagus, and simmer for 5–10 minutes. Drain the asparagus and leave it to cool.

Spread out a large piece of plastic wrap. Brush half the wrap with a little of the olive oil. Arrange 4 langoustines on the oiled wrap and fold over the unoiled half. Beat the 4 langoustines gently until paper thin. Repeat with the others. Place in the refrigerator to chill for 20 minutes.

Juice the oranges and lemon. Pour the juices into a small saucepan and boil for 8 minutes until reduced. Set aside to cool.

with Asparagus

Put the remaining olive oil, finely chopped tarragon, and coarse grain mustard into a small bowl, then beat in the cooled citrus juice to make a dressing. Season the dressing to taste with salt and pepper, and reserve it.

Just before serving, take the langoustine carpaccio out of the fridge and leave it to stand for a few minutes. Remove the plastic wrap and arrange the langoustine slices on a plate.

Cut the asparagus into 3 in/8 cm-long pieces. Check the seasoning in the dressing, adjust if necessary, and pour it over the langoustine slices. Arrange the asparagus decoratively on the plate. Garnish the langoustine slices with a sprig or two of fresh dill. Serve well chilled.

Tuna with

Preparation time: 20 minutes
Cooking time: 15 minutes
Difficulty: ★

Serves 4

3 generous cups/500 g   zucchini
2 cups/500 ml   chicken stock
¾ cup/180 ml   olive oil
                         salt
                         pepper
½ bunch   fresh chives

½ bunch   fresh chervil
1 sprig   fresh tarragon
3½ tbsp/50g   capers
1   shallot
12 oz/350 g   red tuna
2 tbsp   olive oil

For the garnish:
1   leek
                rock salt
                oil for deep frying

Zucchini take the lead in this recipe. They are very popular in Mediterranean countries, especially in the dish, ratatouille. This recipe by Francis Robin is particularly suitable as a refreshing appetizer in summer, because that's when zucchini have the best flavor. Zucchini is one of the oldest varieties of vegetable; it was in use in Mexico as early as the 8th century B.C.

Choose small, firm, dark green zucchini. If they do not seem to have a strong enough flavor for this recipe, you can add a crushed clove of garlic to heighten it. To retain the zucchini's attractive bright green color in the dressing, avoid using too much olive oil as it leaches out color.

The other key ingredient in our recipe is red tuna from the Mediterranean Sea. This big, meaty fish must be very fresh. It is available between May and September. At the end of the 19th century, lookouts drew the attention of Provençal fishermen to shoals of tuna by blowing trumpets. If you cannot find fresh tuna, you could use fresh salmon, which will work just as well.

The tarragon used in this recipe intensifies the flavor of the tuna meat and enriches the dish with its own spicy-sweet aroma, but the dish will work just as well without this herb. The other fresh herbs, chervil and chives, are often used simply as a garnish. In our recipe, on the other hand, they have the important job of lending a special flavor to the tuna tartar.

Wash the zucchini and cut them into chunks. Bring a pan of salted water to the boil, add the zucchini, and simmer for around 5–8 minutes, until they just start to soften.

Rinse the zucchini under cold running water and leave them to drain. Purée the zucchini using a food processor or hand blender, adding the chicken stock and olive oil. Season to taste with salt and pepper, and put aside.

Finely chop the chives, chervil, and tarragon. Drain the capers and chop them finely too, as well as the shallot.

Zucchini Cream

Dice the tuna very finely. Season with salt and pepper, and put aside. Brush 4 small ramekins or molds with a little olive oil.

In a bowl combine the diced tuna, chopped capers, shallot, and herbs with a little oil. Divide the tuna mixture between the molds, press it down well, and put in the refrigerator to chill. Wash the leek and slice a 2–2½ in/6 cm-long white piece into very thin strips.

Heat some oil in a pan and deep fry the leek until crisp and brown. Drain and reserve. Unmold the tuna tartar onto a plate. Pile some of the deep-fried leek on top of the tuna, and sprinkle over a few grains of rock salt. Pour the zucchini cream around the tuna. Serve chilled.

Asparagus Salad

Preparation time: 30 minutes
Cooking time: 8–12 minutes
Difficulty: ★

Serves 4

2¼ lb/1 kg	green asparagus
1 tbsp	rock salt
1½ cups/300 g	fresh fava beans
2	tomatoes
1 bunch	fresh basil

For the balsamic vinaigrette:
6 tbsp	olive oil
2 tbsp	balsamic vinegar
	salt
	pepper

For the garnish:
3½ oz/100 g parmesan

In Rouret, a village in the countryside around Nice, Daniel Ettlinger prepares dishes based on seasonal produce for his guests. Of course, asparagus is on his menu in spring. Ettlinger has a real weakness for this perennial plant and has created an appetizer based on asparagus that is named after his restaurant: asparagus salad "Clos Saint-Pierre."

When buying asparagus it should be firm, bright green, and, when snapped in half, the stem should be shiny with juice. Monsieur Ettlinger suggests you try his favorite asparagus, purple, when it's in season. It's very delicate, but packed full of flavor. Regrettably this variety, which is mainly cultivated in the area around Nice, is seen on the market less and less. For some years it has been grown in glasshouses that retain the heat.

Our chef prefers not to prepare this dish using white asparagus. If he can't get hold of purple, he uses green asparagus, as is the case here. When preparing the asparagus, if the ends are a little dry, snap them off. The rock salt added to the cooking water helps the asparagus retain its bright green color. Be sure to refresh the asparagus in ice water after cooking, as explained in the method.

Tender little fava beans, also a French specialty, are a popular accompaniment to an aperitif. They are in season from May until the end of summer. The beans are eaten with the skin on.

Basil is a highly aromatic kitchen herb that gives a distinctive flavor to this appetizer.

Wash the asparagus and scrape off the scales on the stalk. Peel the asparagus stalks from top to bottom using a vegetable peeler.

Bring a saucepan with 6 cups/1.5 l water and 1 tbsp rock salt to the boil. Add the asparagus and simmer for 8–12 minutes, depending on the thickness of the stalks. Drain and plunge into a bowl of ice water for 10 minutes. Drain again and place on kitchen paper.

Shell the fava beans. Cook in 2 cups boiling water for 5 minutes, drain and reserve. Put the tomatoes in a bowl, pour boiling water over them, and leave for 1 minute. Drain, skin, and deseed the tomatoes. Cut the flesh into thick strips. Wash the basil and finely chop the leaves.

"Clos Saint-Pierre"

To make the vinaigrette, put the balsamic vinegar and olive oil in a bowl, add salt and pepper to taste, then beat well.

Add the fava beans, chopped tomatoes, and basil to the vinaigrette.

Cut the asparagus into finger-length pieces and arrange them on a plate in a criss-cross pattern. Drizzle generously with the vinaigrette. Arrange the tomatoes, fava beans, and basil around the asparagus. Garnish with a few shavings of parmesan.

"Côte d'Azur" Salad with

Preparation time:	30 minutes
Cooking time:	15 minutes
Difficulty:	★

Serves 4

1	small eggplant
2	zucchini
2 cloves	garlic
5 tbsp	olive oil
	salt, pepper
2 sprigs	fresh basil
	leaves from 4 stalks celery
3–4/20 g	scallions
6	fresh peppermint leaves
1 sprig	fresh thyme

2	red bell peppers
1½ oz/40 g	Reggiano parmesan (5 years old)
1	tomato
1 cup/80 g	mesclun

For the balsamic vinaigrette:

4 tbsp	olive oil
4 tbsp	balsamic vinegar
4 tbsp	wine vinegar
1 tbsp	candied stem ginger syrup (optional)
½ tsp	salt
1 pinch	pepper

For the garnish:

¼ cup/30 g	black olives
1 small sprig	fresh lemon thyme (optional)

This salad is a wonderful appetizer from the south that makes the most of eggplant, zucchini, and especially basil. Basil originates from India and its name comes from the Greek *basilikos*, meaning "royal." This is a clear indication of the importance attached to this herb in antiquity.

Basil gives off a strong scent, reminiscent of lemon and jasmine. Basil that has wilted comes alive again if it is plunged into water for a moment, but not for too long, otherwise the leaves turn dark. For our recipe, pinch the top two leaves from each sprig to use as a garnish.

Our chef mainly uses 5-year-old parmesan, because the older it is, the stronger the flavor. Sautéing the vegetables in hot oil is critical to the success of this dish.

Here's another tip from the professionals: To make it easier to remove the skin from bell peppers, after baking them in the oven, wrap them in newspaper or aluminum foil for 3–4 minutes. The garlic should be blanched well to lessen the strong flavor. To do this, peel the cloves, immerse them in cold water, and then in boiling water. Repeat this process three times.

Peppermint is characterized by its small, long leaves with blackish graining. You can substitute ordinary mint for peppermint, and use ordinary thyme if you can't find lemon thyme.

When preparing the balsamic vinaigrette, add a tablespoon of water to prevent the mixture from separating. Ginger syrup is not absolutely necessary, but the sweet and sour flavor lends a very special note to the dressing.

Wash the eggplant and zucchini. Slice them very thinly. Peel the garlic, slice it very thinly, and blanch it by first immersing it in cold water, then in boiling water. Repeat this process 3 times.

Heat the olive oil in a pan and sauté the sliced eggplant and zucchini for 1 minute. Drain the vegetables, season with salt and pepper, and reserve.

Pinch off the top leaves from the sprigs of basil and the tender green leaves from the celery sticks, reserving them for the garnish. Finely chop 2 large basil leaves, the scallions, and peppermint. Strip the leaves from the sprig of thyme. Add the herbs to the vegetables.

Balsamic Vinegar Dressing

Lightly oil a baking sheet, place the bell peppers on it, and broil them for about 10 minutes. When the peppers have cooled, skin and deseed them, then chop them into thin strips. Reserve the chopped peppers.

Using a vegetable peeler, shave off long strips from the parmesan. Wash the tomato, put in a bowl, and pour boiling water over it to blanch it. Leave it for a few minutes, drain, then skin and deseed. Dice the tomato flesh.

Balsamic vinaigrette: Beat together the olive oil, balsamic vinegar, wine vinegar, ginger syrup, salt, and pepper. Toss the salad ingredients with the dressing. Garnish with mesclun, the reserved sprigs of basil and celery, olives, lemon thyme (if used), and parmesan shavings.

Tomato Surprise

Preparation time:	*30 minutes*
Cooking time:	*15 minutes*
Difficulty:	✶

Serves 4

4	beefsteak tomatoes, each around 6 oz/180 g
8	langoustines
3 tbsp	olive oil
⅓ cup + 1½ tbsp/ 100 ml	chicken stock
1 clove	garlic
12 oz/350 g	soft goat milk cheese

1 bunch	fresh chives
3½ tbsp/80 g	black olive paste (or *tapenade*)
	mixed salad

For the balsamic vinaigrette:

	juice of ½ lemon
1 tbsp	olive oil
1 tsp	balsamic vinegar
	salt
	pepper

In this dish Joël Garault has taken his inspiration from the Provençal countryside. Originally farmers stored fresh goat milk cheese, seasoned with chives, wild arugula, olive oil, and pepper, under an olive tree. In fact this summery starter with langoustines pays homage to regional cuisine.

Tomatoes are important in this dish. The most suitable are round, red *Marmande* tomatoes which are available from July to October. The tomatoes should be firm, meaty, shiny, and evenly colored.

Before scooping out the flesh, make an incision on three sides of the tomato, so it retains its attractive shape.

The surprise is the soft goat milk cheese filling. Made solely from goat's milk, this cheese contains a minimum of 45 percent fat. Ask for a *Billy* from the Tarn or a cheese from the Cher department. The cheese must be at peak freshness.

The black olive paste, for which you can use *tapenade* if necessary, is also an unusual ingredient.

You can prepare the tomatoes the day before, but the langoustines should be prepared at the last minute. This tasty, pink-shelled crustacean is available from April to August. When buying, ensure that the shell is shiny, and the eyes bright black. After shelling, the digestive tract must be removed. Joël Garault inserts a wooden toothpick into each langoustine to prevent it from curling up during cooking. Don't forget to remove the toothpick before serving.

Pour boiling water over the tomatoes in a bowl and leave for a few minutes. Drain and skin. Slice the top off each tomato, scoop out the flesh, and reserve. Place the tomatoes upside down on absorbent kitchen paper to drain the juices. Cut the tops to form a fan for the garnish.

Shell the langoustines, reserving the heads and shells for the sauce. Heat 1 tbsp olive oil in a frying pan and sauté the langoustines until golden brown. Season to taste with salt and pepper and put aside.

To make the sauce, put the langoustine heads and shells in a saucepan with the chicken stock. Crush them with a spatula. Add 1 tbsp olive oil, the chopped garlic, and tomato flesh to the chicken stock, bring to the boil, and simmer for around 5 minutes.

with Langoustines

Strain the sauce, beat it well with a wire whisk, and add the lemon juice, olive oil, and balsamic vinegar. Season to taste with salt and pepper, and leave to cool.

To make the filling, mash the goat milk cheese with 1 tbsp olive oil. Finely chop the chives, reserving the tips for the garnish. Stir the chopped chives into the cheese.

Stuff half of each tomato with the cheese mixture, add a layer of olive paste, then finish with more cheese. Slice each langoustine in half lengthwise. Arrange the mixed salad, langoustines, and tomato (showing the filling) on each plate. Garnish with chives, tomato fans, and sauce.

Vegetable

Preparation time:	35 minutes
Marinating:	20 minutes
Cooking time:	45 minutes
Difficulty:	★

Serves 4

2	red bell peppers
	coarse salt
2 tbsp	olive oil
2	eggplants
2	zucchini

For the dressing:

4 tbsp	balsamic vinegar
4 tbsp	olive oil

	salt
	pepper

For the marinade:

	salt
	peppercorns
7 tbsp	olive oil
12	fresh mint leaves
1 tsp	bouquet garni

For the garnish:

	parmesan shavings
	arugula leaves
	cherry tomatoes

Italian cuisine has an endless range of antipasti, which are served as light appetizers. The vegetable dish that we have devised for you in this recipe is easy to prepare—a classic in Italian cookery.

The Italian peninsula is a unique vegetable garden, in which eggplants, zucchini, peppers, tomatoes, and many other types of vegetable flourish. Stroll around the markets and, wherever you go, you will find stalls with beautifully arranged displays and wonderful combinations of colors and aromas. Watch discriminating Italian housewives as they take time to choose the best produce for their families.

Zucchini and eggplants are quintessential summer vegetables and are therefore found in many Mediterranean recipes; here, they are sliced thinly and broiled, then marinated for about 20 minutes in olive oil and seasoned with mint leaves. Mint is rich in calcium, iron, and vitamins and is said to have

remarkable stimulant properties. There are dozens of varieties of this plant, the best known of which is the green mint with long, toothed leaves. It is available all year round and will stay fresh for a reasonable time if kept in plastic wrap in the refrigerator.

The marinade is enhanced with a bouquet garni. This mixture of herbs generally includes bay, rosemary, thyme, and savory and is often used when broiling. As a final touch to this antipasto dish, our chef adds arugula, with its characteristic sharp flavor reminiscent of filberts.

This delicious cold appetizer evokes the finest hot summer days in the Italian countryside.

Lay the peppers on a baking sheet. Sprinkle with a generous pinch of salt and pour over 1 tbsp olive oil. Bake for about 45 minutes, skin the peppers, then remove the seeds and cut into thin strips.

Wash the eggplants and zucchini and cut them into thin, even slices.

Pour the remaining oil into a broiler pan and broil the eggplant and zucchini.

Antipasti

Lay the broiled vegetables in an oven-proof dish. Season with salt and crushed peppercorns. Drizzle over the olive oil with mint and bouquet garni herbs and marinate for 20 minutes.

For the dressing, put the balsamic vinegar, olive oil, and salt and pepper in a small dish and beat well with a balloon whisk.

Shave small rolls of parmesan from a block. Arrange the zucchini and eggplant slices with the strips of pepper on a plate. Pour the dressing over the vegetables. Garnish with a few arugula leaves, cherry tomatoes, and parmesan shavings.

Friulian

Preparation time: 20 minutes
Cooking time: 18 minutes
Difficulty: ★

Serves 4

4	eggs
12 oz/300 g	lamb's lettuce
6 oz/150 g	pancetta (or other smoked slab bacon)
3 tbsp	extra-virgin olive oil
2 tbsp	balsamic vinegar
	salt
1	pomegranate

In his restaurant in Cormons, between Gorizia and Udine in Friuli, chef Paolo Zoppolatti serves his guests a fresh lamb's lettuce salad with eggs and pancetta. He has adapted this traditional recipe to suit modern tastes, separating the yolks and whites of the hard-boiled eggs, slicing the whites and passing the yolks through a sieve, and sprinkling pomegranate seeds over the finished dish.

Buy only fresh, brilliant green lamb's lettuce for this recipe. Lamb's lettuce is a delicate fall and winter vegetable that grows well on sandy soil. Even in its original packaging, it will keep no longer than three or four days in the refrigerator. It should be washed briefly under running water and then left to drain—but not dried. Endive or dandelion can be added to the lamb's lettuce in this recipe.

The charm of this Friulian salad lies in the richly contrasting flavors, ranging from the salty, smoky flavor of the bacon and the acidity of the vinegar through the sweetness of the pomegranate seeds. Although the bacon used in Friuli is first peppered and then either smoked for 12 hours or dried in the cellar for 12 days, ordinary strips of bacon or smoked ham can also be used.

The balsamic vinegar comes from Modena in Emilia-Romagna. It is made from the must of white grapes and is matured in casks for several years. During this time, it is transferred several times to casks made from different kinds of wood. According to connoisseurs, it takes 12 years to achieve perfection. Its sweet-sour character goes wonderfully well with this salad.

Hard-boil the eggs. Wash the lamb's lettuce, drain, and then remove the tiny roots at the base of the leaves.

Leave the eggs to cool and then remove the shells. Remove the yolks with a small spoon and pass through a sieve. Cut the egg white into slices.

Cut the pancetta or bacon into cubes.

Salad

Fry the pancetta cubes in the olive oil in a skillet for 5 minutes, turning frequently.

When the bacon is well done, quench with the balsamic vinegar and season with salt. Fry for another 2 or 3 minutes over a hot flame, while shaking the skillet vigorously.

Cut the pomegranate into quarters and carefully remove the seeds. Place the lamb's lettuce in the middle of a plate and arrange the egg white all around it, then top with the egg yolk, pancetta, pomegranate seeds, and the liquor from the skillet.

Fennel Salad

Preparation time: 15 minutes
Cooking time: 20 minutes
Difficulty: ★

Serves 4

2	fennel bulbs
6 tbsp	olive oil
	salt
	pepper
4	oranges
12	black olives

For the garnish:

fennel seeds
fennel leaves

This fennel salad with oranges, highly regarded by gourmets from Rome to Palermo, is very refreshing and provides a real vitamin boost. It is also very easy to prepare. Fennel grows wild in southern Italy; today, it is cultivated in Apulia and exported all over the world. This aromatic plant, which has a high calcium content, flourishes in the sandy soils around the Mediterranean. It can grow up to 6 feet/2 meters tall, has feathery, dark green foliage, and smells a little like aniseed. It has been eaten since time immemorial as a vegetable, but has also been used for medicinal purposes.

Fennel is sold practically everywhere during the winter. Choose small bulbs that are tender, white, and firm. The fluffy little shoots at the end of the stalks should not be thrown away, because they add flavor to the sauce.

The oranges are a reminder of southern Italy and Sicily, an island that was providing high-quality citrus fruit as far back as the Middle Ages. The Arabian writer, Ibn Zaffir, sang the praises of the orange and lemon trees in the gardens of Palermo: "In Sicily, the trees have fiery heads and stand with their feet in the water." The first orange trees were probably introduced in the 11th or 12th century. Monks subsequently cultivated a number of different varieties of orange on the Palermo plain, which has since been known as the *Conca d'oro*. Seventy percent of Italian oranges still come from Sicily.

For this salad, we recommend either the famous navel oranges or blood oranges, which are very juicy.

Remove the outer layers from the fennel, then cut off the base of each bulb.

Cut the fennel bulbs into even-sized, small cubes. Chop the fennel leaves.

To make the marinade, pour the olive oil into a salad bowl and season with salt and pepper. Add the cubed fennel and fennel leaves and infuse for 20 minutes. Stir gently.

with Oranges

Remove all the peel from the oranges.

Cut the oranges crossways into even slices. Capture and reserve the juice.

Pit the olives. Arrange the fennel with the marinade on the plate first, then place the orange slices and olives on top. Pour over the orange juice and garnish with fennel seeds and fennel leaves.

Chicken Salad

Preparation time:	20 minutes
Soaking time:	1 hour
Cooking time:	30 minutes
Difficulty:	★

Serves 4

4	dried porcini mushrooms (heads)
½	onion
1	carrot
1	stick celery
8 oz/200 g	chicken breast

2 tsp	balsamic vinegar
4 tsp/20 g	pine nuts
1 scant cup/ 225 ml	extra-virgin olive oil
	salt
	pepper

For the garnish:

| | basil (to taste) |

The Garfagnana mountains, around 20 miles/30 kilometers from Lucca, our chef's native city, are revered by Tuscan gourmets, for it is there they can enjoy the tastiest porcini mushrooms, delicious chestnuts, pecorino cheese, and wonderful spelt dishes.

As early as June and July, but especially in late summer, many people go for walks in the forest in search of porcini mushrooms. The most popular is the *Boletus edulis*, or Bordeaux cep, which tastes good in salads, broiled, in fricassees, in omelets, in soup, or in a delicate pasta sauce.

Since it is virtually impossible to find porcini mushrooms out of season, dried ones are often used. Before soaking them, always wash the dried mushrooms carefully under running water.

Even the simplest Tuscan salad is not complete without a good olive oil to enhance its flavor. Sauro Brunicardi prefers extra-virgin olive oil from Lucca. This has a pronounced green color and is rather cloudy, as it is not filtered. It has a very light, fresh taste, reminiscent of a tart, green apple. In this chicken salad it combines wonderfully well with the subtly flavored balsamic vinegar that comes from Modena.

The pine nuts give the salad some bite and a slightly resinous aroma. The umbrella pine, of which they are the seeds, is part of the Tuscan landscape. Before you use them, make sure they are fresh. Because of their high fat content, they go rancid very quickly. Scatter the roasted pine nuts over the salad after you have garnished it with basil leaves.

Soak the dried porcini mushrooms for 1 hour in lukewarm water, then rinse well. Peel the onion and chop finely. Peel and slice the carrot. Wash the celery and cut into thin slices.

Immerse the onion, carrot, and celery in boiling water and simmer for 10 minutes.

Add the chicken breast to the vegetables. Bring to the boil over a high heat and cook for another 15 minutes.

with Porcini Mushrooms

Cook the mushrooms for 3 minutes in salted water to which 2 drops of balsamic vinegar have been added.

Drain the chicken breast and cut into slices with a sharp knife.

Fry the pine nuts in a skillet without any fat. Arrange a slice of meat and a piece of mushroom alternately on a plate and pour olive oil and a few drops of balsamic vinegar over the top. Season with salt and pepper and garnish with pine nuts and basil.

Tuna Bottarga Salad

Preparation time: 10 minutes
Cooking time: 1 minute
Difficulty: ★

Serves 4

11 oz/300 g	fennel bulbs
	juice of 1 lemon
6 oz/180 g	*bottarga di tonno* (salted, dried red tuna fish roe)
4 oz/100 g	pitted black olives

1 tbsp/15 ml	olive oil
1 tbsp/15 ml	white wine vinegar

For the dressing:

4	oranges
2 tbsp/30 ml	olive oil

For the garnish:

	fennel seeds
4 sprigs	fennel tops

Sicily has a distinctive, ancient culture, and the feel of an island where time has stood still. A strong sense of family is only one of the many deeply rooted traditions that survive. In springtime at Favignia, near Trapani, thousands of spectators come to see the annual *mattanza*, when the local fishermen use traditional longboats and huge nets to trap and spear large numbers of tuna fish. A favorite dish in Sicily, these enormous fish can reach up to 12 feet/4 meters in length, and weigh several hundreds of pounds.

Giuseppe Barone's easily-made salad, using *bottarga di tonno*, oranges, and fennel, comes from Porto di Capo Passero, a small fishing village in the far south of the island. With its typically Sicilian ingredients, this cold appetizer is ideal for a summer menu. *Bottarga di tonno*, a local specialty, consists of the salted, pressed, and dried roe of

the female tuna fish. Also known as "Sicilian caviar," it is served sliced. It can be eaten raw, fried, or steamed. In some recipes it is dressed with olive oil, garlic, parsley, and a little red pepper.

This refreshing, vitamin-rich salad is dressed with the sharp juice of oranges and features a delightful mixture of tastes and textures. The aniseed-flavored fennel provides an intriguing contrast to the other ingredients.

Famous since the Middle Ages for its citrus fruits, the countryside around Palermo resembles a magnificent orchard. Originally created by Arab colonizers in the 11th and 12th centuries, these fruit groves benefited from a sophisticated irrigation system. Many varieties of citrus fruit are grown on the island, the best known being the navel, *tarocco* (blood), and oval oranges.

For the dressing, cut away the peel of the oranges, juice them, strain, and put the juice to one side.

Wash the fennel bulbs and slice finely. Place the sliced fennel in a bowl of water to which lemon juice has been added.

Evenly slice the pressed tuna fish roe.

with Orange and Fennel

On a moderate heat, sauté the olives for 1 minute in a frying pan with olive oil. Add the vinegar.

Now finish the dressing: add one tbsp of hot water to the bowl of orange juice, together with the olive oil. Whisk until an emulsion is obtained.

Drain the fennel in a sieve. Arrange it on the plates with the bottarga, the sautéed olives, and the orange dressing. Garnish with fennel seeds and fennel tops.

Isabella Salad

Preparation time: 10 minutes
Difficulty: ★

Serves 4

1	small celery heart
1	small tomato
4 oz/100 g	*bottarga* (mullet roe)

For the dressing:

1	lemon
2 tbsp/30 ml	olive oil
	freshly ground pepper

For the garnish:

	celery leaves

This flavor-filled salad is a variation on a classic of Sardinian cuisine. Created by Amerigo Murgia, he has named it after his daughter Isabella. Very easy to prepare, it makes a delicious summertime appetizer.

Surrounded by a turquoise sea of crystalline purity, Sardinia is the most distant of the Italian islands. The traditional dishes of this ravishingly beautiful island are generally very simple. A particularly well-known specialty is *bottarga di muggine* (mullet roe).

Found and fished mainly off the coast around Cabras in the west of the island, mullet has a distinctive flavor. The *bottarga* is generally prepared in August and September when the female fish are full of eggs. The elongated roe sack is removed, salted, and massaged by hand, before being pressed between wooden planks beneath stone or marble weights. The roe is then air-dried for between four and eight weeks, turning a rich amber in color.

Bottarga is much prized in Sardinian cuisine, often simply eaten in thin slices on fresh bread. It can be mixed with olive oil and scattered in crumbs over pasta. An essential ingredient for this recipe, it can be found in Italian or other delicatessens as well as in specialist grocers. Amerigo Murgia suggests that it is best placed in the freezer for a few minutes to make it easier to slice.

Celery is used to enhance this refreshing appetizer, with its crunchy texture and hint of aniseed. This recipe provides a perfect opportunity to get acquainted with the sun-filled riches of Sardinian cuisine.

Wash the celery heart. Cut it into fine slices.

Place the tomato in boiling water for a few moments, peel, and cut into small, even dice.

Cut the bottarga *into thin slices of equal size.*

with Bottarga

Squeeze the lemon, removing any pits from the juice.

Prepare the salad dressing by first grinding some pepper into a bowl.
Now add the olive oil, followed by the lemon juice. Mix.

Assemble the individual salads using a bottomless circular metal mold placed on each plate: start with a layer of celery. Cover this with some bottarga, then a layer of tomato. Repeat the 3 layers. Remove the circle. Pour over the dressing. Garnish with celery leaves.

Broiled Vegetables

Preparation time: 10 minutes
Cooking time: 20 minutes
Difficulty: ★

Serves 4

2	red bell peppers
2	green bell peppers
2	yellow bell peppers
2	medium eggplants
3	zucchini
	salt
	olive oil
2	sliced tomatoes (optional)

2 cloves	garlic
	flat-leaf parsley
7 oz/200 g	feta
	capers (optional)
1 pinch	dried oregano
	wine vinegar

In their restaurant, which is dedicated to the god Apollo, Konstantinos and Chrysanthi Stamkopoulos invite their guests to discover the delights of traditional Greek dishes. This mix of broiled peppers, eggplants, and zucchini drizzled with olive oil has its near equivalent all around the Mediterranean.

Enjoyed hot or cold, broiled vegetables are a popular summer *mezze* throughout Greece. Food-lovers sometimes add a few well-ripened tomatoes to the griddle pan with some garlic, then use them to top the other vegetables.

The Greek name for the eggplant is *melitzana*, although it was unknown to the Ancient Greeks and Romans. In those days it was only grown in India, arriving in Greece via the Turks. These days this highly dietetic vegetable finds its way into much Greek cooking, whether broiled, puréed, or made into little fritters.

The eggplant that is most highly prized in all Greece is the one grown in Tsakonia. Oblong in shape and pale mauve in color, it was first grown in the Arcadia region of the Peloponnese. This is followed by the popular and widely used eggplant grown in Komotini (Thrace), again oblong, but this time with a dark purple skin.

Unpeeled eggplants and zucchini can be cut into long thin slices and broiled, or grilled over a charcoal barbecue or on a cast iron griddle.

The Greeks usually use long slim peppers to make this dish, which they leave whole after broiling. If you are using big bell peppers, cut them into thick strips instead.

After arranging the vegetables on the plate, all you need to do is add the feta, herbs, vinaigrette, and a few capers for that touch of extravagance.

Wash and dry the peppers. Arrange them on a baking sheet and put them under the broiler for about 20 minutes or until the skins have turned black and wrinkled. In the meantime, cut the unpeeled eggplants and zucchini lengthwise.

Line up the eggplants and zucchini on a cutting board. Sprinkle with salt and brush with olive oil. Sprinkle with salt again, then cook on a cast-iron griddle, with the tomato slices, if using.

When the peppers are done, remove them from the heat and leave to cool before carefully peeling them with your fingers or a small knife.

Konstantinos Style

Split the peppers. Using the tip of your knife, remove all the little seeds and the membrane. Cut the flesh first into big pieces then into strips.

Peel the garlic and cut it into very thin slivers. Finely chop the parsley. On the serving plate, arrange alternating layers of eggplant, strips of multicolored peppers, and the zucchini.

Decorate the vegetables with the slivers of garlic, crumbled feta, and capers, if using. Sprinkle with chopped parsley and dried oregano, then drizzle with vinaigrette made from olive oil and wine vinegar.

Icaria Octopus Cooked

Preparation time: 25 minutes
Cooking time : 30 minutes
Marinating time (octopus): 30 minutes
Difficulty: ★

Serves 6

1	octopus weighing 2¼ lb/1 kg
	salt
scant ½ cup/ 100 ml	red wine vinegar
3½ oz/100 g	red bell peppers
3½ oz/100 g	green bell peppers
3 tbsp	capers

2 cloves	garlic
2 tsp	dried oregano
1 handful	fresh fennel leaves
1 cup/250 ml	extra-virgin olive oil

Located in the eastern part of the Aegean Sea and close to the Turkish coast, the island of Icaria, set in crystal clear waters, has retained its wild landscapes, thermal springs, and numerous vestiges of past civilizations, some of which date back to the Neolithic Age. From April to October the seas around the island teem with all sorts of marine life.

In their natural environment, octopuses live close to the rocks. The locals sometimes spear them in the craggy places where they hide. Since industrial fishing for octopus is unknown on the Greek Islands, the fishermen who capture them sell them direct to local restaurants. There they are made into the famous recipe for octopus that our chef has updated for you.

When choosing an octopus, Miltos Karoubas recommends that you look for one with firm flesh and plump tentacles, weighing less than 5 ½ pounds/2.5 kilograms. It is best, in fact, to avoid the heavier ones, which are older and thus have flesh that has become soggy and spongy.

The addition of vinegar to the cooking water makes the flesh turn a very appetizing deep red color. Note that Greek chefs also use this method for poaching shrimp and spiny lobster. To check whether it's done, you need to prick the flesh of the octopus several times with a fork. When the fork goes in easily, the octopus is cooked.

This recipe is generally served on small plates set out in the middle of the table alongside other small dishes such as *taramasalata* or *tzatziki*. The marinade should fill half the plate so that the octopus is bathed in it. Do as the Greeks do and mop up the sauce with a piece of bread.

Wash the octopus. Plunge it into a large pan filled with salted water. Add 3–4 tbsp red wine vinegar. Bring the pan to the boil and cook for 30 minutes, adding more water if necessary. Drain the octopus and cut it into thick slices.

Slice open the peppers, remove the seeds and white membrane and cut the flesh into fine julienne strips.

In a metal bowl mix the pieces of octopus, the strips of pepper, and the capers.

the Karoubas Way

Add 1 clove of garlic, peeled and finely chopped, to the dried oregano and the chopped fennel leaves and mix.

Make a garlic vinaigrette in a bowl by whisking together the olive oil, remaining wine vinegar, the other peeled and chopped garlic clove, and a pinch of salt.

Pour the garlic vinaigrette over the octopus and the peppers. Mix well. Leave to marinate for 30 minutes, then eat when it has thoroughly cooled.

Greek

Preparation: 25 minutes
Difficulty: ★

Serves 4

4	small cucumbers
4	tomatoes
2	medium onions
1 each	green, red, and yellow bell peppers
1 bunch	flat-leaf parsley
1 bunch	arugula (rocket)
8 oz/225 g	feta

24	black Kalamata olives
	olive oil
	salt
1 pinch	oregano
	capers (optional)

Greek salad, which we present here in its most traditional form, is frequently found among the assortment of dishes that make up the *mezze* served with aperitifs. It is served with *tzatziki*, marinated octopus, broiled bell peppers, or stuffed vine leaves. Everybody likes to relax with these fresh and appetizing dishes, washed down with a glass of ouzo.

In restaurants this salad is always served in copious quantities, but rarely as a dish on its own. As well as an accompaniment to an aperitif, the Greeks enjoy eating this crunchy and juicy salad with broiled lamb.

Cucumbers, or *angouri*, are refreshing and low in calories and are used in many local appetizers. Mixed with yogurt and garlic, cucumber is transformed into *tzatziki*, a flavorsome creamy dip. Greek cooks traditionally use small and highly aromatic cucumbers.

Our salad is enriched with black Kalamata olives, which have a more robust taste. Grown in the Massini area of the Peloponnese, these oval shaped fruits are picked by hand then split in two with a razor blade before being covered with brine to impregnate them with salt. If you prefer, you can use green olives instead.

Greek salad is sometimes known as *horiatiki salata* ("rustic salad"). Cooks from different areas like to add local wild herbs, but romaine lettuce can also be used. Some like to add boiled potatoes or hard-cooked eggs. Likewise the feta can be replaced by fresh goat milk cheese.

Like the Greeks, take care not to mix all the vegetables together and season them in a bowl before you serve them. Instead, arrange your ingredients artistically directly onto the serving plate so as to preserve their color, flavor, and individual crispness. Season and serve immediately.

Peel the cucumbers. Cut them in half lengthwise, then into thin half-moon slices.

Wash the tomatoes, cut them in half and then into segments. Peel the onions then slice into thin rings.

Wash the peppers. Cut them open across the middle. Remove the seeds and the white membrane and slice into fine rings.

Salad

Wash the parsley and arugula and roughly chop with a knife.

On the serving platter, arrange the parsley, arugula, and cucumbers around the edge, then the peppers, tomatoes, and cubes of feta in the center, and the slices of onion around the outer edges.

Scatter over the olives and add a generous drizzle of olive oil, salt to taste, a pinch of oregano, and the capers, if using.

Tonn Immellah with

Preparation time: 30 minutes
Cooking time: 2–2½ hours
Soaking time for
 garbanzo beans: overnight
Difficulty: ★

Serves 4

4 slices	Maltese country bread
7 oz/200 g	salted tuna
7 tbsp/100 ml	olive oil

For the garbanzo purée:

1 cups/200 g	garbanzo beans (chickpeas)
3 cloves	garlic
4	anchovy fillets in oil
½ bunch	flat-leaf parsley
3½ tbsp/50 ml	olive oil
	salt and pepper

For the tomato salad:

2	large tomatoes
8 leaves	basil
½ bunch	flat-leaf parsley
3 cloves	garlic
½	red onion
1 tbsp/15 g	capers
3½ tbsp/50 ml	olive oil
	salt and pepper

Optional garnish:

	arugula leaves (rocket)

Michael Cauchi is the owner and chef of a noted fish restaurant, *Il Re del Pesce*, in Marsacala on the island of Malta. As an appetizer, he suggests these slices of salted tuna served with garbanzo purée, and an anchovy and tomato salad on toasted bread.

Tuna is one of the most commonly-found species of fish caught in the waters around Malta. Michael Cauchi likes to oven-bake the fresh fish, serving it with a caper or sweet-sour sauce. Salted tuna, as used in our recipe, is sold in pieces, either whole or ready-sliced. It is ready to eat and is a perfect accompaniment for cold vegetable dishes.

To make the accompanying garbanzo purée, it is important to soak the dried beans in water overnight and then boil them for two to two-and-a-half hours (or until soft). When blending them in the food processor, add a little of the cooking liquid as necessary to give a creamy consistency.

If you are in a hurry, ready-prepared canned garbanzo beans may be used. Much appreciated in North Africa, garbanzo beans were introduced to the island of Malta by Moorish invaders.

The garbanzo beans, slices of tuna, and tomato salad are made even more delicious by the addition of olive oil, although Maltese cooks often use corn oil as olive trees are scarce on the island, and there is only one brand of local olive oil.

The tomato salad is served on toasted slices of Maltese bread called *hobza*, giving a rather more elaborate version of a Maltese favorite *hobz biz-zejt* ("bread with oil") eaten as a snack or with a drink in bars.

Garnish the dish with arugula leaves and drizzle with olive oil.

To make the garbanzo purée, first soak the beans overnight in water. The next day, rinse them and cook for 2 hours (or until soft) in a pan of boiling water. Drain them, reserving some of the cooking water, and blend them in a food processor with a little of the liquid.

Peel and chop the garlic together with the anchovies and the parsley. Add them to the puréed garbanzo beans. Add a little oil, salt, and pepper. Mix well and set aside in a cool place.

For the tomato salad, peel the tomatoes and cut into small dice. Chop the basil and parsley. Peel and chop the garlic and red onion. Chop the capers. Place all these ingredients in a bowl.

Garbanzo Purée

Pour a little olive oil over the salad and season with salt and pepper. Mix well with a spoon.

Toast the slices of bread and top them with the tomato salad.

Slice the tuna into thin pieces. Arrange 2 or 3 slices on one side of each plate, a piece of toast with tomato salad in the center, and some garbanzo purée on the other side. Drizzle with olive oil and serve cold.

Artichoke

Preparation time: 30 minutes
Cooking time: 40 minutes
Difficulty: ★

Serves 4

4	large artichokes
1	medium carrot
2	potatoes
10	scallions
1 bunch	dill

scant ½ cup/ 50 g	flour
1 tbsp	sugar
	salt to taste
	juice of 3 lemons
scant ½ cup/ 100 ml	olive oil
¾ cup/100 g	freshly shelled peas

Bayrampaşa, which is the district on the European side of Istanbul, used to be known for its artichokes. As the town expanded, however, the areas where they were grown were gradually built on. Today, the main growing region is in the area around Izmir on the Aegean Sea.

First the outer leaves of the artichoke are removed, then the inside leaves are separated from the heart with a knife and the fibrous center scooped out with a small spoon. The artichoke should be rubbed well with lemon juice to prevent it from turning brown. The stems are peeled thinly; they can either be removed from the heart of the artichoke and cut into pieces or left where they are, which is quite decorative and enhances the freshness of the vegetable.

Artichoke hearts are served with peas, carrots, and diced potato. A firm potato that does not turn floury when cooked is best.

The artichokes are cooked gently with the other vegetables in a combination of water, flour, sugar, salt, lemon juice, and olive oil (one of Turkey's best-known olive oils comes from Ayvalık, a small town on the Aegean coast to the north of Izmir). First the pot is sealed well with aluminum foil and then covered with a lid. The peas are added ten minutes before the end of the cooking time.

Like almost all Turkish dishes that contain olive oil, Artichoke Bayrampaşa is usually served cold. If fresh peas are not available, diced celery is a good substitute.

Cut off the tips of the artichoke leaves. Remove the leaves and scoop out the fibrous center with a small spoon. Peel the stalk.

Peel and slice the carrot, and peel and dice the potatoes. Peel the scallions and cut into thick slices.

Half fill a large pot with water and place the artichoke hearts inside.

Bayrampaşa

Add the carrot and potatoes.

Add the sliced scallions and chopped dill.

Combine the flour, sugar, salt, and lemon juice in a bowl with a little water. Add the olive oil and stir well. Pour over the vegetables. Cover and cook for 30 minutes. Add the peas and cook for a further 10 minutes. Serve cold.

Bulgur Salad

Preparation time: 15 minutes
Cooking time: 15 minutes
Difficulty: ★

Serves 4

1¾ cups/360 g	bulgur wheat
	salt
1 bunch	flat-leaf parsley
4	scallions
4 cloves	garlic (very young)
	green lettuce leaves
1	onion
1 tbsp	red pepper paste
1 tbsp	tomato paste

1 tbsp	ground pepper
1 tbsp	paprika
1 tsp	dried mint
1 cup/250 ml	olive oil
2 tbsp	pomegranate syrup

For the garnish:

	fresh mint or
	lettuce leaves

This Antep-style *kısır* is related to Lebanese *tabbouleh*, a reference to the close proximity of the border with the Near East. The gastronomy of this region, where many cultures meet, is strongly influenced by Arabic, Syrian, Armenian, and even Roman cuisine.

The word *kısır* is common throughout Turkey. The addition of pomegranate syrup is typical of *kısır* from Antep, however, where the dish is known as *içkatması* (the first part of the word denotes "stuffing," the second means "addition"). According to Ayfer T. Ünsal, it is a very old dish. To make the syrup, the pomegranate is cooked until it has turned into a sticky, dark-brown mass; it adds a pleasantly tart taste to the dish, similar to that of lemon juice or vinegar. The best substitute is balsamic vinegar.

This dish is based on *simit*, fine bulgur wheat (bulgur is wheat that has been boiled, dried, and then ground). Ayfer T. Ünsal works the soaked bulgur and tomato and red pepper pastes until the mixture is evenly red in color. Bulgur can also be cooked in the microwave. Place the bulgur in a suitable dish together with salt, water, and tomato and red pepper pastes, and cook for 5–7 minutes. The onion can be sautéed in oil in a skillet for a few minutes and then added to the bulgur mixture.

Tomatoes and red peppers, concentrates of which are used to color this dish, have only been grown in the Antep region since World War I. Oddly enough, tomatoes are called "French eggplant" in the local dialect!

Garnish the dish with fresh mint or a few lettuce leaves before serving.

Place the bulgur in a dish, season with the salt, and gradually pour over 2 cups/ 500 ml boiling water. Cover and leave to stand for 15 minutes.

Wash and finely chop the parsley, scallions, and garlic. Thinly slice the lettuce leaves. Peel and finely chop the onion.

Add the tomato and red pepper pastes to the bulgur and combine them well, using your hands.

Antep Style

Add the onion, salt, pepper, paprika, and dried mint, and continue kneading with your hands. Gradually add the olive oil.

Pour over the pomegranate syrup and combine well.

Finally, add the parsley, scallions, garlic, and sliced lettuce. Serve chilled.

Stuffed Vine Leaves

Preparation time:	25 minutes
Cooking time:	45 minutes
Difficulty:	★

Serves 4

1¼ lb/500 g	onions
	oil for sautéing
½ cup/100 g	rice
½ tsp	sugar
	salt and ground pepper to taste

½ bunch	dill
½ bunch	smooth parsley
1 tsp/5 g	dried mint
10 oz/250 g	preserved vine leaves
2 sprigs	fresh mint
1	lemon
scant ½ cup/ 100 ml	olive oil

Stuffed vine leaves are the most typical *meze* dish of the Ottoman palaces. All over the country they are traditionally served cold as a snack, together with other delicacies and plenty of *rakı*, the well-known alcoholic drink.

In Turkey, they are called *zeytinyağlı yaprak sarma* (the first part of the name means "olive oil," the second "vine leaves," and the third "stuffed, rolled"). Stuffed vine leaves belong to the large family of *dolma*. *Dolma* is a mixture that is used to stuff vegetables such as eggplant, bell peppers, tomatoes, and zucchini, or which is rolled up in leaves. You can also use Swiss chard for this recipe; the results will be just as delicious.

Vine leaves are used in a wide range of Turkish specialties. They are picked when still young, then stacked and soaked in brine for a long time. They come predominantly from the wine-growing area around Tekirdağ in the Marmara region,

Tokat in Central Turkey, and from the Izmir region on the Aegean coast.

Before cooking, wash the rice thoroughly in warm water. Dried mint is better for flavoring the rice, as fresh mint can be too acid.

Hüseyin Özoğuz rolls the vine leaves to the thickness of a finger—which is how they are served in the restaurant. In private homes they are rolled up as thin as a cigarette.

Hüseyin Özoğuz gives the dish various intensive flavors: He covers the bottom of the pot with a layer of parsley, dill, mint, lemon slices, and vine leaves. He arranges the stuffed vine leaves in a circle on top, placing them close together. This helps them to keep their shape while they are cooking, and gives them the most wonderful aroma.

Chop the onions and sauté in a little hot oil in a large pot for 5 minutes. Add the rice and stir with a spatula.

Once the rice is evenly coated with the oil, stir in the sugar, salt, and pepper.

Chop three quarters of the dill and parsley, and add together with the dried mint. Pour over about ½ cup/100 ml of water and cover. Simmer gently over a low heat for about 10 minutes, stirring frequently. Remove the pot from the heat and leave it to cool a little.

in Olive Oil

Wash the vine leaves and pat them dry. Place a leaf on a worktop and put a scant tablespoon of the mixture in the middle.

Fold the bottom edge of the leaf over the stuffing, slowly pulling in the sides as you roll the leaf along. The small package should be about the thickness of a finger. Repeat with the remaining leaves, reserving a few.

Place the stuffed vine leaves in a pot on a bed of the remaining chopped parsley and dill, fresh mint, 4 or 5 lemon slices, and the reserved vine leaves. Add the water, a dash of lemon juice, and the olive oil. Cover and simmer gently for 30 minutes. Leave to cool before serving.

Çoban

Preparation time:	15 minutes
Cooking time:	12 minutes
Difficulty:	★

Serves 4

2	cucumbers
2	tomatoes
2	eggs
2	green bell peppers
2	red bell peppers

4	scallions
1	onion
scant ½ cup/	
100 ml	olive oil
3½ tbsp/50 ml	wine vinegar
6 oz/150 g	sheep milk cheese

For the garnish:

| 12 | black olives |
| | parsley |

Çoban is the Turkish word for "shepherd." The pastoral tradition has enriched the multifaceted country's culinary repertoire, adding a number of simple recipes in which Mediterranean aromas dominate.

This colorful, traditional salad, which is also a *meze* dish, is easy to prepare and very refreshing. It consists of fresh, crunchy vegetables and is simply bursting with vitamins—the ideal summer meal.

The cucumber—which is very popular in Turkish cuisine—came originally from the Himalayas. Its high water content means it is very low in calories, as well as an excellent provider of potassium and vitamin C. Cucumbers should be light green, fresh, and crunchy.

Bell peppers are the main ingredients in a Turkish shepherd's salad. Today, easily a dozen different varieties are available on the market. The green bell pepper keeps best, as it is harvested before it is ripe. It is a little stronger in flavor than the red variety, which is popular for its juicy flesh and sweet aroma. Choose firm, smooth specimens with a hard, green stalk.

Tomatoes are one of the main ingredients in Mediterranean cuisine, but did not arrive in Turkey until fairly recently—they came to Europe from their South American home via Spain in the 16th century. These fruits, which prefer a warm climate and lots of water, are grown mainly on Turkey's eastern Mediterranean coast.

This healthy salad is a delightful homage to the life of the shepherd. Black olives and sheep milk cheese (*beyaz penir* or feta) provide it with its typical flavors.

Peel the cucumbers with a paring knife and carefully skin the tomatoes.

Remove the seeds from the tomatoes and chop into even-sized pieces. Chop the cucumbers. Boil the eggs for about 12 minutes until hard. Rinse under cold water and peel.

Wash the red and green bell peppers and remove the seeds, then chop into small, even pieces.

Salad

Wash the scallions and cut into rings. Peel and finely chop the onion. Put all the vegetables in a salad bowl.

Pour the olive oil and wine vinegar over the vegetables. Combine everything thoroughly but carefully with a large spoon.

Cut the eggs into eighths. Arrange the salad on a serving dish, grate over the sheep milk cheese, and arrange the eggs on top. Garnish with olives and parsley.

Olive and

Preparation time:	20 minutes
Chilling time:	2 hours
Difficulty:	★

Serves 4

10 oz/250 g	green olives
¾ cup/85 g	walnut kernels
4	scallions
3 cloves	garlic (very young)
1 bunch	flat-leaf parsley

1 tsp/4 g	paprika
	salt to taste
2 tsp/10 ml	pomegranate syrup
4 tsp/20 ml	olive oil

For the garnish:

| 1 | pomegranate (optional) |

This salad is called *zeytin piyazı* in Turkish, and originated in Gaziantep, an area to the east of the Mediterranean. Its name consists of the words *zeytin* ("olive") and *piyazı* ("onion salad"), from *piyaz* ("onion"). The cuisine in this region was for a long time under the influence of nearby Iran. In bygone days, the ladies would treat themselves to a day together in the *hamam*, the Turkish baths, taking with them whatever their hearts desired, including *zeytin piyazı* or *içkatması*—a kind of *tabbouleh*, also called *kısır*.

The olives that are harvested in the Gaziantep area in the fall are mostly used to make olive oil. Only green olives should be used for this salad, because the consistency and strong aroma of the black variety is less suitable. Gaziantep olives are usually pitted individually with a flat stone as soon as they have been harvested, when they are still very hard, bitter, and inedible. Because fresh ones are hard to find commercially, we have used preserved olives for this recipe.

Ayfer T. Ünsal uses pomegranate syrup to make the salad very slightly sour. This is the juice of sour pomegranates, which are boiled until they have turned into a thick, brown syrup. In Turkey it is used for sauces, salads, and other dishes. You can also use balsamic vinegar or lemon juice with a small amount of sugar as a substitute.

Chill the salad in the refrigerator for at least two hours before serving, to allow the flavors to develop fully. You can then simply enjoy it as it is, or—as is the preference in Gaziantep—place it on a thin flatbread (*lavaş*), roll it up, and eat it like a sandwich.

Using a flat stone, remove the olive flesh from the pit. Discard the pits. Roughly chop the walnuts.

Chop the scallions. Peel and finely chop the garlic.

Wash, dry, and chop the parsley.

Onion Salad

Using a spoon, combine the chopped olives, walnuts, scallions, garlic, parsley, paprika, and salt in a bowl.

Stir in the pomegranate syrup.

Add the olive oil and combine well. Chill in the refrigerator for 2 hours and garnish with fresh pomegranate seeds if desired.

Yogurt

Preparation time: 20 minutes
Cooking time: 2 minutes
Difficulty: ★

Serves 4

For the carrots in yogurt:
2 carrots
4 cloves garlic
2 tbsp/30 ml olive oil
 salt
⅔ cup/150 g set yogurt

For the cacık:
2 cups/500 g set yogurt
 olive oil

4 small cucumbers
4 cloves garlic
1 pinch dried mint

For the hadari:
4 cloves garlic
⅔ cup/150 g set yogurt
½ tsp dried mint
 salt to taste

For the garnish:
 black olives (optional)
 olive oil
 dill
 fresh mint (optional)

In Turkey, a meal with friends always begins with a course of small appetizers, the *meze*. Accompanied by *rakı*, they are intended to stimulate the appetite. The many different dishes that make up *meze* consist mainly of raw ingredients, vegetables, fish, and meat, and are an impressive testimony to the variety of Turkish cuisine as well as an expression of Turkish lifestyle.

The popular yogurt *meze* are refreshing and easy to prepare. They are normally served with *pide* (pitta), which is a flatbread.

Yogurt was inherited from the Turkish nomads, and is today one of the main ingredients in Turkish cuisine. As long ago as the 13th century, the amusing stories of Nasreddin Hodja spoke of the role of this dairy product in everyday life. In the country, yogurt is made at home from cow's, sheep's, or buffalo's milk; heated for a long period of time,

it loses up to 30 percent of its water content. It is then poured into goatskin bags or clay jugs and left to ferment naturally.

The creamy yogurt is ideal for combining with cucumbers. This vegetable, which came originally from the Himalayas, grows in abundance in Turkey. The pale green flesh should be firm and crunchy. Cucumbers contain a lot of water, so they are extremely low in calories. They also contain plenty of potassium and vitamin C. They are better peeled, as this prevents the bitter flavor; use only shiny, firm specimens.

For *cacık*, the cucumber is flavored with garlic and mint. It is a good idea to add a few crushed ice cubes, as this enhances its refreshing effect. *Cacık* is also served as a cold soup, or as an accompaniment to pilaf.

Peel and grate the carrots. Peel and crush the garlic.

To prepare the carrots in yogurt, sauté the garlic in the hot olive oil. Add the grated carrots, season with salt, and cook for 2 minutes. Combine well with the yogurt.

For the cacık, put the yogurt in a bowl and whisk with a little oil.

Meze

Wash the cucumbers, cut them in half lengthwise, and remove the seeds. Chop them finely.

Chop the garlic and add to the yogurt. Add the mint and chopped cucumber to the yogurt, combining all ingredients well.

For the hadari, first chop the garlic. Stir the yogurt, garlic, mint, and salt in a bowl. Pour everything into small bowls. Carrots in yogurt: Garnish with an olive. Cacık: Drizzle over olive oil and garnish with dill. Hadari: Garnish with fresh mint leaves.

Mediterranean

Preparation time: 45 minutes
Soaking time: 12 hours
Chilling time: 5 minutes
Cooking time: 40 minutes
Difficulty: ★

Serves 4

For the hummus:

1	bouillon cube
1¼ cups/300 g	garbanzo beans
4 cloves	garlic
1 tsp	paprika
3½ tbsp/50 ml	tahini (sesame paste)
2 bunches	parsley
1 bunch	mint
¼	green bell pepper
2 tbsp	olive oil
	salt
	ground pepper

For the bean purée with dill:

1¼ cups/300 g	dried fava beans
1	onion
	juice of ¼ lemon
½ tsp	sugar
	salt
6 cloves	garlic
2 tbsp	olive oil
½ bunch	dill

For the eggplant caviar:

4 cloves	garlic
	juice of 1 lemon
4 tbsp/60 ml	olive oil
2	eggplants
	salt, ground pepper
2 tbsp/30 g	set yogurt

These three *meze* are well named, because they are true classics in this sunny region.

They are very easy to prepare, and are almost always served with *rakı*, the popular aniseed alcoholic drink, in Turkey. *Hummus*, the well-known garbanzo bean purée, originally came from the Middle East. Seasoned with garlic, parsley, paprika, mint, green bell pepper, tahini, and olive oil, it is also a delicious main course.

The garbanzo bean came from Central Asia, and is mentioned in Homer's *Iliad*. It is a small, round, pealike pulse. According to legend, the Phoenicians brought them to the Mediterranean region. Garbanzo beans are slightly nutty in flavor, and extremely nutritious. They need to be soaked for 12 hours before cooking.

Bean purée is extremely popular in southern Europe—it is a creamy, intensively flavored specialty. The fava bean is harvested from spring until well into summer, and is related to the garbanzo bean. There is no need to remove the outer skin if the beans are still young. Cooked and cooled, they are also used in salads. It is a good idea to drizzle a little oil over the bean purée before serving, to prevent it from drying out.

There are many different ways of cooking eggplant in Turkey. Their home is India, and they have been known there for over 2,500 years. For this dish, use long, deep purple specimens.

The day before, soak the dried fava beans and the garbanzo beans in water in two separate bowls. Pierce the eggplants several times with a fork and remove the stalks. Hold the eggplants over a flame or roast them in the broiler.

Begin making the eggplant caviar by crushing the garlic. Whisk together the garlic, lemon juice, and olive oil in a bowl.

Peel the eggplants and cut them into the olive oil mixture. Season with salt and pepper. Add the yogurt, and crush everything with a fork.

Meze

To make the hummus, bring the bouillon cube to the boil in 2 cups/500 ml water. Add the soaked garbanzo beans and cook for about 40 minutes until soft. Drain. Purée the garbanzo beans with the remaining hummus ingredients.

To make the bean purée, put the drained beans, finely chopped onion, lemon juice, sugar, salt, whole peeled garlic, and olive oil in a pot of water and cook for 35 minutes until soft. Drain.

Purée the bean mixture and place in a mold. Sprinkle over the chopped dill and chill for 5 minutes. Arrange the meze on a serving dish.

Radhkha

Preparation time: 40 minutes
Difficulty: ★

Serves 4

1³/₄ lb/800 g	tomatoes
5 oz/150 g	mild green chiles
2¹/₂ oz/70 g	tuna in oil
4	garlic cloves
7 tbsp/100 ml	olive oil
¹/₂	a lemon
	salt

For the garnish:
6¹/₂ tbsp/100 g   black olives

When the heat rises above 104 °F/40 °C, the inhabitants of Tozeur eat *radhkha* to cool themselves down. Tunisian women make small crepes of fine semolina, salt, and water, called *rougag*, as an accompaniment to this salad.

The preparation of the *radhkha* is typically Mediterranean. All the ingredients—garlic, tomatoes, mild green chiles, and tuna—are crushed in a mortar with a pestle called a *mihras* in Tunisian. The use of this round container, which varies in size, goes back to ancient times. Whether they're made of olive wood, thick china, marble, or stone, the pestle and mortar have proved to be essential tools in the creation of many North African, Southern European, and Far Eastern dishes.

Garlic brings its own distinctive flavor to this appetizer. Grown for over 5,000 years, this bulb has the reputation of promoting good health. In spring, the new garlic appears in the markets. It's fairly gentle in flavor and easy to peel. Select very hard, plump cloves. Keep them in the fridge in the crisper. However, the ordinary garlic that is available throughout the year must be stored in a dry place. If it gets damp, it tends to sprout.

Chiles, like tomatoes, are essential ingredients of the Tunisian culinary tradition. Discovered in the New World by Christopher Columbus, these plants were introduced into the Tozeur region by the Arab-Andalucians. There are a huge number of varieties of fresh and dried chiles in Tunisia. Their spicy flavor ranges from mild to very strong. To make this recipe, you need to deseed and dice them finely before grinding them up. Remember to rinse your hands after handling them.

Radhkha is a salad with quite a spicy taste and its colorful appearance is most attractive.

Wash the tomatoes and dice them.

Wash the chiles and split them in two. Deseed and dice them. Flake the tuna.

Peel the garlic cloves. Grind them in a mortar.

from Tozeur

Put the diced tomatoes and chiles in a bowl, and grind with a pestle. Add the ground garlic cloves.

Pour 7 tbsp/100 ml of olive oil into the bowl and add the flaked tuna. Mix. Crush the mixture with the back of a large spoon.

Add the salt and squeeze the half a lemon into the mixture, removing any pits that fall in. Arrange the radhkha salad on plates. Garnish with black olives.

Fava Bean Salad

Preparation time:	10 minutes	2 tsp	cumin
Cooking time:	15 minutes		salt
Difficulty:	☆	½ tsp	pepper

Serves 4

4 lb/2 kg	fresh fava beans (broad beans)
1	lemon
2 tsp	harissa
⅔ cup/150 ml	olive oil

Fava bean salad with cumin and harissa is a great favorite with Tunisian families. Locally, it's known as *m'dammes* and is dead easy to make. The fava beans, called *foul* in Tunisian, are grown all over the country. To enjoy them at their best, Mohamed Bouagga recommends preparing this dish with young beans.

The way to recognize older beans is that they have a black thread running around the pod. Young beans have a tender green thread. When you use young beans, there is no need to remove their skin as it's relatively thin, but older beans are better with their skins removed. This is an easy task when the beans are cooked. To keep their fresh green color, Mohamed Bouagga adds lemon to the cooking water, using the zest of the lemon used in the recipe.

Originally, *m'dammes* was served hot, and the cooking liquid was retained. It goes with the traditional tomato sauce with harissa and cumin. If you want to bring out the garlic flavor, add two chopped garlic cloves to this salad.

Many westerners aren't used to eating highly seasoned or very spicy dishes. To get used to the strong flavor we recommend that you add the harissa bit by bit. Taste the dish at each stage of its preparation to gauge its strength, rather than adding the two teaspoons of harissa straightaway.

If you want to make your own harissa, it is very easy. Simply crush 1 lb/450 g *felfel* (small dry red chiles), having deseeded and softened them in cold water. Next grind them in a mortar. Add 4 garlic cloves reduced to a paste and season with two pinches of caraway seed and two pinches of coriander. Finally, add salt to the mixture and put the harissa paste into a container, covering it with olive oil to keep it fresh. Then you can use and abuse it, as most Tunisians like to do.

Shell the fava beans and wash them, but don't remove the skins. Squeeze the lemon and put the juice to one side.

Put the lemon zest into the cooking water and bring to the boil.

Cook the fava beans in the lemon water for 10–15 minutes. When they begin to wrinkle, they're cooked.

with Cumin and Harissa

Drain the fava beans. First, leave them to cool at room temperature. Then put them in a cool place. Discard the lemon zest.

Prepare the seasoning by putting the harissa and olive oil into a bowl. Add the cumin and the reserved lemon juice. Season with salt and pepper.

Season the fava beans with the harissa, cumin, and olive oil sauce (add it bit by bit, tasting, to control how spicy you want it). Serve chilled.

Tunisian

Preparation time: 25 minutes
Cooking time: 45 minutes
Difficulty: ★

Serves 4

2¹⁄₄ lb/1 kg	octopus
¹⁄₂	lemon
5 oz/150 g	fresh tomatoes
1	small onion
3¹⁄₂ tbsp/50 g	chopped flat-leaf parsley
3¹⁄₂ tbsp/50 ml	olive oil
1	lettuce
	salt and pepper

For the garnish:

2 oz/50 g	radish
16	black olives
2	lemons, optional

Octopus salad is a culinary delight from Mahdia, one of the most important ports in Tunisia. These marine animals, also called octopods, have horny mouths and eight tentacles with suckers. The fishermen of Mahdia usually bring back medium-sized fish weighing between 1³⁄₄ lb/800 g and 3lb/1.5 kg. They are not allowed to capture the smallest specimens, and large octopuses have fairly tough flesh and are less sought after.

To catch them, fishermen use containers derived from amphorae known as gargoulettes. The gargoulettes are left in the sea in the evening, and octopuses adopt them as hiding places. Then all the fishermen need to do the next morning is to hoist the lot onto their boats.

The time for the best Tunisian octopus is between September and December. For the rest of the year, salads are made from octopus dried in the sun on nets hanging from walls.

Preserved this way, it can be kept for several months, but it then needs to be rehydrated the night before cooking. Our salad can also be prepared with calamari or cuttlefish.

Octopus must always be tenderized at least 15 minutes before you start cooking it. In Tunisia, cooks either hit the fish a number of times against a wall, or lay it on a board and beat it forcefully with a stick. To check you have tenderized it enough, gently pull the skin at the level of a sucker. It should tear slightly.

When you start cooking the octopus, the flesh and the water you poach it in turn crimson. Do not cook it for more than 45 minutes, as it can become rubbery. Use the point of a knife to prick it to see if it's tender and cooked. When it is ready, remove the octopus from the liquid and plunge it in a container of iced water to prevent further cooking.

Rinse the octopus and cut it into large pieces. Tenderize it by beating it a number of times with a meat mallet or a stick.

Immerse the octopus in a stockpot of cold water. Bring it gently to the boil and cook for approximately 45 minutes, until tender.

Using a slotted spoon, remove the octopus pieces from the cooking juice. Transfer to a saucepan filled with iced water.

Octopus Salad

Meanwhile, squeeze the lemon, placing the juice to one side. Chop the tomatoes. Peel and chop the onion.

Cut the octopus into small strips. Mix the tomatoes, onion, and parsley in a bowl. Add the octopus strips to this salad.

Drizzle the lemon juice and a little olive oil over the salad. Season with salt and pepper. Arrange it on a bed of lettuce leaves. Garnish the salad with black olives, small pieces of radish, and slices of lemon, if using.

Ganaria

Preparation time: 40 minutes
Cooking time: 25 minutes
Difficulty: ★★

Serves 4

3	lemons
6	large artichokes
2	eggs

For the filling:

1	crystallized lemon
3½ oz/100 g	mozzarella
3½ tbsp/50 g	pitted green olives
2 medium-sized	tomatoes
3½ tbsp/50 g	parsley

3 tsp/10 g	capers
1 tsp	harissa
7 tbsp/100 ml	olive oil
	salt and pepper

For the garnish:

	lettuce leaves (optional)

Ganaria salad is a refreshing mixture based on artichokes. A great favorite of the people of Tunis and Nabeul, this cold appetizer is popular in the spring.

Scooping out the artichokes is the tricky part of this recipe. Originating from Sicily, artichokes are hardy plants that belong to the Compositae family. They are often used in Mediterranean cooking. The fleshy, tender heart of the artichoke is served after its choke has been removed. The base of the leaves is also edible. Select large artichokes for this recipe, as they're easier to fill. Avoid artichokes with leaves that have lost their fresh green color. If you want to keep them for a few days, keep their stems in water. After preparing them, they must be kept in water with lemon juice added until they are needed, to stop them going brown.

All the filling ingredients are typically Mediterranean. A prime example is mozzarella, an Italian cheese with a sweet, slightly tangy flavor, made in the Latium and Campanula regions from buffalo milk. Mozzarella is sold in a number of forms, usually preserved in salted water, and when cooked it forms a stringy paste with a barely discernible crust.

This sunshine salad uses capers as a condiment. Capers are the flower bud from the caper shrub, a small tree growing wild in Tunisia, and they are found in many regional dishes. Our chef recommends that you select very small capers, which are valued for their delicate flavor and pronounced scent.

As for harissa, its reputation goes far beyond the boundaries of Tunisia. Harissa is renowned for enlivening a large number of dishes. Harissa is still homemade in some families—a paste made from dried, chopped red chiles, seasoned with salt, garlic, caraway seeds, and olive oil.

In a bowl, squeeze the juice of 2 lemons and add a little water. With a sharp knife, remove the stem and peel the 6 artichokes by scooping them out right down to the heart. Remove the choke with a spoon. Put the artichoke hearts in the lemon water.

Take 2 artichoke hearts and slice into ¼ in (2–3 mm) thin strips and put in the lemon water. Put the 4 remaining hearts in boiling water and cook for approximately 25 minutes. Hard-boil the eggs and shell them.

Prepare the ingredients for the filling by thoroughly peeling the crystallized fruit. Finely dice the skin, the mozzarella, and green olives.

Salad

Chop the parsley very finely; finely dice the tomatoes and hard-boiled eggs.

Put all the filling ingredients into a bowl. Add the artichoke strips and the capers. Mix gently. Squeeze the juice of the remaining lemon into the mixture and stir. Season with salt, pepper, harissa, and the olive oil. Stir together.

Drain the cooked artichoke hearts. Fill them with the ingredients. Arrange the ganaria salad on the plate. Garnish with lettuce, if used, and decorate the plates with a trickle of olive oil, flavored with harissa.

Mosaic Salad

Preparation time: 20 minutes
Cooking time: 25 minutes
Difficulty: ★

Serves 4 to 6

2	potatoes
2	carrots
2	red beets
³/₄ cup/100 g	peas
3¹/₂ oz/100 g	navy beans
2	eggs
2	onions

¹/₂	bunch flat-leaf parsley
7 tbsp/100 ml	Tunisian olive oil
1	lettuce
1 can	sardines in Tunisian olive oil
6¹/₂ tbsp/100 g	black or green olives
	salt and pepper

Mosaic salad from Sfax is a favorite springtime treat in Tunisia. At this time of the year, the markets are full of small, tender, colorful, and tasty vegetables. The spring carrots are juicy and fragrant, and there is a wide variety of vegetables to choose from. As the fancy takes them, gourmets add artichokes and turnips to their salad as well as the seafood.

As prolific producers of sun-ripened fruits and vegetables, Tunisians usually prepare salads according to the season: early produce in spring; tomatoes, onions, and cucumbers in summer. Once the season has finished, the surplus vegetable harvest is dried in the sun and stored for the winter.

Potato cultivation is a fast-expanding industry in Tunisia, and it takes place throughout the year. New potatoes appear from March to May, the height of the season is between June and October, and the end of the season is from November to February.

Olives reach maturity at the beginning of November. Initially green, they turn black when they are very ripe, at which point they are squeezed to produce the highly renowned Tunisian olive oil. In this recipe, green and black olives are equally suitable.

What could be more natural than to add sardines in oil to a salad from Sfax? The ports of Sfax, Mahdia, and Kelibia have long been known for their sardine fishing. Several varieties of sardines are sold in cans, either in vegetable or olive oil, tomato sauce, or sometimes even flavored with harissa. Some families preserve sardines themselves: removing the heads, gutting and cleaning them, the sardines are then dipped in very hot oil and preserved in a hermetically sealed jar of olive oil.

Peel the potatoes, carrots, and the red beets. Cut into small cubes. Shell the peas. Cut the navy beans into 1 in/2 cm lengths. Cook everything separately in boiling water "al dente" (until they're just cooked), or until softer, according to taste.

As soon as they're cooked, use a slotted spoon to transfer the navy beans and peas into a basin of ice water to keep their fresh green color.

Hard-boil the eggs for 10 minutes in boiling water, peel them, and cut into quarters. Peel the onions. Chop the onions and parsley finely.

from Sfax

Mix the potatoes, carrots, peas, onions, navy beans, and parsley in a dish to make a salad.

Season the salad with a trickle of olive oil, salt, and pepper. Separate the lettuce leaves, rinse and spin them. Drain the canned sardines.

Make a bed of lettuce in your serving dish. Arrange the vegetable salad on top. Garnish with cubes of red beet, egg quarters, and olives. Arrange the sardines on the salad. Serve chilled.

Fethi Tounsi's

Preparation time:	20 minutes
Cooking time:	10 minutes
Difficulty:	☆

Serves 4

7 oz/200 g	fresh green chiles
3½ oz/100 g	fresh red chiles
2	tomatoes
⅔ cup /150 ml	olive oil
1 tsp	ground coriander

1 tsp	cumin
2	garlic cloves
4	herring fillets
4 tsp/20 g	capers
	salt and pepper

For the garnish (optional):

| 3½ tbsp/50 g | pitted black olives |
| | mint leaves |

In Arabic, *renga* means herrings. This summer salad bears the name of our chef, who has adapted it. A chef at the president of the Tunisian Republic's residence, Fethi Tounsi is also head chef of the Abou Nawas El Mechtel restaurants in Tunis.

Consisting mainly of chiles and tomatoes, *renga* salad is a very refreshing appetizer. It may seem surprising to find herrings in Tunisian cuisine. However, in the past, the inhabitants of the Goulette quarter, a small seaside resort near Tunis, stored these fish during the month of Ramadan. Although this tradition has tended to disappear, *renga* are still popular for their oily, flavorsome flesh.

According to how long they are soaked or cured, you find semi-salted smoked herrings and mild smoked herrings. The latter constitutes the bulk of the smoked herring market. Herrings have many similarities with sardines and mackerel, which can be used instead of herrings. If this is the case, blanch them first when you prepare this appetizer.

The chef uses capers as the main flavoring. The caper shrub is a spiny small tree growing wild in Tunisia from which the flower buds are picked. The smaller the capers used, the more subtle the flavor and the stronger the aroma.

The presence of the green and red chiles makes this appetizer relatively spicy. In Tunisia, there are numerous varieties of chiles which can be bought fresh or dried. The spicy flavor of these vegetables comes from a substance called "capsine." Capsine makes you salivate and stimulates the digestion. If you prefer a milder flavor, remove the seeds and the whitish membranes inside.

Fethi Tounsi's *renga* salad is simple to make. In this recipe, herrings complement the Mediterranean flavors perfectly.

Wash the green and red chiles. Remove the stalks and seeds. Dice them. Wash the tomatoes, scoop them out and dice.

Brown the diced chiles and tomatoes in 7 tbsp/100 ml of the olive oil.

Season the mixture with salt and pepper. Add the coriander, cumin, and crushed garlic cloves. Simmer for 3 minutes.

Renga Salad

Prepare the herring rosettes by cutting the fillets. Slice them into rectangular shapes. Place the trimmings to one side.

Chop up the herring trimmings and add to the chile and tomato mixture.

Pour the mixture into a salad bowl. Add the capers and the rest of the olive oil. Arrange the renga salad on a plate with a herring rosette in the center. Garnish with the olives and mint leaves, if using.

Seafood

Preparation time: 20 minutes
Cooking time: 45 minutes
Difficulty: ★

Serves 4

1½ lbs/650 g	mussels
1½ lbs/650 g	small shrimp
1	lemon
7 oz/200 g	black olives
	salt

For the chermoula sauce:

1 clove	garlic
1 bunch	parsley
1 bunch	cilantro (coriander)
½	pickled lemon
7 tbsp/100 ml	argan oil
2	fresh lemons
1 pinch	paprika
1 pinch	Moroccan saffron powder for coloring
1 pinch	ground cumin
	salt and black pepper

Nearly all Moroccan salads are made with either cooked or raw vegetables: *chachouka* is made with broiled (roasted) paprika, *zaalouk* with pickled eggplant or pickled pumpkin, and there are also potato salads, beet salads, or carrot salads. For this dish the chef would like to introduce you to a very sophisticated cold entrée; mussels and shrimp cooked in a fine *chermoula* sauce.

In Morocco a great variety of shrimp is available in the markets, but the ones most used are the medium-sized common shrimp. Most of the crustaceans with which the entire country is supplied are delivered to the ports of Agadir and Safi.

The seafood cooked in *chermoula* sauce can then be prepared in many different ways: mixed with Chinese thread noodles, they make a splendid filling for a *dorade*, but also for the famous Moroccan *briouates*.

You can even use them for a savory bake: in a baking dish, alternate layers of *yufka* pastry with the seafood *chermoula* and bake in the oven until golden-brown.

For this recipe, Abdelmalek el-Meraoui has chosen blue mussels. These fat, fleshy mussels are the best currently available in Morocco.

Argan oil comes from the south-west of the country. This is produced from the fruit of the argan tree. The nuts in the fruit flesh are three times as thick as hazel nuts and very hard to crack. The oily "almonds" within are smaller than sunflower seeds.

Peel the garlic. Chop together with parsley, cilantro, and pickled lemon.

Steam the mussels or place them in boiling water until they open. Pour on cold water to stop the cooking process. Remove the mussel flesh. Poach the shrimp in cold water to which lemon slices have been added and then shell them.

Put a little argan oil into a pan. Add parsley, cilantro, garlic, half a pickled lemon, and fresh, pressed lemon juice and stir until a chermoula is created.

with Chermoula

Season the chermoula with salt and pepper. Add paprika, Moroccan saffron, and cumin. Cook for 10 minutes, stirring.

Add shrimp to the chermoula. Fry briefly, stirring.

Add mussels to the sauce and mix in. Cook for 15 minutes and then allow to cool. Serve the salad in little bowls, garnished with pieces of black olives. Serve cold.

Spinach Salad

Preparation time: 30 minutes
Cooking time: 25 minutes
Difficulty: ★

Serves 4

4½ lbs/2 kg	fresh leaf spinach
7 tbsp/100 ml	argan oil
1 bunch	parsley
1 bunch	cilantro (coriander)
1 clove	garlic
1 pinch	saffron threads

1 pinch	ground cumin
1 pinch	paprika
1	pickled lemon
9 oz/250 g	fresh tomatoes
7 oz/200 g	red olives
	salt and pepper

Salads with argan oil are popular all over Morocco. In the country, they are often made with the leaves of the mallow plant, which grows wild in hedgerows and along the roadside. In restaurants, on the other hand, cooks like to use fresh spinach which can easily be bought in the market. This spinach salad is an excellent winter appetizer; Abdelmalek el-Meraoui serves it cold.

Spinach, a vegetable that is widely available all over the world, is eaten rarely in Morocco. If it is served at table, it is usually in the form of a salad or a garnish, for example, for rice dishes. The chef here emphasizes the spinach flavor by serving it with *chermoula* sauce. The salad can be further varied by adding finely diced white fish (bream, rockling, John Dory, or similar), shrimp, or small pieces of beef or lamb.

Argan oil gives this salad its particular flavor, typical of the plain of Sous not far from Agadir in the south-west of Morocco. The oil is produced in the mountains of the Anti-atlas, by families still using traditional methods. It takes the women some 15 hours of hard work to produce four cups/one liter of oil.

First of all, the fruits of the argan tree are harvested and dried. They are then crushed to separate the kernel from the fruit flesh. Then comes the most laborious stage: each kernel is cracked open between two stones to free the little seeds within it. The seeds are toasted, giving them a nutty flavor, and then ground between millstones. The resulting paste is kneaded with lukewarm water and finally pressed. 220 lbs/100 kilograms of dried fruit produce an average of 13 cups/3.3 liters of oil.

Wash the spinach under running water and then chop coarsely with a knife. Steam for around 10 minutes and then allow to cool.

Use your hands to press out the slightly cooled spinach leaves over a bowl, removing as much moisture as possible.

For the chermoula, put argan oil, chopped parsley, and chopped cilantro, crushed garlic clove, salt, pepper, saffron, cumin, paprika, and small cubes of pickled lemon in a pan. Allow to simmer on the stove, stirring.

with Argan Oil

Pour boiling water over 7 oz/200 g tomatoes and skin, halve them and remove seeds. Cut the fruits into quarters and chop them. Also chop the olives.

When the chermoula is well simmered, add the chopped tomatoes. Allow to simmer for around 5 minutes, stirring.

Add the chopped spinach to the chermoula. Bring to the boil on a high heat, stirring. Finally, add the chopped olives. Garnish the salad with the remaining tomatoes and serve as cold as possible.

Salad of

Preparation time:	30 minutes
Cooking time:	45 minutes
Difficulty:	★

Serves 5

2¼ lbs/1kg	tomatoes
½ tsp/2 g	fine salt
1 pinch	Moroccan saffron
	powder for coloring
¼ tsp	saffron threads
5 or 6	cinnamon sticks

2¼ cups/500 g	sugar
7 tbsp/100 ml	orange flower water
⅘ cup/200 ml	peanut oil

The fields and greenhouses of Morocco produce fresh tomatoes all the year round. This amazing salad of fresh tomatoes is easy to prepare and it makes a welcome appetizer. Because of the sugar, the tomatoes turn an intensive red in color. In consistency and taste, they are reminiscent of a compote of dried apricots.

The Moroccans love to eat sweet tomatoes cold or warm as a salad, part of a selection of *kemias*. They are not only distinctive and decorative, but, with the sweet touch to their flavor, simply delicious. They can keep well for three to four days in the fridge. They are also used to garnish tagines of chicken with onions, cinnamon, and ginger.

It is necessary to know that the Moroccans have developed preserving food in the most diverse ways into an art. Red or black olives, lemons, little onions, small peppers, and bell peppers, but also beef (*le khlii*) are cooked and pickled using salt, but sweet sauces are preferred, using tomatoes, dried beans, plums, figs, pears, apples, and similar fruits. Particularly good for sweet preserves is a mixture of sugar and honey.

This appetizer will be most successful if you choose fine, round, deep-red tomatoes of medium size. The fruits should be quite firm and not too juicy, as liquid—in the form of orange flower water and oil—is added during the cooking. The tomatoes should still be fleshy after removing the skin and the seeds.

In Moroccan salads, you often find vegetables combined with orange flower water. Cucumbers, grated and preserved in white vinegar with sugar and orange flower water, are often included among *kemias*.

Remove stalk base from tomatoes. Cut a cross in the flesh at the other end. Blanch in boiling water. When the skin loosens, remove from the water with a slotted spatula.

Immediately place the tomatoes into a container with iced water. Carefully remove the skins with a knife.

Halve all the tomatoes vertically. Remove the seed cores, in one piece if possible.

Sweet Tomatoes

Place all the tomatoes onto a baking sheet, hollowed-out side up.

Distribute salt, Moroccan saffron, saffron threads, and cinnamon sticks over the tomatoes.

Sprinkle with sugar, then drizzle over orange flower water and peanut oil. Cover the tomatoes with a large piece of aluminum foil. Bake in the oven for 45 minutes at 300 °F/150 °C. Serve hot or cold.

Kemia Salad,

Preparation time:	20 minutes
Cooking time:	40 minutes
Difficulty:	★

Serves 4

For the eggplant purée:

2 each	eggplants, tomatoes
2 cloves	garlic
1	onion
	olive oil, paprika, cumin

For the seafood salad:

3½ oz/100 g each	calamaries (small squid), meagre (or other white fish)
1 each	onion, lemon
	saffron, olive oil, salt, pepper

For the tomato and pepper salad:

	oil for deep-frying
2 each	peppers, tomatoes

5 stems each	cilantro (coriander), parsley
2 cloves	garlic
	cumin, olive oil, white vinegar, salt, pepper

For the cucumber salad:

1 each	cucumber, tomato
4 stems	parsley

1	onion
	cumin, olive oil, white vinegar, salt, pepper

For the zucchini salad:

1 each	zucchini, onion
2 cloves	garlic
	saffron, paprika, olive oil

For the bell pepper salad:

2 each	yellow peppers, red peppers, onions
2 cloves	garlic
8 stems	parsley
2 tbsp/30 ml	olive oil
	salt and pepper

For the carrot salad:

2	carrots
4 stems	parsley
4 stems	cilantro (coriander)
1 tbsp/15 ml	white vinegar
	paprika, cumin, olive oil, salt, pepper

Most Moroccans would never receive guests without offering them a selection of fresh and colorful *kemias*, which are served on small plates. The host will arrange the little *kemia* dishes around the table and place the hot dish in the middle. While enjoying the main course, the guests can, just as they wish, help themselves to this or that salad with a small spoon. The indispensable flat, round Moroccan bread is served as an accompaniment.

This ensemble of different salads displays the variety of Moroccan garden vegetables, although it was not until the 16th century that the conquistadors brought tomatoes, chiles, bell peppers, and zucchini from America. The eggplant had long been enjoyed in India and Persia before it reached Morocco in the 15th century.

In our salad, the chef chops the raw calamaries before frying them in oil. They can, however, equally well be poached in boiling water with a dash of lemon juice. Immediately after cooking, immerse the calamaries in ice water to keep them tender. The meagre, a large fish with very delicate flesh, belongs to the croaker family. They are caught in the Atlantic and in the Mediterranean.

As is the case with the cuisine in every part of the Mediterranean, Moroccan cooking is also very strongly influenced by the flavor of olive oil, made from a great variety of types of olive and available in many different qualities. In the traditional oil press, the fruits are crushed by a thick millstone, usually powered by a donkey or a horse.

Eggplant purée: poach the eggplant with tomatoes, garlic, and onions. Purée in a blender until a paste is formed. Fry on a low heat in 2 tbsp of olive oil with a pinch of paprika and cumin.

Seafood salad: clean and gut the calamaries and cut into small pieces. Chop, then sprinkle the onion with salt, pepper, and saffron. Sweat in 1 tbsp of olive oil. Add calamaries and fry till golden-brown. Do the same with the meagre. Add the juice of half a lemon to both.

Tomato and bell pepper salad: fry peppers, skin them and chop. Scald the tomatoes, peel and chop. Finely chop cilantro, parsley, and garlic. Mix tomatoes, peppers, parsley, çilantro, salt, pepper, a pinch of cumin, garlic, olive oil, and vinegar.

Earth and Sea

Cucumber and zucchini salads: mix diced cucumber and tomato with chopped parsley, onion, cumin, salt, pepper, olive oil, and vinegar. Dice the zucchini. Fry the chopped onion and garlic in 2 tbsp of oil. Add diced zucchini, saffron, and paprika.

Bell pepper salad: chop 1 onion and 1 clove of garlic and fry in olive oil. Lightly fry the red bell pepper and sprinkle with half the chopped parsley. Prepare the yellow bell pepper salad in the same way.

Carrot salad: cut the carrots into sticks and poach in salt water. Drain. Mix the carrots with salt and pepper, 1 pinch paprika and cumin, chopped parsley and cilantro, vinegar and olive oil. Serve all salads fresh.

Cucumber Salad

Preparation time: 15 minutes
Difficulty: ★

Serves 4

1 ⅛ lbs/500 g   cucumbers
1 bunch   fresh thyme
½ cup/100 g   sugar
1 tbsp   orange flower water

For the garnish (optional):
½ bunch   fresh mint
                  ground cinnamon

This cucumber salad with fresh thyme makes an extraordinarily refreshing appetizer. The summery recipe is especially popular in Fez. The salad is easy to prepare and also very original, because the savory thyme blends harmoniously with the sugar and the delicate aroma of the orange flower water.

Like zucchini, cucumbers are the fruits of an all-the-year-round plant of the pumpkin family. They originated in the Himalayas and have pale green, crunchy and fresh fruit flesh. Cucumbers contain a great deal of water and only a few calories; on the other hand, they are a useful source of vitamin C.

The fleshy, firm, and cylindrical fruits almost always need to be peeled, as the peel is often bitter. The variety used by the chef comes from a greenhouse. Greenhouse cucumbers can vary in size, but always have a smooth skin and are available all the year round. Garden-grown cucumbers often have warty skins and thick seeds. It is strongly recommended that you try the cucumbers first to avoid the salad turning out bitter.

For his recipe, Abdellah Achiai has chosen exclusively regional ingredients. The thyme used is a variety that grows wild in the Atlas range. The Atlas Mountains with their breathtaking landscape are named after the famous Titan of Greek mythology. The thyme that grows there has a unique aroma. The Moroccans ascribe thousands of qualities to the herb, including the capacity to strengthen the organism. You can also make this appetizer using ordinary thyme.

This wonderfully light salad is particularly delicious when eaten in hot weather.

Peel the cucumbers with a vegetable peeler and keep 3 to garnish the plates.

Grate the cucumbers finely.

Cut the cucumbers reserved for garnish into thin slices.

with Atlas Thyme

Rub the thyme between your fingers over a plate.

To make the salad dressing, put thyme, sugar, and orange flower water into a bowl.

Add the grated cucumbers to the dressing and mix together. Arrange the salad in the middle of a plate and garnish with cucumber slices, mint, and cinnamon (if used).

R'jla Salad with

Preparation time: 20 minutes
Cooking time: 35 minutes
Difficulty: ★

Serves 6

6 bunches	r'jla
3 bunches	flat-leaf parsley
2 bunches	fresh cilantro (coriander)
²/₃ oz/20 g	garlic
²/₃ oz/20 g	sweet paprika
1 oz/25 g	cayenne pepper
	salt and pepper

2 tbsp/30 ml	olive oil
9 oz/250 g	pickled red olives
2	pickled lemons

Moroccan gourmets have a particular liking for salads made from fresh, colorful vegetables or herbs that are readily available in the country. M'hamed Chahid has put together a very original creation based on a wild plant named *r'jla* and flavored with cilantro, parsley, cayenne pepper, and paprika. He also uses the same recipe for mallow, a spring plant often found in cornfields and by the roadside. Out of season, it is best to use Swiss chard or spinach leaves. The salad will then look a little different, as the spinach will collapse after steaming, while mallow and *r'jla* keep their shape better in cooking.

R'jla is always used in salads and belongs to the purslane family. The leaves have a slightly sour, sharp taste. The stalk is fairly thick, striped pale green and red. The stalks bear bushes of thick, smooth, teardrop-shaped leaves, a little less than an inch long and about half an inch wide. *R'jla* grows in wheatfields and vineyards in the spring and summer and is not sold in the markets in Morocco. However, children can be seen offering it for sale to passing drivers along the roadside.

After cooking, the chef garnishes his dish with pickled red olives. The olive fruit, a virtual symbol of Mediterranean countries, goes through several stages of ripeness. At first they are green, they then become red. With increasing ripeness they become purple and finally black. After harvesting, the red olives are kept in a broth of salt, vinegar, and lemon juice for a long time to preserve them. They go wonderfully well with pickled·lemons.

Wash the r'jla stems under running water. Cut off smaller stalks with their leaves.

Place several stems onto a cutting board and chop coarsely with a knife.

Bring water to the boil in a couscous steamer. When it is bubbling, place the chopped r'jla in the strainer part of the steamer and place it above the boiling water. Cover. As soon as the steam rises, steam, covered, for 20 minutes.

Lemons and Olives

Chop parsley, cilantro, and garlic. Fry garlic lightly in a pan with a little oil. Season with salt and pepper. Add paprika and cayenne pepper.

Add parsley and cilantro to the pan. Cook for 5 minutes on high heat, stirring.

Finally, add the steamed r'jla to the mixture. Cook for another 5–6 minutes. Add the olives, pits removed. Allow to cool. Decorate with olives and strips of pickled lemon and then serve.

Hot Appetizers

Tapas

Preparation time: 30 minutes
Cooking time: 15 minutes
Difficulty: ★

Serves 4

For the fritura andaluza:
2 cups/500 g	chanquetes or fresh anchovies
⅞ cup/100 g	flour
2 cups/500 ml	olive oil
	lemon
	salt

For the gambas:
2 cups/500 g	gambas
1	dried chile pod

1 clove	garlic
7 tbsp/100 ml	olive oil
5	parsley stalks
1	small glass white wine
	salt

For the toast with chorizo:
4 slices	baguette
1 clove	garlic
1	ripe tomato
1	small, mild chorizo sausage
4 slices	pork loin, marinated a little native olive oil

The Spanish like to meet up with friends in a café before lunch for a drink and a few little appetizers, called tapas. José-Ignacio Herráiz recommends—in addition to the extremely popular tiny deep-fried anchovies and spicy pork loin with chorizo—tapas "the Granada way."

Chanquetes are tiny young fish that are not usually found anywhere outside Andalusia. You can also use anchovies, small sardines, red snapper, or slices of stockfish (dried salted cod). The chef uses extra-fine wheat meal for the coating, which adheres to the fish in a thin layer, retaining its moisture and aroma. If you only have ordinary household flour to hand, shake off any excess flour in a sieve. Deep-fry small portions of the fish in very hot oil.

Gambas de huelva are the most popular of all Spanish shrimp varieties. Many Spaniards even suck out the heads—although maybe not necessarily in a smart restaurant. To accommodate these connoisseurs, José-Ignacio Herráiz has come up with something really special: he fries the heads in oil, then pushes them through a sieve. He collects the aromatic juices and serves them with the gambas. Incidentally, scampi can also be used for this recipe.

Ready-marinated pork loin is available all over Spain, but it is not difficult to do it yourself at home. Bring the water to the boil with some thyme, oregano, garlic, cloves, and cinnamon, then leave to cool. Cut the pork loin into slices, marinate in the water together with some ground paprika, and leave for two days. If you do not have any chorizo, you can also use a mixture of ground meat, garlic, parsley, and ground paprika as a filling.

Salt the fish for the fritura andaluza. Sprinkle the flour on a plate and coat the fish in it, using your fingers to turn them. Place in a sieve and shake to remove the excess flour.

Heat the oil in a pot until very hot, then deep-fry the fish until light yellow. Remove with a spatula and place on paper towels. Arrange on a plate garnished with lemon slices.

Peel the gambas and cut them open to remove the innards. Crumble the dried chile. Slice the garlic, fry in the oil, then add the chile.

from Andalusia

Salt the gambas and fry in the spiced oil, making sure it is very hot. Sprinkle with chopped parsley and cook for 1 minute, then pour over the white wine and continue cooking.

Toast the bread slices. Peel the garlic. Halve the tomatoes. As soon as the bread is crunchy, rub the surface with the garlic and tomato. Remove the outer skin from the chorizo and dry fry the sausage; reduce the juices a little.

Beat the pork loins until flat, then fry on each side in a skillet with a little oil and garlic for 30 seconds. Place a little chorizo on each side, fold over the other end and secure with a cocktail stick. Repeat with the remaining slices of bread.

Preparation time:	1 hour
Cooking time:	30 minutes
Difficulty:	★

Serves 4

| 2 cups/500 ml | olive oil for deep frying |

For the palillos:

1 oz/25 g	smoked bacon
1	mushroom
½	onion
⅛ stick/15g	butter
1 tsp/5 g	flour
7 tbsp/100 ml	milk
2 tbsp/30 ml	brandy
4	dates
2 slices	bacon
	salt and pepper

For the bread and ham:

| 1 oz/25 g | ham |
| 2 oz/50 g | cepes |

2 oz/50 g	green beans
2 oz/50 g	green asparagus
1 tsp/5 g	baking soda
1 tsp/5 g	butter
2 tsp/10 g	Roquefort
4 slices	white bread
	a little olive oil

For the stuffed eggplants:

2 oz/50 g	mushrooms
1	onion
4 oz/100 g	ground meat
	a little olive oil
2 tbsp/30 ml	brandy
2 tbsp/30 ml	milk
2 tsp/10 g	flour
4	eggplants
3½ tbsp/50 g	grated cheese
	salt

For the Spanish sauce:

4 tbsp/60 ml	olive oil
½	diced onion
½	finely chopped carrot
1	leek
1	tomato
1 glass	port
1 tbsp/15 g	flour
2 tbsp	tomato concentrate
2 tsp	sugar
	salt and pepper

Tapas are the expression of the typically Spanish *joie de vivre*. This also applies to Alicante. Vast selections of tasty tapas are popular all over this holiday resort on the Costa Blanca. *Palillos*, literally "toothpicks," are ideal with an aperitif. These spicy filled dates, wrapped in bacon, are a salty-sweet culinary treat. The fruit is characteristic of the Alicante region. The first date palms were introduced by the Carthaginians. The Arabs continued with the cultivation, and built up their own date plantations. In the 12th century the town of Elche had a date grove that today boasts nearly 400,000 palms, making it one of the biggest in Europe.

Platos gratinados, or gratins are a specialty of Alicante. The eggplants in this recipe, filled with meat and mushrooms, seasoned with garlic, then baked with cheese, are a delicacy. To make the Spanish sauce, heat the olive oil in a pot and sauté first the diced onion, finely chopped carrot, leek, and tomato. Pour over half the port, and leave the vegetables to simmer for 5 minutes. Then season to taste with salt and pepper. Add the flour and tomato concentrate, pour over a little water, and simmer for an hour. In a second pot, caramelize the sugar until light brown, then remove from the heat and pour over the remaining port. Simmer gently for one minute and then add it to the sauce.

For the palillos, finely chop the smoked bacon, mushroom, and onion, and sauté in the butter. Season with salt. Add the flour and milk, and simmer gently for 2 minutes, then pour over the brandy and season with pepper.

Pit the dates, fill with the mixture, and wrap each one in a strip of bacon. Secure with a cocktail stick, and fry in olive oil.

For the bread and ham, chop the ham, cepes, beans, and asparagus very finely. Blanch the beans and asparagus separately in water with a little baking soda. Fry the ham in the butter, add the chopped vegetables, then season with salt and sauté for 3 minutes.

from Alicante

Add the Roquefort, and simmer for 1 further minute. Fry the bread slices in olive oil, and spread liberally with this mixture.

For the eggplant stuffing, finely chop the mushrooms and onion, and combine with the ground meat. Fry the mixture in olive oil, season with salt, and pour over the brandy. Add the milk and flour, and stir well.

Prepare the Spanish sauce as described opposite. Scoop out the eggplants and bake in the oven (350 °F/180 °C). Fill with this mixture, sprinkle over the cheese, and return to the oven for 5 minutes. Arrange the tapas on plates.

Tapas

Preparation time:	1 hour
Marinating time:	5 hours
Cooking time:	40 minutes
Difficulty:	★★★

Serves 4

For the marinade

4 tbsp/60 ml	olive oil
	vinegar
2 tsp	oregano
1 tsp	cumin
	salt and pepper

For the lamb tripe:

2	lamb's tripe
4	vine tendrils
	a little olive oil for frying
1 lb 2 oz/500 g	wholegrain bread

For the almagro eggplant:

²/₃ cup/150 ml	water
²/₃ cup/150 ml	sherry vinegar
1	red bell pepper
1	dried chile pod (guindilla)

2 tsp	cumin
2 tsp	ground paprika (pimiento)
2 tbsp	dried oregano
4	dwarf eggplants
4 tbsp/60 ml	olive oil
	salt and pepper

For the quail in honey sauce:

2	quail
5 tsp/25 g	honey
7 tbsp/100 ml	sherry vinegar
1 sprig	rosemary
2 tbsp/30 g each	bacon and Serrano ham
1	leek (white part)
	oil for deep frying
	salt and pepper

When enjoying the delights of the tapas from the region of La Mancha, it is easy to picture Don Quixote and his faithful Sancho Panza philosophizing over a pitcher of wine and delicacies such as these tapas.

The specialty of Cuerca, the chef's native village, is lamb's tripe. This rustic dish is very popular, and is usually eaten sprinkled with lemon juice. Marinating it for five hours makes the tripe wonderfully aromatic. Make sure the tripe you buy is clean and white, and do not forget to wrap it in vine tendrils.

Like Don Quixote and his manservant, we too are embarking on a culinary voyage to Almagro in the south of La Mancha. The town is as famous for its theatrical festival as it is for its eggplants. Every year, it produces some 5,000 tons of this fabulous vegetable.

The small oval *berenjenas de Almagro* (Almagro eggplants) are prized all over the Iberian peninsula. They are harvested from July to September, after which they are cooked and then preserved. This form of preparation is also recommended by Alberto Herráiz. The reputation of *orza*, eggplant cooked traditionally in a small ceramic pot, extends far beyond La Mancha. They are available as preserves in good delicatessens.

Quail are also an essential part of typical Catalan tapas. They are served with a sweet sauce that typifies the finesse and wealth of the region's cuisine.

For the tripe, stir together 4 tbsp of olive oil, vinegar, oregano, and cumin for the marinade. Season with salt and pepper. Marinate the tripe in this mixture for five hours. Then wrap the tripe in vine tendrils and boil in water for about 15 minutes.

Cut the cooked tripe into slices and fry in the remainder of the oil. Meanwhile, toast the bread in the oven.

For the eggplants, mix together the water and sherry vinegar. Cut the bell pepper into strips and add with the chile and 1 tsp each of cumin, ground paprika, and oregano. Bring to the boil and add the eggplants. Cook for 10–15 minutes.

"Don Quixote"

Skewer the eggplants onto little sticks. Garnish with strips of bell pepper. Make a sauce of olive oil, the remaining cumin, ground paprika, and oregano. Season with salt and pepper.

Joint the quail and remove the legs; season with salt and pepper. For the sauce, put the honey, vinegar, and rosemary in a pot and boil briefly; season with salt.

Wrap the quail drumsticks in bacon and ham. Bake in the oven (400 °F/200 °C) for 10–12 minutes. For the garnish, cut the leek into fine strips and deep-fry. Arrange the tapas on plates and serve.

Asparagus from

Preparation time:	30 minutes
Cooking time:	25 minutes
Difficulty:	★

Serves 4

1 lb 2 oz/500 g	fresh green asparagus
1 lb 2 oz/500 g	fresh white asparagus
4	fresh eggs

For the sauce:

2	eggs
¼ stick/30 g	butter
1 tbsp/15 ml	sherry vinegar
pinch	ground paprika
	salt and pepper

Fresh asparagus is available everywhere in Madrid from April to September. It is usually from Aranjuez, the old royal residence on the banks of the Tagus between Madrid and Toledo. Both green and white asparagus thrives in the fertile soils of the area.

This delicate vegetable was popular with the Greeks and Egyptians thousands of years ago. Clever Roman chefs found ways and means to grow the tender stalks, but after the fall of Rome it sank into oblivion until Louis XIV—whose favorite vegetable it was—started a veritable boom in the 17th century. He demanded to have the tender stems all year round, and so his gardener, La Quintinie, invented the greenhouse cultivation of this noble vegetable. When Louis's grandson, Bourbon King Philip V, ascended to the Spanish throne in 1700 he introduced asparagus to the Iberian Peninsula.

Formerly, the preference in Madrid was for a simple recipe, in which the eggs were cooked together with the asparagus. Creative chefs developed this further into a dish that was served with a sauce made of butter and eggs. Green asparagus must be plunged into iced water after cooking to help it retain its bright green color. It looks very pretty if the stalks are "tied" into small bundles with a strip of leek or chive.

The eggs are soft-boiled in their shells and plunged into iced water so that the white becomes firm but the yellow stays soft, oozing over the asparagus when the egg is cut. The sauce must be beaten very quickly with a balloon whisk over a low heat, otherwise the eggs will curdle and not blend with the butter. Whisk the ingredients over hot water until you have a smooth and velvety sauce that adheres to the back of the spoon.

Peel the green and white asparagus with a vegetable peeler. Only the tips and about 2 in/5 cm of the stalks are used for this recipe.

Blanch the green asparagus in boiling water for 2 minutes, and the white for about 8 minutes. As soon as it is cooked, plunge it into a bowl of iced water.

Slide the eggs into boiling water and boil for 3–4 minutes, then drop them in a bowl of iced water.

Aranjuez with Eggs

To make the sauce, place a bowl in a pot of hot water and beat the eggs. Add the butter, vinegar, ground paprika, salt, and pepper, then whisk well.

Whisk the sauce over hot water for about 10 minutes until it is smooth, bright orange-yellow in color, and has increased considerably in volume.

Bundle together the asparagus stalks and tie them together using, for example, strips of leek. Arrange on plates. Carefully peel the eggs, cut them in half, and place them next to the asparagus. Cover with the egg yolk and the sauce.

Sardine

Preparation time:	30 minutes		2 cups/500 ml	olive oil
Marinating:	half a day		3	tomatoes
Cooking time:	10 minutes		dash	sherry vinegar
Difficulty:	★		2 tbsp	flat-leaf parsley
				salt and pepper

Serves 4

24	large sardines
sprigs	fresh thyme
sprigs	fresh rosemary
	fresh bay leaves
pinch	ground nutmeg

Centuries ago, people who liked eating grilled food had the brilliant idea to slide it onto small sticks, or skewers. And so *espetones* were born. Even today, fishermen and other coastal dwellers skewer five or six sardines on a piece of reed, stick it in the sand, and cook the fish over an open wood fire. Fresh from the skewer, they are the greatest delicacy. Of course, specialists position their skewers according to the wind so that the aroma of the fish is not affected by the smoke.

Because not all of us have a beach close by, our chef thought of something else. He threads five sardines onto thin wooden skewers and bakes them in the oven. Professional chefs usually use a so-called salamander, but most of us do not have one of these appliances, with their impressive top heat, in our kitchen.

Sardines from the Atlantic or Mediterranean are very popular on the Iberian Peninsula. They got their name from the island of Sardinia, where they were already a popular delicacy in Roman antiquity. Today, they are found in vast shoals all over the Mediterranean. Spanish gourmets like to eat them grilled or broiled, usually with a little olive oil and some aromatic herbs.

If the sardines are on the big side, they should be cleaned and boned. To do so, cut into the belly with scissors or a small sharp knife. Very small sardines are best left whole.

Cut off the tip of the tail from each sardine and remove the scales. Cut into the belly with scissors, remove the insides, and wash.

Place the sardines in an ovenproof dish and season with salt and pepper. Add the thyme, rosemary, bay leaves, and nutmeg, plus 1 cup/250 ml of olive oil, then marinate for half a day.

Slide five of the marinated sardines onto a skewer and put them back in the same dish to broil in the oven for 10 minutes, turning them once.

Skewers

Pour boiling water over the tomatoes and plunge them into cold water. Remove the skins, cut the tomatoes into quarters, and remove the seeds. Chop into small pieces.

Pour a little vinegar over the juices in the ovenproof dish. Whisk together the remaining olive oil, salt, and pepper with a fork.

Add the chopped tomatoes and chopped parsley to this sauce. Arrange the sardine skewers on plates, and pour over the sauce. Garnish with rosemary, thyme, and bay leaves.

Vegetable Stew

Preparation time:	35 minutes
Cooking time:	25 minutes
Difficulty:	★

Serves 4

10 oz/250 g	green beans
1	carrot
1	mangold leaf
10 oz/250 g	cauliflower
10 oz/250 g	green asparagus
1 tsp	baking soda

2	artichokes
1 clove	garlic
4 tbsp/60 ml	olive oil
2 slices	Iberian ham (Pata negra)
	coarse sea salt

For the lechada:

1 tbsp/15 g	flour
1 tbsp/15 ml	olive oil
1	lemon, squeezed
	salt

This vegetable stew with ham is served warm, and is a real spring meal. A specialty from Navarre, it is greatly prized all over Spain and part of the culinary heritage of the Iberian Peninsula. It is easy to prepare and makes the most of the vegetables grown around Navarre. The so-called Ribera, which simply means "valley," is famous for its vegetables. Vegetables are the main ingredient in the native cuisine, which is famous far and wide for its finesse.

Thanks to a clever irrigation system, which dates back to the times when Arabs ruled over southern Spain, vegetables thrive particularly well in this region—including, and in particular, green beans and mangold. The vegetables for this *menestra* (stew) are blanched briefly in salted water so they stay crisp. Allow 10 minutes for the beans, 12 for the white of the mangold leaves and the carrots, and 8 minutes for the cauliflower and asparagus.

The secret to this extremely healthy dish is the green asparagus. It is the pride of the vegetable farmers of Navarre, who still use the traditions of their ancestors to grow it. According to the chef, green asparagus is far superior to white. Make sure the tips are still firmly closed. Wrapped in a damp cloth in the refrigerator, asparagus will keep for three to four days. Rinse briefly under running water before cooking. Peel the stalks from the tip down, and cut off the woody stalk.

The artichokes are cooked in a *lechada*—a combination of flour, lemon juice, olive oil, and salt, which prevents them from turning black. Drain the artichokes when cooked and add them to the stew.

Trim the beans, carrot, mangold, cauliflower, and asparagus and—with the exception of the cauliflower—cut into small pieces. Blanch each type of vegetable separately in salted water. Add the baking soda to the water for the asparagus.

Cut off the leaves of the artichokes until only the hearts are left, and cut them in half. In a pot, heat 1¹/₂ cups/350 ml water with the flour, olive oil, lemon juice, and salt. Cook the artichoke hearts in the lechada for 20 minutes.

Peel the garlic and chop very finely. Sauté in olive oil.

with Ham

Drain the vegetables and add to the garlic. Sauté for 2 minutes.

Sieve the lechada, pour over the vegetables, and simmer for 2 minutes.

Slice the ham very thinly and sauté in a little olive oil. Arrange the vegetables on plates. Sprinkle with the ham strips and pour a little of the sauce around them.

Patatas

Preparation time:	25 minutes
Cooking time:	50 minutes
Difficulty:	★

Serves 4

6 medium	potatoes
1¼ cups /150 g	flour
2	eggs
2 cloves	garlic
1	onion
4 cups/1 l	chicken stock (instant)
10	parsley stalks
2–3	chives
	salt and pepper

Potatoes used to be on the menu every day in Spain, and so chefs devised a number of extravagant dishes for variety. One was *Patatas a la importancia*: slices of potato coated in egg and flour, which are first fried and then cooked in a tasty stock. This dish is on the menu in countless restaurants today. Potatoes originally came from Peru. The Incas cultivated them almost 3,000 years ago. Known to them as *papas*, the tuber came to Galicia with the returning Spanish conquerors in about 1570. However, to begin with it was not well received in Spain, the South of France, or Italy. For a long time it was used as animal fodder. But finally, in the 19th century, it was accepted in the kitchen.

Make sure that the potatoes are a firm-cooking variety, so they do not disintegrate in the stock. To coat them, Julio Reoyo cuts them into slices, seasons them with salt and pepper, then coats both sides in flour on a plate. Wait a moment until moisture starts to appear on the surface, then coat them in flour again so it adheres better while they are frying. Gently shake the potato slices to remove any excess flour.

The potato slices must not touch each other while they are frying. Each portion will take about 5 minutes to cook. Use a spatula to remove the potatoes from the hot oil, then continue cooking them in a clear chicken stock, which you can enhance with white wine and saffron threads. These delicious *patatas a la importancia* are ideal either as an appetizer or an entrée, maybe as a side dish with salmon slices or perhaps roast meat.

Peel the potatoes and cut into ⅕ in/5 mm slices. Wash and pat dry with paper towels.

Sprinkle the flour on a plate. Season the potato slices with salt and pepper, and coat well with the flour.

Beat the eggs and dip the potato slices in the eggs.

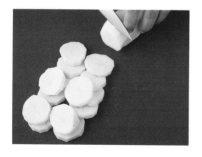

a la Importancia

Deep-fry the potatoes in portions in very hot oil for 5 minutes. Chop the garlic and onion, and sauté in hot oil for 5 minutes. Add 1 tbsp/15 g of flour and stir well. Pour over the stock, then bring to the boil.

Shake any excess off the potato slices, then place the slices in the stock.

Chop the parsley and chives, then add to the potatoes. Press the potatoes down in the stock with the back of the spatula. Simmer gently for 30 minutes.

Pisto

Preparation time:	35 minutes
Cooking time:	35 minutes
Difficulty:	★

Serves 4

2	onions
2	green bell peppers
12 oz/300 g	tomatoes
12 oz/300 g	zucchini

1 cup/250 ml	olive oil
8	eggs
4 slices	white bread
	salt
	white pepper (optional)

For the garnish (optional):

| 1 | dried red chile |
| strips | zucchini skin |

The Basque country on the Atlantic coast has developed an extensive repertoire of tasty dishes. The Basques are proud of their heritage, and of their reputation as connoisseurs. From simple *pintxo* and other tapas served at the bar and eaten "in the hand," to extremely lavish traditional dishes, Basque cuisine always reveals its wholly independent character.

Pisto a la bilbaina is a popular warm appetizer. As the name suggests, the dish—which is similar to the Tunisian *chakchouka*—is typical of the province of Bilbao. It is easy to make, and is a refreshing appetizer in summer when bell peppers, zucchini, and tomatoes are abundant on the markets. Made with generous quantities of olive oil, it is combined with beaten eggs at the end. *Pisto* is a light dish, easily digestible thanks to the zucchini, with plenty of liquid, and low in calories. The zucchini should be small

and a standard dark green in color. This vegetable from the New World is now a firm fixture in Mediterranean cuisine.

For almost two centuries tomatoes were believed to be poisonous, but they were eventually accepted and are now an essential part of Mediterranean cuisine. Almost 4 million tons/3.6 million metric tonnes of the fruit are produced on the Iberian Peninsula every year. Tomatoes should be firm and fleshy with a fine aroma. Our chef uses green bell peppers for this dish, which have the added advantage of keeping well. The aroma is slightly drier and stronger than that of red bell peppers, and therefore it goes extremely well with this dish.

Bread sautéed in olive oil is an excellent accompaniment to *pisto a la bilbaina*, which is excellent as an appetizer or entrée.

Peel the onions. Wash the bell peppers, tomatoes, and zucchini. Peel a few strips of skin off one of the zucchini using a vegetable peeler, and set aside. Roughly chop the vegetables.

Heat 7 tbsp/100 ml of olive oil, and sauté the bell pepper and onions. Cover and simmer for about 10 minutes, stirring occasionally with a wooden spoon.

Add the chopped tomatoes and zucchini, season well with salt and pepper, and stir. Continue to simmer for 15 minutes.

a la Bilbaina

Beat the eggs in a bowl.

Spoon the vegetables over the beaten egg with a skimmer. Sauté the bread in 7 tbsp/100 ml olive oil, then set aside.

Heat the remainder of the olive oil in a large pot until very hot, then pour in the egg and vegetable mixture. Stir with a wooden spatula until it sets. Arrange the pisto on plates with the bread. Garnish with strips of chile and zucchini peel.

Vegetable and

Preparation time:	30 minutes
Cooking time:	40 minutes
Difficulty:	★

Serves 6

2¼ lb/1 kg	potatoes
8 oz/200 g	onions
2 small	zucchini
4 tbsp/60 ml	olive oil
10	eggs
1 cup/200 g	cooked shrimp
1 tsp	salt
½ tsp	pepper

All those whose eyes sparkle at the mention of the word "picnic," but have had more than their fair share of potato chips and sandwiches, will love this appetizing tortilla, which is eaten warm and made to an old Seville family recipe. A tortilla is a kind of omelet, full to bursting with eggs, potatoes, and onions, as well as other ingredients that are left to the chef's imagination.

In Spanish households, the eggs for the tortilla are whipped up on a Saturday night. The tortilla is then baked at the last minute on Sunday, and taken to the beach. The potatoes are peeled, and then diced immediately without patting them dry. Use large potatoes for a truly authentic Spanish touch. The onions and potatoes are cooked in a covered skillet together, making sure they don't turn brown.

Zucchini do not take long to cook if they are to retain some crunch. Large or small, they contain plenty of water,

so they are cooked uncovered to enable some of the liquid to evaporate. Instead of zucchini you could also use eggplant, mushrooms, or tomatoes. For a particularly aromatic tortilla, save the vegetable juices and drizzle them over the tortilla when you turn it. Whatever your preference, one thing always remains the same: the eggs are beaten with a fork.

The olive oil should be very hot, but the tortilla must not burn. Shake the skillet a little to blend the contents well. When you want to turn the tortilla over, place a large plate face down on top of the skillet, turn everything upside down so the tortilla ends up on the plate, then slide the tortilla back into the skillet. As it sets, the tortilla should double in volume.

Peel the potatoes and onions. Cut the onions and zucchini into three lengthwise and, holding them together with your fingers, cut them crosswise into ¾ in/2 cm cubes.

Fry the potatoes in 1 tbsp of hot olive oil. Add the onions and combine well. Cover and simmer gently for 15 minutes. Add the zucchini and cook uncovered for a further 15 minutes. Drain the vegetables in a sieve.

Put the cooked vegetables in a bowl and set aside. Crack the eggs into a large bowl and, using a fork, whisk them gently, then more briskly for 10 minutes.

Shrimp Tortilla

Peel and halve the shrimp. Combine with the vegetables and add everything to the beaten egg. Season with salt and pepper, and stir well.

Heat the remainder of the olive oil in a large, deep skillet, and add the mixture at once. Smooth the surface and fry uncovered over a high heat for 5 minutes.

When the tortilla begins to set, put a plate on top and remove from the heat. Turn the tortilla over, then put the skillet back on the heat and slide the tortilla back into the skillet. Cook over a low heat for a further 5 minutes. Serve warm.

Cod Purée with

Preparation time:	40 minutes
Fish soaking time:	24 hours
Cooking time:	30 minutes
Difficulty:	★

Serves 4

10 oz/300 g	dried stockfish
10 oz/300 g	fresh cod
2 cups/500 ml	milk
	zest of 1 orange, unwaxed
½–1 oz/10 g	fresh root ginger (optional)
3 tbsp	olive oil
4 cloves	garlic

	salt
	pepper
½	baguette

For the garlic cream:

½ bulb	garlic
1 cup/250 ml	milk
1 cup/250 ml	light cream
	salt
	pepper

For the garnish:

2 oz/50 g	black truffle
	ground paprika (optional)

In Nîmes, cod purée is just as important as the Roman amphitheatres, the ancient Maison Carée, or public holidays. This cold-water fish is known as *morue* when it is salted or dried. Fresh, it is called *cabillaud*.

For this recipe it is important to soak the fish thoroughly, to remove as much of the salt as possible. The water should be changed several times. Before using the fish in the recipe, remove the skin and bones. When cooked in milk the fish takes on a pale color.

Christian Étienne uses garlic in all his recipes, and this one is no exception. Garlic originated in Central Asia and is a member of the lily family.

To lessen the intensity of the flavor, the garlic is blanched several times in boiling milk and cold water. Only then should it be added to the sauce.

The orange zest gives a hint of this dish's Provençal origins. The same applies to the ginger, but this ingredient is optional.

The cod purée, or *brandade* as it is known in France, is served hot. The Vaucluse truffle garnish is an elegant touch. Truffles are available in widely varying sizes (you may have to go to a specialty shop for them). They are mostly black or dark brown, but some are gray, or even white. If you want to serve a more rustic dish, dispense with the truffle and use roughly chopped black olives instead. Finish off with a garnish of thyme.

Chop the fresh cod and well-soaked stockfish into large chunks. In a saucepan, bring the milk to the boil; add the orange zest, grated root ginger (if using), and fish. Poach the fish in the milk for around 3–4 minutes.

Drain the fish and transfer it to a heavy-based pan. Mash it with a spatula until it forms a purée.

Heat the pan on low heat. Add a thin trickle of olive oil, beating the fish purée hard with a wooden spoon. Continue heating for 15 minutes, until it forms a smooth mixture.

Black Truffle Slivers

Peel the 4 garlic cloves and crush them with the back of a fork. Fold the garlic into the cod pureé. Season the purée to taste with salt and pepper, but be sparing with the salt. Keep the purée warm.

Garlic cream: Bring the milk to the boil, blanch 3 peeled garlic cloves in the milk, then plunge them into cold water. Repeat 3 times. Stir the blanched garlic into the cream in a saucepan, then heat gently to the boil, and simmer for 20 minutes. Purée in a blender, and season to taste.

Toast slices of baguette in the oven for 3 minutes. Rub the toasted bread with a piece of garlic. Arrange 3 tbsp cod purée in the center of the plate and top with slivers of truffle. Pour a little garlic cream around the fish, sprinkle with ground paprika, and serve with the toast.

Artichoke Hearts

Preparation time: 40 minutes
Cooking time: 25 minutes
Difficulty: ★★

Serves 4

16	globe artichokes
1	lemon

For the vegetable accompaniment:

2	carrots
2	onions
2 cloves	garlic
1 tbsp	olive oil
1 cup/250 ml	dry white wine
1	chicken bouillon cube

For the bouquet garni:

1	bay leaf
2 sprigs each	fresh thyme, parsley
	salt, pepper

For the squid:

1¼ lb/600 g	baby squid (or very small cuttlefish)
⅛ stick/10 g	butter
1 tbsp	olive oil

For the parsley butter:

¼ stick/20 g	butter
1 bunch	fresh parsley
2 cloves	garlic
1 tsp	Pernod (or other aniseed drink)
	salt, pepper

For the garnish:

	fresh chervil

It was Catherine de Médicis, a definite gourmet, who introduced globe artichokes to France. Without them, our chef, Alain Carro, would not have been able to create this dish. In the process he was inspired by the artichoke creations of famous chef Roger Vergé, who lives in Mougins, near Cannes. In this area, globe artichokes are also referred to as "spiny," and the variety is known as *poivrades*. They are cultivated in the Var region, around Hyères, not far from our chef's restaurant.

A good artichoke must feel quite heavy and firm, with hard, tight-packed leaves. They can be stored in your refrigerator's salad compartment for a few days. Note that as soon as they are cooked, they oxidize very quickly, so they are best served immediately after cooking. The purple, Provençal globe artichokes in our recipe have elongated heads, and are green, with purple shading in places.

This vegetable from the thistle family is rich in iron, and is a diuretic.

When prepared, the artichokes in this dish are reminiscent of mushrooms. In rural Provençal cuisine, artichokes are sometimes prepared in the same way as *barigoules*, which belong to the milk-cap family of mushrooms—they are cut off just below the head, drizzled with oil, and broiled.

Cuttlefish is very similar to squid. In southern France, small cuttlefish are called *pistes* or *supions*. This dish incorporates another Mediterranean specialty—*pastis*. In our recipe the skillet is deglazed with Pernod. If you can't obtain baby squid or very small cuttlefish, use the top part of an ordinary squid instead. In this dish Alain Carro succeeds perfectly in combining the aniseed flavor of the Pernod with the flavor of the artichokes.

Pull or cut the leaves off the artichokes. Use only the heart and the upper part of the stalk. Put the artichokes into water acidulated with lemon, so that they don't discolor.

Heat the butter and olive oil in a skillet. Sauté the cleaned and prepared baby squid (or small cuttlefish) for 1–2 minutes, until they are firm. All the liquid from them must evaporate. Drain the squid and put them aside.

Peel the carrots, then score grooves in them lengthwise. Slice them thinly. Peel and thinly slice the onions. Peel and slice the garlic. Heat the olive oil in a skillet. Sauté the vegetables and the bouquet garni herbs for a few minutes in the hot oil. Season with salt and pepper.

with Squid

Drain the artichokes and add them to the pan with the vegetables. Sauté until the vegetables are golden brown. Sweat the vegetables on low heat for 15 minutes.

Deglaze the skillet with the white wine, and braise the vegetables for 5 minutes. Add the bouillon cube and stir until it has dissolved.

Mix the butter with the chopped parsley and finely chopped garlic, then add the Pernod. Add this parsley butter to the squid. Deglaze the pan with the Pernod. Season the squid to taste with salt and pepper, arrange on a plate, and garnish with a little chervil.

Lentils and

Preparation time: 35 minutes
Cooking time: 35 minutes
Difficulty: ★

Serves 4

2	oranges
2	grapefruits
½	lemon
¾ cup/150 g	Puy or green lentils
1 clove	garlic, unpeeled and sliced in half
1 sprig	fresh thyme
1	bay leaf
⅓ cup + 1½ tbsp/ 100 ml	olive oil

	salt
1	shallot
1 bunch	fresh chives
12	scallops
6 slices	Parma ham
1 bunch	wild arugula

For the vinaigrette:

2 tbsp	olive oil
1	grapefruit segment lentil liquor

For the garnish:

8	orange segments
4	grapefruit segments fresh chives

Lentils with scallops and citrus fruit is a fabulous combination! Joël Garault lightens this wintry appetizer with citrus fruit from the area around Menton.

As soon as the lentils start to cook, the grapefruit and lemon give off their slightly acidic aroma. Although citrus fruit are available throughout the year, their main season is November to March. Oranges are especially prized for their high vitamin C and vitamin A content. Depending on the variety, they can be sweet or sour, and more or less perfumed. Look for firm fruit with a smooth skin.

The grapefruit are also rich in these vitamins. Grapefruit vary in sweetness, depending on the color, the palest being the sharpest. If you prefer, the grapefruit can be omitted from this recipe. Lemons are also very rich in vitamin C. Look for very firm, unblemished fruit.

Our chef recommends buying little, green Puy lentils, which is a protected brand name. They grow on the volcanic soil of the Auvergne and benefit from the microclimate there. The dried lentils are not floury. They have a soft skin and delicate flavor. You should only add salt to lentils halfway through the cooking time, to prevent them turning hard.

When you buy the scallops, they should be closed. If they don't close when touched, they are not safe to eat. You can also prepare this appetizer using squid. Because the Parma ham is very salty, season the dish with salt sparingly.

Juice 1 orange, 1 grapefruit, and ½ lemon. Put the lentils into a saucepan. Add the citrus juice, garlic, thyme, and bay leaf. Pour 1¾ cups/450 ml water into the pan with 1 tbsp olive oil. Bring to the boil and simmer for 30 minutes. Season to taste with salt after 15 minutes.

Drain the lentils, reserving the liquor. Fold the chopped shallot and finely chopped chives into the lentils. Open the scallops. Run a finger under the black beard and remove the meat from the shell. Wash the scallops and drain them.

Peel the remaining orange and grapefruit. Cut out 8 orange segments and 4 grapefruit segments for the garnish. Reserve an additional grapefruit segment for the vinaigrette.

Scallops

Juice what is left of the orange and grapefruit. Put 1 tbsp lentil liquor and 1 grapefruit segment in a bowl. Add 2 tbsp olive oil, and purée with a hand blender to form a dressing. Spoon 4 tbsp of this vinaigrette over the lentils.

Cut the Parma ham in half lengthwise and wrap a strip around each scallop. Secure the ham with a toothpick.

Sauté the scallops in olive oil for 1 minute on each side. Make a pile of lentils in the center of the plate. Garnish with orange, grapefruit, and chives. Cut each scallop into 2 slices, and arrange the slices around the lentils. Add arugula leaves with a little dressing.

Braised Snails

Preparation time: 20 minutes
Cooking time: 1 hour 10 minutes
Difficulty: ★

Serves 4

4 dozen	snails
14 oz/400 g	squid
1 tbsp	olive oil
	rock salt
2	tomatoes
1 pinch	saffron
	table salt
	pepper

For the sofregit sauce:

1	onion
1 clove	garlic
5 oz/150 g	ground pork or beef
1 tbsp	olive oil

For the bouquet garni:

	fresh thyme
	bay leaf
	fresh rosemary

In this recipe Jean Plouzennec introduces you to a typical Catalan dish. His mixture of flavors from field and sea is a clear indication that he's at home in the French department of Pyrénées-Orientales. This is also evident from the fact that he has prepared *sofregit*, a pillar of Catalan cuisine. This is a kind of basic sauce, with the ingredients varying according to personal taste. Over the border in Spain, it is known as *el sofrito*. Spain is able to offer another strange ingredient from the sea, the sea cucumber.

Catalonia is often very humid, and this is why the *petit gris* snails, or *escargots*, which are plentiful, are used in this dish. Gathering snails is carefully regulated in France. They taste best in winter, after they have fasted, because the meat is more tender and the flavor less acidic.

We recommend you to use prepared snails. If you buy fresh ones, it is very important that you follow the correct proce-

dure before you include them in this recipe. We have not given the instructions for that here; you will need to consult other sources.

The marine element comes from the white flesh of the squid. If you are using whole squid, slice them in half or into rings. It is possible to buy deep-frozen squid, but it is best to use fresh, as the texture is better. If you are put off by the appearance of squid, ask your fishmonger to prepare them for you. The best season to eat squid is in the early fall.

Try to obtain prepared snails for this recipe.

Prepare the squid by removing the head, the cartilage (quill), and ink sac. Peel the skin, rinse the squid, then squeeze gently to drain out some of the liquid. If too big, cut in half. Cut the squid into rings.

To make the sofregit, peel and chop the onion and garlic. Heat the olive oil in a large saucepan, and fry the onion and garlic. Add the ground beef or pork, and bouquet garni herbs, and fry them for 5 minutes. Remove the bouquet garni.

and Squid

Heat 1 tbsp olive oil in a skillet until very hot. Fry the squid until golden. Add a pinch of rock salt. Add the squid to the sofregit sauce and simmer for 2 minutes.

Put the tomatoes into a bowl. Pour over boiling water and remove them after a few minutes. Skin and deseed the tomatoes, dice finely and add to the squid mixture. Sprinkle the saffron over the squid. Season with salt and pepper, and simmer for 30 minutes on low heat.

Add the snails, cover the pan, and simmer the snails for another 30 minutes. Serve individual portions in mini casserole dishes.

Oyster Fritters

Preparation time:	30 minutes		1 generous cup/	
Chilling time:	1 hour		250 ml	light cream
Cooking time:	20 minutes			salt, pepper
Difficulty:	★		4 cups/1 l	oil for frying

Serves 4

For the batter:

2 dozen	Bouzigues or other		2 scant cups/200 g	flour
	large oysters		3	eggs,
8 oz/250 g	spinach			separated
1 tbsp	olive oil		½ cup/120 ml	beer
1	shallot		1 cup/250 ml	milk
⅓ cup + 1½ tbsp/				salt
100 ml	Noilly Prat			

For the garnish:

fresh chives

Oysters in batter make an original appetizer. These shell-fish are usually eaten raw, or are enjoyed simply with lemon juice, or a vinegar and onion dressing.

Bouzigues oysters are specially farmed in southern France, more specifically in the Thau Basin. They take their name from a little village in Hérault which was known for its oysters even before the Roman invasion. Contrary to the widely prevailing opinion that oysters should only be eaten when there is an "r" in the month, the oyster farmers in the Thau Basin harvest the oysters all year round. Oysters are extremely sensitive. They must be stored in a dark, cool, well-ventilated place at a temperature between 41 and 59 degrees Fahrenheit/5 and 15 degrees Celsius. If you can't find large oysters, you could always use a smaller variety, such as Marennes, which contain less iodine.

After poaching, let the oysters rest in their shells, so that the juices are drawn out. They should be fried at the last minute.

When making the batter, ensure that you don't add too much egg white, otherwise the batter, when cooked, will not hold its shape.

The blanched spinach is wrapped around the oysters in order to protect them during cooking. It also imparts a delicate flavor to the batter. From time to time the chef uses sorrel too.

Because oysters contain iodine, the shallot dressing needs little salt. Noilly Prat is a sun-ripened vermouth with a very intensive flavor. It is typical of the area. You can substitute chardonnay, or even champagne.

Put the oysters in a pan with just enough water to cover them. Bring to the boil and simmer for 8 minutes. Strain, reserving a little of the cooking liquor. Put the oysters into cold water to open, and discard any that do not open. Detach the meat from the shell, then put it back in the shell.

Batter: Beat together the flour, egg yolks, and salt. Beat in the beer and milk. In a separate bowl, beat the egg whites with a pinch of salt until stiff. Carefully fold the egg whites into the batter until a smooth, creamy mixture forms. Leave to rest for an hour in the refrigerator.

Pick over the spinach, removing the stalks. Bring a pan of salted water to the boil and blanch the spinach in it for 1 minute. Refresh the spinach in cold water, then wrap each oyster in a spinach leaf.

with Noilly Prat

Using a fork, dip the oysters in the batter until they are well coated.

Heat 1 tbsp olive oil in a skillet and sweat the chopped shallot for 3 minutes until softened. Add the Noilly Prat and simmer for 5 minutes. Add a little of the reserved oyster liquor and the cream, and simmer for 2 minutes. Season to taste. Blend, strain through a sieve, and keep warm.

Heat the oil in a deep pan until very hot. Fry the oysters for 2 minutes, then drain on kitchen paper. Place a spinach leaf in each oyster shell. Put an oyster fritter on top. Pour some of the sauce into a small bowl for dipping, garnish with chives, and serve with the oyster fritters.

Bouzigues Oysters

Preparation time:	30 minutes
Cooking time:	20 minutes
Difficulty:	★ ★

Serves 4

16	Bouzigues or other large oysters
8 oz/250 g	Swiss chard leaves
½ stick/60 g	butter
1 clove	garlic

3½ tbsp/50 g	poutargue (salted, pressed and flattened mullet roe; optional)
6½ tbsp/100 g	whipping cream
	salt
	freshly ground pepper
	large quantity of rock salt

Nowadays it is possible to enjoy oysters throughout the year. Thanks to advances in oyster farming, oysters are no longer limited to a certain time of year. The village of Bouzigues, in the Thau Basin, produces first-class oysters all year round.

Georges Rousset, Maître Cuisinier de France, prefers slightly bigger oysters. They are hollow and decidedly tasty, juicy, and plentiful. Large oysters are especially suitable for cooking. If you can't find Bouzigues oysters, you could use another kind of oyster or other shellfish, such as scallops. In each case the filling is made from Swiss chard.

To ensure that the oysters open, Monsieur Rousset recommends spreading the oysters on a baking sheet and baking them in an oven preheated to about 320 degrees Fahrenheit/160 degrees Celsius for ten minutes. Don't forget to reserve the juices that are drawn out.

We only use the green part of the Swiss chard in our recipe. You should remove the white ribs. Monsieur Rousset likes to add a hint of garlic to his recipe by spearing a peeled clove of garlic on the fork that is used to turn the Swiss chard during cooking.

This unusual appetizer also introduces another Mediterranean product, *poutargue*: salted, pressed, and flattened mullet roe, also sometimes known as *caviar de Martigues*. Don't add any salt when you use *poutargue*. By the way, this very special ingredient is not essential to this recipe—except for gourmets.

Open the oysters, remove the meat from the shells, and reserve. Collect the liquor and strain it. Clean the oyster shells and wash the Swiss chard. Remove the white ribs, boil a pan of salted water and blanch the Swiss chard for 4 minutes. Drain the leaves and chop them finely.

Melt a scant ⅛ stick/10 g butter in a skillet and add the chopped Swiss chard. Stir with a fork that has a peeled clove of garlic on the end. Add 1 tbsp cream and incorporate it into the chard. Fill the oyster shells with the Swiss chard, making a shallow well in the center.

Carefully place the oyster meat in a saucepan, add the reserved oyster liquor and a little salt and pepper, and poach them in their own juices for 4 minutes on each side, but don't let them boil. When they are almost cooked through, drain them, reserving the liquor.

with Swiss Chard

Put a slice of poutargue (if using) in the middle of the Swiss chard. Place an oyster on top.

To make the sauce, bring the oyster cooking liquid to the boil and reduce it. Season with pepper. Add the rest of the cream and bring to the boil again, until a nice, smooth sauce forms. Beat in the rest of the butter.

Grate the remaining poutargue into the sauce. Warm it on low heat for 2 minutes, but do not let the sauce boil. Cover a deep dish in rock salt. Position each oyster shell securely in the salt so they can't tip over. Carefully spoon the hot sauce over the oysters, and serve immediately.

Artichoke Millefeuilles

Preparation time:	25 minutes
Marinating time:	1 hour
Cooking time:	10 minutes
Difficulty:	★

Serves 4

5 oz/150 g	young goat milk cheese
8	globe artichokes
3 tbsp	olive oil
few sprigs	fresh thyme
2 cloves	garlic
generous ¾ cup/ 200 ml	oil for frying
3½ oz/100 g	arugula (rocket)
	salt, pepper

For the marinade:

2 tbsp	balsamic vinegar
3 tbsp	olive oil

	salt
	pepper

For the balsamic vinaigrette:

½ tsp	salt
1 tbsp	balsamic vinegar
1 tbsp	wine vinegar
1 tbsp	candied root ginger syrup
4 tbsp	olive oil
½ tsp	salt, pinch of pepper

For the garnish:

1	sun-dried tomato
3	celery sticks, with leaves
	parmesan
	rock salt

This appetizer, with young goat milk cheese, is a down-to-earth dish. Our chef prepares it with Gorbio, a goat milk cheese made in the Nice area. You could also use Crottin de Chavignol. Let the cheese marinate for as long as possible, so it takes on the slightly sweet taste of the balsamic vinegar.

If you can find them, buy spiny globe artichokes, with a slightly bitterer taste. These artichokes come from Sicily and are members of the thistle family. The globe sits on the base of the flower and is surrounded by leaves. When the choke is removed, the meaty, soft artichoke heart makes good eating. The fleshy lower part of the leaves is also delicious. The artichoke, introduced to France by Catherine de Médicis, has long been used as a medicine. They will keep for a couple of days if the stalk is put in water, like a flower. Artichoke hearts should be put into water acidulated with lemon immediately, otherwise they discolor. If your artichoke hearts are too big, you can cut them in half.

Garlic tastes sweeter if it is blanched. Peel it and immerse it alternately in cold and boiling water; repeat the process three times. If desired, you can season the sautéed slices of artichoke with celery salt. You can use curly endive instead of arugula.

When preparing the millefeuilles, layer the goat milk cheese and sautéed artichokes on top of each other. Finish off with the fried garlic and one or two parmesan shavings. Then add the celery leaves, the sun-dried tomato, and a couple of grains of rock salt. Prepare the millefeuille in advance if you like more intense flavors, but the salad should only be dressed at the last moment.

Cut the goat milk cheese into slices that are ½–¾ in/1–2 cm thick. Allow 3 slices per millefeuille. Beat together the ingredients for the marinade, pour them over the cheese, and marinate for 1 hour.

Cut off the artichoke stalks and remove the leaves down to the base. Scoop out the choke with a spoon. Cut the artichoke hearts into slices that are about ¼ in/2–3 mm thick.

Heat 3 tbsp olive oil in a skillet and sauté the artichoke slices. Season to taste with salt, pepper, and some rubbed thyme. Drain the slices on kitchen paper.

with Goat Milk Cheese

Peel the garlic and cut into slivers. Blanch the garlic, then drain it. Heat the oil in a pan and fry the garlic, keeping the slivers moving so they don't stick together.

To make the vinaigrette, beat together the salt and balsamic vinegar. Add the wine vinegar, ginger syrup, olive oil, and pepper. Beat again, adding 1 tbsp water.

Build up the millefeuille in 3 layers, alternating a slice of goat milk cheese and a slice of artichoke. Finish off with fried garlic and parmesan shavings. Toss the salad in the vinaigrette, arrange on a plate with the millefeuille, and garnish.

Green Cabbage Rösti

Preparation time:	20 minutes
Cooking time:	50 minutes
Difficulty:	★

Serves 4

12	thin slices bacon
5 oz/150 g	slab of bacon
½ head	green cabbage
1	thin salami
2 tbsp	drippings
1 loaf	rye bread

rock salt
salt
pepper

For the garnish:

1	scallion (optional)
4	cherry tomatoes

This appetizer is a traditional dish from Cerdagne, a region in the Pyrénées-Orientales department of France, which was partitioned by France and Spain in 1659. The farmers originally prepared this meal with Savoy cabbage, a variety of green cabbage traditionally harvested after the first frosts. They cooked it with drippings and pork belly. Jean-Claude Vila has taken this rustic recipe and brought it right up to date.

Pork belly is no longer cooked with the cabbage. Instead it appears in the form of thin, crispy, fried rolls of bacon that are a wonderful complement to the soft cabbage. Sometimes, poverty dictated that the farmers had to use spoilt, blemished cabbages, but you should ensure that your cabbage is firm, with tightly closed leaves without holes.

Before preparing the dish, remove the outer layer of cabbage leaves. Blanch the green cabbage in boiling, salted water for five minutes. Carry out this process three times, changing the water each time. Then let the cabbage drain, and finally refresh it in ice water. According to our chef, sautéing the cabbage is important. It should be nicely browned and all the steam should have evaporated.

Drippings are made from the fat that runs from fried bacon (or pork belly). It is mostly used for long cooking times because of its creamy consistency.

The usual accompaniment to this dish is a slice of rye bread. Rye comes from Anatolia and the area around Turkistan, growing in the mountainous areas on poor soils. Rye flour produces dark, heavy bread. It has a slightly acidic taste and keeps well.

Lay 8 slices of bacon side by side on a baking sheet and cover them with another baking sheet. Preheat the oven to 350 °F/180 °C and bake the bacon for about 15 minutes. Roll up the remaining slices and put them aside for the garnish.

Finely dice the slab of bacon. Dry-fry it in a large skillet, until crisp and brown.

Bring a pan of salted water to the boil. Blanch the cabbage in it for 5 minutes. Change the water and repeat the process twice more. Drain the cabbage, refresh in ice water, and dice.

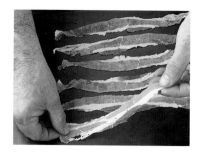

with Bacon Sails

Cut off a few slices of salami for the garnish. Of the remaining salami, dice one half, and very finely chop the other. Add the salami to the pan with the bacon and sauté it for 5 minutes.

Add the cabbage and the drippings to the skillet. Press the mixture down firmly, and sauté it for 10 minutes.

Cut out rounds of cabbage mixture. Transfer to the center of a plate. Arrange the slices of salami and bacon rolls around the cabbage. Arrange a slice of the crisp bacon on top of each cabbage round, like a sail. Add scallion rings and a cherry tomato. Serve with rye bread.

Fried Garbanzo

Preparation time: 35 minutes
Cooking time: 25 minutes
Difficulty: ★

Serves 4

⅓ cup + 1½ tbsp/100 ml   olive oil
1 scant cup/150 g   garbanzo flour
                          oil for frying
                          salt

For the tomato sauce:
5   tomatoes
1   small onion
1   shallot
1 tbsp   olive oil
10   black olives
1 pinch   cayenne pepper
2   anchovy fillets in oil

For the bouquet garni:
2   bay leaves
1 sprig   fresh thyme
2 sprigs   fresh flat-leaf parsley

In the Marseilles of the 1930s, the mobile traders in the Old Harbor loudly proclaimed the popularity of their *panisses*, garbanzo flour pancakes, which were a local specialty at the time. Now they are available the length of the Mediterranean coast. In the south of France they are sometimes called "poor man's bread."

Without doubt, this dish is one of the cornerstones of Mediterranean cuisine. The garbanzo bean is a pulse, which for centuries has formed part of dishes such as couscous, braised beef, stews, ragouts, or *olla podrida*, the Spanish version of French *pot-au-feu*, or one-pot stew. It appears in the form of small balls in the Near East, which are known as *falafel*. *Hummus*, garbanzo bean purée, originated there too.

Garbanzo beans have been known throughout Europe since the Middle Ages. They are available dried or canned. The dried beans are soaked in cold water overnight, with a little baking soda, to soften them, so they are easier to digest.

When using garbanzo flour, make sure it cooks slowly and doesn't form lumps. Georges Rousset says that in the past, garbanzo beans were always cooked with a bay leaf. Our chef recommends that you use aromatic, clear, cold-pressed olive oil.

You could also serve your garbanzo bean dumplings with a side salad. If you have a couple of dumplings left over, simply serve them with a different sauce a couple of days later. They can be served sprinkled with grated parmesan and baked, covered with sliced mushroom, or coated in pesto, a sauce made from basil, garlic, toasted pine nuts, and olive oil.

Pour 2 cups of water into a saucepan with the olive oil and a pinch of salt, and bring it to the boil.

Take the pan off the heat. Gradually stir the garbanzo flour into the saucepan, stirring carefully to prevent lumps from forming.

Put the pan back on the burner on low heat and simmer for 15 minutes. Stir constantly to help the mixture thicken and prevent it burning.

Bean Dumplings

When the mixture has formed a thick paste, use it to fill individual patty tins. Leave them to cool. Tomato sauce: Pour boiling water over the tomatoes in a bowl. Leave for a few minutes, drain, skin and deseed them, then chop the flesh. Peel and finely chop the onion and shallot.

Fry the chopped onion and shallot, add the tomatoes and bouquet garni. When the sauce has combined and reduced, remove the bouquet garni. Purée the sauce and heat it in the pan. Add the chopped olives, cayenne, and anchovies, and simmer for 2 minutes.

Take the garbanzo flour dumplings out of the patty tins. Heat the oil for frying until very hot, and fry the dumplings for 2 minutes, until golden brown. Serve the dumplings hot on a bed of the tomato sauce with olives and anchovies.

Storzapretti

Preparation time: 40 minutes
Cooking time: 25 minutes
Difficulty: ★

Serves 4

11 oz/300 g   Swiss chard leaves
1   *brocciu* (Corsican cheese, weighing about 14 oz/400 g)
2   eggs
3 pinches   *nepita* (peppery wild mint)

⅓ cup/20 g   fresh breadcrumbs (optional)
⅞ cup/100 g   flour
3½ oz/100 g   grated *tomme* (Corsican cheese)
    salt and pepper

For the tomato sauce:
½   onion
2 tbsp/30 ml   olive oil
1 clove   garlic
½ bunch   parsley
4   tomatoes
    salt and pepper

Corsican cooking is both generous and substantial, and traditionally features entirely local produce. *Storzapretti* are a good example. According to legend, the name of this specialty refers to a particularly greedy priest who ate large quantities of these vegetarian dumplings every day. This easy recipe is usually served as a hot appetizer. For a main dish simply double the quantities.

This dish uses the famous Corsican *brocciu*, a mild, creamy cheese. *Brocciu* is made on local farms in the winter and spring; the similar-tasting French cheese known as *brousse* is an acceptable substitute if *brocciu* is unavailable. Another important ingredient is Swiss chard. Blanched for a few minutes and then finely chopped, these leaves combine extremely well with the *brocciu*. Swiss chard, a fresh and nutritious vegetable, is grown in small inland gardens, and sold in large quantities in the springtime. Choose young plants for their milder flavor and wash them carefully before cooking. Spinach leaves can be substituted for the Swiss chard if necessary.

With the addition of *nepita*, a slightly peppery wild mint, these *storzapretti* instantly evoke the *maquis* (wild scrub) that is so important a feature of the Corsican landscape. This very typical dish is finished with the characteristic taste of Corsican *tomme*. *Tomme* is a strong ewe's-milk cheese, the taste of which underlines the rustic origins of this specialty.

Clean the Swiss chard leaves. Heat a pan of salted water to boiling point and add the leaves, cooking them for 2 minutes. Drain and chop.

For the sauce, lightly brown the chopped onion in the olive oil. Add the garlic and chopped parsley. Add the chopped tomatoes with salt and pepper. Cook over a gentle heat for about 20 minutes. Mix together and set aside.

Crumble the brocciu into a bowl and add the chopped Swiss chard and the eggs. Season with salt and pepper. Sprinkle on the nepita and mix in. If the mixture is too liquid, add some breadcrumbs.

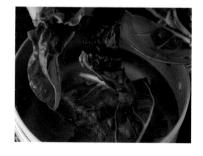

with Corsican Cheeses

Form the mixture into dumplings and roll them in flour.

Heat a pot of salted water to boiling point. Now carefully lower the dumplings into the water with a spatula. When they rise to the surface, lift them out.

Pour the tomato sauce into an ovenproof dish and place the dumplings in it. Sprinkle the grated Corsican tomme over the dish and brown it for 5 minutes in an oven heated to 400 °F/200 °C. Serve.

Artichokes

Preparation time: 20 minutes
Cooking time: 20 minutes
Difficulty: ✷

Serves 4

8	artichokes
1	lemon
1 bunch	fresh mint
2 bunches	parsley

2 cloves	garlic
	salt
8 tbsp	olive oil
scant ½ cup/	
100 ml	white wine

For the garnish:

	fresh fava beans
	pecorino shavings

This artichoke dish, which can be served warm or hot, is a classic in Italian cuisine and is very popular at Easter time. A Roman specialty, it is very easy to prepare. In addition to the numerous varieties of artichoke native to Rome and its environs, the vegetable stalls in the Eternal City also offer regional variations such as the thick *Romanesco*, which is quite round in shape and thornless, the *Catanese* with its spindle-shaped leaves, the *Violetto* from Tuscany and the area around Palermo, small Ligurian artichokes, and many others besides.

Buy the youngest possible artichokes, which are recognizable by their pretty green and purple color and are so tender that you can eat them raw. Make sure that the leaves are neither damaged nor marked, and that the flower head is still tightly closed. Place the artichokes in water with a dash of lemon juice to prevent discoloration, then drain.

Long ago, the ancient Romans set great store by artichokes, which originate from Sicily. They named them *cynara*, for a young girl in ancient Roman folklore who gradually turned into an artichoke. The Italians then named the plant *carciofo*, from the Arabic *kharsufa*. During the Renaissance, scholars believed the artichoke possessed therapeutic powers. Bartolomeo Scappi, the personal chef of Pope Pius V, recommended stuffing the head of this thistle-like plant with lean veal, ham, eggs, spices, garlic, and aromatic herbs.

The Romans opted for a lighter version. In addition to garlic and parsley—extremely common flavorings in Italy—this filling contains mint, the fresh, powerful flavor of which goes outstandingly well with artichokes. Prepared in this way, artichokes are a delight for gourmets everywhere.

Remove the fibrous outer leaves of the artichokes. Cut off the stalk crossways at the bottom and peel.

Cut off the top leaves horizontally. Open out the artichokes and place in a bowl of water containing lemon juice.

Wash and chop the mint and parsley. Peel the garlic cloves and chop finely. Stuff the artichokes with this mixture.

Roman Style

Carefully dip the tips of the artichokes in a dish of salt.

Hold the artichokes by the stalk and place them in a saucepan. Pour over 8 tbsp olive oil. Cover and simmer for 3 minutes.

Pour in the white wine. Cover, turn up the heat, and bring to the boil, then simmer for approximately 15 minutes over low heat. Serve the artichokes garnished with fava beans and pecorino shavings.

Deep-Fried

Preparation time:	30 minutes
Cooking time:	15 minutes
Difficulty:	★

Serves 4

8 oz/200 g	small cuttlefish
20	langoustines
20	fresh shrimp
2 cups/250 g	flour
	oil for frying
	salt

For the sauce tartare:

| 2 | egg yolks |
| | salt |

	pepper
¾ cup+1 tbsp/	
200 ml	sunflower oil
2 tbsp	capers
5 sprigs	parsley
3	gherkins

For the garnish:

| | basil leaves |

To serve:

| | lemons |

The gulf of Naples is world-famous, not only for its beauty, but also for its fishing grounds. The Mediterranean Sea, known in ancient times as *Mare nostrum*, or "our sea," has been supplying the inhabitants of southern Italy with fish, mussels, and crustaceans since time immemorial.

Our deep-fried seafood is quick and easy to prepare. Depending on availability, red mullet or red snapper, anchovies, and sardines can also be used for this recipe.

Langoustines are found in abundance in western European coastal waters. They have very tasty flesh, reminiscent of lobster, and are excellent for broiling or poaching. They are also very good in most recipes featuring crustaceans, and are served with the pincers left on. They are available all year round.

Fresh shrimp are highly prized by connoisseurs for their extremely fine flavor.

Small cuttlefish, related to squid (*calamari*), have succulent, delicate flesh. They can be broiled, fried, or stuffed. Around 20 inches/50 centimeters in length, they have spiral-shaped bodies, dark-colored skin, and two triangular fins at the tail end. There are ten edible tentacles at the head end, two of which are very long.

To enhance our seafood recipe, the chef suggests serving sauce tartare, which has the subtle flavor of capers. The flower buds of the caper bush are harvested in spring. Since capers are preserved in vinegar or brine, they need thorough rinsing before use. In Italy, capers from Lipari and Pantelleria, islands off the coast of Sicily, are especially popular.

Clean the cuttlefish under running water. Carefully remove the head and tentacles, then remove the ink sac and quill. Cut the flesh into even-sized pieces.

Remove the heads from the langoustines and shrimp by giving a slight twist, then peel the tails.

Place the flour in a large dish. Dip the cuttlefish, langoustines, and shrimp in the flour and carefully shake off any excess.

Seafood

Heat the oil and add the cuttlefish, langoustines, and shrimp. Deep-fry the basil leaves (for the garnish) with the seafood.

Remove the cuttlefish, langoustines, and shrimp from the oil, drain on paper towels, and season generously with salt.

Sauce tartare: Mix the egg yolks, salt, and pepper into a creamy sauce. Then, beating constantly, add the oil a little at a time. Stir in the capers, chopped parsley, and diced gherkins. Serve the deep-fried seafood with the sauce and slices of lemon. Garnish with basil.

Liver Guazzetto with

Soaking time:	overnight
Preparation time:	15 minutes
Cooking time:	40 minutes
Difficulty:	★

Serves 4

For the guazzetto:

¾ oz/20 g	dried porcini mushrooms
8 tbsp	extra-virgin olive oil
½ clove	garlic
½ bunch	parsley

	salt
	pepper
4	chicken livers
1	onion

For the polenta:

1 scant cup/	
150 g	cornmeal
	salt

For the garnish:

	parsley
	chives

Guazzetto was once a dish that was eaten mainly by the poor. When a chicken was killed, they naturally could not afford to throw anything away; the liver was therefore used to make a *guazzetto* and the skin was cut into strips and made into a kind of *fettucini*.

In the mushroom season, fresh porcini mushrooms (of which there are several sub-species) should be used if possible. Out of season, dried mushrooms can be used instead; these have to be washed thoroughly and soaked in cold water. Biancarosa Zecchin suggests serving the mixture of liver, onions, and fried porcini mushrooms on a bed of polenta.

Polenta has played a major role in the cuisine of northern Italy for several centuries. Corn was introduced from America by Venetian merchants in the 16th century, and the thick broth prepared from cornmeal, like those previously made from barley, millet, spelt, and garbanzo beans, became very popular soon afterward. Corn, which was a staple food for poor peasant farmers in particular, did a great deal to relieve famines, and eventually cornmeal broth could be found on the table at any time of the day. This extremely restricted diet did, however, result in serious malnutrition.

The classic cornmeal broth for polenta has to be stirred for 45–60 minutes on the stove. We therefore recommend pre-cooked polenta, which is easier to prepare. It is cooked over low heat until it reaches the consistency of oatmeal porridge. It can also be cooked for longer and then poured into a dish; after it has cooled, it can then be turned out and served cut into slices.

Guazzetto is a delicious appetizer, but can also be served as a main course.

Soak the dried porcini mushrooms in lukewarm water for 20 minutes. For the polenta, bring 4 cups/1 l water to the boil in a saucepan and add the cornmeal and salt. Stir for about 20 minutes until the consistency of oatmeal porridge is reached. Set aside.

For the guazzetto, drain the mushrooms and chop with a knife.

Heat 4 tbsp olive oil in a pan and sauté the mushrooms with the chopped garlic, chopped parsley, salt, and pepper for about 5 minutes.

Porcini Mushrooms

Cut the chicken livers into strips.

Peel and chop the onion. Heat the remaining olive oil in another pan and sauté the onion. Add the livers, then season with salt and pepper. Stir with a spoon for 3–4 minutes until browned.

Add the browned livers to the mushrooms. Fry for another 4–5 minutes, stirring constantly. Serve the livers with the porcini mushrooms on a bed of polenta, and sprinkle with chopped parsley and chives.

Gratin of Mussels

Preparation time: 25 minutes
Cooking time: 15 minutes
Difficulty: ★

Serves 4

7 lb/3 kg	mussels
4	large tomatoes
1 clove	garlic
1 bunch	parsley

6 tbsp	olive oil
	breadcrumbs to bind
	salt

For the garnish:

parsley

Today it is almost impossible to imagine Italian cuisine without tomatoes—*pomodori* in Italian—and the bright red tomatoes make this gratin of mussels look particularly appealing. The mussels are easy to prepare and excellent when served as a light appetizer among friends.

Mussels are very delicate and must be eaten within three days of being harvested. Choose them very carefully and avoid those that have broken shells or are slightly open. Fresh mussels are always tightly closed. Before cooking, they must be cleaned by removing the beards and then scrubbing them under running water. The chef suggests substituting Venus clams, with their particularly delicate and flavorsome flesh, for the mussels if necessary. The filling contains garlic, giving the recipe a Mediterranean feel. Garlic has been cultivated for over 5,000 years and is absolutely indispensable in the cuisine of southern Europe.

Parsley goes wonderfully well with garlic, and can be bought all year round. In Italy, people who are held in universally high esteem are described as *come il prezzemolo*, as essential as parsley in the kitchen.

Tomatoes are a staple ingredient in Mediterranean cuisine. Although the conquistadors had brought the tomato to Europe from Peru, it was only in the 18th century that it was cultivated in Campagna. At that time it was called *pomo d'oro* ("golden apple") because of its yellow color. Today, tomatoes are eaten all year round. There are around 5,000 known varieties, including the famous *Roma*, originally from the southern part of the country. Choose firm, fleshy tomatoes with a uniform, brilliant red color.

Clean the mussels and remove the beards with the tip of a knife. Place in a saucepan with water and boil for 3–5 minutes until they open.

Leave the mussels to cool and remove the meat from the shells. Set aside. Blanch and skin the tomatoes, remove the seeds, and dice into small cubes.

For the filling, peel and chop the clove of garlic. Wash the parsley and chop.

with Tomatoes

Transfer the mussel meat with the parsley and garlic to a bowl and pour 2 tbsp olive oil over the top. Add the breadcrumbs. Season with salt and mix carefully.

When the mussels are completely coated, fill the mussel shells with the breadcrumb/meat mixture and press it down lightly.

Lay the filled shells in an ovenproof dish. Scatter the diced tomatoes on top. Season with salt and pour the remaining olive oil and 4–5 tbsp/60–75 ml water over the top. Bake at 350° F/180 °C for 10 minutes. Serve the mussels garnished with parsley.

Baked Eggplants

Preparation time: 40 minutes
Cooking time: 2 hours 20 minutes
Difficulty: ★

Serves 4

3	carrots
2	onions
1 clove	garlic
1 stick	celery
4 tbsp	olive oil

4 tbsp	white wine
1¾ lb/800 g	tomatoes
	salt
8	eggplants
2	buffalo mozzarella cheeses
	oil for frying
3½ tbsp/50g	grated parmesan
1 bunch	basil

For the garnish:

	basil leaves

Baked eggplants with parmesan is a classic dish. It is easy to prepare and there are many local variations. In Sicily, for example, it is served with grated chocolate, while the Neapolitans add sweetbreads.

The flavorsome vegetarian recipe here, in which the eggplant slices are strewn liberally with parmesan cheese before being placed in a hot broiler, is originally from Calabria. In Italian it is called *parmigiana di melanzane*, taking its name from the famous cheese that comes from northern Italy.

The eggplant, a classic summer vegetable, was probably introduced into southern Italy by the Arabs, who called it *badindshan*. A dry climate, silicon-rich soil, and high temperatures are essential for the successful cultivation of eggplants. These three factors prevent bitter substances forming in the flesh of the vegetable and provide favorable conditions for the concentrated, yet mild, flavor to develop. There are a number of varieties, distinguished by their different shape and color.

The various kinds are found in abundance in Italian markets between October and June—*Violetta di Firenze*, *Bellezza nera*, and *Nubia*, for example. When buying them, make sure that the stalks are still intact, the skins are smooth and unmarked, and the flesh is undamaged and firm: in other words, that they are as fresh as possible. Eggplants keep well in the refrigerator.

Parmesan is the typical ingredient in this recipe. True parmesan can only be produced in the provinces of Parma, Reggio-Emilia, Modena, Mantua, and Bologna, where it is still made by hand. Its flavor is unmistakable: highly salted and sometimes sharp.

Peel the carrots, onions, and the garlic clove. Cut the celery and carrots into sticks and slice the onions. Crush the garlic.

Heat the olive oil. Add the carrots, onions, celery, and garlic and sauté for 15 minutes over a low heat. Pour in the white wine and reduce.

Blanch and skin the tomatoes, then add to the vegetables in the saucepan. Cover and simmer for about 1 hour. Season with salt to taste.

with Cheese

Wash the eggplants and cut into even-sized, thick slices. Slice the mozzarella cheeses.

Heat the oil in a skillet and add the eggplant slices. Deep-fry until they are golden brown, remove, and drain on paper towels.

Pour the vegetable mixture into an oven-proof dish. Arrange a layer of eggplant slices on top and sprinkle with parmesan. Layer the mozzarella and basil on the eggplant and repeat, ending with a layer of eggplant. Bake at 350° F/180° C for 1 hour. Garnish with basil before serving.

Caponata

Preparation time:	45 minutes
Cooking time:	40 minutes
Difficulty:	★

Serves 4

4	eggplants
1/3 cup/80 ml	olive oil
1	carrot
1	celery heart
2	onions

2	tomatoes
1 bunch	parsley
1/2 cup/100 g	capers
1 cup/200 g	pitted green olives
1/2 cup/100 g	sun-dried tomatoes
2 tbsp/30 ml	wine vinegar
1 tbsp/15 g	superfine sugar
	salt and pepper

For the garnish:

	parsley

Caponata, a Sicilian specialty made with eggplants, captures the essence of the Mediterranean sun. Similar to ratatouille, this easily made classic uses summer vegetables and has a distinctive sweet-sour taste.

Theories differ as to the origins of the name *caponata*. Some Sicilians believe that it is derived from the word *caupone*, or harbor-side tavern, where dishes of octopus, celery, and eggplant were traditionally prepared in a sweet-sour sauce.

The word may also refer to the fishermen of Naples, the *caponi*, who used to cook a kind of fish and vegetable soup while out at sea in their fishing boats.

One thing is certain: *caponata* is the universally popular trademark dish of Sicily's coastal regions.

Made from summer vegetables, typically the ingredients of *caponata* are tomatoes, onions, celery, and, most importantly, eggplants. Eggplants are particularly appreciated on Sicily and in southern Italy, where they are traditionally said to have been introduced by the Arabs in the 10th century. They can also be served stuffed with tomatoes, or pulped and shaped into balls or patties. *Macaroni alla Norma*, a pasta specialty from the area around Catania, is served with a topping of fried eggplant and ricotta cheese.

Famous for their excellent quality, capers from the nearby islands of Lipari and Pantelleria are another typical Sicilian ingredient. These are the flower buds of the caper bush, and are used in *caponata* to bring out the flavors of the other ingredients. They are usually sold preserved in vinegar, and should be rinsed before use.

Peel and dice the eggplants. Put them in a colander and salt generously. Leave to "sweat" for around 40 minutes, then rinse and pat dry (this removes the bitterness). Cook them in 4 tbsp of olive oil, on a medium heat, for about 10 minutes, stirring occasionally.

Peel and grate the carrot. Wash the celery and chop finely. Peel and chop the onions. Peel and pulp the fresh tomatoes (drop them briefly into a pan of just-boiled water before peeling). Wash and chop the parsley.

Gently brown the onions in a frying pan, in the remaining olive oil. Add the celery and soften over a low heat. Add the pulped tomatoes and mix them in. Add salt and pepper.

Now add the carrots to the mixture, together with the capers, the olives cut into slices, the chopped sun-dried tomatoes, and the parsley. Mix together and cook for about 10 minutes.

Add the diced eggplant and cook for a further 10 minutes.

Mix in the vinegar and the sugar. Cook for about 5 minutes. Serve garnished with chopped parsley.

Feta

Preparation time: 20 minutes
Cooking time: 15 minutes
Difficulty: ★

Serves 4

4	tomatoes
2 cloves	garlic
1 bunch	basil
1 lb 2 oz/500 g	feta
7 or 8	black olives
1	red bell pepper
1 pinch	paprika
1 pinch	oregano
	olive oil

Saganaki are small pieces of grilled cheese, cooked in the oven in a metal dish of the same name. Extremely simple to make, they are both delicious and very colorful.

The internationally famous feta, a cheese made from ewe's milk which has been known to Greeks for several thousand years, is used in this dish. In *The Odyssey*, Homer refers to a ewe's milk cheese similar to today's feta. The Ancient Greek dramatist, Aristophanes, in his play *The Horseman* (400 B.C.) also refers to *chlorotyri* and *trophalyda*. Cut into slices before being packed into barrels, by the 17th century it had taken the name *feta*, a corruption of the Italian word *fette* or "slice." Without its rind, it is white and soft and can easily be cut into small cubes or slices. Providing it is kept well wrapped up and moistened with its brine, feta can keep for about six months in the refrigerator.

This dish is garnished with tomatoes, garlic, basil, feta, pepper, and black olives, and should be generously sprinkled with olive oil, which will lend its flavor and prevent the other ingredients from sticking to the bottom of the cooking dish. For this recipe, our chefs prefer to use the delicious olive oil from Sitia on the island of Crete. Greenish-yellow in color, this virgin oil has a very low acidity level and a fruity flavor. Its quality is due in great part to the amount of sun the crop receives and the specific composition of the local soil. Harvested at the end of November, the olives are pressed within three days of being picked.

Our chefs normally prepare the *saganaki* in small individual dishes and top each serving with a big piece of cheese. But as we have done here, you can also make it for several people in one large dish. The small cubes of golden feta will give the dish a more decorative appearance and provide a good showcase for all the other ingredients.

Wash the tomatoes and pat them dry. Cut each one into 3 thick slices.

Arrange the sliced tomatoes in a small ovenproof dish. Scatter over thin slices of peeled garlic and basil leaves.

Arrange 2 cubes of feta on top of each round of tomato.

Saganaki

Pit and halve the olives. Wash and dry the pepper. Slice it in half and remove the white membrane and seeds. Cut it into strips.

Arrange the strips of pepper among the tomatoes, with the feta on top. Scatter the black olives over the dish.

Sprinkle the top of the dish with paprika and oregano and drizzle with olive oil. Place the dish in an oven preheated to 475° F/240° C for 15 minutes. Garnish with a few basil leaves.

Prasopita

Preparation time:	*20 minutes*
Cooking time:	*50 minutes*
Difficulty:	★

Serves 6

6	leeks
scant ½ cup/ 100 ml	olive oil
1 bunch	dill
2	bay leaves
½ cup/50 g	coarse semolina
	salt
	pepper

3	eggs
1 scant cup/ 100 g	grated Gruyère (or *kasseri* cheese)
2–3 tbsp	dried breadcrumbs
7 oz/200 g	feta

Born in Kozani, a district of western Macedonia, Chrysanthi Stamkopoulos has prepared *prasopita* for you, a sort of "flat cake" made with leeks, which her grandmother used to make. This is a very nourishing dish that is altogether simpler than the pies made with phyllo (filo) pastry.

Since leeks are a winter vegetable, *prasopita* is particularly prized during that season. Within mainland Greece there are still many little villages where everybody cultivates their own vegetable gardens and whose diets therefore follow the seasons. Grown for thousands of years, the leek was highly esteemed by the Assyrians, Egyptians, and the Hebrews. The best warriors of the Pharaoh Cheops were all rewarded—with armfuls of leeks!

Leeks are often used to help shore up the soil and to rid it of various impurities. After cutting the leeks into slices, put them into a colander and wash them in an abundant supply of fresh running water. Raw, leeks keep for five days in the refrigerator, providing that the top part of the leaves has first been cut off.

Enriched with aromatic herbs and eggs, the leeks used for the *prasopita* can also be accompanied with thin slivers of carrot and garlic. The grated cheese, whether Gruyère or *kasseri*, will also add to the flavor, help to bind the mixture, and give it a softer, smoother texture. For a more authentic taste, use *kasseri*, a cheese made from ewe's milk or cow's milk produced in Thessalia, central Greece, and in in the northern Aegean. Pale yellow in color, it has a soft consistency and no rind. The flavor is soft and salty.

Our chef generally pours the mix into a large rectangular mold, the base covered with dried breadcrumbs to prevent the *prasopita* from sticking to the bottom. A circular mold has been used here.

Trim off the tough green part and the root of the leeks. Slice the white and the light green parts into rounds. Rinse them thoroughly in a colander under running water to make sure that any soil is removed.

In a saucepan, gently fry the leeks for 5 minutes in a little hot oil. Add the chopped dill and bay leaves and stir for about 10 minutes over the heat. Remove the bay leaves, add the semolina, and mix again. Season with salt and pepper.

Whisk the eggs in a separate bowl. Add to the leek mixture and stir well.

Kozanis

Reduce the heat to low and stir in the grated Gruyère or kasseri cheese.

Sprinkle the bottom of an ovenproof dish with the dried breadcrumbs and, using a spatula, transfer the leek mixture into the dish.

Arrange small cubes of feta at regular intervals over the surface of the dish. Cook in an oven preheated to 425° F/220° C for 30 minutes and serve piping hot.

Mytilene

Preparation time: 30 minutes
Cooking time: 50 minutes
Total draining time
  (zucchini): 1 hour
Difficulty: ★

Serves 6

4½ lb/2 kg	zucchini
4 or 5	zucchini flowers
3½ oz/100 g	bacon
2	medium onions

scant ½ cup/ 100 ml	olive oil
1 lb 5 oz/600 g	feta
12	eggs
	mint leaves
1 bunch	dill

Many of the poets and musicians of Greek Antiquity were born on the island of Lesbos, also known as Mytilene. These days, the third biggest Greek island still retains vestiges of its past—antiquities, Byzantine ruins, and little picturesque fishing harbors.

In the olden days, the diet of the people living on the Greek islands comprised vegetables, wild herbs, cheese, olive oil, and bread because meat was so rare and expensive. This is reflected in *sfougato*, literally a "flat cake," made from eggs flavored with herbs, enriched with fresh and natural ingredients.

Look for small, tender, and delicately scented baby zucchini that still have their pretty orange flowers. If the flowers have not been "cleaned," remove the central pistil. Some cooks also make *sfougato* with potatoes or spinach.

The feta made on the island of Mytilene is prized throughout the whole of Greece. Although this cheese was made in ancient times, the word *feta* only dates from the 17th-century Venetian occupation. In Venetian, *fette* means "slice" because the cheese is cut into slices before being put into a brine solution. A word of advice: Don't bother with the insipid feta produced on an industrial scale using cow's milk.

The inhabitants of Mytilene also produce a very famous olive oil. Bright golden yellow in color, it has the sort of flavor characteristic of fully ripe olives.

Cooks on Mytilene traditionally cook pork at Christmas. They smoke some parts of the pig, and make full use of any meat left over as a filling for the *sfougato*. This can be replaced by bacon or cubes of pancetta. Unlike an omelet, the *sfougato* is not folded but has the shape of a "flat cake" that is served directly from the dish in which it was cooked.

Quickly grate the unpeeled zucchini using a grater with large holes. Then leave them to drain for 30 minutes in a colander.

Arrange the zucchini flowers on a cutting board. Cut them into pieces measuring about ½ in/1 cm square. Cut the bacon into very small cubes. Peel and chop the onions.

Heat the oil in a skillet, fry the bacon and the onions for 5 minutes, then add the grated zucchini. Leave to cook for 5–10 minutes, stirring all the time, then pour the mixture into a colander and leave to drain for 30 minutes.

Sfougato

Put the mixture into a bowl. Add the pieces of zucchini flower and roughly crumbled feta.

In another bowl, whisk the eggs and add chopped mint and dill. Pour this mixture into the zucchini–feta mix. Mix well with a wooden spatula.

Pour the prepared mixture into a large gratin dish. Cook in a preheated moderate oven at 325° F/170° C for 30–35 minutes. Serve hot or cold.

Canea Lamb

Preparation time:	50 minutes
Cooking time:	1 hour
	20 minutes
Resting time (pastry):	20 minutes
Difficulty:	★

Serves 4

1¾ lb/800 g	leg of lamb (boned)
	salt, pepper
½ bunch	mint
1 lb 2 oz/500 g	*anthotyros* cheese
10 oz/300 g	*malaka* cheese
1 sprig	thyme
1 sprig	oregano
1 tsp	dried marjoram

2	lemons
1 tbsp	olive oil
1	egg yolk (glaze)
2 tbsp	sesame seeds

For the pastry:

¾ cup/200 ml	milk
½ oz/20 g	fresh yeast
	(or 1½ tsp dried)
1 lb 5 oz/600 g	all-purpose flour
2 oz/50 g	lamb suet
2	eggs
	salt

For the garnish:

| | mint leaves |

A favorite in the little coastal town of Canea, this lamb pie is a Cretan specialty. This "puff pastry" dish is particularly popular at weddings.

Cretan cooking is very healthy, and even today it retains many similarities with the Minoan civilization. One text dating from 1800 B.C. was already referring to a dish made from lamb wrapped in pastry.

Renowned for its exceptional taste, lamb has been the meat of choice since the days of Ancient Greece. Sheep are raised in the mountainous regions of the country, where they graze on wild grasses, and the meat takes on a wonderfully aromatic taste. Depending on the season, this recipe can also be made with kid goat.

Carefully thought out, this pie is a wonderful mix of aromatic herbs. It is a reflection of Crete itself, where thyme,

mint, oregano, and rosemary all grow in abundance—this dish only serving to magnify their typically Mediterranean flavors. A close cousin of oregano, the subtlety of marjoram shines through in this puff pastry pie. Originally from Asia, this herb is used in Greece to add extra flavor to various meats and marinades. If you want to dry it, cut the stems just before the plant comes into flower.

A substantial dish, Canea lamb pie is further enriched by a filling made from three different types of cheese. Typically Greek, *anthotyros*, made from ewe's milk or goat's milk, was in the olden days known as *myzithra* in Crete. *Malaka*, meanwhile, is an unsalted, fully skimmed soft cheese that was mentioned as long ago as the 6th century in documents found on the island of Santorini. You can easily replace the *anthotyros* with Gruyère and the *malaka* with mozzarella.

Put the boned leg of lamb into a saucepan. Season with the salt and pepper, cover with water and simmer over moderate heat for about 40 minutes. Strain the stock and set aside. Cut the meat into small pieces.

To make the pastry, first warm the milk. Add the yeast and leave to rise (if using dried yeast, follow maker's instructions). Sift the flour into a large bowl and add the suet, eggs, and salt. Make a well and gradually mix in the milk, then work by hand.

Pour a scant ½ cup/100 ml lamb stock onto the pastry mix. Continue to knead, then leave to rest for 20 minutes.

Pie

On a floured board, roll out the pastry thinly. Finely chop the mint and mix with the anthotyros and malaka cheeses. Season with salt.

Mix the lamb pieces with the herb leaves. Add the lemon juice. Oil the base and sides of an ovenproof dish and line with the pastry, leaving long overhangs of pastry. Spread the mint and cheese filling on the pastry base. Spread the meat evenly on top and moisten with a little stock.

Fold the pastry back over to form a lid for the pie. Beat the egg yolk and use it to glaze the top of the pie. Sprinkle with sesame seeds. Cook in an oven preheated to 300° F/150° C for 40 minutes. Serve garnished with mint leaves.

Two Cretan Dishes

Preparation time: 20 minutes
Cooking time for
  boubouristi *snails:* 30 minutes
Cooking time for snails
  with fennel: 40 minutes
Difficulty: ★

Serves 4

For the *boubouristi* snails with rosemary:
1 lb/500 g   live *petit-gris* snails
²⁄₃ cup/150 ml   virgin olive oil
3¹⁄₂ tbsp/50 g   fresh rosemary

²⁄₃–⁴⁄₅ cup/
  150–200 ml   vinegar
              salt

For the snails with fennel:
1 lb/500 g   live *petit-gris* snails
6   scallions
                (spring onions)
⁴⁄₅ cup/200 ml   virgin olive oil
⁴⁄₅ cup/200 ml   white wine
2 lb/1 kg   fennel tops
4   ripe tomatoes
              salt and pepper

For the garnish:
              fennel tops

Many Cretans still observe the requirement to fast on certain days in the Christian calendar. With meat from warm-blooded animals, eggs, and dairy produce off the menu, the "fast" typically features fresh vegetables, snails, beans, and olives. Archaeological excavations on the neighboring island of Santorini have revealed that snails were already being eaten in the Minoan period. The ancient Greeks also ate these easily harvested delicacies.

The snails of the Cretan mountains favor a habitat of aromatic plants that gives them their celebrated flavor. The Cretans gather them and keep them in boxes containing vine shoots for two weeks. They are then carefully cleaned and, if necessary, the operculum (the bony covering on the snail's "foot") is removed. From among the many Cretan recipes for snails, Ioannis Lappas has selected *boubouristi* (fried) snails, generally served as an appetizer, and snails with fennel, a main dish.

The most popular way of serving snails on Crete is fried. Fried snails are one of the island's favorite *meze*, accompanying a glass of wine or the local brandy, *tsikoudia*. The live snails (in their shells) are arranged in a pan on a thin layer of salt, with the shell openings facing downward. All the shells should touch the bottom of the pan to ensure even cooking. As the cooking proceeds, the snails release their juice and shrink into their shells, but not before their flesh has become impregnated with the salt, resulting in a crisp crust. The Cretans often dip *dakos*, the delicious local bread, into the juices.

In the second recipe given here, the snails are cooked with *marathos*, the fragrant wild fennel that grows in the rocky countryside of Crete. This use of wild herbs is typical of Cretan cooking. If fennel tops are unobtainable, they can be substituted with dill, which has a very similar taste.

Wash the snails thoroughly under running water or in a bowl to clean them of any dirt. Remove the operculum if necessary.

For the boubouristi *snails:* cover the bottom of a heavy frying pan with a layer of salt and place the snails on it, in their shells. Heat the pan quickly until a greenish-yellow "juice" is released. Add the oil and toss over a high heat for 5 minutes.

Add the rosemary. Douse the snails with the vinegar. Continue tossing the snails until the vinegar has evaporated, and serve immediately.

Using Snails

For snails with fennel: fill a saucepan with water and bring to the boil. Immerse the live snails, boil for 2 minutes and drain them.

Chop the onions. In a pan, toss the scallions and snails in oil for 5 minutes over a high heat. Add the white wine, salt, and pepper and stir over the heat for a further 3–4 minutes.

Snip the fennel tops finely and chop the tomatoes into small dice. Add these to the snails and cook for 30 minutes (add a little more water, if needed, during cooking). Serve hot, garnished with fresh fennel tops.

Divan

Preparation time:	20 minutes
Cooking time:	35 minutes
Difficulty:	★

Serves 4

1	chicken breast
3 cloves	garlic
1	onion
	olive oil

½ tsp/2 g	fresh thyme
	salt
	freshly ground white pepper
10 oz/250 g	puff pastry dough
1	egg

For the garnish:

	nigella seeds

A thousand years ago, the Turks lived mainly on flour-based foods, lamb, and milk products. Bugra Khan, a governor of Turkistan, supposedly gave his name to a stuffed dough pocket, *buğra*, which is the direct predecessor of today's *börek*.

Today, *börek* is made of *yufka*, a very thin pastry made of flour, salt, and water. Making perfectly thin *yufka* requires practice, which is why the ready-made version is favored. Phyllo (filo), which is the same as *yufka*, may be more readily available in stores, or thinly rolled puff pastry dough can be used instead.

Minced lamb, onions, and tomatoes or a mixture of herbs and feta are the traditional stuffings for *börek*. Göksal Özçelik's unusual version combines chicken, onions, and herbs. This delicious—yet waistline-friendly—filling is a specialty of the restaurant in Istanbul's Hotel Divan.

This appetizing, golden-yellow *börek* is a small, savory pastry, with the puff pastry dough simply wrapped around the stuffing. You can also, however—as is usual in Turkey—alternate layers of *yufka* and filling in a gratin dish. The top layer is brushed with beaten egg and the dish baked in the oven, before being cut into squares for serving.

Before baking, sprinkle the *börek* generously with nigella seeds. This spice originally came from the Middle East, where it is extremely popular. It is also known as black cumin and onion seed. Sesame seeds are a good substitute.

In Turkey, spicy *börek* is served with natural yogurt thinned with a little water.

Thinly slice the chicken breast. Peel and finely chop the garlic. Peel the onion, then cut in half and slice thinly.

Heat 1 tbsp + 1 tsp/20 ml olive oil in a skillet and sauté the onion and garlic for 3–4 minutes. Add the sliced chicken and sauté on all sides over high heat.

Remove the skillet from the heat. Sprinkle over the herbs, season with salt and pepper, and mix well. Leave to cool.

Börek

Cut circles from the dough of about 6 in/15 cm diameter. Put a little of the chicken mixture in the middle of each circle.

Fold the edge of each dough circle up over the stuffing and shape them into small parcels.

Place the parcels seam-side down on a lightly oiled baking sheet. Combine the egg with a little oil. Brush over the parcels and sprinkle with nigella seeds. Bake in a pre-heated, medium oven for 20–25 minutes.

Rize Beans

Preparation time: 30 minutes
Cooking time: 15 minutes
Difficulty: ★

Serves 4

4½ lb/2 kg	flat green beans
3	eggs
	salt
1 scant cup/	
100 g	cornmeal
¾ cup/200 ml	olive oil for frying

This dish, which comes from the Black Sea area, is called *fasulye tava* ("green beans in the pan") in Turkish. In towns it is mainly served as an appetizer, whereas families with a more traditional lifestyle often serve it with a number of side dishes such as salads and pickled vegetables.

The mild, moist climate of the Black Sea coast is ideal for growing vegetables. The weather is influenced by the near-by sea, with the Pontic Mountains protecting the region from the rough climate of the Anatolian highlands. The town of Rize is situated in the midst of extremely fertile ground, with shady groves, magnificent forests, and large tea plantations.

Of all the many vegetable types grown here, a long, flat variety of green bean is particularly enjoyed by local inhabitants. It is usually served with hot meat dishes, whereas runner beans are used mainly for salads.

The beans must first be washed and trimmed, removing the tips and the strings. Use a small sharp knife or peeler. After blanching the beans, plunge them briefly in ice-cold water. This stops them from cooking any further and also helps them to stay a beautiful green color, as well as retaining their vitamins.

Usually Savaş Özkiliç performs the steps illustrated in the last three pictures without pausing in between. The individual beans are dipped in the egg, turned in the coating, and immediately fried, the whole sequence being completed as quickly as possible.

Using a sharp knife or vegetable peeler, remove the tips and strings from both sides of the beans.

Cut the beans into pieces approximately 4in/10 cm long and blanch in boiling water for about 5 minutes.

Remove the beans with a spatula, plunge them briefly in a bowl of ice-cold water, and drain.

in Batter

Beat the eggs in a small bowl. Season the beans with salt and dip each one individually in the beaten egg.

Coat the beans in cornmeal until they are completely covered.

Meanwhile, heat the oil in a skillet until very hot. Add the beans immediately they are coated and fry until golden brown in color. Serve straight away.

Lahmacun

Preparation time:	45 minutes
Resting time:	30 minutes
Cooking time:	10 minutes
Difficulty:	★

Serves 4

2 tbsp	flour

For the base:

2 cups/200 g	flour
1 tsp	salt
½ tsp	sugar
1 tbsp	olive oil

For the topping:

1 bunch	parsley
1 clove	garlic (optional)
8 oz/200 g	onions
1	tomato
1	green chile
8 oz/200 g	ground lamb
	salt
	ground pepper
1 tbsp	tomato paste
1 tbsp	red pepper flakes (optional)

Lahmacun is Turkey's popular version of pizza. The recipe hailed originally from the southeast of the country and the pizza, which had a very spicy topping, was once the focal point of entire villages. In rural areas, fathers and their children would carry the *lahmacun* to the village ovens.

Lahmacun is also extremely popular in cities, and is usually eaten with the hands. Turks add onions and lemon juice to the base, then roll it up to make it easier to eat. It goes without saying that this practically national dish is served at large family gatherings and celebrations. It is accompanied by *ayran*, a salted, yogurt-based drink.

Lahmacun is easy to prepare. The substantial topping consists of ground lamb, garlic, green chile, and lots of parsley. Parsley, which presumably originated from the Mediterranean, is very popular in the kitchen because of its intensive aroma, and is available fresh all year round.

Make sure that you only use leaves and stalks that look appetizing—they should be green, fresh, and firm.

Onions are much valued in Turkish cuisine and many different varieties are available on the market: mild yellow or Spanish onions, white ones, which are slightly sweeter in flavor, and red ones, which are sweeter still. Onions have been cultivated for some 5,000 years, and originally came from northern Asia. Choose ones that are hard and firm, and not sprouting. To make them easier to peel, put them in the freezer compartment for ten minutes or in the refrigerator for an hour.

Tomato paste is extremely popular in sauces and ragouts in Turkey. It adds color and flavor to a dish.

Base: Sieve the flour onto the worktop. Make a well in the center and sprinkle over the salt and sugar. Pour in the olive oil and knead with the flour, gradually adding ⅘ cup/200 ml water, until smooth. Wrap in a damp cloth and chill in the refrigerator for 30 minutes.

Lightly dust the dough with flour. Using your hands, break off equal-sized pieces.

To make the topping, finely chop the parsley, garlic (if desired), and onions. Peel and finely chop the tomato. Wash and finely chop the chile.

Place the ground lamb in a bowl. Combine with the parsley, garlic, onion, tomato, and chile, and season with salt and pepper. Add the tomato paste and, if using, the red pepper flakes. Add 2 tbsp water, then knead with your hands until smooth.

Dust the worktop with flour. Slightly flatten the dough balls with your hands, then roll out using a rolling pin.

Divide the ground lamb mixture evenly between the circular bases, using your hands. Bake in a preheated oven at 400 °F/200 °C for about 10 minutes. Serve the lahmacun arranged on plates.

Mizyal's

Preparation time:	45 minutes
Resting time:	15 minutes
Cooking time:	35 minutes
Difficulty:	★★★

Serves 4

2 tbsp	flour
3½ tbsp/50 ml	olive oil
½ cup/125 g	set yogurt
1 tbsp	sesame seeds

For the dough:

3 cups/350 g	flour
scant ½ cup/ 100 ml	milk

1	egg
scant ½ cup/ 100 ml	olive oil
1 tsp/5 g	baking powder
	salt

For the stuffing:

3½ lb/1.5 kg	leaf spinach
4 oz/100 g	feta
	salt
	ground pepper
1	onion

Gökçen Adar, an expert on Anatolia and the Aegean, hails from Izmir, and often visits this part of Turkey, collecting traditional recipes from its villages. His passion for cooking started in childhood while watching his mother, Mizyal, an experienced cook. These stuffed puff pastry dough pockets are Adar's homage to his mother.

This delicious, typical Turkish dish is generally served at large gatherings. In a country where families often welcome their loved ones to breakfast, börek is almost always on the table.

Making the dough calls for lots of care and patience, and plays a key role in the success of this traditional delight. It must be rolled out very thinly, and spread with olive oil. The stuffing is then placed on top, and the dough folded over in half.

There are at least five different types of börek in Turkish cuisine, and Mizyal's version is one of the classics. The main ingredient in the stuffing is spinach, a vegetable that is widely used in Turkish cooking; it originated in Persia and is available fresh from spring through fall.

Combined with spinach, feta develops its full, slightly salty aroma. This sheep milk cheese is firm to crumbly in consistency, and is popular all over the Mediterranean region. To make it, the curd is drained in sieves or muslin and then pressed into shapes with whey and brine.

Cacık—plain yogurt with cucumber, garlic, salt, and chopped mint—is often served with these delicious dough pockets.

To make the stuffing, wash the spinach, chop into small pieces with a knife, and blanch in boiling water for 1 minute. Drain. Place in a bowl with the crumbled feta. Season with salt and pepper. Grate the peeled onion, and combine with the spinach and feta.

To make the dough, combine the flour, milk, egg, olive oil, baking powder, and salt in a large bowl, and knead until smooth. Leave to stand for 15 minutes.

Sprinkle the worktop with flour. Divide the dough into evenly sized pieces and shape into balls. Roll the dough balls into very thin circles and brush with olive oil.

Börek

Place a little of the stuffing in the middle of the dough circles and fold them in half. Squeeze the edges together with your fingers, and trim with a pastry wheel.

Brush 2 tbsp/30 ml olive oil over an oven-proof dish and arrange the dough pockets in it, overlapping them slightly and covering them with olive oil.

Stir the yogurt in a small dish. Brush it over the dough pockets and sprinkle over the sesame seeds. Place in a preheated oven and bake at 350 °F/180 °C for 30–35 minutes. Arrange on a dish and serve.

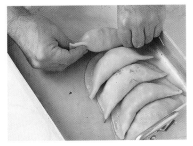

Stuffed Pasta

Preparation time: 50 minutes
Resting time: 45 minutes
Cooking time: 12 minutes
Difficulty: ★★★

Serves 4

2 tbsp	chicken stock
¼ stick/30 g	butter
1 tbsp	vegetable oil

For the dough:

2½ cups/300 g	flour
⅜ stick/40 g	butter
1 tbsp+1 tsp/ 20 ml	olive oil
	salt
1	egg white

For the stuffing:

4 oz/100 g	ground veal
4 oz/100 g	ground lamb
½ bunch	parsley
½	onion
	salt
	ground pepper
1	egg

For the vegetable sauce:

1	onion
2 cloves	garlic
2	tomatoes
3	mushrooms
2	scallions
½	red bell pepper
½	green bell pepper
3½ tbsp/50 ml	corn oil
	salt, ground pepper

For the yogurt sauce:

1 scant cup/ 200 ml	plain yogurt
1 clove	garlic
	salt

For the spicy sauce:

½ stick/50 g	butter
1 tsp	red pepper flakes
1 tbsp	sunflower oil

These delicious *mantı*—meat-filled pasta—are irrefutable proof of the country's culinary skills. According to historical sources, the dish was already popular with the nomads who settled in Turkey. The method of preparing the pasta is supposed to have been copied from the Chinese. After Constantinople was conquered in 1453, cooking developed as an art in the palaces (*seraglio*), taking full advantage of the regional diversity of the vast empire. This resulted in a cuisine that constantly displayed its art and tradition.

Kayseri, the town at the heart of Anatolia, is also called the capital of *mantı* because, since the time of the Ottomans, at least a dozen types of *mantı* have been created. It is also said that there are cooks in the town who are able to scoop 36 *mantı* on a single spoon!

The quality of the dough is the key to the success of this dish. It must be left to rest for 45 minutes. At the time of the Ottomans, the *mantı* were steamed. Sedat Özkan bakes them in the oven for about ten minutes before pouring stock over them.

The *mantı* are always accompanied by lots of yogurt and a spicy sauce. Sedat Özkan also serves them with a dish that harmoniously blends the aromas of red and green bell peppers and onion.

To make the stuffing, place the ground veal and lamb, chopped parsley, peeled and grated onion, salt, pepper, and egg in a bowl, and combine well using your hands.

To make the dough, combine the flour, butter, and olive oil in a bowl, and season with salt. Add a little water and knead until smooth. Shape the dough into a roll, then cover with a clean cloth and leave to rest for 30 minutes. Cut the dough into 6 equal-sized pieces.

Flatten the dough slightly, then leave to stand for 15 minutes. Roll out very thinly, and using a pastry wheel cut 1½ in/ 3 cm-squares.

from the Seraglio

Brush the squares with some egg white, then place a little of the stuffing on top. Fold the squares together, leaving a little opening in the center. Bring the chicken stock and 4 tsp/20 g butter to the boil with 2 cups/500 ml water.

Brush an ovenproof dish with the vegetable oil and place the mantı in it. Bake in a preheated oven for 10 minutes at 300 °F/150 °C. Dot over the remaining butter and pour over the stock, reserving about 1 cup/200 ml.

Vegetable sauce: Dice the vegetable ingredients, sauté in the corn oil, and pour in the reserved stock. Season to taste with salt and pepper. Spicy sauce: Heat all the ingredients until the butter has melted. Yogurt sauce: Combine the ingredients. Serve the sauces with the mantı.

Swiss Chard

Preparation time:	20 minutes
Cooking time:	20 minutes
Difficulty:	★

Serves 4

2½ lb/1 kg	Swiss chard
2	onions
¼ stick/30 g	butter
1 tsp/4 g	fresh mint leaves
	salt and ground pepper
	to taste
4	eggs

Mıhlama is an egg dish that is extremely popular with Black Sea gourmets and is served in a variety of ways. The most common is *kaygana*, an anchovy omelet. Savaş Özkiliç presents these delicious egg nests with Swiss chard, flavored with onion and fresh mint.

Although Swiss chard is a winter vegetable, it is increasingly grown all year round in Turkish greenhouses. This unassuming "poor man's vegetable" is grown all along the Mediterranean coastline. Its large, green leaves have a long, white-green stalk, and—depending on the recipe—the leaves or the stalks, which are also known as "ribs," are used. In this dish, for instance, only the leaves are used. The stalks can be used elsewhere, for example in a sauce or in a gratin.

If you are preparing the dish for no more than four people, you can use a large pot and ideally cover it with a lid so the nests steam from both bottom and top. We have chosen, however, to bake them in the oven. Simply place the Swiss chard nests in an ovenproof dish, and break the egg into the small indentation.

An oval, copper pan with a handle, in which the Swiss chard nests can be served as well as cooked, is best. The eggs are seasoned with salt and pepper before the *pazı mıhlaması* are put in the oven, but the vegetables do not require any further seasoning. Cover the pan with a piece of aluminum foil; oil the foil first so that it does not stick to the eggs.

Remove the stalks from the Swiss chard. Wash and trim the leaves.

Using a large knife, finely slice the Swiss chard leaves.

Peel and chop the onions and sauté in the melted butter for 5 minutes until they are just starting to change color. Add the Swiss chard and, stirring occasionally, cook for 5 minutes until they collapse.

Nests

Chop the mint and add with the salt and pepper. Stir well.

Shape 4 Swiss chard nests in an oven-proof dish.

Break an egg into the center of each nest, and season the eggs with salt and pepper. Oil a piece of aluminum foil and place, oiled side down, on top of the dish. Bake in a preheated oven at 350 °F/180°C for 10 minutes.

Börek

Preparation time: 35 minutes
Cooking time: 50 minutes
Difficulty: ★★

Serves 4

10 oz/250 g	green olives
1	onion
2 tbsp	olive oil
8 oz/200 g	ground lamb
½ cup/85 g	chopped walnuts

½ tsp/2 g	paprika
	salt to taste
2 tsp/10 ml	pomegranate syrup
8	scallions
2 bunches	flat-leaf parsley
1 lb 10 oz/ 750 g	yufka (phyllo) pastry
	flour for dusting

Zeytin böreği, olive-stuffed dough pockets, is a specialty of the Gaziantep area on the border with Syria. This hinterland of the Mediterranean does not immediately spring to mind as a region where green olives are grown, yet these are what give the dish its originality. In Gaziantep the stuffing is normally prepared at home and then taken to a baker, who kneads the dough, stuffs it with the provided mixture, and bakes the dough pockets, which are very popular for picnics. Of course, many housewives also make the dough themselves, and a ready-to-use variety is available.

The stuffing is made of lamb, olives, onion, and chopped walnuts, and is—like so many dishes in this region—well seasoned with paprika. Pomegranates are cooked for a long time to make the syrup, which is dark and sticky in consistency and adds a delicately acid aroma to the stuffing. A suitable substitute for flavor would be balsamic vinegar.

Olives are grown mainly along the Aegean and Mediterranean coasts of Turkey. Gaziantep is the only area away from the sea where they are grown. Most olives from here are used to make cooking oil; only one variety is used for table oil. After harvesting, the pit is removed from every single olive individually, using a flat stone. As the olives are still very hard at this stage they do not get crushed.

The typical Turkish yufka pastry that encases the stuffing is not very easy to make, and it takes a little practice to roll it out as thin as it should be. Phyllo (filo) pastry is the same as yufka. If you cannot get hold of yufka or phyllo, you can use thinly rolled puff pastry instead. To cut out the circles required, you can place a round bowl on the dough and cut around it with a knife if you do not have a suitable cutter. Ayfer T. Ünsal recommends one portion per person.

Cut the flesh of the olives away from the pits using a small knife. Chop the onion and sauté in very hot oil for 5 minutes. Add the chopped olives and combine with the onion.

Add the ground lamb, combine well, and cook for 20 minutes.

Finally, stir in the chopped walnuts, paprika, and salt, and cook for a further 5 minutes over a high heat.

with Olives

Remove the skillet from the heat and stir in the pomegranate syrup.

Cut the scallions into rings and chop the parsley. Combine both well with the cooked meat mixture. Spread the yufka out on a floured worktop and cut out circles of 6 in/15 cm diameter.

Spoon the mixture onto the middle of a dough circle. Fold the circle together and press down on the edges with a fork. Place on a baking sheet lined with baking parchment and bake in the oven at 400 °F/200 °C for 20 minutes.

Shish

Preparation time:	15 minutes
Marinate:	12 hours
Cooking time:	10 minutes
Difficulty:	★

Serves 4

2 lb/800 g	leg of lamb, off the bone
2	tomatoes
4	green chiles
8 oz/200 g	onions
4 tsp/20 g	butter

For the marinade:

	salt and ground pepper to taste
4 tbsp	olive oil
1	onion

For the garnish:

	rosemary

Broiled or barbecued kebabs are called *şiş kebap*, and they are known everywhere as a typical Turkish specialty. Making them could not be easier, and this family dish is a popular item on a summer picnic.

In the Adana and Antep regions, this classic is served with a glass of *ayran*, a slightly salty yogurt drink. Another popular accompaniment is *salgam suyu*, a sour, salty syrup made from beets.

The quality of the meat is the key factor in a successful shish kebab. Leg of lamb, which is preferred for its wonderful flavor, should not be too fatty. It should be cut into even-sized pieces and marinated for about 12 hours. The marinade makes it even more tender, and olive oil, salt, pepper, and onion impart the most wonderful aromas.

These meat skewers are ideal for serving to guests, and make the most of the country's vegetables. Green chiles, which are often combined with lamb, are available in abundance in Turkey's markets. The Turks love this vegetable most of all when it is stuffed. Choose firm, smooth specimens with a firm, green stalk and no blemishes.

Green chiles are juicy and notable for their wonderful aroma. You can, however, also use the sweeter red or yellow varieties.

According to the *kebap* tradition, meat skewers are often served with onions. The varieties of this root vegetable from more southern regions—part seasoning, part vegetable—are milder and more delicate in flavor than onions grown in northern countries.

Trim the meat and cut into cubes.

For the marinade, put the salt, pepper, and olive oil in a large bowl. Peel and grate the onion. Squeeze the juice of the onion into the marinade using your hands.

Put the meat cubes into the marinade and combine well. Cover the bowl with plastic wrap and place in the refrigerator for 12 hours.

Kebab

Wash the tomatoes, then cut into sections and remove the seeds. Wash the chiles, remove the seeds, and cut into even-sized rectangles.

Thread the pieces of meat with the tomato and chile pieces alternately onto the skewers, and broil or barbecue.

Peel and chop the onions, and sauté in the melted butter. Arrange the skewers on a plate and serve the onions separately in a flat dish. Garnish with rosemary.

Eggplant

Preparation time: 40 minutes
Cooking time: 1 hour 5 minutes
Difficulty: ★

Serves 4

1 lb/400 g	leg of lamb, off the bone
3	tomatoes
1	green chile
1	onion
3 tbsp/45 g	margarine
4 tbsp	tomato paste

1 tbsp	flour
	salt
	ground pepper
1 lb/400 g	eggplants
	olive oil for deep frying

For the garnish:

1	green chile
1	tomato
	parsley

Eggplant kebab, with its Mediterranean aromas, is extremely popular in Turkey. This simple dish originally came from the country's south, but today is served all over the country.

The lamb meat really comes into its own here. The (hind) leg is greatly prized for its meat, but you can also make it with meat from the shoulder, which is just as tasty.

The eggplant is Turkey's favorite vegetable, and large quantities of them are available in markets everywhere throughout the summer. The main growing region is around Antep, with its lime-free soil and warm and dry climate.

The eggplant came from India, and has been used as a vegetable in Asia for over 2,500 years. There are many different varieties, although the long, purple one is the best known, and is also used for this recipe. When shopping, make sure that the vegetable is not marked, the skin is firm and unblemished, and the stalk is fresh. Choose specimens that are as small as possible.

Tomatoes are an essential ingredient in Mediterranean cooking. The women of Cappadocia preserve this precious fruit by making it into a sauce in vast cauldrons. This means that even winter dishes have a summery flavor.

Spanish conquerors brought the tomato from the Andes in South America to Europe in the 16th century, although it did not become established in Europe until the early 18th century. Today there are an estimated 5,000 varieties! Use fruity Roma or egg tomatoes for this recipe.

Trim the leg of lamb and cut it into even-sized pieces.

Put the meat in a pot with ⅔ cup/150 ml water and simmer for about 10 minutes. Drain and set aside. Skin and finely chop the tomatoes. Cut the chile into strips.

Chop the onion and sauté in the melted margarine. Add the meat, sliced chile, chopped tomatoes, tomato paste, and flour. Season with salt and pepper. Stir well, cover with water, and simmer for 45 minutes.

Kebab

Cut off the ends of the eggplants. Peel off strips, creating a stripy pattern on the eggplants.

Cut the eggplants in half lengthwise. Cut the halves into thick slices, then thinner ones. Slice the chile that is being used for the garnish.

Deep-fry the eggplant and chile strips in hot oil. Arrange the meat and the sauce on a plate with the deep-fried eggplants. Garnish with chile, sliced tomato, and parsley.

Stuffed Small Vegetables,

Preparation time: 55 minutes
Cooking time: 40 minutes
Difficulty: ★★

Serves 4

4	tomatoes
2	lemons
10¹⁄₂ oz/300 g	zucchini
8³⁄₄ oz/250 g	eggplants
7 oz/200 g	mild green chiles
1¹⁄₄ lb/500 g	potatoes
	salt and pepper

For the stuffing:

¹⁄₄ cup/50 g	rice

1¹⁄₄ lb/500 g	ground beef
1	onion, chopped
6¹⁄₂ tbsp/100 g	chopped parsley

6¹⁄₂ tbsp/100 g	grated Swiss cheese
1 tsp	caraway seeds
1	egg, beaten
1 tsp	harissa
	cooking oil

For the tomato sauce:

1³⁄₄ lb/750 g	tomatoes
2	garlic cloves, crushed
7 tbsp/100 ml	olive oil
1 pinch	saffron strands, in ¹⁄₂ glass water

For the garnish:

	chopped parsley

Known as *doulma*, this mixture of stuffed small vegetables from the Tunis area is typical of the Mediterranean region as a whole. Consisting of zucchini, eggplants, tomatoes, mild green chiles, potatoes, and lemons, this refreshing dish is mainly served in summer.

According to a family's taste, the stuffing is prepared with ground beef or ground lamb. The highly flavored meat goes perfectly with the vegetables. When you fry the vegetables, our chef recommends that you lightly brush the stuffing with beaten egg and all-purpose flour. This way, they'll retain their attractive appearance.

It's best to start by frying the potatoes. These vegetables, originating from Latin America, are eaten throughout the world. Select the hardest potatoes with a smooth skin, unblemished and without any sprouts. They keep perfectly well in a dry, cool place, preferably out of direct light. On contact with the air, the inside of a potato tends to go black. Leave peeled potatoes immersed in cold water while waiting to use them.

The zucchini and eggplants must be added at the same time. These summer vegetables are a great favorite of Mediterranean people. Preferably choose the smaller, tastier vegetables for this recipe. With their strong flavor, eggplants go extremely well with the tomato sauce. They must be unblemished, with a smooth, intact, and firm skin. As for the zucchini, you can judge their freshness by how uniform their color is. They are not usually peeled, but you need to scrape the skins.

In the Tunis region, stuffed small vegetables are often enjoyed as a family meal. According to your preference you can either pour the tomato sauce straight onto the vegetables or serve it separately.

Prepare the stuffing by boiling the rice for about 10 minutes. Mix the ground beef, chopped onion, chopped parsley, grated Swiss cheese, and boiled rice in a bowl. Add the salt, caraway seeds, and harissa. Mix well. Allow to stand for approximately 10 minutes.

For the sauce, wash, peel, and deseed the tomatoes; then reduce them to a purée. Wash the remaining tomatoes and the lemons, zucchini, eggplants, and chiles. Peel the potatoes. Cut the zucchini into chunks. Deseed the chiles. Scoop out all the vegetables.

Prepare the sauce by browning the prepared purée and crushed garlic cloves in 7 tbsp/100 ml olive oil. Add salt and pepper. Add the saffron water. Fry gently until the vegetable water has evaporated. Add a little extra water and cook for approximately 10 minutes.

Tunis-Style

Blanch the scooped out lemons. Fill the zucchini, potatoes, tomatoes, lemons, and chiles with the stuffing.

Heat the cooking oil. Brush the vegetable stuffing with a little beaten egg. Carefully immerse the vegetables in the hot oil.

Place the stuffed vegetables on a dish. Pour the sauce over the top. Bake in the oven at 350 °F/180 °C for 10 minutes. Arrange the small vegetable parcels on a serving dish. Garnish with a little chopped parsley.

T'Bikha

Preparation time: 25 minutes
Cooking time: 55 minutes
To soak the
  garbanzo beans: 12 hours
Difficulty: ★

Serves 4

2	onions
²/₃ cup/150 ml	olive oil
¹/₂ cup/100 g	garbanzo beans (chickpeas), soaked overnight and drained
1 tbsp/17 g	tomato paste

1 tbsp	harissa
1 tsp	paprika
1¹/₄ lb/500 g	squash
2	tomatoes
5 oz/150 g	hot green chiles
5 oz/150 g	fava beans (broad beans)
4	garlic cloves, crushed
	salt and pepper

For the garnish:

	chopped parsley

T'bikha is a typical Tunisian specialty. This hot appetizer is served as the main course for many family meals. Although it varies from region to region, using different vegetables such as zucchini, carrots, or even eggplants, the most popular is most probably t'bikha with squash.

Called kla by the Tunisians, squash is the generic name for the fleshy fruit of any of the various plants of the gourd family (genus Cucurbita). These vegetables originally came from America, and were discovered through the expeditions of Christopher Columbus. At that time, gourd was reputed to be a remedy for "dryness of the tongue" and they were mainly eaten for their moisturizing properties. Spherical and bulky in shape, the gourd is distinguished by the yellow or red color of its skin and flesh.

This vegetarian dish also includes fava beans, which are a very common ingredient in Tunisian cuisine. Originally from Persia and Africa, they have been popular in the Mediterranean region since ancient times. When they are young, the delicate skin of fava beans does not need to be removed.

Fava beans are excellent spring and summer vegetables. They are prepared either hot or cold in a salad. In the t'bikha, their strong flavor is brought out. Our chef advises you to add them to the mixture once the garbanzo beans are cooked.

Don't forget to add a touch of chopped parsley as a garnish. Its aroma and color will give this recipe a dainty touch.

Peel the onions and cut them roughly into thin slices.

Sweat the onions in ²/₃ cup/150 ml olive oil. Add the garbanzo beans and the tomato paste. Mix well.

Season with salt and pepper. Add the harissa and the paprika. Stir and cover with water. Cook for approximately 25 minutes.

with Gourd

Peel and cut the squash and tomatoes into large cubes. Cut the hot chiles in two, deseed and cut into small pieces.

Shell the fava beans. Remove the skin of the beans and add the beans to the mixture.

Stir the pieces of squash, tomatoes, and chiles into the saucepan. Cook for approximately 20 minutes. Five minutes before the end of the cooking time, add the crushed garlic cloves. Pour the t'bikha into a deep dish and garnish with a little chopped parsley.

Trio of Tunisian

Preparation time: 40 minutes
Cooking time: 25 minutes
Difficulty: ★★

Serves 4

4	fritter sheets
1	lemon
	cooking oil

For the basic filling:

1 medium-sized	onion, chopped
4 tbsp/50 ml	olive oil
½ bunch	parsley
1 x 5 oz/150 g	potato, cooked and puréed

3½ tbsp/50 g	capers, chopped
1	egg
	salt and pepper

For the chicken filling:

3½ oz/100 g	chicken breast meat
1 tsp	ground coriander

For the ground meat filling:

3½ oz/100 g	ground beef
1 tbsp	olive oil
1 tsp	ground coriander
1 tsp	turmeric
1 tsp	caraway seeds

For the tuna filling:

½ can	tuna in oil, drained

For the garnish:

	paprika (optional)

When you think of Tunisia you immediately picture beautiful landscapes, fine sandy beaches, and … its delicious fritters! They are a national specialty that is enjoyed at any time of day.

Fritter sheets, which are also called *malsouka*, are a legacy of the Turks' passage through Tunisia. These "crepes," which are sheets of unleavened fine semolina, are traditionally prepared on a tinned copper tray, placed over a stove. Every Tunisian family chooses its own fritter fillings, according to taste, season, or budget. Some families fill them with liver pâté, red snapper, or even shrimp. But for the most part, they're made with tuna, eggs, or meat.

In fact, you can use any ingredients you like for this recipe. However, to make this specialty properly you must include the basic filling, which is always made of onion, chopped parsley, egg, and potato. Some people also like to add ca-

pers, which are young flower buds from the caper shrub and are generally pickled in white vinegar or brine. Used as a flavoring, capers were very popular with the ancient Romans when they occupied Tunisia.

Different shapes of fritters can be served. The chef suggests that you make a trio of triangle, cigar, and half-moon shapes. He suggests that you fill them with tuna in oil, which is a great favorite of the Tunisians, or with chicken breast. If you make them with ground meat, as in this recipe, add a little water and season with spices halfway through cooking. Most importantly, don't forget to add the coriander (which is also called "Arabic parsley"), as its oriental aroma flavors the meat perfectly.

When they are served, the trio of Tunisian mini-fritters are like an invitation to travel and offer a taste of this warm and friendly country.

Prepare the basic filling by browning the chopped onions in the olive oil for about 5 minutes. Stir in the chopped parsley. Allow to cool. Add the potato purée and the chopped capers. Season with salt and pepper. Break the egg into the mixture. Stir and place to one side.

With a pair of scissors, cut 2 fritter sheets into 2½ in/6 cm wide strips to make the triangles; cut another fritter sheet in 2 to make the cigars; using a pastry cutter, cut out circles in the other sheet, to make the half-moons.

Prepare the different fillings by cooking the ground meat in olive oil and spices; cook the chicken in salted water for 5 minutes, and chop it with the coriander. Flake the tuna. Share out the basic filling between each filling. Place a circle of each filling on each fritter sheet.

Mini-Fritters

Spread the chicken filling evenly at the end of the strip. Fold the fritters into triangles by rolling them once to the left, and once to the right, as if you're tucking them in.

Prepare the cigar fritters by placing the ground meat filling at the end of the sheet. Fold it once in a $1/2$ round towards the middle and roll it up to the end. For the half-moons, place a spoonful of the tuna filling on one side and pull the sheet over it.

Fry the fritters, 3 minutes on each side. Soak up any excess oil on a paper towel. Arrange a selection on plates, served with a lemon quarter and dusted with paprika, if using.

Chakchouka

Preparation time:	30 minutes
Cooking time:	1 hour 25 minutes
Difficulty:	★★

Serves 4

2 cups/500 ml	live snails
1 or 2 sprigs	fresh thyme
1 or 2 sprigs	fresh rosemary
2 oz/50 g	garlic cloves
1 tsp	ground caraway seeds
¹/₂ tsp	ground coriander
14 oz/400 g	red squash

10¹/₂ oz/300 g	onions
4	moderately hot green chiles
7 oz/200 g	fresh tomatoes
³/₄ cup/200 ml	Tunisian olive oil
1 tbsp/17 g	tomato paste
1 tsp	North African harissa
¹/₂ tsp	chile powder
	salt and pepper

For the garnish:

parsley (optional)

Chakchouka with Snails graces the tables of the Ksour Essef and Mahdia region in east Tunisia. The dish known as *chakchouka* is very popular across the whole of Tunisia. It's a vegetable ragout consisting of onions, fresh tomatoes, moderately hot green chiles, garlic, caraway seeds, tomato paste, harissa, salt, and pepper. The Mahdian cooks usually add green fava beans to the dish, while those of Ksour Essef supplement it with red squash. Some Tunisians also enrich it with potatoes, peas, or lentils.

Depending on the region and the cook, *chakchouka* can also be garnished with merguez (spicy sausage), octopus, shrimp, or eggs. Chokri Chteoui, a native of Ksour Essef, has an even more original approach and boldly adds snails to the dish. The children of this region take advantage of rainy days to go looking for the small gastropods in the forest, just as our chef did in his youth.

Our chef buys his live snails in the *souk* (the market). He keeps them and feeds them on semolina, thyme, and rosemary for several days, to give them a unique flavor before cooking them.

In his recipe, Chokri Chteoui has used two local varieties of snail: one is quite small with a white shell marked with a chocolate-colored spiral; the second, which resembles a snail from Burgundy, has a gray, finely-streaked shell. The "little grays" variety would also be perfectly suitable. If you use canned snails you won't need to cook them for as long as 45 minutes.

The squash used by our chef is an ordinary pumpkin, which is very easy to find. In Tunisian cookery, it's served with couscous, in *chakchouka*, and also is often reduced in soups for children's meals.

Rinse the snails thoroughly in several changes of water. Cook for 45 minutes in a pan of hot water, adding thyme and rosemary. Meanwhile, crush the garlic in a mortar with the caraway seeds, coriander, and salt and set aside.

Peel the squash and the onions and cut into large cubes. Cut the chiles into strips. Cut the tomatoes in two, de-seed and quarter them and then cut into cubes.

Heat the olive oil in a saucepan. Add the onions to the hot oil and brown them, stirring all the while, to prevent them sticking to the bottom of the pan.

with Snails

Once the onions have started to brown, add the tomato paste, and mix gently. Add the fresh tomatoes, bring to the boil, keep it bubbling, and stir well. Season with salt and pepper.

Sprinkle the mixture with chile powder. Add the harissa, the cubes of squash, the chile, and the reserved garlic and spice mixture. Simmer for 15–20 minutes, until the vegetables are very tender. This mixture is the chakchouka.

As soon as the snails are cooked, drain them. Add them to the chakchouka. Reheat for about 10 minutes, stirring continuously. Serve hot, garnished with the parsley, if using.

Bissara

Preparation time:	*30 minutes*
Cooking time:	*30 minutes*
Difficulty:	★

Serves 4

1	onion, chopped
2	garlic cloves, crushed
3½ tbsp/50 ml	olive oil
1 tbsp/17 g	tomato paste
2	tomatoes

4	eggs
1¼ lb/500 g	green fava beans (broad beans)
	salt and pepper

Tunisian hospitality is recognized all over the world. If you have the good fortune to be invited to share a meal with a family, you might be surprised to find that the appetizers follow one after another.

Bissara with green fava beans is generally offered as the second hot appetizer. It is a traditional peasant recipe. In this farming region, where women work on the land and look after the children, this specialty has the advantage of being nourishing and quick to prepare. Fava beans are an important ingredient in Tunisian dishes. Particularly rich in proteins and vitamins—even when dried—they are very nutritious. They belong to the same family as peas, which can be used instead of fava beans in this recipe.

Originating from Persia and Africa, fava beans have been known and eaten in the Mediterranean region since ancient times. They are both spring and summer vegetables, and are sometimes served cold in salads. When they're young, you don't need to remove their delicate skin.

Onions, which are an ingredient of *bissara*, are found in many Tunisian recipes. According to our chef, they help the body fight against the effects of the heat.

In this farming region, the people tend to live on what the farm produces: eggs, poultry, vegetables, fruit, and so on, so it's no surprise to find a soft-boiled egg as the accompaniment to *bissara*. Eggs have been eaten for their nutritional value and versatility since ancient times. They will keep for a minimum of three weeks in the least cold part of the fridge. Store them pointed end down, and never wash the shells; otherwise the eggs will absorb strong odors.

Although *Bissara* is a traditional appetizer from the Béja region, you can serve it as a main dish.

Brown the chopped onion in 3½ tbsp (50 ml) of olive oil for 3–4 minutes. Add the crushed garlic to the onion. Mix well.

Add the tomato paste to the onion and garlic, and mix well.

Peel the tomatoes and deseed them. Cut them into small cubes and add to the mixture. Season with salt and pepper. Cook for approximately 5 minutes.

Stir and add 7 tbsp/100 ml water.

After shelling the fava beans and removing the skins, add them to the mixture. Cook for 15–20 minutes.

Break the eggs into a ramekin. Then transfer them to the mixture, cover and poach for approximately 8 minutes. Using a skimming ladle, remove. Arrange with the fava beans and the tomato sauce on plates.

Ojja with Shrimp

Preparation time:	15 minutes
Cooking time:	15 minutes
Difficulty:	★

Serves 4

1¼ lb/500 g	mild green chiles
8¾ oz/250 g	tomatoes
2	garlic cloves, crushed
7 tbsp/100 ml	olive oil
2 tbsp/35 g	tomato paste
1 tsp	harissa
1¼ lb/500 g	small shelled shrimp
1 tsp	ground cumin
4	eggs
	salt and pepper

For the garnish:

	ground cumin

Ojja is a traditional Tunisian specialty. It is a hot appetizer that is similar to the Basque *piperade* with its basic ingredients of tomatoes, mild green chiles, and eggs. The dish comes from Nabeul, the pottery capital, in the Cap Bon region, and is prepared in a variety of ways. According to each family's preference, *ojja* can include lamb's brain, dried herring, or merguez. *Ojja* with scrambled eggs and harissa is nicknamed *kadhaba*, which means "untruthful woman!"

For his part, our chef wanted to add a touch of sophistication by making this recipe with small pink shrimp. These crustaceans, highly prized for the delicacy of their flesh, are often sold in their shells. They impart the taste of the sea to this hot appetizer. If you buy pre-cooked shrimp, add them to the mixture at the same time as the chiles.

Tomatoes are closely associated with Tunisian culinary heritage. They must be firm, plump, shiny, and preferably have a uniform color. If the tomatoes are very juicy, there's no need to add the half glass of water.

It's vital to add the ground cumin at the last moment to avoid a bitter flavor. This aromatic plant, which has its origins in Turkestan and has been spreading across the Mediterranean region for centuries, is distinguished by its hot, spicy, and slightly sharp taste. Follow the example of our chef and use it as decoration for your plates too. Its slightly ocher color harmonizes perfectly with the hot colors of the *ojja*.

This simple appetizer is easy to prepare and is quite filling. If you haven't tried it before, it's high time you discovered it.

Cut the chiles into thick slices and the tomatoes into cubes.

Brown the garlic with 7 tbsp/100 ml olive oil in a saucepan. Add the cubed tomatoes and simmer for approximately 3 minutes.

Add the tomato paste and the harissa. Simmer for approximately 3 minutes.

from Nabeul

Add the shelled shrimp. Pour in ½ glass of water and reduce for approximately 2 minutes.

Add the sliced chiles. As soon as the sauce becomes smooth and the chiles have softened, add salt and pepper, and sprinkle the ground cumin into the mixture.

Break the eggs into a bowl and beat to an omelet mix. Stir them into the mixture. Cover the pan and cook them over a low heat for approximately 3 minutes. Arrange on a plate and garnish with a touch of cumin.

Jban Briouates

Preparation time: 30 minutes
Cooking time: 3–4 minutes
Difficulty: ★

Serves 4

3½ oz/100 g   black pitted olives
½ bunch   cilantro (coriander)
2 pieces   jban (fresh goat's cheese)
      white pepper

2   eggs
1¼ lbs/500 g   yufka pastry dough sheets
      (or Phyllo)
      oil for frying

For the garnish:
1   tomato
      leaves of mint

If you travel to the Fez region, you will certainly have the opportunity of tasting the famous *briouates*. In a menu of several courses, these dainty little bites are served as an appetizer or a dessert. Their fillings vary according to what the chef puts in them or what is available on the market. Some prepare them with chicken, pigeon, spinach, or shrimp. Others prefer almond paste or honey.

You can let your imagination run free when preparing the fillings. The chef for this dish has decided on *jban*, the typical Moroccan soft goat's cheese. This cheese is generally used in sweet cookies and cakes, and is made only from goat's milk. It contains less than 45 percent fat and has a sweetish, sometimes slightly sour aroma. If you cannot get hold of it, ricotta is also suitable, but it has a much more neutral taste.

In this recipe the cilantro gives the goat's cheese its special aroma. Cilantro—coriander leaf—is an important ingredient in many Arab dishes, from salads, soups, and ragouts to fish. Black olives are particularly favored in the Mediterranean, and are pickled in brine. Even if they are rinsed, they don't lose their salty taste. Remember this when seasoning!

In Morocco, cooking is unthinkable without sheets of *yufka* pastry. These are made from flour, salt, and water only, and in earlier years families made them themselves. Experience is necessary for their preparation. Wherever *yufka* pastry sheets are still made by hand, this is done by very experienced women who still use the *tabsil dial ouarqua*, a copper tray with a tin-plated surface on which the pastry sheets can be heated.

Dice the black olives into small pieces on the work surface.

Wash the cilantro and chop finely with a large knife.

In a bowl, mix the goat's cheese, diced olives, and chopped cilantro.

with Cilantro

Season with pepper. Break 1 egg into a small bowl, beat and add to the salad bowl. Mix using a wooden spoon.

Using a long knife, cut the yufka pastry lengthways into strips. Break the second egg into a small bowl, beat, and put aside.

Place a little filling onto each strip. Then fold from left to right to make a closed triangle. Stick down the end with beaten egg. Deep-fry for 3–4 minutes. Drain. Arrange on serving platters and garnish with a piece of tomato and fresh mint.

Seafood and

Preparation time:	1 hour
Soaking time:	15 minutes
Cooking time:	35 minutes
Difficulty:	★★★

Serves 4

3 oz/80 g	Chinese thread noodles
10 oz/300 g	button mushrooms
11 oz/320 g	chicken
3½ oz/100 g	calamaries (small squid)
1 tbsp/15 ml	olive oil
7 tbsp/100 ml	peanut oil
4	medium onions
2 cloves	garlic
1 tsp/5 g	saffron threads

½ envelope	Moroccan saffron for coloring
1 pinch	ginger
1½ tsp	paprika powder
2	fillets of white fish
3½ oz/100 g	small shrimp, boiled and shelled
1 bunch	fresh cilantro (coriander)
1 bunch	flat-leaf parsley
½ stick/60 g	fresh (unsalted) butter
1	lemon
1	egg yolk
8 sheets	yufka pastry dough (or Phyllo)
	salt and pepper

Traditionally, *m'hancha* are served as sweet pastries; the sheets of pastry are filled with a sweet almond mixture, rolled up, and formed into a spiral shape. Between 1993 and 1994, Bouchaïb Kama developed a savory version for the Farah restaurant and hotel in Casablanca. This is filled with chicken, seafood, button mushrooms, and Chinese thread noodles. After being promoted on various TV programs, the recipe has motivated other chefs and restaurateurs to serve this dish at weddings and receptions.

The chef recommends using small shrimp for the filling. In the seas around Morocco, there are many varieties of shrimp, and all of them are delicious. Among the best known are the blue shrimp, the fat *bouark*, common shrimp, scampi, and various deep-sea shrimp with bright red shells.

Calamaries (small squid) require careful preparation. Cut off the head, draw out the intestines and the bone, then turn the mantle inside-out like a glove and rinse off any remaining sand.

Your choice of seafood will naturally depend on what is available in the market. It is then up to you whether to use shellfish, such as shrimp, mussels, cockles, scallops, or fillets of fish such as sea bass, shi drum, John Dory, or sole.

When frying the diced chicken together with the button mushrooms, you can add fish or shrimp stock to braise the ingredients and add flavor. Let the filling cool before rolling it up in the pastry sheets, to avoid the *m'hancha* splitting during baking.

Soak the noodles. Dice the mushrooms and chicken. Clean and gut the calamaries. Fry the chopped onions, garlic, and saffron threads in 1 tbsp each of olive and peanut oil. Add the chicken, calamaries, button mushrooms, salt, pepper, saffron powder, ginger, and paprika.

Allow the ingredients to simmer for 8 minutes, then stir in the thread noodles, cut small with a knife. Cook for 6–8 minutes. Add fish fillets and shrimp. Cook for a further 8–10 minutes.

After cooking, add cilantro and parsley, both finely chopped. Stir once more.

Chicken M'hancha

Spoon in the butter to make the filling smooth. Squeeze the lemon over it and mix in the juice. Transfer the filling to a plate and allow to cool. Meanwhile, beat 1 egg yolk in a small bowl.

Spread 2 sheets of pastry out on the work surface. Place a strip of filling on one end of the sheets. Roll up carefully but firmly from top to bottom. Stick down the ends of the roll with the beaten egg yolk.

Spread peanut oil over the roll. Carefully shape it into a spiral (m'hancha). Coat the end, once again, with egg yolk. Form a further 3 spirals in the same way and then bake all of them in the oven on an oiled baking sheet for about 5 minutes at 400 °F/200 °C.

Small Passover

Preparation time: 40 minutes
Cooking time: 40 minutes
Difficulty: ★

Serves 4

3¼ lbs/1.5 kg	potatoes (Bintje if available)
½	unwaxed lemon
1 tsp	sugar
1 pinch	ground cinnamon
5	eggs
¼ cup/50 g	matzo flour or fine semolina
	oil for frying

For the filling:

1	onion
2¼ lbs/1 kg	ground beef
1 tsp	vegetable oil
½ bunch	parsley
2	bay leaves
½ tsp	grated nutmeg
½ tsp	mace
1	pinch saffron threads
	salt and pepper

The Passover festival commemorates the exodus of the Israelites from Egypt and the end of their enslavement. This important festival in the Jewish calendar is celebrated by all families. In remembrance of the event as told in the Torah, Jews, just the same as their forebears, may not eat anything made of leavened dough during the festival.

For the Passover festival, all the rooms of the house are thoroughly cleaned to remove the last particle of yeast, *hamets*. The ritual prescribes the eating of only unleavened bread or *matzo* at the table.

In Morocco, members of Tangier's Jewish community customarily serve little parmentiers at the Passover table. For these, they shape mashed potatoes, prepared without any milk products, into little domes. With their delicious filling of ground beef, onion, nutmeg, mace, bay leaves,

oil, salt, and pepper, they are particularly popular with children.

This very filling Tangier specialty is more than a substitute for unleavened bread. For Passover, the semolina is replaced with matzo flour, ground from grain that has not been in contact with water, and is often used during the festival.

The best type of potato for the mashed potatoes is "Bintje." This yellow, oval variety can be found in season from September to May. Whatever you use, the parmentiers should not be fried until shortly before serving.

The parmentiers are redolent of mace, a little-used spice made from the scarlet husk of the nutmeg that is pressed and dried and sold as powder or in fine flakes.

For the filling, peel and grate the onion. Chop the parsley. Peel the potatoes for the parmentiers and cook them in salted water. Wash the half lemon, grate the peel, and put aside.

Heat the ground beef with 1 tsp of oil, then pour on water to cover. Add parsley, onion, bay leaves, nutmeg, mace, and saffron threads. Season with salt and pepper. Cook until all the water has evaporated.

Mash the cooked potatoes. Add grated lemon peel, sugar, and ground cinnamon. Knead the mixture with your hands. Boil 2 eggs in salted water, shell and put aside.

Parmentiers

Use your hands to make ball shapes out of the mashed potatoes. Hollow these out to form bowls.

Chop the hard-boiled eggs. Fill the shells of mashed potatoes with ground beef and place a piece of egg on top of each. Shape the mashed potato bowls into cones.

Break 3 eggs and beat them. Dip the parmentiers first in egg, then in matzo flour or semolina. Heat the oil in a pan and deep-fry the parmentiers until light brown. Serve the parmentiers in little bowls.

Soups &
Tagines

Preparation time:	30 minutes
Cooking time:	1 hour
Difficulty:	★

Serves 4

2½ tbsp/40 g	dried porcini
1 cup/250 g	fresh chanterelles
¾ cup/200 ml	olive oil
2	onions
2	leeks
3	ripe tomatoes

2 cups/500 ml	chicken stock
2 slices	white bread
	salt

For the picada:

2 cloves	garlic
pinch/0.6 g	saffron
4 tsp/20 g	toasted almonds
pinch	salt

Mushroom gatherers take to the forests of Catalonia in September, so it is hardly surprising that there should be an abundance of recipes for mushroom soup. This soup is a popular everyday dish that owes its full spiciness not only to the mushrooms in it, but also to the addition of onions, tomatoes, and leeks.

Pep Masiques prefers two highly aromatic mushroom varieties: porcini and chanterelles. The latter grow in mixed forests from the end of May to October, at the foot of oaks, chestnuts, and walnut trees, as well as around conifers. The aroma of this mild, slightly peppery, mushroom is reminiscent of peaches or apricots.

In contrast to the chanterelles, which are used fresh, for this recipe Pep Masiques prefers to use dried porcini. These tiny, gray-pink mushrooms have a slightly cone-shaped top and a tough inedible stalk. They grow in abundance in fields and meadows, and by the side of the road, from spring until fall. Remember to drain the mushrooms in a sieve after cooking to remove any excess oil. Instead of using bought chicken stock, you can also "stretch" this soup by using your own chicken stock, which you can make from chicken bones and vegetables.

For the *picada* (spiced paste), chef puts the mortar on the kitchen towel and wraps the ends around the pestle to prevent the contents from escaping. Some families simply purée the soup, but purists insist on straining it through a sieve for an even finer, more homogeneous consistency. If you find the soup too thick, thin it with a little hot water or stock.

Soak the porcini in warm water for 5 minutes and drain. Wash the chanterelles and cut into pieces, reserving 2–3 for garnish.

Heat ⅔ cup/150 ml olive oil in a skillet and sauté the porcini for 5 minutes. Then add the chanterelles, and season with salt. Simmer for 10 minutes until the liquid has evaporated. Drain the mushrooms.

Peel and finely chop the onions. Sauté in the remainder of the oil with the finely sliced leeks for 15–20 minutes. Cut the tomatoes into quarters and add. Simmer for a further 8–10 minutes.

Mushroom Soup

Add the mushrooms, pour over the stock, and stir well. Bring to the boil.

Place the bread slices in the soup, then simmer for 5 minutes.

For the picada, peel and coarsely chop the garlic. Then crush in the mortar with saffron, almonds, and a pinch of salt. Add this paste to the soup and blend with a hand blender. Serve garnished with fried chanterelles.

Palm Sunday

Preparation time: 20 minutes
Cooking time: 30 minutes
Difficulty: ★

Serves 4

2	green bell peppers
2	red bell peppers
16 stalks	green asparagus
4	tomatoes

12 slices	white bread
	a little olive oil
4 cloves	garlic
8 cups/2 l	chicken stock
4–5	flat-leaf parsley stalks
	salt and pepper

In spring, the inhabitants of Málaga love to prepare a selection of fine vegetables in clear stock. This dish is called *sopa de siete ramos*, which literally means "soup of the seven branches." According to history, the name reminds us of Easter week and the custom of consecrating palm or box branches on Palm Sunday.

Red and green bell peppers, tomatoes, garlic, and asparagus are the base for this delicious soup. Try to use wild asparagus if you can find it; according to Javier Valero, this is much better than the farmed variety. The green to lilac-colored stalks are very thin with an extremely characteristic aroma that is much prized in Spain.

However, green farmed asparagus is far more readily available, and can happily be used for this soup. In Spain it is grown primarily in Navarre, and harvested from April to June. The wooden stalk is removed before peeling. After blanching them, plunge the stalks in iced water so they retain their deep green color.

Pour boiling water over the tomatoes, then skin them and remove the seeds. Cut them into quarters; according to Javier Valero they then look like "petals."

The ingredients are all poached in chicken stock. You can make it from bouillon, but home-made stock is much tastier. To make your own, brown a chicken carcass with some soup vegetables (onion, cloves, carrots, bay leaf, celery, leek), then cover with water. Simmer for a good 90 minutes, then strain.

To serve, the vegetables are arranged on small plates with the croutons. The stock is served separately.

Place the bell peppers on a foil-covered baking sheet and broil for about 10 minutes. Using the tip of a sharp kitchen knife, remove the skin and cut the peppers into slices.

Wash the asparagus and pat dry. Peel from top to bottom, then blanch in boiling salted water for 5 minutes.

Place the tomatoes in a bowl, then pour over boiling water. As soon as the skin starts to lift, pour the water away and plunge the tomatoes into iced water. Peel with a small, sharp knife, remove the seeds, and cut the flesh into slices.

Soup

Cut the bread into cubes and sprinkle over a little olive oil. Place on a baking sheet and bake in a preheated oven for a few moments. Then rub each piece with a peeled garlic clove.

Bring the chicken stock to the boil. Add the asparagus, tomatoes, red and green bell peppers, and season with salt and pepper. Simmer for 5 minutes. Scoop the vegetables out of the stock with a skimmer.

Peel the remainder of the garlic and cut into thin slices. Sauté in hot olive oil, then add the parsley and pass through a sieve. Pour the stock into soup bowls. Serve the vegetables and croutons separately, and drizzle the flavored oil over the soup.

Preparation time:	45 minutes
Cooking time:	1 hour
Difficulty:	★

Serves 4

1	white onion
1	red onion
1 clove	garlic
2	tomatoes
7 tbsp/100 ml	olive oil
2	leeks
2 cups/500 g	shrimp
4 tbsp/60 ml	cognac
²/₃ cups/150 ml	white wine

5 tsp/25 g	cornstarch
2 cups/500 g	sieved tomatoes (optional)

1 lb 2 oz/500 g	mixed fish fillets (sole, hake, sea perch, scorpion fish etc.)
2 cups/500 g	clams
	salt and pepper
For the fish stock:	
2¼ lb/1 kg	fish offcuts (heads, tails, bones, skin)
	the green of a leek
1	white onion
3	parsley stalks
For the garnish:	
	parsley
	ground paprika (optional)

Basque cuisine is dominated by the sea, and the range of recipes for fish and seafood is as extensive as it is varied. Because the Basques are very traditional, those throughout northern Spain still use the wonderful recipes devised by their ancestors. The Spanish name for this soup is *sopa de pezcado a la marinera*. It is a standard dish for fishermen's families, who always use whatever is caught. The soup is especially popular in winter.

You can use whatever fish is available. Emilio González Soto likes sole, because the flesh of this fish, which is at home on the sandy bottom of the Atlantic Ocean, is delicate and aromatic. He also likes to include scorpion fish—*rascasse* is a key ingredient of bouillabaisse—which is popular for its white, oily flesh.

Home-made fish stock is essential for the success of this dish. It is made from offcuts (heads, tails, bones, and skin), and is pure flavor. The stock, which also includes parsley, leek greens, and white onions, develops its typical aroma after being reduced and strained.

Basques love all kinds of shellfish, especially clams, usually plain or stuffed. Clams are gathered along the Atlantic coast, but they are also found in the Mediterranean, where another variety, the carpet shell—also known as the *clovisse*—hails from. Mussels can be used instead. The cognac emphasizes the typical aroma of this tasty soup.

You can also add sieved tomatoes—as we have done here—to enhance the color of the soup.

Peel and thinly slice the white and red onions and the garlic clove. Finely chop the tomatoes.

To make the fish stock, bring 8 cups/2 l water to the boil with 1 lb 2 oz/500 g fish offcuts, the green of a leek, a sliced white onion, and the parsley, then boil briskly for around 3 minutes.

Sauté in olive oil the finely sliced white of the leeks, tomatoes, onions, and garlic in olive oil. Simmer for 15 minutes. Prepare the shrimp, and put the heads in the pot. Add the remainder of the fish offcuts, stir, and simmer for 5 minutes.

Fish Soup

Add the cognac and wine, and stir. Strain this liquid through a sieve, add to the fish stock, then simmer for a further 30 minutes.

Blend the cornstarch with 7 tbsp (100 ml) water in a small bowl. Strain the soup through a sieve, then return to the heat and stir in the starch. Return to the boil, stirring continuously. Add the tomatoes to the bubbling soup.

Season with salt and pepper. Remove any foam with a skimmer. Add the shrimp, fish fillets, and clams, then bring to the boil. Remove from the heat and leave to stand for 5 minutes. Pour into deep bowls. Garnish with parsley and ground paprika.

Cold

Preparation time: 10 minutes
Chilling time: 20 minutes
Difficulty: ★

Serves 4

3 cups/750 g	fresh strawberries
1	green bell pepper
1	red bell pepper
1	onion
2 cloves	garlic
2 tbsp/30 g	confectioner's sugar

³/₄ cup/200 ml	olive oil
6¹/₂ tbsp/100 ml	sherry vinegar
1 tsp	salt
1 tsp	pepper

For the garnish (optional):

chopped red bell pepper
chopped green bell
    pepper
croutons

José Luis Tarín Fernández's brightly colored, nutritious and refreshing strawberry soup is proof of the creativity of modern Spanish cuisine. Much is reminiscent of Andalusian gazpacho, the main difference being that this recipe uses sweetly aromatic strawberries instead of tomatoes. The soup is so original that no other fruit can be used as a substitute for the strawberries unless you want something slightly more acidic, in which case add a handful of raspberries.

To make the soup nice and mild, use very ripe summer strawberries with a firm flesh. Choose large, fully ripe specimens with no marks. Strawberries are very delicate and must be handled with care. Wash them quickly under running cold water, then leave them to drain.

Bell peppers are a firm fixture in Spanish cuisine, and can be combined with any number of sauces. Whether a slightly acid green or a mild red bell pepper, the main thing is that the peppers are bright in color with a smooth, shiny skin. The thin white pith and seeds are removed because they are indigestible. The sweet aroma of the red bell pepper can overpower the delicate flavor of the strawberries. Our chef therefore adds a little sherry vinegar for its slight tartness. Vinegar made from sherry is very spicy. It is also quite viscous, and does not readily dissolve. Add the required amount to the soup in several small amounts and stir well. If you do not happen to have any sherry vinegar to hand, use a few drops of balsamic.

The strawberry soup is puréed in the blender, then passed through a sieve. Chill in the refrigerator for a few minutes before serving. Croutons go well with this dish.

Trim the strawberries. Carefully remove the stalks and leaves without damaging the fruits. Wash the strawberries under running cold water, then place in a sieve to drain. Cut into quarters.

Wash the bell peppers and pat them dry, then cut in half lengthwise. Remove the pith and seeds. Cut the peppers into quarters, then cut these into chunks 1 in/3 cm in length. Do the same with the peeled onion. Peel and halve the garlic.

Place the bell peppers, onion, garlic, and strawberries in the blender, then add the salt, pepper, and sugar. Purée carefully for 2–3 minutes until you have a velvety-smooth, well-blended mixture.

Strawberry Soup

Remove the lid from the blender and pour in half the olive oil. Run the machine again at high speed, then add the remainder of the olive oil and run for a further 2–3 minutes.

Place a sieve over a bowl. Ladle the soup into it in several portions and pass through the sieve using the ladle to squeeze as much liquid as possible out of the flesh.

Add the vinegar and stir in well until it has completely dissolved. Check the soup, adding more seasoning if required, then chill for 20 minutes. Serve very cold but not icy. Garnish with diced bell peppers and croutons.

Cold Almond Soup

Preparation time: 30 minutes
Cooking time: 10 minutes
Difficulty: ★

Serves 4

4 oz/100 g	grapes
1½ cups/350 ml	virgin olive oil
1½ cups/350 g	skinned almonds

½	day-old baguette
1 clove	garlic
5 tbsp/80 ml	sherry vinegar
	salt and pepper

For the garnish:

4	chive stalks

There is an old Spanish tradition of enhancing everyday meals with delicious soups. Soups are essential as an appetizer or the main part of a light evening meal. Fresh vegetables are usually used for these simple, delicate soups, so this delightful cold almond soup—a specialty from Málaga—is something of an exception. It is very easy to make, but its charm lies in the quality of the ingredients; the utmost care is taken when choosing them.

The process starts with the almonds. They are used dried rather than harvested fresh. Spain's almond trees flower in the spring, so the almonds used are usually from domestic trees. The growing region extends from Tarragona to Valencia and Málaga, but there are also plantations in Granada and Almería, and on the Canary Islands. There are many different varieties of almonds, all of different shapes which range from long and slender to heart-shaped. These versatile nuts are served with an aperitif or as a satisfying snack, and are used in countless baked goods, candies, and desserts. They are also an important source of protein: a single almond contains 45 percent fat, plenty of iron, calcium, phosphorus, and vitamin B.

The olive oil used should have an acid content of 0.2 to 0.4 degrees.

The soup is passed through a sieve to make it nice and smooth. Traditionally it is served with bread, grapes, and thin slices of sweet melon. Essentially a simple soup, it looks particularly appealing if served in stemmed glasses.

Remove the grapes from the stalks. Carefully cut them in half with a sharp knife and remove the seeds.

Heat 4 tbsp/60 ml of olive oil and sauté the blanched almonds until golden.

Cut the crusts off the baguette and cut the bread into strips, then into 1 in/3 cm squares.

from Málaga

Peel the garlic and remove the core. Purée in the blender, together with the almonds.

Add the diced bread and continue blending, gradually adding the vinegar and the remainder of the olive oil. When the mixture is smooth, add 4 cups/1 l of water, then season with salt and pepper.

Pour the almond soup into soup bowls or stemmed glasses. Garnish with grapes and chopped chives.

Cold Cream of Almonds

Preparation time: 45 minutes
Steeping time for
  vegetables and almonds: 8 hours
Difficulty: ★

Serves 4

2	scallions
1	onion
1 lb/500 g	ripe Mallorcan tomatoes

2	Mallorcan green bell peppers
1 cup/150 g	blanched Mallorcan almonds
1 tsp/5 g	paprika
3½ tbsp/50 ml	sherry vinegar
⁴/₅ cup/200 ml	extra-virgin olive oil
	salt

Trampó is one of the favorite dishes eaten by country people on the Balearic Islands. The classic version consists simply of a refreshing summer salad of bell peppers, tomatoes, onions, and olives, dressed with good quality olive oil and vinegar. Some chefs serve it as an accompaniment to baked fish. Oscar Martínez Plaza has taken this classic recipe and created a marvelous new dish by mixing the ingredients with almond milk. A garnish of diced vegetables remains, however, to remind us of the dish's origins.

Oscar Martínez Plaza uses typical Balearic vegetables for this recipe. Mallorca, the largest of the islands, is famous for its vegetable produce. Since the island is not large, the vegetables are still very fresh when they reach the village markets or the main covered market in Palma, the Mercat Olivar.

The main vegetable crop on Mallorca is tomatoes, grown over an area of more than 2,500 acres/1,000 hectares. The tomatoes are often tied into bunches and sun-dried by hanging against the walls of the houses. Tomatoes dried in this way are known as *tomàtigues de ramellet* in Catalan, or *tomates de ramillete* in Castilian.

The idea of combining *trampó* with almonds is not so surprising, since almonds grow abundantly on the Balearic Islands. The Arabs, who colonized these islands between the 8th and the 13th centuries, introduced and cultivated both almonds and figs. Mallorcan almonds, while irregular in size and so not considered to be of the finest quality, have a fine flavor. Mixed with water and the vegetables, they should be allowed to soak for a long time in order to rehydrate, becoming juicy and easier to mix. The resulting soup is both tasty and elegant.

Wash the vegetables. Chop the scallions, peel and chop the onions, and cut the tomatoes into quarters. Cut open the peppers, remove the seeds, and roughly chop (reserve a half of each type of vegetable for the garnish).

Mix all the vegetables in a bowl. Add the almonds and the paprika, reserving a few almonds for the garnish. Cover with water and leave to soak for 8 hours. Drain.

Tip the ingredients into a food processor and blend until creamy.

with Trampó

Add salt, the vinegar, and ²/₃ cup of olive oil. Blend again.

Sieve the creamed vegetables into a bowl.

Cut the reserved halves of tomato, onion, green pepper, and scallion into small dice. Season with salt and 3¹/₂ tbsp of olive oil. Pour the soup into soup bowls, garnishing it with a few almonds surrounded by a circle of vegetable dice.

Menorcan Crawfish

Preparation time: 45 minutes
Cooking time: 45 minutes
Difficulty: ★★

Serves 4

1	Menorcan crawfish weighing 3 lb/1.5 kg
⁴/₅ cup/200 ml	olive oil
⁴/₅ cup/200 ml	brandy
1	onion
1 clove	garlic
1	tomato
10 cups/2.5 liters	fish bouillon

For the *majado*:

1 cup/150 g	blanched almonds
	olive oil for frying crawfish "coral"
2 cloves	garlic
1 sprig	parsley
1 sprig	fresh thyme
2 or 3 slices	bread
7 tbsp/100 ml	Mallorcan herb liqueur

For the toast:

8 slices	stale bread
1 clove	garlic
¼ cup/50 g	red pork fat

The small island of Menorca is famous for its crawfish soup. Known all over the island, *caldereta de langosta*, as it is called locally, has put the northern bay of Cala Fornells firmly on the culinary map.

Menorcan fishermen catch the crawfish in woven pots placed on the sea floor. The crawfish feeding grounds lie off the rocky shores of the Balearic Islands; here they find the shellfish that give such a delicate flavor to their meat. Strict rules are imposed to protect this valuable natural resource, with fishing restricted to the period from May to September. Any crawfish that are smaller than 8 inches/ 19 cm in length must be returned to the sea.

To prepare the live crawfish, place it on a chopping board and hold its head down firmly with a cloth. With the other hand, cut through the neck with a cleaver. Empty the orange parts found within the head (the "coral") into a bowl.

Chop the head open in order to get at the remaining coral. This will be used to bind, color, and flavor the *majado*, a pounded or mixed paste used to thicken the bouillon.

The bouillon is generally made from rock fish (whole or scrap pieces), lightly browned with tomatoes, onions, and garlic and then covered with water. This mixture is brought to the boil and then simmered. Alternatively, a good quality fish bouillon cube can be used, adding the vegetables and the crawfish shells.

The *majado* used to give body to the bouillon is based on almonds and flavored with a Mallorcan liqueur made of local herbs. This aniseed-flavored digestive has a beautiful green color, perfumed with rosemary, marjoram, lime flowers, chamomile, fennel, and mint. A good-quality Provençal pastis can be substituted if necessary.

Fry the blanched almonds in the olive oil and set aside. Holding the crawfish firmly on a chopping board, sever the head and empty the coral into a bowl for use later. Blanch the crawfish tail in boiling water and then remove the shell.

Heat ⁴/₅ cup of olive oil in a pan. Add the pieces of crawfish head and brown them. Pour over the brandy and flambé it, shaking the pan. Continue for 2–3 minutes until the flames have died down.

Add 1 onion, 1 garlic clove, and 1 tomato to the fish bouillon, bring it the boil and simmer for 10 minutes. Pour the bouillon over the pan containing the pieces of crawfish. Bring it to the boil again and cook for 15 minutes.

Soup

For the majado, *using a mortar, pound to-gether the garlic, parsley, thyme, cubes of bread fried in oil (keep a few to garnish), the fried almonds, and the herb liqueur. Gradually add the crawfish coral, grinding the ingredients until a smooth paste has been obtained.*

Leaving the bouillon on a low heat, add the majado *and mix it in to thicken the liquid. Turn up the heat for a few minutes.*

Toast the slices of bread, rub them with a garlic clove, then spread with red pork fat. Pour the soup into the bowls and place a lump of crawfish head and some of the meat from the tail in the center. Garnish with cubes of fried bread and herbs. Eat with the pieces of toasted bread.

Cream of Pumpkin

Preparation time: 20 minutes
Cooking time: 40 minutes
Difficulty: ★

Serves 4

1	onion
1 tbsp	olive oil
1½ cups/250 g	pumpkin
1 clove	garlic
1 cup/250 ml	chicken stock

1 cup/250 ml	light cream
	salt
	pepper
1 pinch	grated nutmeg
	juice of ½ lemon
1 bunch	fresh chives

For the garnish:

1 tbsp	olive oil

This cream of pumpkin soup with chives is a wonderful way to get children to eat soup. It's easy to prepare, and its sweetness and color are reminiscent of the beautiful Provençal countryside.

The term "pumpkin" covers a wide variety of fruits, such as the calabash, marrow (giant zucchini), and Hokkaido pumpkin. These members of the pumpkin family originate from Asia, Africa, and America. They are round, voluminous, and colored red and yellow, inside and out. They appear on plates in the winter in the form of soup, baked *au gratin*, mashed, or baked as a sweet pie. Provençal pumpkin is brownish and slightly sweet, like the calabash. Our chef cooks pumpkin in chicken stock.

The chef sweats the onions, so that the soup develops a full flavor, but they should not brown. Onions originally came from Asia and have been cultivated for over 5,000 years.

They consist of fleshy, white leaves surrounded by a papery yellow, brown, red, or white skin. Christian Étienne prefers using brown onions.

Ground nutmeg is indispensable in this recipe, because it heightens the pumpkin's flavor. This spice, originating from Southeast Asia, has a very spicy and intense aroma.

Chive, a relative of onions and garlic, has an onion-like taste. It is used fresh, chopped into little rings.

The success of this dish depends on the ingredients. If any of them is omitted, the cream of pumpkin soup will lose its delicious aroma.

Peel and slice the onion. Heat 1 tbsp olive oil in a pan and sweat the onion in it.

Peel the pumpkin, removing the seeds and fibers. Cut the pumpkin flesh into small dice. Crush the garlic. Add the diced pumpkin and crushed garlic to the onion and mix well.

Pour the chicken stock into the pan and simmer for 15 minutes, stirring frequently, until the liquid has evaporated.

Soup with Chives

Stir in the cream and simmer the soup for a further 15 minutes. Season to taste with salt and pepper.

Pass the cream of pumpkin soup through a sieve, so the texture is nice and smooth. Add a pinch of ground nutmeg.

To heighten the pumpkin taste, fold in the lemon juice and chopped chives. Serve in soup cups or deep bowls, garnished with a drizzle of olive oil.

Bouillabaisse

Preparation time:	20 minutes
Cooking time:	1 hour
Difficulty:	★

Serves 8–10

2	onions
4 cloves	garlic
3 tbsp	olive oil
3	tomatoes
1 tbsp	tomato paste
1 piece	dried fennel
	weighing 3½ oz/100 g
3 envelopes	saffron
2¼ lb/1 kg	rock fish
4	large potatoes

2	scorpion fish,
	each 14 oz/400 g
3	gurnard, each 7 oz/200 g
1 lb 10 oz/800 g	monkfish

1 lb 10 oz/800g	conger eel
3	weever fish,
	each 7 oz/200 g
2¼ lb/1 kg	John Dory
4	rock lobster
	salt, pepper

For the garlic mayonnaise (rouille):

3	egg yolks
8 cloves	garlic
2 cups/500 ml	olive oil
	salt, powdered saffron

For the croutons:

1	thin baguette
5 cloves	garlic
2 tbsp	olive oil

Bouillabaisse, a very special fish soup from Marseilles, is famous throughout the world. The word *bouillabaisse* comes from the Provençal *bouïa-baisso*, roughly meaning "cooked on a low flame." In the past, the soup was first boiled up, before continuing to simmer on a low flame.

This soup was a simple fisherman's meal. Sea water was used for cooking, with the fish simmering in the water just as they had been caught. Nowadays bouillabaisse has become a classic dish and is a particular specialty of the "Miramar," our chef's restaurant.

In 1980 this fish soup became the subject of a legal directive, specifying which fish can be used in this recipe: gurnard, weever fish, John Dory, monkfish, conger eel,

scorpion fish, and rock lobster. You can choose whatever is available. Jean-Michel Minguella advises using six varieties of fish, but you can use just four.

Whilst the fish are cooking you should keep your eye on them and take them out of the pan as soon as they are cooked. To enjoy the splendor of this dish, bring the fish to the table whole, and portion it there.

Make the essential hot, red, garlic mayonnaise (*rouille*) in the blender like ordinary mayonnaise. Season the egg yolk with salt, and add finely chopped garlic. To rescue mayonnaise which has separated, add an ice cube to the blender while it is running, and as if by magic, the ingredients will form a smooth, creamy emulsion.

Peel and finely chop the onions and garlic. Heat 3 tbsp olive oil in a large pan, add the onions and garlic, and fry until softened. Cut the tomatoes into quarters and add them with the tomato paste, dried fennel, and 2 envelopes of saffron to the pan.

Add the rock fish and enough water to cover. Season with salt and simmer for 20 minutes. Strain the fish and vegetables, reserving the broth. Purée the fish and vegetables. Strain the soup and return it to the pan. Simmer for a further 10 minutes and put aside.

Peel the potatoes and slice them lengthwise into ¾ in/2 cm-thick slices. Pour some of the reserved fish broth into a long fish kettle and add the potatoes.

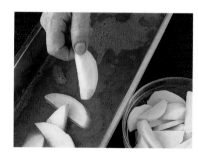

'Miramar"

Place the scorpion fish, gurnard, monk-fish, conger eel, weever fish, John Dory, and rock lobster in the fish kettle, starting with the biggest and finishing with the smallest.

Pour the remaining broth over the fish and season. Add the rest of the saffron. Cook at a rolling boil for 5 minutes, then simmer for 30 minutes on low heat. To make the mayonnaise, beat the egg yolks, add the salt, garlic, and saffron, then beat in the olive oil, drop by drop.

Slice the baguette into ¼ in/1 cm-thick slices. Rub them with garlic and drizzle olive oil over them. Bake the slices on a baking sheet in the oven at a temperature of 400 °F/200 °C. Spread rouille on 4 of them. Float one on each serving of soup. Strain the fish and serve with the soup.

"Nice" Minestrone

Preparation time:	2 hours
Soaking time:	8 hours
Cooking time:	40 minutes
Difficulty:	★★

Serves 4

8 cups/2 l	chicken stock
3½ oz/100 g	baby squid
3½ oz/100 g	macaroni
1 or 2	scallions
4 tsp/20 g	chives
	salt, pepper

For the soup vegetables:

3½ oz/100 g	pearl onions
2 oz/50 g	shallots
3½ oz/100 g	fennel
3½ oz/100 g	carrots
3½ oz/100 g	kohlrabi
3½ oz/100 g	navy beans
3½ oz/100 g	cauliflower
3½ oz/100 g	waxy potatoes

3½ oz/100g	fresh peas
3½ oz/100 g	green beans
3½ oz/100 g	zucchini
3½ tbsp/40 g	sun-dried tomatoes
1 tbsp	olive oil

For the basil sauce (pistou):

3 cloves	garlic, peeled
6	basil leaves
3	sun-dried tomatoes
4 tsp/20 g	pine nuts
4 tbsp	olive oil
	salt, pepper

For the bouquet garni:

	thyme
	bay leaf
	parsley

Minestrone, an Italian vegetable soup, always contains pasta, sometimes rice. Most important are the types of vegetables, which vary from region to region. In Tuscany navy beans are essential. Minestrone is often served with bread rubbed with garlic and olive oil. Elsewhere, the soup is served sprinkled with grated cheese.

You need fresh vegetables for our recipe. The navy beans should not soak for more than eight hours, otherwise harmful byproducts will form. Add the bouquet garni whilst the beans are cooking, but do not add salt, or they won't soften.

Macaroni, which is part of minestrone, is supposed to have originated in Arabia. It can be replaced by tagliatelle, which must be cut into pieces. It was our chef's idea to liven up this

vegetable soup by adding baby squid. Clean the squid thoroughly, removing the head (reserving the tentacles), quill, and skin, before rinsing under running water. To ensure that the squid stay tender, put a couple of wine corks in the water so that the water stays below boiling point.

Pistou, which is only added at the end, is a Provençal seasoning made from fresh, chopped basil, pine nuts, garlic, and sometimes sun-dried tomatoes. The ingredients are crushed in a mortar and beaten together with olive oil.

Parmesan cheese and rice should be omitted from this soup. Depending on the time of year you could add a couple of boletus mushrooms (ceps or porcini).

Wash and prepare the soup vegetables. Dice them finely. Dice the sun-dried tomatoes and shuck the peas.

Heat 1 tbsp olive oil in a deep skillet. Sweat the onions, shallots, fennel, and carrots for 3–4 minutes, but don't let them go brown.

Add the chicken stock. Then add the bouquet garni, plus the kohlrabi, navy beans, cauliflower, and potatoes. Simmer for 15 minutes, then add the peas, green beans, zucchini, and tomatoes, and simmer for another 10 minutes.

with Squid

Prepare the squid as described above. Wash the squid well, and plunge them into boiling water to blanch, then add a couple of wine corks to prevent the water boiling any more. Blanch the squid for 2 minutes, then drain.

Bring a pan of salted water to the boil, add the macaroni and cook until it is "al dente." Drain the macaroni and cut into ¼ in/½ cm rings. In a blender, purée together all the ingredients for the pistou.

Add the squid to the vegetable soup, with the macaroni, chopped scallions, and chopped chives. Remove the bouquet garni. Finally stir in the pistou. Season to taste with salt and pepper, and serve hot.

Mussels in Cream of

Preparation time:	30 minutes
Cooking time:	40 minutes
Difficulty:	★

Serves 4

4½ lb/2 kg	mussels
1 cup/250 ml	dry white wine
6 tbsp	olive oil
2 slices	white bread
3 cloves	garlic
1	carrot
1	leek

1	onion
1 lb/500 g	assorted rock fish
1½ tsp	saffron strands
	salt
	pepper
2 cups/500 g	heavy cream

For the garnish:

	fresh chives
	ground saffron

The Bouzigues mussels in the cream of rock fish soup get their name from a little village in the Languedoc region. Mussels are typically grown on lines in the Mediterranean area. Back in Roman times, mussels and oysters were harvested from natural mussel beds.

Sort the mussels carefully. They must be tightly closed and should not look dried out. Use them within three days of purchase. You should discard mussels with cracked or half-open shells. Before cooking them, the mussels are cleaned by removing their beards. To do this you need to scrub the shells under running water.

For this soup, Angel Yagues maintains that it's worth switching off the burner a couple of minutes before the specified time. The mussels then finish cooking, cool down, and you can remove them from their shells sooner.

Gurnard, weever fish, and scorpion fish are examples of rock fish. Don't forget smaller varieties. If you have problems obtaining these fish, ask your fishmonger for sole trimmings, which will also lend flavor to your soup.

This mussel soup goes wonderfully well with saffron. Whether in the shape of brownish strands, or yellowish-red powder, this famous spice comes from the stamens of a bulbed plant of the crocus family. It is characterized by its piquant smell and bitter taste.

You could substitute chervil or parsley for the chives.

Rinse and clean the mussels. Put them in a pan with the white wine, bring to the boil, cover, and simmer for about 5 minutes. Strain the mussels, reserving the broth.

Take the meat out of the mussels and set it aside to cool. Heat 3 tbsp olive oil in a skillet. Fry the white bread in the oil, and take it out of the skillet. Let it cool, then rub it with one of the peeled garlic cloves. Cut out 4 rounds using a round cookie cutter.

Wash, peel, and dice the carrot, leek, and onion. Chop the garlic cloves.

Rock Fish Soup

Heat 3 tbsp olive oil in a pan. Add the vegetables and sweat them in the oil for 5 minutes. Add the cleaned and gutted rock fish.

To make the fish soup, strain the mussel broth through a very fine sieve to filter out the dirt. Pour the broth over the fish and vegetables and add the saffron strands. Season to taste with salt and pepper. Cook the soup on low heat for 20 minutes.

Pass the soup through a chinoise, or sieve, and return it to the pan. Bring it to the boil, simmer for 5 minutes, then stir in the cream. Season to taste. Arrange a circle of mussels in a dish. Pour in the soup. Put a slice of fried bread in the center. Garnish with saffron and chopped chives.

Shrimp Soup

Preparation time: 40 minutes
Cooking time: 20 minutes
Difficulty: ★

Serves 4

1 bunch	scallions
4 cloves	garlic
1	white onion
3 tbsp	olive oil
scant ⅛ stick/10 g	butter
generous ¼ cup/50 g	medium yellow cornmeal (polenta)

2 cups/500 ml	chicken stock
12	large shrimp
1 pinch	hot ground paprika
	salt

For the garnish:

1	white onion
scant ⅛ cup/10 g	flour
	oil for frying
	olive oil

Because he has settled in the area around Nice, our chef acknowledges his close association with Mediterranean culinary traditions, but because he originally comes from Alsace, he also gets nostalgic about the cornmeal soups of his childhood. He thus hit on the idea of bringing a southern flavor to what was an old Alsatian family recipe.

This soup also hints at nearby Italy, in that our chef, who has worked in Milan, uses polenta in his recipe. Many dishes from Nice use this yellow cornmeal, which is usually eaten salted. When you start preparing this dish, the polenta should always be browned with the onions in oil and/or butter. If you think the soup is too thick, just add a splash more water.

The onions give this soup its characteristic flavor. The onion is a vegetable from Asia and has been cultivated for over 5,000 years. It consists of white, fleshy leaves that are surrounded by yellow, brown, red, or white skin of a papery texture.

The polenta soup is a wonderful accompaniment to shrimp. When you buy shrimp, they should look perfect. You can tell whether they are fresh or not by how curved the shell is, how firm the flesh, and whether they are easy to shell. When you sauté the shrimp in the skillet the oil must be very hot. Depending on what's available, you could also prepare this soup with langoustines or lobster.

A pinch of hot paprika is essential to this dish. Dried *piment d'Espelette* is best. This red chile is available as a dried pepper, as a powder, or paste.

To make the garnish, peel the onion and slice very thinly. Toss the onion rings in the flour and put aside. Wash the scallions and chop the green part into thin rings. Peel the garlic and slice it thinly. Put aside.

Peel the onion for the soup and chop it roughly. Heat 2 tbsp olive oil and a scant ⅛ stick/10 g butter in a skillet, add the onion, and sauté until golden brown, stirring occasionally.

Add the polenta and stir vigorously for 5 minutes, until the polenta has browned.

with Polenta

Add the chicken stock and simmer for 20 minutes. Keep the soup warm. Heat the oil for frying and fry the floured onion rings. Scoop them out with a spatula and leave them to drain on kitchen paper.

Remove the heads of the shrimp. Gradually pull away the sections of shell. Open up the shrimp with the thumb and forefinger and remove the intestines.

Heat the remaining olive oil in a skillet and sauté the shrimp for about 3 minutes. Add the garlic and scallions. Season with a pinch of paprika. Arrange the shrimp in a bowl, and pour over 2 ladles of soup per bowl. Garnish with the deep-fried onion rings and a drop of olive oil.

Vegetable Soup

Preparation time: 50 minutes
Soaking time: 12 hours
Cooking time: 50 minutes
Difficulty: ★★

Serves 4

2	tomatoes
5 oz/150 g	carrots
3½ oz/100 g	potatoes
7 oz/200 g	zucchini
7 oz/200 g	green beans
½ cup/100 g	dried red kidney beans
½ cup/100 g	dried white kidney beans
1	onion
1 clove	garlic
	salt, pepper
	fresh basil

For the bouquet garni:

	thyme
	bay leaf
1 sprig	parsley
2	leek leaves

For the pistou:

2 oz/50 g	garlic
1	tomato
1 bunch	fresh basil
4 tbsp	olive oil

For the baked eggplant purée:

4 cloves	garlic
2	eggplants
7 tbsp	olive oil
2 sheets	phyllo (filo) pastry

For the tomato mousse:

1 cup/250 ml	cream
2 sachets	gelatin
1	onion
2 cloves	garlic
2	tomatoes
2 tbsp	olive oil

This too is a classic Mediterranean soup, traditionally eaten hot, but when you prepare Francis Robin's recipe, you'll be pleasantly surprised how good it tastes cold. You really do need all the vegetables our chef has listed, otherwise it's not a real *soupe au pistou*. Cut the vegetables into even-sized pieces, so they cook at the same speed.

If you can, buy the best quality red and white kidney beans (available from June to September in southeastern France and in Italy). Soak them separately, if possible overnight, so they will cook more quickly. When cooking them, don't salt the water to start with, otherwise the beans will become tough and won't cook properly. Only add salt to the soup once the beans are cooked. Use young, firm zucchini and carrots, because they taste best.

Basil crushed in a mortar is called *pistou* in Provençal. Take the basil out of the refrigerator at the last minute and don't rinse the leaves, otherwise they lose their powerful scent and flavor.

The gelatin helps the tomato mousse to hold its shape. Soften it in lukewarm water in advance, according to the manufacturer's instructions, and then let it melt in hot olive oil. If you want the mousse to be a bit redder, add a teaspoon of tomato paste. The best tomatoes to use are ripe, juicy plum tomatoes. The eggplant patty is placed on top of the soup once it has cooled down a bit, so that it doesn't become soggy too quickly.

Put the tomatoes in a bowl and pour boiling water over them. Leave them for a few minutes, drain, and skin them. Dice the vegetables and tomatoes. If the red and white kidney beans are too big, cut them in half. Preheat the oven to 400 °F/200 °C.

Put 4 cups/2 l water in a saucepan with the onion, garlic, and bouquet garni, and bring to the boil. Add the beans and simmer for 20 minutes. Then add the carrots, potatoes, zucchini and, finally, the tomatoes. Simmer on low heat for 20 minutes, then season with salt and pepper.

Place 4 unpeeled cloves of garlic on a baking sheet with the halved, deseeded eggplants. Drizzle over 4 tbsp olive oil. Bake for 25 minutes. When the eggplants have cooled, remove the flesh from the skin, peel the garlic, and purée both. Add the remaining olive oil and season.

with Pistou

For the pistou, peel the garlic. Skin and deseed the tomato. Put the garlic and tomatoes in a food processor with the basil and olive oil, and purée them. Season to taste. Take the soup off the burner, remove the bouquet garni, and add the pistou to thicken it.

Beat the cream until stiff and reserve it. Dissolve the gelatin in lukewarm water. Cut 8 phyllo circles, 2½–3 in/6–8 cm in diameter. Put a teaspoon of eggplant purée onto 4 of the pastry circles and cover with the other 4 circles. Crimp the edges, and bake for 10 minutes at 400 °F/200 °C.

Chop and fry the onion, garlic, and tomatoes until very soft. Purée the mixture. Melt the softened gelatin in hot oil. Fold the gelatin and cream into the tomato purée. Place an eggplant purée patty on top of each plate of soup, and garnish with tomato mousse and basil.

Bastia Fish

Preparation time:	35 minutes		2 lb/800 g	mussels
Cooking time:	1 hour 45 minutes		¼	fennel bulb
Difficulty:	★		½ bunch	parsley
			4 cloves	garlic
Serves 4			¼ cup/60 ml	olive oil
			1 tbsp/20 g	tomato concentrate
2 lb/800 g	small lobsters (langoustines, Dublin Bay prawns, Florida lobsterettes etc.)		1 pinch/1 g	saffron powder
			1 lb/400 g	fish fillets (sea bass, dentex, rock salmon, dog fish etc.)
1	spider crab		2½ tbsp/40 ml	light cream
3 lb/1.5 kg	mixed fish for soup (gray mullet, whiting, conger eel etc.)		1 stalk	nepita (wild mint) salt and pepper

7 tbsp/100 ml	white wine
4 oz/100 g	fresh scallions (spring onions)

Typical of the Corsican coastal areas, this traditional fisherman's soup is similar to the southern French bouillabaisse. A meal in itself, it is made with whatever fish and seafood are available. Although it is easy to prepare, it requires a long cooking time.

This Corsican specialty comes from the magnificent city of Bastia, overlooking the Mediterranean. Fishing in Corsica is still carried out in small boats equipped with lines and nets, with trawlers rarely being used. The boats return to port with many different types of high quality fish for the market stalls, including John Dory, gurnard, sea bass, red scorpion fish, mullet, and dog fish. In addition to these there are crawfish, caught in pots woven from myrtle or willow branches.

Corsicans have traditionally used small crabs and rock fish to give extra flavor to this soup. Cooked in their shells together with olive oil, garlic, onion, fennel, and tomatoes, the crabs are then liquidized with the bouillon, and strained through a fine sieve, giving a deliciously concentrated aroma. Vincent Tabarani recommends using a spider crab in this recipe. This spiny-shelled crab with delicate legs and long claws is considered by some to be the most delicately flavored of all the crustacea. It is generally poached in a court bouillon (a light, acidic stock used for quick-cooking seafood) and eaten cold.

This soup gains its extra subtlety from the addition of saffron, the most expensive spice in the world and one with a unique taste. It should be used very sparingly, as too much will give a bitter flavor.

Nepita, the peppery-tasting wild mint native to the Corsican *maquis*, is a reminder of this soup's proud origins.

Remove the flesh from the lobsters and set aside, with the heads and shells. Cut up the spider crab. Reserve the juices from the head. Cut the fish for the soup into large chunks.

Pour the white wine into a large saucepan and add half a chopped scallion. Add the cleaned mussels and cook for a few minutes until they have opened. Remove the mussels from their shells. Reserve the cooking liquid.

Wash and chop the fennel, parsley, and the remaining onions. Crush the garlic. Brown these ingredients in a saucepan with the olive oil.

Soup

Add the tomato concentrate, followed by the langoustine shells and heads, the fish for the soup, and the pieces of spider crab. Crush these with a wooden spoon during cooking to release the flavors.

Pour the liquid used for cooking the mussels and the juices from the head of the spider crab into the fish mixture. Cover with water and cook for 1–1½ hours. Season with salt and pepper. Strain the bouillon.

Sprinkle the saffron into the bouillon. Add the mussels, the fish fillets cut into chunks, and the flesh of the lobsters. Cook for about 2 minutes. Pour the cream into the soup, add the chopped *nepita*, and serve.

Fisherman's

Preparation time:	20 minutes
Cooking time:	40 minutes
Difficulty:	★

Serves 4

1½ lb/700 g	small langoustines
12 oz/300 g	small squid
1 lb/400 g	Venus clams
3	tomatoes

1 clove	garlic
4 tbsp	olive oil
	salt
8 oz/200 g	linguini (pasta)

For the garnish:

| | parsley |

This fisherman's soup is ideal in winter, as it combines all the delicious flavors of the Mediterranean. The dish has a long tradition on the Adriatic coast and is simple to prepare. If you enjoy mussels and crustaceans, this soup could become one of your favorite dishes.

Venus clams, *vongole* in Italian, play a major role in Italian cuisine; *spaghetti alle vongole*, for instance, is very popular all over the country. It is actually possible to eat Venus clams raw, with a little lemon juice. They are easy to recognize from their small yellow to dark gray shells, convex in the middle.

Connoisseurs love langoustines, the taste of which is reminiscent of lobster. It is also a very healthy food, containing a lot of calcium, phosphorus, and iron, and can be prepared in various ways. It is important to remember, however, that crustaceans should only be cooked very briefly. To supple-

ment the range of seafood, Maddalena Beccaceci has also added small squid, which are extremely tender. The tentacles and body sacs are edible, but the ink sac should be removed when cleaning the squid.

The fish stock in which the *linguini* (long noodles, like very fine spaghetti) are cooked and which forms the basis for the soup plays a major part in its success. If you wish to give the soup a stronger flavor, you can add the head of a herring when preparing the stock.

The absence in this recipe of pepper or other strong seasoning allows the flavor of the individual ingredients to develop. Even the garlic is used only to enhance the olive oil and is removed after frying.

Pull the heads off the langoustines and shell the meat. Reserve the heads for the stock. Remove the head and tentacles from the squid, as well as the innards. Skin the squid and remove any hard or rough areas. Wash and slice into small pieces.

For the stock, bring 8 cups/2 l water to the boil in a saucepan and add the langoustine heads. Cover and cook for about 30 minutes.

Put the Venus clams in a saucepan and cover with water. Cook for a few minutes until the clams have opened. Remove the meat. Blanch, skin, and dice the 3 tomatoes.

Soup

Fry the whole, peeled garlic clove in olive oil, then remove from the pan. Add the langoustines and fry for about 2 minutes. Then add the squid, Venus clams, and diced tomato. Season with salt and simmer for 5–10 minutes.

Strain the fish stock and bring to the boil. Break the linguini into the pan and cook in the fish stock until the pasta has become "al dente."

Add the seafood and infuse for 1 minute. Pour the soup into bowls and serve sprinkled with chopped parsley.

Spring

Preparation time: 35 minutes
Cooking time: 25 minutes
Difficulty: ★

Serves 4

3½ lb/1.5 kg	small zucchini
1	onion
2 tbsp	olive oil
¾ stick/80 g	butter
	salt
	pepper

4 slices	white, crusty bread
2 cloves	garlic
3	eggs
½ bunch	parsley
	parmesan

For the garnish:

	4 egg yolks (optional)
	mint leaves

Spring soup is traditional farmer's fare and to a certain extent is symbolic of spring. It is very popular in Lazio, and also in Campagna and Calabria. Easy to prepare, this soup can be eaten hot or cold with bread.

Italian cuisine would be much the poorer without zucchini, which can be cooked in so many different ways—braised, broiled, fried, stuffed, or in salads—and are an essential ingredient in this soup. With their high water content and low nutritional value, zucchini grow in abundance in the southern part of the Italian peninsula. When buying, choose small ones, as these are especially tender. Make sure that they are firm at the ends and unblemished. Zucchini can be eaten either peeled or unpeeled, but in any event should be washed thoroughly. Depending on the season, you can substitute white beet or pumpkin.

This soup, which is highly nutritious thanks to the eggs, cheese, butter, and bread, is greatly enhanced by the addition of parsley. This aromatic plant, which is available all year round, is an essential ingredient in Italian cuisine. It should be fresh and crisp, with firm stalks and leaves.

Garlic is also available throughout the year. It tastes milder in spring and is easier to peel. In cultivation for over 5,000 years, garlic belongs to the labiate genus of plants and is said to be very good for the circulation. Only use firm, fat cloves.

In southern Italy, pecorino, an air-dried ewe's milk cheese, is normally used to enhance the flavor of this soup. In this recipe, however, Marco and Rosella Folicaldi prefer to use parmesan.

Wash and dice the zucchini.

Peel the onion and chop coarsely. Sauté in olive oil and butter, then add the diced zucchini. Cover and simmer for 10–20 minutes, adding water if necessary. Season with salt and pepper.

Toast the crusty bread. Rub with the peeled garlic cloves and set aside.

Soup

Beat the eggs in a small bowl. Add the chopped parsley and beat again.

Add the beaten eggs to the zucchini and stir with a wooden spoon.

Grate parmesan over the soup. Season to taste with pepper. Serve the soup in bowls with the bread. If desired, add an egg yolk to each serving and garnish with mint leaves.

Barley Soup

Preparation time: 50 minutes
Cooking time: 55 minutes
Difficulty: ☆

Serves 4

1	zucchini
1	carrot
1	leek
1	radicchio
3 tbsp	vegetable oil
½ stick/60 g	butter
2	bay leaves
	salt
	pepper
1½ cups/300 g	pearl barley
4 cups/1 l	milk
2 slices	bacon

For the croquettes:

12 oz/300 g	grated *Cantal* cheese, mild
3½ tbsp/50 g	grated parmesan
4 tsp/20 g	flour
2	eggs
4 oz/100 g	breadcrumbs
2 cups/500 ml	oil for deep frying

For the garnish:

	parsley

The high plain of Asagio in South Tyrol has been famous for its milk for over 1,000 years. According to Francesca de Giovannini, the Germanic Cimbri tribe brought their herds to graze the pastures and settled there, subsisting mainly on barley and milk.

Our chef is very interested in the history of her region and has therefore provided us with an ancient recipe that is said to date back to the time of the Cimbri. During the course of the centuries, the soup has been enriched with seasonal vegetables. This recipe is also enhanced by the addition of cheese croquettes and slices of bacon, typical specialties of the region.

Barley, a very hardy cereal, is cultivated in Italy mainly in South Tyrol and Friuli. The husks are removed from the long, pointed grains, which are then ground between two millstones into small, round pearls. Pearl barley is especially suitable for soups, but spelt can be used instead.

Francesca de Giovannini's peasant-style soup is almost a vegetable soup. In South Tyrol, the radicchio, a red endive from Treviso, is very popular; connoisseurs even hold events in its honor. This crunchy vegetable can be eaten raw or cooked, broiled or stuffed. It is easily recognized by its violet color and white ribs and is available on all the market stalls from December onward. Zucchini, with their high water content, are also an indispensable ingredient in Mediterranean cuisine, and are grown mainly in southern Italy. When buying, choose those of uniform color.

This nutritious, Cimbri-style barley soup is an ideal dish for the winter months.

Wash and wipe the zucchini, carrot, leek, and radicchio, and then dice very finely.

Heat 2 tbsp vegetable oil and ⅜ stick/50 g butter in a large saucepan. Add the diced vegetables and bay leaves. Season with salt and pepper and sauté for 3 minutes. Mix in the barley.

Pour in the milk and stir. Simmer over medium heat for 40–50 minutes.

Cimbri Style

For the croquettes, mix the Cantal cheese, parmesan, flour, and 1 whole egg in a salad bowl and knead to a smooth dough. Beat the remaining egg in a small bowl.

Roll the dough into a thin roll and cut into pieces about the width of a finger. Roll each piece into a ball in the palms of your hands. Dip in the egg and then breadcrumbs. Deep-fry in oil.

Heat the remaining vegetable oil and butter in a pan and brown the bacon. Serve the soup with the croquettes and bacon, with chopped parsley scattered on top.

Zuppa

Preparation time:	40 minutes
Cooking time:	35 minutes
Difficulty:	★

Serves 4

1¼ lb/500 g	Venus clams
5 cloves	garlic
5 tbsp	olive oil
¼ bunch	parsley
8 oz/200 g	sausagemeat

	salt
	pepper
2 sprigs	rosemary
4 tbsp	white wine
12 oz/300 g	potatoes

For the garnish:

	parsley

Alberto Melagrana thinks that the Marche region must be very like Paradise. He is so much in love with this region that his praise for the variety and quality of the produce here, which the natives of the area are fortunate enough to have in abundance, knows no bounds. The richly endowed region is the source of many sophisticated and original recipes like this one.

Zuppa Picena is a typical soup from the province of Picena and was traditionally prepared on fishing boats. Before they set sail, the seamen took their provisions on board, storing potatoes in the hold and hanging sausages from the mast. Depending on what they caught in their nets, they would prepare a soup that would remind them of dishes they ate at home. Today, *zuppa Picena* is eaten mainly in winter, sometimes with the addition of toasted slices of white bread.

Venus clams are easily recognizable from their small, convex shells. They are highly prized in Italy for their tasty flesh and go wonderfully well with white wine, tomatoes, shallots, and thyme. If they are unavailable, it is possible to substitute Tellini mussels, which should be cleaned the night before.

Farmers in the Marche region used to slaughter their pigs themselves. Surplus meat was distributed among their neighbors or made into sausages. These sausages, which kept for a long time, were also popular with fishermen on the coast. Italian sausage is typically made from coarsely chopped meat and is not highly seasoned. The meat is often used in sauces and ragouts.

Clean the Venus clams under running water. Sauté 4 cloves garlic in 4 tbsp olive oil and add the clams. Cover and simmer briefly until the clams have opened. Scatter the chopped parsley over the top.

Form the sausagemeat into even-sized small balls and brown them in a pan with the remaining olive oil. Season with salt and pepper. Add the remaining garlic and a sprig of rosemary. Sauté for 3–4 minutes before pouring in the white wine.

Peel the potatoes and cut into small even-sized cubes.

Picena

Place the potatoes in a pan of boiling water and cook with the other sprig of rosemary. Drain.

Carefully transfer the Venus clams, potatoes, and meatballs to a saucepan.

Pour over 2 cups/500 ml boiling water and simmer for 5 minutes. Pour the soup into bowls and garnish with parsley.

St Lucy's

Preparation time:	*40 minutes*
Cooking time:	*2 hours 10 minutes*
Soaking time	
for the wheat:	*72 hours*
Soaking time for	
the garbanzo and	
navy beans:	*12 hours*
Difficulty:	★

Serves 4

1 cup/200 g	whole wheat grains
⅓ cup/50 g	garbanzo beans (chickpeas)
¼ cup/50 g	dry navy (haricot) beans

1½ lb/700 g	wild herbs and leaves (or wild chicory, Swiss chard, tarragon etc.)

2 cloves	garlic
1	onion
2 tbsp/30 ml	olive oil
1 oz/25 g	celery
2 oz/50 g	carrot
	salt

For the bouquet garni:

1 sprig	thyme
1 sprig	rosemary
2	marjoram leaves
1	bay leaf

To accompany:

	garlic toast

St Lucy is the patron saint of the magnificent city of Siracusa on Sicily, where she is commemorated with an annual festival. During the city's catastrophic famine of 1600, the inhabitants prayed to St Lucy for help, after which she is said to have caused boats full of wheat to arrive in the port. The starving people rushed to take the precious cargo, still damp with seawater. From it they made a soup flavored with the leaves of wild plants.

A very popular dish in Siracusa, this filling specialty is typically eaten in wintertime. Wheat has been cultivated on Sicily since Antiquity, for baking flour and durum wheat flour (used to make pasta). Sicily became known as the "granary of the Roman Empire" when the Romans converted much of the land there to the cultivation of wheat. Even today, there are villages where Ceres, the Roman goddess of agriculture, continues to be venerated. In preparing this soup, it is important to soak the wheat for a full 72 hours so that the grains can swell up and cook thoroughly.

This is a very simple soup to cook. Garbanzo and navy beans, later additions to the original recipe, make the soup even more nourishing.

The wild herbs and edible leaves are an essential feature of this rustic soup, and are much used in Sicilian cooking. They can be replaced, as they are here, by young Swiss chard and spinach leaves, wild chicory, and tarragon. Tarragon, a strongly aromatic herb, that originally came from Central Asia, adds a slight hint of aniseed and pepper to the dish.

Soak the wheat for 72 hours in a bowl of water. Soak the garbanzo and navy beans for 12 hours in separate bowls. Drain and cook the three items separately in simmering water, the wheat for 1 hour, the garbanzo beans for 1 hour, and the navy beans for 1 hour 30 minutes.

Wash the leaves. Cut up the chicory, Swiss chard, and tarragon. Blanch them in salted water for 3 minutes and drain. Now shred the leaves. Reserve the cooking liquid.

Brown the crushed garlic and chopped onion in olive oil. Add the celery and carrots, chopped into small dice. Cook for 5 minutes.

Wheat Soup

Tip the cooked wheat into the mixture. Add the shredded leaves. Cook for 5 minutes. Transfer the mixture into a large saucepan.

Pour the reserved liquid used for cooking the leaves over the mixture. Bring to the boil and simmer for 10 minutes.

Add the garbanzo and navy beans to the pan with the bouquet garni. Cook for a further 15 minutes. Season with salt. Serve the soup with bread rubbed with garlic and toasted.

Kakavia

Preparation time: 50 minutes
Cooking time: 20 minutes
Difficulty: ★

Serves 4

1	sea bream weighing 1½ lb/600 g
1	scorpion fish weighing 1½ lb/600 g
1	eel
2	onions
1¾ lb/800 g	potatoes
	salt

⅔ cup/150 ml	pepper
	olive oil
2 cups/500 ml	white wine
2	lemons
2	quinces
3–4 cloves	garlic
	fennel leaves

For the garnish:

fresh dill

To serve:

toasted chunks of bread

Kakavia is a delicious soup that is traditionally eaten by fishermen. Extremely popular in Greece, this cousin of bouillabaisse from Marseille in southern France takes its name from the *kakavin*, a cooking pot that was used by sailors in the olden days to cook the different fish they caught in their nets.

Bursting with unrivaled flavors, this soup is still made today on board the small boats that sail around the Greek islands, and they still use seawater! According to our chef, the inhabitants of the Greek islands also traditionally make it once a year when they celebrate their local patron saint.

Kakavia pays homage to the Mediterranean Sea and can be made from all kinds of fish, depending on the catch. Aristedes Pasparakis has used scorpion fish, always regarded as a great delicacy here. Known as *skorpios* in Greek, it is famous for its white, slightly oily flesh.

This soup also stars the sea bream. This fish is most often found around the Mediterranean coast where it is prized for its taste and delicacy. But be extra careful when you cook it because its delicately flavored texture tends to become soft and a bit fluffy.

Over the years, local fishermen have started to introduce products from the New World into this dish. Potatoes, which originated in South America, today enrich the original recipe. On certain islands the appearance is further enlivened with the addition of tomato.

A judicious concoction of flavors, *kakavia* is served with chunks of toasted bread and a dish of *skordalia*, a sort of Greek aioli. Made from garlic, olive oil, quince, lemon juice, fennel leaves, salt, and pepper this "sauce" not only lifts but comes into its own with this tasty soup.

Scale and clean the sea bream and the scorpion fish. Fillet the fish. Reserve the heads for the stock. Cut the prepared eel into thick chunks.

Peel the onions and the potatoes and slice both into regular-shaped rounds.

Layer the onions on the bottom of the pan. Cover these with half the potatoes. Add the fillets of sea bream and the reserved fish heads.

Add the remaining potatoes, eel chunks, and the fillets of scorpion fish. Season to taste and add a scant half cup/100 ml olive oil, the white wine, and 4 cups/ 1 l water. Bring to the boil and cook for 15 minutes. Remove the fish heads and squeeze in the juice of 1 lemon.

Wash the quinces and cut in half. Drop them into a pan of boiling water and cook for about 15 minutes. Drain the quinces.

When cooled, peel the quinces and blend well in a processor with the garlic, juice of the second lemon, salt, and pepper. Add the fennel leaves and the remaining olive oil. Serve the kakavia, the quince sauce, and the toasted bread in separate bowls. Garnish with sprigs of dill.

Ntomatosoupa

Preparation time: 35 minutes
Cooking time: 50 minutes
Difficulty: ★

Serves 4

9 lb/4 kg	ripe tomatoes
2 sprigs	basil
2	onions
1 clove	garlic
2 tbsp	olive oil
	salt
	black pepper
1 pinch	sugar
4½ oz/125 g	kritharaki (Greek noodles)
3–4 tbsp/50 g	Greek, or thick creamy, yogurt

Typical of the sort of food eaten at Greek monasteries, this tomato soup, *ntomatosoupa*, tastes of pure summer. Extremely refreshing, this light dish varies according to the part of Greece in which you eat it. In Athens they add *kritharaki*, typically Greek noodles, or even bulgur wheat. Others prefer simply to serve it with a yogurt sauce.

Extremely easy to make, *ntomatosoupa* awards the starring role to the tomato. Originally from Peru, this fruit was first imported to Spain in the 16th century, although it had to wait more than 200 years before it found its way onto Southern European tables. Tomatoes love the sun so they flourish in Mediterranean countries. In Greece the Cyclades islands produce a very small variety that are bright red and have a distinctive taste. These vegetables, which are ready to use very early in the year, are traditionally grown on non-irrigated land.

For this recipe, try to find the Roma, or plum, tomato. Firm fleshed and with a delicate flavor, this is an excellent "cooking" tomato. When you've removed the seeds, don't forget to keep them. Wrapped up in a cheesecloth with a few sprigs of basil, they can be added to the water used to flavor the soup.

The somewhat delicate flavor of this dish is lifted by the slightly sharp taste of the Greek yogurt. Creamy smooth and with a dense consistency, Greek yogurt is primarily made from ewe's milk. It is the inspiration behind many Greek specialties, including the famous *tzatziki*, a *meze* dish based on cucumber and garlic.

The lovely yogurt sauce is enhanced with the aroma of basil. The leaves of this aromatic herb have been prized for thousands of years. Often served with tomatoes, they generously impart their strong flavor of lemon and jasmine.

Wash the tomatoes and cut into quarters. Remove the seeds, which should be kept to one side. Blend the tomatoes to a purée in the food processor.

Put the reserved seeds into a piece of cheesecloth. Add the basil stalks, stripped of the leaves, and tie the cloth into a pouch shape. Chop, or tear, the basil leaves and keep to one side.

Peel and finely chop the onions. Peel and crush the garlic. Brown both together in 1 tbsp olive oil. Add the tomato purée. Cover with about 4 cups/1 l water, season to taste, and add the sugar. Cook over a gentle heat for about 40 minutes.

Bring some water to a rolling boil in a small pan and drop in the pouch containing the tomato seeds and basil stalks. Cook for 10 minutes, remove the pouch, then pour the flavored water into the tomato soup.

Add the Greek noodles and cook for about 10 minutes.

In a small bowl, mix the Greek yogurt with 1 tbsp olive oil, season, and add the chopped basil leaves. Serve the soup in bowls topped with a spoonful of the yogurt sauce.

Chicken Soup

Preparation time: 35 minutes
Cooking time: 1 hour
    40 minutes
Difficulty: ☆

Serves 4

1	free-range chicken weighing 4½ lb/ 2 kg (rooster, if possible)
1	onion
1	bay leaf

	black peppercorns
	salt
1 generous cup/ 125 g	rice
2	eggs
2	lemons
	black pepper

For the garnish (optional):
    celery leaves

Chicken soup with *avgolemono* sauce is a classic in the Greek culinary repertoire. In Thessalia this dish is traditionally associated with Christmas. It is very filling and is often enjoyed as a main course.

Bursting with typically Greek flavors, the starring role goes to the rooster. This farmyard bird, eaten toward the end of its life, needs a long cooking time. Fans of this dish appreciate its firm flesh, although in some regions they use a boiling fowl instead, which tastes equally good.

This recipe only has a few ingredients but they are used wisely. The stock is flavored with peppercorns and onion and is enhanced with the special aroma of bay leaf. The evergreen bay tree grows wild in the Mediterranean. The leaves are used to give a lift to dishes that are simmered for a fairly long period of time, or are incorporated into mixes for fillings and marinades. After removing the chicken carcass, don't forget to strain the stock and reserve about 2–2½ cups/600 milliliters for the *avgolemono* sauce.

An ideal winter dish, this soup is very filling. The addition of the rice really makes this family dish special. Possibly originating in China, legend suggests that rice was imported to Mesopotamia by the Persians. After his expedition to India, Alexander the Great was keen to encourage the cultivation of rice in Macedonia. Regarded as a luxury in ancient times, today rice is eaten throughout the world.

Avgolemono sauce is found in a lot of Greek cooking, and really lends itself to this dish. It is always made from eggs, lemon juice, and stock, although cooks often add their own special touch. Panagiotis Delvenakiotis suggests adding a teaspoonful of cornstarch to help thicken and bind it.

Using a knife, make an incision in the chicken skin along the spine. Carefully remove the thighs. Cut the main carcass into 4 equal quarters and divide it, cutting the flesh away from the ribs, starting at the top of the breastbone. Discard the breastbone and remove the wings.

Put the chicken pieces into a large pan and add the whole peeled onion, the bay leaf, and a few peppercorns. Cover with water. Put the lid on the pan and cook for 1½ hours, from time to time skimming off any froth that forms on the surface. Add salt to taste.

Remove the chicken pieces and reserve about 2–2½ cups/600 ml stock. Add the rice to the remaining stock and cook for about 10 minutes.

with Avgolemono

To make the sauce, separate the eggs and put the whites into a bowl while reserving the yolks. Add some salt and whisk the egg whites until foaming.

Add the reserved egg yolks to the bowl and whisk.

Pour on the lemon juice. Whisk, and gradually add the reserved stock. Beat the sauce the whole time and add to the rice. Serve the soup in bowls sprinkled with black pepper and serve the meat separately. If desired, garnish both with celery leaves.

Navy Bean Soup

Preparation time:	25 minutes
Cooking time:	1 hour
	25 minutes
Soaking time (beans):	overnight
Difficulty:	★

Serves 4

2½ cups/500 g	dried white navy (haricot) beans
2	carrots
2 or 3 stalks	celery
2	onions
2	tomatoes
1 tbsp	tomato paste

	salt
	pepper
	olive oil
1 tsp	boukovo (flakes of dried red pimento)

To serve (optional):

chopped onion
smoked herring
black olives
red bell peppers

From time immemorial Greeks have come up with tasty recipes based on navy (haricot) beans, which they often serve with meat, vegetables, fish, and aromatic herbs. Navy bean soup, or *fasolada*, is always popular and can rightly be described as one of the country's "national dishes." Comforting and nourishing, it is ideal to serve hot in the winter.

Lots of different varieties of bean, or *fasola*, are grown throughout Greece. The ones that are most commonly used come from Kato Nevrokopi and are of medium size, either cylindrical or flat. A smaller bean is also grown in the Pelion region. Some people love to use the giant very soft beans grown around the Florina area to make this soup. All of them go well with tomato, onions, celery, and oregano.

Tomatoes will add a wonderful aroma and color to your soup. To peel them, use a sharp knife to score a little cross on their base. Plunge them into boiling water for about one minute, until the skin starts to loosen, then transfer to a bowl of iced water to refresh before peeling the skin. Tomatoes from the Cyclades, especially the ones grown on the islands of Syros and Santorini, have an excellent reputation, as have the ones from Nafplion and Argos in the Eastern Peloponnese and from Thessalonika in Macedonia.

The addition of *boukovo* to the soup is entirely optional. These yellow-orange colored flakes are obtained from small very spicy red pimentos that are dried then roughly processed in a special grinder.

This delicious dish, in which the refreshing taste of the olive oil counterbalances the fire of the pimentos, is good served with olives, pearl onions, and smoked herring. Don't forget to put a bottle of olive oil infused with herbs on the table so that each guest can add as much or as little as they want to the soup.

The night before you make the soup, soak the beans in a large pan filled with cold water. The next day, drain them and put into a pan filled with water. Bring to the boil then let the beans simmer briskly for about 15 minutes. Strain and cover again with clean water.

Meanwhile, prepare the other vegetables. Peel the carrots, cut off both ends, and slice into thin rounds. Cut the celery stalks into thin slices and finely chop the onions.

Peel the tomatoes as described above, cut them in half, and chop finely.

with Boukovo

Add the chopped onions, celery, and carrots to the saucepan containing the beans. Cook for 20 minutes.

Now add the fresh tomatoes and the tomato paste. Season and cook for another 30 minutes.

Finally add a trickle of olive oil and the boukovo, check the seasoning, and simmer gently for a further 20 minutes.

Mani-Style

Preparation time:	40 minutes	1 lb 2 oz/500 g	tomatoes
Cooking time:	35 minutes	⅔ cup 150 ml	white wine
Difficulty:	★		salt
			pepper
		9 oz/250 g	potatoes

Serves 4

To serve (optional):
croutons

3½ lb/1.5 kg	pollock (or cod)
1	carrot
1 stalk	celery
1	onion
⅔ cup/150 ml	olive oil
7 oz/200 g	pearl onions

For the garnish:
celery leaves

In Greece, the sea is never very far away. On this land blessed by the gods, Poseidon generously offered all the treasures of his watery kingdom to the inhabitants—fish, shellfish, crustaceans. The cluster of tiny villages in the Mani region pays regular homage to this mythological deity through their cuisine.

Famous throughout the country, Mani-style fish soup is traditionally eaten in winter. Easy to make, this specialty from the coast stars pollock as its main ingredient. Greatly appreciated for its firm white flesh and pleasant consistency, it is often found at fishmongers cut into fillets or steaks. If it is hard to obtain pollock, cod can be used instead. Around the islands of the Aegean Sea, local fishermen sometimes use grouper fish or hake for this dish.

In this recipe, products from the soil also play an important role. Olive oil, also produced in the Mani region, is used to

flavor the pearl onions. Pearl onions, which originally came from Asia, have been cultivated for more than 5,000 years. The flavor of the ones grown around the Mediterranean is particularly subtle.

This dish allows the characteristic taste of celery to shine through. Available all year round on market stalls, this vegetable is esteemed for its fresh flavor and crunchy texture. Used for soups, stews, and sauces, it grows wild in Greece, where it is known as *selino*. Celery is a rich source of sodium chloride. The heads should be bright green, have no blemishes, no signs of wilting, and no yellowing at the base of the stalks. To keep them fresh, stand the base of the celery stalk in cold salted water.

This delicious fish dish is usually served with croutons. Greek families serve the fish and the soup separately at the table.

Use a sharp knife to make an incision into the pollock following the line of the dorsal fin to fillet it. Cut the fish into thick slices and remove the skin. Clean off the fish bones and put to one side.

In a large pan of water, make a stock from the prepared carrot, celery, and onion. Add the cleaned fish bones. Let the stock cook for 20 minutes, skimming off any froth that forms.

Heat the olive oil in a separate pan and add the peeled pearl onions. Peel and chop the tomatoes into small pieces, add to the pan and cook for about 5 minutes.

Fish Soup

Add the white wine, cook for about 5 minutes, and season to taste. Peel the potatoes and, using a melon baller, cut the potatoes into little balls.

Strain the stock and pour half onto the onion and tomato mixture. Cook the potatoes in the rest of the stock.

Lay the slices of pollock on top of the onion mixture and cook for 4 minutes. Serve the strained soup with the croutons (if using) in one bowl, and the fish on another plate with the potatoes and pearl onions. Garnish with celery leaves.

Yalitiki

Preparation time:	20 minutes		2¼ lbs/1 kg	onions
Cooking time:	50 minutes		3½ tbsp	olive oil
Difficulty:	★			

Serves 4

2¼ lb/1 kg	shin of beef, boned
	and rolled
	salt
4	carrots
1 head	celery
	peppercorns

A Venetian fortress has dominated the large harbor at Sitia on the easternmost coast of Crete for several centuries. The Serene Republic, which conquered and governed Crete from 1211 to 1660, also left a number of influences on the local cuisine. This soup of boiled beef prepared by our chef comes into that category. In Greek, it is known as *yalitiki*.

George Anastassakis is anxious to reintroduce this recipe, which he believes is on the brink of disappearing from the Greek culinary repertoire. In the 1970s, when mass tourism was developing in Crete, some cooks were willing to mix carelessly different European styles of cooking. These days, however, traditional dishes are coming back into fashion, and are very much appreciated by tourists anxious to discover original Greek culinary traditions.

When making this dish, our chef normally uses *moschari*, meat from an older calf (or young bullock) in which the flesh is already red. It is easy to replace this with ordinary beef, which is the nearest to it in terms of texture and appearance. Knuckle of veal (*kotsi* in Greece) is the best cut of meat to use for this dish because it contains gelatin, which helps to thicken the soup.

Please note that the stalks of celery are only used to add flavor to the stock and are not eaten as part of the meal itself. Celery can be easily substituted with celeriac that is cut into cubes.

It is up to you whether you want to add the onions raw directly to the beef stock when it is three-quarters cooked. However, as these will be served with the meat, it is better to brown them in a frying pan before adding them to the soup. Also, the flavor of fried onions really enhances the aroma of the stock.

Cut the shin of beef into thick slices of just under 1 in/2 cm.

The slices then need to be trussed. Wrap a piece of cooking string around the outside of each piece of meat, tie it with a knot, and trim off the loose ends.

Put the pieces of meat into a large pan. Fill with water and add salt to taste. Bring to the boil and leave to cook for about 10 minutes.

Soup

If too much froth forms on the surface, skim it off using a slotted spoon.

Peel the carrots, trim the celery stalks, reserving some leaves, and add the stalks and some leaves to the pan with the peppercorns. Continue cooking for about 30 minutes.

Chop the onions and fry in a skillet with a little olive oil. Add them to the pan and cook for a further 10 minutes. Lift out the meat, remove the string, and discard the celery. Ladle the broth into the serving bowls, add the beef, vegetables, and a few celery leaves.

Trachanosoupa

Preparation time: 15 minutes
Cooking time: 35 minutes
Difficulty: ★

Serves 4

7 oz/250 g	small tomatoes
4 tbsp/60 ml	olive oil
5½ oz/150 g	trachana (roughly pounded grains of wheat)
4	eggs
	salt
4 slices	goat milk cheese
1 scant cup/100 g	all-purpose flour
3 tbsp	vegetable oil

Greek families usually eat this traditional soup in winter. It is made from *trachana* (grains of roughly pounded sun-dried wheat), tomato, eggs, and cheese. Easy to make, this extremely popular dish is often served as a main course.

Wheat has been cultivated in Greece for thousands of years. It is an annual cereal, a member of the graminaceous family, the grains used to produce flour and semolina. Highly prized in Ancient Greece, it was used to make flat breads and other types of bread.

Typically Greek, *trachana* can also be turned into a type of pasta. Still made in local villages, the grains of wheat are sometimes soaked in milk before they are dried under the sun on a large cloth. They are used in certain specialties of the country, particularly soups, their slightly sharp taste adding something special. If you can't find it, use bulgur wheat instead.

This national specialty also stars tomatoes. On the Island of Chios, where our chef comes from, the tomatoes are particularly small. Grown primarily in the south of the island on non-irrigated soil, they decorate village balconies during the winter months. When dried they become quite hard and firm.

Brought back from Peru by the Spanish Conquistadors, tomatoes today feature in much Mediterranean cookery. A vegetable that revels in the sun, they can be found in abundance at every market throughout Greece in the summer. For this recipe, try to use the Roma variety, which is very tasty. Choose well-ripened tomatoes that are plump, shiny, and have a uniform color.

The goat milk cheese meanwhile, another favorite ingredient in Greece, adds its own characteristic flavor to this dish and gives the *trachanasoupa* a real lift.

Plunge the tomatoes into boiling water for about 1 minute until the skins loosen. Refresh in ice water. Peel, then pass them through a mouli, or quickly blend, to form a purée.

Pour 4 cups/1 l water into a large pan, add the puréed tomatoes, and blend using a whisk. Add 4 tbsp olive oil. Cook for about 15 minutes.

Add the trachana. Gently mix and cook for about 5 minutes.

Break the eggs into the cooking pan. Let them cook for about 3 minutes. Season with a little salt.

Remove some of the salt from the goat milk cheese by putting the slices into very cold water for a few minutes. Drain and pat dry with paper towels. Coat the slices with flour. Heat the vegetable oil in a skillet and fry the cheese.

Pour the soup into small ovenproof dishes. Top each one with slices of cheese. Cook in an oven preheated to 475° F/ 240° C for 1 minute. Take the trachanosoupa to the table and serve.

Xinochondro

Preparation time:	30 minutes
Cooking time:	1 hours 55 minutes
Difficulty:	★

Serves 4

1³/₄ lb/800 g	leg of goat
1	carrot
1 stick	celery
¹/₂	zucchini
1 sprig	thyme
1	bay leaf

3 oz/80 g	xinochondro
¹/₃ cup/80 ml	olive oil
	juice of ¹/₂ lemon
11 oz/300 g	tomatoes
	salt and pepper
4 tsp/20 g	yogurt
4	fresh mint leaves

Xinochondro soup with goat meat is a dish prepared in many Cretan villages. For centuries, mutton and goat were the favorite meats eaten on the island. The local goats are allowed to range freely over the mountain pastures, which abound in aromatic grasses and herbs. As a result, their meat is healthy, lean, and full of flavor.

While the goat meat is stewing, be sure to skim the froth regularly with a spatula as it rises to the surface of the pot. Set a bowl full of cold water near the cooking pan. Each time you skim the meat, dip the spatula in the water to clean it, leaving behind the scum. If the meat is of good quality, this will be white rather than a suspect brown.

If goat meat is unobtainable, it is possible to make this recipe with pork, but the result will be a greasier dish. Since the soup itself is fairly substantial, some people eat it on its own without meat.

The piquant taste of xinochondro gives this soup its unique flavor. To make your own, as the Cretans do, place 2¹/₂ pints of sheep or goat's milk in a bowl and leave it for 3 or 4 days at room temperature until it curdles. Then boil it with 1 lb of cracked wheat and some salt. When the mixture is thick and smooth, leave it to cool and then break it up with a spoon. Leave it to dry in the sun or in a low oven.

Generally made at the end of August, xinochondro can be eaten immediately, but will remain fresh for several months. It forms into small lumps that can be crumbled when used in the soup.

In the villages of Crete, the soup is served in bowls accompanied by a plate of large pieces of meat. For this recipe Michalis Markakis suggests a less rustic presentation, the meat being cut into small pieces and mixed into the soup.

Remove the fat and gristle from the leg of goat meat. Cut the meat into cubes.

Scrape the carrot. Using kitchen string, make a bundle of small sticks of celery, zucchini, and carrot, together with the sprig of thyme and the bay leaf. Chop the remaining vegetables into small dice and set aside.

Place the goat meat in a large pot. Fill with cold water. Bring to the boil, then reduce the heat, skim, and add the bundle of vegetables and herbs. Simmer for 1 hour 40 minutes, skimming off the froth at intervals.

Soup

When the meat is cooked, remove it from the pot. Now add the crumbled kinochondro to the cooking liquid.

Add the olive oil, the lemon juice, and the chopped tomatoes. Season with salt and pepper.

Lastly, add the diced vegetables. Bring the soup back to the boil and simmer for 15 minutes. Serve in bowls with the meat. Top with a spoonful of yogurt and a fresh mint leaf.

Tal-Grottl

Preparation time:	40 minutes
Cooking time:	40 minutes
Difficulty:	★★

Serves 4

4 sticks	celery
1	carrot
1	onion
12	small rock crabs
4 cloves	garlic
2 tbsp/30 ml	wild fennel tops

7 tbsp/100 ml	olive oil
2 tbsp/40 ml	tomato concentrate
4 or 5 sprigs	parsley
2 small glasses	Maltese anisette
	salt and pepper

A nourishing and delicious soup featuring rock crabs, *tal-grottli bisque* is traditionally a poor man's dish in Malta. Today, celebrated Maltese chefs often serve this type of recipe as an introduction to the island's authentic, traditional cuisine. It is hard to believe that barely a decade ago such delicacies were available only in modest village bars, or for family meals at home. Nowadays, cookery programs on television and radio, and magazine and newspaper articles, are furthering the chefs' efforts to rediscover and promote these dishes.

The name of this soup comes from the Maltese word *grottli*, small rock crabs with a very tough, hairy shell and large claws. They contain only a small amount of flesh and so are usually used for soups. They are cooked whole, in their shells, giving a rich flavor to the cooking liquid. The Maltese catch the crabs on the beaches at night, using a kind of fork.

It is important to strain this soup very carefully after cooking the crabs—either into a bowl or directly into the pan containing the tomato sauce—in order to remove all the pieces of crab shell and the remains of the vegetables. To get the most from the crabmeat and the other flavors, press the ingredients through the sieve with a pestle.

Unless very ripe, well-flavored fresh tomatoes are available, tomato concentrate added to fried garlic will be ideal for this recipe. Do not add the anisette until the last minute, otherwise it will evaporate and its flavor will be lost.

Cut up the celery stems and roughly chop the leaves. Peel and chop the carrot and slice the onion.

Put the crabs in a large saucepan, cover with water, and add the prepared vegetables. Season with salt and pepper. Bring to the boil and cook for 30 minutes.

Transfer the vegetables and crabs to a large plate. Remove the crab claws and set aside.

Bisque

Tip the vegetables and crabs into the bowl of a food processor and mix gradually until a greenish-colored bisque is obtained.

Pass the bisque mixture carefully through a fine mesh sieve, into a bowl or pan.

In another pan, fry the chopped garlic and fennel plumes in the oil. Add the tomato concentrate and chopped parsley. Pour in the sieved bisque and the anisette. Reheat. Serve with a dribble of olive oil and garnished with parsley and the crab claws.

Kusksu

Preparation time:	25 minutes
Cooking time:	1 hour 10 minutes
Difficulty:	★

Serves 4

9 oz/250 g	fresh fava beans (broad beans)
⅔ cup/100 g	fresh peas
2	medium onions
3 cloves	garlic

3½ tbsp/50 ml	corn oil
½ stick/50 g	butter
5 tbsp/100 g	tomato concentrate
1	bay leaf
4 cups/1 liter	beef bouillon
9 oz/250 g	*kusksu* pasta
	parmesan
	salt and pepper

For many centuries, it has been traditional on Malta to serve *kusksu* at Easter, the season when fava beans and peas are green and tender. The name of this soup sounds like "couscous" and although the recipe is very different from the famous North African dish, the word may be derived from the presence of the small, seed-like pieces of pasta, which are similar to coarse couscous grains.

Soup is a popular item on Maltese menus. Light fish soups are eaten in the summer, while in the winter, thick soups made with local vegetables are common. There are many small market gardens on Malta, growing a wide range of vegetables that are offered for sale, freshly picked, in small village shops and on stalls at the big market on Merchants Street in Valletta.

The pasta used in this traditional soup is called *pasta ta'l kusksu* in Maltese. It consists of very small, multifaceted

balls that are made by just one producer on Malta. Used solely in the preparation of *kusksu*, the pasta is only manufactured around Easter time. With such a small level of production, like several other Maltese specialties, it is not exported. A variety of similar types of pasta can be found in Italy, however, including *acini di pepe* ("pepper seeds").

It will be noted that, in this recipe, Johann Chetcuti uses a mixture of corn oil and butter to brown the garlic and onions. This is because, unlike their Mediterranean neighbors, the Maltese do not cook exclusively with olive oil. Olive trees are relatively scarce on the island and olive oil is not produced on a commercial scale.

The soup is delicious served with grated or shaved parmesan. To make the soup even richer, some Maltese add a few spoonfuls of ricotta, or a few of the tiny goat cheeses produced on the island of Gozo.

Shell the fava beans and peas. Peel and chop the onions and the garlic, and brown them for 5 minutes in a large pan in a mixture of corn oil and butter.

Add the tomato concentrate to the pan. Cook for 3 minutes, stirring all the time.

Add the bay leaf and then the bouillon. Bring it to the boil.

When the bouillon has come to the boil, add the beans and peas. Simmer for 30 minutes.

Now add the pasta. Cook for 20 minutes until it is soft. Season to taste with salt and pepper.

When ready to serve, add the grated parmesan and mix well. Garnish with shavings of parmesan.

Chicken and

Preparation time:	20 minutes
Cooking time:	1 hour
Difficulty:	★

Serves 4

1	oven-ready chicken
1	tomato
1 clove	garlic
2 tbsp	olive oil
4 cups/1 l	hot chicken stock
	salt

3½ tbsp/50 g	soup noodles
	juice of ¼ lemon
	(optional)
4 sprigs	flat-leaf parsley

This clear soup with the brightly colored ingredients—noodles, tomatoes, and chicken—may be simple, but it is also delicious. Its Turkish name is *tavuklu domatesli şehriye çorbası*, and it is usually served at family meals.

Soups are extremely popular in Turkey, and they are served as an appetizer before a meal of lamb or chicken, rice or *börek*, vegetables cooked in olive oil, and a dessert.

Chicken has recently seen something of a development in Turkish cuisine. *Tavuk*, as it is called there, is the only type of poultry that is consumed in great quantities in Turkey—far more than turkey or quail. It used to be served on special occasions, but today it is freely available, either whole or in pieces. A young chicken needs to be cooked for about 40 minutes, and up to an hour if it is a large one.

Tomatoes are called *domates* in Turkish, and the best ones are harvested in the late spring and early summer, when cucumbers, bell peppers, and green beans are also at their finest. As in all Mediterranean countries, thanks to greenhouses, tomatoes are available all year round in Turkey. Diced carrots, zucchini, and celery can also be added to the soup to make it more filling and colorful.

Soup noodles, *şehriye*, are ideal in this soup. One of the varieties available in Turkey is called "birds' tongues."

Adding a little lemon juice to the soup just before serving gives it a fruity, slightly acidic flavor.

Boil the chicken for at least 40 minutes. Drain, then remove the breast and chop into small pieces.

Skin and finely chop the tomato. Peel and crush the garlic.

Heat the olive oil in a pot and sauté the garlic. Add the chopped tomato and cook over high heat for 5 minutes, stirring continuously.

Tomato Soup

Add the hot stock, season with salt, and bring to the boil.

When the stock is bubbling, add the chopped chicken and boil again briefly. Lower the heat.

Add the noodles to the soup and simmer for a further 5 minutes. Add the lemon juice, if desired, just before serving, and sprinkle with chopped parsley or garnish with parsley leaves.

Ezo Gelin

Preparation time: 10 minutes
Cooking time: 25 minutes
Difficulty: ★

Serves 4

1¼ cups/300 g	yellow lentils
2	beef bouillon cubes
⅜ stick/45 g	butter
½ cup/100 g	rice
scant ½ cup/ 50 g	flour

1 tsp	dried mint
½ tsp	red pepper flakes
	salt and ground pepper to taste
1 tbsp	tomato paste

For the garnish (optional):
fresh mint leaves

This tasty farmhouse soup is eaten mainly during Ramadan. It is typical of southeast Anatolia, but is very popular all over Turkey. Easily prepared and nutritious, it was named after a young bride (*gelin* in Turkish) who was called Ezo.

The special thing about this soup is the lentil, an ingredient often used in Turkish cooking, also as *köfte* or a purée. The striking thing about this tiny, flat pulse is the bright color. Originally from the Near East, the lentil has been grown for thousands of years, and is notable for its high levels of iron, fluoride, and copper. Its subtly spicy aroma develops fully during cooking. Unlike other dried pulses, the lentil does not require soaking.

Rice is also an important ingredient in this traditional soup. The grain is popular all over the world, and was first cultivated in China in 3,000 B.C., if not earlier. According to

legend, it was the Persians in Mesopotamia and Turkistan who introduced it. Alexander the Great brought the plant to the Aegean coast from his Indian campaign.

Rice is not only the basic ingredient of a pilaf, an internationally known Turkish specialty, but is also often used for stuffing. There are an estimated 8,000 varieties, classified by grain length: short, round, medium, or long. You can also use bulgur wheat instead of rice.

This uncomplicated specialty is exceptionally aromatic. The mint adds a fresh aroma. Mint soothes the nerves, but stimulates the senses. If you want to dry mint, do so in a dark, well-ventilated place.

Wash the lentils in a bowl of water, then pour them out and drain. Put the bouillon cubes, 1 tbsp butter, and the lentils in a pot with 6 cups/1½ l water, and cook for about 10 minutes. Scoop off the foam with a ladle.

Rinse the rice, then drain and add to the lentils; cook for a further 10 minutes.

Melt the remaining butter in a pot and stir in the flour.

Lentil Soup

Combine the dried mint, red pepper flakes, salt, and pepper in a small bowl. Put this mixture in the pot and whisk in with the flour, using a balloon whisk.

Stir in the tomato paste and add ⅘ cup/ 200 ml water.

Stir this mixture into the lentils and rice, and simmer gently for about 5 minutes. Ladle the soup into bowls and garnish with mint leaves.

Preparation time:	30 minutes
Soaking time:	overnight
Cooking time:	1 hour 40 minutes
Difficulty:	★★

Serves 4

⅔ cup/140 g	dried garbanzo beans (chickpeas)
12 oz/300 g	ground beef
1 tbsp	olive oil
1 scant cup/ 190 g	rice
	salt, ground pepper
scant ½ cup/ 100 ml	beef stock

for the yogurt sauce:

1¾ cups/440 g	set yogurt
1 tsp	flour
1	egg

For the garnish:

½ tsp/2 g	dried mint
3 tbsp	olive oil
	coarsely ground black pepper

This yogurt soup is often cooked in the Turkish provinces. It is called *lebeniye çorbası* in Gaziantep, the hinterland of the Mediterranean (*leben* comes from the Lebanese word for "sour milk"). This old, much-loved family dish is especially popular in winter. In other regions it is also called *yayla çorbası* ("soup from the plains"), and wheat grains or bulgur wheat may be used instead of rice.

The consistency and flavors of beef and garbanzo beans blend in the broth. This pulse needs to be soaked and then cooked for an hour, though the garbanzo bean itself might have different views on that: According to the poet Mevlana, who lived in Konya in the 13th century, a dried garbanzo bean once complained to the cook because it did not want to go in the boiling water. The cook patiently explained that this was necessary so that people could eat it.

That was the only way the little garbanzo bean could be part of human life, and thus experience godly love. With this metaphor Mevlana shows how the soul has to suffer before it can go to Paradise.

The combination of beef and garbanzo beans with the aroma of Turkish olive oil is a special delight. The best known olive oils come from Ayvalık and Edremit. Turkey has the third largest olive growing region after Spain and Tunisia. Gaziantep is the only area that is not on the coast.

Yogurt gives the soup a creamy consistency and slightly acid flavor. Never add it directly to the hot soup, as it will curdle. First thicken it with an egg and a little flour, and stir until smooth with a little warm broth.

Soak the garbanzo beans overnight in cold water. Next day, drain them and cook in boiling water for 1 hour until soft. Sauté the ground beef in hot olive oil for 5 minutes until brown, then pour over 1⅔ cups/400 ml water.

Add the boiled, drained garbanzo beans and cook for 5–10 minutes.

Wash the rice and put in the pot. Season with salt and pepper, and cook for a further 10 minutes.

Yogurt Soup

For the sauce, put the yogurt in a bowl and gradually stir in the flour, then the egg. Continue stirring until the sauce is smooth and creamy, then put in a pot.

Gradually blend a little broth from the meat and garbanzo beans with the yogurt sauce, stirring continuously. Heat gently for 10 minutes, until the flavors blend to form a good sauce.

Pour the yogurt sauce into the meat mixture. Add the beef stock and simmer for a further 5 minutes, stirring continuously. Heat the mint gently in the olive oil, then drizzle the oil over the soup and garnish with coarsely ground pepper.

Chorba with

Preparation time: 35 minutes
Cooking time: 30 minutes
Difficulty: ✴

Serves 4

1	onion, finely chopped
4 tbsp/50 ml	olive oil
5 tbsp/100 g	tomato paste
1	celery stick, chopped
1	sprig parsley, chopped

1¼ lb/500 g	sole, red snapper, and bream
1¼ cups/250 g	short pasta (*"langues d'oiseaux"*—"birds' tongues")
	salt and pepper

For the garnish:

	parsley
2	lemons, quartered

In Arabic, *chorba* means a soup. With this recipe, Chedly Azzaz introduces a coastal region specialty. *Chorba* with Mediterranean fish is simply a Tunisian fish soup. Traditionally, this popular dish used less expensive fish such as scorpion fish and whiting, cut into pieces and added to the stock. Occasionally, some families add the head of a grouper fish.

Our chef devised this sole, bream, and small red snapper soup as a *chorba* for feast days. Red snappers have a unique flavor, and their fine, delicate flesh makes them a great favorite. So as not to mask their flavor, no spices have been added. However, in the Sfax region, this dish is made with cumin. If you want a spicier flavor, add a tablespoon of harissa. You can also add lemon juice to the stock.

The strong aroma of the celery stick works its way through the *chorba* during cooking. Its flavor is akin to fennel. Also used for its distinctive fragrance, the characteristic flavor of flat-leaf parsley permeates the soup. This aromatic plant is sold all year round. Parsley must be very green and fresh, and the leaves and stalks rigid.

According to legend, the Arabs expelled from Spain after the fall of Granada took back pasta with them, which was previously unknown in North Africa. This new ingredient, a legacy of the Arab-Andalucian world, has found its place in Tunisian culinary heritage, and in particular in the *chorba*. You can use short macaroni instead of *"langues d'oiseaux"* ("birds' tongues"—short pasta), which are typical of the Orient.

Originally prepared during the month of Ramadan, today *chorba* has become a popular, very fashionable dish. So popular, indeed, that some families may eat it two or three times a week!

Sweat the chopped onions in a pan with the olive oil, without browning, for approximately 4 minutes.

Add the tomato paste, half the chopped celery and half the chopped parsley to the pan. Place the rest to one side. Season with salt and pepper. Sweat for another 2 minutes.

Add cold water to the mixture.

Mediterranean Fish

Wash, scale, gut, and clean the fish. Cut them up into large pieces. Add them to the pan and cook uncovered for 15 minutes. Remove the cooked fish and place to one side.

Pour in a little water. Adjust the seasoning. Add the short pasta and cook for approximately 15 minutes.

Strip the flesh from the fish and remove the bones. Add the rest of the chopped parsley and celery to the soup. Cook gently for a further 2 minutes. Add the fish meat. Serve the chorba in a soup tureen and garnish with parsley. Put the quartered lemons in a separate dish.

Ftir

Preparation time: 1 hour
Cooking time: 40 minutes
Difficulty: ★★

Serves 4

5 oz/150 g	carrots
5 oz/150 g	potatoes
1	celery heart
1	celery stick
8¾ oz/250 g	shoulder of lamb
3½ tbsp/50 ml	olive oil
1 pinch	saffron strands
1	onion, sliced
¾ cup/100g	peas
	cooking oil

1	egg yolk
½	lemon
	salt and pepper

For the cigar fritters:

3½ oz/100 g	ground lamb
2 tbsp/30 ml	olive oil
4 tsp/20 g	chopped parsley
5 tsp/25 g	grated Swiss cheese
2	eggs
2	malsouka sheets (fritter sheets)

Ftir el euch is a very substantial soup. Some Tunisian families eat it in the evening as a main course. Very rich in vegetables, Mohamed Boujelben suggests you serve this original specialty with small, cigar-shaped fritters—*malsouka* sheets filled with lamb.

For a successful soup, our chef recommends that you start by cooking the peas, celery, and carrots. Carrots are thought to have originally come from Central Asia. They are found in many Tunisian recipes and are packed with vitamin A. Select new carrots, which have an excellent flavor. They must be very hard, crunchy, blemish-free, and their tops should be green and fresh. They will keep for about two weeks in the refrigerator.

Ten minutes after you've started cooking, add the potatoes. Wait another ten minutes and remove the celery stick. This

kitchen garden plant is renowned for the wonderful flavor it gives to soups, sauces, and ragouts.

Almost at the end of the cooking time, you must add an egg yolk and lemon juice to the soup. Our chef advises you to blend them off the heat.

Ftir el euch is served with small cigar-shaped fritters. Stuffed with a filling, *malsouka* are closely associated with Tunisian culinary heritage. Made with all-purpose flour, salt, oil, and water, these sheets are used to prepare the famous *brick* (fritters). Our chef wanted to present the cigars in a separate dish. According to a family's taste, the fritters are sometimes cut up and served in the soup.

Ftir el euch is a meal in itself. It is an ideal dish for children as it is not spicy.

Peel and finely dice the carrots and potatoes.

Thinly slice the celery heart. Dice the celery stick.

Trim the shoulder of lamb and cut into cubes.

el Euch

Fry the lamb cubes gently in the olive oil. Soak the saffron in a little water and add the water with the sliced onion. Season with salt and pepper. Cover with water. Bring to the boil. Add carrots, peas, celery, and potatoes. Cook for 30 minutes.

Prepare the cigar fillings by browning the ground lamb in the olive oil. Season with salt and pepper. Add the chopped parsley, grated Swiss cheese, and 1 egg. Mix well. Beat the other egg.

To make the cigars, spread out the malsouka sheets and cut them in half. Place some filling along the curved side, and roll up. Stick down the edge with a little beaten egg. Fry the cigars in the cooking oil. Finally, mix 1 egg yolk and the juice of ½ lemon into the soup.

Hlalem

Preparation time:	30 minutes
Cooking time:	45 minutes
Difficulty:	★★

Serves 4

3½ oz/100 g	lamb
4	artichokes
2	lemons
4 tsp/20 ml	olive oil

1 bunch	celery, chopped
1 bunch	flat-leaf parsley, chopped
4 tsp/20 g	tomato paste
¼ cup/50 g	soaked garbanzo beans (chickpeas)
6½ tbsp/100 g	hlalem pasta
	salt and pepper

The inhabitants of Tunis are great consumers of *hlalem* throughout the year, but in spring they add a few delicious slices of artichoke to it. More often than not, this very substantial soup, using a minuscule type of pasta, is enriched with dried lamb, or *kadid*. To make the recipe easier, Ali Matri has used fresh lamb, but there's nothing to stop you trying beef or veal instead.

The preparation of the *kadid* is actually quite complicated. During the feast of *Aïd*, pieces of lamb are set aside, for example from the low ribs that are cut up into strips. Rubbed with mint, garlic, chile, and salt, the meat is put out to dry in the sun for several days, and then fried in olive oil. Afterwards, it can be kept for several months. In the past, Tunisians didn't eat fresh meat every day, but they laid in reserves so that there was always some *kadid* throughout the year.

Artichokes bring their distinctive flavor to this *hlalem*. Two varieties—the green and the violet—are those favored by Tunisian gourmets. Ali Matri prefers the violet variety, which is more fragrant. When he prepares them, he always leaves the tendril root of the stem under the artichoke heart to flavor the soup. If the stems are very tender, peel them and cut up their hearts into small cubes. Add them to the soup just after the tomato paste. Spring *hlalem* can also be made with early fava beans or peas.

The small variety of pasta—*hlalem*—is the ingredient that gives this soup its character. *Hlalem* are minuscule, like fine grains of rice, and are prepared half with all-purpose flour and half with semolina enriched with brewer's yeast, and separated by hand. After cooking, they should still have the taste of the yeast, and be a little crumbly in the mouth.

Using a sharp knife, cut the lamb into slices, then into small regular cubes ½ in/1 cm across.

Cut the artichoke stems at the base of the head. With a small pointed knife, remove the leaves and the beard. Squeeze half a lemon on to the hearts you have removed, to prevent them discoloring, then immerse in a bowl of cold water.

Rapidly brown the meat cubes in the olive oil in a stockpot. Season with salt and pepper, and stir to prevent it sticking to the bottom of the pan. Add the chopped celery and parsley. Cook for 10 minutes until the juice starts to run.

with Artichokes

Next, add a glass of cold water to the mixture. Boil gently until the herbs are very tender. Incorporate the tomato paste with a spatula. Stir and leave to simmer so that the tomato loses its acidity.

Add a glass of cold water to the saucepan. Bring to the boil, then add the artichoke hearts cut into large strips and the garbanzo beans. Adjust the seasoning. Cook for approximately 10 minutes uncovered.

When the artichokes are nearly tender, add the hlalem pasta. Cook for another 5 to 10 minutes. Adjust the seasoning and serve hot. Serve with the remaining lemon cut into quarters.

Hsou from

Preparation time: 15 minutes
Cooking time: 40 minutes
Difficulty: ★

Serves 4

1	onion, chopped
6½ tbsp/100 ml	olive oil
1 tbsp/17 g	tomato paste
1 tsp	harissa
1 tsp	paprika
1 tsp	caraway seeds
1 tsp	ground coriander

1	celery stick
3	garlic cloves, crushed
A few	rue leaves
½ cup/70 g	medium-sized semolina
1	lemon
	salt and pepper

For the garnish:

A few	rue leaves
	lemon slice

Tunisians generally use the word *hsou* when referring to a liquid mixture. This soup comes from the oasis of Tozeur, in the southwest of the country, and is particularly famous for its spiciness. Eaten with stale bread in the morning by the *ramess*, the date harvesters, *hsou* is an ideal start to the day and helps to keep out the cold.

This popular Tozeur dish is also prepared during the period of fasting—Ramadan. In some families, it is served in the evening after prayers, with milk and a few dates.

This meatless soup is full of spices and aromatic plants. One of them, rue, grows wild in this region, close to the Sahara desert. The small tree, resembling a herbaceous perennial, grows to about 23–29 in/60–75 cm high. Covered in round, serrated leaves, with a green or bluish-green color, rue is recognizable by its strong, bitter scent. Use the leaves sparingly in this recipe, and be aware that some people may have an allergic reaction to it. It's not essential to include it. On the other hand, the celery stick is definitely needed. Finely chopped, it gives this soup a pleasant flavor. Available in the markets all the year round, celery should be very green, perfectly hard, blemish-free, with no yellowish marks at the base. The very tender heart of this vegetable is delicious raw.

Semolina gives body to this peasant dish. After adding it to the saucepan, our chef advises that you skim the vegetable fat off the soup.

Easy to make, *hsou* from the oases will be popular with those who love spicy flavors. Try this dish to discover the culinary traditions of this region of Tunisia.

Gently fry the chopped onion in the olive oil.

Stir in the tomato paste, harissa, paprika, caraway seeds, and coriander. Season with salt and pepper. Stir well with a wooden spatula.

Wash and chop the celery. Add the celery and the crushed garlic cloves to the mixture.

he Oases

Add 4 cups/1 liter water. Stir well and cook for approximately 20 minutes.

Wash the rue leaves and add them to the soup mixture. Add the semolina and stir. Cook for approximately 10 minutes.

Peel the lemon thoroughly. Dice the pulp very finely, remove the pits and add the lemon cubes to the mixture. Cook for a further 5 minutes. Pour the soup into a dish. Garnish with rue leaves and 1 lemon slice.

Bey's

Preparation time:	30 minutes
Cooking time:	20 minutes
Difficulty:	★

Serves 4

2 lb/1 kg	spinach
9	eggs
10 tbsp/150 g	ricotta
10 tbsp/150 g	grated Swiss cheese
6½ tbsp/100 g	parsley, chopped
1 tbsp	olive oil

For the basic filling:

8¾ oz/250 g	ground lamb
7 tbsp/100 ml	olive oil
1	onion, chopped
3	garlic cloves, crushed
1 large pinch	ground coriander
	salt and pepper

In the Tunisian culinary tradition, the tagine resembles a kind of "tart." It is nothing like the Moroccan dish of the same name. According to family and region, this popular dish, made from eggs and grated cheese, is served with various vegetables and meats.

Very easy to make, Bey's tagine is our chef's version. Three fillings, blended separately with the basic filling, make this a sophisticated and original dish. Adopting a similar presentation to the *baklawa el bey*, a tri-colored marzipan sweetmeat, Mohamed Boujelben has reworked the famous tagine by experimenting with colors and shapes.

The name of this recipe is an allusion to Tunisian history, and in particular to the Ottoman presence. The bey, a Turkish governor of a province or district in the service of the sultan, was in charge of administration until the 18th century. Numerous palace conspiracies led to this title becoming hereditary, and later to the foundation of the Husseinite dynasty.

Famous for their gastronomic mores, the beys would no doubt have appreciated their title being given to this tagine. Blended with the basic filling of ground lamb, the spinach forms the first layer of this dish. Originating from Persia, spinach may be eaten raw in a salad or cooked. The leaves must be well-shaped, complete, and unblemished. Before blanching them, our chef recommends washing them in running water, without soaking them.

The central part is cheese-based, making a contrasting white layer, setting off the green of the spinach and parsley layers. Made with grated Swiss cheese and ricotta, this filling brings a light, smooth flavor to the dish.

Make the basic filling by gently frying the ground lamb in the olive oil. Add the chopped onion and the crushed garlic. Season with salt and pepper. Add the coriander. Mix well. Allow to cool and place to one side.

Blanch the spinach in boiling water for approximately 3 minutes then drain. Shape the spinach into small bundles and chop it up.

Separate the basic filling into 3 equal parts. Prepare the spinach filling by mixing it with 3 of the eggs and one part of the basic filling.

Tagine

Prepare the cheese filling by mixing the ricotta and grated Swiss cheese with 3 more eggs and the second batch of basic filling.

Prepare the third filling by mixing the chopped parsley with the remaining 3 eggs and the rest of the basic filling.

Grease the dish with 1 tbsp olive oil and spread the spinach filling over it. Bake in the oven at 350 °F/180 °C for 5 minutes. Spread the cheese filling over. Bake again for 5 minutes. Top with the parsley filling. Bake again for 5 minutes. Cool, and turn out. Cut into diamond shapes.

Eggplant and

Preparation time:	35 minutes
Cooking time:	1 hour 20 minutes
Difficulty:	★

Serves 4

1¼ lb/500 g	boned shoulder of lamb
14 oz/400 g	eggplants
1	large onion, chopped
7 tbsp/100 ml	olive oil
1 pinch	turmeric
½ bunch	parsley, chopped
13 tbsp/200 g	grated cheese
8	eggs
	cooking oil
	salt and pepper

The culinary heritage of Tunisia reflects its history. Invaded several times, the population of this country has assimilated the culinary traditions of its occupying forces over the centuries. Eggplant and lamb tagine is evidence of this cultural integration. This dish, originating from the time of the Ottoman Empire, was mainly served at the tables of the affluent classes in Tunis until the 1960s. Since then, it has become more widely popular and is enjoyed by many families.

The tagine takes its name from the deep, glazed, terracotta pot, with a well-sealed conical lid, in which it is prepared. This pot can be used to cook and serve slow-cooking dishes, keeping them moist and flavorsome. The word "tagine" usually means vegetables, fish, poultry, or meat prepared in this way. But the Tunisian tagine is very different, and is actually a kind of "tart" made from eggs and grated cheese, mixed with meat and various vegetables.

To be designated as lamb, the animal must be no more than 300 days old at the time of slaughter. If you prefer, you can use beef or veal. When you season the meat, try adding a little *harissa* to pep up the flavor.

Eggplants are strongly flavored and are an ingredient of many oriental and Mediterranean dishes. They are thought to originally come from the Indo-Burmese region. For the tagine, cut the eggplants into cubes.

Our chef has used turmeric for its irreplaceable aroma. This herbaceous plant is generally used as a spice or for coloring. The turmeric root, after grinding, has a slightly sharper flavor than saffron.

In Tunisia, eggplant and lamb tagine is mainly eaten during the month of Ramadan. This delicious dish is enjoyed in the evening under the benevolent gaze of the moon…

Trim the lamb and cut it into small pieces. Wash the eggplants and cut them into thin slices.

Brown the chopped onion in 3½ tbsp (50 ml) of the olive oil. Add the lamb pieces. Fry gently. Season with salt and pepper and stir in the turmeric.

Add sufficient water to the mixture to just cover it. Cook uncovered until the stock has completely evaporated. Add the chopped parsley. Allow to cool.

Lamb Tagine

Break the eggs into a bowl and beat them. Stir into the meat mixture. Add 10 tbsp/150 g of the grated cheese. Stir well to combine.

Gently fry the eggplant slices in the cooking oil. Absorb excess oil on a paper towel. Stir them gently but thoroughly into the mixture.

Grease the mold with the remaining olive oil. Empty the tagine into the mold and sprinkle the rest of the cheese over it. Bake in the oven at 350 °F/180 °C for approximately 25 minutes. Turn out the tagine with the help of a spatula and arrange on a dish.

Mediterranean

Preparation time: 20 minutes
Cooking time: 35 minutes
Difficulty: ★

Serves 4

7 oz/200 g	white fish fillets
7 oz/200 g	shelled shrimp
3½ oz/100 g	button mushrooms
2	onions
4 cloves	garlic
7 oz/200 g	calamaries (small squid)
¼ tsp/1 g	saffron threads
1 tbsp/15ml	olive oil

1 tbsp/15 ml	peanut oil
2	fresh tomatoes
4 tbsp	tomato paste
3½ oz/100 g	thin soup noodles
1 bunch	parsley
1 bunch	cilantro (coriander)
1 tbsp	cornstarch
	salt and pepper

Moroccan cuisine includes a great variety of soups, all under the name of *shorba*. There should always be some chopped ingredients in the thick, aromatic stock.

Here, Bouchaïb Kama introduces us to a recipe from the Mediterranean coast, in which he uses seafood and white fish. In Arabic, the soup is known as *shorba belhout*. When it comes to *shorba*, there is no limit to the imagination of Moroccan cooks: *harira* is made with tomatoes, coriander, and lamb, and then there are *shorbas* with vegetables, noodles, and poultry, with shrimp, button mushrooms, soup noodles, and cilantro and so on. There is even a "white *shorba*" made from semolina cooked in salt water, mixed with milk and flavored with olive oil.

Nearly all kinds of fish and seafood can be used for this Mediterranean *shorba*. Morocco's coastline, along the Atlantic and the Mediterranean, is 2,175 miles/3,500 kilo-

meters long. The country therefore has a huge area available for catching fish and for profits from intensive deep-sea fishing. From the Atlantic waters jumbo shrimp, tuna, and turbot come onto the market, while in the Mediterranean the catch is mainly bream or swordfish.

Many different kinds of shrimp compete for the esteem of Moroccan gourmets. The Mediterranean varieties, however, are far smaller than their Atlantic cousins. For this *shorba*, you can also use cockles, scallops, or blue mussels.

In Morocco, soup is accompanied by the traditional flat wheatmeal bread. In earlier times, this bread was prepared in the following manner: an earthenware container, the *farrah*, was placed in a hole dug in the ground. The bread was baked brown in the *farrah* under a platter covered with embers.

Dice the fish fillets, shelled shrimp, button mushrooms, onions, and garlic very finely. Cut off the heads of the calamaries, draw out the intestines and the bone, and remove the skin. Turn the mantle inside out like a glove, rinse, and chop.

In a pan, briefly fry the cubes of onion and garlic sprinkled with saffron in the peanut and olive oil. Add the calamaries. Fry for 3–4 minutes, adding a little water. Season with salt and pepper.

Add the fish, diced shrimp, and button mushrooms. Mix and bring to the boil.

Fish Soup

Scald the fresh tomatoes, skin them, and chop finely. Mix the tomato paste in a bowl with water and add to the soup. Also add the chopped tomatoes. Cook for 10 minutes on medium heat.

Add the soup noodles and the chopped parsley and chopped cilantro. Taste and adjust seasoning. Cook for a further 5 minutes.

Mix the cornstarch with water in a small bowl. Pour into the soup and stir while on the heat until the soup thickens a little. Serve the soup in a handsome soup tureen.

Soup with

Preparation time:	15 minutes
Cooking time:	35 minutes
Difficulty:	★

Serves 4

2¼ lbs/1 kg	sea bass
7 oz/200 g	onions
7 oz/200 g	fennel bulb
3½ oz/100 g	celery sticks
1 bunch	flat-leaf parsley
1 bunch	cilantro (coriander)

1¾ sticks/200g	butter
½ tsp	ground nutmeg
10 cups/2.5 l	fish stock
6 cloves	garlic
½ tsp	salt
1 tsp	pepper

This *shorba* or soup from sun-drenched Essaouira is valued everywhere where fresh fish are unloaded by the fishermen. The originality of this sea bass soup lies in its spiciness: the powerful aroma of nutmeg and the slightly aniseed-like flavor of the fennel.

The making of the *shorba* can vary just as much as that of the bouillabaisse of Marseilles. The flavor differs somewhat if sea bass is replaced by allis shad, a less common fish living in the estuary waters of the rivers. You can in fact find allis shad all the year round in Rabat or Salé, two towns on the banks of the Bou Regreg, which flows into the Atlantic.

Whether you use sea bass or allis shad, the fish is cooked in a sauce or fried in a pan and then served with *chermoula*, a

sauce made of oil, vinegar, cilantro, cumin, and mild or hot red paprika. You can do without the fish stock, but it is not hard to obtain ready-to-use stock in stores. Ideally, you prepare it in larger quantities yourself and keep it in the fridge. It makes a fine supplement to bouillon.

If the dish is prepared using allis shad, the cooking time is a little longer. Sea bass should not cook for longer than five minutes. Its flesh breaks apart very quickly and in any case it tastes better while still firm.

Before you start preparing the soup, prepare some garlic cream. Cook six unpeeled garlic cloves until they are soft. Then peel them and crush them in a little olive oil. Season with salt and stir until a cream is formed; you can simply add this to the soup shortly before serving.

Remove the scales from the fish and rinse under cold water. Slice into thick pieces and drain in a colander.

Peel the onions and clean the fennel. Dice finely, and do the same to the celery sticks. Chop parsley and cilantro. Keep each ingredient in a small bowl.

Melt some butter in a pot and then lightly fry parsley, cilantro, onions, and celery. Brown for 5 minutes on a low heat, stirring from time to time.

Sea Bass and Fennel

Add fennel to the pot and stir with a wooden spatula. Season with salt and pepper and sprinkle with nutmeg. Continue to cook for a further 5 minutes on medium heat, stirring constantly.

Add the fish stock and continue to cook on a medium heat for a further 20 minutes.

Finally, put the fish pieces into the pot and cook for a maximum of 5 minutes—the flesh should not break apart.

Preparation time: 15 minutes
Soaking time: overnight
Cooking time: 1 hour 45 minutes
Difficulty: ★

Serves 8

1¼ cups/200 g	garbanzo beans (chickpeas)
2 oz/50 g	rice
1 bunch	parsley
1 bunch	fresh cilantro (coriander)
1	onion
3½ oz/100 g	celery sticks
7 tbsp/100 ml	oil

5 oz/150 g	chicken breast fillets
2 envelopes	Moroccan saffron powder for coloring
1 cube	chicken stock
9 oz/250 g	tomato paste
6	eggs
⅞ cup/100 g	flour
	salt and pepper

For serving:

lemons
dried figs

During Ramadan, the powerful aroma of *harira*, which is made in all households, wafts through the streets. It is eaten as soon as the fast is broken, immediately after sunset. Moroccans always eat it accompanied by dried dates or figs and various small pastries.

This nourishing soup is made from pulses and flavored with cilantro, parsley, and tomato. It can be enriched according to taste by small pieces of lamb or chicken or meatballs (*kefta*), or simply cooked with a bone to give the bouillon more flavor. The soup is thickened with flour that has first been mixed with water. According to the customs of the region, soup noodles, rice, or eggs are also added.

In Morocco, pulses are a popular winter food, especially in the rough mountain climate. Dried garbanzo beans, lentils,

and beans are then on the daily menu. Like all beans, garbanzo beans ripen in their husks. Fresh garbanzo beans have a rather boring taste, and for this reason, almost the whole harvest is dried before being used as food.

In his restaurant, M'hamed Chahid generally uses short-grain rice for his stew. The rice is grown in the fertile Garb region (near Khénitra).

If the eggs are put into the pot towards the end of the cooking time, they don't need to cook for long. They will continue to cook in the soup when the pan is taken off the heat.

Squeeze the lemon directly before serving and add the juice to the soup or serve it separately. Strings of dried figs are decorative and make a wonderful sweet accompaniment.

Soak the garbanzo beans the evening before cooking. Cook the rice for 20 minutes in salted water. Finely chop the parsley and cilantro. Peel the onion and dice into small pieces. Do the same with the celery.

Heat the oil in a large pot. Lightly fry the finely diced ingredients, stirring. Add the drained garbanzo beans and the diced chicken breast meat.

Add saffron powder, salt, pepper, 1 crumbled chicken stock cube, and tomato paste. Pour on 6 cups/1.5 l water, bring to the boil and simmer for 1 hour.

Rice and Figs

Mix the flour with water in a small bowl. Pour into the pot and, with the pot on the heat, stir in well to bind the soup. Allow to thicken for about 15 minutes.

At the end of the cooking time, add the cooked and drained rice to the soup.

Break the eggs into a bowl and add to the soup. Cook for 2–3 minutes, then take the pot from the heat. Serve with wedges of lemon and dried figs.

Fez Ramadan

Preparation time: 35 minutes
Soaking time: 12 hours
Cooking time: 1 hour 40 minutes
Difficulty: ★

Serves 4

½ cup/100 g	yellow lentils
1¼ cups/200 g	garbanzo beans (chickpeas)
2	onions
1 bunch	cilantro (coriander)
1 bunch	parsley
1 stick	celery
9 oz/250 g	shin of beef
5	tomatoes

1 tsp	smen (preserved butter) or olive oil if not available
1 tsp	Moroccan saffron powder for coloring
1 tsp	ground ginger
1 cube	chicken stock
3½ oz/100 g	Greek noodles (kritharaki)
⅞ cup/100 g	flour
5 oz/150 g	tomato paste
	salt and pepper

For the garnish:

8	dates
8	figs (optional)
	lemon (optional)

It is impossible to imagine the heritage of Moroccan cuisine without *harira*. This traditional soup, made from meat, garbanzo beans, lentils, tomatoes, and celery, is eaten by every family during Ramadan. It is also served to a newly-married bride on the morning after the wedding night.

This nourishing dish, which can perhaps be compared to a Hungarian goulash, varies from region to region and family to family. However, for many Moroccans, the true *harira* is the one eaten in Fez. This royal city, with a culinary tradition going back fourteen centuries, is an upholder of tradition and has brought recipes to Moroccan cuisine that are worthy of their reputation. *Fassia* gastronomic culture is considered noble and elite and is distinguished by its skill and refinement.

This *harira* is easy to prepare and displays a subtle mixture of different aromas. It is therefore essential to cook it for a long time. Celery, *krafece* in Moroccan, gives soups, sauces, and ragouts a wonderful aroma, and is available all year round in the markets. Choose green sticks without wilted patches and no yellowish stains at the bulb end. They keep well in the fridge.

Harira fassia is unthinkable without lentils and garbanzo beans. Garbanzo beans, which originate in western Asia, develop a light nutty flavor. They are very nourishing and keep their shape when cooking. Don't forget to soak them for twelve hours and pull off the little husk that surrounds them. *Harira* is always eaten with a sweet accompaniment such as dates or figs.

Soak the lentils and the garbanzo beans the evening before cooking. Remove the husks from the garbanzo beans. Peel the onions and chop finely. Chop cilantro, parsley, and celery.

Dice the beef into small cubes. Scald the tomatoes and peel them. Cut into small cubes, purée and put aside.

Sweat the onions in the smen. Add diced meat, saffron powder, and ginger. Season with salt and pepper. Dissolve the chicken stock cube in a glass of water and pour into the pan. Add the garbanzo beans. Bring all ingredients to the boil.

Soup

Pour on water. Add cilantro, parsley, and celery. Cook for about 30 minutes. Add the lentils and cook for a further 20 minutes. Stir in puréed tomatoes. Cover and cook for a further 20 minutes.

Add the noodles. Cook for about 5 minutes. Mix flour and tomato paste with water.

Pour in the mixture and allow all ingredients to cook, covered, for about 15 minutes, stirring occasionally. Pour into a soup tureen and serve with dates, figs, and lemon.

Preparation time:	15 minutes
Cooking time:	30 minutes
Difficulty:	★

Serves 4

9 oz/250 g	dried small beans
3	unpeeled cloves of garlic
2 tbsp/30 ml	olive oil
1 tsp	salt

For serving:

ground cumin
paprika
olive oil

In the winter, Moroccans like to warm themselves up with a plate of *bissara*. This intensively aromatic soup of dried beans, salt, and oil may seem a little dull in flavor at first, which is why each guest is provided with little bowls of olive oil, paprika, and cumin to flavor the soup according to taste.

Amina Khayar prepares *bissara* using very small dried beans, about the same size as peas. These have the advantage of cooking very quickly. Of course, the soup can also be prepared using fava beans or peas. Fresh fava beans go very well with pickled lemons, a combination frequently used in lamb tagines. There is also a couscous with green beans and wild figs, known as *kuran*. Small beans are popular poached and marinated in *chermoula* sauce. Dried beans, on the other hand, are always made into soups.

The beans must be rinsed several times to remove even the last traces of dirt. At the same time, this makes them lose some of their excess starch. Stir regularly during cooking to make the beans cook and break apart more quickly. The garlic you put into the soup can be peeled beforehand. Depending on the desired consistency, the soup can finally be passed through a sieve or puréed in a blender.

Amina Khayar's *bissara* also depends on the flavor of Moroccan olive oil. The best olive oil comes from the Berber regions in the south of the country. It is dark green in color and has a slightly bitter taste. In was not until King Hassan II commanded it that large-scale olive plantations were introduced to the country. These are cultivated to this day, covering an area of around 8,650 acres/3,500 hectares.

Pour the dried beans out onto a large plate or onto the work surface. Pick out bits of leaf, beans still in their husks, small stones etc. with your fingers.

Rinse the beans well in a bowl or in a colander under running water. Repeat at least 3 times in order to remove all impurities.

Put the beans into a large pot. Fill the pot three-quarters full with hot water.

Bissara

Put the unpeeled garlic into the bean water. Add a generous splash of olive oil and season with salt. Cover and cook for 20–30 minutes.

Take the garlic out with a slotted spatula. Pour on cold water and then peel carefully with a small knife.

Put the bean soup and the garlic in a food processor and blend to a smooth purée. Taste and adjust seasoning. Serve hot with cumin, paprika, and olive oil to accompany.

Preparation time:	20 minutes
Cooking time:	25 minutes
Difficulty:	★

Serves 4

2	zucchini
2	carrots
2	potatoes
2	tomatoes
½ bunch	cilantro (coriander)
½ bunch	parsley
2 cloves	garlic

1	onion
1 tbsp/15 ml	olive oil
2 oz/50 g	Chinese thread noodles
1	chicken stock cube
1 pinch	saffron threads
4 tbsp/60 g	fine semolina
1 tbsp	butter
	salt and pepper

This vegetable soup was originally eaten in the "valley of the thousand *casbahs*," which lies along the route from er-Rachidia to Ouarzazate in southern Morocco. Almond and olive trees, cactus and reeds grow in this extraordinary landscape, and again and again one comes across one of the numerous *ksours*, castles built out of beaten clay.

In this region, the *casbah* culture has strongly influenced the local character. In earlier years, these mighty fortresses, originally rulers' residences, also served as safe refuges for the people of the villages when invasion threatened. In the *casbah*, the caravans trading between the Maghreb and the southern part of the African continent found a safe place to stay overnight, as well as a secure warehouse for their goods from distant lands.

According to legend it was the nomads who primarily enjoyed this fortifying soup of vegetables, noodles, and semolina. Today this popular dish is served mainly among the Berber families of Ouarzazate. It is easy to prepare and is usually served as a main course. The inhabitants of the region are particularly fond of noodles.

For this recipe, the chef has used Chinese thread noodles made from soy flour and available in long, mother-of-pearl-colored strands. They can be boiled or fried, and used in stews and fillings.

In earlier times, this vegetarian soup was made solely from seasonal vegetables. For example, for the zucchini it was necessary to wait until summer. Zucchini originate in Central and South America, but are now firmly established in Mediterranean cuisine. These vegetables are rich in water but are not overly filling. They should be an even green color.

Wash the zucchini. Peel the carrots and potatoes and grate the vegetables finely. Scald and chop the tomatoes.

Finely chop the cilantro and parsley. Peel and crush garlic cloves. Peel and finely chop the onion.

Lightly sweat the onion and garlic in a saucepan in olive oil. Cut up the thread noodles and add them. Also add the grated potatoes, carrots, and zucchini.

Vegetable Soup

Fill the pan three-quarters full of water. Add the stock cube.

Season with salt and pepper. Add saffron threads, parsley, and cilantro. Cook for about 20 minutes.

Add the semolina. Stir with a wooden spatula to bind the soup. Stir in the chopped tomatoes and the butter. Serve the casbah soup in little bowls.

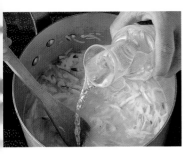

Sabbath Soup

Preparation time:	*20 minutes*
Soaking time:	*12 hours*
Cooking time:	*5 hours*
Difficulty:	★

Serves 4

6 cups/1 kg	large garbanzo beans (chickpeas)
1 tsp	baking soda
2¼ lbs/1 kg	lean beef (shoulder and breast)
3	marrow bones

1	onion
1	potato
2 cloves	garlic
1 bunch	cilantro (coriander)
1 tsp	saffron threads
4 tbsp/60ml	vegetable oil
1 tsp	turmeric
	salt and pepper

Many of the Jews who come from Morocco nostalgically remember the garbanzo bean soup eaten on the evening before the Sabbath. This tasty dish is particularly popular today in Tangier and Meknès and is served on the Sabbath.

It is easy to make but needs some time to cook. In Judaism the use of fire is prohibited during the Sabbath. As a consequence, this specialty is prepared on the Friday afternoon. On the eve of the Sabbath, the family table resembles an altar. For the Jewish community, this is a privileged moment, to be experienced with joy, and also the opportunity of enjoying special dishes.

Garbanzo beans, highly esteemed everywhere in the Mediterranean countries, must be soaked for 12 hours in water before cooking. Victoria Berdugo also adds a teaspoon of baking soda to make them more digestible.

Garbanzo beans originate in Central Asia and are the fruits of a herb-like, annual plant. The pods contain three to four peas, which taste slightly nutty.

Garbanzo beans are very nourishing and keep their shape when cooking. While many Jews in Tangier prefer to crush or even purée them, whole beans, floating in the soup, are popular in Meknès.

This delicious soup contains a wonderful mixture of Middle Eastern aromas. Cilantro—coriander leaf—without which Moroccan cuisine would be unimaginable, gives the soup its characteristic touch. Cilantro is known as *kosbor* in Arabic. It develops the whole power of its flavor in this soup. In order to ensure that the garbanzo bean soup turns out really spicy, add some of the spices right at the end of cooking.

Put the garbanzo beans into boiling hot water (but not on the stove) the evening before. Add 1 tsp baking soda. Cover and soak for 12 hours.

Put the garbanzo beans in clear water the next day and rub them with your hands in order to release the skins.

Put the beef and the bones into a saucepan. Add garbanzo beans, onion, potato, crushed garlic cloves, a tied ½ bunch of cilantro, saffron threads, and oil. Fill the pan with water and cook, covered, for about 4½ hours.

with Garbanzo Beans

Take out the meat and the bones. Purée the garbanzo beans and the other ingredients in a blender.

Finely chop the other half of the bunch of cilantro. Add to the garbanzo bean soup with the turmeric. Taste and adjust seasoning with salt and pepper.

Replace the meat and bones in the soup. Cook for another 30 minutes or so. Take the bones out of the soup. Serve the garbanzo bean soup on plates and serve the meat separately.

Atlas-Style

Preparation time:	45 minutes
Cooking time:	1 hour 5 minutes
Difficulty:	★★

Serves 4

8	quails
2 cloves	garlic
2	onions
1 bunch	parsley
1 bunch	cilantro (coriander)
4 tbsp/60 ml	olive oil
4 tbsp/60 ml	peanut oil

1 pinch	ginger
2 pinches	saffron threads
2 pinches	Moroccan saffron powder for coloring
²/₃ cup/150 ml	chicken stock
1¹/₃ lbs/600 g	fresh spinach
12	quail's eggs
½ stick/50 g	fresh (unsalted) butter salt and pepper

Quail tagines are among the most sophisticated delicacies that Moroccan cuisine has to offer. Bouchaïb Kama is never short of good ideas, and here introduces us to one of his most recent creations; small pieces of quail with delicious balls of spinach and quail's eggs glazed with saffron and butter, in a sauce of saffron and onions.

The tagine owes its name to a container made of glazed earthenware with a cone-shaped lid used for cooking. The Moroccans have retained the custom of cooking over a *majmar*, a ceramic container filled with hot coals. It is difficult to find the handsome tagine pots outside Morocco. If you do not have one, the chef recommends that you at least serve the dish in another earthenware vessel with a colorful border.

The quails used by the chef come from the Atlas Mountains, where there are several farms rearing quails. Quails shot in the wild are not on offer in Moroccan restaurants, as their origin is too uncertain and they are often too full of shotgun pellets. Quails shot by family members are eaten within the family only. Quail farms make it possible for these birds to be available all the year round. For this recipe you can also use turkey, chicken, rabbit, or duck.

The small, rather expensive quail's eggs with their little brown spots are often used to garnish very sophisticated dishes, such as those served at receptions. In provincial parts of Morocco old people still maintain that hard-boiled quail's eggs eaten in the morning help to cure asthma.

Clean and gut the quails and rinse them under running water. Cut off the necks, wingtips, and thighs. Carve the bodies lengthways and cut into 2 parts, giving 6 pieces per quail.

Peel the garlic and the onions and chop. Also chop the parsley and cilantro. Fry the quails in both kinds of oil. Season with salt and pepper. Add garlic, onions, ginger, 2 pinches of saffron threads,s and saffron powder. Fry until the quails are browned.

When the quails have simmered for about 10 minutes on a medium heat, add the chicken stock and stir.

Quail Tagine

Add the parsley and cilantro at once. Cover. Cook for a further 25–30 minutes.

Scald the spinach in salt water. Pour on cold water to keep the green color. Press out the liquid and chop finely. Roll into small balls with your hands.

Boil the quail's eggs for 5 minutes and then shell them. Melt the butter in a small pan. Stir in 1 pinch of saffron powder. Put in the quail's eggs and move them around in the saffron butter until they are yellow all over. Arrange the dish on a serving platter.

Pasta, Rice, Couscous & Co.

Vegetable

Preparation time:	20 minutes
Cooking time:	50 minutes
Difficulty:	★

Serves 4

4 oz/100 g	baby fava beans (broad beans), washed
½ lb/200 g	cauliflower florets
4	artichokes
½	leek
1	red bell pepper

1	carrot
1	zucchini
3	mangold leaves
1	ripe tomato
3 cloves	garlic
7 tbsp/100 ml	olive oil
1 tsp	ground paprika
1½ cups/350 g	rice (ideally "Bomba")
8 cups/2 l	chicken stock
pinch	saffron threads
	salt

Vegetable paella is not really a traditional Spanish dish, but it is something that is enjoyed by many families in the Valencia region. Oscar Torrijos has been lovingly making his own version for 30 years.

Rice has been grown in the marshy region of Albufera near Valencia since the Middle Ages. This is where paella, the pride of all Valencians, hails from. The word "paella" referred originally to the large, shallow pan with two handles in which rice, fish, vegetables, or seafood were prepared. Paella used to be served only on high days and holidays, and was usually eaten outside.

Today, paella may be made from a huge variety of ingredients. Oscar Torrijos recommends bomba rice, which is grown near Valencia. Its advantage is that the grains increase three- to fourfold during cooking without bursting.

They absorb the stock well and develop an incomparable aroma. One kilogram of rice is enough for 10 to 12 people. In Albufera, rice is harvested in September and October. The rice is then dried, peeled, and polished. The grains are considered "young" until the following May. The cooking time for paella is 18 to 20 minutes. Special skillets are available, but a normal skillet or even a casserole will also do well.

The vegetables can be chosen according to what is in season. In Valencia, vegetables come from the Huerta region, a vast fruit and vegetable growing area, where artichokes, bell peppers and chiles, carrots, cabbages, eggplants, potatoes, tomatoes, mangold, onion, beans, and many more varieties are cultivated. Such abundance stimulates creativity, which is confirmed most wonderfully by Oscar Torrijos' paella.

Trim the beans and cut the cauliflower into small rosettes. Trim the artichokes and cut into pieces.

Prepare the remaining vegetables as follows: cut the leek, bell pepper, carrot, and zucchini into 2 in/4 cm pieces. Thinly slice the mangold. Skin the tomato, cut into quarters, then remove the seeds. Peel and chop the garlic.

Combine the vegetables in a bowl. Heat the olive oil in a paella pan, then sauté the vegetables. Add the ground paprika. Continue cooking for about 5 minutes, stirring continuously.

Paella

As soon as the vegetables start to turn brown, add the rice and stir until it becomes transparent.

Pour over the chicken stock and bring to the boil.

Season with saffron and salt, and simmer gently for 20 minutes, stirring continuously. Finally, put the paella in the oven for 8 minutes, and serve very hot.

Potato Gnocchi

Preparation time: 30 minutes
Cooking time: 1 hour
Difficulty: ★★

Serves 4

For the gnocchi:

2¼ lb/1 kg	potatoes
	salt
2 cups/225 g	flour

For the sauce:

| 1 stick | celery |
| 1 | carrot |

1	onion
2 cloves	garlic
1½ lb/700 g	tomatoes
4 tbsp/60 ml	extra-virgin olive oil
	salt
	pepper
20	small thyme leaves

To serve:

| 8 tsp/40 g | grated pecorino |

The restaurant "La Mora" in Ponte a Moriano (the name means "rest" or "pause" in Latin) dates back to 1867. It is a very inviting place to stop after touring the countryside around Lucca. Sauro Brunicardi and his colleague Paolo Indragoli recommend one of its specialties, potato *gnocchi* with a simple, highly piquant vegetable sauce.

Gnocchi—meaning "little dumplings"—have been produced mainly in northern and central Italy since the 18th century, when the parcels of dough were called *ravioli* (ravioli as we know them used to be called *tortellini*). Today, two main types are produced: those made from potatoes and flour, and those made from semolina with spinach and ricotta.

Although gnocchi look easy enough to prepare, a certain amount of skill is needed to achieve an acceptable-looking result. The dough must be light, yet firm, and must not dis-

integrate in the sauce during cooking. Floury potato varieties such as Bintje give the right consistency. Knead the mixture as you would pastry dough. Then cut the gnocchi on a floured surface, so they do not stick.

The sauce should be thick enough to coat the gnocchi well. Italians traditionally serve tomato sauce with basil or pesto with nuts and gorgonzola as an accompaniment to gnocchi. Sauro Brunicardi passes the vegetables for the sauce through a sieve to remove the skins and seeds. The resulting, smooth purée goes wonderfully well with thyme and pecorino, a ewe's milk cheese that gives the dish its typically Tuscan character. After maturing for four months, the cheese is the color of straw; it develops its full flavor in this dish.

For the gnocchi, boil the unpeeled potatoes in salted water for 20 minutes. Drain, peel, cut into large pieces, and pass through a sieve. Leave to cool slowly.

Sprinkle some flour over the work surface. Knead the lukewarm potato with about 1¾ cups/200 g flour, until it no longer sticks to your fingers.

Divide the potato dough into portions, rolling each one into a long tube a finger's breadth in diameter. Cut into pieces about ¾ in/2 cm in length.

'Mora"

For the sauce, clean the celery and carrot, then slice. Peel the onion and garlic and chop finely. Quarter the tomatoes. Put the oil in a pan, add the vegetables, season with salt and pepper, and cook over high heat for 25–30 minutes.

In a large saucepan, bring some salted water to the boil and add a few drops of oil. Cook the gnocchi in the boiling water until they rise to the surface.

Strain the cooked vegetables through a sieve and transfer to a large pan with the gnocchi and a few thyme leaves. Stir well and bring to the boil. Serve with grated pecorino.

Lasagne

Preparation time: 50 minutes
Cooking time: 1 hour
Difficulty: ★

Serves 4

2	eggplants
2	zucchini
2	large onions
2	very young artichokes
1	lemon
4 tbsp	white wine
4 tbsp	balsamic vinegar
4 tbsp	olive oil
	salt
	pepper

10 oz/250 g — lasagne
10 tbsp/150 g — grated parmesan

For the béchamel sauce:
scant ½ stick/
50 g — butter
scant ½ cup/
50 g — flour
2 cups/500 ml — milk
— salt
— pepper
1 pinch — grated nutmeg

For the garnish:
— arugula

Sergio Pais named his restaurant in Paris "La Rucola"—"arugula"—as a result of his love for this Mediterranean salad plant. This recipe, a vegetable lasagne, is one of the specialties on the menu.

The natives of Bologna regard themselves as the unassailable champions when it comes to preparing lasagne. Normally these long, rectangular sheets of pasta, originally from Emilia-Romagna, are layered alternately with minced meat and béchamel sauce. Here is a tip, should you need to serve your lasagne in smaller portions: Leave the prepared dish to cool for about three hours, then you can easily cut it to individual requirements.

This northern Italian specialty is inconceivable without béchamel sauce, which is made from a roux of flour and milk. It was traditionally made with cream, which produced a wonderfully thick, velvety sauce.

When you have cleaned the small, violet artichokes, immerse them in water containing lemon juice to stop them discoloring. If you want to keep them for a few days, leave the stalks on.

Zucchini, a classic summer vegetable, adds color.

Eggplants are popular throughout the Mediterranean region. The most common variety is purple-skinned, and is the one used by Sergio Pais in this recipe.

Give this simple recipe a try—it is sure to be popular with family and friends.

Wash the eggplants and zucchini and cut these, together with the peeled onions, into even-sized cubes. Remove the outer leaves from the artichokes until you reach the hearts, then immerse them in water with a dash of lemon juice.

Pour 2 cups/500 ml water into a saucepan with the white wine and balsamic vinegar and boil the artichokes in this liquid for about 20 minutes. Drain. Remove the "choke" and cut the flesh into small pieces.

Braise the onions, eggplants, and zucchini in the olive oil in another pan, and drain on kitchen paper.

'Rucola"

For the béchamel sauce, melt the butter and stir in the flour. Add the milk, stirring constantly. Season with salt and pepper, and sprinkle with nutmeg.

Add the onions, zucchini, eggplants, and artichokes to the béchamel sauce. Stir carefully and adjust seasoning to taste. Reserve a few of the diced vegetables for the garnish.

Layer the lasagne sheets with the sauce in an ovenproof dish and sprinkle with parmesan. Bake for 30 minutes at 350° F/180° C. Place a serving of lasagne on each plate and garnish with a drizzle of oil, the remaining diced vegetables, and arugula.

Preparation time:	20 minutes
Cooking time:	2 hours 10 minutes
Difficulty:	★

Serves 4

8 oz/200 g	boned breast of lamb
4 leaves	basil
4 tbsp	red wine
	pepper
6 tbsp	olive oil
1	onion
	salt

10 oz/250 g	tomatoes
12 oz/300 g	paccheri di gragniano (pasta)
6 oz/150 g	grated *Caciocavallo* cheese

For the garnish

4 leaves	basil
	oil for deep frying

According to Michelina Fischetti, the actor Eduardo De Filippo spoke often of a famous Neapolitan goulash he had greatly enjoyed, from a very young age. This substantial goulash is traditionally served at weddings. It is simple to prepare and absolutely delicious. The meat from a breast of lamb is braised slowly with tomatoes, onion, and red wine, to which the main accompaniment is pasta—in the Neapolitan region, this is *paccheri*, which is Neapolitan for "a box on the ears." *Paccheri* are small, thick tubes, and it is therefore possible to substitute macaroni in this recipe.

Many historians believe that the Chinese invented pasta, while others attribute the invention to imperial Rome. The Romans are known to have eaten noodles made from flour and water, which they called *langanum*. The Neapolitans like to think that pasta was invented at the foot of Vesuvius. Although this is not entirely consistent with historical fact, given that pasta has only been eaten there since the end of the 18th century, a wide range of ingenious variations have nevertheless originated in Naples. Originally known as *mangiafoglia*, or "leaf eaters," the Neapolitans have subsequently come to be known as *mangia-maccheroni*, or "pasta eaters."

The fresh flavor of tomato plays an important role in the success of this goulash. Tomatoes are an indispensable part of Mediterranean cuisine and can undoubtedly be described as the favorite vegetable of the Italians. They are grown mainly in southern Italy, which supplies the north of the country with tomatoes and, in addition, exports them all over the world. It took some considerable time for tomatoes to find their way onto the table at the Neapolitan royal palace; serious cultivation probably did not begin until the mid-18th century.

Our chef recommends *caciocavallo*, the southern Italian version of parmesan, to go with the *paccheri*.

Cut the meat into small pieces with a knife. Deep-fry 4 basil leaves for the garnish. Tear the other 4 leaves into small pieces and set aside.

Transfer the lamb into a salad bowl and cover with water. Pour in 2 tbsp red wine, mix, and leave for a few moments to infuse. Drain the meat and season with pepper.

Pour the olive oil into a pan. Peel and chop the onion and sauté until transparent. Add the lamb and brown for 5 minutes. Season with salt.

with Lamb Goulash

Add the remaining red wine and reduce. Wash, blanch, and skin the tomatoes and sieve to make a purée.

Add the tomato purée to the meat. Simmer for 2 hours, then add the torn basil leaves.

Boil the paccheri in salted water until cooked "al dente." Drain. Pour the goulash over the pasta and mix. Transfer the paccheri onto plates, sprinkle with the cheese, and garnish with deep-fried basil leaves.

Preparation time: 1 hour
Resting time for
 the dough: 1 hour
Cooking time: 25 minutes
Difficulty: ★ ★

Serves 4

1 lb/400 g cherry tomatoes
3 tbsp olive oil
¾ lb/350 g buffalo mozzarella

For the dough:
5 tsp/25 g beer yeast
4⅓ cups/
500 g flour
  salt

For the garnish:
  basil leaves
  olive oil

To invent pizza, you would probably have had to be born at the foot of Vesuvius. Today there are endless variations on this Neapolitan specialty that is now world-famous. Although the Italians proudly claim that you can use anything you like as a topping—Venus clams, mussels, sausage, ham, arugula, paprika, onions, artichokes, capers, olives, and different types of cheese—purists know that the topping of a *pizza Napoli* consists only of tomatoes, mozzarella, basil, and olive oil. The pizza baker Raffaele Esposito is said to have devised this pizza topping with the colors of the Italian royal kingdom—green, white, and red—in honor of Queen Margherita in 1889.

With the mass exodus from Italy to America, the traditional pizza, as well as many other varieties, reached the New World and achieved hitherto unknown popularity, with the result that the first pizzeria was opened in New York in 1905. *Pizza Napoli* would certainly never have been such a success had it not been for the many years of experience of the Neapolitan pizza bakers, as everything depends on the preparation of the dough. This should be rolled out to about ¼ inch/5 millimeters in depth.

The flavor of the tomatoes used is crucial. During the 19th century, the Neapolitans pioneered various procedures that enabled them to eat tomatoes all year round. Today, we have canned, peeled tomatoes to fall back on.

In Naples, a pizza without mozzarella would be tantamount to heresy. The traditional spherical cheese from Campagna is held in high regard because of its mild, acidic taste.

This southern Italian specialty can be served equally well as an appetizer or a main dish. As the Italians say, it is, quite simply, *buonissima*.

For the dough, stir the yeast into warm water. Put the flour in a bowl and make a hollow in the middle. Pour the yeast mixture into the hollow and add salt.

Using your hands, gradually knead 2 cups/500 ml water into the dough until it is elastic and comes away from the sides of the bowl. Cover with a damp cloth and leave to rise for 1 hour.

Wash the cherry tomatoes and crush between your hands to remove the seeds from them.

Napoli

Roll the ball of dough in flour. Dust the work surface with flour and roll out the dough with a rolling pin until you have a thin, flat circle to fit your baking sheet.

Pour 2 tbsp olive oil over the tomatoes. Grease the baking sheet with the remaining oil. Cover the sheet with the dough and distribute the tomatoes over the top. Bake for about 20 minutes at 450° F/ 230° C.

Remove the pizza from the oven and sprinkle with mozzarella cubes. Bake for a further 5 minutes at 450° F/230° C. Garnish with basil leaves and serve drizzled with olive oil.

Herb Orzotto

Preparation time:	30 minutes
Cooking time:	1 hour 20 minutes
Difficulty:	★★

Serves 4

4	sage leaves
10	mint leaves
12 oz/300 g	spinach
10	basil leaves
2 tsp/10 g	chopped parsley
2 oz/50 g	fennel

12	large shrimp
½	onion
1	carrot
1 stick	celery
3	shallots
2 tbsp	extra-virgin olive oil
1¼ cups/	
250 g	pearl barley
	salt
	pepper
scant ½ stick/	
50 g	butter

This outstanding *orzotto* from Friuli, which is related to risotto, originally from Lombardy, used to be prepared as a soup with pearl barley as the basic ingredient. Paolo Zoppalatti, however, prefers to make it with a less liquid consistency, skillfully seasoning it with a mixture of aromatic herbs and enhancing it with shrimp.

An *orzotto* is cooked in the same way as a risotto: The grains are fried in a pan with the shallots and then quenched with the herb stock that is subsequently reduced. The first step when preparing the dish is to make an original stock from sage, mint, spinach, basil, and fennel. Blanch the herbs and vegetables briefly and transfer to a dish containing ice cubes. This interrupts the cooking process, so that the herbs retain their chlorophyll and hence their beautiful green color. They will be needed again later to give the barley its color and flavor.

In Italy, barley is grown mainly in Friuli and South Tyrol. It dates back thousands of years and flourishes in poor soil and harsh climatic conditions. The grains are of similar diameter and color as grains of wheat, but are rather longer and more pointed. In Friuli, barley is frequently ground and used as flour, but the grains are also used with the husks removed or as pearl barley: in other words, milled until the grains are spherical.

Shrimp play a dual role in this recipe: The heads give flavor to the herb stock and the delicious flesh enhances the *orzotto*. The Friuli and Venezia Giulia regions lie on the northern Adriatic coast, where the fishing industry is still very important. The inhabitants of the lagoons of Grado and Marano continue to catch large quantities of mullet, perch, turbot, and various types of crab. Other crustaceans or mussels can successfully be substituted for the shrimp.

Finely chop the sage, mint, spinach, basil, and parsley. Cut the fennel into large pieces. Blanch all these ingredients in boiling water for 1 minute.

Remove the herbs with a spatula and transfer immediately to a small bowl of ice cubes. Set the herbs and stock aside.

Remove the heads from the shrimp. Peel the tails and dice the flesh, reserving 4 whole tails for the garnish. Set aside.

with Shrimp

Strain the herb stock into a saucepan. Add the onion, carrot, celery stalk and leaves, and shrimp heads. Simmer for about 40 minutes.

Fry the chopped shallots gently in the olive oil for about 5 minutes, until they are soft and transparent. Stir in the pearl barley and sauté for 3 minutes, stirring constantly. Mix in the diced shrimp.

Add a little herb stock to the barley mixture. Cook for 20 minutes. Gradually pour in the remaining stock. Add the blanched herbs. Season with salt and pepper. Leave to infuse for 10 minutes before adding the butter. Serve the orzotto on soup plates, garnished with shrimp tails.

Black

Preparation time: 35 minutes
Cooking time: 2 hours 25 minutes
Difficulty: ★★

Serves 4

12 oz/300 g	cuttlefish
½	onion
⅔ cup/150 ml	olive oil
2 cups/400 g	Arborio rice
4 cups/1 l	fish stock

	salt
	pepper
1 clove	garlic
1	cuttlefish ink sac
4 tbsp/60 g	grated parmesan
⅞ stick/100 g	butter

For the garnish:

	parsley
	cherry tomatoes
	(optional)

This black risotto, which is very popular in Venice, has a long tradition on the Adriatic coast. Today, this delicious cuttlefish dish also has a following in other regions.

Black risotto is very easy to prepare and has a subtle flavor. The cuttlefish are around 12 inches/30 centimeters long, and live on the seabed in coastal waters. They are easily recognized by their gray-beige, oval bodies and large heads with ten irregular tentacles, two of which are very long.

The outer covering of the cuttlefish with the fins has a hard, rough part that must be removed. It is best to wear gloves to do this. The ink sac, if still present, must be removed carefully with the fingers, although it is possible to buy these vacuum-packed in the shops. The ink sac should be kept refrigerated. The ink gives the risotto a distinctive character.

Rice—rich in magnesium and typical of northern Italian cuisine—ranks alongside wheat as the most important source of nutrition in the world. The means by which rice was introduced to the Italian peninsula is disputed. Some historians believe that rice was known to the Romans; others that it was only brought much later to Sicily by the Arabs; and finally the Venetians, who are very proud of their past, insist that it was brought to Italy from the Orient by merchants of the *Serenissima*, the beautiful city of Venice. Whatever its origins, one thing is certain: No rice was cultivated on the Po plain before the 16th century.

Black risotto is a highly original dish and will be very much appreciated by your guests.

Wash the cuttlefish thoroughly under running water. Remove the rough parts and, if necessary, the ink sacs, and set aside. Cut the cuttlefish into small pieces.

Peel and finely chop the onion and cook in a saucepan with 5 tbsp olive oil until soft and transparent. Add the rice and cook for another 2 minutes, stirring constantly.

Gradually add the fish stock to the rice. Simmer for 18 minutes, stirring with a wooden spoon.

Risotto

Heat the remaining olive oil in a pan. Add the cuttlefish and fry until brown. Season with salt and pepper and add the chopped clove of garlic.

Stir the ink into the cuttlefish. Stir with a wooden spoon and add to the rice. Mix very gently.

Sprinkle parmesan over the rice. Stir and add the butter, and adjust seasoning to taste. Serve the risotto garnished with parsley and cherry tomatoes if desired.

Porcini Mushroom Risotto

Preparation time:	15 minutes
Soaking time:	1 hour
Cooking time:	25 minutes
Difficulty:	★

Serves 4

⅓ cup/40 g	dried porcini mushrooms
4 tbsp	olive oil
2	onions
1½ cups/ 300 g	Vialone-Nano rice (or other risotto rice)
7 tbsp	white wine

1 lb/400 g	pumpkin
	salt
1 clove	garlic
½ bunch	parsley
½ tsp/3 g	ground saffron
	pepper
2oz/50 g	grated parmesan

For the garnish:

	parsley
	dried saffron strands

Although the home of risotto is in northern Italy, more specifically Milan, the rest of Italy has also mastered the art of cooking rice. It is fried in oil and combined with local produce, which almost invariably includes butter and parmesan. This porcini mushroom risotto is a well-known specialty of the Marche region. The natives of the Marche region have a reputation for being fond of the pleasures of the table, especially rice dishes.

Alberto Melagrana specifically recommends the Vialone-Nano variety of rice, the grains of which are rather fat, quite firm, and have a high starch content. If you cook the rice in vegetable stock instead of water, the risotto will have an even more piquant flavor.

Saffron is a much sought-after spice and is cultivated in the province of L'Aquila in the Abruzzi region. According to some historians, the Romans were admirers of this valuable plant, using it, among other things, to scent their theaters. Saffron was also used as a strong yellow dye for silk.

The inhabitants of L'Aquila, who traded with Venice, Milan, and Marseille, concentrated on growing saffron in the Middle Ages. Saffron from this region is still highly prized throughout Italy today. In our recipe, the powdered saffron must be dissolved in a little water before use.

Alberto Melagrana loves porcini mushrooms. They are recognizable by their club-shaped stalk and convex heads. According to our chef, the unmistakable taste of porcini mushrooms is ideal for a risotto flavored with saffron.

The addition of creamed pumpkin gives this dish its unique sophistication.

Soak the dried porcini mushrooms for 1 hour in water. Heat 2 tbsp olive oil in a copper saucepan. Sauté 1 chopped onion until soft and transparent, then add the rice and sauté, stirring constantly, until it, too, is soft and transparent.

Add the white wine. When it has reduced, slowly pour in 2½ cups/600 ml water. Simmer for about 15 minutes.

Peel the pumpkin and cut into cubes. Transfer the pumpkin and the remaining peeled onion to a saucepan, add a glass of water, cover, and simmer for 15 minutes. Strain, and purée the pumpkin and onion. Season with salt.

with Creamed Pumpkin

Sauté the whole peeled garlic clove in a pan with 1 tbsp olive oil. Add the diced mushrooms and cook slowly. Stir in the chopped parsley.

Add the mushroom mixture to the rice. Dissolve the ground saffron in half a glass of water and pour into the rice. Season with salt and pepper.

Remove the pan from the stove and sprinkle the grated parmesan over the top. Add 1 tbsp olive oil. Transfer the creamed pumpkin and risotto onto plates and serve garnished with parsley and saffron threads.

Spaghetti with

Preparation time: 20 minutes
Cooking time: 30 minutes
Difficulty: ★

Serves 4

3¼ lb/1.5 kg	small langoustines
1	shallot
7 tbsp	olive oil
	salt
4 tbsp	dry champagne

4	tomatoes
¼	green bell pepper
1lb/400 g	spaghetti alla chitarra
	(or ordinary spaghetti

For the garnish:

strips of green bell
pepper

Every region in Italy has its own variety of pasta. In Abruzzi and Molise, the typical spaghetti is *alla chitarra*, named after the "guitar" (*chitarra* in Italian) that is used to prepare this particular kind of pasta. *Spaghetti alla chitarra* is usually served with meat, but our chef recommends using langoustines instead in this recipe.

The ingenious inventor of the *chitarra*, unfortunately unknown, was undoubtedly a music- as well as a pasta-lover, and would certainly be a household name in Abruzzi and Molise were his identity known.

The *chitarra*, which is indispensable when making spaghetti and macaroni, consists of a rectangular beechwood frame across which very fine metal wires are stretched at regular intervals of ⅕ inch/1 millimeter. Just as in a real guitar, the strings can be tightened up with a special key when they become slack. The pasta dough is

pressed onto the *chitarra*, which cuts it into very fine rectangular strips. You can, however, use ordinary spaghetti or macaroni.

Langoustines are found in abundance off the coasts of western Europe. They resemble small lobsters or large shrimp, either of which can be substituted for the langoustines in this recipe. Langoustines are very popular because of their outstanding meat and are available all year round. When you buy them, make sure they still have their claws, their shells are shiny, and that they still have the characteristic smell of the sea, with its tang of iodine.

This dish is pasta at its most sublime!

Twist off the heads of the langoustines and remove the meat from the shells. Reserve the meat and heads (with claws). Place the shells in a saucepan with 8 cups/2 liters water, boil for 30 minutes. Strain the stock and set aside.

Peel the shallot and chop finely. Sauté with olive oil in a pan. Add the langoustine meat and heads and sauté for 3 minutes. Season with salt.

Pour on the champagne and reduce for 5 minutes. Wash the tomatoes, then blanch, skin, and chop them finely. Cut the bell pepper into thin strips.

Langoustines

Add the diced tomatoes and bell pepper to the pan, cover, and cook slowly for about 5 minutes.

Bring the strained langoustine stock to the boil and season with salt. Add the spaghetti and boil until cooked "al dente." Remove from the water and drain the spaghetti.

Add the spaghetti immediately to the seafood and stir well. Serve on plates with strips of green bell pepper.

Spinosini with

Preparation time:	20 minutes
Cooking time:	15 minutes
Difficulty:	★

Serves 4

4 oz/100 g	broccoli florets
3 oz/80 g	black truffles
8 tbsp	olive oil
1 clove	garlic
1	anchovy fillet

2 oz/50 g	pitted black olives
2 oz/50 g	cherry tomatoes
10 oz/250 g	*spinosini* (or ordinary spaghetti)
	coarse salt
	pepper

For the garnish:

	truffle shavings

In Italy there are as many types of pasta as there are ways of preparing it. Pasta enjoys a status similar to that of soccer, and both are the subjects of passionate arguments. In a country in which pasta is revered, each province claims that it is the birthplace of pasta, marrying it in true ceremonial style with the best produce of the particular region.

Spinosini resembles long, thin spaghetti and is typical of the Campo Filone region. This excellent egg pasta is made using a cherrywood board, which gives it a characteristic flavor. According to our chef, *spinosini* has properties that make it very good for cooking, but traditional spaghetti can also be used in this recipe.

In the Marche region, *spinosini* is traditionally eaten in winter with goulash, while in hot weather it is served with tomatoes and basil. Alberto Melagrana recommends combining *spinosini* with black truffles. This mushroom, which

grows underground, is highly regarded in the province of Pesaro, the native city of composer Gioacchino Rossini. Even in ancient times, the Roman gourmet Apicius described the truffle as "the acme of luxury." Like his contemporaries, he believed that truffles only grew under trees that had been struck by lightning by Jupiter, the god who ruled the forces of nature. When buying truffles, the chef recommends that you look for round, firm ones. If you want to keep them for a few days, they can be wrapped individually in parchment and stored in an airtight container in a cool place.

Broccoli originates from southern Italy and is rich in vitamin C and minerals. It is available from October to April but its close relative cauliflower can be substituted in this recipe if required.

Separate the broccoli florets from the stalk using a knife. Boil the florets for 5 minutes in salted water.

Remove the broccoli from the saucepan and plunge into ice water. Remove after a few minutes and drain.

Grate the black truffles. For the sauce, heat 3 tbsp olive oil in a pan with an unpeeled clove of garlic. Add the grated truffles. Sauté briefly and set aside.

Black Truffles

Pour the remaining oil into a pan and sauté the washed, finely chopped anchovy, finely diced olives and tomatoes, and broccoli florets for 1 minute.

Heat some water in a large saucepan and boil the spinosini until cooked "al dente," then remove from the water and drain.

Transfer the pasta to the pan with the broccoli. Fry briefly, then season to taste with coarse salt and pepper. Serve on plates with the truffle sauce, garnished with truffle shavings.

Culurgioni

Preparation time:	1 hour
Cooking time:	1 hour
Resting time for pasta:	30 minutes
Difficulty:	★★

Serves 4

For the pasta:

1 lb/500 g	flour
1	egg
½ tsp/pinch	saffron powder (optional)
	salt

For the filling:

1	onion
3 tbsp/45 ml	olive oil
4 cloves	garlic
1 bunch	fresh mint
1¼ lb/600 g	potatoes
3½ oz/100 g	grated pecorino
11 oz/300 g	casu aceddu (salty ewe's-milk cheese)

For the tomato sauce:

2 lb/1 kg	tomatoes
1	carrot
1 stick	celery
1 clove	garlic
1	onion
1	bay leaf
3	basil leaves
3 tbsp/45 ml	olive oil
	salt and pepper

For the garnish:

7 oz/200 g	grated pecorino
	basil leaves

Culurgioni are a delicious type of ravioli. A substantial dish, this popular specialty makes use of several typically Sardinian products. Requiring much dexterity and patience, the local cooks are highly skilled in making this stuffed pasta.

Also known as *culurzone*, *culurgioni* can be recognized by their characteristic shape. The ingredients used for the traditionally vegetarian stuffing can vary from household to household. The recipe given here by Amerigo Murgia is one of the classics, using cheeses, potatoes, mint, garlic, onion, and, of course, Mediterranean olive oil.

Sardinian pecorino cheese plays an important role in many of the island's traditional recipes, and is famous for its exceptional flavor. Flocks have grazed on the island of Sardinia for thousands of years. Today, there are more sheep than people. It has been estimated that one third of all the livestock in Italy today is to be found in Sardinia. Animal husbandry is the main source of income for the Sardinians, hence the island's many excellent cheeses.

In addition to pecorino, the filling used in this recipe calls for another typically Sardinian cheese, *casu aceddu*. A specialty of the Ogliastra region, it is similar to "blue" cheese. In the past, shepherds would eat it spread on potatoes baked in the embers of the fire. *Casu aceddu* can be eaten in its soft, freshly made state (similar to yogurt). It can also be salted and kept for about 12 months.

These simple, delicate Sardinian ravioli offer the pasta lover a veritable feast of concentrated flavors, complemented by those quintessential Mediterranean ingredients: garlic and, naturally, tomato sauce.

For the pasta, put the flour in a bowl and add the egg and saffron powder. Gradually add salted water. Work the mixture until an elastic pastry is obtained. Set this aside to rest for 30 minutes.

For the filling, brown the chopped onion in 2 tbsp of olive oil. Add the crushed garlic. Take the pan off the heat and add the chopped mint. Mix and set aside.

Cook the potatoes in boiling water for about 20 minutes. Peel them and then pass them through a potato-press into a bowl. Add the pecorino and casu aceddu. Add the onion mixture and mix everything with your fingers. Add the remaining olive oil.

Form the pastry into a ball and roll out with a rolling pin until it is very thin. Cut out circles.

Prepare the tomato sauce by cooking all the diced vegetables in olive oil, together with the herbs, for 30 minutes. Blend in a food processor and reserve. Using your fingers, make balls of the potato and herb filling, placing one on each round of pasta.

Fold the circles of pasta in half around the filling. Press lightly at one end, pinching the pasta into fan-like folds. Lower the culurgioni into boiling water for about 4 minutes, remove, and arrange on plates with the tomato sauce. Garnish with grated pecorino and chopped basil.

Malloreddus

Preparation time:	25 minutes
Cooking time:	20 minutes
Difficulty:	★

Serves 4

7 oz/200 g	eggplant
1	red bell pepper
1	green bell pepper
1	yellow bell pepper
2	onions
5 tbsp/75 ml	olive oil

1 lb/500 g	malloreddus (pasta)
5	basil leaves
7 oz/200 g	grated ewe's-milk cheese (pecorino, or parmesan)
	salt and pepper

For the garnish:

| | basil leaves |

Sardinian cooking is typically based on fresh local food and is, above all, copious and filling, with pasta every bit as important as bread. *Malloreddus*, also known since Antiquity as *gnocchetti sardi*, are a national specialty that perfectly expresses the richness of the island's ancient cuisine. Featuring sun-ripened Mediterranean produce, this vegetarian dish can be eaten both hot and, the next day, as a cold appetizer.

The Sardinian language is closely similar to Latin, and considered by linguists to be a Romance language in its own right rather than a dialect of Italian. The name *malloreddus* means "little calves" and refers to the elongated, horn-like shape of the pasta pieces.

Still made in the traditional way, the pasta consists of durum wheat flour, warm water, and salt, sometimes enriched with saffron, artichokes, or tomatoes. After prolonged kneading,

it is divided into pieces of equal size and rolled out into fine strings. These are formed into the *malloreddus* using an ancient method that gives them their characteristic ridged appearance. They are available in specialist grocers and delicatessens, but if necessary can be replaced with penne.

This ideal family dish makes use of several typically Mediterranean vegetables, grown in abundance on the island. The sunny colors of the red, yellow, and green bell peppers will brighten up the table. Sardinian eggplants, grown in large quantities on the island's fertile plains, are celebrated for their excellent quality.

This dish is further enhanced by the deliciously perfumed local olive oil and the delicate taste of basil. This herb, very frequently used in mainland Italian, Sardinian, and Sicilian cooking, is an ideal partner for use with tomatoes and pasta dishes.

Wash the vegetables and chop them all into small dice.

Pour the olive oil into a large pan. Heat it, and then add the diced vegetables. Cook for about 10 minutes. Season with salt and pepper.

Heat a large saucepan of water. When it boils, add salt and then the malloreddus. Cook for about 9 minutes. Drain the pasta.

Wash the basil leaves carefully and chop.

Add the malloreddus to the vegetable mixture and mix carefully with a wooden spatula.

Sprinkle the grated cheese and chopped basil over the pasta and serve. Garnish with basil leaves.

Preparation time: 25 minutes
Cooking time: 30 minutes
Difficulty: ★

Serves 4

11 oz/300 g	pane carasau (sheets of durum wheat)
1	bouillon cube
4 oz/100 g	grated ewe's-milk cheese or parmesan
4 tbsp/60 ml	white wine vinegar
4	eggs

For the tomato sauce:

1¾ lb/800 g	tomatoes
1	onion
1 stick	celery
1	carrot
3 tbsp/45 ml	olive oil
2 cloves	garlic
½ bunch	parsley
1	bay leaf
3	basil leaves
	salt and pepper

The Sardinians have a saying that their beautiful island was blessed by God—an earthly paradise providing a rich harvest for its fishermen and shepherds. Strongly influenced by the pastoral tradition, the island's cuisine is characterized by its simple, wholesome specialties. A good example is *pane fratau*, an ancient vegetarian dish.

This popular recipe is easy to make and requires good, fresh vegetables. *Pane carasau*, the thin sheets of durum wheat used in this dish, are a Sardinian specialty. Available from specialist grocers and delicatessens, it is also known as *carta di musica* ("music paper") because of its resemblance to the crisp parchment once used for sheet music.

The laborious task of making *pane carasau* is carried out by skilled bakers. The dough is kneaded several times be-

fore being placed in flat molds and baked twice. For this recipe, do not forget to dip the sheets of *pane carasau* in liquid before use to make them malleable. Sardinian shepherds generally prefer to use a bouillon of mutton or poultry for this.

Full of sun-drenched Mediterranean flavor, *pane fratau* is served with a tomato sauce sprinkled with pecorino, a ewe's-milk cheese.

Sardinia abounds in market gardens, and produces particularly well-flavored vegetables. The juicy Sardinian tomatoes are sold in the markets of Milan and Turin. They have a thin, smooth skin and very few seeds.

With the addition of poached eggs, this is a perfect dish for an informal meal with friends.

For the sauce, dice all the vegetables. Heat the olive oil and add the garlic and parsley. Add the diced tomato, onion, celery and carrot together with the bay leaf. Cook for 30 minutes. Season with salt and pepper. Add the chopped basil and blend the sauce in a food processor.

Break the pane carasau into rough pieces. Dissolve the bouillon cube in a saucepan of hot water.

Gently dip the pieces of pane carasau into the bouillon to soften them. Place half of them on a serving dish, reserving the rest.

Fratau

Pour half the tomato sauce over the pieces of pane carasau.

Sprinkle the dish with some of the grated cheese. Cover with the rest of the pane carasau and then with another layer of tomato sauce and cheese.

Heat 2 cups/500 ml of water. When boiling, add the vinegar and break the eggs into the liquid. Poach them for about 1 minute, then lift them gently with a spatula and place them on top of the dish of pane fratau.

Preparation time: 40 minutes
Cooking time: 25 minutes
Difficulty: ★

Serves 4

2	onions
2 cloves	garlic
1 stick	celery
1 bunch	parsley
1 bunch	basil
1¼ oz/30 g	sun-dried tomatoes
11 oz/300 g	tomatoes
3½ tbsp/50 ml	olive oil

1	small dried chile
1 tbsp/20 g	tomato concentrate
3½ tbsp/50 ml	white wine
1 lb/400 g	*bavette* (flat, slightly convex type of spaghetti about ⅛ inch/½ cm in width)
	salt

For the garnish:

cherry tomatoes (optional)
parsley
basil

A wide variety of pasta dishes are eaten on Sicily, at all occasions. An intrinsic part of the local culture, some of these delicious recipes have become classics, exemplifying all that is best in Sicilian cuisine. Notable specialties include *macaroni alla Norma*, made with eggplants, and *pasta con le sarde*, served with fresh sardines.

Pasta alla scarpara is a well-known summery vegetarian dish that originates from Caltagirone, the inland village where Angelo La Spina was born. He learned the recipe from the wife of the village cobbler (*scarparo*), who was fond of this easily made dish. It is important not to overcook the *bavette* (it should be served *al dente*: "with bite").

The invention of pasta is a claim proudly advanced—with numerous and varied historical proofs—by every region of Italy. The Sicilian theory credits the introduction of pasta to the island's Arab invaders in the 9th–11th centuries. Pasta was quickly adopted by the locals and became an essential part of the Sicilian diet. A work written in the 15th century mentions *maccheroni* being placed out in the August sun to dry.

Angelo La Spina uses *bavette*, a flat, slightly convex type of spaghetti, for this recipe. It is made equally well with tagliatelle or fettuccine.

This well-balanced and colorful dish is full of the flavors of the Mediterranean. Celery, a vegetable much employed in Sicilian cooking, combines deliciously with the tomatoes, onions, garlic, and basil. *Pasta alla scarpara* is quite simply *buonissima*.

Finely chop the onions. Crush the garlic cloves. Chop the celery, parsley, and basil. Cut up the sun-dried tomatoes. Peel the fresh tomatoes, remove the seeds, and mash them.

Brown the onions and garlic in the olive oil. Add the celery and cook for 5–6 minutes. Add the basil, parsley, and the dried tomatoes. Cook for a further 10 minutes. Season generously with salt and sprinkle on the ground chile.

Add the fresh tomato pulp to the mixture and mix with a wooden spatula. Add the tomato concentrate. Cook for about 5 minutes.

Scarpara

Pour over the white wine and mix in with a wooden spatula. Cook for another 5 minutes or so.

Heat a large saucepan full of salted water. Bring to the boil, add the bavette, and cook for about 12 minutes, stirring occasionally with a fork. Drain the pasta.

Transfer the pasta to the sauce and mix together over the heat. Serve the pasta alla scarpara garnished with cherry tomatoes, parsley, and basil.

Preparation time:	1 hour
Cooking time:	2 hours 35 minutes
Difficulty:	★★

Serves 4

1 piece	lamb bone (shank)
2	carrots
1 stick	celery
1	onion
3	bay leaves
½ stick/50 g	shortening

1 lb/500 g	ricotta
4 oz/100 g	3-month-old pecorino, grated
3½ tbsp/50 g	fresh marjoram
	salt and black pepper

For the *cavatini*:

2 cups/350 g	durum wheat flour
1¼ oz/30 g	dry pecorino, grated
1	egg
1 tbsp/15 ml	olive oil
	salt and black pepper

For Catholics, the rhythm of life on Sicily is marked by religious festivals, many of which are associated inextricably with traditional dishes of food. Easter is celebrated in fine style, and *turtera* (literally, pie) is traditionally associated with this time of year. A substantial pasta dish, *Turtera* is eaten as a hot appetizer.

Pasta, eaten with an almost infinite variety of sauces, is taken seriously on Sicily. The famous *cavatini* are made of durum wheat flour, egg, pecorino cheese, olive oil, salt, and pepper. Giuseppe Barone suggests that the name may be derived from the verb *cavare*, meaning to scrape or hollow out. The original *cavatini* had a grooved appearance, created by hand. They are available in Italian grocers, or instead use *cavatielli* or *garganelli*.

Full of rustic Sicilian flavors, the filling for these *turtera* also requires ricotta, a cheese made from the whey of cow's, ewe's, or goat's milk. If possible, do as the Sicilians do, and use the dry, stronger-tasting *ricotta dura* (hard ricotta) for pasta dishes, stuffings, and with vegetables.

Sicily is the setting for an episode of Homer's *Odyssey* where it is described as a land of shepherds. The importance of the island's flocks of sheep is underlined by the famous passage in which Odysseus and his companions are taken prisoner by Polyphemus, one of the Cyclopes. The resourceful Greek hero manages to escape from his jailer by clinging to the underside of a sheep. Giuseppe Barone has made a study of the history of Sicilian food and believes that the Sicilians of Antiquity made a cheese very similar to the modern ricotta.

The flavors of this dish are enhanced by the use of the delicately scented herb marjoram. Similar in taste to mint or basil, it is much used in Mediterranean cooking.

For the pasta, mix the flour, salt, pepper, pecorino, egg, and olive oil in a bowl. Gradually add 7 tbsp/100 ml of water. Knead the mixture for about 15 minutes until it has formed into a dough. Leave it to rest for 5 minutes.

Cook the lamb bone with the roughly-chopped carrots, celery, and onion in a medium oven (350 °F/180 °C) for 30 minutes. Transfer these ingredients to a large saucepan filled with salted water and the bay leaves. Simmer for 2 hours. Strain the liquid and set aside.

Roll out the pasta dough on a flat surface to a thickness of ½ inch/1.5 cm. Cut it into strips. Cut these into small rectangles of equal size.

Place a rectangle on the upturned prongs of a fork, and press down as you roll it up, giving it a fluted appearance.

Bring the reserved bouillon to the boil and add the pasta. Cook for about 5 minutes. Remove it when cooked, reserving the bouillon.

Place half of the cooked pasta in a greased dish. Arrange some sliced ricotta on top. Season with pepper and then scatter on the grated pecorino. Add the marjoram and then a second layer of pasta. Pour the bouillon around the pasta and cook at 350 °F/180 °C for 30 minutes.

Trachanas, Onion, and Min

Preparation time: 40 minutes
Cooking time: 1 hour
  5 minutes
Resting time (pastry): 30 minutes
Difficulty: ★★

Serves 6

For the phyllo (filo) pastry:

2⅔ cups/300 g	all-purpose flour
1 tsp	salt
1 tsp	bicarbonate of soda
2 cups/500 ml	very cold water
1 cup/250 ml	olive oil
1	egg

For the filling:

1¾ cups/400 ml	milk
3½ oz/100 g	trachanas
1 lb 5 oz/600 g	shallots
3 tbsp	olive oil
4	eggs
7 oz/200 g	feta
1 bunch	fresh mint
	salt
	pepper

This recipe for *trachanas*, onion, and mint pie made with phyllo (filo) pastry comes from the ancient city of Thebes. It represents an interesting blend of ingredients that typify Greek cuisine: onions, mint, *trachanas*, and olive oil.

Greeks have been cooking with phyllo pastry for thousands of years. The first reference dates right back to the 3rd century B.C. in Macedonia. Inventive pie-makers found a way of replacing heavy yeast-based pizza-type pastry with a light flaky pastry made with lard.

This type of pastry is known throughout Greece as *phyllo*, the Greek word for leaf. The word accurately describes the action of rolling out the pastry into tissue-thin sheets. If the mix is too soft, don't hesitate to add a bit of flour. Always leave it to rest for a while so that everything blends smoothly. This also makes it easier to roll.

Trachanas are very small dried, yellowish colored pulses that add both flavor and texture to the pie filling. They are based on a mixture of crushed wheat or flour, salt, and either goat's milk or ewe's milk, which is then kneaded, crumbled, and dried for one week. There are two sorts available: *xinos trachanas* (bitter, made with sour milk) and *glykos trachanas* (sweet). They keep for a long time and are widely used in phyllo pastry pies and soups.

The pie filling is subtly flavored with the fresh taste of mint, but basil could replace the mint.

Our chef decorates his pie with little shavings of fried carrots, tomato, and mint. He suggests you do as the Greeks do and serve it with a bowl of natural Greek yogurt.

To make the pastry, put the flour, salt, and bicarbonate of soda into a bowl, make a well, and gradually add the water and ¾ cup/200 ml of the olive oil. Add 1 egg. Knead the dough well and leave it to rest for 30 minutes.

Sprinkle your work surface with flour. Divide the pastry into 6 balls and sprinkle them with flour. Roll each one out until you end up with 6 tissue-thin sheets of pastry. Cover with a damp cloth.

To make the filling, pour the milk into a pan and bring it to the boil. Stir in the trachanas and cook for about 5 minutes.

Pie made with Phyllo Pastry

Peel and finely chop the shallots. Heat the olive oil in a skillet and fry the shallots. Stir the fried shallots into the cooked trachanas.

Whisk the eggs in a bowl then add cubes of feta, chopped mint, and season with salt and pepper. Pour the contents of the bowl into the trachanas and stir everything together over the heat for another 5 minutes.

Line the bottom of a greased ovenproof dish with 3 sheets of phyllo, ensuring the edges of the pastry hang over the side of the dish. Add the filling and cover with the 3 remaining sheets of pastry, sealing the edge firmly. Bake in an oven preheated to 350° F/180° C for 50 minutes.

Chiropoiita Macaron

Preparation time:	50 minutes
Cooking time:	15 minutes
Soaking time	
(garbanzo beans):	12 hours
Resting time (pasta):	15 minutes
Drying time (macaronia):	2–8 hours
Difficulty:	★★

Serves 4

2 oz/55 g	goat milk cheese (finely grated)

For the sauce:

¾ cup/85 g	garbanzo beans (chickpeas)

1 tsp	bicarbonate of soda
3	fresh white onions
2 sprigs	dill
3½ oz/100 g	baby zucchini
2¼ lb/1 kg	tomatoes
5 tbsp	olive oil
	salt
	pepper (optional)

For the pasta:

9 oz/250 g	all-purpose flour, sifted (or pasta flour)
3 tbsp	olive oil

For the garnish:

	dill

In the northeast Aegean, there is a trio of extraordinary islands, Lesbos, Samos, and Chios (where our chef comes from). Each has its own individual cultural, historic, and gastronomic charms. Typical of the little villages in the southern part of Chios, our *macaronia chiropoiita*, served here with tomato sauce, is made from garbanzo beans and fresh vegetables. Reasonably easy to make, this festive vegetarian dish is full of unforgettable flavors.

Still made by local families, *macaronia chiropoiita* takes its name from the Greek *chiro*, or "hand," and *poiita*, which comes from the verb *poio*, "to create." The pasta dough, which is made into long tubes, is usually shaped around twigs from a bush called *sparto* which grows naturally on Chios. You can easily substitute the *sparto* with long toothpicks. Don't forget to leave the *macaronia* to rest before plunging it into the boiling water. The Greeks usually put them into a cloth and leave them out in the sun to dry

for two hours before cooking them. You could also leave them under artificial light for about eight hours.

This traditional recipe is very filling thanks to the addition of the garbanzo beans. These originated in the Mediterranean basin, but later became widespread in this part of the world thanks to Phoenician traders. Homer, who it seems was born on Chios, even mentions them in *The Iliad*.

These days they are primarily grown on the island of Sifnos in the Aegean Sea. Garbanzo beans are the seeds of an annual herbaceous plant. Recognizable by their cream color, they are highly prized for their underlying taste of hazelnut. In accordance with the culinary customs of the Greek Orthodox Church, they are associated with the many days and periods on which the faithful are prohibited from consuming either meat or fish, and they also play an important role in monastic cuisine.

Fill a bowl with water and let the garbanzo beans soak for 12 hours. Drain but reserve the water. Sprinkle the garbanzo beans with bicarbonate of soda. Leave for 5 minutes, then cook them in the soaking water for 20 minutes, then drain.

Peel and finely chop the onions, together with the dill. Dice the washed, but unpeeled, zucchini. Chop the tomatoes and reduce down to a purée by cooking in 2 tbsp of olive oil for about 5 minutes. Season to taste and set the purée to one side.

Heat the remaining olive oil in a skillet and fry the onions. Add the zucchini, garbanzo beans, and dill. Season with salt to taste and cook for 5 minutes.

with Tomato Sauce

To make the macaronia (pasta), put the flour into a bowl and pour over the olive oil. Work them together adding about 1¼ cups/300 ml water a few drops at a time. Knead until a pliable dough is obtained. Leave to rest for 15 minutes.

Sprinkle some flour on the work surface. Roll strips of dough into a long cigarette shape then cut it into little cubes. Holding these in the palm of the hand, roll them around a toothpick to create the macaronia, then slide out the toothpick. Leave to dry for 2–8 hours.

Put the macaronia into a pan of salted boiling water and boil for 5 minutes. Drain well and add to the garbanzo bean mixture. Stir well. Serve the pasta topped with the tomato sauce and scattered with finely grated goat milk cheese. Garnish with dill.

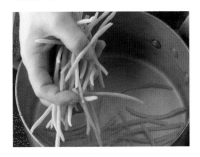

Stuffed Tomatoes and

Preparation time:	30 minutes
Cooking time:	1 hour
	25 minutes
Difficulty:	★★

Serves 6

6	very ripe tomatoes
6	large green
	bell peppers
1 cup/100 g	pine nuts
¾ cup/100 g	chopped almonds
1	onion
1 cup/250 ml	extra-virgin olive oil

½ cup/100 g	rice
1 cup/125 g	golden raisins
2 cloves	garlic
3½ oz/100 g	scallions
1 tsp	ground cinnamon
1 cup/250 ml	tomato juice
¾ oz/20 g	fresh mint
	salt
	freshly ground
	black pepper
1 tbsp	sugar
1 oz/30 g	flat-leaf parsley

Tomatoes and peppers stuffed with rice, pine nuts, almonds, golden raisins, and herbs are one of the specialties of the island of Samos. Situated in the eastern Aegean, just a few nautical miles from Turkey, this island still retains a tradition of the sweet-salted dishes that are typical of Asia Minor. The Greeks love fresh stuffed vegetables: They eat tomatoes, bell peppers, eggplants, zucchini, or potatoes filled with rice and herbs during meat-free religious days, and incorporate finely chopped meat the rest of the year.

To prepare the vegetables, first slice a bit off the base so that they will stand upright in the cooking dish, then cut off a little "lid." Our chef suggests you use the following method for hollowing out the tomato: Stick the tip of the knife half-way up and slice around the tomato so that you cut the flesh inside it at the same time. Use a melon baller to scoop out the flesh.

The amount of rice you will need for the stuffing depend on the size of the tomatoes and bell peppers. Try to use fine white rice that doesn't swell too much during cooking. I will only need to be half cooked in the tomato sauce as i will continue cooking inside the vegetables.

In their version of this dish the inhabitants of Samos use *samiotiko*, locally grown tiny pale yellow grapes dried into golden raisins. Samos has 5,685 acres/2,300 hectares o vines planted in terraces. Local vine growers produce grapes for one of the most famous dessert wines in the world, Samos Muscat, with its mellow, refreshing flavor.

The sugary taste of the stuffing comes from the dried fruits However, don't hesitate to smear a little powdered sugar around the inside of the vegetables. During the cooking time, this will amalgamate with the juices and be transformed into a tasty caramelized layer.

Wash the tomatoes and peppers. Cut a small slice off the base and cut off little "lids." Use a melon baller to scoop out the tomatoes and reserve the flesh. Then remove the seeds and membranes from the peppers.

Dry-fry the pine nuts followed by the chopped almonds. In another skillet, fry the chopped onion for 3 minutes in 3½ tbsp oil. Add the rice, stir rapidly, then add the raisins, chopped garlic, chopped scallions, cinnamon, pine nuts, and almonds.

Add the reserved tomato flesh and stir. Pour in just enough water and diluted tomato juice to cover the mixture. Leave to cook for 10–12 minutes, stirring regularly to prevent it from sticking.

Peppers from Samos

Chop the mint and add to the rice when it is tender and the juices have been absorbed. Season to taste, and give the mixture a final stir.

Arrange the tomatoes and peppers in an ovenproof dish. Smear the insides with a little sugar, then fill them with the rice stuffing.

Put the "lids" back on the stuffed peppers and tomatoes. Pour a generous dash of olive oil over each one. Place in an oven preheated to 375° F/190° C for 50–60 minutes, basting regularly with the oil and the cooking juices. Serve hot or cold scattered with chopped parsley.

Okra

Preparation time: 30 minutes
Cooking time rice: 25 minutes
Cooking time vegetables: 25 minutes
Difficulty: ★

Serves 4

1¼ sticks/ 150 g	butter
1 cup/200 g	rice
2 cups/500 ml	chicken stock
8 oz/200 g	okra
2	tomatoes

3½ tbsp/50 ml	red wine vinegar
2	scallions
	salt and ground pepper to taste
	juice of ½ lemon

Asude was created long ago in the palaces of the sultans and aristocrats. Today, this delicious pilaf of rice, tomato sauce, and okra is sinking into obscurity, but Hüseyin Özoğuz has "dusted it off" for you and adapted it to suit today's tastes.

The rice, the basic ingredient for this dish, is prepared traditionally: sautéed first in a little butter, then cooked in chicken stock. In a covered pot, it takes about 20 minutes for the rice to absorb all the stock. If the liquid is being absorbed too quickly, just add a little more.

Rice (*pirinç*) is grown in Turkey. Whichever variety of rice you use for your pilaf, the grains should stay fluffy while cooking and not stick together. The *toysa* variety, which is grown in Kastamonu on the Black Sea coast, is white and

round; *kızılcahaman* rice comes from the Ankara region and is golden-brown in color; *persani* rice has long, white, thin grains and comes from the region of Central Anatolia.

Gently melting okra is called *bamya* in Turkish. It comes from the Tropics and is a member of the mallow family. The pods are green, slightly ridged, and can be long and pointed or short and thick. Okra (or gombo) is found in Yalova, the bay of the Sea of Marmara near Izmit, in summer and fall. The Turks are very fond of the vegetable, and dry the pods so they have supplies for the winter.

Okra contains a gelatinous substance that is used to thicken sauces and soups, but you should remove it for this recipe. To do so, simply pour vinegar over the pods and then rinse them under running cold water.

Melt 1 stick/100 g butter in a pot. Sauté the rice in it for a few minutes until it is glassy. Pour over the stock, then cover with a lid and simmer over a medium heat for 20 minutes.

Remove the stalks from the okra.

Skin and dice the tomatoes.

Pilaf

Place the okra in a bowl, pour over the vinegar, and stir the okra carefully so they are covered. Then rinse the okra thoroughly under running cold water.

Chop the scallions. Melt the remainder of the butter and sauté the scallions for 5 minutes. Add the okra.

Add the chopped tomatoes, salt, pepper, lemon juice, and a little water, and cook for 20 minutes. Arrange the rice in a serving dish and garnish with the okra and tomato mixture.

Chicken Pilaf

Preparation time: 35 minutes
Cooking time: 1 hour 35 minutes
Difficulty: ★★

Serves 4

For the pilaf:

1	chicken weighing about 2¼ lb/1 kg
½ stick/50 g	butter
2 scant cups/ 380 g	rice
1 tsp	sugar

	salt to taste
¾ cup/100 g	blanched almonds
2 tbsp	olive oil

For the pastry:

	butter for the mold
8 oz/200 g	yufka pastry (or phyllo)
1	egg yolk
2 tbsp	olive oil

This recipe came directly from the kitchens of the Ottoman sultans' palaces. It features a very clever, but sadly, little known dish consisting of a *pilav* (pilaf) of rice, chicken, and almonds (*bademli*) concealed behind a pastry "curtain" (*perde*). The chefs in the sultans' palaces used to compete against each other to create the most original pilaf.

Hüseyin Özoğuz washes the chicken thoroughly under cold running water before he cooks it. He also suggests adding onions, carrots, parsley, bay leaves, and finely chopped scallions to the stock to improve its flavor. This is even more important because the stock is used to cook the rice.

Once the chicken is cooked, it is removed from the stock and placed on a plate to cool slightly, before being divided up: thighs, wings, and finally the breast. The skin and bones must all be removed, which is best done with a meat fork and a sharp knife.

Only very experienced cooks attempt the *yufka* pastry that encases the filling. Phyllo (filo) pastry is the same as *yufka*, alternatively, you can use puff pastry that is rolled out very thinly. To ensure the pilaf is properly covered, fold the pastry three times, place it over the mold, and trim off any excess. Then unfold the pastry, put it back on the pilaf, and press the edges together firmly.

To vary the recipe a little, Hüseyin Özoğuz suggests substituting pistachios or even pea-sized meat patties (*köfte*) for the almonds. You could also enhance the pilaf with currants, pine nuts, or pieces of fried liver.

Cook the chicken in salted water for about 40 minutes, drain, and place on a plate to cool slightly. Allow the stock to cool slightly. Melt the butter in a pot. Add the rice and cook for 5 minutes, stirring continuously.

When the rice has turned glassy, pour over 1¾ cups/450 ml of the chicken stock. Add the sugar and salt. Bring to the boil and cook for 15 minutes.

Meanwhile, joint the chicken. Remove the meat carefully from the bones and cut into thin slices.

in Pastry

Brush a deep, conical gratin dish (charlotte mold) with melted butter. Cut the yufka sheets in half and line the mold with them.

Sauté the almonds in the olive oil for 5 minutes. To make the filling, combine the rice, almonds, and chicken, and spoon into the mold.

Top the filling with a sheet of pastry, and squeeze the edges together. Whisk the egg yolk with the olive oil and brush over the surface of the pastry. Bake in a preheated oven at 400 °F/200 °C for 45 minutes. Tip the cooked pastry out onto a plate and serve immediately.

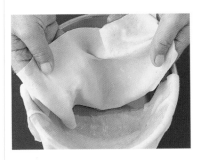

Preparation time:	15 minutes
Soaking time garbanzo beans:	12 hours
Soaking time tomatoes:	3 hours
Standing time:	15 minutes
Cooking time:	1 hour
Difficulty:	★

Serves 4

1 scant cup/ 150 g	garbanzo beans (chickpeas)
¾ cup/150 g	dried tomatoes
1	onion
4 tbsp	olive oil
2 cups/500 ml	chicken stock
⅛ stick/15 g	butter
	salt
1½ cups/300 g	rice

For the garnish:

dried tomatoes
flat-leaf parsley

This garbanzo bean pilaf is a very popular Turkish specialty. In a country where gastronomy is considered to be a form of art, some dishes—such as this one—are an important part of everyday life.

Garbanzo bean pilaf was originally a dish eaten by the farmers of Central Anatolia, but today it is also extremely popular in the cities. The dish is often available at fast-food stalls, and is enjoyed at any time and occasion.

This pilaf, for which the grains of rice should be loose and not too sticky, is prepared traditionally. The rice is cooked in olive oil or butter until transparent, then covered with stock and cooked with the garbanzo beans. For best results, it really should be left to stand for about 15 minutes before serving.

The garbanzo beans make this simple dish highly nutritious. This pulse is extremely popular in Central Anatolia and is known for its high content of copper, calcium, magnesium, phosphates, and potassium. Originally from the Mediterranean basin, it is even mentioned in Homer's *Iliad*. The round, beige-colored seeds maintain their shape while cooking, and do not disintegrate.

Dried tomatoes enhance the aroma of the other ingredients beautifully. Depending on the season, Savaş Özkiliç suggests you also try this dish with fresh tomatoes.

This garbanzo bean pilaf can be served as a main dish, or as a side dish with meat.

Place the garbanzo beans in a bowl, cover with water, and leave to stand for 12 hours. Put the dried tomatoes in another bowl, cover with water, and soak for 3 hours.

Drain and chop the tomatoes. Dice the onion and sauté with the tomatoes in 2 tbsp hot olive oil for about 4 minutes. Cook the drained garbanzo beans in water for about 40 minutes until done.

Pour the chicken stock over the onion and tomato mixture, bring to the boil, and then simmer for 4–5 minutes. Remove the pot from the heat.

Garbanzo Bean Pilaf

Heat the remaining olive oil and the butter in a pot, add the rice, and stir until transparent. Season with salt.

Purée the tomato stock and add it to the rice.

Add the drained garbanzo beans. Bring to the boil, then cook for 15–20 minutes over low heat. Cover with a lid and leave to stand for 15 minutes. Put the pilaf in a serving dish and garnish with strips of dried tomato and chopped parsley.

Bulgur Pilaf

Preparation time: 20 minutes
Cooking time: 55 minutes
Difficulty: ★

Serves 4

1 cup/200 g	brown lentils
	salt
1 tbsp	paprika
	ground pepper
1 cup/200 g	fine bulgur wheat
1	large onion
4 tbsp	olive oil
4	eggs

Bulgur pilaf with lentils is one of the most popular dishes in the Gaziantep area, where it is known as *mercimekli pilav*. It is also very inexpensive. Over the centuries, countless pilaf variations have been developed. Some are made with rice, others with bulgur wheat. Bulgur is boiled, dried, and ground, and is greatly prized in the countries of the Near East.

Two types of bulgur are used in Turkish cuisine: a somewhat finer one for stuffing, pilaf, salads, and soups—Ayfer T. Ünsal recommends this variety for this recipe—and a coarse one, which is served with meat skewers and dishes made from ground meat, or as a main dish with vegetable and meat ragouts.

In this pilaf, the bulgur is combined with green lentils (although Ayfer T. Ünsal prefers yellow ones at home). Lentils have been known in the Near East for thousands of

years, and archeological finds have confirmed that they were already used in ancient Mesopotamia. A recipe similar to *mercimekli pilav* is recorded in the writing of Marcus Gavius Apicius, who lived in the first half of the first century A.D.

As well as the skin, the outer layer is also removed from the onion. It is then washed, cut into thin strips, and sautéed in aromatic olive oil, which is still made using traditional methods in Gaziantep.

This pilaf is usually served with onions or a fried egg. To make the dish slightly more nutritious, Ayfer T. Ünsal has opted for both here. While cooking the egg, press slightly on the yolk with a wooden spoon, then top the pilaf with the egg like a crown.

Place the lentils in a pot and season with salt. Cover with water to 1 in/3 cm above the top, and cover the pot with a lid. Bring to the boil and simmer for about 10 minutes.

Stir in the paprika, put the lid back on, and bring to the boil again. Then cook for 25 minutes over medium heat. Season with salt and pepper.

Add warm water, then the bulgur to the lentils. Cover with a lid and cook for about 10 minutes until the bulgur has absorbed the water.

with Lentils

Peel and wash the onion, dry, and cut into thin rings. Sauté in 2 tbsp hot olive oil for 5 minutes.

Top the pilaf with the onion rings in the cooking oil.

Heat the remaining olive oil in a small pot, and fry one egg for each portion. Arrange the pilaf on plates and top each serving with a fried egg.

Holiday

Preparation time: 20 minutes
Soaking time: 30 minutes
Standing time: 20 minutes
Cooking time: 30 minutes
Difficulty: ★

Serves 4

2 cups/400 g	rice
8 oz/200 g	lamb's liver
4 oz/100 g	lamb bones
⅜ stick/75 g	butter

4 tsp/20 g	pine nuts
4 oz/100 g	scallions
	salt
	ground pepper
1 tsp/5 g	ground star anise
1 tsp/5 g	ground cinnamon
5 tsp/25 g	sugar
¼ cup/40 g	currants

For the garnish:

½ bunch	mint
½ bunch	dill

Today, the farming families in tiny Central Anatolian villages still serve their guests this holiday pilaf. The luxurious meal with its salty-sweet aromas is also served at weddings and circumcisions.

This traditional dish is very easy to prepare, and bears testimony to the impressive variety of Turkish cuisine. Next to rice, wheat is the most grown grain in the world, and is particularly highly prized in Turkey. Originally from China, the Persians brought it to Mesopotamia and Turkistan. According to legend, Alexander the Great brought it to Greece in about 320 B.C.

Pilaf is a typically Turkish dish in which the buttered or oiled rice has a particularly soft consistency. For best results it should be left to stand for 20 minutes before it is served.

This pilaf is enhanced with lamb's liver and currants, and is an absolute delight. Currants are particularly sweet and contain only a few seeds. The grapes are dried either in the sun or in hot air, which causes them to lose 90 percent of their moisture, which in turns concentrates the sugar content of the fruit.

The aroma of the pine nuts further enhances the flavor. These are the highly nutritious seeds from the cone of the pine that is found all over the Mediterranean region. Their slightly resinous, spicy flavor is reminiscent of that of the almond, which you can use as a substitute, if you prefer.

Put the rice in a bowl of warm water. Run your hands through it a few times, then leave to stand for 30 minutes. Drain.

Finely chop the lamb's liver into even-sized pieces. Boil the lamb bones in 2 cups/500 ml water for about 20 minutes. Strain the resulting stock, and set aside.

Melt the butter in a pot and stir-fry the pine nuts until golden brown, stirring continuously. Cut the scallions into thin slices, add to the pine nuts, and fry for a further 5 minutes, stirring occasionally.

Pilaf

Add the drained rice. Season with salt, pepper, star anise, cinnamon, and sugar and combine well.

Add the currants and the strained stock.

Add the chopped lamb's liver. Bring the pilaf to the boil, then simmer gently over low heat for 10 minutes. Remove from the heat. Cover with a lid, and leave to stand for 20 minutes. Put the pilaf in a serving dish and garnish with mint and chopped dill.

Preparation time:	25 minutes
Soaking time:	30 minutes
Standing time:	15–20 minutes
Cooking time:	2 hours 30 minutes
Difficulty:	★

Serves 4

2¼ lb/1 kg	octopus
2 tbsp/30 ml	white wine
2¼ cups/450 g	rice

2¼ lb/1 kg	Swiss chard
1 bunch	scallions
3½ tbsp/50 ml	olive oil
	salt
1⅔ cups/400 ml	chicken stock
⅔ cup/150 ml	cream
	ground pepper

The dishes from the Aegean coast are as healthy as they are delicious, and are typical of the Mediterranean cuisine that has been influenced over the centuries by the Turkish, Greek, Armenian, and Jewish cuisines.

This easy pilaf from the Aegean is a traditional family dish. The juicy octopus meat adds its very special aroma.

Octopus is available from fishmongers all year round. Below its head it has—as the name "octopus" implies—eight tentacles armed with suckers. When freshly caught, octopus has no odor, and beating the flesh well makes it extremely tender. You can also use squid, shrimp, or mussels for this dish, depending on what is available at the time.

The Turkish olive oil that is produced mainly on the Aegean coast is essential in the cuisine of this region. It is very fruity and adds a wonderful aroma to the flavor of Swiss chard.

Swiss chard is a highly fortifying, stimulating vegetable. It contains plenty of magnesium, potassium, and the vitamins A and C. Choose Swiss chard with firm, richly colored leaves and stalks with no soft areas, and wash it thoroughly. You can also use spinach as a substitute.

Pilaf is a typical Turkish rice specialty. The full aromas of the Mediterranean are able to develop in this unusual method of preparation. When ready, the pilaf should be left to stand for 20 minutes.

Cook the prepared and washed octopus, covered, over very low heat for 90 minutes. Pour over the white wine, and continue cooking for a further 5 minutes.

Cut the octopus into small, even-sized pieces. Put the rice in a bowl, pour over 1⅔ cups/400 ml salted water, and leave to stand for 30 minutes.

Wash the Swiss chard. Cut off the stalks, then slice the leaves. Wash the scallions and cut into thin rings.

Pilaf

Drain the rice. Sauté the scallions in hot olive oil. Add the Swiss chard and sauté for 8–10 minutes, stirring continuously.

Add the rice and chopped octopus to the Swiss chard. Season with salt and pour over the chicken stock. Cover with a lid and cook for about 10 minutes.

Mix together the ingredients. Add the cream, season with pepper, and stir well. Cook for a further 5 minutes, then remove the pot from the heat. Cover with aluminum foil and leave the pilaf to stand for around 15–20 minutes. Arrange on a serving dish.

Preparation time:	20 minutes	4 tsp/20 g	tomato paste
Cooking time:	55 minutes	¼ cup/50 g	garbanzo beans
To soak the			(chickpeas),
garbanzo beans:	12 hours		soaked overnight
Difficulty:	★	1½ cups/300 g	large bulgur wheat
		¼ cup/70 g	fresh peas
			salt and black pepper

Serves 4

1¼ lb/500 g	shoulder of lamb
6 tsp/30 g	ground turmeric
3½ tbsp/50 g	ground paprika
4	garlic cloves, crushed
7 tbsp/100 ml	Tunisian olive oil
2	onions, thinly sliced

For the decoration:

4	green mild or hot chiles, fried

A very popular dish, the *borghol bil allouche* is a great favorite throughout Tunisia. It is very similar in appearance and flavor to lamb risotto, but with one crucial difference—locally produced *borghol* is cooked with the lamb instead of rice, which has to be imported.

Made from blanched wheat, *borghol* is widely eaten in Tunisia. The fertile plain of Mateur, in the north, as well as the governorships of Jendouba and Béja in the northwest produce most of the country's cereals. After an initial grading, the grains of wheat are cooked in boiling salted water, then drained and dried in the sun. Next, they are ground in a mortar, or crushed in the village mill. Finally, the grain is sieved. Nowadays, these complex preparations are increasingly carried out on an industrial basis.

Fine *borghol* is used to make delicious soups, while the larger-grained version is cooked in a meat sauce and served

as a main course. *Borghol* is also frequently served as par of a salad, where it is mixed with tomatoes, olive oil, salt and pepper, and many Tunisians eat it for breakfast, sprinkled with milk and liquid honey.

Cooking *borghol* is similar to cooking rice for a risotto: allow two volumes of water to one volume of cereal. Following a method passed down from his grandmother, Mohamed Boussabeh adds water to the spices that remain at the bottom of the dish in which he has coated the meat. Then he pours this flavored liquid into the *borghol*, which is much better than simply adding a glass of water!

Also, our chef advises that cooking a few lamb bones with the meat will strengthen the flavor of the dish. Of course, the same recipe can be produced with pieces of rabbit or free-range chicken.

Bone the shoulder of lamb. Cut up the meat into large cubes of approximately 1¾ oz/50 g and place in a large dish.

Sprinkle salt, pepper, turmeric, paprika, and ground garlic over the meat. Sprinkle olive oil liberally over the mixture. Turn the meat thoroughly with your hands so that the meat is well covered with the spices.

Pour a trickle of olive oil into a stockpot, add the onion slices, tomato paste, spicy lamb pieces, and the garbanzo beans.

Bil Allouche

Pour approximately 2 glasses of water into the saucepan. Bring to the boil.

When the mixture has come to the boil, add the borghol. Stir well and cover. Cook for approximately 35 minutes. Stir occasionally during cooking.

Finally, add the fresh peas. Stir in. Pour the contents into a gratin dish and finish cooking under the oven broiler for 10 minutes. Decorate with fried green mild or hot chiles.

Steamed Chorba

Preparation time: 20 minutes
Cooking time: 1 hour 15 minutes
Difficulty: ★★

Serves 4

2¹⁄₂ lb/1 kg 200g	leg of lamb
4 tbsp/60 ml	olive oil
1 large	onion, thinly sliced
2 tbsp/35 g	tomato paste
1 tsp	harissa

2	carrots
2	potatoes
2	green bell peppers
2¹⁄₂ cups/500 g	*chorba* or large *"langues d'oiseaux"* ("birds' tongues" short pasta)
	allspice
	salt and pepper

Chorba m'faoura is a Tunisian culinary classic. Translated as "steamed chorba with lamb," it's often served at family gatherings. The short variety of pasta, shaped like grains of rice, which makes this hearty dish, is called *chorba*, or more poetically *"langues d'oiseaux"* ("birds' tongues").

This minuscule variety of pasta is a legacy of the Italians, but it has become a common feature of Tunisian cuisine. The pasta, made from durum wheat flour, is rolled and very carefully kneaded between the fingers. This process, requiring the dexterity of a clockmaker, is industrialized nowadays, much to the relief of busy cooks! It is widely available and can be bought in several sizes. The smallest variety cooks very quickly.

In the past in Tunisia, this lamb dish would cook slowly over the charcoal of the traditional *kanoun*—a terracotta

brasero—which was used in every household. If you are unable to get lamb, it can be substituted with veal or chicken. Make sure that you always cut the meat into small pieces; Tunisian families have a keen sense of sharing!

Lovers of strong flavors will probably want to increase the amount of harissa, but don't be tempted to overdo it as you will mask the other flavors. Garbanzo beans can be among the vegetables served with the *chorba*, which will give body to the dish. Garbanzo beans will cook in the meat sauce. Remember to soak them overnight, as they'll cook quicker. To save time with the preparation, you can buy them pre-cooked in cans.

The allspice should be added halfway through the cooking and not right at the beginning. If it is cooked for too long, it can give the dish a sharp flavor.

Cut the meat into 2 in/5 cm pieces and cook gently in the lower part of the couscous steamer with 4 tsp/20 ml of the olive oil, the onion slices, harissa, and tomato paste.

Cover the meat with water. Cook gently for 30 minutes. Season with salt and pepper, and a pinch of allspice.

Peel the carrots and potatoes. After the 30 minutes, add the carrots, then the potatoes, and the bell peppers. Finish cooking over a low heat.

with Lamb

P Coat the pasta in the remaining olive oil in
c a container. All the pasta must be well
u coated with oil.
n

Put the pasta into the couscous steamer
basket 15 minutes before the meat has
cooked. After 10 minutes, trickle several
drops of water over the pasta.

When the pasta has cooked, separate the
grains thoroughly using your hands.
Transfer the pasta onto the serving dish.
Pour the meat sauce over the pasta. Cover with tinfoil and let it soak up the sauce.
Arrange the meat and vegetables over the
pasta. Serve hot.

Bil Meslene

Preparation time:	20 minutes
Cooking time:	45 minutes
To soak the garbanzo beans:	12 hours
Difficulty:	★

Serves 8 to 10

2	onions, thinly sliced
7 tbsp/100 ml	olive oil
4	garlic cloves, crushed
3	tomatoes
12 tbsp/200 g	tomato paste
1	boned saddle of lamb
¾ cup/150 g	garbanzo beans (chickpeas), soaked overnight
3½ tbsp/50 g	harissa
1¼ lb/500 g	carrots with stalks, halved
1¼ lb/500 g	potatoes, peeled and halved
2	green chiles
5 cups/1 kg	fine semolina
	salt and pepper

The dish *bil meslene* couscous, usually served with a whole saddle of lamb, is peculiar to Siliana. In this north-west region of Tunisia, Bedouins have preserved the ancestral traditions. During marriage ceremonies, saddle of lamb is set aside for the guests.

Before polygamy was banned in 1958, there were stories of how wives in Siliana would compete to try to win favors from their husband. *Bil meslene* couscous became the stake in these feminine rivalries. The whole saddle of lamb was presented on the dish, and then cut up in front of the husband. Taking it in turns, the women of the harem used to carry out this ritual, intensifying the seduction.

If you want to cut up the lamb, our chef recommends browning the pieces before adding them to the vegetables. To make life easier, the saddle can be cut up before it's served on the plates.

The chiles can be fried in strips to reduce their spiciness. Chedly Azzaz suggests that you also replace pepper with cinnamon, as it has a more powerful aroma. If you wish, you can follow this example and make a *kemia* (a selection of colorful small dishes) to accompany this dish.

The success of a couscous dish depends on the preparation of the semolina. Allow approximately 1¼ cups/300 ml of hot water to 5 cups/1 kg of semolina. Olive oil prevents the grains from sticking. To test whether the semolina is completely cooked, our chef crushes some grains between his fingers. If, on the other hand, you use semolina that is not pre-cooked, it must be steamed initially for 20 minutes, then carry out the moistening and molding process. Cook for a further 20 minutes.

In Tunisia, *bil meslene* couscous is a very substantial dish. Why not present the whole saddle of lamb as in the past…?

Sweat the onions in ⅓ cup/80 ml of the olive oil in a saucepan without browning for 3 minutes. Add the crushed garlic. Mix with a wooden spatula.

Skin and deseed the tomatoes. Cut them up roughly and add them to the onion and garlic mixture, together with the tomato paste. Season with salt.

Trim the saddle of lamb. Place the whole saddle in the saucepan. Drain the garbanzo beans and add to the pan.

Couscous

Stir in the harissa. Cover the ingredients with cold water and cook for 40 minutes. Three-quarters of the way through cooking, add the carrots and potatoes. 5 minutes before the end of cooking, add the chiles.

Pour the semolina into a dish. Moisten it with the remaining olive oil. Season with salt. Mix with your hand and pour 1¼ cups/300 ml hot water into it. Allow to soak.

Rub the semolina between your palms, then pour into the couscous steamer's colander. Cook covered for 10 minutes. Remove the lid, and cook for a further 10 minutes. Add pepper to the stock. Arrange the semolina in a dish, moistening it with the stock, and cut up the meat.

Couscous with Cherkaw

Preparation time:	15 minutes
Cooking time:	1 hour
Difficulty:	★ ★

Serves 4

2	onions, chopped
7 tbsp/80 ml	olive oil
3¹/₂ tbsp/50 g	harissa
5 tbsp/100 g	tomato paste

4	green chiles
1¹/₂ lb/700 g	cherkaw
2¹/₂ cups/500 g	couscous
4	potatoes
7 oz/200 g	pumpkin
	salt and pepper

"Couscous with cherkaw from Monastir" is the top dish of the region. Delicious small silvery fish nicknamed *cherkaw* take center stage. The locals are so proud of them that they celebrate them every year. A multitude of these fish appears from spring onward. Apparently, these *cherkaw* are so plentiful that the coast seems like a gigantic mirror. According to the locals, these fish are only caught around Monastir…

Cherkaw look like the small fish called smelts found in France, but they have a distinct advantage over them as they're much tastier than their French counterparts! They taste more of the sea and are very meaty. If *cherkaw* from Monastir are unavailable, in Europe you can substitute other small fish called whitebait, or indeed smelts. Usually, the heads of these small fish are removed and sometimes even their tails so that they're easy to eat. Other recipes call for the fish to remain intact, for the delight of their utter crunchiness when they're fried.

As for the stock for the couscous, it frequently consists of a very red and very spicy tomato sauce. Pumpkin is grown in the Monastir region; its very pleasant, sweet flavor tempers the fieriness of the harissa in this dish. Select a pumpkin with a very smooth skin. The seeds should still be moist. It can be kept for several days in the crisper of the refrigerator, but make sure that the pulp doesn't become too soft.

For the defining decoration, use a pastry cutter on the pumpkin. If you don't like the strong flavor of the chiles, use bell peppers instead. You can also serve the stock separately with its vegetables; and for a fiendishly hot sauce, don't forget the traditional harissa pot! You'll be enjoying a little more sunshine…

Blanch the chopped onions in 2¹/₂ tbsp/ 40 ml of the olive oil. Add half the harissa and the tomato paste. Season with salt and pepper. Add the whole chiles. Stir in 4 cups/1 liter water.

Season the fish with salt and pepper and the rest of the harissa.

Moisten the couscous grain with ²/₃ cup/ 150 ml water and add the remaining olive oil. Stir well. Arrange the small fish in the bottom of the couscous steamer basket.

from Monastir

Cover the fish with the couscous grain and place the basket over the couscous steamer cooking pan. As soon as steam rises from the couscous steamer basket, allow 30 minutes' cooking time.

Peel the potatoes and the pumpkin. Cut 4 pieces of pumpkin of equal size. Cook the vegetables in the couscous steamer cooking pot by immersing them in the stock with the chiles.

Remove the fish from the couscous. Separate the couscous with a fork, pile it on the serving plate and moisten it with a little stock. Place the vegetables of your choice and small fish on the top. Serve hot. Serve the rest of the stock with its vegetables separately.

Farfoucha

Preparation time: 25 minutes
Cooking time: 40 minutes
Difficulty: ★

Serves 4

7 tbsp/100 ml	olive oil
4	fresh onions, sliced
2	tomatoes, roughly chopped
2 tbsp/35 g	tomato paste
2	garlic cloves, crushed
1 tbsp	harissa
4 dried	red chiles
1 cup/200 g	medium-sized semolina

1 tbsp	ground coriander
1 tbsp	ground caraway seeds
1¼ lb/500 g	fennel leaves
	salt

For the garnish:

1	fennel bulb (optional)

In Tunisia and Morocco, couscous is a popular dish. Each family has its own recipe, passed down the generations. This recipe has its origins in the Cap Bon region. Featuring fennel leaves, this vegetarian couscous turns out to have a subtle and very refreshing flavor.

The term *farfoucha* means "to mix up." In this recipe, once the fennel leaves are cooked they're mixed into the semolina. The semolina must be moistened and cooked in the couscous steamer for fifteen minutes.

Fennel, called *besbes* in Arabic, is grown in the Nabeul region. During the harvest, trucks overflow with these winter vegetables, and they perfume the roads with their aniseed aroma. For this recipe, you must use only the leaves. It's better to order them in advance from your greengrocer. If you have difficulty obtaining them, fresh dill is an adequate substitute.

The spices or condiments that flavor this dish, such as harissa, are vital and should not be substituted. Harissa is a purée made of dried and chopped red chiles, seasoned with salt, garlic, caraway seeds, and olive oil. Coriander, also called Arabic parsley, is an ingredient of many Mediterranean dishes. Caraway, which is mainly grown for its oblong, brown, and dried seeds, is an ideal spice to flavor dishes.

Farfoucha couscous is an easy dish to make. This specialty of farmers from the Nabeul region is a highly original dish and should captivate more than one gourmet!

Heat the olive oil and add the tomatoes and onions. Stir and add the tomato paste, crushed garlic cloves, and harissa. Brown for approximately 5 minutes.

Soak the red chiles in water for 5 minutes. Drain and add them to the sauce. Moisten the semolina with cold water.

Season the sauce with salt, coriander, and caraway seeds. Add a glass of water. Simmer over a low heat until the water has completely evaporated. Remove the chiles and reserve for the garnish.

Couscous

Wash the fennel leaves thoroughly and cut them into small pieces. Fill the bottom part of the couscous steamer with water, bring to the boil and steam the fennel leaves in the top part for 10–15 minutes.

Pour the semolina over the fennel leaves and continue to steam for 15 minutes. At the end of cooking, remove the lid and allow to stand.

Pour the semolina and the fennel leaves into a container and mix with two wooden spatulas. Sprinkle the sauce over them and mix well. Arrange the farfoucha couscous in a dish. Garnish with the chiles and fennel bulb (if using).

Macaron

Preparation time:	20 minutes
Cooking time:	30 minutes
Difficulty:	★

Serves 4

2 cups/150 g	fresh peas, shelled
2	eggs
1 x 2 lb/1 kg	chicken
4 tbsp/50 ml	olive oil
1 tsp	caraway seeds
1 pinch	saffron strands

1	onion, chopped
1	garlic clove, crushed
1 tsp	harissa
10½ oz/300 g	macaroni
1	tomato, cubed
5 tsp/25 g	chopped parsley
3½ tbsp/50 g	grated Swiss cheese
	salt and black pepper

To describe macaroni au gratin, Tunisians use the term *mjamra*. In the Tunis region, recipes based on pasta are a particular favorite, and, as such, pasta may be eaten two or three times a week.

Tunisia has an excellent, sophisticated cuisine, and has made the most of the diverse Mediterranean influences. This recipe is a worthy homage to the Italian peninsula, lying just to the north. After cooking the macaroni in boiling water, it must then be mixed with the other ingredients. This tube-shaped pasta is reheated in the oven and covered with grated Swiss cheese. The cheese preserves all the smooth texture and flavor of the gratin. You can serve it straightaway in an attractive dish.

This fairly rich dish includes peas, which have been a favorite of Mediterranean people since ancient times. A wonderful spring vegetable, the pods of this kitchen garden plant are easy to shell. Select peas with a fresh green, intact, and full pod. They will keep two or three days in the refrigerator, but it is better to use them soon after you've bought them.

To give a special flavor to this dish, our chef adds saffron water to the mixture. Called *za'farân* in Arabic, this colorful spice is irreplaceable. Its distinctive flavor finds its way into many Tunisian recipes. The upper ends of the saffron are made up of the pistil or stigmas, which are dark red, velvety, and vivid.

Our chef suggests that you season the chicken with a cinnamon stick and add the carcass and giblets to the sauce.

Macaroni au gratin is a family dish that is easy to make. It's quite rich and can be eaten at lunchtime or in the evening.

Blanch the peas in salted water for approximately 6 minutes. Drain and place to one side. Hard-boil the eggs. Shell and chop them, then place to one side.

Cut the chicken into pieces. Brown the pieces in the olive oil. Season with salt and pepper. Add the caraway seeds.

Soak the saffron in ½ glass water. Add the chopped onion, crushed garlic, and harissa. Pour in the saffron water. Stir well.

u Gratin

Cover the ingredients with water and cook with the lid on for approximately 15 minutes. Cook the macaroni separately in salted water for approximately 10 minutes. Drain. Place to one side.

Remove the chicken pieces. Cut the meat off the bone and dice it. Return the meat to the mixture.

Add the peas, chopped eggs, cubed tomatoes, and chopped parsley. Add the mixture to the macaroni in a bowl and mix well. Arrange in an ovenproof dish and sprinkle Swiss cheese over. Broil in the oven for 5–10 minutes.

Preparation time:	20 minutes
Cooking time:	40 minutes
Difficulty:	★★

Serves 4

4	lamb cutlets
2	chicken legs
7 tbsp/100 ml	olive oil
2 slices	grouper fish, cubed
8 large	shrimp
3	calamari, cleaned and sliced
1	onion, thinly sliced
2	garlic cloves, chopped
3	tomatoes, cubed

| 4 | mild green chiles, sliced |

2 tbsp/35 g	tomato paste
½ tsp	ground cinnamon
½ tsp	dried rosebuds
10½ oz/300 g	cooked mussels
1 cup/200 g	medium-sized semolina
	salt and pepper

For the garnish:

| | slice of lemon |
| | pitted black olives (optional) |

Couseïla is a fun word, created by Rafik Tlatli: "I took bits of the words 'couscous' and 'paella' to give a new name to this recipe. Actually, it's made with semolina, lamb, chicken, fish, and seafood." Living in Nabeul, this influential Tunisian chef spends time making his own creative versions of traditional dishes. With more than one string to his bow, he's also a writer, and television and radio host.

Passionately fond of his region's products, our chef only uses ingredients from the Cap Bon area, such as dried rosebuds, which are typical of the town of Nabeul.

The Tunisian coastal waters offer a huge variety of seafood. Pink shrimp with their exceptionally delicate taste are a great favorite, and bring their subtle, slightly marine flavor to the *couseïla*. The grouper is a peaceful fish found in warm seas, and is available all year round at fishmongers. Its white, very dense flesh retains its texture well dur-

ing cooking, and has a pleasantly light flavor. If you want a stronger flavor, our chef suggests that you season the grouper with lemon juice and a teaspoon of cumin before cooking it.

The mussels decorating the plates are already cooked. If you opt for fresh ones, be especially choosy when you select them: they must be completely closed and not dried out. Discard mussels with broken or half-open shells.

Semolina replaces the traditional rice in this oriental-style paella. The semolina must be moistened and then cooked in the couscous steamer for fifteen minutes, before being sprinkled with water.

Rafik Tlatli's *couseïla* is an original creation which brings the flavors and aromas of the Mediterranean region to your table.

Brown the lamb cutlets and chicken legs in the olive oil in a heavy-duty, deep frying pan for approximately 5 minutes. Place the chicken and lamb to one side.

Brown the cubed grouper fish, the shrimp, and cleaned and sliced calamari separately in the frying pan for approximately 5 minutes. Place to one side.

In the same pan, brown the sliced onion, garlic cloves, tomatoes, and the green chiles. Let them gently simmer, then add the tomato paste. Continue cooking over a low heat.

Couseïla

Pour a glass of water into the mixture and simmer for approximately 3 minutes. Return the chicken, lamb, fish, calamari, and shrimp to the pan.

Season with the salt, pepper, cinnamon, and rosebuds. Before reducing the mixture, remove the shrimp and place to one side for the garnish. Prepare the semolina by moistening it with cold water, then cook in the couscous steamer for approximately 15 minutes.

Sprinkle the semolina over the mixture. Stir well. Reheat the mussels. Serve the couseïla on a dish decorated with the shrimp, mussels, lemon slice, and black olives, if using.

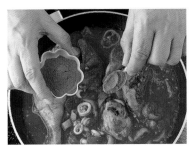

Masfouf with

Preparation time: 15 minutes
Cooking time: 45 minutes
Leave the semolina to stand: 15 minutes
Difficulty: ★

Serves 4

2¹/₂ cups/500 g	fine couscous
1 tbsp/15 ml	olive oil
8 tbsp/100 g	unsalted butter
4 tbsp/30 g	sugar

1 tbsp	attar of rose oil
³/₄ cup/100 g	"Deglet Nour" dates, halved
2¹/₂ cups/150 g	white and purple grapes

This couscous, by Sabri Kouki, is a very sweet dish. The term *masfouf* is usually used in Tunisia and Algeria, meaning a sweetened couscous. It is also known in Morocco as *seffa*. The two terms refer to the generic word "grain." The difference between this sweet recipe and the salted, savory couscous is that it doesn't require any seasoned stock; it is the steam rising from the water in the couscous steamer's pan that cooks it. *Masfouf* is a dry mixture, but has a generous amount of unsalted butter. It is served during the month of Ramadan, often eaten before going to bed, accompanied by a refreshing glass of milk or tea. Occasionally, some Tunisian families even moisten it with milk and supplement it with dried fruits. Served in this way, it's a great favorite during this fasting period because of its nutritional value.

The famous Tunisian dates that top the *masfouf* with sunshine fruits are also called *deglet nour*. In Tunisian, this name means "fingers of light," because they acquire a certain amber-colored transparency when they ripen. These dates are simply the best! They are a product of superior quality and are often sold in the shops under the label "deglet nour of Tunis." Being the only dates that can be presented attached to their stems, you'll easily recognize them.

Grapes are grown in the Cap Bon region and in the Sahel. The white and purple grapes in the recipe are extremely sweet and can also be replaced by the delicious pomegranate. *Masfouf* supplemented by this classical fruit is a very great favorite of the Tunisian middle class. The pulp from the translucent, iridescent pomegranate is a fitting accompaniment to the geranium-attar extract (rose oil), which is distilled in the Cap Bon region and flavors many pastries. This couscous is very often served as a light meal rather than as a dessert.

Moisten the couscous with cold water and cover it thoroughly. Soon after, remove the excess water from the semolina, leaving the semolina to stand for 15 minutes. Preheat the drained water in the bottom part of the couscous steamer ready to cook the semolina.

The couscous is ready when the surface crackles. Stir in 1 tbsp of olive oil and separate the grains with your fingertips. Roll it between your hands and crumble all the small lumps, removing any that do not crumble.

Put the semolina into the couscous steamer and cook it for 20 minutes. Take it off the heat; if it seems dry, moisten it by splashing some water onto it with your fingertips.

Sunshine Fruits

As soon as the couscous is cooked and very hot, add the unsalted butter with your fingers, and the sugar. Remove the grains with the whisk and add a few drops of attar of rose oil.

Transfer the couscous to the savarin mold. Press it down thoroughly.

Turn out the masfouf and top it with halved dates. Put the green and purple grapes into the center of the crown and serve warm.

Couscous with

Preparation time: 1 hour 30 minutes
Cooking time: 4 hours
Difficulty: ★★

Serves 8

6½ lbs/3 kg	onions
1 stick	cinnamon
2 cups/500 ml	vegetable oil
½ cup/100 g	sugar
2 tsp	saffron powder

6 cups/1 kg	golden raisins
⅓ oz/10 g	honey
1 bunch	flat-leaf parsley
1 bunch	cilantro (coriander)
4½ lbs/2 kg	beef (rump)
6 cups/1 kg	medium coarse semolina
	salt and pepper

This couscous, cooked with onions and raisins, is extremely delicious. This recipe is of Jewish origin but with a strong Moroccan influence and requires some time to prepare. It is mainly served at religious festivals.

The onions, cooked with sugar and honey, are a genuine oriental delicacy. Their fine aroma comes to perfection when combined with saffron and cinnamon.

Onions are used in many recipes, as a flavoring as well as a vegetable. The onion originates in north Asia and has been cultivated for more than 5,000 years. It gives a wonderful aroma to ragouts. Moroccan onions are especially known for their fine, sweet flavor.

For this recipe, we recommend that you use large, firm-fleshed onions, undamaged and not sprouting.

If this dish is carefully prepared, the delicate aroma of saffron can also be detected. In Arabic, this spice is known as *sa'faran*. The name contains the root *asfar*, yellow. Saffron, the most expensive spice in the world, is cultivated in the south of Morocco. Every year, from October onwards, the fields of purple crocus blooms that produce saffron extend to the horizon. Two hundred thousand flowers are needed to make a single pound/500g of saffron.

The raisins added to the onions in cooking are definitely nourishing. They are often used in Moroccan cuisine for flavoring.

The greatest difficulty in making this recipe lies in preparing the semolina. You must work in the oil and water by hand, and this stage in the process must be repeated between each steaming.

Peel the onions and set one aside. Cut the others into fine slices and put in a pot. Add cinnamon. When the onions begin to sweat, add 7 tbsp/100 ml oil, sugar, salt, and 1 tsp saffron. Cook for 2 hours.

Once the onions have lost their liquid, add raisins and honey to the pot. Cook for a further hour, then put aside. Bind parsley and cilantro into 1 bunch.

Put the beef into the couscous steamer. Add parsley and coriander, the reserved onion, cut into two halves, and the remaining saffron. Season with salt and pepper. Pour on ⅔ cup/150 ml oil and 8 cups/2 l of water. Cook for 4 hours.

356 Victoria Berdugo, Morocco

Raisins and Onions

Moisten the semolina with water and rub it between the palms of your hands.

Carefully knead the semolina and add oil. Continue to rub between the palms of your hands.

Cook the semolina for 1 hour in the strainer of a couscous steamer and repeat the process of rubbing with oil and water 6 times. Arrange the couscous with the onions and the meat on a serving dish. Serve the meat broth separately.

Lobster Couscous

Preparation time:	*50 minutes*
Cooking time:	*1 hour*
Difficulty:	★★

Serves 4

3 tbsp/45 ml	oil
3 cups/500 g	fine semolina
1	onion
1 bunch	cilantro (coriander)
1 bunch	parsley

2 bunches	watercress
2	lobsters each 3⅓ lbs/1.5 kg
9 oz/250 g	spring onions
1¼ sticks/150 g	butter
1 pinch	ground ginger
2 cups/500 ml	cream
	salt and pepper

Lahoussine Bel Moufid has very close links to the culinary heritage of his home country. At the same time, he lets himself be inspired by regional characteristics to create dishes with a special sophistication. This great Moroccan chef is ever increasing the gourmet's pleasure with his new inventions. He always uses national dishes as the foundation for these and has created a repertoire of recipes in which Middle Eastern and Mediterranean aromas are delightfully combined.

Lobster couscous with watercress cream is a perfect example. The idea for this sophisticated dish came from the Atlas Mountains. The Berber region of Imouzzer des Ida is famed for the purity of its waters. The people there pick the watercress, which grows wild, mix it with cream and serve it as an accompaniment to couscous. To make the vegetarian couscous a bit more nourishing, the chef came up with the idea of adding crayfish from the local rivers.

In the end, he replaced the crayfish with lobster, an elite crustacean from the sea, highly esteemed by gourmets. Lobsters have a hard shell surrounding the abdomen, and tasty firm white flesh. The first set of legs has developed into claws with plenty of muscle flesh. Remember to remove the stomach where the head meets the body and the intestines at the tail end. In the fishmongers, lobsters are always sold live. Before preparing them, you must immerse them head first in bubbling, boiling water, in order to kill them. Take the lobster out again after one or at maximum two minutes. According to taste and budget, you can use spiny lobster or crayfish.

The watercress should be a strong green color and fresh, with undamaged stems and leaves. Watercress can only be kept for one day in the fridge before it starts to fade. The plants should be thoroughly sorted through, washed, and drained.

With your hands, rub 3 tbsp of oil into the semolina and then work in a little water.

In a couscous steamer, heat water with finely chopped onion, and half the cilantro and parsley (chopped). Add salt. When the water boils, cook the semolina for 15 minutes in the strainer. Work in a little fluid. Cook for another 15 minutes. Repeat both stages once more.

Wash the watercress. Take the leaves off one bunch and crush them with a mortar and pestle. Strain the liquid from the couscous steamer and put aside.

with Watercress Cream

Split the cooked lobster lengthways, starting from the head, into 2 halves. Break open the claws. Peel the spring onions, chop, sweat with 7 tbsp/100 g butter. Add the remaining cilantro and parsley (chopped), with the ginger and crushed watercress. Season with salt and pepper.

Place the halves of lobster in the mixture. Add the liquid from the couscous steamer and cook for 5 minutes. Take out the lobster and put aside.

Add the cream and the bunch of watercress. Reduce the sauce to three-quarters of its volume. Replace the lobster. Stir the remaining butter into the semolina. Arrange the lobster couscous on a plate with the watercress cream.

Dchicha

Preparation time: 1 hour
Cooking time: 50 minutes
Difficulty: ★★

Serves 6–8

1⅛ lbs/500 g	carrots
1⅛ lbs/500 g	turnips
1⅛ lbs/500 g	white cabbage
1⅛ lbs/500 g	zucchini
9 oz/250 g	pumpkin
1⅛ lbs/500 g	onions
4½ lbs/2 kg	dchicha (barley semolina)

2 cups/500 ml	argan oil
1	boned shank of veal
1 pinch	ginger
1 pinch	Moroccan saffron powder for coloring
1⅛ lbs/500 g	tomatoes
1 bunch	flat-leaf parsley
1 bunch	cilantro (coriander)
	salt and pepper

Cooks from Sous like to prepare *dchicha* with vegetables, thus creating an original and colorful couscous. The plain near Agadir is very fertile and famed for its cereals, vegetables, and olive groves.

The name of this recipe is due to the semolina used for the couscous. The grains of *dchicha*, a barley semolina, are finely pounded. After steaming, the people of Sous mix hot milk with the *dchicha* to make a gruel, or mix it with *lben*, soured milk. They also prize *barkouk*, a couscous served with honey or *amelou* sauce made from honey, almonds, and argan oil.

Argan oil, with its powerful scent, comes from the fruits of the argan tree, which grows wild. The fruits are yellow or beige and the size of olives. The argan tree grows to 25 or 30 feet, has a knotty trunk with numerous bulges and dense

foliage. Argan trees can be found in the south-east of Morocco in isolated areas stretching north-west from Essaouira and up as far as the vale of Sous.

Giant pumpkins are also often used to enrich Moroccan couscous dishes. Their shape, whether elongated or round, is of no importance. What counts is their deep orange color. The best pumpkins come from the Doukhala region.

First of all, use your fingertips to knead a little lukewarm water into the semolina until all the grains are moistened and begin to swell. Only then should you add the argan oil. Let the semolina rest a little so that it can absorb enough liquid. Meanwhile, prepare the meat. In between cooking stages, twice work cold salt water and argan oil into the *dchicha*.

Scrape the carrots and halve them lengthways. Peel the turnips and quarter; also quarter the cabbage. Cut the zucchini into sticks. Peel the pumpkin and cut into large pieces. Slice the onions thinly.

Put the dchicha on a plate. Using your fingertips, gradually work in a little hot water. Pour some argan oil into your hand and spread it through the dchicha. Once more, rub the semolina through your hands.

Fry the shank of veal briefly in the lower part of the couscous steamer. Add the onions and cover with water. Bring to the boil.

Soussia

Put the dchicha into the strainer part of the couscous steamer. Put the strainer onto the pan below, cover, and steam the dchicha for 15 minutes.

At the end of 15 minutes, season the meat with salt, pepper, ginger, and saffron. Add carrots, turnips, and a large glass of water. Steam the dchicha in 2 further stages of 15 minutes each and between the stages work in a little cold salt water and oil.

Once the vegetables are half-cooked, add zucchini, halved tomatoes, pumpkin, cabbage, parsley, and cilantro. Continue to cook the dchicha as described. Arrange in a dome on a serving platter, place the meat on top and garnish all around with pieces of vegetable.

Fish &
Seafood

Eels

Preparation time: 45 minutes
Cooking time: 1 hour 15 minutes
Difficulty: ★★

Serves 4

8 oz/200 g	potatoes
2¼ lb/1 kg	large eels
4–5	parsley stalks
7 tbsp/100 ml	olive oil

3 cloves	garlic
1	dried red chile
1 tsp	mild ground paprika
	salt and pepper

For the picada (spicy paste):

20	almonds, skinned
2 tbsp/30 ml	olive oil
2	parsley stalks
½ clove	garlic

After paella, eels with *salsa all i pebre* (garlic and paprika sauce) is the second best-known specialty from Valencia. However, because the preparation requires the skill of an experienced chef, it is only ever found on menus at the best restaurants near the coast of Albufera.

The preparations for eels with *salsa all i pebre* usually begin with the sauce. Braise the potatoes, paprika, and eels together to make a kind of ragout. Oscar Torrijos cooks each one of the main ingredients separately, and combines them just before serving. This way each ingredient retains its consistency, color, and flavor.

Eel is extremely popular in Spain. Over the course of its life this unusual fish migrates from saltwater to freshwater, from sea to river, returning to its spawning ground thousands of miles from Europe in the Sargasso Sea between Florida and the Azores in the south-west Atlantic. The tiny

elvers are then transported by the Gulf Stream to Europe, where they swim upriver.

Oscar Torrijos cuts the potatoes into ½ in/1.2 cm thick slices, and cuts evenly sized circles out of the slices. He boils the circles in salted water, to which he adds a little olive oil to prevent them from falling apart.

If the sauce separates during preparation—if the oil fails to combine with the firm ingredients—then simply blend everything together to make a smooth purée.

Oscar Torrijos arranges the eel fillets and potatoes on plates, and serves the sauce separately. We do things slightly differently in this recipe by putting a little sauce on the plates. You can also dress the potatoes in olive oil and sliced almonds, thinly sliced chile, pine nuts, and ground paprika.

Peel and slice the potatoes, then boil in salted water for 20 minutes. To make the picada, fry the almonds for 5 minutes in a skillet in olive oil. Chop the parsley. Peel the garlic, and crush everything in a mortar.

Cut the eel into 4 in/10 cm pieces, and remove the insides. Wash under running cold water, then pat dry, and remove the fillets along the middle bone. Skin the fillets, reserving the bones. Place the fillets on a plate.

Using a pair of tweezers, remove all the bones from the fish. Season the fillets with salt and pepper, and sprinkle with chopped parsley.

from Valencia

Heat the olive oil in a pot, then fry the eel bones and chopped garlic over a high heat for 5 minutes. Cover with water and simmer the stock for about 30 minutes. Sieve and filter.

Quickly fry the dried chile in oil in another pot. Add the picada, ground paprika, and finally the fish stock, then simmer for 20 minutes—and you have your Salsa all i pebre.

Heat a little oil in a large non-stick skillet and fry the eel fillets over a high heat for 10 minutes. Serve the pieces of eel with the sliced potatoes and the sauce.

Stockfish with

Preparation time:	30 minutes
Soaking time for garbanzo beans and stockfish:	24 hours
Cooking time:	1 hour 15 minutes
Difficulty:	★★

Serves 4

2¼ lb/1 kg	stockfish
1 lb 2 oz/500 g	garbanzo beans (chickpeas)
½	onion, finely chopped
8 tbsp/120 ml	olive oil

3½ tbsp/50 g	flour
1 tsp	mild ground paprika
8 oz/200 g	fresh spinach
2	eggs
2 slices	bread
4 tbsp/60 ml	sunflower oil
2 cloves	garlic

For the bouquet garni:

	green of 1 leek
1	thyme stalk
2	bay leaves

In Spain, people like to eat stockfish with garbanzo beans in the *Semana Santa* (the week before Easter), which is treated liked a public festival. Every day there are long pilgrimages in the towns. Believers carry heavy statues of saints and draw lavishly decorated wagons through the streets. After the procession, family and friends meet up and share their favorite dishes. These include stockfish in various guises, especially around Córdoba and Jaén in Andalusia.

Cod has been fished in all the world's cold oceans for centuries. It is dried to make stockfish; strictly speaking, the fish that is dried and preserved with salt is called "klipfish." In bygone days, stockfish used to be prepared in many different ways in rural Spain; most people could afford this inexpensive, extremely long-lasting fish.

Stockfish can be bought in advance, but should be kept in a sealed container in the refrigerator.

The fish is soaked in cold water a day before it is needed to make it nice and tender. The water needs to be changed several times during the 24-hour soaking period. The tail of the fish is cut off and added to the cooking liquid for the garbanzo beans. Depending on the size and hardness of the garbanzo beans, they will take about 50 minutes to cook on the hob, but only about 10 in a pressure cooker. Keep scooping off the froth from the top as they cook.

Some chefs enhance the dish with bread that has been coated in parsley and garlic to make the dish more nutritious. As well as the various vegetables, fried potatoes can also be served as an accompaniment.

Soak the pieces of stockfish and garbanzo beans overnight. Put a pot of water on to boil with the stockfish tail, the garbanzo beans, and the bouquet garni. Bring to the boil and simmer for about 50 minutes.

Cook the onion in 4 tbsp/60 ml of olive oil in a small pot until transparent, but do not let it turn brown. Add the flour and ground paprika with a little water and sweat, stirring briskly.

Drain the garbanzo beans as soon as they are just firm to the bite. Reserve the cooking liquid, adding some to the onion mixture to make a slightly thick flour-based sauce. Add the garbanzo beans.

Garbanzo Beans

Trim and wash the spinach. Simmer in 4 tbsp/60 ml of olive oil in a large skillet until the leaves collapse. Boil the eggs for 10 minutes until hard, then peel and remove the yolks. Chop the whites.

Fry the slices of bread in sunflower oil in a skillet. Peel and crush the garlic in a mortar with the egg yolks and fried bread until smooth.

Add the spinach, bread-and-egg paste, chopped egg whites, and the pieces of stockfish to the garbanzo beans. Boil vigorously for 5 minutes.

Fish Stew

Preparation time:	40 minutes
Cooking time:	40 minutes
Difficulty:	★★

Serves 6

3	tomatoes
2	potatoes
2	onions
4 cloves	garlic
2	green bell peppers

2	red bell peppers
2 cups/500 ml	olive oil
6½ tbsp/100 g	ground almonds
	saffron threads
2 tbsp/30 ml	dry white wine
2¼ lb/1 kg	prepared clams
1²/₃ cups/400 g	thin Spanish noodles (fideos)
8 cups/2 l	fish stock (see page 402)
	salt and pepper

Stews made of vegetables, seafood, and thin noodles are prepared by many fishing families along the coasts of Spain. Noodles often used to be a substitute for rice when none was available.

The vegetables for this colorful dish—which melts on the tongue—are cut into tiny pieces called *brunoises*. The potatoes are first cut into thin strips, then diced. The bell peppers are cut in half lengthwise to remove the seeds and pith, then the strips are diced. The tomatoes are dipped in boiling water, skinned, and the seeds removed before being cut into eighths and chopped. The vegetables are all cooked over a low heat for 3 to 4 minutes without browning, so they need to be watched constantly. The tomatoes are added at the end. For this recipe, the Spanish use a flat paella dish with two handles that distributes the heat evenly.

The clams need to be washed thoroughly before using to remove all traces of sand. Dispose of any clams that are open. When the vegetables are cooked and you have added the almond paste, add the clams and cook at high heat; they will open very quickly.

The main ingredient in this dish is thin noodles known as *fideos*, which can be thick or thin, straight or curvy. They are added uncooked to the vegetables and shellfish, then everything is cooked—like paella—in hot oil. The fish stock enhances the aroma.

Aioli—a sauce made of garlic, salt, egg yolks, and oil—goes extremely well with this dish, as does a sauce made of olive oil, flat-leaf parsley, and chives.

Pour boiling water over the tomatoes and skin them. Wash and/or peel the potatoes, onions, garlic, and bell peppers. Cut the bell peppers in half, and remove the pith and seeds. Finely dice the bell peppers, tomatoes, and potatoes. Finely chop the onions and garlic.

Heat 1²/₃ cups/400 ml olive oil in a paella pan, and sauté the garlic and onions over a low heat for 3–4 minutes. Add the chopped potato and bell peppers, then simmer for 10 minutes. Add the tomatoes, then season with salt and pepper, and simmer for a further 2–3 minutes.

Crush the almonds in a mortar together with 7 tbsp/100 ml olive oil, the saffron threads, salt, and pepper, then blend in the white wine.

with Thin Noodles

Add spoonfuls of this paste to the vegetables.

Add the clams to the vegetables and cook over a high heat for 1–2 minutes.

Add the noodles. Combine well and simmer gently for 2 minutes. Pour over the fish stock and continue simmering gently for 10–15 minutes. Serve very hot.

Lobster with

Preparation time: 1 hour
Cooking time: 2 hours
Difficulty: ★★★

Serves 4

3¼ lb/1.5 kg	lobster
⅔ cup/150 ml	olive oil
1 lb 2 oz/500 g	rockfish (sea perch, scorpion fish, etc.)
4 oz/100 g each	mushrooms, carrots, leeks, zucchini
1	tomato
1	red bell pepper
2 oz/50 g	thin noodles
	salt

For the roast vegetables:

4 oz/100 g	onions
8 oz/200 g	leeks
8 oz/200 g	carrots
2 cloves	garlic

For the bouquet garni:

2 sprigs	thyme
3–4 sprigs	parsley
1	bay leaf

For the herb mayonnaise:

2	eggs
⅔ cup/150 ml	olive oil
⅔ cup/150 ml	groundnut oil
1	lemon
1 tbsp each	dill, chives, chervil
	salt

According to the story, one day the fishermen of Gandia were out on their boat and realized they had run out of rice for their paella. Necessity being the mother of invention, they used some leftover thin noodles—and the results were so good they passed on the recipe. Today, this "leftover" dish is known as *fideuà*, and has become a firm fixture on menus in Valencia and Gandia. There is even an annual international competition!

Oscar Torrijos transforms this popular dish into a culinary experience that leaves nothing to be desired: a feast for every one of the senses. The juicy pieces of lobster lie on nests of thin noodles and vegetables cooked in a stock of crustaceans and iodine-rich fish. The latter are usually used as a garnish for the noodles, and are cooked slowly in a spicy stock. Small scorpion fish, rainbow wrasse, and tiny, boney red mullet add flavor and consistency to the stock.

Lobster is the crowning glory on the noodle nests. Formerly in abundance in Spanish waters, crustaceans now have to be imported. Lobster, which is as tender as it is expensive, can easily be replaced by langoustine, mantis shrimps, or scampi. Oscar Torrijos starts by sautéing the garlic to add flavor to the fish stock from the beginning. He then adds the lobster head and fries it until it is bright red and aromatic. Next, he adds the vegetables, followed by the fish and a bouquet garni.

Before he puts the claws in the pan he breaks them open with a meat tenderizer. The fried lobster pieces are plunged into cold water, which ends the cooking process abruptly, enabling you to remove the meat without burning your fingers. Then it takes just 10 minutes to finish cooking the lobster in the stock.

Cook the lobster in boiling water. Remove the head, and cut the tail in half lengthwise. Heat 6½ tbsp/100 ml olive oil in a pot. Fry the lobster head and the finely chopped roast vegetables for 10 minutes. Add the finely chopped rockfish, bouquet garni, 8 cups/2 l water, and cook for 1 hour.

Trim and wash the onions, then cut them into thin slices. Thinly slice the carrots, leeks, and zucchini. Finely chop the tomato and bell pepper.

Heat a little oil in a pot until very hot. Fry the salted lobster tail and claws over a high heat for 5 minutes until they are red, turning them once. Plunge into cold water. Remove the meat from the shells and set aside.

Thin Noodles

Heat the remainder of the oil in a skillet. Fry the sliced mushrooms, chopped bell pepper, and tomato for 10 minutes until the liquid has evaporated. Season with salt, then add the noodles and continue cooking for 5 minutes, stirring continuously.

Add the zucchini, leek, and carrot strips. Season with salt and cook for a further 10–15 minutes, stirring continuously. Add ³/₄ cup/200 ml of the fish stock and lobster meat. Simmer for a further 10 minutes, adding a little more of the stock.

Make the herb mayonnaise. Place round molds on a serving dish and fill with the noodle and vegetable mix, then garnish with the lobster meat. Remove the molds. Serve the noodles and lobster with the herb mayonnaise.

Angler Fish

Preparation time: 40 minutes
Cooking time: 50 minutes
Difficulty: ★

Serves 4

2¼ lb/1 kg	angler fish
1⅔ cups/400 ml	olive oil
1¾ lb/800 g	potatoes
⅞ cup/100 g	flour
¾ cup/200 ml	fish stock
3 cloves	garlic
2	eggs
	salt

Pep Masiques likes to use his mother's recipe for angler fish. Fish medallions and slices of potato are covered in *alioli*—a sauce made of garlic, salt, egg yolks, and oil—and then baked in the oven.

Angler fish, or sea-devil—*rape* in Castilian—is a deep-sea fish that prefers a sandy sea bottom near the coast. Rather than scales, it has a firm skin that is hard to remove. To fillet the fish, use a knife to cut along the middle bone. Then separate the skin from the head to the tail with your hands. Now put the fish on its back, and repeat on the abdominal side. Cut the fish into medallions and fry them quickly in olive oil. Finish cooking the medallions in the oven. Cook the bones, skin, and fins together with some aromatic vegetables (carrots, celery, leeks) and seasoning to make a delicious home-made fish stock that can be used to cook the fish.

Peel and slice the potatoes, then put them in cold water to stop them from turning brown. Drain them before cooking, and pat them dry, then brown them in a very hot skillet. The skillet should be large enough for the potatoes to spread out and cook evenly.

The sauce adds spice and color to the dish. *Alioli*, known as *all i oli* in Catalan, means "garlic and oil." Originally it was made by crushing garlic in a mortar with a pinch of salt, and then gradually adding oil. Today, most recipes also include egg yolk. The eggs should not be too cold, otherwise the sauce will not thicken properly. So remember to take them out of the refrigerator in advance. You can whisk the sauce with a balloon whisk or an electric stick blender. If it is too thick, just add a few drops of water to make it smooth and thin, and it will coat the fish pieces evenly.

Skin the angler fish and cut off the fins. Cut the meat into medallions and coat in flour. Fry in olive oil for 5 minutes, then set aside.

Heat some more olive oil in the same skillet. Cook the peeled, sliced potatoes for 10 minutes at high heat.

Pour over the fish stock and cook for 25 minutes.

with Alioli

Place the cooked potatoes in a clay pot, then pour over the stock and season with salt. Arrange the fish pieces on top.

Peel and slice the garlic. Put in a bowl with salt and 2 egg yolks, and blend, gradually adding the oil, until you have a nice, velvety sauce.

Spoon the sauce over the fish pieces, then broil in a preheated oven for 10 minutes until golden. Serve in the clay dish.

Hake with

Preparation time: 20 minutes
Cooking time: 30 minutes
Difficulty: ★

Serves 4

6½ tbsp/100 g   filberts (hazelnuts)
1 lb 6 oz/600 g   hake
1½ cup/150 g   flour
7 tbsp/100 ml   olive oil

4 cloves   garlic
2 cups/500 ml   fish stock (see page 402)
1 bunch   fresh parsley
4–5   chive stalks
                 salt and pepper

This specialty from Madrid combines hake and filberts. It is available in numerous restaurants in the Spanish capital. The slices of fish are coated in flour, then fried with garlic and filberts, and finished off in a fish stock.

Hake is one of the most popular types of fish of the Spanish coast. The long, rounded body is gray along the back with golden spots, and white on the belly. The fish grows to a length of between 12 inches and 3 feet/30–100 cm. It has a large mouth full of sharp teeth but no beard threads, two back fins, and one rear fin. The meat contains just a few bones, which are easily removed. The Spanish call this fish *merluza*. In winter, predatory hake gather in large groups off the coast to gorge themselves on vast shoals of sardines. They spend the days in deep waters, coming to the surface at night to hunt. They eat quickly, and large amounts, so

they soon become heavy and slow, which makes it easier for fishermen to catch them. Hake are also caught off the Basque coast. The quality is very much prized—but they are priced accordingly, so they are usually only found on menus in the best restaurants. For this recipe, you can substitute angler fish, perch, or turbot.

Filberts are cousins to hazelnuts, which can be used instead. If the filberts for the sauce are very dry, they can be difficult to skin. You may find it easier to scrape them with a sharp knife.

After adding the stock, the thickness of the fish slices will determine the remainder of the cooking time. The sauce is quite thin at the end of the cooking time; add a little flour to make it thicker if you like.

Blanch the filberts in boiling water, then skin and roughly chop them. Cut the fish into slices and season with salt and pepper. Peel and thinly slice the garlic.

Pour the flour onto a plate and coat the fish on both sides until completely covered.

Heat the olive oil in a skillet. Fry the garlic and filberts for 3 minutes until golden, then push them to the side of the skillet.

Filbert Sauce

Fry the hake for about 5 minutes on each side in the same oil.

Add the fish stock, bring to the boil, and simmer for 15 minutes.

Sprinkle chopped parsley and chives over the fish. Pour over a little stock from the skillet and serve immediately.

Tuna Fillet

Preparation time:	30 minutes
Cooking time:	40 minutes
Difficulty:	⋆

Serves 4

1	carrot
1	white turnip
1 whole	garlic bulb
1	onion
1	green bell pepper
1	leek

7 tbsp/100 ml	sherry vinegar
7 tbsp/100 ml	white wine
2	bay leaves
1 bunch	thyme
pinch	dried oregano
1 tsp	ground cumin
4	cloves
4 slices	red tuna, each weighing 6 oz/150 g
¾ cup/200 ml	virgin olive oil
	salt and pepper

For centuries, Spanish chefs have tried many different ways of preserving tuna without impairing its consistency or flavor. In a break from preserving fish in salt, they had the idea of preserving tuna in a marinade of vinegar, vegetables, and spices—*escabeche*. This cold sauce is used with every possible kind of fatty fish in Spain—including red tuna, sardines, and mackerel, as well as tuna. The abundance of fish oil in these varieties helps to preserve them, as well as enhance the flavor. Over time, this method of preservation has found its way, under various names, into the culinary traditions of other countries—including North Africa, Italy, South America, and even Belgium, which was once under Spanish rule.

Julio Reoyo recommends tuna in a delicious *escabeche*. At the time of the Moors, lookouts were positioned on towers to watch for the vast shoals of tuna. As soon as they were spotted in the vicinity of the coast, fishermen set sail and caught them in huge nets. For this recipe, Julio Reoyo likes to use fatty red tuna.

Escabeche always contains delicious vegetables. The vast, sun-drenched expanses of Castile provide the markets of Madrid with onions, garlic, bell peppers, tomatoes, eggplants, and much more. Garlic is a typical product of La Mancha. The Spanish consume nearly 3½ lb/1.5 kg of it per person per year.

When you have put the sautéed tuna in the *escabeche*, transfer everything into a glass or plastic container. Sealed so it is airtight, the fish will keep for two or three months in the refrigerator. Serve cold or warm.

Peel and slice the carrot. Peel and dice the turnip. Peel and roughly chop the garlic and onion. Cut the bell pepper and leek into chunks.

Put all the vegetables in a pot of water, and simmer gently for 15 minutes, stirring frequently. The vegetables should be well cooked.

Add the vinegar and white wine, and bring to the boil.

n Escabeche

Now put the spices in the pot: bay leaves, thyme, oregano, cumin, cloves, salt, and pepper. Add 2 cups/500 ml cold water, and return to the boil.

Skin the tuna and cut into large chunks. Heat some oil in a skillet until very hot, then cook the tuna all over.

Put the tuna chunks into the boiling escabeche, and cook for 8 minutes. Then remove with a slotted spoon and leave the liquid to cook. Serve the tuna in the warm escabeche.

Fish Platter

Preparation time: 45 minutes
Marinating time
  fish and squid: 1 hour
Cooking time: 10–15 minutes
Difficulty: ★★

Serves 6

12	anchovies
6	sole fillets
3	red barbel
3	medium squid
2 cups/500 ml	milk

1³/₄ cups/200 g	flour
2 cups/500 ml	peanut oil
2 cloves	garlic
3¹/₂ tbsp/50 ml	olive oil
4–5 stalks	flat-leaf parsley
5	lemons
2	tomatoes (optional)
	salt and pepper

For the garnish (optional):

3–4	chive stalks

Málaga is practically in the center of the Andalusian Mediterranean coast, and it has a major fishing harbor. The inhabitants love fried fish and seafood, and serve them in very many ways, either as hot entrées or delicious tapas.

Certain rules have to be observed when preparing the squid for this dish. Start by removing the head, which is connected to the abdominal organs. It is important that you also remove the transparent triangular support mechanism. Then wash the mantles thoroughly in running cold water, and rub them with your fingers to remove any residual sand or dirt. The mouth opening is situated in the middle of the tentacles. Press hard on the "beak" to push it out, and then cut it off. When filleting the red barbel, do not forget to remove the thin colored stripe. The very thin reddish skin, which is hard to remove, remains on the fish, and turns wonderfully crispy when fried.

Marinating in milk for an hour before cooking makes the fish fillets and squid wonderfully tender, and stops them from drying out when they are fried. However, it is important to pat them dry afterwards, otherwise hot fat will splash when they are frying. The flour coat should form only a thin layer around the fish. Shake off any excess flour when you turn it.

You can use groundnut oil or olive oil, or a combination of both, for deep frying. The advantage of groundnut oil is that it can be heated to a higher temperature, so the fish fillets turn beautifully yellow and crispy. Place the fried fish on paper towels to absorb the excess oil, and serve as hot as possible. Diced tomato adds color and a delicate sour touch to the garlic sauce.

Cut the heads off the anchovies. Clean the fish and remove the bones. Remove the sole fillets. Cut deeply into either side of the middle bone of the red barbel and fillet from head to tail.

Remove the heads from the squid and take out the insides. Empty the mantles completely using your fingers and draw out the hard supporting mechanism. Skin and wash everything thoroughly under running cold water.

Cut the squid crosswise into rings and cut off the tentacles.

from Málaga

Season the anchovies, squid rings, tentacles, sole, and red barbel with salt and pepper. Then place in a bowl of milk and marinate for an hour. Remove from the milk and pat dry with paper towels. Coat in flour.

Heat the peanut oil in a pot until very hot. Deep fry the fish, squid, and tentacles for 6–7 minutes until golden.

Fry the thinly sliced garlic in olive oil for 5 minutes. Add the chopped parsley, salt, lemon juice, and skinned, chopped tomatoes. Arrange the fish fillets, sliced squid, and tentacles on plates. Serve garnished with chives and garlic sauce.

Rock Lobster

Preparation time:	20 minutes
Cooking time:	1 hour
Difficulty:	★★

Serves 4

1	rock lobster, approx. 2³⁄₄ lb/1.2 kg
2	dried red chile pods (pimiento ñora)
pinch	saffron threads
1 lb 2 oz/500 g	rockfish (scorpion and gurnard, for example) and fish offcuts

1	fish stock bouillon cube
2 whole	garlic bulbs
²⁄₃ cup/150 ml	olive oil
4 tbsp	tomato paste
3 cloves	fresh garlic, chopped
10 oz/250 g	tiger shrimps, cleaned
2 cups/400 g	rice
	salt

For the garnish:

	flat-leaf parsley

This clever recipe "in the style of Santa Pola" is typical of the town near Alicante, where there are numerous ways of preparing fish and seafood. This special dish combines lots of special aromas. Gourmets value rock lobster for its firm yet tender white flesh. If you can, choose a medium-sized specimen.

For the dish to be a complete success, the stock must be prepared correctly. In the Alicante region, it is usually made from small, aromatic rockfish such as scorpion fish, gurnard, and various types of perch. Make sure you also take the offcuts (head, skin, tail, bones) when you buy your fish, as they will make the stock even tastier.

The Moors introduced rice-growing to Spain in the 8th century, and because of the proximity to the Ebro Delta the practice became widespread in the area around Alicante.

Cesar Marquiegui particularly recommends Bomba, the variety grown in Calasparra, as the grains absorb plenty of liquid and yet retain their bite.

Saffron, the tiny stigma of a type of crocus, is essential for rice dishes such as this one, because it adds both aroma and color. The spice was introduced to Spain by its Arab occupiers. Today, more than 70 percent of the world's production is harvested in Castilia alone! October brings with it an incomparable sight, when entire fields of the mauve fall crocuses are in flower. The blue fields stretch as far as the eye can see, from Toledo to Albacete. Migrant workers gather to harvest the precious flowers. Often it is men who pick them, flower by flower. It is left to the women to remove the red stigma from the flowers, after which the stigma are roasted.

Using a sharp knife, cut the rock lobster in half from head to tail, then cut diagonally into pieces. Remove the seeds from the chile and crush the saffron threads in a mortar.

To make the fish stock, set a large pot of water on to boil and add the rockfish, fish offcuts, and the bouillon cube. Bring to the boil, then cook for about 20 minutes.

Fry the whole garlic and the chile in 7 tbsp/100 ml olive oil. Stir well, then add to the stock. Add the tomato paste and saffron, and cook for 15 minutes. Sieve and season with salt.

Rice Santa Pola

Heat the remainder of the olive oil in a paella pan. Fry the rock lobster pieces, then remove and set aside.

Fry the 3 chopped garlic cloves and the prepared shrimps in the paella pan for about 2 minutes. Add the rice and combine well.

Pour over 3¹/₄ cups/800 ml fish stock and simmer for about 18 minutes. Check the seasoning, then arrange the rock lobster pieces on the rice. Bake in the oven/480 °F/250 °C for 10 minutes, then leave to stand for 2 minutes. Garnish with parsley.

Paella with

Preparation time: 40 minutes
Cooking time: 55 minutes
Difficulty: ★★

Serves 4

For the paella:

2	leeks
1	carrot
1	head of celery
1 bunch	scallions (spring onions)
6 stalks	green asparagus
¾ cup/150 g	tomatoes
16	crayfish
4 tbsp/60 ml	olive oil
1 clove	garlic
1 tsp	ground paprika

pinch	ground saffron
1 cup/200 g	rice (ideally Bomba)
	salt

For the river crayfish stock:

	green of 2 leeks
1	carrot
2	scallions (spring onions)
1	head of celery
1	tomato
4 tbsp/60 ml	olive oil
1 clove	garlic, halved
3 sprigs	parsley
1	bay leaf
4	crayfish

For the garnish:

	flat-leaf parsley

This paella with crayfish is an absolute delight; the original combination of delicate flavors make it the perfect highlight of a special meal shared with friends and family.

Every Spanish province along the Mediterranean has its own recipe for paella. Originally, the name *paella* referred only to the large skillet with two handles that was used for preparing rice. Rice, which is very popular in Spain, has been cultivated for about 6,000 years, and it was the Moors who brought it from India and China to the Iberian Peninsula.

The success of this recipe is determined by the quality of the rice and the olive oil. As a purist, Alberto Herráiz recommends round-grained Bomba, which absorbs lots of liquid without losing its bite. This variety of rice comes from Calasparra, and it can absorb up to five times its own weight of liquid without bursting.

You really should make the stock for this recipe yourself using some crayfish, because this will provide the aroma that makes the charm and flavor of the paella. Watch out for the measurements: always use twice as much liquid as rice.

Crayfish, which grow to between 5–6 inches (12–15 cm), are freshwater crustaceans. They used to be abundant in rivers and streams, but are quite rare today. Their delicate, aromatic meat is ideal for this dish. Depending on your preference and wallet, you can also use shrimp or lobster. Whatever you use, this Castilian feast will delight and impress your guests.

Trim and roughly chop the vegetables for the stock. Cut the leeks, carrot, celery, and scallions into fine strips for the paella. Peel the asparagus. Purée the tomatoes.

Clean all the crayfish. Pull sharply on the middle tail fin, and remove the black thread from the inside.

To make the stock, fry the halved garlic clove in a large pot, and add the vegetables, parsley, and bay leaf. Add 4 of the crayfish and simmer. Break the crayfish with a pestle. Cover with water and simmer for 30 minutes. Strain.

Crayfish

To make the paella: heat 4 tbsp/60 ml of olive oil and fry 1 whole garlic clove in it. Add the vegetable strips and halved asparagus stalks. Brown. Remove the garlic. Add the tomato purée. Stir well. Remove the skillet from the heat and stir in the ground paprika.

Return to the heat and pour over the strained stock. Stir in the saffron and plenty of salt. Stir in the rice. Cook over a high heat for 5 minutes. Lower the heat as soon as the rice rises to the surface.

Continue cooking the rice and vegetables in the oven (480 °F/250 °C) for 10 minutes. Place the crayfish on the rice and cook for a further 5 minutes. Serve the paella garnished with parsley leaves.

Red Barbel

Preparation time: 35 minutes
Cooking time: 30 minutes
Difficulty: ★

Serves 4

4	small red barbel
¾ cup/200 ml	olive oil
1	red bell pepper
2	potatoes
2	tomatoes
pinch	saffron thread
½	onion

4 tbsp/60 ml	white wine
2 tbsp/30 ml	pine nuts
1 clove	garlic, chopped
1 sprig	parsley
2	bay leaves
4	shrimp
	salt

For the fish stock:

1	tomato
1	leek
	offcuts from the red barbels (heads, tails, bones)

This dish is typical of the town of Alicante. It is easy to prepare and yet contains a mixture of aromas. It is usually served in a clay dish called *rustidera* in Spanish.

There is a lively fishing industry around Alicante. There are fishing villages everywhere, in which the culinary traditions are handed down from generation to generation. Red barbel is a rockfish, and its tasty firm flesh has many fans. The fish, which is easily identified by its pink to dark-red scaly skin, is available all year round from good fishmongers.

Red barbel has lots of small bones, but the meat is lean, fine, and extremely delicious. The smaller the fish, the more aromatic they are. If red barbel is not available, you can use turbot, another popular, high-quality fish, instead.

The village of Dénia is near Alicante. It is famous for its excellent, dark-red "gambas." These wonderful shrimp are usually served simply *a la plancha*, on a red-hot skillet brushed with olive oil, and eaten as tapas. In this recipe, though, they are baked in the oven with the other ingredients. If you are unable to obtain shrimp, you can substitute clams.

The sophisticated and independent culinary tradition of the region of Alicante is also evident in the addition of pine nuts, a popular ingredient in many local dishes. These long kernels are the fruit of various pine trees that grow around the Mediterranean. Their resinous, nutty flavor is similar to that of almonds, but the mild aroma and softer consistency make them ideal for use in all kinds of fish dishes.

Clean the red barbel and scrape off the scales. Cut off the heads and tails, and set aside for the stock. Cut crosses into the flesh on one side of the fish. Season with salt, brush with olive oil, then broil quickly under the broiler.

Roughly chop the tomato and leek for the stock. Cook the leek, tomatoes, and red barbel offcuts in a large pot of water for about 20 minutes. Then strain the stock.

Remove the seeds from the bell peppers and cut into strips. Peel and thinly slice the potatoes. Slice the tomato. Crush the saffron in a mortar.

from Alicante

Peel and thinly slice the halved onion and fry in a pot with 7 tbsp/100 ml olive oil. Fry the bell pepper strips, sliced potatoes, and tomatoes separately in the remainder of the oil.

Add the potatoes, bell pepper, and tomatoes to the onions, and pour over the white wine. Add the saffron threads and season with salt.

Add the pine nuts, chopped garlic, parsley, and bay leaf. Arrange the cleaned shrimp and the pre-cooked red barbel on the vegetables. Pour over the stock. Bake in the oven (350 °F/180 °C) for 8 minutes. Arrange on plates.

Tiznao

Preparation time: 25 minutes
Soaking time for
    the stockfish: 24 hours
Cooking time: 2 hours
Difficulty: ★

Serves 4

2¼ lb/1 kg   stockfish
1 lb 14 oz/800 g   onions
1 lb 14 oz/800 g   red bell peppers
1 clove   garlic

For the spicy sauce:
6½ tbsp/100 ml   olive oil
2 tbsp/30 ml   sherry vinegar
1 tsp   dried oregano
½ tbsp   ground paprika
                 (pimientón)
                 black pepper

For the garnish:
                 fresh oregano
                 ground paprika
                 (pimientón)

To the Castilians of La Mancha, *tiznao* (literally translated as "glowing embers") is always associated with stockfish. The traditional recipe is usually cooked on a Friday (the day on which devout Catholics refrain from eating meat), and of course during Lent. The period of abstinence between Ash Wednesday and Easter Sunday has always been taken seriously in Spain.

The deeply religious Spanish have therefore made stockfish—*bacalao*—a Lent dish par excellence. Salted, dried coldwater cod has been at home on the Iberian Peninsula since the 17th century, and is used in many delicious dishes.

It is important to soak the stockfish for 24 hours. Alberto Herráiz advises covering the dish with plastic wrap and putting it in the refrigerator, and changing the water several times during the soaking period.

Tiznao is an ancient recipe. The ingredients used to be cooked over an open fire. The glowing embers helped to remove the salt from the stockfish, and smoked the other ingredients at the same time.

This very healthy dish with lots of Mediterranean flair is based primarily on red bell peppers. These garden fruits which are pampered by the sun, are delicious raw or cooked, with or without their skins. The skin is easy to remove if you broil the bell peppers first. Red bell peppers contain a great deal of vitamins A and C, and the flesh is crunchy and mildly aromatic. Make sure the peppers you choose are firm and smooth with a hard, green stalk.

The aroma of the *tiznao* is produced by the onions, liliaceous plants that have been cultivated for over 5,000 years and came originally from northern Asia. The large, yellow onion—or Spanish onion—is particularly mild.

The evening before, cut the stockfish into pieces. Soak in cold water. Wrap the peeled onions, bell peppers, garlic, and stockfish individually in aluminum foil, and bake in the oven (300 °F/150 °C): stockfish and bell peppers for 15 minutes, garlic and onions for 2 hours.

Remove the bones from the stockfish and separate the flesh into pieces. Reserve some of the flakes for the garnish.

Combine the olive oil, sherry vinegar, dried oregano, ground paprika, and black pepper, and whisk with a balloon whisk.

Using a sharp knife, skin the bell peppers and remove the seeds. Cut the flesh into thin slices.

Thinly slice the onions. Cut the roast garlic cloves in half lengthwise, and, using the knife blade, squeeze out the soft flesh.

Combine the stockfish, bell peppers, onions, and garlic in a bowl. Pour over the sauce, and combine well. Arrange on plates. Put a few flakes of stockfish on each plate. Garnish with oregano and dust with ground paprika.

Stuffed Squid with

Preparation time:	1 hour
Cooking time:	1 hour 30 minutes
Difficulty:	★★★

Serves 4

For the stuffing and vegetable sauce:

16	giant shrimp
7 tbsp/100 ml	olive oil
2	leeks
2	large onions
2 heads	spinach
1 head	Swiss chard
1	cauliflower
2 or 3	eggs
2	tomatoes
4 cups/1 liter	fish stock

1³/₄ lb/800 g	whole squid
⁷/₈ cup/100 g	flour
	oil for frying

For the basil sauce:

2 bunches	basil
¹/₄ cup/50 g	pine nuts
2 cups/500 ml	olive oil
	salt

For the shrimp sauce:

	shrimp shells and trimmings
3¹/₂ tbsp/50 ml	brandy
3¹/₂ tbsp/50 ml	olive oil

Bartolomé-Jaime Trias Luis has never forgotten his grandmother's vegetable-stuffed squid. Dishes of this type are very popular on Mallorca, although the stuffing is more usually made with a mixture of pork, herbs, and eggs. For a special occasion, Bartolomé-Jaime Trias Luis has suggested a recipe using giant shrimps with two sauces: one of basil (known as pesto, which can also be bought ready-made), and another of seafood.

Closely related to the cuttlefish, squid range from about 8 to 16 inches/20 to 40 cm in length. They are sharp-eyed hunters which capture their prey using two long tentacles armed with suckers that emit a paralyzing poison. To escape its own predators, the squid is able to change color, and to move through the water at a speed of some 7 miles/11 km an hour. These remarkable creatures gave rise in the past to many myths about sea monsters. More recently, scientists have discovered a type of giant squid, known as *architeuthis*, living at depths of 10,000–13,000 feet/3,000–4,000 meters and reaching up to 20 feet/6 meters in length, with tentacles extending to 39 feet/12 meters.

Squid are caught on summer nights, when they are attracted to the surface by dragnets to which lights are attached. They make delicious eating once they have been thoroughly cleaned, and with the innards and skin removed.

This recipe uses a great range of vegetables. Some, mixed with the squid tentacles and the eggs, are used to stuff the squid pockets. The rest, with the addition of tomatoes and fish stock, are used for the sauce.

To prepare the giant shrimp used in this recipe, shell them by first removing the head and then the top two sections of the shell. Now press gently on the sides; the whole body will come out without breaking. Keep the shells and trimmings to flavor the delicious shrimp sauce.

Shell the shrimp and reserve the shells and trimmings. Remove the innards from the squid. Chop the tentacles and brown for 15 minutes in oil with the chopped leeks, onions, spinach, Swiss chard, and cauliflower. Halve this mixture and add the eggs to one half to make a stuffing.

Meanwhile, continue to cook the other half of the vegetables. Add the chopped tomatoes and the fish stock and cook for 30 minutes. Fill each of the squid pockets with some stuffing and one shelled shrimp. Close the end of the squid body with a cocktail stick.

Flour the squid and fry them in a pan of very hot oil for 5 minutes, turning to ensure even browning. Remove them from the oil and place them in the pan containing the vegetable sauce. Cook them gently in the sauce for 35 minutes.

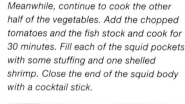

Vegetables and Shrimp

For the basil sauce, briefly poach the basil leaves, strain and reserve. Toast the pine nuts in the oven, then blend with the basil leaves, a little water, and salt. Press the mixture through a sieve, with a little more water if necessary. Finally add a little olive oil and mix thoroughly.

Place the cooked squid on a chopping board. Cut them into evenly-sized pieces about 1 inch/2–3 cm thick.

Sauté the shrimp trimmings and shells for 5 minutes in an oiled pan. Deglaze with brandy and flambé it. Now add a little water and cook for a few minutes. Strain the sauce. Arrange the pieces of stuffed squid on plates with the shrimp and basil sauces and the strained vegetables.

One-Pot Stew with

Preparation time: 30 minutes
Cooking time: 1 hour 15 minutes
Difficulty: ★

Serves 4

4	potatoes
	saffron threads
2¼ lb/1 kg	baby squid
1 tbsp	olive oil
1 cup/250 ml	fish stock
1 cup/250 ml	light cream
	salt
	pepper

For the sofregit:

1 clove	garlic
1	onion
2 oz slab/50 g	back bacon (or Catalan *sagi*)

For the aioli (garlic mayonnaise):

1 clove	garlic, unpeeled
1	egg yolk
6 tbsp	olive oil
	salt

The boats of Catalan fishermen rock against their moorings on the Mediterranean's gentle waves. We are in Port-Vendres... it was a good catch and it's all been sold. Now all that remains is to prepare the delicious baby squid, or very small cuttlefish (*supions*), which are similar. With them the fisherman fry up *sagi*, a rancid white bacon that gives a nutty flavor, especially in the traditional *bullinada de supions*. You can replace the *sagi* in our recipe with regular bacon, or a good olive oil.

Jean Plouzennec's recipe can be served as an appetizer, but you should use more squid. If you can't obtain baby squid or very small cuttlefish, you can use squid rings. *Sofregit*, one of the basic recipes of Catalan cuisine, forms the basis of this dish, with its caramelized onions and sometimes tomatoes as well. The precise ingredients vary from family to family.

Bullinada is served with *aioli*, a strong garlic mayonnaise extremely popular in southern French cuisine. All of the ingredients must be at the same temperature for it to be successful. Our chef suggests that you put in the salt at the beginning.

You need the best garlic that you can find for *aioli*. You can use the white or the pink variety. Your dressing will have the best flavor if the bulbs are young, and you have removed the cores from the cloves. The garlic should be crushed well. Sweated, soft garlic is also easier to work.

The olive oil should be perfumed and slightly cloudy; if it is, the *aioli* will taste even better! We're less demanding about the variety of potato, also an integral part of *bullinada*, but you should definitely use a waxy variety.

To make the sofregit, peel the garlic and onion and chop them finely. Chop the bacon finely too. Put half the bacon in a deep saucepan and fry it until the fat runs. Then fry the garlic and onion in the bacon fat. Put aside the remaining chopped bacon for the next step.

Peel the potatoes and cut them into ¼ in/3 mm-thick slices. Put the potatoes in a pan of boiling, salted water, adding the remaining bacon and 10 strands of saffron. Simmer for 15 minutes, then drain the potatoes, reserving 1 tbsp potato liquor. Add a little pepper.

Clean and gut the squid and squeeze them gently to remove excess moisture. Fry all the squid and tentacles in olive oil in a skillet for 2 minutes until all the liquid has evaporated and the squid is pale golden brown.

Baby Squid and Bacon

Add the browned squid to the pan with the onion, garlic, and bacon. Add the fish stock and sprinkle on some saffron. Bring to the boil. Add the cream. Bring to the boil again. Simmer for 45 minutes.

To make the aioli, roast one clove of garlic in the oven, peel it, and crush it with salt and the egg yolk. As with a mayonnaise, using a wire whisk, beat in the olive oil. Add 1 tbsp potato liquor.

Add the aioli to the pan with the squid. Stir to form a smooth mixture. Arrange a circle of potato slices around the edge of the plate. Pour the squid into the middle and serve immediately.

Baked Porgy

Preparation time: 30 minutes
Cooking time: 40 minutes
Difficulty: ★

Serves 4

2	large onions
3 cloves	garlic
7 tbsp	olive oil
1 sprig	fresh or dried dill

1	porgy weighing 2¼ lb/1 kg
8	medium new potatoes
1 tbsp	chopped fresh thyme
2	bay leaves
4	tomatoes
2	lemons
⅔ cup/150 ml	dry white wine
	salt
	pepper

Here is a dish that is one of the most popular Sunday meals among families in southern France, and it is one of the easiest fish recipes ever. To make preparation even easier, ask your fishmonger to scale, gut, and clean the porgy for you. This fish is easy to identify because of the pale stripes on its cheeks.

Our dish is seasonal. Porgy is only available between March and October. If you can't find it, use bass.

The porgy's eyes should be bright and the gills red, signs that the fish is fresh. Take care not to cook it for too long, otherwise it will become dry. Here's a gourmet tip: This dish tastes even better the next day. The potatoes will have soaked up the delicious juices—a fantastic treat for the taste buds—and the flavors will have married perfectly.

We decided to use new potatoes for this dish because they are well suited to baking in the oven. You could use other kinds of potato, though. Whilst in the oven the fish must be well covered from head to tail, otherwise it will burn.

The splendid porgy is easy to prepare and eat, because it doesn't have too many bones. Even novice cooks will enjoy this recipe. It's so simple that nothing can go wrong. The red tomatoes and yellow lemons are all that is needed by way of a garnish. The fish is the star.

Sauté the sliced onions and garlic in 2 tbsp olive oil until golden brown. Put the onions and garlic in an oven-proof dish large enough to take the porgy.

Insert the sprig of fresh or dried dill into the prepared porgy's belly cavity. Drizzle 1 tbsp oil over the porgy.

Cut the peeled potatoes into ¼ in/5 mm-thick slices. Sauté them in olive oil, with 1 tbsp chopped thyme and 2 bay leaves, until golden brown. Season with salt.

with Vegetables

Layer the fried potato on top of the onion and garlic in the oven-proof dish. Arrange the tomatoes, cut into ¼ in/5 mm-thick slices, and the lemon slices, on top, putting some aside for later.

Put the porgy on top of the vegetables and garnish with slices of lemon and tomato. Season with salt and pepper and drizzle the remaining olive oil over the fish.

Pour the white wine over the fish and vegetables. Cover with aluminum foil and bake for 30 minutes in an oven preheated to 400 °F/200 °C, basting every 5 minutes with the cooking juices. Serve hot, straight from the dish.

Fillet of Sea Bass

Preparation time:	40 minutes
Cooking time:	30 minutes
Difficulty:	✶

Serves 4

2¼ lb/1 kg	sea bass
15	baby carrots
2	zucchini
1 tbsp	olive oil
	salt
	pepper

For the fish stock:

	sea bass trimmings
3 tbsp	olive oil

1	leek
1	onion
1 bunch	fresh parsley
1 sprig	fresh thyme
1	bay leaf
⅓ cup + 1½ tbsp/ 100 ml	white wine
6 tsp	aniseed seeds

For the zabaglione:

3	egg yolks
⅓ cup + 1½ tbsp/ 100 ml	light cream

For the garnish:

1 bunch	fresh chervil

Sea bass is a member of the serranid family and is an extremely popular edible fish. Get your fishmonger to fillet it for you if possible, but ask him to save you the bones and head, minus the gills, because you need them for the fish stock. Wash the fish carefully and, above all, do not salt it. Depending on the time of year, you can substitute porgy or John Dory.

Zabaglione is really an Italian dessert. In this dish it is served hot. Our chef advises that you move it to the edge of the burner when you beat it, so that it doesn't go lumpy. The zabaglione will remain liquid if you don't add the cream until the end. Purée the sauce in a blender and then strain it through a sieve to remove the aniseeds. Just before serving, pour enough zabaglione into the base of an oven-proof plate to cover it, and bake it in the oven for two minutes at 465 degrees Fahrenheit/250 degrees Celsius, so that the sauce turns golden brown.

Aniseed originated in the Orient and is a member of the umbelliferous plant family. In ancient China, aniseed was regarded as a holy herb and the Romans valued it too. In Europe, aniseeds were used in baking from the earliest times. For this recipe you could use fennel seeds instead.

Our chef cooks the carrots first, then the zucchini. Briefly blanch the vegetables in cold water afterwards, so that they retain their attractive color. You could make a soup with the remaining vegetables.

Use a griddle to broil the fish fillets. The ridges make an attractive pattern on the fish. You can serve boiled potatoes with this dish.

Make an incision in the fish along the backbone, from head to tail, and then make another incision behind the gills. Cut off the full length of the fillet by working the knife along the length of the fish against the backbone. Remove the second fillet in the same way.

Fish stock: Put the fish bones, fish head, and olive oil in a saucepan. Add a little water, followed by the washed and chopped leek, chopped onion and parsley, thyme, and bay leaf. Simmer for 10 minutes. Add the white wine. Simmer for 10 minutes, then sprinkle in the aniseeds.

Starting at the tail, cut the fish fillets into equal chunks, then refrigerate them. Slice the carrots and zucchini on the diagonal to form oval slices and boil them (carrots first, see above) for 5 minutes in salted water.

on Aniseed Zabaglione

To make the zabaglione, strain the fish stock and beat in the egg yolks.

Beat the egg yolks hard with a wire whisk over heat so that the mixture thickens.

Add the cream and season to taste. Purée the zabaglione on the highest setting, so that it emulsifies, and strain. Fry the fish for 5 minutes in 1 tbsp olive oil. Season the sea bass with salt. Arrange the zabaglione sauce, fish, and vegetables on a plate. Garnish with chervil.

Red Mullet Fillets

Preparation time:	2 hours
Cooking time:	45 minutes
Difficulty:	★★★

Serves 4

4	red mullet, each 8 oz/250 g
1 tbsp	olive oil
1 bunch	fresh dill
	salt, pepper

For the fish soup:

1	onion
1	carrot
1 clove	garlic
1	bouquet garni
2 tbsp	olive oil
1 lb/500 g	assorted rock fish
generous ¾ cup/200 ml	Pernod/aniseed drink

1 sprig	fresh dill
1 large pinch	ground saffron
2 tbsp	tomato paste
	salt, pepper

For the ratatouille:

2	zucchini
1	large eggplant
1	onion
1 clove	garlic
1	red bell pepper
1	green bell pepper
2 tbsp	olive oil
1 sprig	fresh thyme (optional)
	salt, pepper

For the red garlic mayonnaise (rouille):

1	egg yolk
1 tsp	Dijon/mild mustard (optional)
generous ¾ cup/200 ml	olive oil
1 pinch	ground saffron
1 pinch	harissa/chilli powder, salt

This recipe is a complete homage to the south of France! Alain Carro has given this creation the same name as his restaurant, "Le Castellaras," after the prehistoric fortifications on the peaks of the Maritime Alps. If you visit this area, take a little time before you eat to enjoy a traditional aperitif in the form of the aniseed alcoholic drink, *pastis*.

All of the ingredients in this recipe come from an area that basks in the sun. It is an extremely refined dish, both in taste and presentation. For this specialty to be a total success, the ratatouille vegetables should be chopped into fine dice, as it is important for the finished appearance.

Remove the bell pepper cores and chop all the vegetables into evenly sized dice. Get your fishmonger to fillet the red mullet (red snapper can be used if red mullet is unavailable). If you want to make the effort yourself, clean and gut the fish carefully and fillet it with a sharp knife. Don't for-

get to remove the smallest bones with a pair of tweezers. Rock fish don't need to be gutted and filleted, they just need to be rinsed well. The small fish should be very fresh.

You'll recognize them all again—the little green and black striped white sea bream, the green and brown hog fish, the delicate, long, red and black striped rainbow wrasse, the red and green spotted bass, and the scorpion fish. When the catch is exceptional, the fisherman may sometimes find small crustaceans in his nets, known as rock lobster (*cigalons de mer*).

Rouille is based on a simple mayonnaise. To help it emulsify, add a small teaspoon of mustard or a splash of water. This will also help if the mayonnaise separates.

Peel and dice the onion, carrot, and garlic for the soup. Add the bouquet garni and sweat everything in the olive oil.

When the onions are translucent, add the rock fish to the pan and sauté them too.

Add the aniseed drink, sprig of dill, saffron, and tomato paste. Add enough water to cover the ingredients. Simmer for 20 minutes. Season the soup. Remove the dill and bouquet garni from the pan. Pour the soup into a food processor, purée it, then pass it through a sieve.

"Castellaras"

To make the ratatouille, dice the zucchini, eggplant, onion, garlic, and bell peppers very finely. Sweat them in the olive oil for 10 minutes until the onion is translucent. The vegetables should still be crisp. Add the thyme (if using). Season with salt and pepper.

To make the garlic mayonnaise, beat together the egg yolk, mustard, and olive oil until creamy. Beat in the saffron, harissa powder, and salt.

Season the red mullet fillets. Fry in olive oil for 2 minutes on the skin side and 3 minutes on the flesh side. Sandwich the ratatouille between two fillets. Make a pool of soup around the fish. Put a spoonful of rouille in the soup. Garnish with sprigs of fresh dill.

Monkfish with a

Preparation time:	30 minutes
Vegetable cooking time:	30 minutes
Monkfish cooking time:	15 minutes
Difficulty:	★★

Serves 4

2	monkfish tails weighing
	1½ lb/800 g
8	baby carrots
4	potatoes
8	baby turnips
4 bulbs	baby fennel
7 cloves	garlic
2	bay leaves
10 slices	white bread

| 1 bunch | fresh parsley |
| ½ bunch | fresh thyme |

	salt
	pepper
2	eggs
2 tbsp	olive oil
7 tbsp	peanut oil
scant ⅛	
stick/10 g	butter
1 cup/100 g	pitted black olives

For the garlic mayonnaise (aioli):

4 cloves	garlic
1	egg yolk
1 cup/	
250 ml	olive oil
1 pinch	saffron
	salt

In this recipe by Francis Robin, the tender, delicate flesh of the monkfish is dressed in a golden robe, which gives it an incomparable flavor. This fish is easy to prepare and also very suitable for children, because the fish only has one large backbone. Fishmongers often sell it in pieces, but it is rarely displayed with the head. When choosing monkfish, the flesh should be snow white. If you can see yellow fibers, choose another, fresher fish.

The unusual thing about this dish is that it looks like a leg of lamb, spiked with slivers of garlic. In fact, garlic is used in every Mediterranean dish. *Aioli*, the special mayonnaise from the south of France, is an integral part of our recipe, and garlic is the main ingredient in it. To ensure that your garlic mayonnaise is a success, we recommend crushing the garlic, then salting it. Only then should you add the egg yolk and very gradually beat in the olive oil, a drop at a time.

The vegetable accompaniment should have a very subtle taste. Francis Robin therefore recommends that you omit tomatoes, eggplant, and zucchini. Use waxy potatoes, such as Charlotte, that don't break down when cooked.

Normal vegetables can of course be used instead of the baby vegetables. Buy fennel that is white and plump, with a nice, bright green stalk, but try to get small bulbs, because they are sweeter than the big ones. Fennel will keep for several days in the refrigerator. The carrots and baby turnips should have smooth, shiny skins.

Clean the monkfish tails, removing any skin and fat. Peel the carrots, potatoes, baby turnips, and fennel, leaving a little bit of stalk on the carrots and baby turnips. Cook each vegetable separately in boiling salted water, with a clove of garlic and half a bay leaf.

A day in advance, pass the bread through a wide-meshed sieve to make breadcrumbs, and leave them uncovered, to dry. Put the breadcrumbs into a bowl. Stir in 4 chopped cloves of garlic, chopped fresh parsley and thyme. Season with salt and pepper.

Peel 2 cloves of garlic, cut them into slivers, and insert them all over the monkfish tails. Beat together the eggs and olive oil.

Herb Crust

Dip the monkfish tails in the beaten egg, then coat them in the herbed bread-crumbs. To make the aioli, crush the peeled garlic in a mortar. Season with salt and add the egg yolk. Gradually beat in the olive oil and a pinch of saffron.

Preheat the oven to 400 °F/200 °C. Melt the peanut oil and butter in a large, oven-proof skillet. Fry the fish in the butter and oil until crisp and golden brown. Then transfer the pan to the oven and bake for 10 minutes.

Keep an eye on the baking fish, basting it frequently with cooking juices. Arrange the vegetables and olives around the fish, and serve the aioli separately.

Red Mullet on a

Preparation time: 10 minutes
Cooking time: 10 minutes
Difficulty: ★

Serves 4

4	plum tomatoes
3 tbsp	olive oil
2	shallots
1 clove	garlic
1 cup/100 g	pitted black olives

4	red mullet, each 8 oz/250 g, filleted
	salt
	pepper

For the balsamic vinaigrette:

1 tbsp	balsamic vinegar
3 tbsp	olive oil
	salt
	pepper

Christian Étienne is very fond of Provence, where he was born and grew up. The restaurant that bears his name is located in the center of Avignon, beside the Pope's Palace, and the building once belonged to the Papal Vice-Legate. Inside the restaurant, 15th-century frescoes are a reminder of these splendors.

Red mullet from the Mediterranean Sea is prized above all for its delicate flesh, which is tender and yet firm. In this recipe, you can use red snapper instead, or you could use monkfish or cod. Ask for the fish to be filleted for you.

In summer, the chef's menu revolves around tomatoes. Tomatoes came from Peru originally. They were imported to Spain in the 16th century, where they were regarded initially as poisonous. It took almost 200 years for tomatoes to be common on the tables of Europe.

Roma, a variety of plum tomato, is also known by the name *olivette*. Plum tomatoes are cultivated mainly in Provence and Languedoc-Roussillon, and they are available between July and October. When you buy them, the flesh should be firm, the skin shiny, and they should be a uniform color. You can use other varieties of tomato, but they must be able to withstand frying in very hot oil.

Christian Étienne never fails to use garlic, and he gives the place of honor in this recipe to shallots. This relative of onion and garlic gives the tomatoes a fine flavor.

You could serve rice with the red mullet, or potato mashed with olive oil.

Wash the tomatoes and cut them into slices ¼–½ in/1 cm thick.

Fry the tomatoes in 2 tbsp hot olive oil for 2 minutes.

Peel the shallots and garlic and chop them finely. Sprinkle them over the tomatoes and sweat them briefly. Season with salt and pepper, turn off the burner, and leave the tomatoes to infuse.

Bed of Pan-Fried Tomatoes

Coarsely chop the black olives. To make the balsamic vinaigrette, beat together the salt, pepper, and balsamic vinegar. Beat in the olive oil, then add the chopped olives.

Using a spatula, lift the tomato slices out of the skillet and arrange them on a plate. Season the red mullet fillets with salt and pepper.

Fry the red mullet fillets in the remaining olive oil for 2 minutes on the skin side and 1 minute on the flesh side. Arrange the red mullet fillets on the bed of tomatoes, and dress them with the balsamic vinaigrette with olives.

Sea Bass

Preparation time: 30 minutes
Cooking time: 30 minutes
Difficulty: ★

Serves 4

3½ lb/1.5 kg	sea bass
2 bulbs	fennel
5 tbsp	olive oil
2 cups/500 ml	fish stock (see below)
	salt
	pepper

For the garnish:

	fennel tops
1 pinch	saffron strands

Sea bass on braised fennel with saffron-scented fish sauce is one of the classics of Provençal cuisine. This fish is a member of the serranid family and is prized above all for its fine, firm flesh that contains little fat and tastes delicious. You could use red mullet, red snapper, cod, or monkfish instead.

If you find it difficult to fillet fish, ask for the fish to be filleted when you buy them. Try to get a large fish with skin, because this browns slowly during frying.

The fish stock is prepared as follows: Sweat a finely chopped onion in 1 tablespoon of olive oil. Then add 1 tablespoon of tomato paste and cook everything for one minute so that the acidic flavor of the tomato paste softens. Then add 2¼ pounds/1 kilogram of rock fish that have been cleaned and gutted, as well as any fish trimmings from the sea bass (see main method, below). Peel a bulb of garlic, crush the cloves, and add them to the fish. Season the fish well. Add enough water to cover, 1 scant ounce/20 grams saffron strands, a sprig of thyme, and a bay leaf. Simmer the stock ingredient for 20 minutes, then strain the stock back into a pan. Continue to boil the stock until it turns syrupy, then beat in 3 tablespoons of olive oil.

As an ingredient, fennel is just as important as the fish stock. Its aniseed flavor is a wonderful accompaniment to fish. Fennel is a wide bulb of tightly packed leaves and is eaten as a vegetable. When you buy it, it should be firm and white, well rounded, with no blemishes.

The sea bass with braised fennel and saffron-scented fish sauce develops a delicate flavor of the sea in combination with a fresh aroma.

Scale and fillet the fish. To do this, position the knife at gill height and work backwards from the head along the stomach to the tail, freeing the fillet from the backbone. Remove any remaining small bones with a pair of tweezers.

Reserve the fish trimmings for the fish stock. Cut the fish fillets into 4 thick pieces.

Wash the fennel and slice it thickly, reserving the stalk.

Fry the sliced fennel in 2 tbsp olive oil for 1–2 minutes, until golden brown.

Braise the fennel in the fish stock for about 20 minutes. Drain and cut out the root. Season the stock to taste with salt and pepper.

Season the sea bass fillets with salt and pepper. Fry them in the remaining olive oil for 5 minutes on each side. Pour a pool of sauce onto the plate. Place a slice of fennel in the middle, and put a fish fillet on top. Garnish with the fennel tops and saffron strands.

Eel Ragout

Preparation time:	30 minutes
Cooking time:	25 minutes
Difficulty:	★★

Serves 4

3 lb/1.2 kg	eel
2 oz/50 g	onions
3 oz/75 g	shallots
2	tomatoes
2 cloves	garlic
2 tbsp	olive oil
¼ cup	wheat flour
	salt
	pepper
	cayenne pepper

| 1 cup/250 ml | white wine |
| ⅓ cup + 1½ tbsp/100 ml | fish stock |

For the herbs:

1 bunch	fresh chervil
1 bunch	fresh chives
1 bunch	fresh flat-leaf parsley
1 sprig	fresh tarragon

For the croutons:

| 4 slices | bread |
| ⅛ stick/15 g | butter |

The eel is truly a special fish. It can grow up to around 3 feet/1 meter, and its smooth body is slippery to the touch. Eels hatch in the Sargasso Sea near Bermuda, and the larvae migrate to Europe, which takes two to three years. On arrival, they swim upriver, where they reach sexual maturity. All eels are born female, then some change sex in the course of their lives. Eels swim back to the sea to return to their breeding grounds, and it is at this stage that fishermen catch them. Only female eels are sold as food.

This dish is a classic from the Sète region, close to the Thau Basin, where eels are plentiful. Because they spoil quickly they are sold very fresh and the skin removed at the last minute. You should consume the eel on the day of purchase. Ask your fishmonger to prepare the eel for you, because it's laborious work. At least the spine can be removed with a single incision. If you buy pre-skinned and pre-cleaned eel, you need to check how fresh it is. Eel is also available frozen, jellied in cans, or smoked.

In ancient times the Romans regarded eel as a delicacy and the epitome of refined taste, which is why they were often served at splendid banquets. Nowadays they are found in many French recipes, especially along the west coast. Exports from the Languedoc region are flourishing, because the greatest eel lovers live abroad: The Japanese, Scandinavians, and Italians seem to be almost obsessed with them.

Eel is considered a fatty fish, but it is very high in vitamins A and D, and is an excellent source of protein.

This hearty fish ragout is often prepared with red wine and herbs.

Obtain an eel that has been skinned, cleaned, and gutted. Cut the eel into 2 in/5 cm chunks.

Plunge the eel chunks in boiling, salted water for 1 minute to remove the fat. Refresh them immediately in cold water. Drain the eel chunks and put to one side. Peel and chop very finely the onions and shallots. Skin the tomatoes and chop the flesh. Peel and crush the garlic.

Heat 1 tbsp olive oil in a pan. Sweat the shallot, onion, garlic, and chopped tomato for 6 minutes until very soft and well combined.

à la Palavasienne

Dust the eel chunks with flour. Put them in the tomato sauce. Season to taste with salt, pepper, and cayenne pepper. Simmer the eel for 8–10 minutes.

Add the white wine and simmer until reduced by one third. Add the fish stock and boil for 5 minutes. While the stock is boiling, cut the bread into triangles and fry them in the butter. Wash the herbs and chop them finely.

Add the remaining olive oil to the sauce. Add the chopped herbs to the sauce at the last moment. Check the sauce seasoning and adjust as necessary. Serve the eel chunks with the tomato sauce. Garnish with the croutons.

Monkfish o⟩

Preparation time:	30 minutes
Time to preserve the garlic:	35 minutes
Cooking time:	45 minutes
Difficulty:	★

Serves 4

3½ lb/1.5 kg	monkfish
2 tbsp	olive oil
	salt
	pepper

For the eggplant purée:

3½ lb/1.5 kg	eggplant
5 tbsp	olive oil

⅙ cup/20 g	pine kernels
	salt
	pepper

For the bell pepper sauce:

1	shallot
1 tbsp	olive oil
1 lb/500 g	red bell peppers
8 oz/250 g	tomatoes
1 tbsp	tomato paste
1 clove	garlic
2 cups/ 500 ml	fish stock
4–5/5 g	star anise
	salt, pepper

For the garnish:

4 cloves	garlic
3½ tbsp/50 ml	olive oil
1 sprig	fresh chervil

Monkfish medallions is one of the most popular dishes in the south of France. Our head chef has refined this recipe in his Monte Carlo restaurant, saying, "Here the firm flesh of monkfish marries with the sun-drenched flavor of red peppers and the soft smoothness of the eggplant purée, accompanied by toasted pine kernels."

In the Mediterranean, monkfish is commonly known as *baudroie*, but is also called *lotte de mer*. Despite its unattractive appearance, it is highly prized—on account of its firm flesh. If you have trouble filleting fish, ask the fishmonger to do it for you when you purchase the fish. Depending on what is available at the time, many French people use little mackerel, known as *lisettes*, instead.

When prepared as a sauce, as it is in this recipe, the red bell pepper develops its full flavor. This fruit, used as a vegetable, is very closely related to the spicy, elongated pep-

pers from which it differs in size and shape. Red peppers are the most difficult to keep. You should buy firm, smooth fruit with a green stalk that is securely attached to the pepper.

The fish blends extremely well with the eggplant purée. Don't use big eggplants because their flesh is often fibrous and there are too many seeds. When you are buying eggplant, ensure that the fruit has a smooth, tight, shiny skin without blemishes. If the flavor of eggplant is too strong for your taste, you could serve puréed zucchini with the fish instead.

Clean and gut the fish and make a cut in the outer skin with a pair of scissors. Remove the remaining skins. Cut off the ventral and dorsal fins, and the tail in the opposite direction. Cut the fish into 12 medallions.

Using a vegetable peeler, peel strips of skin off the eggplant, keeping them for later. Cut the eggplant in half lengthwise and scoop out the seeds. Season the eggplant. Drizzle each half with 2 tbsp olive oil. Place on a baking sheet and bake for 45 minutes at 320 °F/160 °C.

To make the eggplant purée, scoop out the cooked flesh. Chop it finely with the pine kernels. Season to taste with salt and pepper and set to one side. Fry the cloves of garlic in olive oil and keep them for the garnish.

Bell Pepper Sauce

To make the bell pepper sauce, sauté the finely chopped shallot in the olive oil. Add the diced red peppers and tomatoes, tomato paste, crushed garlic, fish stock, and star anise. Simmer for 15 minutes. Purée with a hand blender and pass through a sieve. Season to taste.

Cut the strips of eggplant skin into diamonds. Fry them in the remaining olive oil. Put them to one side for the garnish.

Season the monkfish medallions. Fry them in olive oil for 3 minutes. Arrange 3 tbsp eggplant purée on a plate, each with a monkfish medallion in the center. Spoon the bell pepper sauce around the fish and eggplant. Garnish with chervil, fried eggplant diamonds, and fried garlic.

Pot-au-feu

Preparation time: 30 minutes
Soaking the
   marrow bones: 24 hours
Cooking time: 35 minutes
Difficulty: ★

Serves 4

For the vegetables:
2	carrots
2	baby turnips or kohlrabi
2 sticks	celery
1	potato
4	baby onions

¾ cup/200 ml	fish stock
1 lb/500 g	green asparagus

4 pieces	sea bass, each 5 oz/150 g
4 pieces	marrow bone, 1 in/3 cm in diameter
4 tsp	truffle juice
1	bay leaf
1	small truffle
1	potato
	oil for frying
	rock salt
1 tsp	olive oil
	salt, pepper

For the garnish:
	celery leaves (optional)

A *pot-au-feu* is very specifically French. What was once a farmer's stew consists of broth, meat, and vegetables. Although there are countless recipes for this dish, our chef has had an idea for an innovative version, replacing the meat with fish.

Mediterranean sea bass is a member of the serranid family. This is a fish that is very popular in the region. Ask your fishmonger for wild sea bass, which has a much better flavor than the farmed fish. If you can't find sea bass, you could always use porgy instead.

The use of truffles gives this dish an added attraction. These highly coveted and expensive fungi were known in ancient times. The Ancient Egyptians liked them best surrounded in goose fat and baked, and the Greeks and Romans ascribed extraordinary aphrodisiacal powers to them.

The fungus itself is an irregular, rounded lump. It's usually black or dark brown, sometimes gray, or white.

When you buy the vegetables ensure that you buy large specimens. After cooking the vegetables, refresh them in ice water so they retain their attractive green color. Marrow bone is often used in *pot-au-feu*. It must be soaked for 24 hours in cold water, changing the water frequently.

When serving, first arrange the vegetables on the plate and then put the fish on them. The broth is poured over the top. You could also drizzle a few drops of olive oil over the dish if you like.

Wash and peel the vegetables. Leave a small piece of stalk on the carrots and turnips. Cut the celery into pieces and carefully remove any stringy bits.

Put the fish stock in a pan and add 3 cups/750 ml water. Season with salt and pepper. Add the vegetables. As soon as they are cooked, remove them, and set them aside. Cook the asparagus separately in salted water for 10 minutes.

Cook the pieces of fish and marrowbone in the vegetable liquor for 7–8 minutes. Add the truffle juice, the bay leaf, and half the truffle cut into small dice.

with Sea Bass

Heat the vegetables in the broth and add the other half of the truffle, sliced.

Wash the potato, do not peel it. Cut it into wedges lengthwise. Blanch the potato in boiling, salted water, then refresh it in cold water for 2 minutes. Pat the wedges dry, then fry them.

Drain the potato wedges on kitchen paper and dredge them in the rock salt while still warm. Arrange the drained vegetables on the plate, then the drained fish and marrow bone. Pour over the broth. Drizzle a little olive oil over the dish, and garnish with celery leaves, if using.

Scallops with

Preparation time:	1 hour
Soaking the scallops:	45 minutes
Cooking time:	5 minutes
Difficulty:	★

Serves 4

12	medium scallops
5 oz/150 g	mesclun
	rock salt

For the stuffing:

2 cloves	garlic
1 bunch	fresh flat-leaf parsley
½	fresh chile

1	large shallot
1	scallion
1 stick/100 g	butter
2 slices	white bread
2 tbsp	olive oil
	juice of ½ lemon
	salt

For the balsamic vinaigrette:

3 tbsp	olive oil
1 tbsp	balsamic vinegar
	salt
	pepper

For the garnish:

	rock salt

What is original about this recipe is the way in which the scallops are prepared. Our chef cooks the meat in the shell. No great culinary skills are required for this dish and yet, because of its ingredients, it is representative of the delicious ingredients from the south of France.

Scallops, *coquilles Saint-Jacques* in French, are a large mussel that lives on the floor of the Atlantic Ocean and the Mediterranean Sea, and which moves by opening and closing. It's flat on one side and corrugated on the other. The ridged shell measures 4–6 inches/10–15 centimeters across. You should only buy scallops that are tightly closed. Ask your fishmonger to prepare the scallops without cutting through the muscle. Don't forget to soak them at home. The rock salt is used to support the scallops so that they don't tip over.

The firm, white flesh of this shellfish, which is very popular in France, has a delicate flavor. Scallop fishing is regulated in Europe, and usually takes place between the end of September and beginning of May. In the past, a scallop-shell badge was a sign that a pilgrim had made the journey to the shrine at Santiago de Compostela, in Spain.

The savory stuffing is an important component of this dish and gives the scallops a slightly acidic flavor. Depending on what is available, our chef says you can also enrich the stuffing with black olives, diced lemon, or capers.

Mesclun consists of baby salad leaves from the south of France. These include winter frisée, radicchio, Belgian endive, corn salad, dandelion, chervil, oak leaf lettuce, and purslane. You can buy ready mixed bags of mesclun.

Open the scallops. Run a knife blade along between the shells without cutting through the muscle. Remove the flat side of the shell.

Clean the scallops by gripping beneath the dark pouch and pulling out the membrane and beard. The meat should stay attached to the shell. Soak the scallops for 45 minutes to rinse out sand and other contaminants.

To make the stuffing, chop the garlic, parsley, chile, shallot, and scallion very finely. Dice the butter and bread.

Mixed Salad Leaves

Mix together the diced bread and butter. Add the other stuffing ingredients and the olive oil. Add the lemon juice and stir well to combine.

Season the scallop meat with salt, and gently lift it with a spoon without completely dislodging it. Fill each scallop shell with 1 tbsp stuffing and place the shell on a baking sheet filled with rock salt. Bake the scallops in the oven for 5 minutes at 465 °F/250 °C.

Rinse the mixed salad leaves. Beat together the vinaigrette ingredients. Place a scallop shell on a bed of rock salt and serve accompanied by the mixed salad.

Stuffed Sardines

Preparation time:	30 minutes
Cooking time:	45 minutes
Difficulty:	★

Serves 4

12	sardines, 5 oz/150 g each
1 bunch	mint
1	brocciu (Corsican cheese, approximately 14 oz/400 g
2	eggs

5 oz/150 g	Corsican tomme (cheese)
	salt and pepper

For the tomato sauce:

1	onion
3½ tbsp/50 ml	olive oil
½ bunch	parsley
1 clove	garlic
1 lb/500 g	tomatoes
3½ tbsp/50 ml	white wine
	salt and pepper

For the garnish:

	mint leaves

Typical of the Corsican coast, this dish of sardines filled with *brocciu* cheese would have been a regular favorite at any fisherman's family table. A wonderful combination of ingredients from the sea and the mountains, this specialty is easy to prepare, and is often served accompanied by spinach or Swiss chard.

Traditional fishing methods are still used on Corsica. Renowned for their delicious flavor, the sardines that abound in the waters of the Mediterranean in the spring and summer are caught in trawl nets. Fairly large fish should be used for this dish, as these are the most suitable for stuffing. Whole squid "pockets" are a delicious alternative.

Many Corsican dishes involve the use of *brocciu* in a stuffing. Traditionally made by shepherds from the whey of goat's or ewe's milk, mixed with whole milk, water, and

salt, this cheese is creamy, light, and mild, and much used in cooking. It has been awarded a coveted French *appellation d'origine contrôlée*, guaranteeing its quality and authenticity.

The taste of the sardines in this summery dish is enhanced by the refreshing flavor of wild mint, commonly found throughout the Mediterranean. Believed in Antiquity to have calming properties, we know today that it is rich in calcium, iron, and vitamins. Choose mint with firm stems and a good green color. If you have more than you need, you can dry it by placing it in a well-ventilated place away from the light. It can then be chopped finely and stored in a glass jar.

The finishing touch to this colorful and delicious dish is the tomato sauce, usually made from home-grown vegetables.

Prepare the sardines. Break off the head, then remove the innards and central bone. Rinse in running water (whole fresh, filleted sardines can also be bought at good fishmongers).

Wash the bunch of mint. Detach the leaves and slice finely with a knife.

Put the brocciu in a bowl and mash it together with the eggs and the chopped mint. Season with salt and pepper. Mix well.

with Brocciu

For the sauce, brown the chopped onion in the olive oil. Add the chopped parsley and garlic. Add the pulped tomatoes and season with salt and pepper. Pour over the white wine and cook the mixture for about 15 minutes. Blend the sauce in a food processor.

Place the filleted sardines on the work-top. Using a spoon, fill them with the cheese stuffing, propping them up one against the other on a plate, to prevent the sauce from spilling out.

Pour the tomato sauce into an ovenproof dish. Arrange the sardines in the dish. Scatter with shavings of Corsican tomme cheese. Cook at 350 °F/180 °C for about 30 minutes. Serve the sardines on plates with the sauce. Garnish with the mint leaves.

Tians of Sea Bass with

Preparation time:	40 minutes
Cooking time:	40 minutes
Difficulty:	★

Serves 4

| 12 | spinach leaves (to wrap the tians) |
| 1¼ lb/600 g | sea bass fillets salt and freshly ground pepper |

For the stuffing:

7 oz/200 g	spinach leaves
11 oz/300 g	brocciu (Corsican soft cheese)
½ bunch	parsley
1 sprig	persia (wild marjoram)

| 1 | egg |
| | salt and pepper |

For the tomato coulis:

12	basil leaves
1	scallion (spring onion)
5 sprigs	parsley
2 cloves	garlic
3½ tbsp/50 ml	olive oil
11 oz/300 g	ripe tomatoes
	salt and pepper

This elegant dish of sea bass with *brocciu* and a tomato coulis uses typically Corsican ingredients. Vincent Tabarani has created a truly delicious recipe that combines the best of the island's seas and mountains. Corsica's popular *brocciu* cheese stuffing is combined here with fish. Easy to prepare, this is a convivial dish to share with friends.

In the old days on Corsica, a young bride would be welcomed by her mother-in-law with a gift of a bowl of *caghiatu*, milk curds. This country custom emphasizes the importance attached throughout history to the local cheese, *brocciu*. Still made using traditional methods from a mixture of the whey and whole milk of goats or ewes, the cheese now holds a coveted *appellation d'origine contrôlée*, guaranteeing its authenticity and quality. It has a very mild taste, and can be used in cooking, for both sweet and savory dishes.

Stuffing made with *brocciu* and a hint of *persia* (wild marjoram) is a classic of Corsican cuisine. It is most commonly used as a filling for pasta envelopes, but marries equally well with fish, as will be seen here. Sea bass, much prized by the people of the Mediterranean for its delicate, firm flesh, is also found in the Atlantic. Other fish that can be used for this recipe are dentex or trout, the latter being common in Corsican streams.

The fish tians are parcels of stuffed fish wrapped in spinach leaves. Coming originally from Persia, spinach can be found on the market stalls in both spring and fall. Swiss chard leaves may also be used. With their accompanying tomato coulis, these fish tians make a most attractive and colorful dish.

Wash the spinach leaves. In salted water, blanch the spinach for the stuffing, followed by the 12 leaves to be used to wrap the tians. Refresh the latter in iced water.

Prepare the coulis by browning the basil and chopped scallion, the chopped stalks of the parsley (reserve the leaves), and the crushed garlic in the olive oil. Add the chopped tomatoes and season with salt and pepper. Cook for about 30 minutes, then blend in a food processor.

For the stuffing, mix together in a bowl the brocciu, parsley leaves, persia, and chopped spinach leaves. Add salt and pepper and then the egg. Mash the mixture together with a fork.

Brocciu and Tomato Coulis

Check the bass fillets for bones and re-move these. Cut the fish into thin pieces weighing about 2 oz/50 g each.

Spread the 12 spinach leaves on a flat surface. Place one fillet of fish on each leaf. Season. Cover with stuffing. Place a second piece of fish on top.

Wrap the fish in the spinach leaf. Place the completed parcels in a dish and pour over the tomato coulis. Cook in a medium oven (350 °F/180 °C) for 8–10 minutes. Serve the tians with the tomato coulis on plates.

Stockfish Frecole

Preparation time: 30 minutes
Desalting
  the fish: 48 hours
Cooking time: 20 minutes
Difficulty: ★

Serves 4

1¼ lb/500 g	stockfish
1⅓ cups/	
150 g	walnut kernels
10 oz/250 g	stale bread
1 clove	garlic

2 tsp/10 g	dried oregano
	salt (optional)
	pepper
3 tbsp	olive oil

For the garnish:

	walnuts
	oregano leaves

The word *frecole* is Italian dialect for the crumb of a loaf of bread, which in this region is often used instead of fine breadcrumbs. This typical, dried-cod dish from Avellino is traditional Christmas fare.

Cod, which is highly regarded by other nations as well as the Italians, is one of the most frequently caught fish worldwide. In Norway, it is made into stockfish: In other words, it is cut into two and heavily salted before being left to dry in the open air. It is therefore absolutely essential to soak it thoroughly for 48 hours before use.

Thanks to its lean, tasty flesh, *baccalà*, as the Italians call stockfish, is a gourmet food. In this recipe, it is possible to substitute sole or gold bream, in which case Michelina Fischetti recommends that you add tomatoes and parsley to round off the dish.

The *frecole* mixture consists of garlic, oregano, olive oil and walnuts. The nuts give the dish bite, as well as being healthy and nutritious. Walnuts should always be kept in an airtight container in a cool, dry place. In order to "rejuvenate" them, soak them for a few hours in hot milk. The skins will then fall off practically by themselves and the nuts will be fresh and crunchy again. You can of course use filberts or almonds as an alternative.

Oregano is a wild variety of marjoram with a rather stronger taste. It is indispensable in Italian cookery, especially as a seasoning in many tomato dishes.

Stockfish *frecole* is an excellent dish for festive occasions, not just at Christmas time.

Using a large knife, cut the stockfish into even-sized pieces and remove the bones.

Lay the pieces of fish in a bowl of water. Soak the fish for 48 hours to remove the salt, changing the water several times.

Crush the walnuts with a pestle and mortar.

with Nuts

Rub the bread into crumbs with your hands. Peel and crush the garlic.

Place the breadcrumbs, garlic, oregano, and crushed walnuts in a salad bowl. Season with salt (if desired) and pepper. Add 2 tbsp olive oil and combine the ingredients, using your hands.

Oil an ovenproof dish with 1 tbsp olive oil, place the fish in it, and sprinkle over the nut mixture. Bake in the oven for 20 minutes at 350° F/180° C. Serve garnished with whole walnuts and a few oregano leaves.

Preparation time:	1 hour
Cooking time:	55 minutes
Difficulty:	★★

Serves 4

8 oz/200 g	eel
8 oz/200 g	salmon trout
4	live crayfish
12 oz/320 g	swordfish
1	small, dried chile
	olive oil
1 clove	garlic
1 tbsp	chopped parsley
1 scant cup/	
200 ml	white wine

11 oz/300g	tomatoes
	salt
	pepper

For the fish stock:

	head, bones, and fins
	of the trout
1	small stick celery
½	carrot
½	onion
3	basil leaves
	salt

To serve:

toasted slices of
farmhouse bread
extra-virgin olive oil
chopped parsley

The Serchio river, with its plentiful supply of fish and crustaceans, flows past Sauro Brunicardi's restaurant, "La Mora." This has given the chef the idea of transforming a traditional recipe from Livorno, on the coast of the Tyrrhenian Sea, and adapting it to use freshwater fish from the Serchio. Legend has it that, a long time ago, a poor widow from Livorno used to beg for the waste from fish and mollusks in order to make a thin soup, which is how *cacciucco* originated. With time, the list of ingredients grew somewhat, to include fish from the region as well as crustaceans. The tasty sauce in this *cacciucco* consists of tomatoes, garlic, parsley, white wine, and herbs.

With the exception of the swordfish, the fish used by Sauro Brunicardi are mainly freshwater fish. Freshwater fish are seldom eaten in Italy, because their flesh is considered insipid, but eels are certainly an exception to this. They are

caught in southern Tuscany in the Bay of Orbetello when they swim down the Albegna River toward the sea.

When you buy fresh eels, make sure that they have been killed and prepared by the fishmonger on the day of purchase; they should be as fresh as possible. Eels are also sold smoked, canned, or frozen.

When preparing the salmon trout, be sure to remove all the bones, or ask the fishmonger to fillet it for you. Sauro Brunicardi serves his *cacciucco* with Tuscan bread baked in wood-fired ovens, which has a very firm crust. The bread is first toasted and then drizzled with oil; it is wonderful for soaking up the sauce.

Obtain prepared eel. Cut the eel into pieces 1–1½ in/3–4 cm long.

Make a cut along the lower edge and gut the salmon trout. Slice along the backbone and make a horizontal cut just above the tail. Run the knife along the backbone to loosen the fillets. Cut these into strips 1½–2 in/4–5 cm wide and 4 in/10 cm long.

Place the head, bones, and fins of the salmon trout in a saucepan of salted water. Add the celery, carrot, peeled onion, basil, and salt to taste. Simmer for 30 minutes over low heat. Strain and set aside.

Add the crayfish to a pan of bubbling boiling water and cook for 2 minutes. Cut along them lengthways. Slice the swordfish. Cut the chile and remove the seeds.

Fry the peeled and sliced garlic in oil in a large skillet. Add the parsley and finely chopped chile and sauté for 1 minute. Add the swordfish, eel, crayfish, and salmon trout and cook for 5 minutes, stirring constantly. Quench with white wine.

Add the chopped tomatoes and cook for 5 minutes over high heat. Season with salt and pepper. Pour over the fish stock and simmer for 10 minutes. Transfer the fish, crayfish, sauce, and the slices of bread drizzled with olive oil onto plates and garnish with chopped parsley.

Preparation time: 45 minutes
Cooking time: 45 minutes
Difficulty: ★★

Serves 4

2 lb/800 g	cuttlefish
6 oz/150 g	sliced bread
9 tbsp	extra-virgin olive oil
1¼ lb/500 g	cherry tomatoes
1	small chile
1 clove	garlic
	salt
1 scant cup/ 200 ml	rosé wine

The "Taverna del Capitano" in the Bay of Naples is the restaurant of Alfonso Caputo, who has made a specialty of fish and seafood dishes. When preparing stuffed cuttlefish, the filling traditionally consists of the tentacles, minced pork or veal, and sliced bread. The chef suggests a lighter filling, however, mixing the tentacles with cherry tomatoes, bread cubes, garlic, and chile.

Cuttlefish belong to the cephalopod family and are classed as marine mollusks. They have a dark skin, but their flesh is tender and extremely tasty. They are fished from the depths of the sea, using dragnets and are a particular favorite of Neapolitan cooks, who either stuff them or serve them in soups or with pasta. Sliced bread is the perfect filling. After you have carefully removed the crusts, stack the slices of bread on top of one another and cut into cubes.

The strong, red color and mildly acidic flavor of the cherry tomatoes make a huge contribution to the success of this dish. They go extremely well with both the cuttlefish and the subtle acidity of the rosé wine used for cooking. Alfonso Caputo recommends a Lacrima Christi from Campagna, but any other rosé wine, or even white wine, can be used.

Cooking the cuttlefish so that the outside and the filling are equally tender is the only difficulty with this recipe. When the sauce has reduced and started to thicken, the cuttlefish are just right. Cut through them carefully, so that the filling does not fall out of the outer rings. Place three medallions and a little sauce on each plate and then garnish with a little chopped parsley.

Cut off the heads of the cuttlefish and remove the innards. Pull off the skin and rinse thoroughly under running water.

Dice the tentacles. Cut the bread into small cubes.

Heat 2 tbsp olive oil in a pan and fry the tentacles. Add half the cherry tomatoes, the bread cubes, the finely sliced chile, and the sliced garlic. Cook over high heat.

Cuttlefish

Add the cuttlefish to the pan. Spoon in the filling and seal with a wooden skewer.

Pour the remaining olive oil into an ovenproof dish. Add the remaining cherry tomatoes and season with salt. Lay the cuttlefish in the dish and pour over the wine. Arrange the remaining filling around the cuttlefish and cover the dish with aluminum foil. Bake in the oven for 40 minutes at 340° F/170° C.

When the cuttlefish and stuffing are both cooked, set aside in a warm place. Sieve and purée the vegetables from the baking dish, using some of the liquor, sufficient to make a smooth sauce. Slice the cuttlefish into 3 rings and arrange on plates in the sauce. Serve very hot.

Red Mullet Fillet

Preparation time:	40 minutes
Resting time for the polenta:	1 hour
Cooking time:	10 minutes
Difficulty:	★

Serves 4

4	red mullet, each 8 oz/200 g
12	cherry tomatoes
	salt
	pepper
4 tbsp	sunflower oil

For the nut pesto:

8 oz/200 g	walnut kernels
2 cloves	garlic
1½ oz/40 g	fresh basil
1⅔ cups/ 400 ml	olive oil
	salt
	pepper

For the polenta:

2 cups/500 ml	milk
½ stick/60 g	butter
⅔ cup/100 g	cornmeal
	salt
	pepper

World-famous *pesto genovese* is made with basil and pine nuts, and eaten with pasta. Here, Sergio Pais introduces his own variation on this classic dish. Instead of pine nuts he uses walnuts and, being a fish lover, serves his pesto with red mullet fillets, which are highly regarded in Liguria.

Red mullet, with its characteristic three scales beneath the eyes, was popular even in ancient times. Its firm, tasty flesh requires only brief cooking. Even if the fishmonger has filleted the fish for you, do not forget to remove any remaining small bones with tweezers. Depending on availability, you can substitute red snapper, gold bream, or herring for the red mullet.

In Ligurian cooking, walnuts are used mainly for *salsa dei noci*, a nut sauce. Walnuts originated in Asia and were introduced to Italy by the Romans in ancient times.

The most important ingredient in any pesto is the basil, with its strong fragrance and brilliant green color. A particularly fine-tasting variety of basil flourishes in the gardens of Genoa. This aromatic plant is an import from India and its name is derived from the ancient Greek word *basilikos*, meaning "royal." In the kitchen, basil is added mainly to tomato and pasta dishes.

These red mullet fillets are served with polenta. Polenta is a specialty from the Veneto region that is now available all over northern Italy. Culinary purists still cook polenta over wood fires, then cut it on a wooden board using the wetted blunt edge of a knife.

For the polenta, heat the milk, add the butter, and pour in the cornmeal. Stir with a wooden spatula and cook for 3–4 minutes. Season with salt and pepper.

Spread out a damp dish cloth and spread the polenta on it. Fold up the cloth securely and leave to stand for 1 hour.

Remove the scales from the mullet and cut into the fin. Make a cut from the head along the backbone as far as the tail. Turn the fish over and repeat the process on the other side. Cut off the fillets and remove the small bones. Make an indentation in the fillets at one end.

with Nut Pesto

For the pesto, mix the walnuts, garlic, basil leaves, and olive oil in a blender and season to taste with salt and pepper.

Lay the fish fillets in a skillet, skin side down. Brush the fillets with pesto. Add the halved cherry tomatoes. Season with salt and pepper. Bake in the oven for 3 minutes at 350° F/180° C (if necessary, unscrew the skillet handle beforehand).

Unwrap the polenta and cut into regular slices. Pour the sunflower oil into a pan and fry the polenta slices until golden yellow. Season with salt and pepper. Serve the fish fillets with polenta and some of the pesto.

Turbot Fillet

Preparation time: 20 minutes
Cooking time: 1 hour 15 minutes
Difficulty: ★★

Serves 4

salt	
1¼ cups/ 200 g	white cornmeal
1	turbot weighing 2¼–2¾ lb/1–1.2 kg
2 cloves	garlic
6 tbsp	extra-virgin olive oil
1½ tbsp	white wine vinegar pepper

1 scant cup/ 200 ml	white wine salt

To serve:

	coarse ground black pepper

We owe *boreto*, a fish sauce consisting of vinegar, white wine, black pepper, and garlic, to the fishermen of Friuli and Venezia Giulia. It is used to enhance eel, turbot, and perch dishes. Paolo Zoppolatti serves his turbot in *boreto* on a bed of white polenta.

Turbot, with its lozenge-shaped body, is found both in the Atlantic and the Mediterranean. With its tender, succulent white flesh, it is one of the finest fish. Our chef recommends frying the fillets briefly before pouring the *boreto* over them.

White polenta, which has a more subtle flavor than the yellow variety, is very popular in Friuli as an accompaniment to broiled or fried fish. Since the 17th century, when corn was introduced by Venetian merchants, this sumptuous dish has numbered among the culinary treasures of the Adriatic region.

Paolo Zoppolatti uses classic cornmeal, which means that 40–45 minutes are required for preparation. Pre-cooked polenta, which is ready in 20 minutes, however, is also available. Polenta is traditionally cooked in a copper cauldron over a wood fire (copper is a very good conductor of heat). The water must be heated until it is nearly boiling. In order to determine whether it has reached the correct temperature, test with a pinch of cornmeal: If a whirlpool is formed, then the rest of the cornmeal can be added. Stir well with a wooden spoon, constantly reversing direction, until the consistency of thick oatmeal porridge has been reached. To make the polenta smoother, cook the cornmeal in a mixture of milk and water.

To serve, you can add a little olive oil to bind the fish sauce. Garnish the fish with a few fried cherry tomatoes.

In a saucepan, bring 3½ cups/800 ml salted water to just under boiling point. Add the cornmeal and cook for 40 minutes, stirring constantly, until the consistency of thick oatmeal porridge is reached.

Cut open the turbot along the backbone and fillet it. Chop the bones and the other off-cuts of the fish.

Fry the peeled, halved garlic cloves in 2 tbsp olive oil in a skillet. Add the bones and other off-cuts of the fish, remove the garlic, and fry over high heat for 5 minutes.

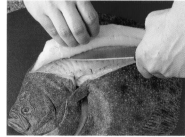

with Polenta

Add the vinegar and scrape around the bottom of the pan with a wooden spatula to incorporate all the browned ingredients. Season with pepper. Reduce over medium heat for 5 minutes.

Quench with white wine, scrape the bottom of the pan again, and add some water. Reduce for another 10 minutes, season with salt, then strain.

Season the turbot fillets with salt. Fry in the remaining olive oil for 5 minutes on each side. Serve each fillet on a bed of polenta, pour the fish sauce all round, and sprinkle with ground black pepper.

Stockfish

Preparation time: 25 minutes
Desalting the fish: 48 hours
Cooking time: 30 minutes
Difficulty: ★

Serves 4

1¼ lb/500 g	stockfish
4 oz/100 g	potatoes
1	onion

1 stick	celery
8 oz/200 g	tomatoes
4 tbsp	olive oil
	salt
	pepper

The Fischettis are a good example of a typical, close-knit, southern Italian family.

The family's restaurant, "L'Oasis," is poised like a beehive high up in Vallesaccarda in the countryside around Avellino. On their magnificent estate, the 13 members of the Fischetti clan welcome their guests and experiment with traditional regional recipes, creating variations on them as a labor of love.

Stockfish is very popular, especially in the area around Naples. It can be prepared in many different ways. In bygone times, stockfish was important for a very specific reason: Salting and drying was the only method of preserving fish. With abundant supplies ensured, the population was even able to survive famines.

This colorful dish devised by the Fischetti family is typical of the Mediterranean. It owes its characteristic flavor to celery leaves; this plant is in plentiful supply in autumn and winter and is particularly appetizing when added to soups, sauces, and goulash.

The tomatoes add a classic Neapolitan accent to this dish. In Italy, tomatoes are eaten almost daily. The tomato, a member of the solanum family, used to be grown in gardens for home consumption, but now tomatoes are cultivated on a grand scale, especially in southern Italy, and are exported all over the world.

This stockfish recipe from the Fischetti family is simple to prepare, yet highly sophisticated!

Using a large knife, cut the stockfish into even-sized pieces and remove the bones.

Place the pieces of fish in a salad bowl full of water for 48 hours to remove the salt, changing the water several times.

Peel and chop the potatoes and onion. Wash the celery and cut the leaves into small pieces. Blanch, skin, and dice all the tomatoes.

'Casa Fischetti"

Heat the olive oil in a pan and sauté the onion for 5 minutes. Add the potatoes and cook for a further 5 minutes. Add the tomatoes and season with salt and pepper. Cook for another 5 minutes, stirring several times with a wooden spatula.

Drain the stockfish and remove the remaining bones. Add the pieces of fish to the vegetables in the pan and simmer for about 5 minutes.

Add the chopped celery leaves. Simmer for 10 minutes, stirring, then transfer the cod and vegetables onto plates to serve.

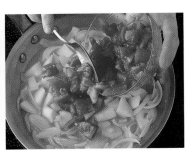

Preparation time:	40 minutes
Cooking time:	50 minutes
Difficulty:	★

Serves 4

4½ lb/2 kg	mussels
1	onion
1 scant cup/ 200 ml	white wine
1 scant cup/ 200 ml	light cream
2 tsp/10 g	butter
1 bunch	marjoram
	salt
	pepper

2	coarse salt
2	eggplants
	large onions
	sunflower oil for frying
1–1¼ cups / 125–150 g	capers
scant ½ cup/ 100 ml	white wine
scant ½ cup/ 100 ml	balsamic vinegar
	salt and pepper to taste

For the salad:

| 2 | red bell peppers |
| 2 tbsp | olive oil |

For the garnish:

| | marjoram |

This sophisticated dish is one of Sergio Pais' creations. The creamed mussels are served with a salad that tastes of sunshine and the south. This colorful dish is easy to prepare and will delight your guests. The Gulf of Taranto, which lies between the "heel" and "sole" of the boot of Italy, is famous for its mussel beds. The inhabitants call it *Mar piccolo*, or "little sea." The clear waters of the gulf are ideal for the cultivation of mussels.

When buying, choose only tightly closed mussels. They should be eaten within three days of harvesting. If any of them have broken shells or are slightly open, throw them away. The beards and any seeweed must be removed from the mussels. They should then be brushed thoroughly under running water.

The marjoram sauce is excellent and quite outstanding with the mussels. Marjoram is often used in cooking in

the Mediterranean. Originally from Asia, it is a relative of oregano but has a milder, subtler flavor reminiscent of mint and basil. It is used to flavor tomato dishes, salad dressings, stuffings, fish, and soups.

The salad consists of eggplants, onions, red pepper, and capers, and is enhanced with a dash of olive oil. Balsamic vinegar is made by reducing grape must, just as it was 900 years ago by the Duke d'Este and other noblemen in the area around Modena. Although regarded as a medicinal product, it was presented as a gift among the higher social echelons. High-quality balsamic vinegar is very expensive and, for this reason, is used very sparingly.

Lay the bell peppers on a baking sheet, pour over the olive oil, and sprinkle with salt. Roast in the oven for about 45 minutes, then remove the skin and seeds and cut into thin strips. Dice the eggplants and peel and slice the onions.

Pour the sunflower oil into a pan and sauté the eggplant cubes. Remove from the pan and drain. Brown the onions in another pan.

Transfer the eggplants, onions, and bell pepper strips to a salad bowl and add the capers.

Marjoram Sauce

Pour the white wine and balsamic vinegar into a small pan and reduce by half. Pour the reduced liquid onto the salad and stir carefully, then add salt and pepper.

Clean the mussels and remove the beards. Chop the onion. Heat the onion in a saucepan with the white wine. Add the mussels, cover, and infuse for 10 minutes. Remove the meat from the mussel shells.

Stir the cream, butter, and marjoram leaves together over a low heat. Season with salt and pepper and mix thoroughly. Add the mussel meat. Simmer for 3–4 minutes. Serve the salad with the mussels and sauce and garnish with a few marjoram leaves.

Sardines

Preparation time: *30 minutes*
Soaking time: *1 hour*
Marinating: *12–48 hours*
Cooking time: *30 minutes*
Difficulty: *★*

Serves 4

⅓ cup/50 g   raisins
1½ lb/600 g   sardines
1 scant cup/
100 g   flour

1⅔ cups/
400 ml   extra-virgin olive oil
12 oz/300 g   onions
scant ½ cup/
50 g   pine nuts
scant ½ cup/
100 ml   red wine vinegar
   salt

For centuries, the natives of the Veneto region have been enjoying sardines—known as *sarde in saor* in the local dialect—cooked in the same way that Biancarosa Zecchin prepares them. They are first coated in flour, then fried in oil, and finally marinated in a mixture of vinegar and onions. The nobility in the Veneto region used to enhance the dish with raisins and pine nuts to distinguish themselves from ordinary folk, who could not afford these ingredients. The dried fruit makes the dish more nutritious and gives it a festive touch. Sardines *in saor* are served in restaurants in Venice both as a small appetizer and as a main course.

In those parts of the lagoons around Venice where there are less *vaporetti* and motor-boat traffic, sardines are still plentiful. They used to constitute the majority of the day's catch, and were affordable by ordinary families as well as by the more affluent.

Medium-sized and smaller sardines are perfect for this recipe. When preparing these small fish, just remove the head and nothing else. After you have dipped them in flour, tap them with your finger to remove any excess. The oil used for frying the sardines is then used to sauté the chopped onion.

Biancarosa Zecchin recommends marinating the sardines for at least 12 hours before eating them. If they are marinated for as long as 48 hours, they will develop an even stronger flavor.

Serve three or four sardines per person. Spread the onion mixture on top and sprinkle with raisins and pine nuts, if desired.

Soak the raisins for 1 hour in lukewarm water. Remove the fish heads, then cut open and gut the sardines. Rinse them thoroughly under running water and pat them dry carefully.

Coat the sardines in flour.

Heat the olive oil in a large skillet. Fry the sardines for 5 minutes on each side. When they are golden yellow, drain them on paper towels. Reserve the oil.

n Saor

Peel and slice the onions.

Sauté the onions for 5 minutes in the oil used for frying the sardines. Stir frequently to ensure they cook evenly. Add the pine nuts, drained raisins, vinegar, and salt to taste. Cook for 15 minutes.

Arrange the sardines on a plate and spread the onion mixture on top. Leave to absorb the flavors for at least 12 hours. Serve cold, with a little strained marinade.

Salmon Trout

Preparation time:	35 minutes
Cooking time:	10 minutes
Difficulty:	★★

Serves 4

2	salmon trout, each 1 lb 6 oz/600 g
⅓ cup/50 g	wheat flour
	salt
scant ½ stick/ 50 g	butter
scant ½ cup/ 100 ml	white wine
1	unwaxed orange

For the fish stock:
1 carrot
1 onion

3	tomatoes
1 stick	celery
	trout heads, bones, and fins
3	basil leaves
	salt to taste

For the garnish:

1	orange
1	tomato
	chervil

For centuries, the major rivers draining the water from the Apennine Mountains and the Alps contained trout, perch, carp, sturgeon, and Allis shad (alosa alosa) in abundance. Industrial development and also, of course, environmental pollution have put an end to this plentiful supply of fish, and today most trout are farmed.

Although stocks of salmon trout have declined dramatically, some still remain in River Serchio, near Sauro Brunicardi's restaurant in Ponte a Moriano. They were customarily broiled or fried; here, however, our chef serves them in an orange sauce.

Sauro Brunicardi uses trout weighing 1 pound 6 ounces/600 grams each. If you use larger fish, the fillets will need dividing. After filleting the fish, carefully remove all the bones with tweezers.

It is of course easier to ask your fishmonger to fillet the fish for you, but ask him to save the heads, bones, and fins for the fish stock. You will also need celery, onions, carrots, and basil for the fish stock. Tomatoes can also be added if desired.

First, Sauro Brunicardi fries the fish—with the skin on—in a coating of flour. The skin side should be fried first; this holds the fish together while it is cooking and the fat makes the fillets brown and crisp on the outside. Then turn the fish and fry on the other side.

This recipe is also excellent for trout, swordfish, or turbot—the flavor of all these fish will develop fully in the orange sauce.

Cut the trout along the underside and gut them. Cut along the backbone and then cut horizontally just above the tail. Remove the fillets and reserve the heads, bones, and fins for the fish stock.

For the fish stock, peel the carrot and cut into pieces. Peel and quarter the onion and quarter the tomatoes. Cut the celery into small sticks.

Add the heads, bones, and fins of the trout with the vegetables, basil, and salt to a saucepan of boiling water. Leave to infuse for 1 hour over a low heat, then strain and set aside.

with Orange Sauce

Place the flour on a plate with a little salt. Turn the fish fillets in the flour to coat them, first the flesh side, then the skin side. Tap with your finger to remove any excess flour.

Melt the butter in a large skillet. When it is hot, transfer the fish fillets to the skillet, skin side down. Turn and cook for about 6 minutes until golden brown. Pour off the fat.

Pour the white wine into the pan. Add the juice from the orange, the orange peel cut into strips, and the strained fish stock. Reduce for 5 minutes over a high heat. Transfer the fillets to plates and pour over the sauce. Garnish with small pieces of orange, orange slices, tomato, and chervil.

Swordfish

Preparation time:	40 minutes
Cooking time:	25 minutes
Difficulty:	★

Serves 4

4 slices	swordfish
⁷/₈ cup/100 g	flour
⅓ cup/80 ml	olive oil
1 knob	butter (optional)
5	tomatoes
1	celery heart
1 bunch	basil

1 bunch	parsley
1	onion
2 cloves	garlic
½ cup/50 g	pitted green olives
⅓ cup/40 g	capers
2 tbsp/30 g	raisins (if possible, from *Sultanina* or *Italia* grapes)
	salt and pepper

For the garnish:

	celery leaves

Sicilian cuisine has been enriched throughout the island's history by encounters with other cultures. The Arabs, who settled on Sicily between the 9th and 11th centuries, introduced many delicacies that added a touch of sweetness to the local dishes. Dried fruit, sugar, and spices soon became an integral part of Sicilian cooking. Dishes evolved with a combination of sweet and sour or savory flavors, many of which are still enjoyed today.

This recipe for swordfish prepared *alla ghiotta* (*ghiotto* means "greedy") originates from Messina and Palermo. It is a traditional but delicate dish, easily prepared and suitable for any occasion.

Sicilians have always looked more to the sea than to the land for their livelihood, so it is not surprising that they have a particular fondness for fish and seafood. The very popular swordfish is still caught by traditional methods i the Ionian Sea and the Straits of Messina. Armed with fearsome "sword," this fish can reach up to 12 feet/4 me ters in length, and weigh as much as 440 lbs/200 kilos. A song by the Italian singer Domenico Modugno immortal izes the dangers involved in catching them. Known for th tenderness of its flesh, swordfish is generally sold slice into steaks. Similar to tuna, which can also be used for thi recipe, swordfish is equally delicious broiled, braised steamed, or marinated.

This recipe features two typically Sicilian flavors: th slightly acidic capers and the sugary raisins, with their hin of Oriental cooking. Raisins are a nourishing foodstuf generally made from seedless grape varieties. Angelo L Spina suggests using locally produced, large, ovoid *Itali* or *Sultanina* raisins.

Dip the pieces of swordfish in flour. In a pan, heat 3¹/₂ tbsp/50 ml of the oil with the knob of butter. Lightly brown the fish steaks in the pan for 3–4 minutes on each side. Remove them to a plate and soak up any excess oil with a piece of paper towel.

Peel the tomatoes and discard the seeds. Reduce them to a pulp. Wash the celery, basil, and parsley. Chop small, together with the onion and garlic cloves. Chop up the green olives.

In the pan used to cook the fish, heat the remaining olive oil and brown the onion and garlic. Add the celery, capers, and raisins. Season with salt and pepper. Cook for 5 minutes, then add the tomato pulp.

Alla Ghiotta

Add the chopped green olives to the vegetable mixture and mix carefully with a wooden spatula.

Sprinkle on the chopped parsley and basil. Mix, then cook for about 5 minutes.

Arrange the slices of swordfish in an ovenproof dish. Cover the fish with the vegetables and cook in the oven at 350 °F/180 °C for about 10 minutes. Serve the fish garnished with a few celery leaves.

Sea Perch with

Preparation time:	40 minutes
Cooking time:	1 hour
Difficulty:	★★

Serves 4

4 portions	sea perch
	salt
	pepper
3	onions
3 cloves	garlic
4	potatoes

8	ripe tomatoes
2	zucchini
2	eggplants
1	leek
	olive oil
1 bunch	dill
1 bunch	parsley

Konstantinos and Chrysanthi Stamkopoulos have been running a restaurant for many years that they have named after Apollo, the Greek god of the sun. They share with you now one of their own recipes, oven-baked sea perch surrounded by tasty, juicy, colorful vegetables. This generous dish is popular with families, and is just right for sharing.

In Greece, sea perch (known as sea bass in the Atlantic) is almost always served broiled, accompanied by vegetables that are cooked separately. This noble fish is particularly prized along European coasts. It has a long head, a big mouth, and a tapered body. The back is grayish-black, the sides are silver, and the belly is white. Measuring 16–40 inches/40–100 centimeters, the average weight is 3½ pounds/1.5 kilograms, although it can weigh as much as 26 pounds/12 kilograms! Found in shallow waters, this solitary fish swims around the coastline and estuaries in the summer. You could also use sea bream, mackerel, or any

other fish, providing the flesh will hold its shape in the liquid from cooking the vegetables.

Eggplants, potatoes, tomatoes, zucchini, onions, garlic, and leeks are all used in this dish. The Greeks eat more vegetables than anybody else in Europe. Their hot sunny climate and the many meat-free days stipulated by the Orthodox religious calendar have encouraged cooks to be inventive. They like to serve their vegetables with a range of different sauces. The addition of pickles, a generous dash of olive oil, and long simmering times are usually all it takes to show off these colorful, tasty vegetables.

To make sure the dish looks appetizing and that each ingredient is uniformly browned, we have fried them separately in just a very small quantity of oil. They could, however, all go into one big skillet or ovenproof dish so that they all brown at the same time.

Scrape the scales off the sea perch using a small knife. Using scissors, slit the belly of the fish lengthwise, gut and clean it. Turn the hard interiors of the gills inside out and cut them off. Wash the fish thoroughly.

Season the sea perch with salt and pepper both inside and outside.

Peel the onions, garlic and potatoes and cut them into slices. Set the onions to one side. Next wash and slice the tomatoes, zucchini, and the unpeeled eggplants, together with the leek. Fry each vegetable separately in a small amount of oil.

Vegetables—Apollo Style

Fry the onion rings in oil and when they start to turn brown add chopped dill and parsley. Set to one side.

Put slices of fried eggplant and tomato on the bottom of an ovenproof dish. Lay the fish on top, then arrange the slices of fried potato, zucchini, and leeks around the fish.

Scatter the onions and herbs on top of the fish, finishing with more slices of tomato. Sprinkle with any chopped parsley or dill that is left over. Put into an oven preheated to 350° F/180° C for 30–40 minutes.

Angler Fish and Mussels

Preparation time: 30 minutes
Cooking time: 10 minutes
Difficulty: ★

Serves 4

1 lb 2 oz/500 g	angler fish (monkfish)
4 tbsp	olive oil
1	onion
1	small green chile
2 cloves	garlic
	salt
	pepper
2 tsp	flour

10 oz/300 g	mussels
3 tbsp	white wine
⅓ cup/20 g	breadcrumbs
½ bunch	parsley
½ bunch	dill (optional)
4 oz/115 g	zucchini
1 tbsp	sweet mustard
1	lemon

For the garnish (optional):

thin slivers of red
bell pepper

Thessalonika, also known as Salonika, is a magnificent city with a prestigious past, its Mediterranean-style façades looking out to sea. In this city founded by Cassander, King of Macedonia, 325 years before Christianity arrived in Greece, fish dishes have always been particularly popular with the locals. Angler fish (monkfish) and mussels fried with zucchini is a traditional, succulent dish in this part of Greece, usually eaten as a hot appetizer.

Every day boats from the little fishing villages dotted around Thessalonika bring in their catches of top quality fish to be sold in the local markets. The angler fish is very highly prized in Greece. It lives on the sandy and clayey seabed around the coast. Its dense, delicate, and juicy flesh, which tastes like lobster, can be cooked in lots of different ways. Depending on the time of year, our chef says you could also use whiting or even cod.

This particular specialty also stars mussels. Known as *mydia* by the locals, most are collected in the Pieria area of Macedonia. Famed for their tasty flesh, these mollusks are often served as part of a *mezze*, accompanied by an aperitif. Cleaned and shelled by hand, great quantities of Pieria mussels can be found in the markets in Athens and Thessalonika. If you are using fresh ones, be particularly careful when you sort through them, making sure you discard any that have broken shells or that are half open. Before cooking mussels, remove the beards and any filaments then scrub them under plenty of running water, discarding any that are open or don't shut after a sharp tap with a knife.

This bright and cheerful looking dish pays homage to the flavors of summer. Zucchini, so loved by Mediterranean people, are complemented with the distinctive flavors of parsley and dill, which all blend wonderfully with the angler fish and the mussels.

Skin the angler fish. Using a knife, remove the central bone, then slice the flesh into medallions of equal thickness.

Heat 2 tbsp olive oil in a skillet and fry the finely chopped onion, finely sliced chile, and 1 crushed clove of garlic. Season the medallions of fish with salt and pepper, sprinkle with 1 tbsp flour and fry in 2 tbsp olive oil until golden. Set aside.

Clean the beards off the mussels and tip them into the onion, chile, and garlic mixture. Add the medallions of angler fish.

Fried with Zucchini

Pour over the white wine, cover, and cook for 3 minutes. Remove the mussels, discarding any unopened ones. Cook for 2 minutes, then remove the fish and strain the stock. Shell the mussels.

Mix the breadcrumbs, remaining crushed garlic, and 2 sprigs each of chopped parsley and dill. Spread over the fish. Cut the zucchini into very thin slices and blanch in boiling salted water for about 1 minute.

Add a little water and 1 tsp flour to the reserved stock and blend with a whisk. Add the mustard and lemon juice. Stir well, then sprinkle with the remaining chopped parsley and dill. Arrange the angler fish, mussels, and zucchini on a plate. Pour over the sauce and garnish.

Squid Stuffed with Mastelo

Preparation time:	15 minutes		
Cooking time:	5 minutes		
	+ barbe-		
	cuing time		
Difficulty:	★		

Serves 4

4	red Florina peppers
4 slices	*mastelo* cheese (or mozzarella)
4	large squid
	salt
1 tbsp	olive oil

For the sauce:

1 clove	garlic
3–4 tbsp	olive oil
1 tbsp	all-purpose flour
2	lemons
	salt
½ bunch	parsley

For the garnish:

	lemon zest

In the traditional religious calendar of the Greek Orthodox Church, there are many days on which the faithful are prohibited from eating meat, and in order to honor this ruling, Greek families often eat squid instead. The recipe for this dish comes from the island of Chios.

Squid are found in huge numbers around the Aegean coast. Usually measuring about 20 inches/50 centimeters long, they are recognizable by their spindle-shaped bodies covered with blackish membranes. They are usually eaten broiled, fried, or stuffed. Cousins of the cuttlefish, which you could alternatively use, they are valued for their flesh.

This carefully planned seafood recipe awards an equally important role to red Florina peppers. Grown exclusively in the Florina area of western Macedonia, they are very sweet and the Greeks love them. In earlier times they were used primarily in the manufacture of powdered red peppers

which used to be exported throughout Europe and the Balkans. These days they are steeped in vinegar and sold in jars. If you can't find Florina peppers you can use fresh red bell peppers instead. Before stuffing them, broil them for about 10 minutes so you can peel the skins. You also need to carefully remove the seeds and membrane, making sure the peppers retain their original shape.

In this summer dish, *mastelo* cheese adds the finishing touch. This cheese is produced in the plains around Chios and is still made by hand. Our chef suggests you use mozzarella if you can't find *mastelo*.

Serve with a sauce made from parsley and olive oil. Stefanos Kovas wanted to introduce an additional touch of color, so he has added some strips of lemon zest pared from the rind. Don't forget to blanch the strips in two lots of boiling water.

Prepare the Florina peppers as outlined above. Cut the cheese into 4 triangles, stuffing one inside each pepper.

Cut off the head and tentacles from the squid and gently empty out the innards and cartilage from the mantle. Set aside the tentacles. Peel off the skin and wash the mantles and wings.

Insert the stuffed peppers into the squid mantles. Add the chopped tentacles.

Cheese and Florina Peppers

Pick up the squid in your hand and insert toothpicks at intervals to close the opening. Salt it, brush lightly with olive oil, and grill over a barbecue. For the garnish, pare off the lemon peel with a zester or sharp knife and blanch it twice.

To make the sauce, brown the whole, peeled garlic clove in the olive oil. Remove the garlic clove, add the flour, and blend with a whisk. Add ⅔ cup/150 ml water, whisking constantly, and add the juice of the lemons and a little salt.

Sprinkle chopped parsley into the sauce. Cut the squid into thick rounds. Serve with the sauce poured round the squid, garnished with the lemon zest.

Squid Stuffed with

Preparation time:	40 minutes
Cooking time:	45 minutes
Marinating time (squid):	30 minutes
Difficulty:	★★

Serves 6

6	squid, each about 10 oz/300 g
1	lemon
3 oz/85 g	onions
3 oz/85 g	tomatoes
3 oz/85 g	red bell peppers

3 oz/85 g	green bell peppers
4 oz/115 g	kefalotyri cheese
	salt
	pepper
¾ cup/175 ml	extra-virgin olive oil

By filling the squid with peppers and cheese, Miltos Karoubas is sharing one of the Greek's most favorite ways of enjoying these mollusks. A delight for the eye and the taste buds, the stuffing enhances the slightly bland taste of the squid and helps to soften them.

Squid are part of a culinary heritage that dates back to Ancient Greece. When cooking them, Greek cooks usually pull off the head and the organs come away at the same time. Our chef, however, uses a knife to make a cut high up on the mantle, then cleans out the squid and removes the translucid central bone at the same time. After skinning them, and washing them carefully to remove any sand or impurities, rub a slice of lemon into the mantles and the tentacles. Leave to marinate for 30 minutes so that the flesh absorbs the flavor of the lemon, the acidity of which also turns the flesh white.

The squids in this recipe are garnished with a savory mix of bell peppers, tomatoes, onions, and cheese. Bell peppers are closely associated with Mediterranean cookery these days, and were first imported from the Americas in the 16th century. They are available in a wide range of colors and varieties, from green to bright red, orange, or pale yellow. Choose peppers that are firm to the touch and that have unwrinkled, bright shiny skins. You can keep them for eight days in the refrigerator.

The *kefalotyri* used to stuff the squid is one of the most popular cheeses in Greece. Hard and salty, it works well in stuffings and with pasta, and is a great addition to pie fillings.

The stuffed squid are usually served whole, each guest eating them as they like. A more elegant way of serving them is to slice them into medallions so that all of the ingredients used to stuff them are on view.

Cut the tentacles off the squid. Make a cut around the mantles, then remove the head, internal organs, central bone, and the gray skin. Rinse the mantles and tentacles under running water.

Rub the squid mantles and tentacles with slices from half the lemon and leave to marinate for 30 minutes.

Peel and finely chop the onions. Cut the tomatoes into small half-moon sections. Cut open the bell peppers, remove the seeds and membranes, and cut the flesh into thin strips.

Vegetables and Kefalotyri

Lay out the squid mantles on a cutting board. Stuff them with the strips of bell pepper, finely chopped onions, then the sections of tomato and sticks of kefalotyri cheese.

When the squid are filled, close the ends using 3 or 4 toothpicks. Season them and place under a broiler for 45 minutes on moderate heat, turning them from time to time.

In a bowl whisk the olive oil with the salt and pepper and the juice of half a lemon until it turns into a sauce. Put one stuffed squid on each plate and pour over the sauce.

Sea Bream with Celery

Preparation time: 20 minutes
Cooking time: 35 minutes
Salting time (sea bream): 15 minutes
Difficulty: ★

Serves 4

4	gray sea bream, each about 1 lb 9 oz/ 700 g, cleaned and gutted
	salt
1 scant cup/ 100 g	all-purpose flour

scant ½ cup/ 100 ml	virgin olive oil
1	medium red onion
1 head	celery
1	small celeriac root
	freshly ground black pepper
3	eggs
3	lemons

Located to the south of Epirus, the port of Preveza opens onto the Gulf of Amvrakiko, a particularly famous fishing area. An enormous choice of fish and shellfish is available at Preveza market, some from the Gulf of Amvrakiko and some from the Ionian Sea. Our chef is pleased to bring you this recipe for gray sea bream flavored with celery and coated in *avgolemono*, a popular sauce made from eggs and lemons that Greeks add to a whole range of dishes.

Since royal sea bream is unknown in Greece, cooks use the gray variety instead. This coastal fish, a member of the sparid family, measures 8–16 inches/20–40 centimeters in length and weighs 10 ounces–4½ pounds/300 grams– 2 kilograms. Its white lean flesh is highly prized by gourmets. Smaller sea bream weighing 10–12 ounces/ 300–350 grams are known as *kotses* in Greek. The big ones, which is what we are using in our recipe, are known as *tsipoures*.

Only the leaves from the celery stalk will be used to add flavor and color to the recipe. You can choose either a white or red variety of onion, although our chef prefers the red ones which he thinks taste better.

When the sea bream is being cooked with the celery and onion, use some of the cooking juices to baste the fish at regular intervals so that it doesn't dry out. This will also impregnate the flesh with the flavor of the vegetables.

The *avgolemono* sauce poured over the fish at the last minute takes its name from the words *avgo* ("eggs") and *lemoni* ("lemon"). Particularly popular in the Ionian region, it is used to coat fish or meat, and is also added to soups. Our chef recommends that you don't pour it cold over the fish, because it will curdle. Warm it up a little instead by blending in some of the warm cooking liquid so that it is the same temperature as the fish.

Wash the sea bream. Place in a colander, salt them and leave to rest for 15 minutes. Then coat in flour.

Heat 3–4 tbsp oil in a heavy-bottomed pan. Put the fish into the hot oil and fry on one side for 5 minutes, then turn with a palette knife to brown on the other side.

In a large, shallow pan, fry the chopped red onion in olive oil. Add the celery leaves, the peeled and cubed celeriac, a cup of water, salt, and pepper. Cover and cook for 15 minutes (moving the mixture around while it is cooking to prevent it from sticking to the bottom of the pan).

and Avgolemono Sauce

Lay the fried sea bream on top of the vegetables and bring to the boil (add a little water if necessary). You may have to do this in batches, depending on the size of the fish and your pan.

Meanwhile whisk the eggs in a bowl until they are foaming, add the juice of 3 lemons and a little of the warm cooking juices and whisk rapidly.

Pour the sauce over the fish, check the seasoning and serve hot.

Kalkani with

Preparation time: 45 minutes
Cooking time: 30 minutes
Difficulty: ★★

Serves 4

1	turbot weighing 4½ lb/2 kg
1	bay leaf
1	carrot
1	onion
1 stalk	celery
10 oz/300 g	fennel bulbs
⅔ cup/150 ml	olive oil
5 oz/150 g	pearl onions

1 clove	garlic
	salt
	pepper
1 sprig	thyme
¾ cup/200 ml	white wine
1	egg yolk
2	lemons

For the garnish:
fennel leaves

A particularly popular fish among Cretans and the inhabitants of northeastern Greece, this recipe marries turbot (*kalkani*) and fennel with great flair. An extremely elegant summer dish, it is ideal to share with friends.

Greek cookery provides a wonderful showcase for fish and shellfish caught in local waters. Even when just broiled and served with a dash of olive oil, aromatic herbs, and lemon juice, the taste is outstanding.

Kalkani with fennel is a perfect illustration of this. Enjoyed since the days of Ancient Greece for its white, firm, and particularly delicate flesh, turbot is regarded by Greeks as the king of flat fish. Depending on the catch, however, you could replace it with any other sea fish provided it has a more robust taste than farmed fish. You could also replace the turbot with tilapia. Don't forget to keep the head and the trimmings for making the stock.

This subtle and carefully thought out dish allows the aniseed flavor of the fennel to shine through. This umbelliferous plant can grow up to 6 feet/1.8 meters tall and it flourishes in the sandy soil of the Mediterranean coast. Widely available in Greek markets in winter, fennel is renowned for its high vitamin C content.

In ancient times, Hippocrates and Dioscorides recommended it to their patients! Try to find small ones because they will be more tender, white and crisp. Our chef suggests you also try this recipe with young Swiss chard leaves.

The crowning touch to this dish of turbot with fennel is an *avgolemono* sauce. Typically Greek, the sauce is made from beaten egg, olive oil, lemon juice, salt, pepper, and a little of the reserved fish stock, which should be added while still warm. Rich and smooth, it is traditionally added to soups and a wide range of seafood dishes.

Using a sharp knife, gently fillet the turbot. Remove the trimmings and the head and set aside for the fish stock.

Pour 4 cups/1 l water into a pan with the bay leaf and peeled and roughly chopped carrot, onion, and celery. Add the turbot trimmings and head and cook for 20 minutes, then strain the stock and put to one side.

Wash the fennel bulbs and cut into equal slices with a knife.

Fennel

Heat 2 tbsp olive oil in a pan and brown the chopped pearl onions and crushed garlic clove. Add the fennel, seasoning, and scatter the mixture with thyme leaves. Pour on the white wine and top up the liquid with stock so that it just covers the vegetables. Cook for 3 minutes.

Season the turbot fillets. Heat 1 tbsp olive oil in a skillet and brown the fillets on their skin side. Add the fish (with the skin side uppermost) to the fennel mixture. Cook for 2 minutes. Reserve the cooking liquid.

In a bowl, beat the egg yolk then add the remaining olive oil and the lemon juice. Season. Add a little of the reserved cooking liquid. Stir well, pour around the turbot and fennel and serve garnished with fennel leaves.

Preparation time:	45 minutes
Cooking time:	45 minutes
Difficulty:	★★

Serves 4

	salt
2	carrots
2	onions
1 head	celery
	red wine vinegar
2	bay leaves
2	lobsters, each 2½ lb/1 kg

scant ½ cup/ 100 ml	olive oil
10	scallions
1 lb 5 oz/600 g	button mushrooms
2½ lb/1 kg	tomatoes
	pepper
1 bunch	flat-leaf parsley
1	lemon

In choosing this typical dish from Mytilene, George Anastassakis brings together seafood, the gift of Poseidon, the god of the sea, and vegetables, the gift of Demeter, the goddess of the harvest. Greeks are particularly fond of dishes that use crustaceans and fresh vegetables.

In May, the fishermen from Mytilene bring back their catches of wonderfully succulent lobsters from the Aegean Sea, and cook them with scallions and other spring vegetables from their gardens. Hence the name they have given this recipe—*astakos mayatikos* or "May-time lobsters."

The Greeks have been eating fish and seafood for thousands of years. Even in the days of Pericles (450 B.C.), lobster was already on the menu at Athenian banquets, as were oysters, shrimp, mussels, and sole. In Greece, lobsters are these days often poached in a *court bouillon* and served with mayonnaise, or simply grilled over the barbecue.

There are several ways of cooking a lobster. Our chef puts it onto a long flat metal tray (supplied with the fish kettle) and firmly attaches it by winding string around both lobster and tray. Using the handles, he can then plunge the lobster into the hot *court bouillon* without it moving, then easily lift it out again. You can, however, just put it into boiling water without any kind of support. When it is removed from the stock it will need to be left to cool down before being shelled. (Before they cook it, other cooks prefer to plunge the blade of a sharp, heavy knife in the cross-hatch right behind its head. After doing so, the lobster should be placed in the freezer for a few minutes while muscular contractions "empty it out.")

The mushrooms and onions are simmered in just a single glassful of the cooking liquid, and any that is left over will be reused as a delicious base for a fish soup or sauce.

In a fish kettle, add water, salt, peeled and sliced carrots and onions, stems and leaves of chopped celery, dash of wine vinegar, and 1 bay leaf. Cover, bring to the boil, then drop the lobsters into the liquid and let them cook for 20–25 minutes.

Remove the cooked lobsters from the liquid, put them onto a cutting board, and leave them to cool down before you remove the shells.

Cut the 2 tails into medallions.

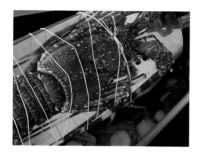

Lobsters

Put the olive oil, ¾ cup/200 ml strained stock from cooking the lobsters, chopped scallions and mushrooms into a pan, and leave to simmer for about 10 minutes.

Peel and chop the tomatoes. Add to the mushrooms with salt, pepper, and chopped parsley and cook for about another 5 minutes.

Add the medallions of lobster to the vegetables. Reheat for 3 minutes over a brisk heat. Arrange a bed of vegetables on the serving dish with the medallions on top. Decorate with the bay leaf and some lemon.

Broiled Sea Perch with

Preparation time:	35 minutes
Cooking time:	25 minutes
Difficulty:	★★

Serves 4

4	large artichokes
1	lemon
12	small potatoes
12	small carrots
12	pearl onions
3½ oz/	
100 g	peas
1	sea perch (sea bass)
	weighing 2½ lb/1.2 kg
	salt, pepper

For the sauce:

3 cloves	garlic
3	basil leaves
½ tsp	sweet mustard
	salt
	pepper
1 pinch	saffron
2 tbsp	white wine
1	lemon
2 tbsp	olive oil
3	blood oranges

For the garnish:

	capers
	dill sprigs
	basil leaves

Extremely light to digest, this recipe is an invitation to discover the riches of Greek cuisine. A particular favorite on the islands, sea perch (known as bass in the Atlantic) is traditionally flavored with olive oil and lemon. Easy to make, this summer dish concentrates several Mediterranean flavors in a marvelous way.

Worthy heirs of Ulysses, the Greeks always have their eyes turned to the sea. Sought out by fish lovers for its fine, dense but delicate flesh, the Mediterranean sea perch has great character. Relatively fragile, it needs only a short cooking time. When bought fresh, it should still be rigid, have shiny scales, and pink gills. Depending on the catch, you could replace it with sea bream.

This delicate recipe is served with spring vegetables. Our chef likes to enrich the original recipe with artichokes.

Usually cooked with lemon, olive oil, and dill, they are eaten either as a hot appetizer or a main course.

Peas, another of the spring vegetables used in this dish have been enjoyed since the days of Ancient Greece. They are grown in many vegetable gardens and can be found in the market in summer. Look out for ones that have a bright green pod that is intact, hard, and plump. They keep for two or three days in the refrigerator, but it is best to use them as quickly as you can. You could also use some fresh fava beans, or English broad beans.

Aristedes Pasparakis is passionate about Greek produce and had the idea of serving the broiled fish with a sauce made from blood oranges flavored with basil. These oranges are grown widely in the Peloponnese, their slightly tart taste adding a real lift to this wonderful fish dish.

Peel the artichokes, removing the leaves until you get to the choke. Holding onto the stem, remove the choke with a melon baller. Dip the artichoke hearts into a bowl of water to which slices of lemon have been added.

Peel the potatoes, carrots, and pearl onions. Shell the peas. Cut the carrots into batons.

Heat a pan of salted water, then add the potatoes and carrots. Cook for 5 minutes before adding the pearl onions and sliced artichoke hearts. Cook for a further 5 minutes, add the peas, and cook for another 5 minutes. Drain and refresh the vegetables in iced water.

Blood Orange Sauce

Clean out and fillet the sea perch. Season the fillets, then dry-fry them in a nonstick skillet.

To make the sauce, put finely sliced cloves of garlic, chopped basil leaves, and the mustard into a salad bowl and season. Add the saffron to the white wine, lemon juice, and olive oil. Stir well and add to the mustard sauce.

Squeeze the oranges. Heat the sauce mixture, add the juice from the blood oranges and allow the sauce to reduce a little. Pass the sauce through a strainer. Pour the sauce and the vegetables around the fish and garnish with capers, dill, and basil leaves.

Octopus with

Preparation time:	20 minutes
Cooking time (octopus):	55 minutes
Cooking time (pasta):	10 minutes
Difficulty:	★

Serves 6

1	octopus weighing 2½ lb/1 kg
	salt
scant ½ cup/ 100 ml	white wine
⅔ cup/150 ml	extra-virgin olive oil
2	onions
3 cloves	garlic
1½ lb/650 g	chopped tomatoes
1 stick	cinnamon
15	black peppercorns
	freshly ground black pepper
½ bunch	parsley
4½ cups/500 g	small macaroni

Located on the very edge of the easternmost island of Chalkidiki in Macedonia, Mount Athos is home to about 20 monasteries and nearly 1,700 Orthodox monks. This octopus stew with small pasta shapes is a recipe that has been adapted for those days on which no meat may be consumed. Having no blood, mollusks can be eaten on these days and this dish has become one of the monks' culinary specialties. It is also enjoyed on the nearby islands.

Octopus, known as *oktapodi* in Greek, means it has eight feet. In fact it has eight tentacles with suckers, all of them the same length, which join at the head. It is particularly abundant in the Aegean Sea. In summer the fishing boats always return with quantities of octopus, squid, and cuttlefish, which are then cooked in lots of different recipes. As the flesh of the octopus is very tough, the fishermen traditionally beat it 44 times against a wall or a rock to tenderize it. The bigger ones are cut into small dice, then used in

salads or stews, while the little ones are particularly popular broiled. One very old custom involves hanging them on wires to dry so they can be kept for "no meat" days.

Octopus are quite a lot simpler to cook than squid or cuttlefish because they don't need to be gutted. However, make sure you wash any sand out of the sac if this has not already been done by the fishmonger.

Simmered in a pleasantly spicy tomato sauce, our octopus is served with small pasta shapes. Dozens of different sorts of pasta can be bought at Greek markets, all of them called some variety of *macaronia*. The type used by our chef is *macaronia kofta*, "cut macaroni," which looks like small rings. Add these cooked pasta shapes to the stew just before it is served.

Wash the octopus. Put it into a large pan filled with salted water and add the white wine. Bring to the boil and leave to cook for 30 minutes. Drain immediately.

Put the octopus onto a chopping board and cut it into small cubes.

In a pan, briskly fry the pieces of octopus in olive oil, together with chopped onions and garlic. Add the chopped tomatoes.

Small Pasta Shapes

Next add the stick of cinnamon, pepper-corns, salt, and ground pepper. Add a little oil if necessary and cook for 15–20 minutes. When the octopus is tender add chopped parsley and stir.

During this time cook the pasta for 10 minutes in a separate pan filled with boiling salted water. Drain well.

Add the cooked pasta to the octopus stew. Stir for a moment or two over the heat, then serve as quickly as possible.

Saffron Rice with Mussels

Preparation time: 30 minutes
Cooking time: around
25 minutes

Difficulty: ★★

Serves 4

2¼ lb/1 kg	mussels
2 or 3	carrots
1	zucchini
1	onion
2 cloves	garlic
½ cup/125 ml	olive oil

scant ½ cup/100 ml	white wine
scant ½ cup/100 ml	ouzo
3 cups/800 ml	fish stock
1	bay leaf
3 g	saffron
	salt
	pepper
1¾ cups/350 g	long grain rice
1 bunch	arugula (rocket)
2 tbsp	wild dill

In the port of Thessalonike and along the beach at Aretzo, the little restaurants all serve succulent plates of mussels. Comprising of rice, mussels, and vegetables flavored with saffron, the dish our chef is sharing with you is somewhat similar to a Spanish paella.

For thousands of years Greeks have collected mussels off the coast, which they cook with basil, saffron, or just fry. Mussel farms were first developed about 20 years ago in the Pieria region of Macedonia and these days tasty mussels are produced on floating lines.

To cook them, use a knife to scrape off any incrustations that have formed on the shell, then cut off the little black beards. It is vital that you discard any mussels that are still open (they are dead). You can also buy mussels that have already been cleaned and vacuum-packed. Failing this, you could use other shellfish or shrimp for our recipe.

These mussels are cooked with a lot of different flavors, such as ouzo and saffron. This spice was already known in Santorini and Cretan cookery as long ago as 2000 B.C. The poet Homer recounted how the god Jupiter would lie on a bed of saffron, hyacinths, and lotus blossom. Today, 15 percent of the world's production comes from Kozani in western Macedonia. However, always use the threads if you can because the powder is often cut with cartham, curcuma, or marigolds.

The ouzo lends its strong aniseed flavor to this recipe. This Greek spirit flavored with aniseed and fennel is consumed at any time of day.

Long grain (Carolina) rice suits this dish well. The Greeks, who themselves grow a little rice in the Larissa district of Thessalia, also import it from different parts of the world. You can choose your favorite from the many varieties.

Scrape the mussel shells to get rid of any incrustations and remove the beards. Cut the ends off the carrots, peel and slice into small batons. Wash the zucchini and cut into batons.

Peel and finely chop the onion and garlic. Heat the olive oil in a large skillet and gently fry the onion, garlic, and carrots.

Arrange the mussels on top of the bed of vegetables in the frying pan and leave them to simmer for 5 minutes.

nd Baby Vegetables

Next add the zucchini batons.

Keeping the pan over the heat, stir in the wine, ouzo, fish stock, bay leaf, saffron, and season with salt and pepper. Leave to cook for 4–5 minutes—the liquid should be only just bubbling.

Finally, turn up the heat and add the washed rice. Stir, then leave to cook for about 10 minutes at a rolling boil. Serve hot, garnished with arugula leaves and sprigs of dill.

Grouper with

Preparation time: 35 minutes
Cooking time: 50 minutes
Salting time for the okra: 1–2 hours
Difficulty: ★

Serves 4

1¼ lb/600 g	fresh okra
	juice of 1 lemon
2 lb/1 kg	grouper
4 oz/100 g	onion
1 clove	garlic

7 oz/200 g	tomatoes
⅓ cup/80 ml	extra-virgin olive oil
	salt and pepper

To garnish:
2 tbsp/30 g	flat-leaf parsley

The Cretans living in the coastal areas of the island are skilled in adapting the harvest of the sea to their daily menu. One of the favorite dishes in Malia, Sitia, and Rethymnon is fish with okra, known locally as *psari me bamiès*.

For this version of the recipe, Michalis Markakis has used fillets of grouper fish, but sea bream or red snapper would be equally suitable. The grouper is a large fish with delicate flesh. Its sides are brown with brownish-yellow patches, and it has a protuberant mouth. On Crete, they are sold when still quite small (2–4 lb/1–2 kg) and can be cooked whole. The fish can be served whole and eaten without difficulty, as the central bone lifts out easily.

Much enjoyed all over Greece, okra or *bamya* are long, green vegetables, about the size of a small gherkin. Other names for this vegetable are "Greek horn" and "ladies' fin-

ger." Okra is also a distinctive feature of African and Caribbean cooking. Its flavor combines especially well with tomatoes and onions.

The flesh of the okra produces a gelatinous substance, which is useful for thickening sauces. To eliminate this when it is not needed, Cretan cooks sprinkle the okra with salt and lemon juice, vinegar, or green grape juice, depending on the time of year. This draws out the gelatin, shrinking the vegetables and making them less likely to fall apart when cooked. The acidity of the lemon juice or vinegar also makes them slightly quicker to cook in the oven. They should be rinsed before using.

This dish is usually sprinkled with parsley before being placed in the oven. Michalis Markakis recommends adding the parsley after cooking, however, thus preserving its bright green color, flavor, and vitamins.

Rinse the okra. Clean them by scraping off the tiny pointed leaves at the tip and the prickly hairs.

Place the okra on a dish and pour over the juice of half a lemon. Salt generously. Leave them to give up their gelatin for 1–2 hours, then rinse them in running water.

Cut the fish fillets into individual portions. Peel and chop the onion and garlic. Peel and blend the tomatoes to make a pulp.

Okra

In a frying pan, brown the chopped garlic and onion for 5 minutes in the olive oil. Deglaze with lemon juice. Add the puréed tomato to the pan and season with salt and pepper. Simmer the sauce for 15 minutes.

Place the okra and pieces of fish in a shallow ovenproof dish. Pour over the tomato sauce. Cook in a moderate oven (340 °F/170 °C) for 30 minutes.

When the fish and vegetables are cooked, sprinkle the dish with chopped parsley and serve piping hot.

Cuttlefish in

Preparation time:	20 minutes
Cooking time:	35 minutes
Difficulty:	★

Serves 4

2 lb/1 kg	small, cleaned, and gutted cuttlefish
⁴/₅ cup/200 ml	virgin olive oil
7 tbsp/100 ml	red wine vinegar
2 level tbsp/50 g	honey
3¹/₂ tbsp/50 g	fresh rosemary
	salt and pepper

A traditional dish served on Crete, cuttlefish in *oxymeli* sauce is served during *megali sarakosti*, the period of seven weeks' fasting leading up to Easter. While meat and its derivatives (butter, milk, eggs, and cheese) may not be eaten on fast days, fish is permitted.

To speed up the preparation of this dish, it can be made with ready-prepared cuttlefish bodies, either fresh or frozen. If these are not available, remove the head and innards of the fresh cuttlefish, followed by the skin and the hard inner "bone." Rinse the mantles in running water, turning them inside out like the finger of a glove, but taking care not to tear them.

After rinsing the cuttlefish, dry them well with paper towels to prevent them from spitting when put in the hot oil. Even so, stand well back from the pan, or cover it, when frying.

Cuttlefish is ideal for this recipe since the flesh remains firm even when cooked. Squid can also be used but should be floured beforehand so that they will brown without collapsing in the pan.

Oxymeli sauce is commonly used on Crete with seafood, fish, snails, and salads of wild herbs and leaves. The Cretan honey, *meli Kritis*, gives it a delicate, sweet-sour flavor. According to legend, Zeus spent his childhood on Crete, hidden on Mount Ida. He was fed on goat's milk and honey that the bees brought to his lips. Honey has been an essential ingredient of Cretan cooking for centuries, and is used as a sweetener and in medicines.

In this sauce, the rosemary blends perfectly with the virgin olive oil so characteristic of many Cretan dishes. The small, needle-like leaves of this herb, used in Greek cuisine since Antiquity, will enliven the *oxymeli* sauce.

Open out the cuttlefish bodies and cut them into large rectangles.

Heat the olive oil in a pan. Add the pieces of cuttlefish and brown them for 10 minutes over a high heat.

Remove the pieces of fried cuttlefish and arrange them in a shallow ovenproof dish. Retain the pan with the cooking oil.

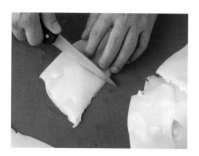

Oxymeli Sauce

To the oil used for cooking the cuttlefish, add the vinegar, honey, salt, pepper, and rosemary leaves. Raise the heat and allow the liquid to evaporate for 3–4 minutes, stirring all the time.

Pour the sauce over the cuttlefish pieces. Put the dish in a hot oven (430 °F/220 °C) for 10 minutes.

Remove the dish from the oven and turn over the pieces of cuttlefish. Return it to the oven for another 10 minutes. Serve hot.

Preparation time:	40 minutes
Cooking time:	50 minutes
Difficulty:	★★

Serves 4

8	mackerel
⁷/₈ cup/100 g	flour
1 cup/250 ml	olive oil
12	tomatoes
2 cloves	garlic
1²/₃ cups/400 ml	white wine
1 sprig	fresh mint
2 tbsp/30 g	capers
	salt and pepper

Michael Cauchi and his wife have been running their famous restaurant in Marsascala, *Il Re del Pesce*, for eight years. Here, they have developed many delicious recipes, including this one of fish fried and simmered in a tomato and caper sauce.

Fishing on Malta is still carried out in the traditional way, using the brightly painted boats known as *luzzu*, so frequently seen on posters and postcards, and in travel books and advertisements. An eye painted on either side of the prow of each boat is believed to bring luck and ward off the evil eye.

The cream of the day's catch can be admired and bought in the fish market at Marsaxlokk. Michael Cauchi originally created this recipe using the Mediterranean fish known as bogue, or *vopa* in Maltese. This is a long, golden-colored fish with large eyes, sharp spines along the dorsal fin, and tiny pectoral fins. Here, Michael suggests using mackerel (which is much more readily available) instead. On Malta, a particularly favored variety is "Spanish mackerel" or *kavall*, which has white flesh. Unlike common mackerel, it has a striped dorsal fin, gray-blue spots over the sides and underside, and a translucid area between the eyes. Michael Cauchi suggests squeezing a lemon over the fish after frying to bring out the flavor of the flour coating.

To prepare the tomato sauce, first cut the tomatoes into quarters. Remove the skin with a knife, and chop the flesh into a pulp. This sauce will have the additional flavor of capers, which are traditionally harvested from bushes growing in the Maltese countryside.

The fish can either be covered with the tomato sauce or served on a bed of sauce to offset their appetizing browned skin.

Split the mackerel open along the underside and remove the innards.
Be sure to slice open and clean away the dark red substance running along the fish's backbone too. Rinse thoroughly, and dry the fish with paper towels. Salt the insides of the fish.

Place the flour, seasoned with salt and pepper, on a plate. Carefully coat the fish with flour on both sides.

In a frying pan, fry the floured mackerel for 5 minutes in ⁴/₅ cup/200 ml of hot olive oil, turning them to brown on both sides.

Kavalli

Peel the tomatoes, remove the seeds, and chop small. Peel and crush the garlic and brown it in a pan in the remaining oil. Add the tomato to the pan with the white wine and stir vigorously over a high heat.

When the sauce is well blended, add the chopped mint leaves and capers.

Arrange the mackerel on an ovenproof dish and pour the tomato sauce over them. Cook in the oven at 320 °F/160 °C for 25 minutes.

Sea Perch

Preparation time: 10 minutes
Cooking time: 40 minutes
Difficulty: ★

Serves 4

2 lb/800 g	sea perch
2	tomatoes
8 oz/200 g	mushrooms
½	green bell pepper
1	onion

2 cloves	garlic
⅓ cup/80 ml	olive oil
2	bay leaves
¾ cup/200 ml	fish stock
	salt
	ground white pepper
	juice of ½ lemon
1 bunch	dill
2 tsp/10 ml	*rakı*

Sea perch with *rakı* is easy to prepare. It is a traditional fish dish with typically Turkish aromas, and is a delight at any time of year.

Sea perch is also known as bass and loup de mer, and is extremely popular in Turkey, especially for its delicate, very lean flesh. The white flesh tends to disintegrate, however, so steaming is the best method of preparation. It is also delicious poached, flambéed, or stuffed. Freshly caught sea perch is firm and shiny, and smells of iodine. Depending on what is available, you can also substitute sea bream.

This wonderful fish dish is delicately enhanced with *rakı*, an aniseed alcoholic drink made mainly in Tekirdağ, between Istanbul and Gallipoli, and is practically Turkey's national drink. It is common practice to have a bottle of *rakı* on the table during a meal of several courses and for

glasses to be topped up frequently. Traditionally, *rakı* is produced in state-owned distilleries from fermented figs and raisins; the first distillation is produced with aniseed. The first *rakı* distillery was founded in Izmir in 1912.

Thanks to the healthy vegetable accompaniment, this dish is very light. Green bell peppers are harvested before they are fully ripe. Make sure the specimens you buy are firm and smooth and have a healthy stalk with no marks or soft areas on them.

Mushrooms are available from supermarkets all year round. Use small mushrooms if at all possible, as they are more highly flavored.

Fillet the fish. Cut around the gills and run the knife along the middle bone toward the tail fin to loosen the fillets.

Skin and dice the tomatoes, and peel and slice the mushrooms. Finely chop the bell pepper. Dice the onion and finely chop the garlic.

Heat the olive oil in a skillet and sauté the finely chopped garlic. Add the chopped onion and sauté for 3–4 minutes, then add the bay leaves.

with Rakı

Add the vegetables, pour over the stock, and simmer for 2 minutes.

Season the fish fillets with salt and pepper, and place on top of the vegetables. Simmer for about 4 minutes. Chop the dill.

Check the seasoning, and add more salt and pepper if required. Add the lemon juice, chopped dill, and rakı, and simmer for 2 minutes. Arrange the fish and vegetables on a serving dish.

Bonito

Preparation time:	20 minutes
Marinating time:	30 minutes
Cook:	on the barbecue
Difficulty:	★

Serves 4

2 lb/800 g	genuine bonito; use tuna or mackerel as a substitute
2	tomatoes
2	green bell peppers
1	yellow bell pepper
1	lemon

For the marinade:

	juice of ½ lemon
16	bay leaves
scant ½ cup/ 100 ml	olive oil
	salt and ground pepper to taste

Surrounded by tiny fishing villages on the banks of the blue Bosphorus, Istanbul is famous all over Turkey for its seafood specialties. In this city, whose inhabitants are known as seafood enthusiasts, there is a wide range of fish and seafood dishes. Bonito kebabs are extremely popular because they are easy to make and consist of a combination of wonderful Mediterranean aromas.

Skewers are called *şiş* in Turkish, are quick and easy to make, and the people of Istanbul love them. There is a long tradition behind this method of preparation: Kebabs are considered a very sociable way of eating, and are therefore popular all over the country. Bonito is one of the biggest-selling fish varieties in Turkey. At home in the Aegean Sea, it is absolutely delicious. You can use tuna or mackerel if bonito is not available.

In Turkish cuisine, fish is often marinated before cooking, which makes it more tender and aromatic. Aybek Şurdum recommends enhancing the marinade with onion juice. If you do, do not marinate the fish for longer than 30 minutes.

Bonito kebabs are cooked on the barbecue, and so are ideal for summer. The flesh falls apart quite easily, so watch it closely while it is cooking. Of course, you can also cook the kebabs in the broiler, in which case they will take about seven minutes.

The fish is complemented by colorful pieces of bell pepper. This extremely versatile vegetable is greatly prized in Mediterranean cuisine. Red and yellow bell peppers are sweeter than the green ones, and the flesh is not as thick.

Cut the fish into even-sized pieces.

Wash the tomatoes and bell peppers. Cut the lemon in half lengthwise and then into thin slices; likewise the tomatoes.

Remove the seeds from the bell peppers and cut them into even-sized rectangles.

Kebabs

Place the fish pieces in a deep bowl and pour over the ingredients for the marinade. Marinate for 30 minutes.

Slide the fish pieces onto metal skewers, alternating with the bell peppers, tomatoes, and lemons. Brush the skewers with the marinade.

Cook the kebabs on the barbecue, then arrange on a serving dish.

Karaburun-Style

Preparation time:	10 minutes
Cooking time:	25 minutes
Difficulty:	★

Serves 4

1	zucchini
2	large potatoes
	salt
	ground pepper
4 tbsp	olive oil
4 oz/100 g	firm goat milk cheese
2 tsp	paprika
4	sea perch fillets
4	sprigs dill

For the sauce:

2⅛ cups/250 g	flour
8 tbsp	olive oil
	salt
	juice of ½ lemon

For the garnish:

	paprika
	dill

The village of Karaburun (literal translation: "black peninsula") on the Aegean coast near Izmir is known all over the country for its light, healthy seafood cuisine.

The sauce that the fish is cooked in for this recipe consists of olive oil, flour, salt, water, and lemon juice; use milk instead of water for a slightly more nutritious version. This delicious dish is prepared mainly by women who are working in the fields, and it has the added advantage of being quick and easy to prepare and cook.

Sea perch, also known as sea bass and loup de mer, is valued for its firm, lean, delicate flesh, and can be prepared in many different ways. Gökçen Adar advises keeping an eye on it while it is cooking, as the flesh does tend to disintegrate. Freshly caught sea perch is firm with shiny scales, and smells slightly of iodine. You can also use gurnard.

We recommend a potato and zucchini gratin as a side dish. Both vegetables come from Central or South America, and are firm fixtures in Mediterranean cuisine. Zucchini is a classic summer vegetable, as it contains lots of water and few calories. Whether you choose light- or dark-green ones, make sure they are small, as they will be far more tender, and check that the skin is not damaged.

You can use Gruyère or any other well-flavored cheese instead of goat milk cheese. The paprika is essential, however, as it provides a pretty color contrast.

To make the sauce, sieve the flour into a bowl and, using a balloon whisk, combine with 2 cups/500 ml water and the olive oil. Season with salt, and stir in the lemon juice.

Peel and thinly slice the zucchini and the potatoes.

Layer the zucchini and potato slices in an ovenproof dish. Season with salt and pepper and spoon over the olive oil. Bake in a preheated oven at 400 °F/200 °C for about 15 minutes, then pour over half the sauce, reserving the rest, and return to the oven for a further 5–6 minutes.

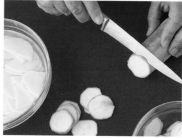

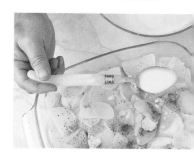

Sea Perch

Grate the cheese and sprinkle over the vegetable mixture, then dust with 1 tsp paprika. Return to the oven until the cheese browns.

Skin the fish fillets and season with salt. Break up the dill sprigs and stir into the reserved sauce. Pour enough sauce into an ovenproof dish to cover the bottom. Place the fish fillets in the dish and pour over the remainder of the sauce.

Dust the remainder of the paprika over the fish mixture, and return to the oven for 10–15 minutes. Arrange the fish and the gratin on a plate, and garnish with more paprika and dill.

Bonito

Preparation time:	50 minutes
Cooking time:	25 minutes
Difficulty:	★

Serves 4

2 lb/800 g	genuine bonito or tuna
2	potatoes
2	carrots
1	onion
4 cloves	garlic

scant ½ cup/ 100 ml	olive oil
2	tomatoes
2	bay leaves
	juice of ½ lemon
	salt
	ground pepper
½ bunch	flat-leaf parsley

Bonito *pilaki* is a much-loved cold appetizer in Istanbul, and is served mainly in the *meyhane*, the *rakı* bars. This delicious dish has a long history, and is ideal for all social occasions.

Striped bonito is found in the waters around the Bosphorus, and is in great demand all over Turkey. Its aromatic flesh is incomparable and can be cooked in many different ways.

Pilaki is a typically Turkish cooking method, incorporating olive oil from the Aegean coast along with onions and tomatoes.

Flat-leaf parsley adds a characteristic aroma to this seafood specialty. The herb is available all year round, but do make sure that the leaves and stalks are green, fresh, and firm.

Bay leaves are used in many Mediterranean specialties, either whole or crumbled. They were used to crown the heads of many poets and victorious army leaders in antiquity. Aybek Şurdum is of the opinion that they are also a pretty garnish.

Bonito *pilaki* is a colorful fish specialty that is lent a wonderfully bright orange color by the carrots. This root vegetable came from the Middle East and Central Asia, and is known and prized for its high content of vitamin A. Depending on the season, young, crispy carrots will be available, which are to be preferred. Make sure that they are firm and undamaged, with fresh, green leaves.

Potatoes are grown and consumed on every continent. Put them in water when you have peeled them to stop them from discoloring.

Remove the skin of the fish (if preferred), and cut the meat into medallions.

Peel the potatoes and carrots. Scoop out balls with a baller. Chop the onion and garlic cloves.

Heat the olive oil and sauté the garlic. Add the onions. Skin and finely chop the 2 tomatoes.

Pilaki

Add the vegetable balls, chopped tomatoes, bay leaves, and lemon juice to the onions and garlic. Season with salt and pepper. Stir briefly, and simmer for 3–4 minutes.

Top up the vegetables with water and simmer for about 10 minutes.

Season the bonito medallions with salt and pepper, then place on the vegetables and cook for 3 minutes. Sprinkle with chopped parsley, then arrange on a serving dish.

John Dory

Preparation time: 40 minutes
Cooking time: 20 minutes
Difficulty: ★

Serves 4

2	John Dory, each 1¼ lb/500 g
	salt
	ground pepper
4 tbsp/60 ml	olive oil
1	onion
2	bay leaves

scant ½ cup/ 100 ml	fish stock
2 tsp/10 g	flour
1 pinch/2 g	saffron threads

John Dory with saffron sauce really does melt in the mouth. The recipe is very old; it dates back to Ottoman times. Today it is served mainly on special occasions.

Fish is extremely important in Turkish cuisine; after all, the country is surrounded by four seas, so there is always plenty of freshly caught fish and seafood available.

John Dory, which is available in fall and winter, can be recognized by its oval shape and the dark round patches on both sides of its body. It is greatly prized for its firm, white flesh, and the offcuts make excellent fish stock.

Fresh John Dory can be identified by its lovely fins and shiny scales. If you find filleting a nuisance, ask your fishmonger to do it for you. You can also use bream or sea salmon as a substitute.

The word "saffron" comes from the Arabian *za'farân*, which comes from the word *asfar* ("yellow"). Saffron is grown mainly in the region of the border with Iran. The most expensive spice in the world is obtained from a type of crocus: 200,000 flowers are needed for 2 pounds/1 kilogram of saffron. Dried saffron threads not only give this dish its pretty yellow color, but also add a unique aroma. Add the saffron at the end of cooking to prevent it from becoming bitter.

The bay leaf is an important herb in Turkish coastal regions. Whole or crushed, it enhances soups and braised dishes, stuffings, and marinades.

Fillet the fish and remove the skin. Season the fillets on both sides with salt and pepper.

Heat two-thirds of the olive oil in a skillet and fry the fillets on each side for 1 minute. Remove the fish from the skillet and set aside. Leave the oil in the skillet.

Peel the onion and slice into thin rings, then sauté in the skillet. Add the bay leaves and fish stock, and cook until reduced by half.

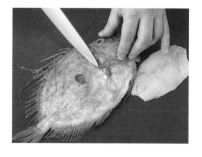

with Saffron Sauce

Strain the stock and pour into a pot. Reserve the bay leaves. Combine the flour with the remainder of the olive oil in a small bowl, then add to the fish stock.

Carefully place the fish fillets in the stock. Add the bay leaves.

Sprinkle over the saffron threads, and season the sauce with salt and pepper. Arrange the fish fillets on a serving plate and pour over the saffron sauce. Garnish with a bay leaf.

Preparation time:	25 minutes
Cooking time:	25 minutes
Difficulty:	★

Serves 4

2¼ lb/1 kg	mullet
⅔ cup/150 ml	olive oil
1 tsp	cumin
1 tsp	turmeric
1	onion, sliced
1¾ lb/750 g	potatoes

2	tomatoes
2	mild green chiles
1 pinch	saffron strands
1½ tbsp/20 g	salted butter
1	lemon, cut into slices
	salt and pepper

For the garnish:

| | parsley (optional) |

The old port of Bizerte, in the north of Tunisia, is as popular as ever, with its outdoor cafés where locals come to enjoy a mint tea and to admire the small, brightly colored fishing boats, aboard which the fishermen prepare their nets.

One of the most popular fish is probably the mullet. Called *bouri*, it is renowned for tasting strongly of the sea and for its firm flesh. When you go to your fishmonger, choose a firm specimen with brilliant scales, a plump belly, and bright eyes. If mullet is not available, our chef recommends "denti" or a pink bream instead.

The preparation of this traditional dish is typically Mediterranean. The mullet is baked in the oven at the same time as the potatoes, tomatoes, lemon slices, and onion. It is easy to make, yet delicious. According to our chef, the seasoning plays a critical part in the success of this recipe:

"In Tunisia, we have a popular saying which goes: 'Don't prepare fish without cumin.' *Kamoun*, as we call it, makes all the difference. This word also appears in many songs, because it personifies a person's charm!"

The precious cumin is an aromatic plant that originally came from Turkestan, but now is found all over the Mediterranean region. With its warm, spicy, and slightly bitter flavor, there is no substitute for this major spice in Tunisian cuisine.

Saffron strands, which need to be soaked in water, are also closely associated with the preparation of fish. Tunisians mainly use turmeric for its intense orangey color.

Bouri from the Old Port is a delicious dish which is eaten throughout the year. When you serve it, we suggest that you add a touch of green by decorating it with chopped parsley.

Scale, gut, and clean the mullet. Cut the fish into steaks.

Pour the olive oil into a dish. Season the mullet steaks with the salt, pepper, cumin, and turmeric, and put them into the dish with the sliced onion.

Peel the potatoes. Slice some and leave the others whole. Wash the tomatoes and cut them into quarters.

Old Port

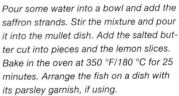

Transfer the mullet steaks to an oven dish.

Add the potatoes, tomatoes, and mild chiles.

Pour some water into a bowl and add the saffron strands. Stir the mixture and pour it into the mullet dish. Add the salted butter cut into pieces and the lemon slices. Bake in the oven at 350 °F/180 °C for 25 minutes. Arrange the fish on a dish with its parsley garnish, if using.

Stuffed Bream

Preparation time: 30 minutes
Cooking time: 20 minutes
Difficulty: ★

Serves 4

4	bream
14 oz/400 g	potatoes, peeled
pinch	saffron strands
2 oz/50 g	veal liver
	olive oil
2 oz/50 g	onion, chopped
3½ tbsp/50 g	chopped flat-leaf parsley
1	lemon
	salt and pepper

Bream stuffed with veal liver is saved for special occasions and distinguished guests. Surprisingly, those living in the capital don't cook a great deal of fish, with the exception of mullet, which abounds in the nearby still waters. Bream and bass are the fish most commonly stuffed by Tunisians. Ali Matri enjoys serving bream stuffed with mussels and clams, or even fennel, lemon, and melted butter, to his clientele.

Tunisians are extremely fond of bream. It is a migratory fish that is commonly caught along the 800 mile/1,300 km stretch of coastline. The people of Sfax and the Kerkenna Islands eat vast quantities of it. The three species, royal, gray, and pink, are available in the markets. Medium-sized bream are ideal for stuffing, and the larger ones—up to 11 lb/5 kg—usually end up being cut into steaks and cooked in a couscous.

When Tunisian cooks open a bream in order to stuff it, they make a single cut through the back. If they split it through the belly, the fine bones of the rib cage would hamper the neat removal of the backbone and spoil the flesh. When the backbone is removed starting with the tail, the main difficulty is with the head. You need to pull very hard to break the backbone, or cut it with the end of your scissors.

Be cautious when adding the saffron, because the delicate flavor of the bream is easily drowned by the powerful flavor of these crocus pistils. In Tunisian cuisine, which spice is added depends on the method of cooking and not on the fish selected. Thus, saffron would lose its relevance in a fried fish recipe.

Slices of potato cook in the oven alongside the fish. Make them more interesting by cutting them out with a mandoline.

Make an incision in the back of the bream, from head to tail. With the end of a knife, go along either side of the backbone and detach the fillets gently. Pull the backbone out of the fish, cut it at the level of the head, and remove it.

With a mandoline or a zester, cut the potatoes into fluted slices. Sprinkle a pinch of saffron strands over them and place them to one side. Cut the veal liver into small cubes.

Heat a trickle of olive oil in a high-sided frying pan. Add the cubes of liver to the hot oil and fry gently, stirring with a spatula so that they are browned well all over.

from the Tunis Region

Open the fish into two halves. Season the inside with salt, pepper, and a few saffron strands.

Fill the inside of the bream with chopped onion, parsley, and browned cubes of liver. Close up the fish.

Arrange the stuffed bream on a baking sheet. Surround with potato slices. Sprinkle with a little water and a trickle of olive oil. Bake in the oven at 350 °F/180 °C for 10–15 minutes. Serve with lemon slices.

Fillet of Bass with Olives

Preparation time:	30 minutes
Cooking time:	30 minutes
Difficulty:	★

Serves 4

4	fillets of bass, 6¾ oz/ 190 g each
4	tomatoes
1	onion, thinly sliced
1	garlic clove, thinly sliced
7 tbsp/100 ml	olive oil
1	pickled lemon
10 tbsp/150 g	pitted green olives
½ bunch	parsley, chopped

1 tsp	harissa
½ tsp	turmeric
	salt and pepper

For the garnish:

2 sprigs	fresh mint
4 sprigs	parsley, chopped

Fillet of bass with olives and pickled lemon is a typically Mediterranean dish. Our chef's recipe originates from the Tunisian coast, which is well-stocked with fish. A favorite fish since Roman times, the bass, also called sea bass, is noted for the fine quality of its flesh, which is firm, very lean, and delicate. The Tunisians breed them in offshore fish farms and export about 550 tons/500 tonnes a year to Italy, France, and Spain.

To make this recipe, you need some pickled lemon. The acidic, juicy pulp of this citrus fruit, noted for its high vitamin C content, is protected by a yellow, fragrant, and relatively thick skin. If you want to pickle your own lemons, wash them thoroughly and make an incision at the top in the shape of a cross. Then steep them in a mixture of water, salt, and white vinegar for about two months. Allow 7 tbsp/100 ml of white vinegar to 4 cups/1 liter of water.

Our chef suggests following the traditional method used by the villagers to gauge the correct amount of salt: take an egg and clean it. Then immerse it gently in a container holding 4 cups/1 liter water. Add an amount of salt necessary to bring the shell back up to the surface. Then you'll have the ideal amount!

You can also use this steeping method to preserve green olives. In addition, our chef recommends it for blanching them to get rid of any bitterness and excess salt. You can also slice them thinly for a more attractive presentation.

Tunisia has more than 60 million olive trees, distributed over 4 million acres/1.6 million hectares. The production of olive oil, renowned all over the world, is an undeniable part of the heritage of this country, and an economic resource of primary importance.

Cut the bass into steaks with a sharp knife.

Peel the tomatoes and deseed them. Chop them into small cubes. Brown the thinly sliced onion and garlic in 2 tbsp (30 ml) of the olive oil. Add the chopped tomatoes. Season with salt. Fry gently for approximately 10 minutes.

Cut the pickled lemon into short thin strips and remove the pulp. Soak the strips in water to remove the taste of the vinegar and salt.

and Pickled Lemon

Blanch the olives by immersing them in boiling water for 10 minutes. Drain and allow them to cool.

Add the lemon strips, olives, and chopped parsley to the tomato mixture. Mix together gently. Simmer over a very low heat for 2 minutes.

Add salt and pepper to the bass steaks. Brush them with harissa, turmeric, and the remaining olive oil. Cook for 4 minutes on each side. Arrange them on plates and add the tomato mixture and olives. Garnish with mint leaves and chopped parsley.

Preparation time:	25 minutes
Cooking time:	35 minutes
Difficulty:	★

Serves 6

1	potato
1¼ lb/500 g	whiting fillets
1	onion, chopped
1 tbsp	olive oil
½ bunch	flat-leaf parsley, chopped
3½ tbsp/50 g	ground cumin
3½ tbsp/50 g	ground turmeric
1	lemon

2	eggs
¾ cup/50 g	breadcrumbs
1¼ cups/150 g	all-purpose flour

2 cups/500 ml	cooking oil
	salt and pepper

For the tomato sauce:

1	onion, chopped
4	garlic cloves, chopped
3½ tbsp/50 ml	olive oil
5 tbsp/100 g	tomato paste
6 tsp/30 g	sweet paprika
4 or 5 sprigs	parsley, chopped
6 tsp/30 g	cumin

Garnish:

	parsley leaves

As with children of all nationalities, Tunisian children don't like picking over a fish full of bones, and therefore turn their noses up at it. A long time ago, mothers devised a clever way to get them to eat it: simply mix flaked fish and potato purée, add some eggs to hold it together when it's being fried, and then make small balls from the mixture. Children thoroughly enjoy these flat *kefta* browned in oil. They're usually flavored with cumin. When Tunisians invite guests to their homes, they always serve *kefta* alongside the varied dishes, croquettes, and delights made using fritter sheets.

For this recipe, the chef has chosen whiting fillets, but *Kefta* can also be made with other fish such as large sardines.

When the fish is steamed, it remains relatively dry and the resulting filling is easy to mold into small croquettes. If you poach it, take care to drain it well before mixing it with the other filling ingredients. As you flake it, make sure you remove all the bones, both the small and large ones, and separate the flesh as delicately as possible. Your *kefta* will acquire a certain sophistication by doing this.

Two different spices, cumin and turmeric, are combined to season the *kefta*. After the harvest, cumin, coriander, caraway seeds, and fennel are dried in the sun. After that, Tunisians only grind the amount they need for their meals that week, in order to preserve the maximum flavor. If ground too far in advance, cumin loses its volatile aroma, and takes on a bitter taste that will completely change the flavor of the *kefta*. Originating from India and China, turmeric is available in the form of dried rhizomes. Often used instead of expensive saffron, turmeric gives an orangey color to food.

Peel the potato and cut into quarters. Put it on to boil. Poach the whiting fillets over a low heat for 3 minutes, or steam them.

Fry the chopped onion in the olive oil until golden brown. Sprinkle it with chopped parsley and remove from the heat. Stir with a spatula.

Flake the fish and remove all the bones. Place in a bowl and sprinkle with onion and parsley, cumin, turmeric, salt, pepper, a squeeze of lemon, and the cooked potato. Break the eggs into the center of the mixture. Use a fork to mash it finely. Thicken it with the breadcrumbs.

Kefta

Take portions of the mixture and mold into small balls. Flatten them out with the palm of your hand.

For the sauce, brown the chopped onion and garlic in the olive oil. Add the tomato paste thinned with water, the paprika, salt, pepper, and a little water. Cook for 10 minutes. At the end of cooking, add chopped parsley and cumin.

Heat the cooking oil in a frying pan. Roll the croquettes in all-purpose flour and fry them in the oil until brown. Remove with a slotted spoon, then drain on a paper towel. Pour a circle of sauce in the center of the plates, and place the kefta croquettes on top of parsley leaves.

Malthout

Preparation time:	25 minutes
To cook the garbanzo beans:	50 minutes
To cook malthout with grouper fish:	1 hour 35 minutes
To soak the garbanzo beans:	12 hours
Difficulty:	★★

Serves 4

1¼ cups/200 g	garbanzo beans (chickpeas)
10½ oz/300 g	onions, chopped
7 tbsp/100 ml	olive oil

2 oz/50 g	garlic
1 tsp	ground cumin
2 pinches	ground paprika
12 tbsp/200 g	tomato paste
2 lb/1 kg	grouper fish
1 pinch	ground turmeric
7 oz/200 g	mild green chiles
2½ cups/500 g	malthout (broiled barley)
14 oz/400 g	potatoes
14 oz/400 g	pumpkin
7 oz/200 g	zucchini
	salt and pepper

Moez Ksouda's mother has passed this recipe down to her son. She cooks the fish in a *taklia* sauce, which is peculiar to this region: a blend of tomato paste, onions, and spices browned in olive oil, reduced and then simmered with salted mild chiles, which flavor the sauce.

Made with barley, *malthout* is one of the numerous types of Tunisian cereal. Unrefined barley is sorted, broiled, and then pounded to remove the husk. It is then winnowed and ground in a mill. Through several sieving operations, the large grains called *malthout* are initially collected, next the medium-sized grains or *chicha*, and finally the flour. The *malthout* is steamed, the *chicha* is used in soups, and the flour is used to prepare the barley bread made in Sfax.

In the Tunisian countryside, the treatment of durum wheat, barley, and sorghum takes place once a year after the harvests: this is the *Aoula* season. Green barley is turned into

the *chorba frik*; the ripe grains are crushed to make *asmar* couscous, or broiled to obtain *malthout*.

Tunisians can choose between red or white grouper fish. Our chef's advice is to use white grouper, which has a more tender flesh. Very plentiful, but a little expensive, this large fish is considered noble and is served to welcome guests. To spice up the flavor of the sauce, moisten the paprika, tomatoes, salt, pepper, and cumin mixture, and then add the fish head and bones and cook gently for 30 minutes. Filter the sauce by passing it through a small conical strainer.

Rinse the chiles, then make an incision 1 in/2–3 cm in length above the stalk; salt is placed on the tip of a knife and inserted into the incision. When they've cooked in the sauce, don't forget to remove them, before cooking the grouper. Serve the sauce and chiles separately.

Boil the garbanzo beans for 50 minutes. Sweat the chopped onions in 3½ tbsp (50 ml) hot olive oil in the bottom part of the couscous steamer. In a mortar, pound the garlic with 1 pinch cumin, and add to the onions. Brown over a high heat. Add a little cold water.

Stir in the paprika, tomato paste, salt, pepper, and a pinch of cumin. Moisten slightly, then reduce this tomato sauce for 15 minutes over a low heat.

Cut fillets from the fish and remove the skin. Cut into steaks 4 in/10 cm long. Season with turmeric, paprika, salt, pepper, and cumin.

with Grouper Fish

Cut off the stalks of the chiles. Make an incision above the stalk, put some salt on the tip of the knife, and insert the salt into the chiles. Add them to the reduced tomato sauce. Reduce again over a low heat until the chiles are cooked, then set aside.

Rinse the malthout. Mix thoroughly with the remaining olive oil. Pour it into the couscous steamer's colander. Put it all on top of the tomato sauce cooking pot. Cook for 10 minutes.

Immerse the grouper fish steaks into the sauce. Cook for 20 minutes. Remove the fish, and set aside. Cook the potatoes in the sauce for 10 minutes, then 20 minutes more with the pumpkin and zucchini. Serve the fish on top of the malthout, surrounded by the vegetables and beans.

Stuffed Sardines

Preparation time:	*35 minutes*		12	large sardines
Cooking time:	*35 minutes*			salt and pepper
Difficulty:	★★			

Serves 4

For the tomato sauce:

12 oz/350 g	fresh tomatoes
7 tbsp/100 ml	olive oil
½ tsp	caraway seeds
½ tbsp/8 g	tomato paste
½ tsp	harissa
2 cloves	garlic, thinly sliced
	salt and pepper

For the stuffed sardines:

1	whiting fillet
1	cod fillet
2 oz/50 g	onion, chopped
1	clove garlic, chopped
7 tbsp/100 ml	olive oil
1 pinch	ground cumin
1 pinch	ground chile powder
1 bunch	flat-leaf parsley, chopped
1 pinch	ground coriander
¼ cup/20 g	breadcrumbs
2 or 3	eggs

For the fried vegetables:

4	potatoes
4	red and green chiles
	cooking oil

Gourmets in the Sousse region enjoy creating fillings for large, very plump sardines. The third largest town in Tunisia, Sousse is one of the 40 or so ports in the country, and among the dozen which are equipped to fish at sea. Similar to Mahdia, Sfax, and Gabès, it is renowned for its blue fish, sardines, mackerel, anchovies, and bonito. For about a century, a large quantity of sardines has been caught at night by lamplight, using a very powerful lamp pointed at the waves to attract the fish.

From May until August, Tunisian waters abound in the most delicious sardines. Tunisians buy them as soon as the boat arrives at the quay, to ensure their freshness. They are cooked as quickly as possible—either broiled, fried, cooked in the couscous steamer, or baked in the oven, together with chiles, fresh tomatoes, garlic, onion, and turmeric. The port

of Mahdia has important canning factories that pack the little silvery fish in olive oil, vegetable oil, or tomato sauce.

In his recipe, Chokri Chteoui prepares the sardine stuffing from a mixture of small fish, anchovies, mackerel, or whiting. But you could simply stuff them with a mixture of onions, garlic, parsley, breadcrumbs, eggs, and spices.

These sardines can be fried or baked in the oven. If you find the method of filling the sardines too fiddly, open them up through the belly and fill them with stuffing. If you can't buy sardines large enough to stuff, cut them open instead, spread an open sardine on its back and top its flesh with the stuffing. Cover it with another open sardine, placed in the opposite direction from the first. Then all you need to do is fry these small fish "sandwiches" in a pan.

Poach the whiting and cod in salted water for 10 minutes. Chop the flesh. Brown the onion and garlic in 3½ tbsp (50 ml) of the olive oil. Remove from the heat and add the fish, cumin, ground chile pepper, chopped parsley, coriander, breadcrumbs, eggs, salt, and pepper.

Cut the heads off the sardines. Make an incision towards the end of the tail. Massage the sardine along its backbone to loosen it, then pull the tail gently until you can remove the backbone. Fill each sardine with stuffing, pushing it gently in with a spoon handle.

Heat the rest of the oil in the bottom of a large frying pan. Transfer the stuffed sardines to the hot oil and brown on both sides, turning them carefully. Put them to one side on a paper towel.

Sousse-Style

Prepare the sauce: peel and deseed the tomatoes. Cut into small cubes, then pass through a vegetable mill. Peel the potatoes and cut into slices.

Heat the oil in a frying pan. Using a slotted spoon, immerse the chiles in the hot oil. Allow them to brown, then drain on a paper towel. Next fry the potato slices.

In a saucepan, blend the tomato purée with the olive oil. Add caraway seeds, salt, pepper, tomato paste, harissa, and thinly sliced garlic. Simmer for 10 minutes. Arrange 3 sardines, some tomato sauce, and strips of fried chile on each plate.

Grilled Essaouira

Preparation time:	35 minutes
Marinating time:	2 hours
Cooking time:	20 minutes
Difficulty:	★

Serves 4

1⅓ lbs/600 g	swordfish
2	green bell peppers
2	red bell peppers
½ stick/50 g	butter
1 cup/200 g	rice
1 tsp	paprika powder
1 tbsp/15 ml	vegetable oil
	salt

For the marinade:

6 cloves	garlic
1 bunch	parsley
1 bunch	cilantro (coriander)
1 tsp	chile powder
½ tsp	cumin
1 tsp	paprika powder
1	lemon
	salt and pepper

Essaouira, which is well protected by its red and ochre fortifications, is determined to preserve its grand houses with their blue shutters. This charming Phoenician town with its square grid of streets is well known for its maritime life.

You should go to the harbor of an evening to watch the fishing boats tie up. The quays, which seemed quite sleepy beforehand, suddenly come to life. Many people gather there, attracted by the cries of the market-stall holders advertising their wares. Business is at its height at the fish stalls wedged in between the colorful boats and trawlers. Tempting odors of broiled skewers of fish arise from the *kanouns* and *braseros*. Essaouira is full of life.

The people of Essaouira love everything the sea offers them as food, and miss no opportunity of enjoying it. The swordfish skewers are sometimes grilled directly by the shore. They are very popular and also suitable for a meal with guests. At the same time, they are easy to make.

Swordfish live in great numbers in warm ocean waters and are impressively big. They are very popular as they have excellent, tender flesh, but tuna is just as suitable for this recipe. Generally, swordfish are sold in cut pieces. The tail and the fins are also edible.

Grilling the skewers over hot coals is one of the oldest methods of cooking this fish. Some people add a little lamb fat to give the fish additional aroma. Wait until all the charcoal is glowing before you start grilling the fish.

For the marinade, put the crushed garlic cloves, chopped parsley, chopped coriander, chile powder, cumin, and paprika into a salad bowl. Squeeze the lemon and add the juice. Season with salt and pepper and mix together all the ingredients.

Cut the swordfish into strips and then into regular cubes. Place these in the marinade and stir carefully. Marinate for at least 2 hours.

Wash the green and red bell peppers and remove seeds. Cut into very small cubes.

Fish Skewers

Melt the butter in a pan. Add the rice and the cubes of pepper. Sweat for about 3 minutes.

Add 1 tsp of paprika powder and season with salt. Cover with water and cook, covered, for 12–15 minutes.

Take the swordfish cubes out of the marinade and put onto skewers. Drizzle with oil. Cook on the grill and then arrange on plates with some of the rice.

Tangier-Style

Preparation time:	30 minutes
Cooking time:	30 minutes
Difficulty:	★★

Serves 4

2¼ lbs/1 kg	calamaries (small squid)
1¼ cups/250 g	rice
1 bunch	flat-leaf parsley
1 bunch	cilantro (coriander)

3½ oz/100 g	garlic
4 tbsp/60ml	olive oil
2 pinches	cayenne pepper
	salt and pepper

For the garnish:

| 1 | green lemon |

The calamaries introduced here by M'hamed Chahid are filled with a mixture of garlic, herbs, and rice and served in a savory red sauce. In his restaurant, the chef often serves them on a bed of parsley and pours sauce over them.

All year round, Moroccan fishermen supply the country with numerous mollusks such as calamaries, octopus, and squid. They are all available in the markets: the smallest are known as *chipirons, puntia,* or *supions.* For this traditional dish, the chef uses medium-sized calamaries seven to eight inches/20 centimeters in length. It is possible to find large specimens up to two feet/60 centimeters in length.

The Moroccans particularly prize calamaries with a filling of whiting and *chermoula.* The little harbor restaurants also offer these broiled to passers-by.

After removing the head, you should also take out the beak-like jaws in the center of the tentacles. To do this, open the ring of tentacles, press on the head with two fingers so that the "beak" comes into view, and then firmly draw it out.

The rice is first cooked in boiling water, but it should be taken off the heat once it is soft but not quite cooked through. It will then continue to swell inside the calamaries while these simmer in the sauce.

The chef recommends serving this dish with green lemon; its taste refines the strong aroma of the calamaries. In the old quarters of many Moroccan cities there are still houses with courtyards where lemon trees grow. All those living in the house can help themselves as they wish.

To clean the calamaries, hold the head and carefully draw out the innards. Remove the bone. Thoroughly rinse the mantle. Cut off the tentacles and remove the "beak." Blanch the tentacles for 5 minutes in boiling water. Put the mantles aside.

Bring salted water to the boil in a pot. Add the rice and cook for 10 minutes.

Chop the parsley, cilantro, and poached tentacles, one after the other. Peel the garlic and chop finely.

Stuffed Calamaries

Pour a little olive oil into a pot. Add the rice, three-quarters of the cilantro and the parsley, 3 oz/80 g of garlic and the tentacles. Stir while on the heat.

Season the rice filling with pepper, salt, and 1 pinch of cayenne pepper. Fry for 3–4 minutes, stirring.

Fill the mantles with the rice mixture. Close the opening with a toothpick. Fry the calamaries in olive oil with the cilantro, parsley, and garlic that has been kept aside and add salt, pepper, and 1 pinch of cayenne pepper. Cook for 10 minutes in the sauce. Serve.

Sea Bass with

Preparation time:	30 minutes
Marinating time:	15 minutes
Cooking time:	25 minutes
Difficulty:	★★

Serves 4

4	sea bass, each about 12 oz/350 g
4 cloves	garlic
1¼ lb/560 g	onions
1 bunch	parsley
1 bunch	cilantro (coriander)
	salt and pepper

2	lemons
1¾ cups/320 g	large *majhoul* dates
1⅔ cups/200 g	shelled walnuts
4 tbsp/60 ml	olive oil
4 tbsp/60 ml	peanut oil
½ envelope	saffron threads
½ envelope	Moroccan saffron powder for coloring

For the garnish:

| 2 | lemons |
| 4 | medium tomatoes |

Several chefs have taken part in creating this dish. In keeping with tradition, they have combined sweet flavors with savory, but have developed the traditional recipe a stage further. The result is a combination of marinated sea bass with a mixture of herbs and spices and the sweet dates filled with walnuts.

There are two types of sea bass living in Moroccan waters: one with a dark back, and a spotted one that is especially widespread in the Mediterranean. With its fine white flesh, the fish is used for many delicacies in Morocco: skewers, fillets, rolled in beaten egg with herbs and spices (parsley, cumin, cilantro, salt, and pepper) and fried, or in tagines with fresh vegetables (potatoes, olives, pickled lemons).

In Morocco, guests are offered dates and milk as an expression of hospitality. The chef recommends *majhoul* dates for

this dish, as they are large, fleshy, and very sweet. Morocco is not so well known as Tunisia as a producer of dates, yet innumerable different varieties of dates ripen here: the relatively small and pale *boussekri* or the somewhat yellowish *bleuh* are only two examples.

Far south, there are almost a million date palms in the luscious green, water-rich oases of the Tafilalet. Their fruit is harvested at the end of September. In early October, the date festival is held in Erfoud. For three days, Berber tribes, hoteliers, dealers, and tourists all celebrate this small desert fruit.

In his restaurant, Bouchaïb Kama drizzles a sauce of onions and saffron over the sea bass. In this version, he has distributed the sauce around the fish to show off the fish and dates to better effect.

Cut off the fins and the tip of the tail from the sea bass with fish scissors. Cut into the fish at the gills and a little on the belly. Clean and gut, and rinse under running water.

Chop the garlic, onions (put 10 oz/280 g of these aside afterwards), parsley, and cilantro. Mix with salt, pepper, and lemon juice. Stuff the fish with this mixture and allow to soak in for 15 minutes.

Open the dates carefully along one side (without cutting them in two) and remove the pits. Fill each date with a walnut kernel.

Majhoul Dates

Heat both types of oil in a deep pan. Add the reserved onions and fry briefly. Add saffron threads and saffron powder. Sweat the onions, stirring, on a low heat.

Place the stuffed sea bass on this bed of onions and saffron.

Arrange the filled dates around the fish. Add the remaining marinade and a little water. Cover the pan with a piece of aluminum foil and place in the oven for 15 minutes. Reduce the sauce a little and then beat with butter. Garnish, if you wish.

Stuffed

Preparation time: 1 hour 10 minutes
Marinating time: 2 hours
Cooking time: 40 minutes
Difficulty: ★★

Serves 4

1	sea bass, weighing approximately 4½ lbs/2 kg
2	lemons
2¼ lbs/1 kg	tomatoes
1⅛ lb/500 g	green, red, and yellow bell peppers
7 oz/200 g	onions
7 tbsp/100 ml	olive oil

For the chermoula sauce:

6 cloves	garlic
1 bunch	parsley
1 bunch	cilantro (coriander)
1 pinch	chile powder
1 tsp	paprika
½ tsp	cumin
7 tbsp/100 ml	white vinegar
1 tsp	tomato paste
	salt and pepper

For the filling:

1 cup/200 g	rice
4 tbsp	tomato paste
7 oz/200 g	shelled shrimp
3½ oz/100 g	pickled lemons
2 oz/50 g	purple olives, pitted

For the garnish:

2 oz/50 g	shelled shrimp

This stuffed sea bass is a delicacy, usually served only at major festivals. It is a specialty of the royal city of Fez.

Sea bass are plentiful in the Mediterranean. The fish is highly prized for its firm, lean, and delicious flesh. It can be poached, flambéed, fried, or stuffed. Keep an eye on it while cooking, as the flesh can fall apart rapidly. When fresh, its body is firm, smelling slightly of iodine, its scales gleam, the eyes protrude slightly, and its gills are pink. Depending on what is available in the market, you can also replace it with common pandora, dorade, or sea bream.

In this recipe the fish is flavored with *chermoula*. The mixture of garlic, parsley, cilantro, paprika, cumin, tomato paste, chile powder, salt, pepper, and white vinegar not only acts as a flavoring but also makes the flesh more

tender. *Chermoula* also makes the fish keep longer. If the fish is very large, prick it lightly to allow the marinade to soak into the flesh.

Shrimp are of particular importance for the filling. There are hundreds of different varieties of shrimp. The bodies of these crustaceans grow longer the colder the water is in which they live. When fresh, the small common shrimp have a lovely mild scent, and also smells slightly of iodine. They combine harmoniously with the rice, that is also part of the filling. The rice must be cooked before mixing in the other ingredients.

The sea bass is served with tomatoes, lemons, onions, and bell peppers of various colors. These varieties of vegetable are the ingredients of many Mediterranean dishes.

For the chermoula, place the crushed garlic cloves, chopped parsley, chopped cilantro, chile powder, cumin, and paprika in a bowl. Then pour on vinegar and mix all ingredients. Season with salt and pepper, then stir in tomato paste.

Hold the sea bass by the belly and cut from the head to the tail fins. Lift first 1 fillet, then the other. Loosen and remove the backbone with scissors. Marinate the fish for 2 hours in the chermoula in the fridge.

Peel both lemons. Wash tomatoes and bell peppers and remove seeds from the latter. Cut all fruits into slices, and do the same for the onions. Put aside.

Sea Bass

Blanch the rice for the filling. Add tomato paste, shrimp, and diced pickled lemons, and olives. Add 2 tbsp of chermoula. Dilute the remaining chermoula with a glass of water and put aside.

Carefully stuff the sea bass with the filling. Sew closed using a needle and kitchen thread, starting from the head.

Fill a deep baking pan with slices of tomato, lemon, and onion. Place the sea bass on the slices. Pour on the diluted chermoula, olive oil, and shrimp to garnish. Bake for 40 minutes at 350 °F/180 °C. Then remove thread and serve with vegetables and shrimp.

Preparation time:	25 minutes
Marinating time:	24 hours
Cooking time:	25 minutes
Difficulty:	★★

Serves 4

3 lbs/1.4 kg	pandora
5 oz/150 g	green bell peppers
4½ oz/125 g	red bell peppers
4½ oz/125 g	medium tomatoes
2 tbsp/30 ml	vegetable oil
2 tbsp/30 ml	olive oil
3 oz/75 g	button mushrooms
½ oz/15 g	tomato paste
3 oz/90 g	shelled shrimp
1	pickled lemon

For the chermoula sauce:

| 2 oz/50 g | fresh cilantro (coriander) |
| 2 oz/50 g | flat-leaf parsley |

1 oz/30 g	garlic
7 oz/200 g	onions
¼ tsp	ground cumin
½ tsp	paprika
1	lemon
7 tbsp/100 ml	olive oil
	salt and pepper

For the garnish:

2 oz/50 g	red olives
2 oz/50 g	pickled lemon
⅔ oz/20 g	flat-leaf parsley (optional)

In many of Morocco's regions, fish are cooked in a sauce of tomatoes, bell peppers, and olive oil. Mohammed Aïtali, who comes from Rabat, has modified these dishes by adding button mushrooms and shrimp to the sauce. His savory and colorful recipe for pandora is, however, reserved for festive occasions. For everyday meals, Moroccans find it sufficient to broil a few economical sardines, small sole, or whiting. Although the chef has decided on pandora, that doesn't mean you can't choose dorade or shi drum.

The delicious *r'bati* fish are supplied by small fishing boats anchoring in front of the old houses of the Oudaïa casbah in Rabat. The Bou Regreg River, which flows into the Atlantic not far away, separates Rabat from the ancient city of Salé. At the mouth of the Bou Regreg, however, there is a maritime "barrier" that has always prevented large ships from entering the harbor. The nearest large port is Casablanca, and most of the fish eaten in Rabat comes from there.

The only mushrooms used in Moroccan cuisine are finely sliced button mushrooms, used equally in fillings for fish and pastries or *briouates*. Wild mushrooms are eaten only rarely. In the markets of the Atlas, the Central Atlas, and the Shoul region (near Rabat), there is, however, a local variety of mushroom on sale, very similar to the button mushroom.

Mohammed Aïtali strongly recommends marinating the fish for a day in the *chermoula* to allow it to develop its full aroma. If you are in a hurry, marinate it for at least an hour. The *chermoula* gives the fine flesh of the pandora a wonderful flavor.

Make a cut in the pandora behind the head at the height of the gills. Carefully lift off the fillets by moving the knife from head to tail along the backbone.

For the chermoula, chop the cilantro, parsley, garlic, and onions and mix with cumin, salt, pepper, and paprika. Add a little lemon juice and a splash of olive oil. Stir to a smooth paste.

Place the fish fillets on a platter. Cover each fillet with chermoula, pressing the marinade down somewhat with the back of a spoon, to allow the fish to take up the aroma. Chill and leave to marinate for 1 day.

Pandora

On the next day, cut the bell peppers open lengthways. Remove the white pith and the seeds. Halve the tomatoes, remove seeds, and cut into quarters. Cut the bell peppers and tomatoes into thin strips.

Heat a mixture of olive oil and vegetable oil in a pan. Add finely cut bell peppers, tomatoes, and mushrooms and sweat all the above on a high heat, stirring. Add tomato paste mixed with a little water, shrimp, and diced pickled lemon.

Add the marinated fish to the vegetables in the pan. Pour on a little water. Cook in the oven for 15 minutes. Arrange the fish on a bed of vegetables and garnish with red olives, slices of pickled lemon, and parsley.

Jewish-Style

Preparation time: 30 minutes
Cooking time: 25 minutes
Difficulty: ★★

Serves 4

1	pandora, 2¼ lbs/1 kg in weight
1 bunch	cilantro (coriander)
10	ñoras (dried, mild peppers)
6 cloves	garlic
10	thin sticks of reed
7 tbsp/100 ml	vegetable oil
	salt

This Jewish-style fish is typical of Tangier. An inviting family dish, it is usually eaten on Friday evenings at the family meal and was a very widespread dish in earlier times. It was also eaten for lunch as *kemia* on the following day.

Thanks to the balance of its flavors, this dish can also be prepared using dorade. Pandora and dorade, both Mediterranean fish, are suitable for several different methods of cooking.

The pandora can easily be recognized by its shape and is distinguished from the dorade mainly by its reddish coloring. Both fish have white, lean, and very tasty flesh and do not require much cooking. Don't forget to line the bottom of the pan with reeds. This will prevent the fish from sticking.

In this recipe, the cilantro develops its full aroma. The plant is also known as "Arabian parsley" and is used primarily to flavor salads, soups, and sauces. The seeds—coriander—can be recognized by their smell, reminiscent of nutmeg and lemons. Garlic, so prized in those countries bordering on the Mediterranean, is an essential ingredient here. This plant of the onion family can be found all year round in the markets. In spring, buy garlic that is as young as you can get. This is milder and easier to peel. It is best kept in the vegetable compartment of your fridge.

In Morocco, this traditional meal is also known as "fish in red sauce." The color is due to the ñoras—mild peppers from Spain. Christopher Columbus brought these fruits back from the New World and introduced them as a flavoring. The peppers are dried and will keep for at least a year. Don't forget to soak them before using them.

Remove scales from the pandora, gut and wash. Cut into slices of equal thickness.

Wash the bunch of cilantro and chop finely. Soak the ñoras in cold water.

Peel the cloves of garlic. Crush half of them with a fork and put the others aside.

Fish

Place the stems of reed on the bottom of a pan.

Pour on the oil and the drained ñoras.

Add cilantro and crushed garlic cloves to the pan. Season with salt. Add slices of fish. Mix. Add ½ glass of water and whole garlic cloves. Cook, covered, for 25 minutes. Arrange on a plate and garnish with ñoras and garlic. Pour on a little of the sauce.

Meat &
Poultry

Rack of Lamb with

Preparation time:	1 hour
Cooking time:	1 hour 30 minutes
Difficulty:	★

Serves 4

2	racks of lamb, each with 12 cutlets
1	carrot
1	onion
1	tomato
1	leek
²/₃ cup/150 ml	olive oil

³/₄ cup/200 ml	red wine
1 sprig	rosemary
3½ tbsp/100 g	honey
4 tbsp/60 ml	red wine vinegar
	salt and pepper

For the garnish:

8	mini carrots
8	mini turnips
8	mini zucchini
4 oz/100 g	sugar peas

Way back in the 15th century, the Muslim population of Córdoba used to cook roast lamb with honey and aromatic herbs on special occasions. Following the Reconquista in 1492, the region found itself under Spanish-Christian rule once again, but this recipe has survived until today.

Alberto Herráiz is proud of his home, and he chooses high-quality, award-winning lamb of controlled origin for this dish. The animals roam free in La Mancha in the heart of Spain. The method described here does credit to the quality of the meat. The chef believes that the rack is the best cut for this recipe, but the loin is an excellent substitute.

To make the most of the sauce, our chef adds red wine from La Mancha to the cooking juices and vegetables. It is a fairly heavy wine, and so is ideal for reducing the sauce.

Alberto Herráiz uses a wine vinegar based on a Cabernet-Sauvignon, which can also be replaced by a mild red wine vinegar. The vinegar for this sauce should not be too acidic. One further enhancement to the delicate rosemary aroma of the rack of lamb is rosemary honey. If you find the sauce has not reduced sufficiently after braising the vegetables and bones, the chef advises straining the liquid through a sieve and boiling it again until reduced. You can also dust the bones in flour before putting the roasting pan in the oven.

A good winter side dish to go with the rack of lamb is steamed potatoes, whereas spring vegetables are ideal in that season.

Peel the baby carrots and turnips, and pare the zucchini in strips. Blanch the sugar peas until just firm to the bite, then plunge them in cold water. Blanch the zucchini on their own, then blanch the carrots and turnips together.

Trim the meat from between the top of the bones of the racks of lamb. Using a small knife, cut into the meat along the spine, then use a cleaver to separate it from the rack. Set aside the racks. Cut off the fat.

Trim and peel the carrot, onion, tomato, and leek. Chop the lamb's backbone into pieces. Put the vegetables and bones in a casserole with a little oil, and brown for 15 minutes.

Honey and Rosemary

As soon as the vegetables start to change color, pour over the red wine, then add the rosemary, salt, and pepper. Put the casserole in the oven (480 °F/250 °C) for about 1 hour, until the vegetables and meat are very soft.

Season the racks with salt and pepper, and brown on all sides in a skillet. Put the skillet in the oven. Cook for a further 6 minutes, turning occasionally.

Remove the casserole from the oven. Stir in the honey and vinegar, strain, then reduce to thicken the sauce. Slice the racks of lamb. Serve the cutlets with the blanched mini-vegetables, honey and wine sauce.

Young Goat Cutlets

Preparation time: 25 minutes
Cooking time: 15 minutes
Difficulty: ★

Serves 4

2¼ lb /1 kg   rack of baby goat
1 bunch   fresh garlic
1⅔ cups/400 ml   olive oil
3   large potatoes
   salt

The village of Villena near Alicante is famous for its garlic production. The Spaniards love the bulb for its piquancy, and so it is hardly surprising that it should appear in so many dishes.

This dish was invented by goatherders. The main ingredient is young goat. Goats are bred mainly in the Verga Baja region near Murcia. The meat from these young animals is usually available from mid-March to early May. Young goat tastes a little like milk-fed lamb, which makes a perfect substitute.

The olive oil, in particular, gives the baby goat cutlets in this recipe the most wonderful aroma. Olive oil is used everywhere in Spanish gastronomy. The Iberians are great lovers of the fine oil and know everything there is to know about the various qualities and flavors.

In this sun-drenched country, the oil is usually a little tart, but always very mild and fruity. Anyone who values a high-quality product needs to look out for three things: that it is produced in olive groves, that it is harvested by hand, and that it is pressed appropriately. The most renowned is *aciete de oliva virgen extra*—that is to say, the extra virgin oil from the first cold pressing.

Olive oil must be kept cool and out of the light, ideally in a glass bottle or clay jug. Direct sunlight will shorten its shelf life, and reduce the levels of vitamins and nutrients.

Potatoes are grown along the entire Mediterranean coast, from Gerona to Málaga. This root vegetable, which came originally from South America, is one of the staples in the modern diet. Choose ones that are firm and smooth with no obvious shoots.

Trim the meat, cutting the meat off the ribs along the entire length, and cutting out the meat between the ribs. Scrape all the meat off the bones.

Chop off the outer end of the ribs with a cleaver. Divide the rack into cutlets with a sharp knife.

Peel the garlic, then cut it into pieces. Season with salt and fry in olive oil. Set the garlic aside and use the oil for the cutlets.

from Villena

Peel the potatoes. Slice very thinly using a mandoline, then cut these slices into matchsticks.

Fry the potato strips in the remainder of the olive oil and drain on paper towels to absorb the excess oil. Season with salt.

Season the young goat cutlets with salt and fry in the garlic-flavored olive oil. Arrange 2 cutlets with a little garlic and some of the potatoes on plates.

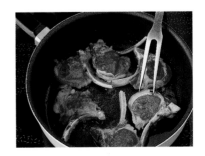

Meatballs

Preparation time: 45 minutes
Cooking time: 1 hour
Difficulty: ★

Serves 4

1¼ cups/300 ml	olive oil
⅛ cup/15 g	flour
½	green bell pepper
½	red bell pepper
1 each	carrot, tomato, onion
1 clove	garlic
1 sprig	thyme
1	bay leaf
8 oz/200 g	squid
4 tbsp/60 ml	white wine
1 tsp/5 ml	Spanish brandy
	salt

For the meatball mixture:

1¼ lb/600 g	ground veal
7 oz/200 g	ground pork
1	unwaxed lemon
1 bunch	chives
10	pine nuts
1 clove	garlic, chopped
1 slice	light country bread
1	egg
	freshly ground nutmeg
	salt and black pepper

This braised dish of meatballs and squid, called *estofado* in Spanish, is a specialty of Catalonia. It cleverly combines the aromas of land and sea, and is well known and loved beyond the borders of Catalonia. In Alicante on the Mediterranean coast, this hearty dish is particularly popular in winter.

Squid, or *sepia*, is identified by its sack-like, gray-beige body, its sides ending in a thin fin seam. Inside is a hard calcium shell, the cuttlebone, which has to be removed before the squid is cooked. Ten tentacles grow from the relatively large head, two of which are considerably longer than the other eight. Depending on what is available at the time, you can also use smaller ones.

Tomatoes and bell peppers are grown in the area around Alicante, and add strong aromas to a dish. These are complemented by the onion, which came originally from Northern Asia. Buy milder Spanish onions. A tip to spare your eyes: put the onions in the refrigerator for an hour, then pour boiling water over them to make them easier to peel.

Cesar Marquiegui combines squid with meatballs made of ground veal and pork. The ground meat is flavored with lemon peel, garlic, egg, and bread, and seasoned with ground nutmeg. This spice, which came from the East Indies, is always used freshly ground, and should be stored in an airtight container.

Another ingredient is chives, which adds a gentle peppery note to the dish. Chives contain lots of vitamins and are available fresh from spring to fall. The stalks should be bright green and firm, and not yet flowering.

Combine the ground meats. Season with grated lemon peel and salt. Add the chopped chives, pine nuts, and chopped garlic. Remove the crust from the bread, then soak the bread. Add it and the egg to the meat. Season with nutmeg and pepper. Knead until smooth.

Oil your hands lightly, then shape small balls from the meat mixture. Coat them in flour.

Heat ¾ cup/200 ml oil in a skillet and fry the meatballs until brown. Remove, place on paper towels to absorb excess oil, and set aside.

with Sepia

Finely chop the bell peppers, carrot, tomato, onion, and garlic. Fry in a pot in the remainder of the oil. Add the thyme, bay leaf, and salt.

Clean the squid and remove the cuttlebone. Cut the body and tentacles into pieces and add to the vegetables. Season with salt and stir.

Add the white wine and brandy. Cook for 2 minutes. Sprinkle over 1 tbsp of flour and stir. Pour over water to cover and bring to the boil. Simmer for 40 minutes. Add the meatballs and continue cooking for 10 minutes. Arrange on plates and serve.

Fricassee with

Preparation time: 30 minutes
Cooking time: 1 hour 15 minutes
Difficulty: ★★

Serves 4

1	oven-ready chicken
1¼ cups/150 g	flour
¾ cup/200 ml	olive oil
1	onion, finely chopped

¾ cup/200 ml	dry white wine
½ cup/50 g	walnuts
1 bunch	parsley, chopped
¾ cup/200 ml	milk
4 cups/1 l	chicken stock
1 whole	garlic bulb
2	eggs
½	baguette
	salt and pepper

Chicken fricassee, with its appetizing sauce of walnuts and parsley, chopped eggs, and croutons, is a popular dish on the menus of luxury restaurants. The walnuts in this dish make it typical of Madrid; other parts of the Iberian Peninsula use chopped almonds instead.

Julio Reoyo finds that light meats work best in this dish. However, you could also use a large, fattier poularde—or even a spring chicken. With this dish, it is not so much the weight classification that matters, especially as Spanish chickens don't usually end up in the pot until the end of their egg-laying careers. Just make sure the bird has plenty of tender meat.

Singe off any feathers left on the skin with a gas torch. Our chef separates the wings and quarters, then divides the

latter into thighs and drumsticks. The carcass is cut in half. Finally, everything is coated in flour so it turns nice and crisp when frying. The flour will also thicken the sauce a little.

As is customary in Spain, the slices of bread are deep-fried in plenty of oil. As soon as they are golden on one side, turn them over and fry the other side. Remove from the oil and place on paper towels to absorb the excess.

This traditional dish from Madrid is one of the so-called *guisos*, as ragouts are called in Spanish. Like all braised dishes, it tastes even better reheated the next day.

Place the chicken on a chopping board and cut into 8 pieces with a large knife. Season with salt and freshly ground black pepper.

Sprinkle the flour on a plate, then coat the chicken pieces completely.

Fry the chicken in a casserole in 6½ tbsp/ 100 ml oil over very high heat, turning each piece so they all brown evenly. Set aside. Sauté the finely chopped onion in the same oil for 5 minutes. Return the chicken to the casserole and pour over the white wine.

Walnut Sauce

Crush the walnuts and chopped parsley in a mortar, then pour in the milk. Pour this mixture over the chicken.

Add the chicken stock. Bring to the boil and cook for about 45 minutes.

Boil the eggs for 10 minutes, then run cold water over them, and peel. Slice the bread and fry in the remaining olive oil for 5 minutes. Serve the fricassee very hot. Garnish with the bread and chopped hard-boiled eggs.

Veal Cheeks

Preparation time: 45 minutes
Cooking time: 4 hours
Difficulty: ★

Serves 4

4	veal cheeks
¾ cup/200 ml	olive oil
1 tsp	veal stock concentrate
2	red onions
2	tomatoes
2	leeks
1 bulb	garlic

4	mild chile peppers (*pimientos choriceros*)
1 75 cl bottle	Rioja
1 lb 2 oz/500 g	peas
	olive oil for deep-frying
	salt and pepper

For the accompaniment (optional):
potatoes
noodles
rice pilaf

For the garnish:
the whites of 2 leeks

When the first winter frosts set in, it is customary in the Basque Country to prepare veal cheeks in Rioja. Emilio González Soto gave some thought to this hearty satisfying dish, and decided to make a few changes.

The preparation of this recipe is easy, and yet the result is an absolute delight, thanks to the fine flavor of the tender veal cheeks. You can also make this dish with beef or pork, if you prefer.

Like all traditional dishes, this one also offers a wide range of different aromas. Depending on the size, the cheeks need to braise in the wine for 3 to 4 hours. Wine from the Rioja region goes particularly well with this dish, and that is what the chef uses. The controlled mark of origin is known all over Spain to represent quality and lifestyle. What's more, the landscape, with its vineyards and wine villages, is as

unique as its excellent wines. Of course, you can also use any other red wine you happen to have to hand.

The mild chiles are an essential ingredient in Basque cuisine, and in this case they provide the spiciness for the sauce. The *pimientos choriceros* can be recognized by their long shape and dark red color. They are also ground and used to make the chorizo sausage.

To add a little more color to this traditional dish, our chef decided to use fresh peas. Ensure that the pods are a rich green and firm with no blemishes. Fresh pods will keep in the refrigerator for two or three days. Shelled peas do not need to be washed.

The leek makes the wine sauce wonderfully mild. The fried white part is used as garnish.

Trim the veal cheeks, then cut off the tendons and fat.

Heat ²/₃ cup/200 ml olive oil in a pot and fry the veal cheeks. Dissolve the veal stock in 4 tbsp/60 ml water and add to the pot. Peel the red onions. Wash the tomatoes and leeks.

Thinly slice the onions, tomatoes, and leeks, then put in the pot. Add the unpeeled garlic cloves and the whole chiles. Cover, then simmer gently for about 10 minutes, stirring occasionally. Season with salt and pepper.

in Rioja

Pour over the red wine and stir. Simmer gently for 3–4 hours, depending on the size of the cheeks. Shell the peas, boil in salted water for 6–8 minutes, and set aside.

Remove the veal cheeks, then strain the sauce through a sieve. Heat for 5 minutes, then add the cooked peas. To make the garnish, cut the white of the leeks into thin slices and fry in olive oil. Set aside.

Cut the cheeks into evenly sized pieces and arrange on plates. Pour over the sauce and arrange with the deep-fried leeks.

Partridge in

Preparation time:	50 minutes
Cooking time:	1 hour 40 minutes
Difficulty:	★

Serves 4

2	partridges, each weighing 1 lb/450 g
1 cup/250 ml	olive oil
4 cloves	garlic, thinly sliced
2¼ lb/1 kg	onions, finely chopped
1 tbsp/15 ml	chicken stock concentrate

2	bay leaves
1 sprig	thyme
1 sprig	rosemary
2 sprigs	parsley
1 cup/250 ml	red port wine
1 cup/250 ml	white wine (Albariño)
1 cup/250 ml	sherry vinegar
1 lb 2 oz/500 g	savoy cabbage
7 oz/200 g	smoked ham
4	small potatoes
	salt

The landscape of the Galician coast is marked by so-called *rias*—expansive, shallow estuaries a little like fjords. The inhabitants of the Atlantic coast in the north-west of Spain are passionate about their homeland, and they hold the customs of their ancestors—not least the culinary ones—in the highest esteem. Hunting is of particular importance to them, so it is hardly surprising that there are many dishes that include game. Partridge, which is greatly prized in Galicia, is a very precious quarry.

Here, María Lourdes Fernández-Estevez presents a recipe from her homeland. The spicy partridge in wine from the Rías Baixas region is particularly popular during the hunting season, in fall and winter.

Partridge has almost cult status on the Iberian Peninsula. In the Middle Ages, this little bird was reserved for princes and church dignitaries. In Spain, many children's fairy stories end with the phrase "they were happy and ate partridge," which is equivalent to "and they all lived happily ever after." Although partridge flesh is similar to that of chicken, it is served only on special occasions. Apart from young birds—no older than a year—the flesh of adult red or grey partridges is very firm and tasty. It is essential to observe the cooking times.

In this creation, the chef allows the wine to develop its full aroma. Albariño, which is renowned in Spain, is similar to a Riesling, which can also be used in its place.

Savoy cabbage, a typical winter vegetable, goes extremely well with partridge. Its firm bite and mild spiciness considerably enhance the dish. Make sure that your cabbage is firm with no tears or hard spots.

Gut the partridge and cut in half lengthwise. Clean and rinse under running cold water. Truss each half—that is, tie the drumsticks and wings to the body. This way, the birds will turn an even brown when frying.

Heat ⅔ cup/150 ml olive oil in a large pot and sauté the thinly sliced garlic and finely chopped onions for about 5 minutes.

Remove the garlic and onions, and blend in a blender. Put the partridge halves and the onion and garlic purée in the pot and fry, stirring continuously. Dissolve the chicken stock in ⅔ cup/150 ml hot water.

Albariño Wine

Add the bay leaf, thyme, rosemary, and parsley. Pour over the port, $^2/_3$ cup/150 ml white wine, and sherry vinegar, then add the chicken stock. Cover and simmer gently for about 1 hour and 30 minutes. Add a little salt.

Wash the cabbage and cut into strips. Finely dice the ham. Peel and deep-fry the potatoes.

Cook the cabbage in boiling water for 35 minutes. Drain. Heat the remainder of the oil in a casserole. Fry the cabbage and diced ham. Add the remainder of the white wine. Continue cooking for 3 minutes. Arrange the partridge on a serving dish. Serve with the cabbage and potatoes.

Hen Pheasant

Preparation time:	35 minutes
Cooking time:	1 hour 15 minutes
Difficulty:	★

Serves 4

2	hen pheasants, each weighing 1³⁄₄ lb/800 g
4	bay leaves
1	carrot, part cut into strips and part cut into round slices
2 sprigs	fresh rosemary

4 tsp/20 g	flour
6¹⁄₂ tbsp/100 ml	olive oil
1³⁄₄ oz/40 g	scallions (spring onions), halved lengthways
1¹⁄₂ cups/300 ml	sherry vinegar
	salt and black peppercorns

For the garnish:

	bay leaves
	fresh rosemary

Hen pheasant in *escabeche* (a marinade) is a specialty from La Mancha. In this area, which is extremely popular with huntsmen, game of all kinds features in countless guises.

This tasty dish is usually eaten cold. *Escabeche* used to be used to preserve and season foods, and it remains an essential part of Spanish cuisine today. Alberto Herráiz even believes that the success of this dish is determined by the quality of the oil and vinegar! The chef uses bay leaves to season the *escabeche*. This evergreen laurel thrives in the Mediterranean region. Its aromatic leaves are used in many braised dishes and casseroles, stuffings, and marinades.

This dish is easy to make and will keep well, because it is cooked in a preserving jar in a *bain-marie* (water bath). This means it can be enjoyed all year round, and not just during the hunting season. A *bain-marie* is used to cook certain dishes very gently, or to melt foods without the risk of burning.

Hen pheasants are greatly prized for the delicacy of their flesh. The bird, which is recognized by its gray-brown feathers, originally came from Asia, but became widespread throughout Europe in the Middle Ages. During the hunting season, from October to February, it is often available with its feathers still in place. If this is the case, ask the retailer to make the bird oven-ready for you.

Wild pheasant is quite literally a different kind of bird from the farmed variety, whose flesh is fattier and lacks the typical "gamey" flavor. The partridge, which is also highly prized in Castile, is an excellent substitute.

Bone the hen pheasants and truss them, using kitchen yarn to bind the drumsticks and wings to the body. Slide a bay leaf, a little carrot, and rosemary under the yarn. Season with salt and dust with flour.

Heat the olive oil in a casserole and brown the birds carefully; remove.

Brown the halved scallions, peppercorns, carrot strips and slices, unpeeled garlic, and the bay leaves in the same oil for 3–4 minutes.

n Escabeche

Pour over the sherry vinegar and reduce. Add 1¹/₄ cups/300 ml water.

Put the pheasants back in the pot and simmer gently for 35 minutes, turning occasionally.

Put the hen pheasants and accompaniments in a preserving jar and cook in a bain-marie (water bath) for about 30 minutes. Slice the birds and arrange on plates with the vegetables and sauce. Garnish with bay leaves and rosemary.

Paella

Preparation time: 15 minutes
Cooking time: 30 minutes
Difficulty: ★★

Serves 4

1³/₄ lb/700 g	rabbit
4	chicken quarters, ideally from free-range chickens
²/₃ cup/150 ml	olive oil
6 oz/150 g	sugar peas
1 clove	garlic
6 oz/150 g	runner beans
8	small artichokes
²/₃ cup/150 ml	tomato sauce
¹/₂ tsp	mild paprika
pinch	ground saffron
2 cups/400 g	rice (ideally bomba)
1 sprig	rosemary
¹/₄ cup/50 g	pre-cooked white cannellini beans
¹/₄ cup/60 g	shelled snails, cooked

There are as many recipes for paella in Spain as there are towns and villages. The dish was named after the large pan in which it is cooked: the pan ensures an even distribution of heat, and has metal handles on either side. Originally, paella was a dish eaten by laborers in the region of Valencia, but soon it was enhanced by the addition of vegetables and snails, and rabbit and chicken on special occasions. In Spain, the men usually prepare the paella on a Sunday, so it is considered a holiday dish. Every village, every family, has its own recipe, using whatever they happen to have at the time: fish on the coast, meat and sausage inland, and vegetables, herbs, and spices.

The main and essential ingredient for paella is rice, ideally the round version called bomba, which absorbs lots of liquid without bursting. It is grown in some parts of Spain, such as Calasparra, where it also has a protected mark of origin. Bomba rice absorbs lots of liquid, yet remains *al dente* (firm), and nice and fluffy. It also absorbs the aromas from the paella pan. And therein lies the secret of a good paella. The best-known versions of this dish are paella Valenciana, in which the rice is cooked in a stock made of rockfish, and paella with squid and ink. In this recipe, Alberto Herráiz uses cannellini beans as well as meat, rice, and artichokes.

Paella cooked to all the rules is also served in Herráiz's restaurant, "Fogón." Not only does Herráiz practice his craft, but he is also involved in the theory of cooking, and is a keen exponent of the retention of Spanish culinary traditions. He recommends serving a red Valdepeña from La Mancha with paella.

Using a sharp knife, cut the rabbit and chicken quarters into small pieces.

Heat the olive oil in a paella pan and brown the meat all over. Meanwhile, trim the sugar peas and cut them into pieces. Chop the garlic.

Put the runner beans and peas in the pan with the meat. Cut off the artichoke stalks and leaves. Cut the artichokes into quarters and remove the "hay." Put in the pan and brown over a high heat. Add the garlic.

Preheat the oven to 480 °F/250 °C. Add the tomato sauce to the meat and vegetables, then sprinkle over the paprika. Pour on 5 cups/1.5 l water, and reduce by a third.

Add the saffron and stir well.

Add the rice and stir in evenly. Add the rosemary, cannellini beans, and snails. When the rice has absorbed the liquid, it will rise to the surface. Now cook the paella in the oven for a further 10 minutes.

Rabbit with Creamed Onions

Preparation time:	1 hour		3 or 4	chive stalks
Cooking time:	1 hour 50 minutes		3 or 4 sprigs	parsley
Difficulty:	★★★		1¼ cups/300 ml	brandy
			3	Mallorcan tomatoes
Serves 4			1 tbsp/15 g	paprika
			12	large Sóller shrimp
1	rabbit weighing			salt and pepper
	3 lb/1.5 kg			
⅞ cup/100 g	flour		**For the *majado*:**	
	olive oil		½	rabbit liver
1	dried *ñora* pepper			olive oil
½ bulb	garlic		2 cloves	garlic
4	large onions		4 or 5 sprigs	flat-leaf parsley
1	bay leaf		1 sprig	fresh thyme
1 sprig	thyme			

The Balearic Islands were conquered in 1229 by James I, king of Aragon and ally of the Catalan counts of Barcelona. The latter introduced their language and culture to the islands. Even today, the local cuisine and foodstuffs recall those of Barcelona. Chef Oscar Martínez Plaza, based in Palma de Mallorca, has created a dish combining Sóller shrimp with rabbit in a sauce of creamed onions.

Although the most commonly eaten meat on the Balearics is pork, rabbit-based dishes are much enjoyed. For a professional touch when presenting this dish, Oscar Martínez Plaza suggests pressing the meat of the rabbit thigh down the bone, to allow it to "sit" attractively on the plate. This recipe can also be made with skinned chicken thighs and drumsticks, which combine equally well with the flavor of shrimps.

The sauce in which the rabbit is cooked consists of vegetables and herbs. These give color and flavor to the meat. On

Mallorca, *ñora* peppers and tomatoes are traditionally prepared in the same way: strung together, they are hung up on the walls of the local houses to dry in the sun. The *ñora* peppers become very dry and need to be rehydrated before use. Once soft, they should be cut open and scraped with a knife.

The magnificent natural harbor of Sóller is in north-west Mallorca. The fishermen of this quaint old seaside city, with its Art-Deco architecture, devote half of their fleet to catching the shrimp that will put the finishing touches to this dish.

The usual method when making this recipe is to cook all the rabbit pieces in the oven. Oscar Martínez Plaza prefers to cook the saddle separately, so as to preserve its tenderness and delicate taste. When sliced up, it can be used to garnish the dish along with the fried onions and some chives.

Prepare the rabbit by jointing into legs, ribs, and saddle. Put the saddle to one side. Using a cleaver, chop the rest of the meat (on the bone) into smaller pieces. Coat these with seasoned flour and brown in the oil for 10 minutes. Remove the meat from the pan and set aside.

Put the ñora pepper in water to soak. Brown the garlic in the oil used to cook the meat. Add the chopped onions (reserving half an onion) and a bouquet garni of bay, thyme, chives, and parsley. Add a third of the brandy and heat until the alcohol evaporates.

Drain the softened ñora pepper and scrape the flesh with a knife. Add it to the softened onions with 2 peeled and blended tomatoes and the paprika. Cook for a few minutes.

and Sóller Shrimp

Add the pieces of fried rabbit to this mixture. Cover with water. Cook for 45 minutes until the rabbit is quite tender. In another pan, sauté the rabbit liver in oil. Grind it to make a *majado* paste with garlic, parsley, and thyme. Add this to the rabbit.

Peel the shrimp, and reserve the flesh. Sauté the shrimp heads and shells in oil for 5 minutes. Add 1 blended tomato and the remaining two thirds of the brandy. Cook for 10 minutes over a high heat. Strain this shrimp sauce through a sieve.

Slice the reserved half onion into thick rings. Blanch them, dip them in cold water, and dry them. Dip them in flour, and fry. Season the saddle of rabbit with salt and pepper, brush with oil, and cook it in a pan. Brown the shrimp meat in a separate pan. Serve everything piping hot with the sauce.

Loin of Lamb

Preparation time: 45 minutes
Cooking time: 1 hour 15 minutes
Difficulty: ★

Serves 4

2	white onions
2 tbsp	olive oil
1 sprig	fresh thyme
1	bay leaf
2	loins of lamb, each
	1½ lb/700 g
1	zucchini
1	eggplant
3	beefsteak tomatoes, each
	2 ½ oz/60 g
	salt, pepper

For the herb crust:

1 bunch	fresh chives
1 bunch	fresh chervil
1 bunch	fresh tarragon
2	egg yolks
7 oz/200 g	prepared mustard

For the lamb gravy:

1	carrot
1	onion
1 sprig	fresh parsley
3½ tbsp/50 ml	white wine
1 tbsp	olive oil

For the garlic oil:

4 cloves	garlic
1 sprig	fresh thyme
1	bay leaf
⅔ cup/150 ml	olive oil

For the garnish:

4 sprigs	rosemary, 1 clove garlic

With this recipe Joël Garault, chef at the restaurant in the "Hermitage" hotel, Monte Carlo, pays homage to the Principality and its famous cliffs.

Loin of lamb with a herb crust is a traditional dish from the Provençal countryside. It's a very popular cut of lamb. According to our chef, each piece, when trimmed, should weigh 1½ pounds/700 grams. If you can't obtain lamb you could serve veal or poultry with the vegetable rosettes.

Spicy mustard plays an important role in the golden herb crust. The seeds of the mustard plant, indigenous to the Mediterranean region, are used to make the yellow condiment of the same name that can be mild or hot. The mustard combines with the flavor of the lamb to produce a characteristic taste.

Of course herbs are also part of the herb crust. Sometimes our chef uses basil instead of tarragon, or flat-leaf parsley instead of chervil. The slightly peppery flavor of chives is, on the other hand, an essential component. Fresh chives are available from spring to fall. They should not be in flower and the blades should be slender and dark green.

To save time you can prepare the vegetable rosettes a day before you need them. They will be nice and juicy when reheated. Choose zucchini, eggplant, and tomatoes that are roughly the same size. Reserve the olive oil in which you fry the unpeeled garlic, because the vegetable rosettes are coated in it too.

Loin of lamb with a herb crust is very simple. The only garnish required is garlic and rosemary.

Peel and chop the onions and sweat them in olive oil for 10 minutes on low heat. Season with salt and pepper. Add the chopped thyme and the bay leaf.

Remove the back bones, belly flaps, and fat from the lamb. Separate the lower part to a depth of 2 fingers wide, and free the ribs. Keep the scraps. To make the garlic oil, sweat the garlic, thyme, and bay leaf in olive oil on low heat for 35 minutes. Drain and keep the oil.

Slice the vegetables. Soak in the cooled garlic oil. Place round ring molds on a baking sheet. Divide the onions between the ring molds, then layer the sliced vegetables on top in a rosette shape. Season, drizzle over a little olive oil. Bake at 320 °F/160 °C for 20 minutes.

with a Herb Crust

To make the herb crust, finely chop the chives, chervil, and tarragon. In a bowl, combine them with the egg yolks and mustard.

Season the loins of lamb and scraps. Bake in the oven at 400 °F/200 °C, together with the chopped gravy ingredients, except for the wine, for 20 minutes. Deglaze the pan with the white wine. Spread the herb paste over the loins and roast at 465 °F/250 °C for 3 minutes.

Strain the gravy and season to taste with salt and pepper. Leave the loins of lamb to rest for 5 minutes. Then cut them into chops. Arrange 3 chops and a vegetable rosette on each plate. Garnish with rosemary, a halved clove of garlic, and a spoonful of gravy.

Preparation time: *1 hour*
Cooking time: *2 hours 40 minutes*
Difficulty: ★★★

Serves 4

For the stuffed rabbit thighs:
4	young rabbit thighs
1	pig's caul
2 cloves	garlic
4	zucchini
4 cups/1 l	olive oil
	salt
	pepper

For the rabbit gravy:
	rabbit bones
1 tbsp	olive oil
1	onion
1 clove	garlic

3 sprigs	fresh parsley
2 sprigs	fresh thyme
⅛ stick/20 g	butter

For the caramelized onions:
3	medium onions
2 sprigs	fresh thyme

2 tbsp	olive oil
	salt, pepper

For the garlic cream sauce:
1 bulb	garlic
⅞ cup/200 ml	milk
1¼ cups/300 ml	cream
	salt, pepper

For the garbanzo flour batons:
1 cup/200 g	garbanzo bean flour
3 tbsp	olive oil
	olive oil for frying
	salt

For the braised tomatoes (optional):
1	onion
2 cloves	garlic
2 sprigs	fresh thyme
4	small tomatoes
¾ cup/200 ml	chicken stock
	olive oil

In rural southern France, rabbit is often on the menu. The little rodents, found everywhere, are normally farmed. Wild rabbits only appear at the butcher's during the game hunting season. Check for top-quality meat that is firm, but not too fatty, and is a deep pink color.

This creation by Francis Robin demands a certain know-how. The rabbit thighs must be prepared carefully. The temperature of the olive oil is also very important. It's best to use a meat thermometer, because the temperature of 160 degrees Fahrenheit/70 degrees Celsius must be accurate for a guaranteed result. Before serving, the stuffed rabbit thighs should be broiled briefly to cook off any unnecessary fat.

Garlic is another popular ingredient. Ensure you select very firm bulbs, preferably of pink garlic, and store it in the driest place in your kitchen. When preparing it, you should remove the core from each clove, because that way it is easier to digest.

This celebration dish not only takes on a colorful note, but an acidic one, when served with braised tomatoes. To make them, sauté chopped onion, crushed garlic, and two sprigs of thyme in olive oil. Then add skinned, deseeded, and diced tomatoes. Add the chicken stock and simmer until reduced. Arrange the tomatoes on a plate as an accompaniment, next to the fried garbanzo flour batons. The dish should be served piping hot.

To make the caramelized onions, peel and finely chop the onions. Sweat the onions with the chopped thyme in 2 tbsp olive oil. Season with salt and pepper, and leave to sweat down for 5–10 minutes. Let the onion mixture cool, then refrigerate it.

Bone the rabbit thighs to create a pocket. Season the inside with salt and pepper. Reserve all the bones. Stuff the thighs with the caramelized onions, wrap them in the pig's caul, and place them in little ring molds.

Heat the olive oil to 160 °F/80 °C in a large saucepan. Add 2 unpeeled cloves of garlic. Fry the rabbit thighs in hot oil at 160 °F/70 °C for one hour. Score grooves down the length of the zucchini, then slice them. Blanch them in boiling, salted water, and put them to one side.

Rabbit Thighs

To make the rabbit gravy, chop the bones and sauté them in 1 tbsp olive oil with chopped onion, garlic, parsley, and thyme. Add 4 cups/1 l water. Simmer on low heat for 1 hour, stir frequently. Boil the broth until reduced, then strain it and beat in a generous ⅛ stick/20 g butter.

Beat together the garbanzo bean flour, 1 cup/250 ml cold water, and 1 tbsp olive oil. Gradually add the garbanzo batter to 3 cups/750 ml boiling salted water, with the remaining olive oil. Leave the resulting dough to cool. Cut into batons and deep fry them in olive oil.

For the garlic cream sauce, peel the garlic and remove the cores. Blanch three times, then drain. Simmer for 25 minutes in the milk and cream. Season, purée, and sieve. Arrange the rabbit along with the garbanzo batons on a bed of zucchini. Drizzle gravy and sauce onto the plate.

Stuffed Shoulder

Preparation time:	2 hours
Cooking time:	1 hour 10 minutes
Difficulty:	★★★

Serves 4

2	rabbit torsos
1	onion
2 cloves	garlic
1	carrot
1	bouquet garni (thyme, bay leaf, parsley)
generous ⅛ stick/ 20 g	butter
1 cup/250 ml	dry white wine
1	pig's caul
¼ stick/30 g	butter for frying

For the stuffing:

	rabbit liver and kidneys
1 strip	back bacon

2 oz/50 g	lean veal
7 oz/200 g	button mushrooms
1	onion
2 cloves	garlic
1 bunch	fresh parsley
generous ⅛ stick/ 20 g	butter
	salt, pepper

For the apricot gypsy toast:

2 tbsp	milk
1	egg
few sprigs	fresh rosemary
1	stale baguette
scant ⅛ stick/ 10 g	butter
1 cup/200 g	dried apricots

We have chef Alain Carro to thank for this recipe, which won a prize at the renowned Marseilles *Mangez du lapin* ("Eat Rabbit") competition in 1998. The unusual way in which the rabbit is filleted and the dual method of preparation—pan-fried and oven-roasted—will astound your friends.

Filleting the loin requires great care, and only in the case of superb quality rabbits are the bones sufficiently strong. Free-range rabbits, preferably from Angers, are best. It's even better if you buy only the front part of the rabbit. Our chef wraps the rabbit's shoulders in a pig's caul to keep them moist and help them retain their shape. If you can't obtain a pig's caul, you will need to hold the meat together with toothpicks.

The apricot gypsy toast adds a touch of acidity and a stylish, exotic, sweet-and-sour note. If you want to emphasize this, our chef suggests you cook some orange zest with the gravy. These flavors are found throughout the Mediterranean region, especially in some Moroccan stews, known as tagines. Finally, rosemary grows throughout the Mediterranean region, wherever there is chalky soil and lots of sunshine. Where you find *garrigue*, the southern scrubland, rosemary will be there too.

If your guests particularly value attractive, colorful presentation, our chef suggests you garnish the plates with a sprig of cherry tomatoes. If they are briefly pan-fried, the skin swells upwards very elegantly.

Separate the rabbit shoulders and bone out the shoulder blades. Carefully remove all the flesh from the bones, and spread it out for stuffing later. Reserve the head and bones.

Make an incision in the little loins and bone out the ends of the rib bones. Only cut through the first ribs again.

Sauté the rabbit bones and meat scraps, finely chopped onion, sliced garlic, chopped carrot, and bouquet garni in butter for 10 minutes. Add the white wine and let it evaporate. Add enough water to cover the meat and vegetables. Simmer for 15–20 minutes, then strain the gravy.

# of Rabbit

To make the stuffing, dice the rabbit liver and kidneys, bacon, veal, and mushrooms. Peel and chop the onion and garlic, chop the parsley. Sauté them with the butter. Season with salt and pepper.

Stuff the rabbit shoulders and wrap them in the pig's caul. Sauté in an oven-proof skillet with a scant ⅛ stick/10 g butter for 5 minutes. Add the gravy, transfer to the oven, and roast the shoulders at 400° F/200 °C, basting regularly with the pan juices. Sauté the rabbit loins.

Beat together the milk, egg, and some chopped rosemary, and dip slices of bread in the egg mixture. Fry the egg-soaked bread in the butter. Top each slice of bread with sliced apricot and rosemary. Arrange the rabbit and toast on a plate. Pour gravy over the loins only.

Haunch of Kid

Preparation time: 35 minutes
Time to
   freeze garlic: 10 minutes
Chichoumay
   cooking time: 30 minutes
Cooking time
   for meat: 60 minutes
Difficulty: ★

Serves 4

2 cloves	garlic
3 lb/1.2 kg	haunch of kid/leg of lamb
16	juniper berries
3 tbsp	olive oil
1	onion

5 cloves	garlic
2 sprigs	fresh thyme
	salt
	pepper

For the chichoumay:

1	eggplant
1	zucchini
3	tomatoes
6	scallions
6 tbsp	regular olive oil
2 cloves	garlic
1	bay leaf
3	basil leaves
6 tbsp	highly aromatic olive oil
	salt, pepper

Kid is very popular in the Languedoc region, especially meat from 7-week-old animals. The dish is dependent on the time of year and child's play to prepare; it's best between February and April.

Relatively firm, low-fat kid meat has a strong flavor. If you can't find kid, you could use leg of lamb instead. The juniper berries give the dish all the flavor of the *garrigue*, the perfumed scrubland of Languedoc. These aromatic berries, with their slightly resinous taste, grow on the thorny juniper bush. They are a superb complement to game.

Chichoumay is ratatouille minus the bell peppers. The eggplant, which originated in India, had found a home in Provence as early as the 12th century. Choose fat, firm specimens. Because eggplant, like poisonous belladonna, is a member of the nightshade family, it was initially called *mala insana,* "mad apple." Nowadays eggplant is popular

in combination with zucchini and tomatoes. If you can, buy tomatoes on the vine, available between June and October, as they have a better flavor.

The famous trio from southern French cuisine is completed by zucchini, which, like the marrow or cucumber, is a member of the pumpkin family. Baby zucchini are best; they should feel firm. The pumpkin is one of the oldest varieties of vegetable known. Once again it was the Italians who brought us this delicious vegetable. In the 18th century they hit on the idea of stewing unripe pumpkins ... and so the zucchini took its place in the kitchen.

Peel 2 cloves of garlic, cut them into slivers, and freeze them for 10 minutes in the deep freeze. Pierce the meat all over with a sharp knife, and insert the garlic slivers and juniper berries into the holes. Season the meat with salt and pepper.

Place the leg of lamb in a baking dish brushed with 2 tbsp olive oil. Preheat the oven to 350° F/180 °C. Add the finely chopped onion, whole unpeeled garlic cloves, and thyme to the meat, and roast it for 60 minutes. Turn the meat frequently and baste it with the pan juices.

Wash the eggplant and zucchini. Cut them into 1½ in/4 cm batons. Blanch each separately for 2–3 minutes and drain. Pour boiling water over the tomatoes, skin and deseed them, and dice the flesh. Wash the scallions and cut them into 1¼ in/4 cm pieces.

on Chichoumay

Heat the regular olive oil in a pan. Fry the zucchini, eggplant, and scallions separately in the olive oil for 5 minutes each. Then put them all in the pan together.

Add 2 crushed cloves of garlic and the bay leaf to the vegetables and season. Sweat for 5 minutes (the vegetables should still be crisp). Toward the end of the cooking time add the diced tomato, finely chopped basil, and aromatic olive oil. Sweat the vegetables for 5 minutes.

When the leg of lamb is done, take the baking dish out of the oven. Deglaze the dish with a little water. Just before serving, baste the meat again with the juices and a tablespoon of olive oil. Arrange the hot chichoumay around the lamb.

Rabbit with

Preparation time: 1 hour 30 minutes
Cooking time: 1 hour
Difficulty: ★★

Serves 4

1	rabbit weighing 3 lb/1.2 kg
1	red bell pepper
1	green bell pepper
generous ¾ cup/200 ml	olive oil
1 can	peeled tomatoes
2 sprigs	thyme
5	potatoes

8 oz/250 g	green beans
⅓ cup + 1½ tbsp/ 100 ml	milk
2 cloves	garlic
1 tbsp	chopped parsley
8 oz/250 g	carrots
1	onion
1 cup/250 ml	white wine
	salt
	pepper

For the garnish:

4 sprigs	fresh thyme
4	vine tomatoes

Hachis parmentier is a rustic French dish of chopped meat and potatoes. It takes its name from Antoine-Augustin Parmentier, a famous military doctor and agronomist. He made a significant contribution to the potato being recognized as a healthy, cheap, basic source of food. For a long time it was regarded as cattle fodder, or at best food for the poor. The olive oil gives the mashed potato flavor.

When you bone the rabbit, cut off all the fat. We recommend frying the liver and kidneys in advance, to obtain the juices. If you dust them with flour before frying them they will brown well, but they should stay nicely pink inside. Instead of rabbit you could use baby partridge for this recipe. To make it easier to prepare the meat, fry it first, then chop it. You should not use a food processor to do this,

however, otherwise the meat will have an unpleasant consistency. Angel Yagues stresses that in this recipe it should be possible to identify the pieces of meat when mixed with the peppers.

Chop the bones to make the rabbit gravy. When you serve this dish, the gravy is poured over the variety meats.

Bell peppers are popular as a cooked vegetable and raw in salads. When you buy them make sure the skin is shiny. Thyme grows wild in the *garrigue*, the Languedoc scrubland. This tough, aromatic herb, with its little green-gray leaves, is picked in May and will keep for a whole year.

Cut off the rabbit thighs using a meat cleaver. Bone the thighs carefully using a sharp knife. Reserve the rabbit's rump and all the bones for the gravy. Refrigerate the thigh meat, liver, and kidneys.

Wash, core, and very finely dice the bell peppers. Sweat them in a little olive oil. Drain the can of peeled tomatoes and reserve the juice. Add the tomatoes with a sprig of thyme, and simmer for approximately 10 minutes. Crush the mixture with a spatula.

Wash and peel the potatoes. Place them in cold, salted water, bring them to the boil, and simmer for about 20 minutes. Boil the green beans in salted water for 8 minutes. Drain the potatoes and mash them with the milk. Beat in 5 tbsp olive oil and season with salt and pepper.

Thyme

Chop the rabbit meat. Cut the kidneys in half lengthwise and fry them, with the liver, in 1 tbsp olive oil for 5 minutes. Fry the meat in the same pan for 5 minutes. Season with salt and pepper. Add the chopped garlic, chopped parsley, and a sprig of thyme.

To make the gravy, brown the rabbit bones and rump in 1 tbsp olive oil. Add the diced carrots, finely chopped onion, and other sprig of thyme. Deglaze the pan with the white wine. Add the tomato juice. Simmer the gravy for 20 minutes, strain it, and season with salt and pepper.

Using a ring mold, layer the chopped meat, tomato and bell pepper mix, and mashed potato. Arrange the sliced kidneys and liver, green beans, and cooked vine tomatoes on the plate. Pour the gravy over the variety meats, and garnish with a sprig of thyme.

Pigeon on

Preparation time: 1 hour
Cooking time: 25 minutes
Difficulty: ★★

Serves 4

2	pigeons, each 1 lb/500 g
3 tbsp	olive oil
1	medium onion, peeled, (keep skin)
2 sprigs	fresh thyme
⅔ cup/150 ml	chicken stock
4	medium new potatoes
4	baby carrots

5 oz/150 g	peas, shucked
5 oz/150 g	fava beans, shucked
	rock salt
	salt, pepper

For the stuffing:

2 slices	baguette, cubed
⅓ cup + 1½ tbsp/ 100 ml	milk
1	small onion
1 tbsp	olive oil
4 cloves	garlic
2	Perugine sausages
1 bunch	fresh flat-leaf parsley
1 sprig	fresh thyme
	salt

Stuffed pigeon on a bed of seasonal vegetables is a rustic dish from the area around Nice. Originally it was cooked simply, braised over low heat. In our chef's recipe it gets a spicy filling.

Tender, tasty pigeon makes a delicious meal of this poultry dish. Wild pigeon is available from spring to the end of summer; the rest of the year farmed pigeon is on the market. If you have difficulty jointing the pigeon, ask your butcher to remove the wings from the body. You need the tips of the wings and the rump, though, for the gravy. Daniel Ettlinger advises leaving the pigeon to rest for a few minutes before removing the fillets. Put the stuffed pigeon carefully in the pan so the skin doesn't tear.

The stuffing must cool a little before inserting it under the pigeon skin. The stuffing gets its characteristic taste from the slightly spicy Perugine sausages, so you don't need any

additional pepper. Before making the stuffing, you should remove the skin from the sausage. Then, when you sauté it, it will marry with the other stuffing ingredients and be cooked at the same time as the pigeon. The cubed bread must be softened thoroughly in the milk so that it is easy to incorporate into the stuffing. Keep the onion skin for the gravy.

The accompanying vegetables are dependent upon the time of year. In spring you could use tender fava beans in the pod, you could also use sugar snap peas, or green beans. Salt the vegetables at the start of cooking, so they retain their color. In winter you could serve turnip or chicory if available.

Soak the cubed bread in the milk. Peel and dice the small onion and sweat it in 1 tbsp olive oil. Stir in the finely chopped garlic, Perugine sausages, softened, drained bread, chopped parsley, and thyme. Season the mixture with salt.

Take the wings off the pigeon without damaging the skin on the breast. Cut off the wing tips and fillet the breast. To do this, cut along each side of the breastbone.

With your finger, gently ease the skin away from the meat and insert the stuffing. Reshape the pigeon breast.

Seasonal Vegetables

Sauté the bones and wings in 1 tbsp olive oil, and season them with salt. Add the onion skin with 1 sprig thyme, and sweat them for 10 minutes. Deglaze the pan with the chicken stock. After 10 minutes, remove the wings and simmer for another 15 minutes. Strain the gravy.

Sauté the peeled and quartered potatoes and sliced onion in 1 tbsp olive oil for 5 minutes. Season with salt and pepper. Add the remaining sprig of thyme, as well as the carrot sticks, and sweat them for 10 minutes.

Blanch the peas in boiling water, salted with rock salt, for 6 minutes. Add the peas and the beans to the other vegetables. Roast the pigeon in the remaining olive oil at 465 °F/250 °C. Let the pigeon rest for 3 minutes. Arrange the pigeon on a plate with the vegetables and gravy.

Guinea Fowl

Preparation time:	15 minutes
Cooking time:	1 hour
Difficulty:	★★

Serves 4

1	free-range guinea fowl
4 strips	back bacon
1 tbsp	olive oil
3	unwaxed lemons
3½ tbsp/50 ml	Banyuls (or other fortified wine)
¾ cup/200 ml	veal stock

	zest of 1 Seville orange
30 cloves	garlic
	salt
	pepper

For the bouquet garni:
fresh thyme
bay leaf
fresh parsley

For the garnish:
fresh chives

If you open any Catalan cookery book, you're sure to find this recipe, which was originally prepared with partridge. Our chef recommends that you buy a free-range guinea fowl, then you can be sure that this classic bird will have firm, tasty flesh.

The meat of these birds is most delicious when they are very young, and guinea fowl are available all year round. In Europe, most of them come from France or Italy. The guinea fowl reached France from Rome, and from there spread all over Europe to wherever there is a temperate climate. Jean Plouzennec wraps strips of bacon around the guinea fowl to prevent the meat from drying out. This is made from belly pork that is soaked in brine for around ten days, then rubbed with pepper, and hung up to dry.

Banyuls is a sweet dessert wine (*vin doux naturel*) whose fermentation is stopped by adding alcohol, so that the grapey flavor and sweetness are maintained. Together with the acidic orange zest, it gives the sweet-and-sour taste common to many Catalan gravies.

The main areas of lemon cultivation in Europe are found in Italy and on the Iberian peninsula, but they are also cultivated in the south of France, mainly in Menton. Buy relatively large fruit with a deep yellow color.

Sticking with tradition, you could prepare this dish with the best young partridge joints, which are more tender than older birds. Allow one baby partridge per person. The meat is a slightly grayish color. New potatoes and, depending on the season, boletus (porcini) or chanterelle mushrooms are a suitable accompaniment.

Preheat the oven to 400 °F/200 °C. Season the guinea fowl inside, and out. Wrap bacon around both thighs. Lay the remaining strips of bacon on the breast and tie the legs together with kitchen thread. Drizzle olive oil over the guinea fowl and roast for 35–40 minutes.

Baste the guinea fowl with the juices throughout cooking. Remove the peel from the lemons in one piece and remove the pith. Fillet two lemons into segments and slice the third.

Remove the bacon from the guinea fowl and put aside. Joint the guinea fowl in the classic manner, separating the thighs, breasts, and wings (cut through the latter). For the gravy, put the carcass back into the roasting pan. Deglaze the pan with the Banyuls and the veal stock.

with Garlic

Add the bouquet garni and the orange zest, season with salt and pepper, and simmer for about 10 minutes. Strain the gravy through a sieve, making sure you squeeze out all the goodness.

Blanch the whole cloves of garlic twice in boiling water. Add them to the gravy with the lemon segments. Bring to the boil, cover, and simmer for 10 minutes. Add the sliced lemon and season to taste with salt and pepper.

Add the guinea fowl joints to the gravy and heat them through. Arrange the guinea fowl joints on a plate with the lemon slices, bacon strips, and garlic cloves. Garnish with a couple of blades of chives.

Fillet of Beef with

Preparation time:	*1 hour*
Time for soaking the bones:	*24 hours*
Time for resting the batter:	*1 hour*
Cooking time:	*1 hour*
Difficulty:	★★

Serves 4

20	fresh anchovies
	oil for frying
12 pieces	bone marrow
2 cloves	garlic
1 sprig	fresh thyme
1	bay leaf
4 slices	fillet of beef weighing 6 oz/180 g
2 tbsp	olive oil
¾ cup/200 ml	red wine
¾ cup/200 ml	port

1⅔ cups/400 ml	beef stock
	salt, pepper

For the tempura batter:

¼ cup/30 g	all-purpose flour
10	ice cubes
	salt
	pepper

For the pissaladière dough:

1 tsp/5 g	salt
1 envelope/5 g	active dry yeast
2⅛ cups/250 g	all-purpose flour
1	small egg

For the topping:

2¼ lb/1 kg	onions
⅓ cup + 1½ tbsp/100 ml	olive oil
	fresh thyme
	bay leaf
	fresh parsley
4	anchovies in oil
1	tomato
8	black olives
	salt, pepper

For the garnish:

	fresh parsley
	rock salt

Nice and its *pissaladière*! This flatbread, lavishly topped with anchovy fillets and black olives, whose name dates back to the 14th century, is equally tasty hot or cold. Originally, before it was baked in the oven, it was spread with *pissalat*, a Provençal seasoning paste that is made with puréed anchovies, thyme, star anise, bay leaves, pepper, and olive oil.

The first main ingredient in Laurent Broussier's original recipe is the anchovies. These saltwater fish, a maximum of 8 inches/20 centimeters long, have yellowish-green backs and silvery bellies. If you use fresh fish that take a little longer to cook, buy ready-filleted fish. Preserved sardines are already salted, so remember this when seasoning your dish.

To make the *pissaladière* dough you will need around ⅔ cup/150 milliliters of water. Put half into one container with the salt, and the other half into another with the yeast. Make a circle of flour on the work surface. Put the egg in the middle, with the salt water and yeast water. Knead the dough by hand until it no longer sticks to your fingers. Then leave it to rest for an hour. If you don't want to go to the trouble of making the dough, bought bread rolls are an alternative.

Soak the bone marrow well so that any blood and toxins are eliminated. The marrow is heated through again briefly just before serving. The marrow is served sprinkled with rock salt and chopped parsley.

To make the tempura batter, put the flour and ice cubes in a bowl. Beat with a whisk until the ice cubes have melted and a fluid batter has formed. Season the batter with salt and pepper.

If making the pissaladière dough, see above. Shape it into rolls. Bake for 20 minutes at 425 °F/220°C. To make the topping, peel the onions and slice them into rings. Sweat them gently in some olive oil. Add the chopped thyme and season sparingly.

Add the bay leaf, roughly chopped parsley, and anchovy fillets. Sweat over low heat for 30 minutes until the anchovy fillets have melted. Add the diced tomato and season with salt and pepper.

Tempura Anchovies

Immerse the fresh anchovies in the tempura batter and fry them for 1 minute in very hot fat. Drain them on kitchen paper.

Slice the bread rolls in half and toast them. Layer the onion mixture, olives, and fried anchovies on the bottom half of the roll, and top with the other half.

Poach the bone marrow in salted water with pepper, garlic, thyme, and bay leaf for 3–4 minutes. Fry the fillets of beef in olive oil. Take the fillets out of the pan and deglaze with the red wine and port. Add the beef stock, stirring all the time, and boil until reduced by one third.

Pigeon and

Preparation time:	55 minutes
Cooking time:	1 hour 5 minutes
Difficulty:	★★

Serves 4

2	pigeons, each 1 lb/500 g
1 stick/100 g	butter
2	shallots
⅔ cup/150 ml	port
4	carrots
	rock salt
2	shallots
1 clove	garlic
1½ cups/300 g	Arborio rice

generous ¾ cup/200 ml	
scant ½ cup/100 g	chicken stock parmesan

1 sprig	flat-leaf parsley
6 oz/160 g	chanterelles
3 tbsp	olive oil
	salt, pepper

For the pigeon gravy:

1	carrot
1 stick	celery
1	onion
generous ⅛ stick/20 g	butter
⅓ cup + 1½ tbsp/100 ml	red wine
⅓ cup + 1½ tbsp/100 ml	chicken stock
1	bay leaf
1 sprig	fresh thyme

Joël Garault works in Monte Carlo. His recipe is a homage to the *Gallia Transalpina* of antiquity. The risotto is directly connected with Italy and the other ingredients come from the department of Alpes-de-Haute-Provence.

Wild pigeons are available from spring to the end of summer, the rest of the year you can buy farmed pigeons. When jointing the pigeon, remember to reserve the wing tips and rump, as you need them to make the gravy. You could also use quail or baby guinea fowl in this recipe.

The yellow chanterelle mushrooms give this dish a special Provençal flavor. These mushrooms are available from June until the fall. In damp weather they flourish in the Provençal countryside and their delicious scent is reminiscent of apricots. Garnish the chanterelle mushrooms with a little chopped parsley.

Joël Garault values Italian cuisine. He uses Arborio rice for his risotto. This high-quality rice has the advantage that the grains don't stick together when cooked. If you want to make this dish a little richer, add puréed garlic braised in olive oil to the risotto, but still add the butter and the parmesan cheese.

In our recipe, the parmesan is in the form of chips baked on a non-stick baking sheet. The king of Italian cheeses is a certified product from semi-skimmed cow's milk, which is heated into a malleable mass, pressed, and which develops a natural rind. It tastes slightly smoky (because of the lactic acid), fruity, salty, and sometimes piquant.

Separate the pigeon thighs with a knife by cutting through the joint. Take off the legs and wings. Take out the spine and breastbone, and keep all the trimmings and bones for the gravy.

To make the gravy, finely dice the carrot, celery, and onion. Fry the pigeon rump and scraps in butter. Add the vegetables and sauté them with the pigeon. Add the red wine and leave it to evaporate completely. Add the chicken stock, bay leaf, and thyme, and simmer for 25 minutes.

Sauté the pigeon thighs in a generous ⅛ stick/20 g butter. When they are golden brown, add 2 sliced shallots. Deglaze the pan with the port and reduce the liquid. Strain the gravy and add it to the pan. Simmer for 25 minutes. Take the thighs out of the pan and strain the sauce.

Chanterelle Risotto

Peel the carrots and boil them for 1 minute in water salted with rock salt. Drain the carrots, and slice them so they form a fan shape. Peel and finely chop 2 shallots and the garlic. Sweat them in a pan with ½ stick/50 g butter. Stir in the rice.

To make the risotto, add the chicken stock and simmer for 15 minutes. Fold in ¼ stick/30 g butter and 4 tsp parmesan. Season and add the chopped parsley, reserving a little for the garnish. Spoon the remaining parmesan on a baking sheet. Broil so that it melts to form chips.

Sauté the chanterelles for a few minutes. Season the pigeon, fry it for 3 minutes on each side, then bake it for 3 minutes at 350 °F/180 °C. Remove the fillets, slice them diagonally. Arrange the fillets with the thighs, chanterelles, and parmesan chips. Pour the sauce over the top.

Chicken in Red Wine

Preparation time: 40 minutes
Cooking time: 45 minutes
Difficulty: ★

Serves 4

1	free-range chicken weighing 3 lb/ 1.4 kg
14 oz/400 g	tomatoes
1	onion
14 oz/400 g	red bell peppers
14 oz/400 g	green bell peppers

8 cloves	garlic
¼ cup/60 ml	olive oil
1 bottle/750 ml	red wine
1	bouquet garni (thyme, bay leaf)
½ bunch	parsley
	salt and freshly ground pepper

Stews occupy an important place in Corsican cooking. This type of tasty home cooking uses nothing but locally produced ingredients. Chicken in red wine with peppers is a traditional dish, enjoyed throughout the island.

Chef Vincent Tabarani is an ardent promoter of the fine local produce marketed by the *Cucina Corsa* (Corsican Cooking) Association. Never one to compromise on ingredients, he insists on free-range chickens for this recipe, fed on wheat and other grains. These have a particularly tender and flavorsome meat. The city of Linguizetta, lying on the eastern plain to the south of Bastia, is famous for its excellent local poultry. As an alternative to chicken, this recipe can also be made with veal.

Wine is often combined with meat and game in Corsican cooking. For this recipe, Vincent Tabarani suggests a full-flavored and well-balanced, young Corsican wine.

Characteristic of the inland cooking of Corsica, this dish is filled with Mediterranean sunshine. Combined with olive oil, garlic, onion, and herbs, the chicken's flavors are enhanced by those of the tomatoes and bell peppers. Peppers, introduced originally from the New World, are now regarded as an intrinsic part of Mediterranean cuisine.

The flesh of red bell peppers has a soft and sweet flavor that is retained even when cooked. Green peppers, on the other hand, are picked before full maturity and so are sharper in taste and more crunchy. Often eaten raw in salads, sometimes peeled, the reds, greens, yellows, and oranges of bell peppers bring a brilliant splash of color to the stalls in Corsican markets. Choose peppers that are firm, smooth, and unmarked, with a stalk that is still green and rigid.

This inviting meal is suitable for any occasion.

To joint the chicken, first slit it down the back. Detach the legs. Detach the oyster and the tendons. Starting from the tip of the breastbone, cut through the ribs. Remove the breastbone and detach the wings (ask your butcher to do this for you if you prefer).

Peel the tomatoes by immersing them briefly in just-boiled water to loosen the skins. Crush them. Chop the onion. Remove the seeds from the red and green bell peppers and slice them into thin strips. Stab the garlic cloves with the point of a knife.

Heat the olive oil in a saucepan. Add the chicken pieces and cook for a few minutes. Season with salt and pepper.

with Bell Peppers

Add the chopped onion to the chicken pieces. Mix together and brown for about 5 minutes.

Deglaze with the red wine. Put in the garlic cloves, still in their skin, and the bouquet garni. Add the crushed tomatoes. Cook over a high heat for about 20 minutes.

Add the bell peppers and check the seasoning. Cook gently for about 15 minutes. Sprinkle on the chopped parsley. Serve the chicken on plates with the pepper and wine sauce.

Lamb

Preparation time:	25 minutes
Cooking time:	30 minutes
Difficulty:	★

Serves 4

3¼ lb/1.5 kg	leg of lamb
4 tbsp	olive oil
1 clove	garlic
	salt
1 sprig	rosemary
2	peppercorns

4 tbsp	white wine
1	lemon
2	eggs
1 tsp/5 g	grated parmesan

For the garnish:

	rosemary
	cherry tomatoes

There are many typical regional meat dishes in Abruzzi, including this lamb dish, which is particularly popular at Christmas and Easter.

Maddalena Beccaceci's Abruzzi-style lamb has a pronounced rustic character. Today, shepherds still drive their flocks of sheep up to the Alpine pastures when the warm weather begins. On the high plains, the animals live entirely on fresh grass and herbs, which is why the meat is supremely tasty and so sought-after all over Italy. Shoulder of lamb is just as good as leg of lamb in this recipe.

The rural population in Abruzzi once lived mainly on eggs and cheese, so this festive dish naturally contains both these ingredients. Parmesan, which is still made by hand, is the king of Italian cheeses. It was probably first produced in Tuscany in the 11th century, and a certain Bartolomeo Riva was apparently responsible for introducing the first

parmigiano reggiano to the people in 1612. Today, parmesan can only be produced in the provinces of Parma, Reggio Emilia, Modena, Mantua, and Bologna. It is made from cow's milk from which some of the cream has been removed. It is called *vecchio*, meaning "old," after maturing for one year. The designation *stravecchio*, "extremely old," can only be used after the parmesan has matured for three years.

Rosemary is indispensable in this recipe. This typically Mediterranean herb has a mild, piquant taste and its fragrance evokes the sun-drenched countryside. Both the fresh and dried leaves of this evergreen shrub are used for flavoring, but they must be used sparingly.

Cut the lamb into cubes. Heat the olive oil and the chopped clove of garlic in a pan and add the meat. Season with salt, then brown the meat all over. Add the chopped rosemary leaves and crushed peppercorns. Braise the mixture for about 10 minutes.

Pour in the white wine and boil for 10 minutes to reduce.

Squeeze the lemon and pour the juice into a bowl. Add the eggs and parmesan and season with salt.

Abruzzi Style

Beat the lemon juice, eggs, and cheese thoroughly with a fork.

Pour the mixture carefully over the meat.

Shake the pan and stir with a wooden spoon until the eggs are set. Serve the meat garnished with the rosemary and cherry tomatoes.

Veal Cutlets

Preparation time:	45 minutes
Cooking time:	15 minutes
Difficulty:	★

Serves 4

1½ lb/600 g	veal fillet
6 oz/150 g	Parma ham
12	sage leaves
1¼ lb/500 g	broccoli
	coarse salt
2	zucchini

1 cup/250 ml	milk
1 scant cup/	
100 g	flour
	olive oil for deep frying
1 tbsp	sunflower oil
1 scant cup/	
200 ml	white wine
1 cup/250 ml	meat stock
1½ tbsp/20 g	butter
	salt
	pepper

These veal cutlets with sage have a real flavor of Italy, and are simply delicious. They are prepared for festive occasions, especially in Lazio.

Knuckle, shoulder, or leg cutlets are easily recognizable by their regular, oval form. In Italy, *scaloppine* are normally cut from the fillet. They are hammered with a meat mallet, which is sometimes notched on one side, and are suitable for frying or braising. The favorite way of cooking them in Milan is with a coating of breadcrumbs.

For this nutritious dish, Sergio Pais must have Parma ham, made from the leg of the pig. In Tuscany, it is flavored with garlic, cloves, and pepper and, after being preserved in this way for four weeks, has to be kept for a long time to mature. After six months, the part not covered by skin is spread with pig fat, and the ham is then left to mature for another six months, during which time it is carefully ob-

served. The crown of the Duchy of Parma is stamped on the skin of every ham as illustrious proof of its origin.

The slightly piquant taste of sage, which is frequently used in Italian cuisine, gives this dish its characteristic flavor. Sage grows in temperate zones and, although mainly used to flavor meat, it is also used for bean and pasta dishes.

Broccoli comes from southern Italy and is cultivated mainly in Apulia. This brassica is rich in vitamins and minerals and is in season from April to October. Its name comes from the Greek *brotrytis*, the approximate meaning of which is "to form a grape." The broccoli florets should be firm and dense and the stalk should be very firm. Broccoli needs to be cooked for 10–15 minutes.

Cut the veal fillet into even-sized pieces and hammer into cutlets.

Cut the Parma ham to the same length as the cutlets. Lay the meat on a work surface. Place a slice of ham and a sage leaf on each cutlet and secure with a wooden cocktail stick.

Remove the broccoli florets from the stalk. Simmer the florets for about 10 minutes in a pan of water with a good pinch of coarse salt. Drain, and cool in ice water.

with Sage

Cut the zucchini into small sticks. Dip in milk, then roll in flour to coat. Deep-fry in olive oil, then drain.

Heat the sunflower oil in a pan and fry the cutlets for about 3 minutes. Remove the wooden cocktail sticks and quench the cutlets with the white wine. Add the meat stock and cook for another 3 minutes.

Add the butter. Shake the pan back and forth. Season with salt and pepper. Serve the cutlets on plates with the deep-fried zucchini sticks, broccoli, and sauce.

Loin of Suckling

Preparation time: 25 minutes
Cooking time: 55 minutes
Difficulty: ★

Serves 4

4 tbsp   extra-virgin olive oil
2¼ lb/1 kg   loin of suckling pig
                 salt
1 tbsp   bouquet garni herbs
1 scant cup/
50 g   breadcrumbs

For the garlic sauce:
5 cloves   garlic
                 salt
2 cups/500 ml   light cream
1 tbsp   cornstarch

For this recipe, Sauro Brunicardi has drawn inspiration from a traditional Tuscan dish of roast pork with herbs (*arista di maiale*). The chef has additionally enhanced the pork by coating the edge of each piece of meat with a thick garlic and herb sauce and sprinkling it with a mixture of breadcrumbs and bouquet garni herbs known in Italian as *pan alle herbe*.

Suckling pig has been regarded as a delicacy since the Middle Ages. The piglet is slaughtered before it reaches two months of age and should then weigh at least 33 pounds/ 15 kilograms. The meat is white, tender, and tasty. For this recipe, choose a loin consisting of 4–5 loin chops; these are not divided until they have been cooked in the oven. A loin of lamb can be prepared in exactly the same way.

For frying the meat, Sauro Brunicardi prefers to use extra-virgin olive oil originating from Lucca. This oil has a wonderfully luminous, green-yellow color and has the taste and smell of green apples.

The loin chops with their coating of garlic and herb sauce are wrapped in aluminum foil, before being cooked in the oven for the second time in such a way that only the edge with the sauce is exposed. This results in a deliciously fragrant, crisp crust.

As an accompaniment, Sauro Brunicardi recommends braised vegetables: for instance, a medley of spinach, broccoli, and cauliflower with potatoes, to add a touch of color. You can also serve poached vegetables with it, if you prefer. Serve the loin chops with carrots, zucchini, potatoes, and the garlic and herb sauce, and decorate the plates with a drizzle of sauce from the meat juices.

Remove the outer, papery covering of the garlic cloves. Using a small knife, cut off both ends and remove the skin, as well as any green shoots.

Put the garlic cloves and salt to taste in a saucepan with the cream. Bring to the boil and simmer for 5 minutes, then mix in a blender.

Return the blended sauce to the saucepan. Mix the cornstarch with a little of the sauce, add to the contents of the pan, and continue to stir for 5 minutes until the sauce is smooth and thick.

Pig with Herbs

Pour the olive oil into an ovenproof dish. Place the meat in the dish and season with salt. Bake in the oven for 40 minutes at 430° F/220° C.

Transfer the meat to a chopping board and separate the cutlets. Mix the bouquet garni herbs and the breadcrumbs.

Spread garlic cream over the fatty edge of the cutlets and sprinkle with the herb mixture. Wrap the cutlets in aluminum foil so that only the coated edge is showing. Return to the oven for a further 5 minutes before serving.

Pork Fillet

Preparation time:	*40 minutes*
Cooling time:	*30 minutes*
Cooking time:	*15 minutes*
Difficulty:	★

Serves 4

1½ lb/600 g	pork fillets
1 tsp	flour
3 tbsp	olive oil
2¼ lb/1 kg	broccoli
	salt
3 cloves	garlic

Dough for crust:

12 oz/300 g	sliced bread
1½ tbsp/20 g	butter

2	egg whites
3 stalks	parsley
2 tsp/10 g	chopped thyme
2 tsp/10 g	chopped marjoram
2 tsp/10 g	chopped rosemary
2 tsp/10 g	chopped savory
1	bay leaf
	salt and pepper to taste

For the basil sauce (optional):

½ bunch	basil
5 stalks	parsley
4 tbsp	olive oil

The inhabitants of the Marche region are justifiably proud of their area. The countryside with its medieval towns and centuries-old oak forests is rich in history and a popular tourist destination.

The cuisine of the Marche region also has much to offer. The aromatic herbs that grow there in abundance are excellent with meat, fish, or vegetables.

This traditional dish of pork fillet with a herb crust is a fine example of the sophistication of the regional cuisine. It is easy to prepare and a classic dish for Sunday lunch.

Pork is the Italians' favorite meat and they are consequently very demanding as far as its quality is concerned. According to our chef, extremely tender meat is obtained from the livestock in the Marche region that are for the most part raised in free-range conditions. Alberto Melagrana rolls the pork fillet in a herb-flavored dough before putting it in the oven.

Wild marjoram, known in the dialect as *persichina*, is typical of the region. It tastes and smells like a mixture of mint and basil. Marjoram has a milder taste than its close relative, oregano.

To enhance the pork, Alberto Melagrana suggests serving a truffle sauce, provided fresh truffles are available. If you opt for this, be sparing with the other flavorings. Cauliflower can also be substituted for broccoli.

For the dough, combine the bread, butter, egg whites, parsley, thyme, marjoram, rosemary, savory, and bay leaf with salt and pepper in a blender. Leave the dough to stand in a cool place for 30 minutes.

Dust the pork fillets lightly with flour. Fry in 1 tbsp olive oil until nearly cooked. Leave to cool.

Roll out the dough thinly. Using plastic wrap, roll the fillets in the dough. Remove the wrap and bake the rolled fillets in the oven at 340° F/170° C for about 6 minutes.

with a Herb Crust

Remove the broccoli florets from the stalk. Simmer the florets for about 5 minutes in salted water. Drain, and cool in ice water.

Heat the unpeeled garlic cloves with the remaining olive oil in a pan. Add the broccoli florets and sauté.

Cut the rolled pork fillets into medallions. Prepare the basil sauce, if using. Serve the fillets in their herb crust with the broccoli, using the basil sauce as garnish.

Rabbit

Preparation time: 25 minutes
Soaking time: 30 minutes
Cooking time: 1 hour
Difficulty: ★

Serves 4

1 good pinch	saffron threads
1	rabbit weighing 2 lb 3 oz/1 kg
3 cloves	garlic
4 tbsp	olive oil
1 sprig	thyme
2	sage leaves
2	black peppercorns
	salt
4 tbsp	white wine

When October arrives, Navelli, in the province of L'Aquila, becomes a hive of activity. Seasonal workers from all over Italy descend on the Abruzzi region in fall when the harvesting of saffron, the most expensive spice in the world, begins. A large number of men and women are employed to complete the harvest within two weeks, and to remove the precious stigmas (threads) from the blossoms by hand. Saffron from L'Aquila is internationally renowned and the Italians obviously enjoy cooking with this fine spice too.

Maddalena Beccaceci flavors her rabbit dish with saffron from Navelli. This traditional dish is easy to prepare and an unforgettable culinary experience.

Rabbit is highly regarded in Italy because of its firm, very tasty flesh. Rabbits should have a well-rounded back and a pale liver without any spots. When preparing the dish, be careful that the meat does not dry out, as this can easily happen. It is also possible to use a chicken instead of the rabbit in this recipe.

This rabbit dish would not be the same without fresh herbs. In particular, Mediterranean cuisine is scarcely imaginable without thyme, a member of the labiate family. Sage is used for the widest possible range of specialties in Italy; with its strong, slightly bitter flavor, it is used for sausages and other meat dishes. This plant, which grows in temperate zones, has been treasured since time immemorial for its healing powers—not least because it makes rich food more easily digestible.

This wonderful rabbit with saffron recipe is an exquisite dish for a festive meal.

Place the saffron threads in a small bowl and pour over 4 tbsp warm water. Soak for 30 minutes.

Divide the rabbit in two and carefully cut into joints.

Peel the garlic and fry in the olive oil. Add the thyme, sage, and peppercorns.

with Saffron

Add the rabbit joints to the skillet. Turn several times, to cover in oil and herbs. Season with salt and then fry for about 30 minutes.

Pour in the white wine and stir with a wooden spoon. Reduce the liquid for about 15 minutes.

Add the saffron. Simmer for another 5 minutes. Serve the rabbit portions on plates with some of the sauce.

Ossobuco

Preparation time:	30 minutes
Cooking time:	1 hour 50 minutes
Difficulty:	★

Serves 4

4 slices	leg of veal
1 scant cup/	
100 g	flour
3 tbsp	sunflower oil
½ cup/120 ml	white wine
2	unwaxed lemons
2	anchovy fillets
scant ½ stick/	
50 g	butter
	salt
1 bunch	pepper parsley

For the saffron risotto:

1	small onion
3 tbsp	olive oil
1 cup/200 g	Arborio rice
3 cups/750 ml	chicken stock
½ tsp/3 g	saffron powder
	salt
	pepper
4½ oz/125 g	grated parmesan
¾ stick/90 g	butter

For the garnish:

| | saffron threads |

Ossobuco alla Milanese is a classic in the cuisine of Lombardy and is eaten on the widest variety of occasions in northern Italy. Literally translated, the name means "bone with a hole," and refers to the slices of veal knuckle. They are cooked for a long time in white wine, which makes them extremely tasty. The chef has introduced a personal note into this recipe, adding anchovy fillets and lemon peel to the list of ingredients.

Veal knuckle, a favorite with gourmets, is found between the foot and shoulder of the calf. Only buy veal of the best quality that is reddish pink in color. Ask your butcher to cut slices from the leg of veal that are about 1 inch/2.5 centimeters thick.

Rice is so important in the cuisine of Lombardy that meat—in contrast with the rest of Italy—is pushed into second place. There are about 8,000 known varieties of rice, distinguished by the type of grain—short, long, or medium.

Rice, which originally grew on dry, sandy soil, was being cultivated in China in 3,000 B.C. Arabian travelers are supposed to have brought it back with them to Europe, where it was first cultivated in Sicily. It was only in the 19th century that rice began to be grown on a grand scale in Italy, on the Po plain. In Milan, saffron risotto is also called *risotto giallo,* "yellow risotto." This specialty, featuring generous quantities of butter and parmesan, is now justifiably internationally famous.

Saffron, which has been cultivated in Abruzzi for many years, is obtained from the flower of a species of purple crocus. In the 13th century, according to historical anecdote, Pope Celestin IV revered saffron above all else and, despite its high cost, the Milanese are supposed to have perfumed his bathwater with it.

Coat the slices of leg of veal in flour and fry for 10 minutes in sunflower oil.

Pour in the white wine and simmer everything for about 1 hour 30 minutes. Remove the zest from the lemons and squeeze them.

For the risotto, peel and chop the onion. Sauté in olive oil. Add the rice and cook slowly for 2 minutes until it is transparent, then gradually pour in the chicken stock. Simmer for about 16 minutes.

alla Milanese

Stir in the saffron, season with salt and pepper, and infuse for 2 minutes.

Add the parmesan cheese and butter, and stir.

Add strips of lemon zest to the meat and pour in the lemon juice. Add the anchovy fillets and butter, then season with salt and pepper. Simmer for 10 minutes. Sprinkle with chopped parsley and place the meat on the risotto to serve. Garnish with saffron threads.

Partridge

Preparation time: 50 minutes
Cooking time: 40 minutes
Difficulty: ★★

Serves 4

2	partridge or red-legged partridge
6 oz/150 g	peeled chestnuts
6 oz/150 g	small onions
	salt
	pepper
4 tbsp	vegetable oil
10	sage leaves

2 tbsp	white wine
6 oz/150 g	porcini mushrooms
1½ tbsp/20 g	butter
1 tbsp	sugar
2 tbsp	white wine vinegar
½ bunch	parsley

For the polenta:

1¼ cups/ 200 g	polenta
	coarse salt

For the garnish:

	sage leaves

In the countryside around Vicenza, where there is still a lot of hunting, there is a long tradition of cooking with wild game fowl, and you can enjoy the most wonderful dishes in the regional cuisine there, especially in winter.

Partridge or red-legged partridge, the flesh of which is reminiscent of tender chicken, is highly regarded by gourmets. Francesca de Giovannini fries the partridge first and then pours white wine over it. Depending on availability, quail, which is smaller, can be substituted for the partridge or red-legged partridge.

Francesca de Giovannini has added a personal touch to this traditional recipe by adding porcini mushrooms. These are very popular in the region and because of their strong flavor make excellent accompaniments to meat or poultry. They are frequently used in the preparation of tasty sauces.

In this recipe they combine wonderfully well with the small onions and chestnuts.

Chestnuts grow particularly well on the granite soils of southern Europe. The trees bear fruit until they are 50 years old. If you want to use fresh chestnuts, cut a cross in the shells and put them in a saucepan of boiling water with a few bay leaves; they will then be easy to peel.

In the Veneto region, serving a wild game dish without polenta would be almost unimaginable, but cornmeal is used in many other combinations as well. This is why the natives of the Veneto region and northern Italy as a whole have earned the name *polentoni*. Polenta is eaten hot, cold, boiled, or baked, and there are endless ways of preparing it. Purists still cook polenta in a copper cauldron over a wood fire.

For the polenta, heat 2 cups/500 ml water with some coarse salt in a saucepan. As soon as the water is boiling, trickle in the cornmeal. Stir with a balloon whisk and cook for about 40 minutes, stirring constantly.

Cut into the partridge along the breastbone on both sides and then divide into two pieces. Steam the chestnuts with the peeled onions for about 10 minutes.

Lay the halved partridge on a high-sided baking sheet. Season with salt and pepper. Pour over 2 tbsp vegetable oil and sprinkle over the sage leaves. Roast for 10 minutes at 400° F/200° C. Pour over the white wine and return to the oven for a further 10 minutes.

with Polenta

Heat 1 tbsp vegetable oil in a skillet and sauté the chopped porcini mushrooms for about 3 minutes.

For the sauce, heat the remaining vegetable oil in a pan with the butter and sugar, stirring with a wooden spoon.

Add the chestnuts, porcini mushrooms, and onions to the caramel sauce. Stir for 1 minute. Pour in the vinegar and continue stirring. Sprinkle with chopped parsley. Serve the partridge portions with the sauce and polenta. Garnish with sage leaves.

Pigeon Supreme

Preparation time: 50 minutes
Cooking time: 50 minutes
Difficulty: ★★

Serves 4

2	oven-ready pigeons, each 1¼ lb/500 g
8 oz/200 g	potatoes
	salt
	pepper
5 tbsp	olive oil
2 oz/50 g	black truffles
⅞ stick/ 100 g	butter

For the game stock:

	remains of the pigeon
1 tbsp	flour (optional)
1 tbsp	olive oil
3	shallots
1	carrot
1 sprig	rosemary
3 cloves	garlic
⅔ cup/ 150 ml	white wine

For the garnish (optional):

	pomegranate seeds

In the Marche region, pigeon stuffed with potatoes was once a classic dish for serving at big family gatherings. Liver, pork, chicken, and truffles were served as an accompaniment to pigeon, which was flavored with cinnamon.

Alberto Melagrana has drawn inspiration from this traditional dish. His delicious pigeon supreme is a dish that emphasizes the refinement of Italian cuisine.

Connoisseurs love the fine, delicate flesh of wild pigeon, which is made into very sophisticated dishes. Wild pigeon is available in markets in Italy from spring to late summer; at other times of the year you will need to substitute commercially reared pigeon.

"Supreme" designates the breast of a bird, with the skin removed, together with the wing bone. If you find it difficult to joint the pigeons into supremes, ask your butcher to do this for you. Save the remains of the birds for the stock. If you think they look too fatty, add a little flour.

In Italy, and in the Marche region in particular, truffles are regarded as the "diamonds" of gastronomy. There are many different kinds of truffle, but for the sauce in this recipe our chef recommends that you choose the black variety. Brush them carefully to remove any particles of earth and then soak for a few minutes in lukewarm water. They should be cooked in extra-virgin olive oil over low heat to retain their incomparable flavor.

To garnish this luxurious dish, Alberto Melagrana has chosen the fruit that bears his name: the pomegranate or, in Italian, *melagrana*!

Remove the legs and tips of the wings from the pigeons. Joint the birds into supremes by cutting along the breastbone on both sides. Reserve the rest of the pigeons.

For the stock, sauté the remaining meat from the pigeon with a little flour in 1 tbsp olive oil. Add the shallots, carrot, rosemary, and garlic. Pour in half the white wine. When this has reduced, add the remaining wine, top up with water, and simmer for 40 minutes.

Peel the potatoes and cut into thin slices. Cook in boiling water for 15–20 minutes. Mash with a fork. Add 2 tbsp strained stock and season with salt and pepper.

"Melagrana"

Heat 2 tbsp olive oil in a skillet. Add the mashed potatoes and fry gently.

Heat the remaining olive oil in a saucepan and brown the pigeon supremes, then transfer them to the oven and bake for 3 minutes at 340° F/170° C. Cut into slices.

Heat the strained game stock in a saucepan with the finely sliced truffles. Season with salt and pepper. Remove from the heat, add the butter, and beat with a balloon whisk. Arrange the supremes on plates with the potatoes and sauce and garnish with the pomegranate seeds.

Rabbit

Preparation time:	50 minutes	11 oz/300 g	tomatoes
Cooking time:	40 minutes	4½ tbsp/70 ml	olive oil
Difficulty:	★	1	small dried red pepper
		1 knob	butter
Serves 4		3 tbsp/50 g	flour
		2 oz/50 g	capers
1	rabbit weighing 2 lb/1 kg	5 oz/150 g	pitted green olives
2	carrots	7 tbsp/100 ml	red wine
1	celery heart	7 tbsp/100 ml	white wine
1 bunch	parsley		salt
1 bunch	basil		
2	onions		

For the garnish:

basil leaves

Rabbit *Angelino*, a delicious family dish, is a particular specialty of chef Angelo La Spina's birthplace, Caltagirone. Famous for its pottery, this inland town retains its old Sicilian charm. Angelo La Spina has improved this traditional recipe with the addition of two typically Mediterranean ingredients: olives and capers.

Much enjoyed on Sicily, rabbit is normally broiled or stewed. At Easter, it is often served in rich, sweet-tasting sauce featuring pine nuts and raisins. Rabbit meat is firm and tasty, and combines well with other ingredients. Choose a rabbit that is not too long, with a rounded saddle, and a liver that is pale and free of blemishes. In season, select for preference the richer-flavored wild rabbit.

With its wonderful flavors, this dish is a good illustration of the subtlety of Sicilian cooking. Used in many of the is-land's specialties, Sicilian celery or *sedano* is chosen for its freshness and crisp texture. Cooked in combination with carrots and onions, also locally produced, celery is an essential ingredient. Available all year round, the exterior of the celery should be green, firm, and without black or brown marks.

Angelo La Spina's reworking of rabbit *Angelino* is a treat. The highly prized Mediterranean olive finishes this typical southern Italian dish to perfection. Olive trees have grown in abundance on Sicily and the Aeolian Islands since Antiquity, particularly in the Biancavilla region near Catania. During the Roman Empire, olive oil began to be produced on a vast scale. The industry was controlled by the *arca olearia*, an official body that set the prices in this lucrative market.

Remove the rabbit liver and set aside. Divide the ribcage from the hindquarters at the point where the bottom of the ribs meets the saddle. Remove the legs and cut them into smaller pieces on the bone. Divide the saddle into pieces of equal size.

Prepare the vegetables. Peel the carrots and cut them into rounds. Wash and chop the celery, parsley, and basil. Peel and chop the onions. Wash, peel, and mash the tomatoes (plunge them into just-boiled water first, to loosen the skins).

In a pan, heat 2 tbsp of the oil with the butter. Flour the pieces of rabbit meat, and fry them in the oil. Cook until golden, for about 10 minutes. Pat the pieces with a paper towel to remove excess oil and set aside.

Angelino

In the remaining oil, brown the chopped onions. Add the celery. Cook for about 5 minutes. Add the carrots, capers, parsley, and basil. Mix them all together. Sprinkle over the ground red pepper and add some salt. Add the tomatoes.

Mix the vegetables together. Add the sliced green olives. Cook for about 5 minutes.

Place the pieces of rabbit in an ovenproof dish. Cover them with the vegetable mixture. Add the red and white wine. Cook in the oven at 340 °F/170 °C for about 20 minutes. Serve the rabbit on plates accompanied by the vegetables and garnished with basil.

Lamb Stew with

Preparation time: 30 minutes
Cooking time: 1 hour 20 minutes
Difficulty: ★

Serves 4

1¼ lb/600 g	fresh fava beans (broad beans)
2 lb/1 kg	leg of lamb
5 tbsp/75 ml	olive oil
2	onions
1 cup/250 ml	lamb bouillon
6	mint leaves
	salt and pepper

For the tomato sauce:

1 clove	garlic
1	onion
2 tbsp/30 ml	olive oil
7 oz/200 g	tomatoes
1	carrot
1 stick	celery
1	bay leaf
3	basil leaves
	salt and pepper

For the garnish:

	mint leaves

No special event can be celebrated on Sardinia without a festive meal. Lamb stew with fresh fava beans is traditionally eaten on family occasions. Distinctive and full of flavor, this dish makes use of locally grown produce.

Once essentially a nation of sheep-farmers, the Sicilians' pastoral roots are reflected in their cuisine. In the past, when the men took the flocks to their summer grazing grounds, they lived on basic foods such as cheese, bread, and olive oil. If they ate meat at all, it was always roasted on a spit. On their return home, their wives would welcome them with a substantial and tasty stew.

The easily-made recipe given here uses leg of lamb, one of the best-flavored and favorite cuts. It is stewed with olive oil and onions, and given an extra freshness with the addition of mint. Believed to help digestion, this highly scented herb grows wild all over Sardinia.

Fava beans are central to this substantial stew. Fava beans originated in Persia, but have been eaten in the Mediterranean area since ancient times, and they are enjoyed for their unique and delicate flavor. Even when dried, fava beans are rich in proteins and vitamins. Fresh garden peas (from the same family of vegetables) can be used as an alternative if desired.

Pomodori (tomatoes) are essential for the rich color and flavor of this stew. Select those that are firm and plump with shiny skins and a uniform color. Grown in irrigated fields, and thriving in the island sunshine, Sardinian tomatoes are a favorite ingredient on the Italian mainland.

Shell the fresh fava beans and blanch them in a pan of salted water for about 4 minutes. Plunge them in a bowl of iced water and then drain.

Bone the leg of lamb and cut into equal-sized pieces (ask your butcher to do this if you prefer).

Brown the pieces of meat in very hot olive oil. Cook for a few minutes and then remove and set aside.

Fresh Fava Beans

In the same pan, brown the 2 chopped onions. Return the meat to the pan and add the bouillon. Bring to the boil and simmer for about 25 minutes.

For the sauce, brown the garlic and diced onion in the olive oil. Add the diced tomatoes, carrot, celery, and a bay leaf. Season with salt and pepper. Cook for 30 minutes. Add the basil. Blend the sauce in a food processor, then pour it over the lamb.

Season the lamb mixture. Add the chopped mint and the fava beans. Cook for about 10 minutes. Serve the stew on plates with a garnish of mint.

Veal Escalope

Preparation time:	20 minutes
Cooking time:	15 minutes
Difficulty:	★

Serves 4

1	eggplant
6 tbsp/90 ml	olive oil
4	veal escalopes
½ cup/120 ml	white wine
4 slices	uncooked ham

2 tbsp/30 g	tomato sauce
8	basil leaves
4 slices	young pecorino cheese
	salt and pepper

For the garnish:

	basil

Invaded many times in the course of their history, even as late as the 19th century Sardinians regarded the sea with suspicion. It was the sea that had brought Phoenicians, Carthaginians, Romans, Vandals, and Spanish invaders to their shores. Retreating to the mountainous regions inland, the local people survived by rearing animals. Many local dishes still feature ingredients reflecting this pastoral life. Veal escalope *alla barbaricina* is a dish typical of the Barbaria or Bargagia region, in the eastern part of the island. It is usually eaten at family meals on a Sunday or other festive occasion. A simple and delicious dish, it is ideal for serving to guests.

Veal escalopes are cut from the most tender parts of the animal, the cushion or the chump end. In this tasty recipe, the meat is covered with a slice of raw ham, a piece of fried eggplant, and some pecorino. About half of the total area of

Sardinia is given over to animal husbandry. The local people are skilled cheese-makers, *pecorino sardo* being a particular favorite. Its mellow taste combines wonderfully with the meat in veal *alla barbaricina*. Made from pure ewe's milk, it is much loved by all Italians.

The tomato sauce served with the meat is a typically Sardinian touch. To make this, dice two tomatoes, half an onion, one stick of celery, and half a carrot. Heat a tablespoonful of olive oil in a pan, and brown one garlic clove and some chopped parsley. Add all the other vegetables together with a bay leaf, and cook for about half an hour. Season with salt and pepper, and sprinkle with basil. Blend the sauce in a food processor.

If you have not tried this deliciously flavored dish before, now is the time!

Wash the eggplant. Remove the stalk and cut the eggplant lengthwise into thin slices.

Heat 4 tbsp of olive oil and gently fry the slices of eggplant. Pat them with a paper towel to remove any excess oil.

Heat the rest of the olive oil in an ovenproof dish. Add the veal escalopes and fry them for 2 minutes on either side.

Alla Barbaricina

Pour the white wine over the veal.
Season with salt and pepper.
Cook for about 4 minutes.

Place the slices of ham on the veal.
Then pour over some tomato sauce
and sprinkle with chopped basil.

Place the pieces of eggplant on the ham.
Cover them with the pieces of cheese.
Transfer the dish to the oven and cook at
400 °F/200 °C for 4–6 minutes. Serve the
escalopes on plates with a drizzle of
tomato sauce. Garnish with basil.

Oven-Baked

Preparation time: 20 minutes
Cooking time: 1 hour
                15 minutes
Difficulty: ★

Serves 4

2 whole bulbs	garlic
3¼ lb/1.4 kg	leg of lamb (or mutton)
2	onions
3–4 tbsp	olive oil
	salt
	pepper
2	lemons

1 sprig	thyme
1 sprig	rosemary
1	bay leaf
3¼ kbs/1.5 kg	potatoes
2	tomatoes
2 tbsp	butter (optional)

For the garnish:

	bay leaves
	rosemary

The symbol of reunions, oven-baked *arni* is a dish to be shared with family and friends. This traditional recipe, typical of the Greek hinterland, is usually served to the family on Sunday. In olden days the villagers would take the dish to the local bakehouse to be cooked!

A land of shepherds, Greeks have a special fondness for lamb and for *arni* in particular. Sheep have been raised in the mountainous areas of Greece for centuries and are prized for their delicious meat. You could sometimes ring the changes and use kid goat or pork instead, which are also favorites with the Greeks.

Characteristic of rustic cuisine, oven-baked *arni* is simplicity itself to make and is full of the Mediterranean flavors so loved by Greeks: thyme, rosemary, onion, and bay leaf, which all add flair to the other ingredients.

Lending its own piquancy, cloves of garlic, a plant that grows wild in Greece, are inserted into the meat before cooking. Athletes in Ancient Greek used it as a "stimulant" as it was reputed to add strength and vitality! According to the beliefs of that time, it had to be eaten in the morning. Today the Cyclades are famous for the quality of their garlic. Available all year round on market stalls, the cloves should be hard and firm.

This copious dish also stars vegetables. Potatoes, popular all over the world, soak up the fruity flavor of the olive oil. Originally from the New World, potatoes have been grown in Greece since the beginning of the 20th century. The Livanates region specializes in producing them and today supplies the country's markets.

This succulent oven-baked *arni* is quite simply the Mediterranean sun on a plate!

Break up the garlic bulbs and peel the cloves. Make small slits in the lamb with the tip of a knife and insert individual cloves.

Peel and chop the onions and arrange them in a large roasting pan, sprinkled with a dash of olive oil.

Season the lamb on both sides. Put it on top of the onions and squeeze over the juice of 1 lemon. Add the thyme, rosemary, and bay leaf. Add 1½ tbsp olive oil and ¾ cup/200 ml water. Bake in an oven preheated to 350° F/180° C for about 40 minutes.

Arni

Peel the potatoes and cut into big cubes. Place in a bowl with the remaining olive oil and lemon juice. Season and mix.

Add the potatoes, with their olive oil and lemon juice, to the meat and add ¾ cup water. Cook at the same temperature for about another 20 minutes.

Wash the tomatoes and cut into quarters. Add them to the pan with the meat, together with the butter, if using. Transfer the lamb and vegetables onto a serving dish and garnish with bay leaves and rosemary.

Greek Meatballs

Preparation time: 40 minutes
Cooking time: 30 minutes
Difficulty: ★★

Serves 4–6

For the meatballs:

3	onions
4 cloves	garlic
1 bunch	parsley
7–8 slices/200 g	stale white bread
2¼ lb/1 kg	ground beef
1 tsp	cumin
	salt
	pepper

4	eggs
	flour
	oil for frying

For the tomato sauce:

10	tomatoes
4 cloves	garlic
4 tbsp	olive oil
1 tbsp	sugar
	salt
	pepper
⅔ cup/150 ml	white wine
1 tbsp	flour

Known as *soutsoukakia*, these beef or pork meatballs coated with a tomato sauce are popular throughout Greece. Rolled into plum-sized portions, they are always the same shape—oblong and slightly flattened at each end.

The classic recipe uses ground meat, onions, herbs, and spices, bound with eggs and bread. Always use stale bread with the crusts removed, because fresh bread would be too mushy once it is mixed with the other ingredients. Week-old bread is ideal. If when you mix the meatballs the ingredients are still too wet to be shaped into balls, add a few dry breadcrumbs and that will solve the problem.

It's not always easy to find tomatoes on market stalls that are as ripe as the ones you pick off the vine. You can improve the color and the flavor of the sauce, however, by adding a tablespoon of tomato paste. Likewise, a pinch of sugar will offset any sharpness from tomatoes that are not quite ripe. Chrysanthi Stamkopoulos is also happy to pass on this tip for improving the flavor of the sauce—just add one or two bay leaves and a stick of cinnamon while the sauce is cooking.

Depending on their size, two or three meatballs will be required for each guest. Rice or pasta make the ideal accompaniment. You can serve the meatballs and sauce separately, or use a mold to make a small dome-shaped mound of rice in the middle of each plate with the *soutsoukakia* arranged around the sides and the hot tomato sauce poured over the top. Your guests will be delighted with these little succulent, flavor-filled meatballs.

Meatballs: Peel and finely chop the onions and garlic and combine. Wash and chop the parsley, reserving a few leaves. Remove the crusts from the bread and break it into chunks. In a bowl, mix the ground beef, onions, garlic, parsley, bread, cumin, salt, pepper, and eggs.

Combine all the ingredients with your hands until they are uniformly blended. Shape into oval balls that are about 2–2½ in/5–6 cm long, flattening them slightly at each end.

Coat the meatballs with flour, tapping off the surplus. Heat the oil in a skillet and brown the meatballs for about 10 minutes, turning them so that they become a uniform color.

with Tomato Sauce

To make the sauce, peel the tomatoes, blend to a purée and transfer to a large skillet. Add finely chopped garlic, olive oil, sugar, salt, pepper, and white wine. Bring to the boil and simmer for around 10 minutes.

In a bowl, mix the flour to a smooth paste with a little water and add to the tomato sauce. Stir for 5 minutes over heat to thicken the sauce.

Arrange the fried meatballs in an oven-proof dish. Pour over the tomato sauce and place in an oven preheated to 350° F/180° C for 5 minutes. Serve hot garnished with parsley leaves.

Loin of Lamb with

Preparation time:	40 minutes
Cooking time:	1 hour
	15 minutes
Soaking time (beans):	12 hours
Difficulty:	★

Serves 4

1 cup/200 g	dried white navy (haricot) beans
1	carrot
1 stalk	celery
1	onion
2	tomatoes
1	bay leaf

	salt, pepper
⅔ cup/150 ml	olive oil
2	loins of lamb

For the herb crust:

2 cups/100 g	breadcrumbs
1 clove	garlic (optional)
½ bunch	parsley
½ bunch	dill
1 sprig	rosemary
1	lemon

For the garnish:

	cilantro leaves (coriander)
	cardamom leaves

Full of unrivaled flavors, this loin of lamb with white Kastoria navy (haricot) beans is a traditional recipe from Thessalia and eastern Macedonia. It has a subtle combination of flavors from the land and is mainly served at weddings.

Raised in the mountainous regions of the country, lamb is an essential part of Greek cuisine. Its highly flavored meat is particularly popular when broiled. Our chef suggests you try kid goat, which is also highly prized in Greece.

Wonderfully appetizing to look at, the cutlets are topped with a herb crust made from breadcrumbs, garlic, parsley, dill, and rosemary, flavors that are so characteristic of the Mediterranean.

Known since the days of Homer, parsley was used by the warriors in *The Iliad* to feed their horses. This plant, a native of Southern Europe, is available on Greek market stalls all year round and is used to give a lift to many dishes. Choose parsley that has bright green leaves and firm stems.

Dill, meanwhile, or *anithos* as it is known in Greek, is also highly regarded in Greece and Turkey for its aniseed taste. Famous for its culinary and medicinal properties, this plant has a soft and slightly bitter flavor and is often associated with fish and dairy products.

This recipe from the Greek hinterland is simplicity itself to make and also uses navy beans from Kastoria. Famed for its production of pulses, this lovely city in northern Greece is also famous for its furriers' workshops.

Extremely nourishing, dried beans formed part of the staple diet in the Byzantine Age. They need a long cooking time but have the advantage of absorbing the flavors of the other ingredients.

Put the dried beans into a bowl, cover with water, and soak for 12 hours. Drain.

Put the drained beans into a pan of water and simmer briskly for about 1 hour.

Add the carrot, celery, onion, and tomatoes, all cut into small pieces, along with the bay leaf. Season to taste and cook for 10 minutes. Add 3–4 tbsp olive oil and cook for a further 2 minutes.

White Kastoria Beans

Trim the loins of lamb, season, and brown in a scant ½ cup/100 ml olive oil. Roast in an oven preheated to 400° F/200° C for 10 minutes.

To make the herb crust, put the breadcrumbs, garlic, if using, parsley, dill, and rosemary into a food processor and blend. Moisten with lemon juice if dry.

Cover the lamb with the herb crust mixture. Return to the oven for 1 minute. Divide into chops and serve with the beans, garnished with cilantro and cardamom leaves.

Giouvetsi

Preparation time: 35 minutes
Cooking time: 1 hour
Difficulty: ★

Serves 4

1¾ lb/800 g	shoulder of veal
6	tomatoes
5–6 tbsp	olive oil
1	meat bouillon cube
3–4 tbsp	white wine

3	bay leaves
6	allspice berries
2	onions
	salt
10 oz/300 g	chilopites (Greek pasta)
1½ tbsp	grated Pecorino cheese

The word *giouvetsi* comes from the name of the earthenware dish in which meat was left to simmer in times gone by. A very popular dish in major Greek cities, this veal stew is enriched with *chilopites*, handmade pasta shapes. This tasty dish can be enjoyed on any occasion.

Greek cuisine traditionally does not use much veal. In this Mediterranean country the scrubland has left its wild imprint on the landscape and has gradually eroded the meadowland. As a result, since the days of Ancient Greece the locals have preferred to eat lamb and mutton.

In olden days cattle were raised for the sole purpose of helping man to work in the fields. Only an animal that had been blessed could be killed and eaten. According to Nicolaos Katsanis, the villagers would club together and buy the meat from the owner in order that he could purchase another animal.

This recipe allows the delicate flavor of the shoulder of veal to emerge, a meat appreciated for its delicacy and smoothness.

Simmered with olive oil, onions, white wine, and tomatoes, it is further enhanced with the distinctive flavor of bay leaf. Known as *dafni* in Greek, this plant owes its name to the pretty nymph Daphne. According to mythology, Daphne was changed into a laurel bush by the gods of Olympus to help her escape the unwanted attentions of the handsome Apollo. Used whole or crumbled, the leaves of this bush are used sparingly. They give an admirable lift to stews, stuffing mixes, and marinades.

Served with pasta shapes, *giouvetsi* is a filling dish. If you have difficulty finding *chilopites* you can use macaroni. Depending on your personal taste, you can also try this recipe with pork without compromising the finished result.

Using a sharp knife, trim the shoulder of veal and cut the meat into cubes of equal thickness. Cut one tomato into thin slices and set aside. Peel and chop the rest.

Heat 4 tbsp olive oil in a pan and add the cubes of veal. Brown them quickly over a high heat for a couple of minutes. Crumble the meat bouillon cube into a cup of water and set aside.

Add the white wine to the veal, 2 bay leaves, 3 allspice berries, and the prepared stock. Top up with water to cover the meat. Cook for 35–40 minutes.

Heat the remaining olive oil in a deep pan and brown the diced onions. Add the chopped tomatoes, remaining allspice berries, and bay leaf. Cook for 10 minutes. Transfer the meat and the stock it was cooked in to the tomato mixture. Season with salt and cook for 10 minutes.

Bring a pan of salted water to the boil and add the chilopites. Cook for about 3 minutes then drain.

Transfer the meat mixture to an earthenware dish and add the chilopites. Top with the reserved tomato slices. Cook in an oven preheated to 350° F/180° C for 20 minutes. Serve the giouvetsi scattered with grated Pecorino.

Moussaka

Preparation time:	45 minutes
Cooking time:	1 hour
	30 minutes
Sweating time (eggplants):	30 minutes
Difficulty:	★★

Serves 4

3½ lb/1.5 kg	ripe eggplants
	salt
	olive oil
1	large red onion
1¼ lb/ 550 g	ground lamb
4 tbsp	virgin olive oil
1 stick	cinnamon

1 pinch	nutmeg
1 cup/250 ml	tomato juice
	pepper
2 cups/100 g	breadcrumbs

For the béchamel sauce:

2 oz/55 g	butter
½ cup 60 g	all-purpose flour
2 cups/500 ml	milk
	salt
	pepper
1 pinch	nutmeg
2	eggs
2 tbsp	grated parmesan

A Greek dish that is now internationally known and loved, moussaka can be traced as far afield as the Middle East and Iran. The origin of the name is not known, but a virtually identical recipe is shared by Greeks, Turks, Iranians, and their neighbors. The Greek version, though, has only been smothered in a layer of béchamel sauce for the past 90 or 100 years. Before that, cooks would arrange the layers of tomatoes or eggplants on the bed of meat to prevent it from drying out during cooking. In Greek families, moussaka is usually eaten as a main course, although some restaurant owners, who really have tried making it in many different ways, have been serving it as an appetizer for the past 20 years or so.

You can sprinkle the slices of eggplant with salt and wait until they "sweat," in other words until their somewhat bitter juice forms into droplets on the surface of the cut slices. Then rinse them under cold running water and blot dry.

When they are fried, don't forget to blot them again on kitchen paper to soak up the excess oil (for maximum drainage, our chef recommends you do this the night before). If you put a bed of breadcrumbs on the bottom of the gratin dish this will also soak up the oil.

Moussaka is usually made with lamb, although some Greeks prefer to use mutton. In fact in the countryside, some lambs weigh up to 12–15 pounds/5–7 kilograms. Greek cooks prefer to bake their tender flesh, essentially the leg and shoulder, in the oven with potatoes.

Moussaka comes in many different varieties, according to the cook's mood. You can add slices of potato or fried zucchini. Our chef sometimes cuts the meat into fine strips and alternates it with mushrooms. It is even possible to replace lamb with beef. Just before serving, cut the moussaka into portions and garnish with the green parts of the scallions.

Cut the eggplants into slices, put them in a colander, sprinkle with salt, and leave for 30 minutes. Blot dry and fry in olive oil until brown.

In another skillet fry the chopped onion and meat in 4 tbsp olive oil over a fairly brisk heat for 10–15 minutes, breaking the meat up with a fork until it has a uniform consistency.

Stir in the cinnamon stick, nutmeg, tomato juice, salt, and pepper. Add water just to cover the contents and continue cooking over a brisk heat for 10 minutes or until the liquid has evaporated.

For the béchamel sauce: Melt the butter and stir in the flour until it forms a roux. Whisk in the milk and continue whisking over low heat to achieve a thick, smooth sauce. Add seasoning and nutmeg.

In a separate bowl, whisk the eggs. Take the béchamel off the heat and beat in the eggs, together with the grated cheese. Adjust the seasoning.

Oil a gratin dish and sprinkle in half the breadcrumbs. Layer the eggplants and meat, cover with béchamel sauce and the remaining breadcrumbs. Cook for 50 minutes in an oven preheated to 400° F/200° C.

Lachanosarmades

Preparation time:	40 minutes
Cooking time:	55 minutes
Difficulty:	★

Serves 4

1	large white cabbage
1	meat bouillon cube
5 tbsp	olive oil
	salt

For the stuffing:

1 lb/450 g	ground pork
1 lb/450 g	ground beef
3	onions
3	scallions

| 1 bunch | parsley |
| scant ½ cup/85 g | Arborio rice |

1 pinch	boukovo (dried flakes of red pimento)
	salt
	pepper
1	egg

For the avgolemono sauce:

1 tbsp	cornstarch
1	lemon
2	egg yolks
	salt
	pepper

For the garnish:

| | lemon zest |
| | boukovo |

A very popular dish throughout the whole of Greece, these stuffed, rolled cabbage leaves, known as *lachanosarmades* or even *lachanodolmades*, are particularly popular in winter. Originally from the town of Kozani in the north of the country, this adaptation is full of incomparable flavors.

Highly regarded in both Greek and Turkish cooking, the cabbage has been known in Europe for more than 4,000 years. Cabbage production spread across the whole of the continent during the Middle Ages. Rich in vitamins A and C, it has a fairly sweet taste. Choose a white cabbage that is a hard, densely packed ball, free of blemishes. If you want to make this recipe with a savoy cabbage instead, because the leaves have an embossed texture, you will need to keep a close watch on it while it is cooking. Rolled into cigar shapes, the leaves should not start to unravel when they are being cooked. Our chef recommends that you wedge them firmly into the dish by putting a plate on top of them.

Greeks love vegetables and have poured all their talents into the art of cooking them: Fried, broiled, puréed, they are also very often served stuffed. In this recipe, the beef and pork used for the filling are combined with onions, parsley, eggs … and rice.

Eaten now throughout the whole world, rice was first imported to Ancient Greece via Mesopotamia and the Persians, and reached Greece in the 4th century B.C. when Alexander the Great introduced it to the country. Initially regarded as a luxury, rice is today part of the staple diet.

These succulent *lachanosarmades* are coated at the last minute with an *avgolemono* sauce, which is made from eggs, lemon juice, stock, cornstarch, salt, and pepper. It provides a lift to many dishes, and is served in generous portions. It is vital that you use a whisk when you are making it to ensure all the ingredients are thoroughly blended.

Use a sharp knife to remove the tough cabbage stalk. Plunge the trimmed cabbage head into a large pan of boiling salted water and let it blanch for about 10 minutes.

Drain and cool the cabbage, then using your fingers tease apart the leaves. Make up the stock with the bouillon cube and set it aside.

For the stuffing: Mix the two meats, chopped onions and scallions, chopped parsley, and rice. Sprinkle on the boukovo, salt, and pepper, add the egg, and stir well.

Cut away the central rib from the cabbage leaves and cut the leaves in half, if large. Add the stuffing, fold in the sides and roll up firmly.

Line the bottom of a deep skillet with some cabbage leaves, and put the rolls on top, wedging them in. Cover with more leaves. Add the stock and olive oil. Cover and cook over moderate heat for about 45 minutes. Pour off the cooking liquid into a bowl.

Pour half of the partially cooled cooking liquid into a pan. Whisk in the cornstarch and lemon juice. Now add the remaining cooking liquid and egg yolks. Season, and pour over the rolls. Garnish with lemon zest and boukovo.

Rabbit with

Preparation time: 35 minutes
Cooking time: 35 minutes
Marinating time (rabbit): 5 hours
Difficulty: ★

Serves 4

1	rabbit weighing 3 lb/1.4 kg
3–4 tbsp	olive oil
10–12	pearl onions
1 clove	garlic
	salt
	pepper

scant ½ cup/ 100 ml	vegetable stock
1¼ lb/550 g	green olives, pitted

For the marinade:

2 cloves	garlic
1 sprig	thyme
2 sprigs	rosemary
2	bay leaves
1 stalk	celery
½	onion
⅔ cup/150 ml	red wine

For the garnish:

	rosemary

Rabbit with green olives is a specialty from Chalkidiki. Forming an enormous peninsula in the shape of a foot from which three "toes" jut out into the Aegean Sea, this hunting and fishing area of northeastern Greece is famous for its traditional cuisine. This exquisite family dish can be enjoyed on any occasion.

In the Greek culinary repertoire, rabbit is a particularly popular meat. It is usually cooked in olive oil with vegetables, which make the perfect foil. In this recipe the firm flesh of the rabbit takes up the flavors of the marinade. If you can, use a short stocky rabbit, with a plump saddle and a pale, unblemished liver. During the hunting season, rabbit can be easily be replaced by hare or wild rabbit.

A mirror image of the landscapes in the Greek hinterland, this dish is a marvelous melting pot for a range of different aromas. Always used very sparingly, thyme, bay leaf, and rosemary really complement the wine used to marinade the meat. Celery, or *selino* as it is known in Greece, grows wild here and is similar to flat-leaf parsley. It has a very distinctive taste that is also popular in soups and stews.

Wonderfully colorful, this dish confirms its Mediterranean origins thanks to the use of green olives. As Greek as Greece itself, these fruits of the olive tree originally came from the Orient. Recognizable by their oval shape, the generous flesh encases a torpedo shaped stone. They are used for the production of olive oil and as a table condiment.

Picked before they are fully ripe from mid September to the end of November, green olives are then preserved in oil or brine. The olives grown in Chalkidiki are quite big and are often stuffed with walnuts, almonds, or peppers.

Remove the liver from the rabbit and split the chest cage from stem to stern at the junction of the ribs and saddle. Pull off the legs and cut them up. Divide the saddle into equal pieces.

For the marinade: Put the crushed cloves of garlic, thyme, rosemary, bay leaves, celery, and the chopped onion into a bowl. Add the pieces of rabbit, pour over the red wine, and set aside for 5 hours.

Heat the olive oil in a pan and brown the rabbit pieces. Add the thyme, the bay leaf from the marinade, the peeled pearl onions, 1 crushed clove of garlic, and some seasoning.

Green Olives

Add the wine from the strained marinade to the rabbit. Cook for 5 minutes, add a scant ½ cup/100 ml vegetable stock and cook for 20–25 minutes.

Add the olives to the rabbit. Cook for 3 minutes, then lift out the olives, pearl onions, and the meat.

Strain the sauce. Serve the rabbit with the green olives and pearl onions. Pour over the sauce and garnish with rosemary.

Rabbit

Preparation time:	45 minutes
Cooking time:	1 hour
	35 minutes
Difficulty:	★★

Serves 6

1	rabbit weighing 3½ lb/ 1.5 kg, skinned and cleaned
3 cups/300 g	cauliflower florets
1¼ lb/600 g	pearl onions
7 oz/200 g	oyster mushrooms
5 oz/150 g	carrots

1	leek
½ cup/125 ml	olive oil
1	cinnamon stick
3 or 4	cloves
4 or 5	allspice berries
	salt
	pepper
4 tbsp	red wine vinegar
½ cup/125 ml	red *brusco* wine
2 cloves	garlic
2	bay leaves
1 sprig	rosemary
8	small plum tomatoes

Braised rabbit, or *lagos stifado*, is traditionally simmered in the middle of an assortment of fresh colourful vegetables and is always rightfully appreciated on Greek tables. Characteristic of many local dishes, the abundance of vegetables and herbs gives this recipe its individual flavor.

In the mountainous and arid country that is Greece, the inhabitants generally eat only a little meat from farmed animals (lamb, goat, rabbit) or game (hare, partridge, etc). Ask your butcher to prepare the rabbit or choose prepacked ones that are ready to cook. This recipe is equally good when made with hare, lamb, or beef.

When garnishing the dish, oyster mushrooms can be easily replaced by stronger-flavored wild ones or even button mushrooms. *Brusco* is a sweet and delicate red wine from Patras in the Peloponnese.

Our chef usually adds a few sun-ripened Greek baby tomatoes, which are very tasty, and much prefers these to the sort of insipid tomatoes that are grown under glass. But if you can't find these, choose small plum tomatoes instead, or even peeled tinned ones. Tomatoes are yet another vegetable introduced relatively recently to Greece. Brought back from the Americas in the 16th century by Portuguese sailors, it would be a couple of centuries before they were grown in Hellenic gardens.

If you need to cook the dish quickly, you can put all the ingredients into an oiled heavy-bottomed pan and cook it on top of the stove. For a better flavor and color, though, it's best to first fry the rabbit with the mushrooms, carrots, leek, onions, and the seasoning (cinnamon, cloves, allspice, and garlic). Pour on the wine and vinegar, then add the other vegetables and herbs and braise the dish in the oven.

Cut the rabbit into 3 large pieces, then cut it again into pieces of about 3–4 in/8–10 cm.

Blanch the cauliflower florets and refresh. Peel the onions. Cut the mushrooms into big pieces, peel the carrots and slice thinly. Trim and wash the leek, slice into thin rings.

Heat a little oil in a heavy-bottomed casserole dish and sauté the rabbit, mushrooms, carrots, pearl onions, leeks, cinnamon stick, cloves, allspice berries, salt, and pepper.

Stifado

Pour the vinegar and red wine over the rabbit and vegetables and mix well.

Add peeled garlic, bay leaves, rosemary, and chopped tomatoes.

Add the cauliflower florets to the casserole. Cover and braise in a moderate oven for 1½ hours, adding water if necessary.

Yiaourtlou

Preparation time:	35 minutes
Cooking time:	20 minutes
Rehydration time (raisins):	10 minutes
Difficulty:	★

Serves 4

1¼ lb/600 g	pork fillet
	salt, pepper

For the yiaourtlou:

3 cloves	garlic
1	onion
3–4 tbsp	olive oil
10 oz/300 g	peeled tomatoes
	salt, pepper
1 tsp	cumin
3 tsp	dried cilantro
1 tsp	boukovo (flaked dried pimento)

¾ cup/150 g	Greek, or thick creamy, yogurt

For the pilau:

2 tbsp	raisins
2 tbsp each	brandy, olive oil
3	small onions
1	leek
	salt, pepper
½ cup/100 g	Arborio rice
3–4 tbsp	white wine
1	lemon
2 tbsp	toasted pine nuts
4 sprigs	dill

For the garnish:

	dill

This ancient recipe has its roots firmly planted on the banks of the Bosphorus and illustrates the flair and refinement of the cuisine of Constantinople. Its wonderful Eastern flavors make it an enchanting experience for the taste buds.

In this recipe our chef wanted to pay homage to Jean Moshos, a monk and great traveler who crossed the known world in the 6th century A.D. Starting from Mount Athos with the goal of reaching the Sudan, this man of the church crossed Libya, Syria, and Egypt. During the course of his odyssey he discovered a range of precious spices. A deeply erudite man, he recorded his experiences in a book of recipes entitled *Spiritual Valleys*.

This cookery book is full of anecdotes and offers a wonderful insight into the tastes of people living at that time. Among the recipes he brought back with him was one for a pilaf, a dish that was very popular in Constantinople.

Aristedes Pasparakis has used exactly the same ingredients here, but has combined the pilaf with pork *yiaourtlou*.

This dish is made extra special by its use of spices and aromatic herbs. This pilaf, a rice-based preparation, uses dill that releases its own particular sweet, aniseed flavor. Dill grows wild all around the Mediterranean basin, and was valued in Ancient Greece for its digestive and stimulating properties. In Greece, as well as in Turkey, it is used to give a lift to dishes made from fish or dairy products.

The *yiaourtlou* sauce, meanwhile, is made with Greek yogurt. The pork is added to the sauce, which is redolent of Eastern flavors, including dried cilantro and cumin, which are given the chance of expressing themselves to the full.

Use a sharp knife to cut the pork into equal sized medallions. Soak the raisins in the brandy for 10 minutes to rehydrate them.

For the pilaf: Trim the small onions and leek and chop finely. Fry in the olive oil, season, stir in the rice. Add the white wine and cook until the liquid has evaporated.

Add lemon peel and the raisins in brandy. Cook for 5 minutes then add the pine nuts, chopped dill, and lemon juice. Cover with water and cook for 10 minutes. Season.

Pork

To make the yiaourtlou sauce: Fry chopped garlic and onion in olive oil. Add the peeled tomatoes and cook for about 10 minutes. Season, then stir in the cumin, cilantro, and boukovo.

Take the pan off the heat and add the Greek yogurt. Stir gently and set aside.

Season the medallions of pork and dry-fry in a nonstick skillet. Arrange them on 4 plates with the pilaf and yiaourtlou sauce, garnished with dill.

Greek-Style

Preparation time: 1 hour
Cooking time: 45 minutes
Difficulty: ★★★

Serves 4

1	chicken weighing 4½–5½ lb/2–2.5 kg
	salt
1	carrot
1 stick	celery
3 cloves	garlic
1	onion
1	potato
½	leek
4 tbsp	olive oil
3–4 tbsp	red wine
2	tomatoes

For the stuffing:

5	scallions
4 tbsp	olive oil
½ cup/100 g	yellow rice
1 clove	garlic
3–4 tbsp	white wine
1 lb/450 g	peeled chestnuts
½ cup/60 g	pine nuts
½ cup/50 g	raisins
1	apple
1 sprig	oregano
	salt

For the sauce:

2 tbsp	sugar
½	lemon
1 tsp	cornstarch

This extremely elegant Greek-style stuffed chicken is usually served as part of the New Year celebrations. Its sweet-salty flavors make this dish a real joy for the taste buds.

Prized for its firm meat, chicken needs a longer cooking time. Our chef recommends that after stuffing it, you insert the pulp from a lemon into the cavity before baking it. And when you come to deglaze the pan with the red wine, don't forget to sprinkle a little water over the chicken so that it doesn't burn or dry out too much. Then cover the dish with sheets of cooking foil. If you prefer you can use turkey instead for this recipe.

The extremely rich stuffing is made from rice, apple, pine nuts and is a classic in the Greek culinary repertoire. Chestnuts go wonderfully well with poultry. They are very filling and highly prized for their delicate taste. If you want to use fresh chestnuts instead, cut a cross on the base with a

sharp knife then plunge them into boiling water that will enable you to peel them more easily.

The stuffing mixture also uses Corinthian raisins from the Ionian islands. They have a distinctive taste and dark color, and are sold with their seeds removed. They come from a very sweet grape variety and are dried either in the sun or artificially, then packed individually or in whole bunches.

This festive dish is given a special lift by the addition of a caramelized sauce. Put the sugar, one tablespoon of water, and three drops of lemon juice into a pan, heat, then add a little liquid from cooking the chicken, which you will need to strain first. Bring it to the boil while blending with a whisk. Add a little salt and incorporate the cornstarch mixed to a smooth paste with a little water. Continue stirring over a gentle heat until the sauce is smooth and thick.

Using a sharp knife, bone the chicken, following the line of the breast bone to keep the rest of it whole. Reserve the giblets.

For the stuffing: Chop the scallions and brown in 4 tbsp olive oil. Stir in the rice, chopped garlic, white wine, and ½ cup/100 ml water. Cook for 10 minutes or until the liquid starts to reduce.

Next add the peeled, finely chopped chestnuts, pine nuts, raisins, and peeled and finely diced apple. Add chopped oregano, a little salt, stir and set aside.

Stuffed Chicken

Salt the chicken generously. Spoon the stuffing into the cavity until it is completely full.

Neatly sew the edges of the cavity together with kitchen string. Chop the carrot, celery, garlic, onion, potato, and leek. For the sauce: Heat the sugar in 1 tbsp water and the juice of ½ lemon. Set aside.

Put the giblets, vegetables, and chicken in a roasting pan. Add olive oil, salt, then cook in an oven at 465° F/240° C for 15 minutes. Add red wine, chopped tomatoes, and cook for 30 minutes. Blend the sauce with the strained cooking juices and thicken with cornstarch.

Chicken with

Preparation time:	30 minutes
Cooking time:	20 minutes
Difficulty:	★

Serves 4

1	chicken weighing 2¼ lb/1 kg
1 tbsp	olive oil
	salt
	pepper
1 tbsp	sweet mustard
3–4 tbsp	white wine
1 tsp	dried oregano
½ bunch	parsley
1	lemon
5½ oz/150 g	graviera cheese (Cretan Gruyère)
4	potatoes

To serve:

	arugula (rocket) leaves

Chicken with *graviera* is a very popular dish, especially in Crete. This nourishing dish, which is simple to make, can be enjoyed on any occasion.

These days chicken is eaten all over the world, but it was probably introduced to Greece by the Persians. Known as *kotopoulo* in Greek, chickens are raised in a free-range environment in villages across the hinterland. Choose chickens with plump lean flesh. A male bird can also be used in this recipe.

This judiciously flavored recipe uses the sort of simple produce so loved by Southern European cooks, and uses them in generous quantities. The indispensable olive oil adds warmth to the other ingredients as it releases its full fruity flavor.

According to mythology, there was a great battle between Athena, the goddess of war and wisdom, and Poseidon for the domination of Attica, which Athena won by making olive trees grow there, the symbol of peace. In the 1st century A.D. Dioscorides was already proclaiming the virtues of the olive tree in his writings: "The oil pressed from the green olive is perfect in the extreme and very good for the health."

The very image of Greek cuisine, chicken with *graviera* is a light dish. Oregano grows very well in this part of the world and is found in abundance around Ebaros in Crete. It is a close cousin of marjoram, but has a stronger taste.

Graviera, meanwhile, is a firm-textured cheese made from ewe's milk. It is a sort of Greek equivalent of Swiss Gruyère or Emmenthal, which you can use instead.

Use a sharp knife to cut off the white meat from the chicken into slices. Wash the arugula leaves and set aside.

Heat the olive oil in a skillet and brown the chicken, season. Put the mustard and white wine into a bowl, scatter on the oregano, and add to the chicken.

Cook over a low heat until all of the wine has evaporated.

Graviera

Add the chopped parsley and the lemon juice to the skillet with the chicken. Stir in the cubes of graviera.

Peel and grate the potatoes. Add some salt and leave to drain.

Cover the entire bottom of a nonstick skillet with the grated potato and dry cook. Turn the galette of potatoes onto the serving plate, spoon the chicken and the sauce into the middle and serve with arugula leaves.

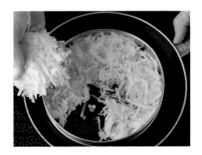

Kid with Askolibri

Preparation time:	20 minutes
Cooking time:	55 minutes
Difficulty:	★

Serves 4

2 lb/1 kg	askolibri (scolymus hispanicus)
2	onions
⅔ cup/150 ml	virgin olive oil
2 lb/1 kg	kid cutlets

7 tbsp/100 ml	white wine
2	eggs
	juice of 1 lemon
	salt and pepper

For the garnish:

1 bunch	dill

Generally eaten in the springtime, this festive dish combines the tender meat of goat kid with the fresh stalks of a species of thistle, *scolymus hispanicus*, in a typically Greek sauce made with eggs and lemon juice.

As long ago as the Minoan period, 4,000 to 5,000 years ago, sheep, goats, and cattle were reared on the island of Crete. Today, lamb and goat are the Cretans' favorite meats. Since both are particularly good at Easter time, either is suitable for this recipe. The meat of Cretan goats has an especially fine flavor, doubtless due to their pastures in the high mountainous areas, where they graze on a number of different herbs and aromatic plants. The recipe calls for cutlets, since these look attractive when served, but other cuts of meat can be used.

Askolibri give great individuality to this dish. These wild plants have long, prickly stems that are slightly curved and furnished with very small toothed leaves. Resembling miniature artichokes, they grow as bushes in the mountains of Crete. They were already known as a foodstuff some 3,000 years ago, at the time of Homer. Several centuries later, the scholars Pliny and Dioscorides recommended boiling their roots in wine to make a body wash. Today, the leaves and roots are generally boiled and then eaten as a salad. They are even cultivated on a small scale on Crete, to sell in the local markets. For this recipe, dandelion leaves or wild chicory can be used as a substitute.

Avgolemono sauce, used in the preparation of many Greek soups and stews, should be made with care to prevent the eggs from curdling in the lemon juice. Once it has been added to the meat, place the pan on the heat, shaking it as you do so. Then serve without delay.

Cut off the bases of the askolibri stems. Scrape off the prickles and small leaves, keeping only the curving stems. Cut them into small pieces.

Peel and chop the onions. Brown them in the olive oil, then add the cutlets, browning them on both sides. Pour on the wine and let it bubble to evaporate for 5 minutes over a high heat.

Blanch the askolibri stems for 5 minutes in boiling water, then drain.

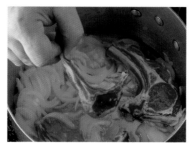

in Avgolemono Sauce

Add the askolibri to the cutlets and season with salt and pepper. Mix together and cook for 5 minutes. Pour in just enough water to cover. Put a lid on the pan and cook for 30 minutes.

Beat 2 egg whites until firm. Beat the yolks in a separate bowl, then combine them with the whites. Add the lemon juice, then gradually add some of the liquid in which the meat was cooked, beating the sauce all the while.

Just before serving, pour the sauce into the pan containing the meat and mix vigorously. Garnish with dill and serve immediately.

Knuckle of Pork with

Preparation time: 30 minutes
Cooking time: 2 hours 40 minutes
Soaking time for the
  garbanzo beans: overnight
Difficulty: ★

Serves 4

2 cups/300 g	garbanzo beans (chickpeas)
2 lb/800 g	boned knuckle of pork
4 oz/100 g	onions
⅓ cup/80 ml	olive oil
4 oz/100 g	very ripe tomatoes
	salt and pepper

In the area around Mount Psiloriti (the ancient Mount Ida) in central Crete, marriage celebrations traditionally began the day before the wedding, when the parents of the bride-to-be would serve their future son-in-law a dish of pork and garbanzo beans, washed down with a good red wine. This custom is still observed, but the food offered today is more likely to be herb fritters or cakes.

Of the various cuts of pork, knuckle is the most suitable for this recipe. An alternative is chine, on or off the bone. The meat should be tender, without being too fatty. Bay leaf and cumin can be added to this delicious Cretan dish, greatly enhancing the flavors of the pork and tomatoes. The recipe also works well with lamb or beef shank.

Pork frequently features in Cretan cooking. In the old days, every family kept a pig, killing it just before Christmas. After the pre-Christmas fast, traditionally observed by Greek

Catholics (or Melkites), the sudden abundance of meat and sausages was a cause of celebration. While some cuts of the meat were eaten fresh, the legs were smoked over the fireplace and other parts preserved in fat. These delicacies would then be eaten throughout the year, on Sundays or other religious festivals.

Easy to store and highly nourishing, beans have always been an important part of the Cretan diet. Garbanzo beans are a particular favorite, and make a perfect accompaniment to cereals, fresh vegetables, and meat. They are enjoyed with tomato sauce, or in a mixture of flour and lemon juice. They also appear as *meze* accompanied by a glass of ouzo, puréed with olive oil and lemon, boiled in salads, or broiled and salted.

A garnish of chopped dill or parsley will add the finishing touch to this dish of pork and garbanzo beans.

Soak the garbanzo beans overnight in a bowl of cold water. The next day, drain them and blanch them rapidly in clean water. Drain again, then cover them with cold water and cook them for 2 hours (or until soft), removing any foam that comes to the top of the boiling water.

Cut the meat into cubes. Peel and chop the onions.

Brown the chopped onions in the olive oil in a saucepan for 5 minutes. Add the pieces of meat and brown them on all sides.

Garbanzo Beans Cretan Style

Cut the tomatoes in half and grate them on a vegetable grater over a bowl.

Pour the tomato pulp over the meat. Add salt and pepper. Cook for 20 minutes.

Now add the cooked, drained garbanzo beans. Continue to cook the meat and beans for about another 10 minutes, adding water if necessary. Serve hot.

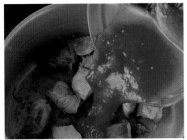

Sautéed Rabbit in Garlic

Preparation time: 35 minutes
Cooking time: 30 minutes
Marinating time for rabbit: 6 hours
Difficulty: ★★

Serves 4

2	small rabbits
7 tbsp/100 ml	corn oil
6 cloves	garlic
3 sprigs	rosemary
3	bay leaves

1²/₃ cups/400 ml	white wine
1¹/₄ cups/300 ml	beef bouillon
1¹/₂ cups/250 g	fresh shelled peas

For the marinade:

1	bay leaf
2 cups/500 ml	white wine
2 cloves	garlic
	salt and pepper

Every year since 1530, the Maltese have celebrated the festival of St Peter and St Paul on June 29. This religious holiday is also known as *Imnarja* (a word derived from the Latin *luminaria* or festival of lights). Mdina Cathedral, in the former capital city of Malta, is arrayed with illuminated decorations for the occasion. On the eve of the festival, on June 28, many families go to the Buskett gardens and the small woods surrounding Mdina, where they stay up all night and the following day, dancing, singing, and eating. This is traditionally an occasion for a *fenkata*: a meal based on rabbit, starting with pasta in rabbit sauce (*spaghetti bizzalza tal-fenek*), followed by sautéed rabbit in garlic and white wine (*fenek moqli*). The food will be washed down with plenty of the local wine.

Rabbit, *fenek*, is highly prized by Maltese food lovers. At one time, large numbers of rabbits lived wild in the countryside on the islands of Malta and Gozo. Today, most of the rabbits sold for eating are farmed chinchillas. The meat is served in many different ways: fried, stewed, in pies, or as a sauce for pasta.

The flavors of the marinade used in this recipe are taken up by the meat, making it tender and fragrant. When it is removed from the marinade, the meat should be carefully drained, and then dried with a cloth. This is to prevent the oil from spitting when the meat is browned.

When the meat is fully cooked in bouillon and wine (red or white), some cooks cover it with pastry to make a delicious pie.

This dish of sautéed rabbit goes well with French fries or just some crusty bread.

Chop the rabbit into small portions with a butcher's cleaver (ask your butcher to do this if you prefer).

For the marinade, arrange the meat in a shallow dish. Add the bay leaf, white wine, peeled garlic, salt, and pepper. Cover the meat with water. Place the dish in the refrigerator and leave the meat to marinate for 6 hours.

After 6 hours, drain the pieces of meat in a sieve. Then dry them well, rubbing them with a large cloth.

and White Wine

Heat 7 tbsp/100 ml of oil in a pan. When it is really hot, add the pieces of rabbit and turn them in the oil for 10 minutes until they are well browned. Pour off some of the oil. Add the chopped garlic and brown for 5 minutes.

Add the rosemary, bay leaves, and white wine to the rabbit in the pan. Cover and simmer for about 10 minutes, stirring from time to time until the wine has been absorbed.

Now add the beef bouillon and the peas. Continue cooking for about 5 minutes until the rabbit is tender, adding more bouillon if necessary.

Quince

Preparation time: 20 minutes
Cooking time: 1 hour 50 minutes
Difficulty: ★

Serves 4

1¼ lb/500 g	leg of lamb
1¼ lb/500 g	onion
1¾ sticks/ 200 g	butter
1¼ lb/500 g	quince

1 tbsp/15 ml	grape syrup
1½ tsp/8 g	ground cinnamon
1 tbsp/15 g	salt
	ground pepper

For the garnish (optional):
flat-leaf parsley

Ayva yahnısı is the Turkish name for this quince ragout. The recipe dates back to Ottoman times, and is a typical example of the versatility of the country's culinary traditions. Today, the dish is served mainly in eastern Turkey.

This simple ragout is a veritable delight for the palate. The tender lamb is braised slowly for a long time, with the onions adding their delicate flavor. Onions have been cultivated for more than 5,000 years; they came originally from northern Asia.

The special thing about this ragout, however, is the quince (*ayva*). These yellow fruits—either apple- or pear-shaped, depending on the variety—are from the quince tree from the Caucasus and Iran, which is a member of the rose family. It has been known since antiquity. The Greeks, for instance, removed the seeds from the quince, filled it with honey,

wrapped it in pastry, then baked it. If quince happen to be out of season, you can use dried apricots or prunes instead.

Syrup is often used in cooking in Eastern countries. The dark, viscous grape syrup with its sweet-sour flavor is ideal for enhancing the flavor of meat and fish dishes.

Cinnamon (*tarçın*) is mostly used in its powdered form in Turkey. The dried bark of this relative of the laurel has a strong aroma, and was irreplaceable in the sultans' kitchens for its sweet yet piquant aroma.

This delightful ragout is an ideal Sunday meal that can be enjoyed by all the family.

Cut the lamb into even-sized pieces. Peel the onion, then cut in half and slice thinly.

Melt half the butter in a casserole, then brown the pieces of meat on all sides. When the juices begin to flow, reduce the heat, cover with a lid, and cook for about 15 minutes.

Add the onion slices and cook for 5 minutes. Pour over 2 cups/500 ml water, cover with a lid, and simmer over a low heat for about 1 hour.

Ragout

Peel and quarter the quince. Remove the seeds and core, and cut each quarter in half. Melt the remainder of the butter in a pot and fry the quince in it.

Add the fried quince to the meat.

Stir in the grape syrup and cinnamon. Season with salt and pepper. Simmer gently over a low heat for a further 30 minutes. Arrange the ragout on plates and garnish with parsley.

Stuffed

Preparation time:	1 hour
Cooking time:	1 hour 50 minutes
Difficulty:	★

Serves 4

| 1 | savoy cabbage |

For the stuffing:

1 bunch	scallions
1 bunch	parsley
scant ½ cup/ 100 ml	olive oil

10 oz/250 g	ground lamb
10 oz/250 g	ground veal
	salt and ground pepper to taste
1 tsp	paprika
¾ cup/150 g	rice
1 tbsp	red pepper paste
3 tbsp	tomato paste
	juice of 1 lemon

For the garnish:

| | flat-leaf parsley |

Stuffed savoy cabbage is a particularly popular winter dish on the Aegean coast and in Istanbul.

The stuffing is full of Mediterranean aromas. The preparation of this satisfying and extremely traditional dish does, however, require a little patience, because the cabbage has to be hollowed out before it can be stuffed with the delicious ground meat mixture.

Cabbage has grown wild in Europe for over 4,000 years. As a cultivated plant it spread all over the continent in the Middle Ages, and soon became a basic essential, not least because of its healthy constituents—including lots of vitamins A and C.

Cabbage is also used a great deal in Turkish cuisine. Savoy is just one of many varieties. Its curly leaves are dark to pale green with a delicate, spicy flavor. Make sure when

buying that the leaves are firm and undamaged and that they have no soft areas.

The delicious, light stuffing is a most impressive testimony to the finesse of the Aegean cuisine. The fruity olive oil—the only oil that is used in this region—refines and enhances the flavor of the ground meat. As an alternative, you could also use finely chopped chicken.

Paprika is ideal for enhancing the flavor of the stuffing. *Kırmızı biber*, as it is called in Turkish, is made from the dried, ground pods of the paprika plant, and is one of the main spices in Turkey. In the villages of the Turkish hinterland, the pods are threaded onto pieces of string and hung up on walls to dry.

Discard the outer leaves of the cabbage. Reserve one leaf for cooking. Cut out the hard core, and hollow out the cabbage using a melon baller.

Finely chop the inside of the cabbage. Trim and wash the scallions, and cut into thin slices. Chop the parsley.

Sauté the scallions in olive oil. Add the ground meat and cook for 10 minutes. Break up any lumps of meat with a wooden spoon. Add the salt, pepper, paprika, parsley, and rice, and stir well. Remove the pot from the heat.

Cabbage

Heat ⅘ cup/200 ml water in a second pot, and cook the finely chopped cabbage together with 2 tbsp tomato paste and the red pepper paste for about 8 minutes. Season with salt. Add the cabbage to the ground meat and stir well.

Fill the hollowed-out cabbage with the meat mixture, and close the opening with the reserved cabbage leaf.

Pour water into a tall pot, and set the cabbage inside. Combine the remainder of the tomato paste with ⅘ cup/200 ml salted water and lemon juice, and pour over the cabbage. Cover with a lid and cook for 1 hour 30 minutes. Lift the cabbage out onto a serving dish and garnish with parsley.

Cabbage

Preparation time:	20 minutes
Soaking time:	30 minutes
Cooking time:	50 minutes
Difficulty:	★

Serves 4

1	savoy cabbage

For the stuffing:

¼ cup/50 g	rice
4 oz/100 g	onions
1 tbsp/15 g	salt
	ground pepper
1 tsp/5 g	dill
1 tsp/5 g	tarragon
10 oz/250 g	ground lamb

These tiny cabbage roulades are called *lahana sarma* in Turkey. They are very popular, easy to make, and highly nutritious, and are often served as treats on festive occasions, generally in winter.

The coarse cabbage leaves that envelop the ground meat stuffing contain lots of vitamins A and C, and have a delicately spicy flavor. Cabbage has been known throughout Europe for over 4,000 years, although it did not become widespread until the Middle Ages. Choose specimens with firm, crunchy leaves that are not marked or damaged. Feridun Ügümü advises: you can also use vine leaves, very popular in Aegean cuisine, as a substitute.

In Turkish cuisine, vegetables are often served as *dolma*, that is to say, stuffed. The cabbage leaves wrapped around the stuffing must not, however, be allowed to disintegrate when they are being cooked.

The stuffing consists of ground lamb, onions, and rice. Tarragon adds a strong, aniseed-like, peppery aroma. The herb came originally from Asia, and is ideal for cooking. Its therapeutic properties have been known since time immemorial, and it was a popular remedy for the treatment of animal bites in antiquity.

Dill is one of the most popular herbs in Turkey. Its delicate, dark-green leaves are used to enhance fish dishes, yogurt, and cucumber salads. It came originally from the East, and has been known in Europe since antiquity. Its aroma is reminiscent of fennel.

Remove the outer leaves of the cabbage. Place it in a pot of boiling water and blanch for 10 minutes, then plunge in a bowl of ice water. Soak the rice in water for 30 minutes.

Drain the cabbage and cut off the leaves. Flatten the leaves out on a worktop and cut out the center ribs.

Peel and finely chop the onions, and place in a bowl with the drained rice. Season with salt and pepper, and knead by hand. Stir in the chopped herbs.

Roulades

Add the ground meat and knead again.

Open the cabbage leaves out on the worktop. Make small sausages out of the meat mixture and place on the cabbage leaves.

Roll up the cabbage leaves, folding the ends to the inside as you go along. Place in a pot, pour over ⅘ cup/200 ml water, and cook for 40 minutes. Arrange on a serving dish.

Anatolian

Preparation time: 10 minutes
Cooking time: 25 minutes
Difficulty: ★

Serves 4

2 lb/800 g	leg of lamb
scant ½ stick/ 50 g	butter
	salt
	ground pepper
1 tsp/5 g	dried thyme

Side dish (optional):
rice with dill

For the garnish:
flat-leaf parsley

This wonderfully aromatic lamb dish is a specialty from the Anatolia region with plenty of tradition. It is cooked in this delightful region on the occasion of the Muslim Festival of Sacrifice. It is usually served with rice and a glass of *ayran*, salty yogurt diluted with water.

A typically Turkish dish, it is also ideal for families and guests. In contrast with Aegean cuisine, which uses only olive oil, Anatolian cookery features plenty of butter.

Meat-lovers adore the flavor of leg of lamb. Thyme, which is at home in the Mediterranean region, is excellent with it, and is often used to enhance marinades, barbecued dishes, and stews. Thyme, *kekik* in Turkish, adds an unmistakable southern flair to any dish. Dried or fresh, it is excellent in cooking. There are two main varieties: summer thyme and winter thyme; the latter has a slightly drier flavor.

Our chef recommends rice as a side dish. Heat 2 tablespoons of olive oil and 1 tablespoon of butter. Add 1 cup/200 grams rice and stir until transparent. Season with salt and pour over 1⅔ cups/400 milliliters chicken stock. Bring to the boil, then simmer gently for 20 minutes. Remove the pot from the heat and leave it to stand for 15 minutes. Garnish with chopped dill.

Anatolian lamb is ideal for any occasion, as well as being a culinary voyage into an ancient cultural landscape.

Trim the leg of lamb and cut the meat into several pieces.

Melt the butter slowly in a pot.

Add the meat and brown all over for 5 minutes. Cover with a lid and cook for about 15 minutes.

Lamb

Season generously with salt and stir with a wooden spoon.

Sprinkle pepper over the meat and stir in. Cook the rice for the side dish (see instructions top left).

Sprinkle the thyme over the meat and stir in. Cover with a lid and cook for about 5 minutes. Then leave to stand for 10 minutes. Arrange the meat on serving plates and garnish with parsley. Serve the dill-garnished rice separately.

Chicken and

Preparation time: 25 minutes
Cooking time: 1 hour 5 minutes
Difficulty: ★

Serves 4

1 lb/400 g	chicken quarters
	olive oil
12	shallots
4 cloves	garlic

	salt
	ground pepper
4	tomatoes
⅞ cup/200 ml	chicken stock
4 oz/100 g	mushrooms
1	eggplant
1	carrot
1	zucchini
4	small chiles (green or red)

This chicken specialty is called *sebzeli piliç güveç* in Turkish. Traditionally, it is cooked in a high-sided clay pot known as a *güveç*. It is also used for cooking lamb, fish, shellfish, and vegetables, and even some milk desserts (*muhallebi*).

First, remove the bones from the quarters. Cut into the legs lengthwise and remove the flesh from the bone with small movements of the knife. Then fold the meat outwards and chop it into pieces. Fry the meat in hot oil, then place it on paper towels or in a sieve to remove any excess oil.

The small selection of vegetables that is served with the meat includes eggplant, the royal vegetable of the Turks. When it was first introduced from India several thousand years ago, it was still white and oval in shape, which is why English explorers traveling to India gave it its name. The

Turkish name is *patlıcan*, and it is frequently combined with all kinds of meat.

Four different varieties are available in the markets: *kemer patlıcan*, a long, slender eggplant, used for stuffing; *bostan patlıcan*, which is rounder, more fleshy, and slightly bitter-tasting, and used for eggplant caviar; *beyaz patlıcan*, the white eggplant; and a fourth variety, also white, which is quite bitter in flavor and used in ragouts. Peel the eggplant to create an attractive striped pattern.

When cut into chunks and arranged around the meat, the eggplant, zucchini, carrot, mushrooms, and chiles form a brightly colored, tasty wreath.

Remove the bones from the chicken quarters, and cut the meat into large pieces. Heat the olive oil and fry the meat at high heat for 5 minutes. Take the chicken out of the oil and set aside.

Chop the shallots and garlic, and sauté in the hot oil. Add the meat and season with salt and pepper. Cook over high heat for 3–4 minutes. Chop the tomatoes and add to the meat mixture.

Pour over the hot stock. Bring to the boil briefly, then remove from the heat.

Vegetable Stew

Peel and halve the mushrooms. Peel the eggplant and carrot, and cut them and the zucchini into chunks. Remove the seeds from the chiles and quarter.

Deep-fry the vegetables, one type after another, in plenty of oil for 3–4 minutes.

Arrange the meat in the center of an ovenproof dish (ideally ceramic). Arrange the vegetables around the meat, and pour over the meat juices. Bake in a pre-heated oven at 320 °F/160 °C for 10 minutes. Garnish with the strips of chile.

Veal Ragout

Preparation time: 40 minutes
Cooking time: 45 minutes
Difficulty: ★

Serves 4

1 lb/400 g	knuckle of veal
2	shallots
4 oz/100 g	mushrooms
½ stick/50 g	butter
2 tbsp	olive oil

3	red bell peppers
2	tomatoes
1 tsp	flour
1 tbsp	red pepper paste
	salt
½ tsp/2 g	mastic
1 pinch	dried thyme
4 oz/100 g	pistachios

Gaziantep, Turkey's "pistachio capital," still known by the Turks by its old name of Antep, is famed throughout the country for its culinary wealth. Spicy *kebap* and braised dishes come from this region (which is quite far from the Mediterranean coast) as do countless specialties that include pistachios.

This simple veal ragout with pistachios is a specialty with lots of different flavors. Knuckle of veal is the recommended meat, because it is highly aromatic and is ideal for braising. Make sure that you choose high-quality meat that is light pink in color.

Mastic is used a lot in Turkish cuisine, and it gives this dish its incomparable aroma. The tiny, amber-colored resin crystals are obtained from the terebinth tree (*Pistacia terebinthus*), a type of pistachio, which grows on the Aegean coast. It should be used sparingly. The Odalisques—the slaves in the sultan's harem—are said to have chewed mastic to make their breath sweeter.

But it is the pistachios that make this brightly colored dish so special. These tiny green nuts, mild and delicate in aroma, are a firm part of Mediterranean and Eastern cuisine. The pistachio tree came from Syria, and is grown in the area around Gaziantep. The seeds are full of potassium, copper, and magnesium, and are used in stuffings, sauces, desserts, and baked goods.

If you are using unblanched pistachios, place them in boiling water for two minutes; this makes them easier to skin.

Trim the knuckle of veal and cut the meat into very small pieces. Peel and finely chop the shallots and the mushrooms.

Heat the butter and the olive oil, and fry the meat all over for about 10 minutes. Add the shallots and sauté for 10 minutes. Add the mushrooms.

Remove the seeds from the bell peppers. Finely chop the bell peppers and tomatoes and stir into the ragout. Simmer for 5 minutes.

with Pistachios

Sprinkle the flour over the ragout and add the red pepper paste. Stir well with a wooden spoon.

Stir some water into the ragout. Season with salt, and add the mastic. Add the thyme and simmer for 10 minutes.

Add the skinned pistachios, then cover with a lid and simmer for about 10 minutes. Transfer the ragout to a serving dish and serve.

Potato and Lamb

Preparation time: 30 minutes
Soaking time: 12 hours
Cooking time: 1 hour 25 minutes
Difficulty: ★

Serves 4

⅔ cup/140 g	garbanzo beans (chickpeas)
1¼ lb/500 g	lamb, off the bone
	salt
2¼ lb/1 kg	potatoes
	ground pepper

For the yogurt sauce:

2¾ cups/660 g	set yogurt
1	egg
1 tbsp	flour

For the garnish:

1 tbsp	olive oil
½ tsp/2 g	saffron threads

Turkish gourmets have been enjoying yogurt for centuries. Nomadic shepherds were the first to make the milk from their herds last longer by this healthy and easy means. The method was widespread in Anatolia by the 11th century.

Today, *yoğurt* is made from cow's, sheep's, or buffalo's milk. Special lactic acid bacteria are added to the milk, and left to "breed" for several hours. This makes the yogurt firm and gives it its pleasant, slightly acidic flavor.

In Turkish cuisine, yogurt is usually served with mixed or stuffed vegetables, as a sauce, or as a salty yogurt drink that is diluted with water. What makes these specialties from Gaziantep so individual is that the yogurt is cooked along with the dish. In this recipe, juicy lamb, garbanzo beans, and diced potatoes are cooked in a creamy, slightly acidic yogurt sauce.

Although lamb and garbanzo beans have been a part of the tradition of Turkish cuisine for as long as yogurt, the potato is a relative newcomer. Spanish conquerors brought it to Europe from America in the 16th century, although it was a long time before it spread throughout the Mediterranean. For this dish, choose a yellow, firm variety that will not disintegrate during cooking.

The Turks use a small vessel called a *cezve* for the saffron oil. This pot is otherwise used to make coffee or boil eggs. The saffron threads turn the oil a bright orange-yellow as they heat up. A few drops of this oil sprinkled over the cooked dish are a delight for the eyes—and the taste buds.

Soak the garbanzo beans overnight in cold water. Cut the lamb into pieces ½–1in/1–2 cm in size. Place in a pot, cover with water, and bring to the boil. Scoop off the foam and season the meat with salt.

Add the drained garbanzo beans. Cover with a lid and cook for 1 hour.

Peel and chop the potatoes, and rinse.

Casserole with Yogurt

Add the diced potatoes to the meat. Season with pepper and cook over high heat for a further 20 minutes.

To make the yogurt sauce, stir together the yogurt, egg, and flour until smooth, and gradually add to the meat. Simmer for 2 minutes.

Gently heat the olive oil and saffron threads in a small pot. Drizzle the saffron oil over the meat stew, and serve very hot.

Aknef

Preparation time:	1 hour
Cooking time:	1 hour 30 minutes
Difficulty:	★★

Serves 4

8	artichokes
juice of	1 lemon
2 lb/1 kg	leg of lamb
½ tsp	saffron
1½ oz/40 g	crushed garlic
2 oz/50 g	carrots

1 oz/30 g	celery
1 bunch	parsley
1	small onion
6½ tbsp/100 g	fresh rosemary
2½ cups/500 g	chorba "langues d'oiseaux" ("birds' tongues"— short pasta)
2 tbsp/30 ml	olive oil
1 tsp	corn starch
	salt and pepper

A Tunisian dish, *aknef* appears on the menu of one of the most important Muslim feasts called the *Aïd el Kebir*. During these festivities, associated with the Mecca pilgrimage rituals, each family kills a lamb. For one week, the animal is savored in all forms imaginable, and if possible in a different dish every day. *Aknef* is a piece of lamb steamed on a bed of rosemary, accompanied by *chorba* with saffron.

When buying the meat, select a leg, shoulder, or cut of lamb that can be cooked for a long time. Our chef prepares *aknef* with the "knuckle-joint," found at the end of the leg. It has a delicate flavor, and when it is finally presented on the plates, it looks perfect. In Tunisia, lamb comes either from local breeds ("beldi" sheep), or breeds of foreign origin ("rharbi" sheep).

Preparing the lamb with artichokes evokes the beginning of spring. The production of this vegetable is expanding within Tunisia, for the export of fresh or canned artichokes. In the country, they're served in a variety of ways: in salads, boiled to accompany lamb, and also cooked in ragouts and some couscous recipes.

"*Langues d'oiseaux*" are served separately. Based on noodles made from durum wheat semolina, they look like grains of rice which have been tapered at the ends. These *chorba lsen asfour*, as they say in Tunisia, come in two sizes: the medium-sized are usually cooked in a sauce to garnish lamb dishes, and the smaller ones are immersed in a court-bouillon with a lot of vegetables, to make soups. When you cook the "*langues d'oiseaux*," stir constantly so that the pasta doesn't stick to the bottom of the pan.

Peel the artichokes and remove the hearts. Peel the stems, keep the heart, and place all to one side in water with lemon juice added. Bone the leg of lamb. Cut it up into large cubes, approximately 2 oz/50 g. Season with salt, pepper, saffron, and crushed garlic.

Pour some water into the bottom pan of the couscous steamer. Add a little saffron. Bring to the boil. Immerse an aromatic mix of carrot sticks, celery, parsley, and a small onion, in the boiling water.

Arrange the rosemary branches in the colander of the couscous steamer. Place the pieces of lamb on top. Put the colander over the pan filled with flavored water.

Surround the lamb with the artichoke hearts and stems you placed to one side. Cover. Steam the contents for 1 hour 15 minutes.

Filter the saffron and vegetable stock through a muslin strainer over a saucepan (keep $^3/_4$ cup/200 ml of the juice, and put to one side). Cut the carrot from the aromatic mix into slices and put them in the saucepan.

Add the chorba and the oil. Cook for 10 minutes over a high heat. Blend the reserved vegetable juice with the starch and reduce over the heat. Serve the meat on a bed of saffron sauce, surrounded by artichokes, and serve the chorba in a separate bowl.

Basine with Rabbit

Preparation time:	30 minutes
Cooking time:	45 minutes
Difficulty:	★★

Serves 4

For the osbène:

	rabbit offal
3¹/₂ oz/100 g	rabbit meat
2 oz/50 g	onion, chopped
1 bunch	flat-leaf parsley, chopped
3¹/₂ tbsp/40 g	bulgur wheat
1 pinch	allspice
1 pinch	dried mint
1 bunch	Swiss chard
1 trickle	olive oil
	salt and pepper

For the rabbit in sauce:

2³/₄ lb/1.2 kg	rabbit
³/₄ cup/200 ml	olive oil
2 oz/50 g	chopped onion
2 small sprigs	thyme, chopped
1 tsp	harissa
1 pinch	ground coriander
1 tbsp	dried tomatoes
3 cloves	garlic, crushed
2 tbsp/35 g	tomato paste

For the basine:

18 tbsp/250 g	ground sorghum
	salt

Sorghum purée or *basine* forms the basis of this dish. The sorghum from Redjiche, a town some 3 miles/5 km from Mahdia, on the east coast of Tunisia, is particularly well known. The *basine* resembles a dense, gray-colored potato purée. Our chef has embellished it with rabbit in tomato sauce, and parcels wrapped in Swiss chard leaves.

Also called "large millet," sorghum is a small-grained cereal, grown all over Africa. After reducing it to a grayish powder, Tunisians blend it with sugar, milk, and orange-flower water; this cream is called *sohleb* and is eaten at breakfast. *Bsissa* is another mixture, made by mixing sorghum, broiled wheat, garbanzo beans, coriander, and sugar.

When preparing the rabbit, remove all the fat, and always seal it well before adding the onion. If the onion is added at the beginning, it may well be burned before the rabbit is browned. The sauce is seasoned with North African harissa, a condiment made of fresh red chiles, steamed and crushed with garlic, caraway seeds, and salt.

The *osbène* accompany the *basine* in a very original way. Usually, cooks make a stuffing of fresh or dried lamb or beef offal. They insert this into pieces of animal gut, and sew them up. These small "andouillettes" (small sausages made from chitterlings) often accompany couscous dishes when guests are invited. In our recipe, the chef has prepared his stuffing with rabbit, thickening it with blanched wheat or *borghol*, and replaced the tripe with a Swiss chard leaf.

After wrapping the tinfoil around the *osbène*, prick it in several places with a knife. This way, the sauce will penetrate during cooking. When the rabbit is cooked, you can be sure that the *osbène*, which are well wrapped in their sheet of tinfoil, will be ready too.

For the osbène, remove the rabbit offal and the piece of meat found on the stomach. Cut it all into very small cubes. Transfer to a bowl.

Add the chopped onion to the cubes of meat, then the parsley, bulgur wheat, allspice, dried mint, salt and pepper to taste, and a trickle of olive oil. Blend well to form a stuffing.

Cut the Swiss chard leaves into large rectangles. Take a small ball of meat stuffing in your hand and place it in a Swiss chard leaf. Wrap the leaf around the stuffing, then wrap this package in a piece of tinfoil. Prepare the other osbène in the same way.

from Redjiche

Cut up the rabbit into 8 portions. Heat the olive oil in a stockpot, and turn the rabbit in the hot oil to seal it. Then add the chopped onion, salt and pepper, and brown the mixture.

Next add the chopped thyme, harissa, ground coriander, dried tomatoes, crushed garlic, and tomato paste to the rabbit. Mix well. Cook for approximately 10 minutes. Add a little water to dilute the sauce, and then add the osbène. Cook for 20–25 minutes.

Add 1 cup + 1 tbsp/250 ml of water to the sorghum. Add salt. Cook over a medium heat for 10 minutes, while stirring briskly to form a thick purée. To serve, arrange a circle of sorghum purée, topped with an osbène and surrounded by the rabbit in its sauce on each plate.

Lamb Cutlets

Preparation time:	20 minutes
Cooking time:	50 minutes
Difficulty:	★

Serves 4

2 lb/1 kg	loin of lamb
2	onions
2 branches	thyme
2 branches	rosemary
½ bunch	parsley
1 tbsp	harissa
3½ tbsp/50 ml	olive oil

| 4 small | potatoes |
| | salt and pepper |

For the garnish:

| | fresh rosemary |

Lamb cutlets steamed with rosemary is a traditional dish enjoyed by the Tunisian middle class. In Tunisian this recipe is called *allouche fil kiskaisse*, meaning "lamb cooked in the couscous steamer."

Some families in the north-west of Tunisia add a tablespoon of tomato paste to the stock and turn it into soup. Then the following day, they add "*langues d'oiseaux*" (short Tunisian pasta) to make a substantial soup.

Loin of lamb is a particularly succulent, tender part of the animal. The cutlets are delicious when steamed. When you serve the food, sprinkle the meat with its own juices. This dish must be served immediately.

In Tunisian cuisine, herbs and spices, used in a marinade, give a wonderful flavor to the meat. The climatic diversity of the country enables it to grow a substantial range of aromatic plants. You can identify rosemary by its evergreen leaves—dark green on top and whitish underneath—and its sharp flavor. You don't need very much for this recipe.

Our chef suggests you could try using fresh mint instead of rosemary and thyme. Add it to the couscous steamer colander straight away and place the meat on top.

However, don't miss out the harissa when you make this dish. This chopped, dried purée of red chiles, seasoned with salt, garlic, caraway seeds, and olive oil, is an integral part of Tunisian cuisine. It is best kept in the fridge.

Our chef suggests small potatoes to accompany this dish. This very light meal is mainly eaten in summer when the sun is at its highest.

Trim the loin of lamb and cut up the cutlets by gently breaking the knuckle bone. Place the trimmings and bones to one side to make the stock.

Remove the skins from the onions, and slice thinly.

Prepare the aromatic ingredients—chop the thyme, rosemary, and parsley.

Steamed with Rosemary

Season the meat with the aromatic ingredients. Add the sliced onions and mix. Add the harissa and olive oil. Season with salt and pepper.

Put the bones and lamb trimmings into the couscous steamer. Half fill with hot water. Add the flavored cutlets to the colander. Steam for 40–45 minutes. 15 minutes before the end of cooking, add the peeled potatoes.

Sprinkle the cooking juices over the meat. Cover the colander for approximately 5 minutes. Arrange the lamb cutlets and potatoes on the plates. Garnish with a sprig of rosemary.

M'Chalouat

Preparation time:	10 minutes
Cooking time:	1 hour
To steep the saffron orange-flower water:	12 hours
Difficulty:	★

Serves 4

1 pinch	saffron strands
7 tbsp/100 ml	orange-flower water
2 lb/1 kg	lamb shoulder, neck, and liver
1 tbsp	turmeric
1 tbsp	sweet paprika
1	cinnamon stick
1 tsp	ground rosebuds
7 tbsp/100 ml	olive oil
1	lemon
	salt

For the garnish:

	mint sprigs
1	potato
¹/₂	lemon

Tunisians sacrifice a lamb on the Muslim feast day *Aïd el Kebir*, and the different pieces are shared out among the neighbors. The people of the Nabeul region make *m'chalouat*. This traditional dish is made of liver, heart, neck, or shoulder of lamb. It is very easy to make and is usually served at midday.

The day before this important ceremony, the women of Nabeul buy orange-flower water, which is a local specialty. The flowers from the bitter orange tree are distilled to make this preparation, used in so many Tunisian dishes. For this recipe, the orange-flower water must steep for at least 12 hours with the saffron strands, which have been broiled and then ground. This slightly reddish liquor gives the cuts of lamb a wonderful flavor.

In Arabic, saffron is called *za'farân*, derived from the word *asfar*, meaning a yellow dye, and is the most expensive spice in the world. There is no substitute for its color and very distinctive flavor.

In the culinary tradition of Tunisia, meat is always seasoned before cooking. Turmeric is a herbaceous plant, used as a spice or colorant. Curcumin is extracted from it to dye milk products, candy, drinks, and mustards. It's ground to a powder, and the root is slightly bitter. The lamb in this recipe is also flavored with rosebuds, which are another specialty of Nabeul. Dried and then reduced to powder, rosebuds are used as a spice and give a hint of sweetness to this dish.

M'chalouat is a sociable dish, usually served when friends and neighbors get together. An excuse to celebrate, it's the first hot dish eaten at midday after the long period of Ramadan. Served in deep dishes, it usually has a generous helping of sauce.

The day before, brown the saffron strands in a frying pan with no oil to give them a crunchy texture. Reduce them to powder using a pestle. Add them to the orange-flower water, and steep for 12 hours.

Cut the different pieces of lamb into portions and season with the salt, turmeric, paprika, cinnamon stick, and ground rosebuds.

Add the olive oil, and the saffron and orange-flower water.

With two wooden spoons, mix the meat in the spices until well coated. Cook the potato in salted water. Place to one side for the garnish.

Cook the meat over a high heat for 10 minutes.

Add 2 glasses of water and cook for approximately 40 minutes until you have a yellowish, smooth sauce. Before serving the meat, sprinkle it with lemon juice. Garnish with the potato and the pieces of liver, 1 mint sprig, and a slice of lemon.

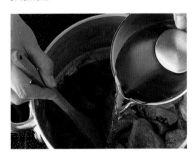

Tunisian

Preparation time:	15 minutes
Cooking time:	30 minutes
Refrigeration of the olives:	10 minutes
Difficulty:	★★

Serves 4

1³/₄ lb/800 g	fillets of beef cut into 4 slices
2	pinches allspice
1 tbsp/15 ml	vinegar
5 oz/150 g	ground beef
5 oz/150 g	large green olives
2	eggs, beaten
5 tbsp/15 g	all-purpose flour cooking oil
1 tbsp	capers
	salt and pepper

For the tomato sauce:

2	garlic cloves, crushed
1	onion, chopped
2¹/₂ tbsp/40 ml	olive oil
1 tbsp	harissa
18 oz/500 g	can of peeled tomatoes

For the garnish:

| | parsley |

This Tunisian dish could just as easily have originated from Sousse or Sfax, because the famous olives grown near these towns are its star attraction. Although the vast majority of olives harvested are destined to produce the precious golden oil, some of the plumper fruits called *akhdar* are intended for direct consumption.

For a Tunisian, owning olive trees is an incalculable blessing. There are about 50 different varieties of olives in this fertile region. Olives are harvested around the month of November. When they're destined to be served for the famous *kemia* (a colorful collection of small dishes), strong flavors and often peppers can be added to them. In our recipe, the olives are blanched earlier to remove the brine and their acrid flavor.

Tunisians name their dishes according to the vegetables or the pasta used, not the meat or fish, in contrast to the Euro-pean custom. In the north of the country, however, the vegetables or starchy food are often described as accompaniments.

In North African countries, meat is usually served in small amounts. The Tunisian title of the recipe says it all: *zitoune mehchi* or "stuffed olives" is a clear indication of how sparingly the locals use meat. Sabri Kouki's recipe is a sumptuous variation with the inclusion of slices of meat.

You can increase the quantity of olives and ground meat and dispense with the fillets of beef if you wish, and this would be more traditional. Don't forget the bread that goes with this dish. Buy barley bread, Italian bread, or semolina crepes to enjoy with this dish. Remember that this is a sociable dish and it's sometimes served on a single plate. Guests use their bread to carry a stuffed olive to their mouths. But first, dip your bread in the sauce. It's exquisite!

First make the tomato sauce: brown the garlic and onion in 2 tbsp/30 ml of the olive oil, and add the harissa and the peeled and chopped tomatoes. Cook for 10 minutes. Tenderize the slices of meat.

Add the slices of meat to the tomato sauce, and 1 pinch of the allspice. Season with salt and pepper. Add ³/₄ cup (200 ml) of water. Cover and cook gently until the oil rises to the surface. At the end of cooking, remove the pan from the heat and stir in the vinegar.

Season the ground beef with the remaining pinch allspice, salt, and pepper. Stir thoroughly to coat the meat. Set aside.

Stuffed Olives

Blanch the olives in boiling water for 2–3 minutes and drain them. Rinse in cold water, then dry on a paper towel. Cut in 2 on one side. Fill them with ground meat. Roll in the palms of your hands. Refrigerate for 10 minutes.

Cover the olives in the beaten eggs, then roll in the all-purpose flour. Allow 5–6 olives per person.

Fry the olives in very hot cooking oil. The oil must be smoking. Arrange the olives with the meat and sauce. Soak the olives in the sauce. Sprinkle the mixture with capers and garnish with parsley, then serve hot with bread.

Lamb Ragout

Preparation time:	30 minutes
Cooking time:	45 minutes
Difficulty:	★

Serves 4

1½ lb/700 g	leg of lamb
7 oz/200 g	tomatoes
7 tbsp/100 ml	olive oil
1	onion, thinly sliced
2	garlic cloves, crushed

1 pinch	saffron strands, soaked in ½ glass water
1	lime
1	lemon
2	mild red chiles
2	mild green chiles
	salt and black pepper

For the garnish:

| | chopped parsley (optional) |

Tunisians are great consumers of lamb. It is used in many of the country's traditional dishes, where it brings its own characteristic flavor. In the Tunis region, lamb ragout with lemon is generally served as a main course. Easy to make, it is prepared all year round.

Well known for its unique jasmine, Tunisia also offers its visitors the most magnificent landscapes with rows and rows of orange and lemon trees as far as the eye can see.

Lemons have the distinctive characteristic of sharpening the flavor of food. This sour citrus fruit is liberally used to flavor soups, sauces, vegetables, ragouts, and pastries. Although some people consider it to have thirst-quenching properties, it is mainly known for its high vitamin C content. It is best to select unwaxed varieties, or wash the lemons thoroughly in hot water and rub them vigorously.

For this recipe, the lemon peel and chiles must be cut into very fine julienne strips. In the first instance, you need to cut them into regular slices of between ½ in and ¾ in/ 1–2 cm thick; then stack them and slice them thinly into filaments of 1¾–2 in/3–5 cm long.

Tunisians grow a great variety of chiles and use them as a flavoring or a vegetable. Their spicy, or even burning, flavor comes from a substance called capsine. Capsine activates the saliva glands and stimulates the digestion. They are often dried, marinated, or cooked. If you prefer a milder flavor, remove the seeds and the whitish inner membranes.

Lamb ragout with lemon is a dish full of Mediterranean flavors. Add an extra touch of color by garnishing your dish with chopped parsley.

Trim the meat off the leg and then cut the lamb into pieces. Peel, deseed, and reduce the tomatoes to a thick pulp.

Brown the pieces of lamb in the olive oil. Season with salt and pepper. Add the onion, garlic, tomato pulp, and the ½ glass of saffron water. Simmer for approximately 10 minutes. Add water until the mixture is just covered; then cover and cook for approximately 15 minutes.

Thoroughly peel the lemon and lime. Cut the peel into julienne strips.

with Lemon

Blanch the peel strips separately in boiling water for approximately 10 minutes. Drain well.

Wash the red and green chiles. Deseed them and slice into julienne strips.

Add the chile strips to the mixture. Cook for 5 minutes. Add the lemon and lime strips. Cook for a further 5 minutes. Arrange the lamb ragout with lemon on plates, garnished with chopped parsley, if using.

Tunisian Ragout

Preparation time:	30 minutes
Cooking time:	50 minutes
Difficulty:	★★

Serves 4

2	eggs
7 oz/200 g	potatoes
1¼ lb/500 g	ground beef
3½ oz/100 g	chopped onion
2 oz/50 g	crushed garlic
3½ tbsp/50 g	chopped flat-leaf parsley
1 pinch	tabil (see below)

4 tsp/20 ml	olive oil
5 tbsp/100 g	tomato paste
½	pickled lemon, rinsed and peel cut into strips
4 tsp/20 g	capers
4	mild green peppers, cut into strips
generous 1 cup/250 ml	cooking oil
	salt and pepper

For the garnish:

	chopped parsley

When he prepares this typical Tunisian dish, Ali Matri makes his own *merguez*, a kind of beef meatball, molding them into the shape of calissons (lozenge-shaped candies made of marzipan). In the past, *merguez* were specifically made from lamb for the feast day of *Aïd-el-Kebir*. In our recipe, the spiced tomato sauce doesn't spoil the flavor of the beef, while it would completely mask the very subtle flavor of *merguez* made with lamb.

Ali Matri flavors his croquettes with a combination of Tunisian spices called *tabil*. During summer, cooks blend three-quarters dried coriander seeds with caraway seeds, dried garlic, paprika, or hot chile pepper. This renowned seasoning spices up beef ragouts. When it comes to kneading the *merguez*, make sure you keep hands wet so that the meat doesn't stick and the surface of the *merguez* will remain perfectly smooth.

Avoid browning the tomato paste in the oil straight away, because it will break down into noxious products and spoil the result. It is better to mix it with the *merguez* cooking juices and water.

At the end of cooking, add a few strips of pickled lemon. Any Tunisians with a lemon tree in the garden will still prepare pickled lemons in salt. The best come from winter lemons which are oblong at both ends and are very fragrant. They bring a very subtle bitter flavor to the dish, but must not cook in the sauce as they might dominate the other ingredients.

In the traditional recipe, the potatoes that accompany the dish are fried first, and then simmered in the sauce. Our chef recommends that you simply fry them instead, and then arrange them around the dish.

Hard-boil the eggs for 10 minutes. Peel the potatoes, and cut them into French fries and reserve. Mix the meat, onions, 1 oz/25 g of the garlic, and parsley in a bowl with your fingertips.

Add salt and pepper to the meat filling. Sprinkle with tabil. *Mix well. Heat a little olive oil in a sauté pan.*

Dip your hands in cold water. Take a little filling and make the meatballs by squeezing a small amount gently in your hand to produce small, oblong merguez.

with Merguez

Seal the merguez in the hot olive oil, turning them over so that they brown on all sides. Remove from the frying pan and place to one side in a dish.

Now put the remaining chopped garlic and the tomato paste into the frying pan. Blend over a low heat, while scraping the cooking juices with a spatula. Deglaze with a glass of water. Simmer the sauce to remove the tartness of the tomatoes.

Return the merguez to the sauce. Add salt, water, and cook for 30 minutes. Finally, add the lemon strips and capers. Cook the french fries. Serve the merguez surrounded by pepper strips, egg slices, lemon strips, french fries, and garnished with chopped parsley.

Sabbath

Preparation time: *1 hour*
Resting time: *30 minutes*
Cooking time: *50 minutes*
Difficulty: ★

Serves 4

1 stick	celery
2 pinches	saffron threads
2	lemons
12	small spring artichokes
4½ lbs/2 kg	peas
2	onions
7 tbsp/100 ml	vegetable oil
	salt and pepper

For the meatballs:

1 slice	bread
2¼ lbs/1 kg	ground beef
1	egg
1	onion
1 bunch	parsley
1 pinch	ground ginger
1 tsp	turmeric
1 tsp	mace
1 pinch	nutmeg
	salt and pepper

The Sephardi Jewish community in Morocco, especially in the city of Tangier, has a culinary repertoire rich in Middle Eastern flavors. There are specific dishes for festivals and special occasions.

The Sabbath, the rest day of the week, is on a Saturday and is a day of prayer when families gather together. The celebrations start the evening before: for this occasion the table is covered with a white cloth with two candelabra on it. A carafe of wine, known as the *kiddouch*, is placed on the table, together with *halot* loaves covered by a cloth.

For the Sabbath, which is celebrated with joy and pleasure, many delicious and popular dishes have been developed. People eat heartily on the Sabbath, and religious traditions

determine exactly what food is cooked and how it is prepared. Beef meatballs are very popular in Tangier and they are often prepared for the eve of the Sabbath.

The meatballs are made exclusively from kosher meat. The term "kosher" comes from Hebrew and is used for foodstuffs that can be eaten without any problems complying with the religious rules. A celery sauce or peas and artichokes are served as an accompaniment.

The meat, mixed with parsley, onion, egg, bread, mace, nutmeg, ginger, turmeric, and salt and pepper, is very aromatic. If you decide to make a celery sauce, take the meat out of the sauce and reduce it. You can also make the meatballs with lamb.

For the meatballs, soak the bread in water. In a bowl, mix the meat with the soaked bread and the egg. Add chopped onion, finely chopped parsley, ginger, turmeric, mace, and nutmeg. Season with salt and pepper.

Mix all ingredients using your fingers, then allow to rest for 30 minutes. Meanwhile, wash the celery. Cut the stick into fine matchsticks and put aside, with the pulled-off leaves. Mix the saffron threads with 1½ glasses of water.

With moistened hands, form evenly sized meatballs. Squeeze the 2 lemons and put the juice into a bowl with cold water. Remove the leaves of the artichokes down to the bottom. Remove the fibers and put the artichoke bottoms in water.

Meatballs

Shell the peas. Peel the onions and sweat in 2 tbsp of vegetable oil. Pour on ¹/₂ glass of saffron water. Add the peas and artichoke bottoms. Season with salt and pepper. Cover all the above with water and cook for 10–15 minutes.

Place half the meatballs into a pan. Pour on 3 tbsp of vegetable oil and ¹/₂ glass of saffron water. Cook, covered, for about 15 minutes.

Place the celery in a pan. Add the remaining meatballs, 2 tbsp oil, and the remaining saffron water. Season. Cover with celery leaves. Cook for 20 minutes. Arrange the meatballs on a serving platter alongside the meatballs cooked with peas and artichokes.

Quails with

Preparation time: 40 minutes
Cooking time
   for quails: 30 minutes
Cooking time
   for couscous: 1 hour
Difficulty: ★★

Serves 4

8	quails
9 oz/250 g	onions
⅓ oz/10 g	garlic
⅓ oz/10 g	flat-leaf parsley
⅓ oz/10 g	fresh cilantro (coriander)
1 pinch	saffron threads
1 pinch	ground cinnamon
5½ tbsp/80 ml	olive oil
1 splash	orange flower water
	salt and pepper

For the filling:

2⅓ cups/400 g	couscous semolina
1 splash	olive oil
7 oz/200 g	slivered almonds
1 tsp/5 g	ground cinnamon
2 oz/50 g	caster sugar
1 splash	orange flower water
	salt

For the garnish:

2 oz/50 g	slivered almonds
1 oz/30 g	fresh cilantro (coriander) (optional)

In Morocco, there are many delicious and rich dishes with quails. Mohammed Aïtali simmers the quails in a bouillon flavored with herbs, onion, and saffron. He then fills them with a heavenly stuffing made from crushed roasted almonds, sugar, semolina, cinnamon, and orange flower water. As a precaution, fry the quails first on the side where they have the most meat, not necessarily, therefore, on the breast side. They are turned later.

In Morocco, quails are particularly prized among gourmets. Among the finest creations of the chefs from Fez, famed for their sophisticated dishes, is the quail *pastilla* with almonds, liberally sprinkled with icing sugar and cinnamon. Quails are also cooked with roast almonds, chicken livers, or a mixture of fine noodles, cinnamon, and orange flower water.

Many festive dishes in Morocco contain almonds or raisins, symbols of luxury and wealth. Stuffed quails, *tajines, mêchouis,* and *pastillas* are unthinkable without these two ingredients. The region around Agadir, with its hot climate, is famous for the quality of the almonds grown there, known in Moroccan as *louz.* They are hardly ever used fresh, but when dried they enrich many dishes.

The large Moroccan *louz* are much less in demand than the sweet, small *bled* almonds. Blanched or slivered (flaked) almonds are best for quail filling. Slivered almonds are easier to roast and chop.

For the filling, place couscous semolina in a shallow bowl and work in a little oil and water by hand. Pour the grains into the strainer on the top of a couscous steamer. Steam 3 times for 20 minutes at a time; between steaming stages, work in a little salt and water.

Cut off the necks of the quails. Clean the birds, then rinse them, and dab dry from the inside with kitchen paper. Trim off the wingtips.

Peel and chop the onions and garlic and also chop the parsley and cilantro. Put a splash of oil and one of orange flower water, the chopped herbs, and the quails into a pan. Sprinkle with saffron, cinnamon, salt and pepper. Cover with water. Cook for 30 minutes on a high heat.

Almond Stuffing

Dry-roast the slivered almonds in a frying pan. Chop in a food processor. Mix well with cinnamon and sugar. Put the cooked couscous into a bowl and fold the almond mixture in thoroughly with a spoon.

Sprinkle the mixture with orange flower water. Mix with a spoon until a brown, homogeneous mass is formed.

Take the quails out of the cooking liquid and allow to cool slightly. Fill the quails with the stuffing. Dry-roast the slivered almonds for the garnish without adding fat. Serve the quails in the cooking liquid sprinkled with roast slivers of almond and garnished with cilantro.

Shoulder of Lamb

Preparation time:	25 minutes
Cooking time:	1 hour 5 minutes
Difficulty:	★★

Serves 4

²/₃ cup/100 g	dried apricots
2	shoulders of lamb
4 tbsp/60 ml	peanut oil
2	onions
3 sticks	cinnamon
½ tsp/2 g	saffron threads
½ envelope	Moroccan saffron powder for coloring

2 tbsp/30 ml	olive oil
½ tsp	ground ginger
1 bunch	fresh parsley
1 bunch	fresh cilantro (coriander)
⁴/₅ cup/150 g	prunes
1	lemon
¼ cup/50 g	sugar
½ stick/40 g	butter
	salt and pepper

Shoulder of lamb, or *delaa* in Arabic, is top of the list of favorite Moroccan dishes. The chef here cooks it in a rich saffron sauce and further refines it with cinnamon, lemon, poached prunes, and apricots cooked in butter. If desired, it can also be cooked with prunes stuffed with nuts, artichokes, and peas.

One shoulder of lamb is considered to serve two people. Before cooking, the meat is rinsed thoroughly to meet the requirements of religious rules. An animal slaughtered according to the Muslim *hallal* rite has to be completely free of blood, as blood is considered unclean.

Do not forget to score the surface of the shoulder of lamb lightly, so that the shallow cuts form criss-cross lines. This helps the meat to cook and makes it easier to carve once it is done. Bouchaïb Kama also pricks the meat several times

in different places with the point of the knife to allow the spices to penetrate better and to allow the aroma and flavor to soak thorough into the meat. If you wish to brown the shoulder of lamb to make it more attractive and crispy, complete the cooking process in the oven on the highest temperature.

Apricots are grown on a large scale in Morocco and are the most widespread fruit in the country. They are either preserved in syrup or dried. Fresh apricots are often eaten with cinnamon, honey, and orange flower water as a dessert. Dried, they are rarely used in savory dishes, except for lamb tagines. Prunes are also added to mutton or beef dishes in Morocco. In earlier times, *gasaa* couscous, garnished with prunes and hard-boiled eggs, was served to newlyweds after the wedding night.

Soak the apricots in a bowl with lukewarm water. Rinse the shoulders of lamb. Score lightly with a knife to make a criss-cross pattern of cuts.

Heat 2 tbsp of peanut oil in a large saucepan. Add chopped onions, 2 cinnamon sticks, saffron threads and powder, salt and pepper. Sweat over a high heat. Turn the shoulders of lamb several times to cover them completely with the spices.

Pour 2 tbsp of olive oil and 2 tbsp of peanut oil over the meat and dust with ginger. Cover with water and cook for 30 minutes.

with Apricots

At the end of this cooking period, scatter chopped parsley and chopped cilantro over the meat. Cook for at least another 30 minutes.

Prepare the prunes: place some water, 1 cinnamon stick, slices of lemon, sugar, and the prunes into a saucepan. Poach until the prunes are soft. Drain the apricots and sauté in ¹/₄ stick/20 g butter.

Place the lamb on a serving platter. Simmer the meat juices and reduce on a high heat. Add the rest of the butter and stir in well, then continue to reduce. Cover the meat with the sauce and garnish with apricots and prunes.

Chicken

Preparation time: 45 minutes
Cooking time: 40 minutes
Difficulty: ★★

Serves 4

8	chicken fillets, 5 oz/140 g each
8	chicken thighs
1 bunch	parsley
1 bunch	cilantro (coriander)
	salt and pepper

2 pinches	saffron threads
2 large	onions
4 cloves	garlic
1 tbsp/15 ml	olive oil
1 tbsp/15 ml	peanut oil
½ envelope	Moroccan saffron powder for coloring
⅓ oz/10 g	ginger
11 oz/320 g	button mushrooms
11 oz/320 g	spring onions
2 cups/500 ml	chicken stock
½ stick/40 g	butter

Kourdass are a type of roulade, already invented by the forefathers of the Moroccans. In the traditional recipe, the filling is made from liver and heart of lamb, herbs, and spices, held together with lamb tripe. Bouchaïb Kama has adapted it to modern eating habits and uses chicken. His filling is a delicate combination of chicken, parsley, cilantro, and saffron, rolled up in chicken fillet beaten very thin. Other chefs are no less inventive and also make *kourdass* with fish.

In Morocco, chicken and lamb are eaten with about the same frequency. Many poultry farms have been set up between Casablanca and Rabat, where most of the consumers live, so poultry is now much more economical. It is also less fatty than lamb, as all Moroccans who are watching their weight know.

For this recipe, you should use the ready-to-cook fillets and boned thighs of four whole small chickens. After cutting off and boning fillets and thighs, make your own stock out of the carcasses. Put them into a pan with parsley stems, finely chopped onions, carrots, and twigs of thyme. Cover with water and cook for one to one and a half hours. You can, of course, prepare your *kourdass* with instant chicken stock. If after the preparation you still have some filling left over, make it into little meatballs in a tomato and herb sauce.

Our chef adds button mushrooms to the sauce. The mushrooms are locally produced: they grow in Imouzar in the Atlas Mountains in caves. All the mushrooms known in Europe also grow in the undergrowth of Moroccan forests: chanterelles, hedgehogs, morels, and ceps.

Place a chicken fillet on a piece of plastic wrap. Cover with a second piece of plastic wrap and beat until flat. Do the same to the other fillets.

Bone the chicken thighs. Place the meat on a chopping board. First dice, then grind finely in a food processor.

Add salt, pepper, half the chopped parsley, and half the chopped cilantro plus 1 pinch of saffron threads. Mix by hand until the mixture is smooth.

Kourdass

Put a little of the filling on the end of a fillet. Roll up to make a roulade. Fasten the ends with a wooden toothpick. Prepare another 7 kourdass in the same way. Peel and chop onions and garlic.

Fry onions and garlic briefly in olive and peanut oil. Add kourdass and turn while frying. Add 1 pinch saffron threads and the saffron powder, and also ginger, cilantro, parsley, quartered mushrooms, and peeled spring onions.

Cook the kourdass for about 40 minutes until tender, gradually adding the chicken stock. Once the kourdass are cooked, reduce the sauce and beat in butter. Halve each kourdass and serve in the sauce with the onions.

Rabbit with

Preparation time: 25 minutes
Cooking time: 1 hour 10 minutes
Difficulty: ★★

Serves 4

1	rabbit, 4½ lbs/2 kg
4 tbsp/60 ml	olive oil
2 envelopes	Moroccan saffron powder for coloring

1 tsp/5 g	ginger
7 oz/200 g	onions
1 bunch	parsley
1 bunch	cilantro (coriander)
2¼ lbs/1 kg	Swiss chard
1	fresh lemon
	salt and pepper

Rabbit meat is much esteemed, especially in southern Morocco, and is often steamed. In Marrakesh, chefs sometimes use the thighs in a *tangia*, a kind of ragout, simmered for a long time in an amphora-like container. M'hamed Chahid has decided to cook the rabbit in a sauce of onions, ginger, and herbs, to which he adds Swiss chard stalks.

The recipe he presents here is based on a dish with a long tradition in Morocco: hare with wild cardoon thistle. In the mountains, it is easy to catch one of the many hares that live there. In most countries, however, hares are available only in the hunting season. It is therefore easier to replace them with rabbit.

Swiss chard belongs to the same botanical family as spinach. In his restaurant, the chef generally prefers to use wild cardoon thistle with its prickly stems and slightly bitter taste.

The leaves and stems of Swiss chard are edible. The latter replace the cardoon thistle in this dish. You can, however, also vary the recipe a little by replacing them with okra or even with small, sour-flavored quince. The cut-off green chard leaves can be cooked like spinach.

In Moroccan cooking, vegetables are a dish in themselves and by no means only an accompaniment. Respecting this tradition, M'hamed Chahid cuts the Swiss chard stems into pieces and cooks them in the meat sauce. This makes them an integral part of the meal and they deliciously absorb the flavors of the herbs and spices.

Remove the head of the rabbit and trim excess fat. Cut the body into 6 or 8 pieces using a carving knife.

Heat some oil in a pan and place the rabbit pieces in it. Season with saffron powder, ginger, salt and pepper. Add peeled and chopped onions.

Chop the parsley and cilantro and add to the pan. Allow to fry for about 10 minutes. Cover with water, cover the pan and cook gently for 45 minutes on a low heat.

Swiss Chard Stems

Cut the Swiss chard leaves off the stems. Clean the stems and scrape with a knife to remove fibers.

Halve the chard stems lengthways, then cut into sticks. Rinse with plenty of water and then place in water mixed with lemon juice.

At the end of the cooking period, add the chard stems to the rabbit sauce. Pour on a little water. Cover the pan and cook for a further 15 minutes.

M'rouzia

Preparation time:	25 minutes
Soaking time:	overnight
Cooking time:	1 hour 55 minutes
Difficulty:	★

Serves 6

1½ cups/250 g	golden raisins
2¼ lbs/1 kg each	shank, shoulder, and leg of lamb
4	onions
2 tbsp	ground ginger
1 pinch	saffron threads
1 pinch	Moroccan saffron powder for coloring
2 tbsp	smen (preserved butter)
2 tbsp	honey
2 cups/500 ml	oil
1½ cups/200 g	blanched almonds

This lamb dish, known as *m'rouzia*, was created behind the fortifications of the ancient city of Fez. Before there were fridges, this method of cooking allowed the meat to be kept for several months. After spices and preserved butter (*smen*) had been added, the pieces of mutton or lamb were simmered for many hours over the coals of the *m'jmar*, a charcoal oven. After that, all the ingredients were placed in a terracotta container: the meat right at the bottom, the raisins and almonds above and finally the sauce. When cooling, the sauce would set, forming a protective layer covering the meat. Finally, the container was covered with a piece of oiled paper tied down with cord.

Today, *m'rouzia* is often prepared for *'Aid el-kebir*. At this festival, Moroccans eat a great deal of mutton and lamb. Nowadays, however, the meat is cooked in a pan over a gas flame. *M'rouzia* can be kept for three or four months in large glass jars in the fridge.

The flavors of *m'rouzia* can be varied according to personal taste. Many people season it with cinnamon or *ras el-hanout* (a Moroccan spice mixture), or with dried and ground coriander. It is sweetened with either sugar or honey. The chef definitely prefers the latter, as the honey holds the meat together better, and gives it a glaze and an attractive golden-brown color.

Not everyone likes the intense flavor of *smen*, which can be replaced by olive oil. To make *smen*, butter is first allowed to soften at room temperature. Then, over a period of one and a half hours, fine salt and hot water are worked into it on a plate. In an airtight Mason jar, *smen* will keep for several years.

Soak the raisins the evening before in a bowl of cold water. Cut the shank, shoulder, and leg of lamb into large pieces.

Peel the onions and cut into very thin slices.

Place the meat in a large saucepan. Cover with finely sliced onions. Add ginger, saffron threads, saffron powder, and smen. Brown for 10–15 minutes, turning the pieces of meat from time to time.

from Fez

Pour water over the meat until the pan is three-quarters full. Cover. Cook for 1 hour 30 minutes, until the meat begins to loosen off the bones.

Towards the end of the cooking time, add the honey and the drained raisins to the meat. Stir. Cook for another 5–10 minutes, until the sauce has a slightly syrupy consistency.

In a pan, fry the blanched almonds in the oil. Sprinkle the almonds over the meat and serve.

Pastilla

Preparation time:	*1 hour*
Cooking time:	*1 hour 15 minutes*
Difficulty:	★★

Serves 4

1⅛ lb/500 g	onions
4	pigeons, each 1lb/450 g
1½ sticks/150 g	butter
½ tsp	ground ginger
1 tbsp	ground cinnamon
1 pinch	saffron threads
1 bunch	parsley
1 bunch	cilantro (coriander)

1	cinnamon stick
1 tbsp	orange flower water
⅞ cup/200 g	sugar
10	eggs
1¾ cups/250 g	blanched almonds
1⅛ lb/500 g	*yufka* pastry dough sheets (phyllo)
	salt and pepper

For the garnish:

	powdered sugar
	ground cinnamon
	almonds
	mint leaves (optional)

Recipes for *pastilla*, which are widespread and exist in many versions, clearly demonstrate the sophistication of Moroccan cuisine. Depending on the family recipe, *pastillas* are made with chicken, offal, or fish. However marvelous they all taste, they pale in comparison with pigeon *pastilla*, the most delicious and most famous of all *pastilla* recipes. However, you do need some time and patience to make this dish.

According to Lahoussine Bel Moufid, Moroccans feel a positively emotional tie to *pastilla* or *ourqa* dough. It is made from flour, water, and salt and reached the country some 1,300 years ago with the Arab conquerors. It originally came from Isfahan in Persia, but it was the Arabs who over the centuries influenced Moroccan cuisine. Brush the sheets of dough with butter while you work with them. This prevents the dough from drying out.

The *pastilla* grants the pigeon a place of honor. Pigeons are highly prized in Morocco because of their meat. In Arabic, the pigeon is known as *hamam* and represents cunning and subtlety. The almonds in this dish are irreplaceable. Almonds originated in Asia. The fruits of the almond tree contain one or two nuts surrounded by a hard shell. Dried, almonds are a common ingredient in Middle Eastern dishes.

The presentation of this dish is also part of its charm. The *pastilla* is always sprinkled with powdered sugar and cinnamon, adding an extra refined touch. It is indeed the garnish that distinguishes this luxurious dish. Many chefs, such as Lahoussine Bel Moufid, become true artists with this task. For example, you can make a flower out of almonds in the center of the *pastilla* and garnish this with leaves of mint.

Peel the onions and slice finely. Cut the pigeon into pieces. In a large pot, sweat the onions in ½ stick/50 g of butter. Add the pieces of pigeon, ginger, ground cinnamon, saffron threads, salt and pepper. Pour on 2 cups/500 ml of water and cook for 30–40 minutes.

Add finely chopped parsley and cilantro, as well as the cinnamon stick, orange flower water, and ⅔ cup/150 g sugar. Cook for 10 minutes. Take out and bone the pigeon pieces. Reduce the sauce for about 15 minutes. Beat 8 eggs and stir in.

Dry-roast the almonds without adding fat, and crush them. Melt the rest of the butter and brush a round baking dish with some of it. Cover with 1 sheet of yufka pastry dough. Place 4 further sheets in a rosette pattern, overlapping slightly. Brush with a little melted butter.

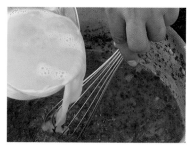

with Pigeon

Put in the pigeon meat. Add the sauce with the eggs, then add the almonds. Sprinkle with the remaining sugar.

Separate the 2 remaining eggs and keep the yolks. Cover the pastilla with 2 sheets of *yufka* pastry dough. Fold over the protruding edges and brush with egg yolk.

Place one last sheet of pastry dough on top and stick down with egg yolk. Bake in the oven, between 2 baking trays, for 10 minutes at 350 °F/180 °C. Drizzle butter over the pastilla and sprinkle with powdered sugar and cinnamon. Garnish with almonds and mint leaves.

Pigeon

Preparation time: 40 minutes
Cooking time: 1 hour 10 minutes
Difficulty: ★

Serves 4

4	squab pigeons, 1 lb/450 g each
2/3 cup/150 ml	olive oil
1 tsp	*smen* (preserved butter) or salted butter
8	eggs
1/2 bunch	parsley
1 tbsp/15 ml	vegetable oil
	salt and pepper

For the marinade:

1/2 bunch	parsley
1/2 bunch	fresh cilantro (coriander)
4 cloves	garlic
9 oz/250 g	onions
1 pinch	saffron threads
1/2 tsp/3 g	mastic gum
1 tsp	ground ginger
	salt and pepper

For the garnish:

2	pickled lemons
	purple olives (optional)

In Moroccan, *m'fenede* more or less means hidden or concealed. You simply have to try this dish to discover the pigeon hidden under the omelet. In the mountains of the High Atlas in southern Morocco, or more precisely in Tafilalet and Sijilmassa, this dish is offered to young mothers in particular. Pigeon *m'fenede* is a highly symbolic dish, and it is said that it improves mother's milk and thereby encourages the growth of the newborn infant. To keep up the tradition, some Moroccans even today serve the dish to a woman shortly after giving birth.

Pigeon *m'fenede* is also part of the heritage of fine cuisine in Morocco and is therefore frequently cooked for ceremonial occasions. The tender flesh of the pigeons and their delicious taste make them an ideal ingredient for luxury dishes. Wild pigeons can be found in the markets from spring to the end of summer; for the rest of the year, you will have to be content with farmed pigeons. You can, however, make this recipe using other poultry such as chicken, for example.

There are various methods for preparing pigeon *m'fenede*. Khadija Bensdira suggests simply folding the pigeon into a fine omelet just before serving. Others prefer to cook the pigeons first in hot oil, and to then take them out and dip them in beaten egg before frying them again. The third method, inherited from the Alawit dynasty, is the most difficult. The pigeon is put in a large pan with a little sauce. When it is hot, beaten eggs are added and the pot is covered once again. As soon as the pigeon is cooked, it must be removed from the pan without the protective layer of egg falling off. However you prepare the pigeons, the intention is that your guests must not suspect what is hidden in the omelet!

In a bowl, prepare the marinade from chopped parsley, chopped cilantro, crushed cloves of garlic, and finely diced onion. Add saffron threads, mastic gum, and ground ginger. Season with salt and pepper. Pour on a little water.

Hold the pigeons over an open flame to singe off any remaining down. Cut off the feet and the tips of the wings. Gut the pigeons and rinse under running water. Tie the thighs and wings tightly to the body with kitchen twine.

Place the pigeons in the marinade. Cut the pickled lemons into pieces and put aside for the garnish.

M'fenede

In a saucepan, bring the pigeons to the boil in the marinade. Cover with water. When this boils, add olive oil and smen. Turn the pigeons. Cook for about 1 hour, then take out the pigeons and reduce the sauce.

Place the pigeons in the oven for about 3 minutes at 350 °F/180 °C. Break the eggs and beat with the chopped parsley. Season with salt and pepper. Fry 4 omelets in oil in a frying pan.

Untie the twine from the pigeons and wrap each pigeon in an omelet. Arrange on plates. Garnish with pieces of pickled lemon and purple olives.

Chicken

Preparation time: 40 minutes
Marinating time: 1 hour
Cooking time: 40 minutes
Difficulty: ★

Serves 4

1	chicken weighing 2½ lbs/1.2 kg
6 tbsp/90 ml	vegetable oil
1⅛ lb/500 g	onions
1¾ cups/250 g	blanched almonds
	salt

For the marinade:

1 bunch	parsley
1 tbsp	red food coloring
1 tsp	saffron threads
1 tsp	smen (preserved butter) or olive oil
4 tbsp/60 ml	vegetable oil
	salt and white pepper

For the garnish:

	parsley

In Moroccan cooking, the term *kedra* refers to a specific method of cooking based on cooked onions and almonds. In the Fez area, chicken is usually served with this slightly sweet accompaniment.

This traditional and sophisticated dish is generally eaten at the family table. According to Abdellah Achiai, even today it is almost always prepared by grandmothers. It is easy to cook, but does take some time.

Many Moroccans are very choosy when it comes to picking the right chicken. All over the country, the *beldi* free-range chickens that can be recognized by their multi-colored feathers are highly prized. On market days, farmers from the surrounding villages make their way to town, loaded down with cages in which they transport their live chickens.

Gourmets in the market choose their *beldi* chicken, which is slaughtered and plucked on the spot. For this recipe, choose a free-range chicken with firm flesh and little fat. These chickens usually need to cook for some time.

The *kedra*, made from onions, is used as a flavoring but also eaten as a vegetable, and is typically Moroccan. The onions have a sweetish flavor if grown in a sunny place. This bulb, of the lily family, has been cultivated for 5,000 years and originated in northern Asia. Choose onions that are not sprouting, with a firm, hard bulb.

The almonds in the onion mixture also come from Asia. The Romans knew them as "Greek nuts." You should use blanched almonds for this recipe.

Cut off the wings and legs of the chicken and divide the body into 2 parts. Cut off the fillets.

For the marinade, place chopped parsley, food coloring, saffron threads, and smen in a bowl. Pour in the oil. Season with salt and pepper. Marinate the chicken pieces for 1 hour.

Fry the chicken pieces briefly in the marinade and 1 tbsp vegetable oil. Cover with water and cook for about 30 minutes.

Kedra

Peel the onions and slice thinly. Cook slowly in the rest of the vegetable oil on a low heat. Season with salt.

Once the chicken is cooked, place aside. Blanch the almonds for about 10 minutes in boiling water.

Place the almonds in the saucepan with the onions and stir carefully. Arrange the chicken meat with the accompaniment on plates. Garnish with chopped parsley.

Oxtail

Preparation time:	20 minutes
Soaking time:	overnight
Cooking time:	2 hours 15 minutes
Difficulty:	★

Serves 4

1¼ cups/200 g	garbanzo beans (chickpeas)
4 tbsp/60 ml	vegetable oil
4 tbsp/60 ml	olive oil
3 lbs/1.4 kg	oxtail, in pieces
⅔ oz/20 g	flat-leaf parsley
1 oz/30 g	fresh cilantro (coriander)

12½ oz/350 g	onions
2 oz/50 g	garlic
½ tsp	ground cumin
¼ tsp	paprika powder
⅘ cup/150 g	golden raisins
	salt and pepper

For the garnish:

⅓ oz/10 g	flat-leaf parsley
1 oz/25 g	sesame seeds

Oxtail with garbanzo beans and raisins is a very popular dish in Morocco. Oxtail is much prized in Morocco, and it is also sometimes cooked in an onion sauce with raisins, or it may be cooked with vegetables for many couscous dishes. However, mutton tail is generally more commonly eaten in Morocco. Dried, it enriches a delicious couscous served at the Ashura festival.

Oxtail is considered a poor quality meat. To make it tender and aromatic, it needs to cook for a long time over a low heat in a highly flavored broth. In many countries, especially in France, the meat is cooked until it comes off the bone. The delicious pieces of meat cooked in this way are used for fillings, stews, or casseroles with ground beef, mashed potato, or similar ingredients. Here, the chef serves the oxtail still on the bone. Moroccan cooks are of the opinion that the taste and consistency of the meat is of the

same order as that of the neck, which can be used to replace it in this recipe. Choose a large piece with plenty of meat on the bone.

Garbanzo beans, cultivated in Morocco, are almost always dried before they are sold. When fresh, they have hardly any flavor of their own. In regional cuisine, they are found in couscous dishes, as an accompaniment to oxtail, in salads, and in dishes with shank of veal.

The raisins, allowed to swell in the sauce, give a touch of sweetness to the dish. They are produced in the wine-growing regions around Meknès, Fez, and Marrakesh, and are available on the market in golden, reddish, or almost black variations. Weddings, official occasions, and religious festivals are almost unthinkable without raisins and almonds.

Soak the garbanzo beans the evening before. In a large pan, heat both types of oil. Place the pieces of oxtail into the hot oil.

On a chopping board, chop the parsley, fresh cilantro, peeled onion, and garlic with a knife. Add to the meat. Fry for a few moments, on a high heat, stirring.

Season with salt and pepper, cumin and paprika. Stir for a few moments on the heat, to allow the spices to develop their full aroma.

with Raisins

Drain the garbanzo beans and add them to the pan with the meat.

Cover all ingredients with water. Cover the pan and simmer for at least 2 hours on a low heat, until the meat begins to loosen off the bones.

15 minutes before the end of the cooking time, add the raisins to the meat. Bring to the boil. Arrange the meat on plates with the garbanzo beans and raisins. Garnish with parsley and sesame seeds.

Tride with

Preparation time: 30 minutes
Cooking time: 1 hour 25 minutes
Difficulty: ★★

Serves 4

1	free range corn-fed chicken
7 tbsp/100 ml	olive oil
2	onions
5	saffron threads

1 envelope	Moroccan saffron powder for coloring
1 tsp	ras el-hanout (spice blend)
6 cups/1.5 l	chicken stock
	salt and pepper

For the tride pastry:

4⅓ cups/500 g	flour
1 pinch	salt
1 tbsp/15 ml	oil

Tride with chicken is a feast. It is often served in the country at harvest festivals. It is also frequently offered to new mothers shortly after giving birth.

Tride pastry is similar to yufka pastry, but somewhat thicker and about the size of a crepe. The traditional style of making the dough is rather interesting. First of all, a dough is formed from flour, salt, oil, and water, then kneaded and shaped into a ball. It is then divided into several smaller balls. On a well-oiled work surface, the dough is teased out with the fingertips as thinly as possible. Charcoal is heated in a brasero, a kind of small barbecue, and a large, rounded pitcher is heated on it. As soon as this is very hot, the sheets of tride dough are slapped onto the walls of the pitcher until they are cooked. Some Moroccans make their task easier by preparing the tride sheets in a frying pan. This is the method the chef has chosen.

M'hamed Chahid recommends choosing a free-range, exclusively corn-fed chicken for this recipe. In Morocco, these chickens are known as beldi. Despite their grayish or yellowish skin and their not over-plentiful, very firm flesh, many Moroccans think they taste far better than factory-farmed chickens, although these may have paler and more succulent meat. Fry the chicken with the spices to make it deliciously golden-brown, cook the onions well and allow the flavors to penetrate deeply into the chicken. Only then should you pour on the chicken stock.

Don't forget to season the sauce with ras el-hanout. This complex spice mixture sometimes consists of up to a dozen different ingredients. Unfortunately, the use of this spice is today limited to recipes from the regional cuisine.

For the dough, place the flour in a bowl. Add salt, a glass of water, and oil. Knead the dough until you can form a ball. Divide the ball into several smaller balls.

Use your fingertips to stretch each small ball until thin, almost transparent discs are formed. Cook like crepes in a frying pan. Put aside.

Cut off both legs from the chicken. Do the same with the wings. Cut the carcass into four.

Chicken

Fry the chicken pieces in a pot in olive oil. Add the onions, cut into rings, saffron threads, saffron powder, salt, pepper, and ras el-hanout. Allow to fry for 10 minutes.

At the end of these 10 minutes, pour the chicken stock over the chicken pieces. Cover and cook for 1 hour.

Break up the trides by hand into large pieces and place them on a decorative serving platter. Place the chicken pieces on top and pour the sauce over everything.

Desserts &
Pastries

La Mancha

Preparation time: 40 minutes
Cooking time: 40 minutes
Difficulty: ★★

Serves 4

1 tsp/5 g	butter
1	unwaxed lemon
4	eggs
½ cup/100 g	sugar
¼ cup/25 g	confectioner's sugar
1⅓ cups/125 g	cake flour

For the sauce:

1	unwaxed lemon
2 cups/500 ml	milk
⅞ cup/200 g	sugar
2 sticks	cinnamon
1	vanilla bean

For the garnish:

	ground cinnamon

The Castilians are widely regarded as absolute gourmets. Every town, every village, in this delightful region in central Spain has its own sweet specialties. The recipe for La Mancha sponge cake is from Alcázar de San Juan.

These cakes are served, with milk to drink, for breakfast. Sponge is a very light and airy cake dough. Sieve the flour before mixing it, and brush the baking parchment with melted butter. Do not open the oven door while the cake is baking, otherwise the cake will collapse.

The lemon plays a special role in this dessert. This sun-drenched fruit is always associated with Spain, and is greatly prized for its high vitamin C content. If you want to use the peel, choose unwaxed specimens when shopping; otherwise wash them thoroughly in hot water.

The vanilla used in this recipe gives the milk an unmistakable aroma. The beans are the fruit of a climber from the orchid family, and first came to Spain with the Conquistadors. It is said that they first saw this spice when offered cocoa by the Aztecs. Impressed by the exceptional aroma of vanilla, they called it *vanillia* ("little bean"). Soon, the aromatic beans embarked on a triumphant march beyond the borders of the Iberian Peninsula, and conquered all of Europe.

Alberto Herráiz adds a cinnamon stick to the milk to counter the sweetness, as it provides a slightly tarter note. The rind of the cinnamon tree, it has a warm, mild sharpness. This tropical woody plant is grown primarily in Sri Lanka and China, and the plantations are scented by its penetrating, intoxicating scent.

To make the sauce, first peel one of the lemons. Heat the milk, sugar, cinnamon, vanilla, and lemon peel in a pot. Simmer over a low heat for 40 minutes until reduced by a quarter. Reserve the cinnamon, vanilla, and peel as garnish. Leave the sauce to cool.

Line a baking sheet with baking parchment. Brush the parchment with melted butter. Grate the peel of the second lemon.

Separate the eggs. Whisk the egg yolks with a balloon whisk. Add the lemon peel and sugar, and combine well. Add the confectioner's sugar, and whisk until foamy.

Sponge Cake

Beat the egg whites until stiff in a second bowl with a clean balloon whisk.

Using a spatula, scoop the beaten egg whites onto the egg yolk mixture, and fold in. Add the flour and combine.

Spoon the dough into a forcing bag and, using a wide round nozzle, pipe strips onto the baking parchment. Bake (320 °F/160 °C) for about 10 minutes. Leave to cool. Put on plates, and pour over the sauce. Garnish with the lemon peel, cinnamon, vanilla bean, and ground cinnamon.

Turrón

Preparation time: 50 minutes
Parfait freezing time: 3 hours
Chilling time
   crème anglaise: 30 minutes
Cooking time: 12 minutes
Difficulty: ★★

Serves 4

For the turrón parfait:
4 cups/1 l	cream
9	egg yolks
1⅛ cups/250 g	sugar
9 oz/250 g	turrón (Spanish nougat)

For the crème anglaise:
2 cups/500 ml	milk
1	unwaxed lemon
1	vanilla bean
4	egg yolks
⅜ cup/100 g	sugar
1 tsp	cornstarch
1 cup/250 ml	cream

For the garnish:
	mint leaves
5 tsp/25 g	ground almonds
	red berries (optional)

This exquisite dessert is typically Spanish. It is easy to make, and smells wonderfully of almonds and honey.

Turrón, probably Spain's most famous confectionery, is made in Jijona, about 12 miles/20 km from Alicante on Spain's Mediterranean coast. The creamy, caramel-colored nougat is made during six months of the year only, because it is usually eaten at Christmas. The age-old recipe is yet another example of the country's Moorish heritage. The Moors ruled over Spain in the High and Late Middle Ages. It was they who introduced the Iberians to delicious sweets made of honey and almonds.

Almond trees have been growing in Alicante for about 12 centuries now, and the plantations stretch as far as the eye can see. The Marcona variety is used to make *turrón*, famous for its delicate, slightly bitter flavor and aroma.

The almonds are roasted whole, then ground and finally combined with orange blossom honey, egg whites, and confectioner's sugar to make the nougat. The extremely short cooking time takes place under the watchful eye of the *turronero* (the master confectioner), who is the only person able to take into account even apparently insignificant climatic changes on the day!

For this recipe, the egg yolks need to be heated with the sugar and *turrón* in a *bain-marie* (water bath) before the mixture is folded into the cream. This helps to prevent major changes in temperature, which would cause the cream to separate.

Cesar Marquiegui serves the parfait with crème anglaise. This delightful dessert is a great success at parties—and with children!

To make the turrón parfait, pour the cream into a bowl and whisk with a balloon whisk until stiff.

Beat together the egg yolks and sugar until foamy, then stir in the crumbled turrón. Whisk in a bain-marie (water bath) for about 5 minutes until everything is combined. Then leave to cool, still stirring.

Pour the egg and nougat mixture into the cream, and fold in gently using a spatula.

Parfait

Pour the mixture into a tin lined with plastic wrap. Freeze for at least 3 hours.

To make the crème anglaise, bring the milk to the boil with the lemon peel and vanilla bean. Beat the egg yolks with the sugar and cornstarch. Strain the milk through a sieve onto the beaten egg yolks. Then leave to stand for 2–3 minutes.

Whip the cream until just holding its shape, then fold into the egg milk. Chill for 30 minutes. Arrange slices of the turrón parfait on plates, and surround them with a little crème anglaise. Garnish with ground almonds, mint leaves, and berries.

Crema Catalana

Preparation time: 30 minutes
Chilling time: 2 hours
Cooking time: 25 minutes
Difficulty: ★

Serves 4

1	unwaxed lemon
4 cups/1 l	milk
⁷/₈ cup/200 g	sugar
1 stick	cinnamon
1	vanilla bean
7 tsp/35 g	cornstarch
8	egg yolks
2 cups/200 g	strawberries

Many Catalonian families make *crema catalana* on March 19, which is St. Joseph's Day. Hens lay more eggs at this time of year than any other, so the large number required for this recipe are readily available. The tradition is so deeply rooted that, in Catalan, the dessert is called *crema de Sant Josep*.

Pep Masiques' choice is an authentic Catalonian dessert: the milk is flavored with cinnamon, vanilla, and lemon, and added hot to the egg cream. Then the crème is thickened slowly over a low heat until nice and smooth, and light yellow in color.

The combination of cornstarch and eggs thickens the crème. Rice flour used to be used for this purpose in Catalonia, but that took more time and was quite complicated.

Today, most Catalonians—and chefs in other regions—pour the crème into individual bowls, and sprinkle it with sugar when it is cool. The surface is caramelized with a hot iron, which does not take long because the sugar forms a very thin layer that soon melts and turns brown. However, Pep Masiques believes this makes the dessert far too sweet—and the caramel overpowers the delicate balance of aromas.

Chef serves the crème with fresh strawberries, whose fruity sweetness combines perfectly with the mild crème. The best Catalonian strawberries, or *maduixes*, come from the greenhouses of Maresme, the area to the north of Barcelona. Of course, wild strawberries—such as the ones found in the Pyrenees—are even better!

Peel the lemon. Pour 3 cups/750 ml milk into a pot, then sprinkle over the sugar. Add the cinnamon, vanilla bean, and lemon peel, then bring to the boil. Lower the temperature, and leave the milk to steep.

Dissolve the cornstarch in 1 cup/250 ml milk in a bowl. Beat together 8 egg yolks, and fold into the milk.

Strain the flavored milk through a sieve.

with Strawberries

Pour the milk into a large pot and gently heat on the hob, gradually adding the egg yolk mixture, and stirring continuously.

Continue heating the milk, still stirring continuously, until it is thick and creamy. Remove from the heat, cool, and put in the refrigerator.

Wash and top the strawberries, and cut into quarters. Whisk the cooled cream again, then pour into a serving bowl. Garnish with the strawberries.

Mallorcan

Preparation time: 40 minutes
Standing time
dough: 10 minutes
Cooling time snails: 24 hours
Rising time snails: 3–4 hours
Cooking time: 15 minutes
Difficulty: ★★

Serves 4

$^1/_3$ cup/70 g	sugar
1	egg
3 cups/300 g	flour
4 tsp/20 g	fresh yeast
9 tbsp/130 g	pork lard
	oil to grease worktop and baking sheet

The Mallorcans are proud of these wonderful snails, which they call *ensaimadas*. Sometimes they are little appetizing squiggles, sometimes spirals the size of a wagon wheel. Visitors to Mallorca will be able to sample the vast array on offer—and take them home as edible souvenirs.

This delight is made with lard, which is spread onto the rolled-out pastry, and prevents the spirals from sticking together. Before ready-made yeast was available, people used a little fermented pastry as a rising agent.

The dough can sometimes be a little stiff if made in the food mixer, in which case a few drops of water will solve the problem. Some confectioners use milk instead of water. If the dough is too runny, add a little more flour.

Spread the lard carefully onto the dough with your fingers so it does not tear. When rolling out the triangles, make sure the dough stays in one piece. It is important to leave it to stand before rolling. Grease the triangles quickly and lightly using your fingertips, then roll them up like horns. It is easier if you brush a little oil on the worktop.

After chilling, the dough needs to rise for 3 or 4 hours. Check regularly to make sure it is not rising too much, but keeping its shape—especially if you are using fresh yeast and the room is warm.

The snails are popular at breakfast, served with hot chocolate or coffee. Gourmets like to enjoy their snails with honey, pumpkin jelly, cream, or even chocolate sauce.

In the mixing bowl of the food mixer, combine the sugar with 6$^1/_2$ tbsp/100 ml water, the egg, flour, and crumbled yeast. Knead with the kneading hook until the dough is smooth and sticking to the hook. Shape the dough into a ball, then leave to stand for 10 minutes.

Oil the worktop. Break the dough ball into pieces weighing about 2 oz/60 g each. Knead them individually on the worktop, and shape them into balls again.

Using the pastry roller, roll each dough ball out into an oval. Beat the softened lard thoroughly in a bowl using a balloon whisk until it looks like meringue. Spread it over the dough, using your fingertips.

Snails

Using your hands, carefully shape each oval into a triangle.

Roll the triangles up, starting at the long side, so you have several thin dough rolls in front of you. Line the baking sheet with baking parchment.

Draw out the dough rolls and shape into snails. Cover with plastic wrap, and chill for 24 hours. Next day, leave the snails to rise at room temperature for 3–4 hours. Bake (350 °F/180 °C) for 15 minutes. Leave to cool, and dust with confectioner's sugar.

Easter Week

Preparation time: 20 minutes
Cooking time: 15 minutes
Difficulty: ★

Serves 4

2 cups/500 ml	milk
²/₃ cup/150 g	sugar
1	vanilla bean
8 slices	light bread with a thin crust
3	eggs
2 cups/500 ml	sunflower oil

For the garnish:

confectioner's sugar
ground cinnamon

The Spanish take to the streets in the days before Easter. The Easter Week processions are elaborate folk festivals, with repentants touring the streets in hooded garments, lavishly decorated carts with statues of the saints, and monks clad in habits. After this spectacle, families meet up for feasts of food special to Easter Week—*Semana Santa*—which differ from region to region. One is *torrijas*, not unlike fritters, which are served at the end of a delicious meal.

Use high-quality white bread with a dense crumb and thin crust, ideally a day or two old. Some countries call this dish "Poor Knights," because stale bread is, of course, something that poor people eat—in this case, as a delicious treat. You can also use toast, but the end result will taste completely different.

José-Ignacio Herráiz scents the milk with a vanilla bean, but you can use a cinnamon stick, or grated orange, or lemon peel, if you prefer. The chef moistens each side of the bread with milk, making sure not too much is absorbed. In other variants of this dish the bread is soaked in honey, or even wine.

As soon as the bread is golden, it is sprinkled with cinnamon and sugar. The sugar melts on the hot surface, providing an intensive aroma. In La Mancha, our chef's home town, the milk-dipped bread is shaped into balls, dipped in egg, then deep-fried. It is served as a typical Easter Week dessert.

Pour the milk into a pot and add the sugar and vanilla bean. Bring to the boil, then leave to stand, and sieve.

Cut the bread into thick slices and cut off the crusts so the slices are more or less square.

Place the bread on a plate and ladle over a little of the vanilla milk. Turn the bread in the milk, so it is well soaked.

Fritters

Beat the eggs and pour onto a plate. Coat each slice of bread in the egg, then place on a second plate.

Heat the oil in a skillet and fry the bread until golden, turning halfway.

Combine the sugar and cinnamon for the garnish on a plate. Coat the torrijas in it while they are still hot. Serve warm.

Tarta

Preparation time: 20 minutes
Cooking time: 20–25 minutes
Cooling time: approx. 1 hour
Difficulty: ★

Serves 4

7 tbsp/100 g butter
1⅓ cups/150 g confectioner's sugar
2 eggs
1½ cups/200 g ground almonds
    butter and flour for the
    cake pan

Since the 9th century, millions of pilgrims have traveled to Santiago de Compostela in Galicia from all over Europe to see the grave of James the Apostle. They still visit the town's confectioneries for refreshment in the form of *Tarta de Santiago*, an exceptionally appealing cake decorated with the sign of the cross. Nobody knows whether the recipe for this culinary delight was first provided by a sweet-toothed pilgrim, or the invention of a local confectioner, and then named after Spain's patron saint.

Santiago Pérez-García is an expert on Spain's confectionery. Here he presents a recipe that he has perfected over the years. Apparently the cake was originally made without butter, but it complements the oil in the almonds beautifully, and makes the cake wonderfully soft. It is first whisked until frothy; if the dough is a little too hard it can be lightened with a little egg white. If the dough is too soft,

add a little confectioner's sugar. There are several different variants of this cake; some contain milk or cream. Some confectioners use cinnamon or lemon peel for added flavor.

The bottom and sides of the cake pan are brushed with melted butter and dusted with flour. The chef then chills the pan for a while. This makes the butter harden again, and helps the flour to stick to the pan without either combining with the dough. Shake the pan to remove excess flour after chilling.

A template is used for the decoration on the *Tarta de Santiago*. Place a St. James cross made of wood, metal, or cardboard on the middle of the cake. Then dust the top of the cake with a thin layer of confectioner's sugar, and remove the cross.

Beat together the butter and ⅞ cup (100 g) confectioner's sugar in the bowl of the food mixer until the mixture turns yellow and thickens.

Add the eggs and continue beating until the mixture is creamy.

Fold in the ground almonds.

de Santiago

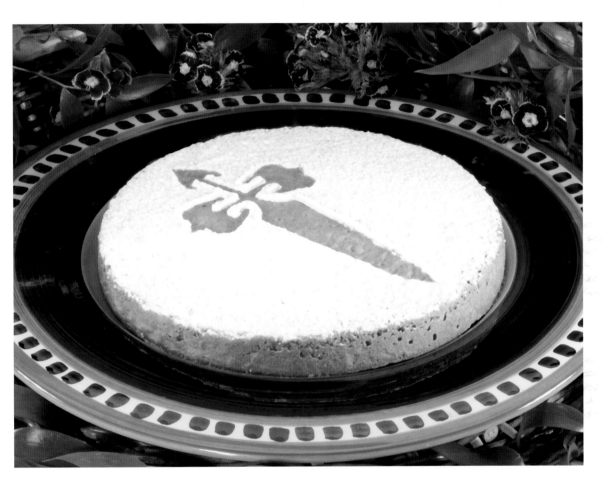

Brush a round cake pan with melted butter, and dust with flour. Chill the pan for a few minutes.

Pour the dough into the pan and bake in a preheated oven (350 °F/180 °C) for 20–25 minutes. Turn the cake out of the pan, and leave to cool.

Place the cake on a baking sheet. Put a St. James cross on the middle of the cake, and dust the surface with confectioner's sugar. Carefully remove the cross, leaving its impression on the cake.

Tocinillos

Preparation time: 20 minutes
Cooking time: 30 minutes
Difficulty: ★

Serves 4

10	egg yolks
4	eggs
⁷⁄₈ cup/200 g	sugar
	glucose for the pans (optional)

When the nuns in Madrid's convents used to treat themselves to something special on Sundays, they were presumably thinking of the heaven that awaited them at the end of their earthly lives. *Tocinillos de cielo*—"Heaven's little pigs"—is one of Spain's oldest and most popular desserts.

The recipe for this flan is not complicated. Whole eggs are blended with egg yolks and sugar syrup. Santiago Pérez-García has dozens of variants in his repertoire. Why not flavor it with orange or lemon juice? Or add a coating of chocolate, or a dusting of cocoa powder? Some chefs use milk instead of water for the syrup.

To make it easier to remove the flans from the molds, chef brushes them with warm glucose, but caramel is a good substitute. Savarin molds can be used for a different shape of the *tocinillos*.

When adding the syrup to the beaten eggs, stir continuously while doing so to combine the ingredients thoroughly. However, do not beat the mixture; it must not become frothy. The water must be bubbling before the molds are put in the steamer insert, because the mixture has to set as quickly as possible or the sugar will sink to the bottom—it is heavier than water and egg yolks.

Before he steams the flans, our chef places a tea towel between the pot and the lid. The cloth absorbs the rising steam, preventing water from dripping on the flans and causing unsightly holes.

For the garnish, a pattern of caramel or chocolate is drawn on the bottom of the serving plate, the *tocinillos* arranged on top. Garnish with mint.

Put the egg yolks and the whole eggs in a bowl. Brush a little warmed glucose on the flan pans with your fingers. Bring some water to the boil in a steamer.

To make the syrup, put the sugar in a pot and add 7 tbsp/100 ml) water. Bring to the boil briefly, then remove instantly from the heat.

Beat the eggs. Add a little of the hot syrup, stirring continuously. Combine well, and strain through a sieve if necessary.

de Cielo

Use a small ladle to pour the crème into the prepared pans.

When the water in the steamer is simmering, place the custards in the insert. Cover with a lid and cook for 15–20 minutes. Remove from the pot and leave to cool.

Carefully shake the pans to remove the custards, and tip them onto a plate. Serve as soon as possible.

Yemas

Preparation time: 30 minutes
Chilling time: 1 day
Cooking time: 10 minutes
Difficulty: ★

Serves 4

1⅛ cups/250 g sugar
15 egg yolks
1 lemon
confectioner's sugar
for the worktop

The Castilians have always had a penchant for desserts of all kinds. A 17th-century confectioner in Ávila, to the west of Madrid, first invented these little balls of baked dough that are dipped in sugar and caramelized. His son had the brilliant idea of naming the *yemas* after a famous local saint: Teresa of Ávila, the founder of the Order of Carmelites. The sweet-toothed saint was famous for saying: "God is everywhere—even in our cooking pots."

Today, the recipe for *yemas de Santa Teresa* is honored in a number of different versions. In this variation, the balls are coated in fine sugar and singed with a hot iron to become *yemas de Léon*. The standard Madrid version is coated in caramel.

The eggs, sugar, and lemon juice are whisked for a long time over a low heat. Santiago Pérez-García recommends that you scrape the bottom and sides of the pot frequently so that the ingredients all cook evenly. Towards the end of the cooking time the mixture looks like thick, yellow mayonnaise. It is then whisked again hard with a balloon whisk until it comes away from the sides of the pot, like choux pastry.

The chef adds a few drops of lemon juice to the mixture, but does not believe that any further aromas are required. If the cooled mixture is too soft to shape into balls, a little sugar can be added to make it firmer.

How the *yemas* are finished varies from region to region, and chef to chef. If you do not have an iron to brown them, you can caramelize them under the broiler, or grill. However, they look and taste equally good just dipped in confectioner's sugar or cocoa powder.

Place the sugar in a pot and add the egg yolks and a few drops of lemon juice. Whisk with a balloon whisk and heat over a low heat until you have a fairly thick dough.

Using a spatula, spread the mixture over a high rectangular tin and smooth off. Cover with plastic wrap and chill for one day.

Next day, dust the worktop with confectioner's sugar and knead the dough with your fingers. Shape into a ball.

de Léon

Using your hands, roll the dough out into an evenly shaped roll.

Cut the roll into pieces, shape each piece into a plum-sized ball, and coat all over in the remainder of the confectioner's sugar.

Place the yemas on a baking sheet and briefly singe the top of each ball with the red-hot iron to caramelize. You can also do this under the broiler.

Oscar's

Preparation time: 50 minutes
Cooking time: 40 minutes
Setting time for the
orange soup/freezing
time for the granita: 12 hours
Difficulty: ★★

Serves 4

For the lemon ravioli:
⅝ cup/140 g   sugar
2   eggs
   juice of 1 lemon
1½ sticks/150 g   butter
4 sheets   fresh ravioli pasta

For the orange sauce:
3 sheets   gelatin
⅔ cup/150 g   sugar
4 cups/1 liter   orange juice

For the herb liqueur granita:
2 sheets   gelatin
¼ cup/50 g   sugar
1⅔ cups/400 ml   Mallorcan herb
   liqueur

For the garnish (optional):
   mint leaves
   fresh raspberries
   cinnamon sticks
   lemon thyme

Oscar Martínez Plaza has based this attractive dessert on typically Balearic ingredients: the filling for the ravioli is flavored with lemons, the sauce is made with oranges, and the granita is full of the fresh aromas of a local herb liqueur. In spring, the mass of blossoming orange, lemon, and almond trees in the Mallorcan countryside is a beautiful sight.

The ravioli can be made with fresh Italian pasta or the Chinese pastry used to make wontons. Alternatively, it can be home-made using 2⅝ cups/300 g flour, 3 eggs, 2 tbsp/30 ml olive oil, and a pinch of salt. The ingredients are kneaded together into a dough and rolled out until very thin or, if possible, passed through a pasta maker.

The lemon filling is simple to make: the lemon juice should be blended cold with the sugar and eggs and then heated gently until it thickens. Do not try to fill the ravioli until the lemon mixture has cooled down. Allowing half a tablespoonful of filling for each parcel, use a teaspoon to slide it onto the center of each rectangle of pasta.

This dessert is topped with an unusual granita of Mallorcan herb liqueur. Known locally as *licor de hierbas dulces*, it is a beautiful olive green in color. Drunk as a digestif, many Mallorcans make it at home by adding flavorings such as fennel, thyme, rosemary, mint, green walnuts, and coffee beans to an aniseed-based spirit.

Beat the orange sauce with an electric mixer before pouring it over the ravioli. The fresh, contrasting tastes of ravioli, granita, and orange sauce make this an ideal dessert for a summer meal.

First prepare the lemon filling. Beat together the sugar, eggs, and lemon juice in a bowl, then heat gently for about 10 minutes, beating constantly until a thick, smooth cream is obtained.

Allow the lemon mixture to cool to a temperature of 130 °F/55 °C. Now add the butter cut into pieces and mix it in thoroughly as it melts. Leave the mixture to cool.

Briefly cook the pieces of pasta in boiling water, then refresh them with cold water. Drain the pasta and carefully cut each piece in half. Place a tsp of lemon filling on each piece of pasta and fold to make a square shape. Make 8 raviolis like this, then set them aside.

Ravioli

To make the orange sauce, soak the gelatin in a bowl of cold water. Place the sugar and a little water in a saucepan and heat until it caramelizes. Cool it by adding the orange juice. Add the softened gelatin, mixing until it has dissolved. Refrigerate overnight.

To make the granita, first soak the gelatin in cold water. Mix the sugar and herb liqueur together in a saucepan, heating them until they form a syrup. Dilute with 2 cups/500 ml water, then heat again, stirring the mixture.

When it boils, add the softened gelatin, beating with a whisk until it has dissolved. Allow the mixture to cool then freeze overnight at −4 °F/−20 °C. Serve the ravioli on a bed of orange sauce, topped with granita, mint, raspberries, cinnamon sticks, and lemon thyme.

Apricot Soup with Terrine

Preparation time: 40 minutes
Cooking time: 45 minutes
Cooling time for terrine: 3–4 hours
Difficulty: ★★

Serves 4

For the terrine:

²/₃ cup/150 ml	milk
¹/₃ cup/75 g	sugar
²/₃ cup/150 ml	light cream
5 oz/150 g	egg yolks
2 sheets	gelatin
	grated peel of 1 lemon
1 tsp/5 g	ground cinnamon

1 cup/200 g	fromage frais (or 1 cup cream cheese beaten together with ¼ cup lemon juice)

For the apricot soup:

1³/₄ lb/800 g	fresh apricots
²/₃ cup/150 g	sugar
⁴/₅ cup/200 ml	triple-sec (orange liqueur)
1 cup/250 ml	orange juice

For the garnish (optional):

chocolate
fresh mint leaves
red berries (any variety)

The inhabitants of the Balearic Islands enjoy desserts made of mild, fresh cheeses served with honey, sprinkled with sugar, and brûléed. Many types of fruit are grown on the islands, and another favorite dessert consists of apricots toasted on a flat sheet of heated metal called a *plancha*. In this recipe, Bartolomé-Jaime Trias Luis first toasts the apricots in this way, then cooks them in a mixture of caramel, triple-sec, and orange juice. Finally, he blends the ingredients together in a food processor. The resulting "soup" has a wonderful color and taste, its sweetness offsetting the slightly acid cheese.

The cheese terrine is a mixture of a light custard flavored with grated lemon peel and cinnamon, gelatin, and cream cheese. The mixture is poured into individual molds and placed in the refrigerator to cool. When set, the terrines can be easily slid out of the molds by dipping the bottoms of the containers into a bowl of hot water.

Apricots are one of the major fruit crops on the Balearic Islands. For this recipe, they can be toasted on top of the stove, in a metal pan, or browned in the oven. In all cases, they should be carefully watched, as they burn easily.

The apricot soup is given added flavor with the addition of orange juice and triple-sec. This is a liqueur made of orange peel, generally drunk with ice or used as an ingredient in cocktails, fruit salads, and ice creams. Kirsch makes a good substitute if triple-sec is unobtainable. When the apricots have been thoroughly cooked in this fragrant mixture of liquids, they are blended in a food processor. They should be sieved after this to remove any bits of skin.

Pour some apricot soup into each plate. Place a terrine in the middle, decorated with some halved blackberries and a mint leaf. Reserve a few apricots, and add these as a garnish together with a few blueberries.

To make the cheese terrine, heat the milk, sugar, and cream in a saucepan. Beat the egg yolks in a bowl. Pour a little warm milk over the eggs, then add them to the saucepan. Heat gently until the mixture thickens. Remove from the heat and add the softened gelatin.

Add the grated lemon peel and cinnamon to the custard, then carefully mix in the cheese. Pour the mixture into individual molds. Leave these to cool for 3 or 4 hours.

To make the apricot soup, cut the apricots in half and remove the pits. Toast them on both sides in a very hot pan.

# of Cream Cheese

Heat the sugar with a little water until it caramelizes. When it is a pale golden color, add the toasted apricots.

Pour the triple-sec over the fruit. Cook rapidly for about 10 minutes, stirring so that the apricots do not stick.

Add the orange juice. Cover the saucepan and simmer for 10 minutes. Set aside 2 or 3 apricots, blending the rest in a food processor. Leave to cool. Surround each terrine with the soup. Decorate with quartered apricots, mint, and red berries.

Crème Brûlée

Preparation time:	40 minutes
Time for custard to cool:	3 hours
Cooking time:	2 hours 20 minutes
Difficulty:	★

Serves 4

¾ cup/200 ml	Muscatel wine
8 oz/250 g	white Muscatel grapes

For the crème brûlée:

2 cups/500 ml	milk
1	vanilla bean
1 tsp	vanilla extract

6	egg yolks
⅔ cup/150 g	superfine sugar
	confectioner's sugar

For the vanilla ice cream:

1 cup/250 ml	milk
4	egg yolks
scant ½ cup/ 100 g	superfine sugar
1 tbsp	vanilla extract

For the garnish:

1 punnet	raspberries
	redcurrants
	fresh mint

Crème brûlée with Muscatel wine is a typical dessert from the Languedoc region, where the grapes for this sweet white wine ripen in vineyards on slopes below the Mediterranean scrub. It is drunk as an aperitif and is also popular for use in cooking. The grapes grow in small bunches with pale, perfumed, firm berries. When preparing this dish, the grapes are skinned and deseeded before being heated briefly in the wine. You could use a dessert wine such as Beaumes de Venise, or a liqueur such as Grand Marnier or Cointreau, in this easy-to-prepare dessert instead.

During cooking, the aluminum foil prevents the water from boiling. To save time, our chef recommends that you prepare the custard a day in advance.

Vanilla is the dominant flavor in this recipe. The vanilla bean, whose essence is used, is a climbing plant from the orchid family. It was originally cultivated in Mexico, but now grows in the Antilles, in Madagascar, and on the Comoro Islands. The ripe vanilla beans are harvested, boiled in water, and then dried in the sun. In the process they turn dark brown and are covered in a layer of crystals that look like frost, which is what gives vanilla its characteristic perfume and flavor.

The Muscatel wine sauce is made using melted vanilla ice cream, but really it's a crème anglaise, or custard. To make it, bring the milk to the boil. Beat together the egg yolks and sugar until frothy, then fold in the vanilla extract. Pour on the hot milk and mix well. Return the mixture to the pan and simmer for two minutes, then pour it into a container and put it in the freezer. If you're short of time you could melt ready-made vanilla ice cream to make the sauce.

To make the crème brûlée, put the vanilla bean and the extract in the hot milk, and leave to infuse for 15 minutes. Strain the milk.

Beat together the egg yolks and sugar until very frothy. Pour on the flavored hot milk and mix well. Strain through a sieve.

Pour the mixture into ramekins. Line a deep baking sheet with aluminum foil, pour a little water into the base of the sheet, and place the ramekins on the baking sheet. Bake the custards for 2 hours at 250 °F/120 °C until set.

with Muscatel Wine

Pour the wine into a saucepan and add the skinned and deseeded grapes. Heat gently for 2 minutes, so that the grapes are infused with the flavor of the wine. Then remove the grapes and reserve for the garnish.

Run the tip of a knife carefully around the rim of the ramekins and turn out the custards onto a plate. Sprinkle confectioner's sugar over the top of the custards and cook under the broiler at 465 °F/250 °C.

Let the wine cool a little, then add the vanilla ice cream (see top left for method). When the ice cream has melted completely, spoon a pool of sauce around the custards. Garnish with the Muscatel grapes, raspberries, redcurrants, and mint leaves.

Figs in Red Wine

Preparation time:	30 minutes
Cooking time:	30 minutes
Difficulty:	★

Serves 4

8	figs
⅔ cup/150 ml	red wine
⅔ cup/150 ml	port
5 generous tbsp/70 g	superfine sugar
1 pinch	cinnamon
1	lemon
1	orange
½	vanilla bean
½ lb/250 g	mascarpone
2	meringues

This is a very simple recipe from the Nice area. The only thing about it that is difficult is choosing the figs which, as our chef stresses, do not keep well. They can only be stored for a day in the refrigerator. When they are ripe, small cracks appear in the surface and when you squeeze them gently with your fingers they give a little. They should definitely not be overripe though. A fresh stalk is an indication of fresh fruit. Daniel Ettlinger recommends the Belonne variety, which is especially sweet. When the figs are cooked in port the flavors soften a little. This fortified wine, whose fermentation is stopped by the additional of alcohol, is a popular aperitif. A sweet dessert wine (Banyuls or Beaumes de Venise) can also be used.

Cinnamon is also important in this recipe. This spice is obtained from the bark of an exotic shrub and in this case is used when poaching the fruit. Cinnamon is recognizable by its sweetish, pervasive aroma and piquant flavor.

On the Côte d'Azur, which is imbued with Italian culture, mascarpone is a popular ingredient. Lovers of tiramisu are likely to be familiar with this rich cheese. You could use heavy cream instead.

The figs poached in red wine with mascarpone cream are sprinkled with crushed meringue. To make meringues, egg whites are beaten together with lots of sugar until very stiff, and dried in the oven. Depending on how long they are baked, the meringues can be squishy, soft, or crisp. If you buy meringues, choose the crisp type.

This dessert takes little time to prepare, but our chef stresses that it should then be served immediately for perfect results.

Wash the figs and carefully make a cross-shaped incision in the top with a small sharp knife.

Place the figs in a shallow baking dish and add the red wine and port.

Sprinkle over 3 heaped tbsp/50 g superfine sugar and a pinch of cinnamon.

with Mascarpone

Cut the lemon and orange into quarters, slit open the vanilla bean, and scrape out the seeds. Add one orange and one lemon quarter, and the vanilla seeds, to the figs. Bake the figs in the oven for 30 minutes at 400 °F/200 °C.

Beat together the mascarpone and remaining sugar.

Pour the wine from the baked figs into a deep plate. Arrange scoops of mascarpone in the sauce. Slice the figs in half and arrange 4 fig halves on each plate. Sprinkle crushed meringues over the top and garnish with the remaining orange and lemon quarters.

Goat Milk Cheese

Preparation time:	15 minutes
Cooking time:	40 minutes
Difficulty:	★

Serves 4

1	eggplant
⅝ cup/140 g	sugar
7 oz/200 g	carrots
⅓ cup + 1½ tbsp/100 ml	milk
1	vanilla bean
2 tbsp/70 g	rosemary honey

4	young soft goat milk cheeses, each 5 oz/120 g

For the garnish:
few sprigs flowering rosemary

Mel y mato is Catalan for "honey and soft cheese." Jean-Claude Vila has taken his inspiration from this traditional recipe and changed it a little. "I have discovered that some vegetables taste wonderful with sugar, which is why I use eggplant and carrot in my recipe."

The goat milk cheese should be at least 45 percent fat. Its very bland taste is similar to that of soft cheese made from cow's milk. For this recipe buy four individual cheeses, each weighing around 5 ounces/120 grams.

This dessert is sweetened by honey, described in ancient times as the food of the gods. Honey, made by bees from the nectar in flowers, is stored in the honeycomb cells. Honey provides much more energy than sugar. The bees produce rosemary honey from the flowers of this Mediterranean herb that flourishes in the Catalan region. In addition, our chef uses rosemary as a garnish.

Preparing carrots with sugar is a sure-fire way to bring many a child round to liking this vegetable, which contains a lot of vitamin A. Buy fresh baby carrots if you are able, and adjust the cooking time according to the size and the quality.

Don't forget to keep the vanilla bean. After using it in this recipe, slit it open lengthwise, scrape out the seeds, and add them to the carrot and honey mixture.

The eggplant slices also make this recipe one of our chef's signature dishes. Beautifully crisp, as they are in this recipe, they make an ideal accompaniment and garnish on the plate.

Wash the eggplant and carefully slice it thinly lengthwise.

To make the syrup, bring 1 cup/250 ml water to the boil with the sugar. Soak the eggplant slices in the hot syrup for about 3 minutes.

Drain the eggplant slices a little and spread them on a baking sheet lined with baking parchment. Bake them in the oven for around 8 minutes, at 340 °/170 °C, until browned.

with Honey

Put the peeled and sliced carrots into a saucepan with the milk, 1 cup + 1½ tbsp/100 ml water, and the vanilla bean. Boil, cover, and simmer for 15 minutes. Then take off the lid and continue cooking until the liquid has evaporated. Purée the carrots, then add the vanilla seeds.

Stir 1 level tbsp/30 g rosemary honey into the puréed carrot and cook on low heat for about 10 minutes.

Arrange the drained goat milk cheeses on a plate. Garnish with sprigs of flowering rosemary. Warm the remaining rosemary honey and drizzle it over the cheeses. Arrange a spoonful of puréed carrot and caramelized eggplant slices next to the cheese.

Canebière

Preparation time: 1 hour
Cooling time: 1 hour 30 minutes
Cooking time: 15 minutes
Difficulty: ★★

Serves 4

4   physalis

For the caramel base:
⅓ oz/10 g   semisweet chocolate
1 tsp/5 g   cocoa butter
3 oz/80 g   nougat
3½ oz/100 g   wafers

For the liquorice mousse:
2   egg yolks
3 tbsp/50 g   superfine sugar

1 dash   liquorice extract
2 envelopes   gelatin
¾ cup/200 ml heavy cream

For the Italian meringue:
2   egg whites
3 scant tbsp/
40 g   superfine sugar

For the chocolate mousse:
¾ cup/200 ml   heavy cream
3 tbsp/50 g   superfine sugar
1   egg yolk
3½ oz/90 g   milk chocolate
1½ oz/40 g   semisweet chocolate

For the custard with liquorice:
2   egg yolks
3 tbsp/50 g   superfine sugar
2 cups/500 ml milk
1 drop   liquorice extract

This dessert is a specialty of the "Miramar," Jean-Michel Minguella's restaurant. His pastry chef, Fabrice Vaquer, created this delicious dessert and named it in honor of a famous avenue, the Canebière, which runs through Marseilles and terminates at the Old Harbor. Our dessert's name is a reminder that it was once a cobbled road.

This delicious liquorice-flavored dessert incorporates part of the city's history. In the past there was a liquorice factory not far from Avenue Canebière. Did you know that liquorice is obtained from a bush? The roots are called liquorice and are also available as sticks that can be chewed. The extract obtained from the bush is used to flavor alcohol and beer, and for liquorice candy. Because the flavor is very strong, you should use it extremely sparingly and ensure that it doesn't slip from your hands when you are adding it to a dish.

All the flavors that one might encounter when dining at the "Miramar" are connected with the port city. Every element in this dessert recreates the ancient city, and the chocolate adds an exotic, cosmopolitan note.

Physalis, the fruit that crowns this dessert, originates from Peru and is sometimes also known as Cape gooseberry. Depending on the time of year, you could use other acidic fruit such as star fruit, kiwi fruit, or pineapple. Jean-Michel Minguella has chosen physalis not just for the beauty of the orange berries, but also because of the delicate acidity which revives the taste buds after the sweetness of the sugar. The acidity balances the chocolate and the sweetness of the dessert.

Melt the chocolate, cocoa butter, and nougat. Custard: Beat together the egg yolks and sugar until foamy. Heat the milk and add half of it to the egg mixture. Heat the other half on low heat, stirring all the time, until it boils. Then add the liquorice extract.

Pour the custard through a sieve and refrigerate it. Crumble the wafers and add them to the chocolate and nougat mixture. Spread this mixture over baking parchment until it is about ¼ in/½ mm thick. Put it in the freezer for 10 minutes to set.

Liquorice mousse: Beat the egg yolks and sugar until foamy. Add the liquorice extract and the gelatin dissolved in 2 tbsp hot water. Meringues: Beat the whites until very stiff. Heat ⅓ cup + 1½ tbsp/100 ml water and the sugar to 250 °F/120 °C. Slowly beat the syrup into the egg whites.

"Cobblestones"

Fold the meringue mixture into the liquorice mousse. Add the stiffly beaten cream and spread the mixture over the chocolate nougat mixture. Freeze for about 20 minutes.

Chocolate mousse: Beat the cream until stiff and put aside. Melt the sugar (230 °F/110 °C) and beat into the beaten egg yolk, using a hand mixer, then let it cool. Melt the milk and semisweet chocolate separately in double boilers or bowls over a saucepan of simmering water.

Mix the chocolate into the egg and sugar mixture, then carefully fold in the beaten cream. Spread this over the set liquorice mousse. Refrigerate for 1 hour. Pour some of the custard into a deep plate. Cut out four "cobblestones" from the set dessert and garnish each with a physalis.

Pear

Preparation time: 15 minutes
Resting time: 30 minutes
Cooking time: 20 minutes
Difficulty: ★

Serves 4

2	pears
1 handful	raisins
⅛ stick/15 g	butter
1 tbsp	sugar
2 tsp/10 ml	pear brandy (e.g. Poire William)
½ cup/50 g	flaked almonds

For the pancake batter:

1 generous cup/125 g	all-purpose flour
1 pinch	salt

3 tbsp/50 g	superfine sugar
3	eggs
2 cups/500 ml	milk
	grated zest of 1 unwaxed orange
	grated zest of 1 unwaxed lemon

For the custard:

1 cup/250 ml	milk
3	egg yolks
3 heaped tbsp/ 55 g	superfine sugar

For the garnish:

1	unwaxed orange

Francis Robin's recipe for pear pancakes (*pannequets*) is a reminder of his past. Even as a novice chef, this *Maître Cuisinier de France* shone at preparing pancakes.

Pannequet was originally the term used for a sweet or savory pancake filled with ground meat or poultry, fruit purée, or custard. They often appear on menus, whether as appetizers, hot hors d'oeuvres or, as we suggest, a sweet dessert, because they are perfect for guests and are very easy to prepare.

Francis Robin lets the batter rest for 30 minutes, but you could leave it for an hour. Use a non-stick pan to prevent the pancakes sticking. After you have made each pancake, wipe out the skillet with kitchen paper coated with oil.

Because pears and almonds are a marriage made in heaven, it is only natural that they both appear in Francis Robin's

recipe. The best variety of pear for this dessert is Conference, available in the fall. It is not very rounded, and has a smooth, green skin with a pale reddish tinge. The slightly acidic flavor of the pear emphasizes the sweetness of the custard. If you can't find Conference pears, use Williams instead.

Francis Robin suggests that you prepare this dessert during the Christmas and New Year holidays using filberts, chopped almonds, pine nuts, or dates. Omitting the alcohol will not impair this recipe. Our chef's final tip for success is to cook the pancakes at the very last minute, because they taste best hot!

To make the custard, bring the milk to the boil. In the meantime, beat together the egg yolks and sugar until foaming. Pour the hot milk onto the egg mixture, stirring all the time. Pour the custard into a saucepan, and cook on gentle heat, stirring all the time, until it thickens.

To make the pancake batter, put the flour in a bowl with a pinch of salt. Add the sugar and 3 eggs and beat in the milk. Stir in the grated orange and lemon zest. Leave the batter to rest for 30 minutes before cooking the pancakes.

Peel and core the pears. Dice the flesh finely. In the meantime soak the raisins in hot water to plump them up.

Pancakes

Melt 2 tsp butter in a skillet. Sweat the diced pear with the sugar and pear brandy, if desired.

As soon as the alcohol has evaporated, add the drained raisins and flaked almonds, and stir them into the pear mixture. Cook the pancakes in the remaining butter in another skillet.

Fill the pancakes with the pear mixture. Shape the pancakes into a little parcel and tie the top with a strand of orange zest. Spoon the custard onto the plate and sit the warm pancakes on top of the custard.

Red Berry Compôte with

Preparation time: 30 minutes
Time for the
  ice cream to infuse: 4 hours
Cooking time: 20 minutes
Difficulty: ★

Serves 4

For the red berry compôte:
½ cup/100 g   pine nuts
2 cups/200 g   strawberries
1 generous cup/
125 g   raspberries
scant ½ cup/50 g blackberries
scant ¼ cup/20 g redcurrants
4 tsp/20 g   honey

generous ⅛ stick/20 g   butter
⅓ cup + 1½ tbsp/
100 ml   maraschino

For the syrup:
1 generous cup/
250 g   superfine sugar
1   vanilla bean

For the lemon verbena ice cream:
3   egg yolks
3 heaped tbsp/
50 g   superfine sugar
⅔ cup/150 ml milk
1 sprig   fresh lemon verbena
⅓ cup + 1½ tbsp/
100 ml   heavy cream

For the garnish:
4   mint leaves

Provençal red berry compôte with lemon verbena ice cream is an original recipe by our chef. This recipe, redolent of summer, is a true delicacy.

All small, red berry fruit are soft and bruise easily. They must be handled carefully and can only be transported in rigid, closed containers. Choose fruit that are not overripe and use them soon after purchase. Depending on the time of year, you could also use wild strawberries, strawberry tree (or arbutus) fruit, cranberries, or cherries.

Maraschino is a liqueur made from sweetened brandy produced from the pits of maraschino cherries. Maraschino is used predominantly for confectionery, quality desserts, and pastries. You could use a cherry liqueur instead.

Joël Garault got the idea of making lemon verbena ice cream one day when his mother-in-law gave him a lemon

verbena plant as a present. Our chef wanted to find a culinary use for this plant from the verbena family, primarily known for its medicinal properties. The leaves and flowers of perfumed verbena are used to make a herb tea that prevents liver and kidney problems. If you're lucky enough to have lemon verbena growing in your garden, garnish the ice cream with verbena flowers rather than mint leaves, depending on the time of year. You can also finely chop a couple of the flowers and cook them with the berries.

The dessert gets texture from the toasted pine nuts. They are rich in carbohydrates and lipids and are therefore a good source of energy. Their spicy, resinous flavor is reminiscent of almonds. You could also use dry cookies to add crunch to the dish.

To make the lemon verbena ice cream, beat together the egg yolks and sugar until frothy. Bring the milk to the boil, and add the lemon verbena and egg mixture. Bring the custard to the boil, stirring all the time, and stir in the cream. Leave the custard to infuse for 4 hours.

Strain the custard and transfer it to an ice cream maker. To make the sugar syrup, bring 2 cups/500 ml water to the boil with the sugar and vanilla bean, then leave it to cool. Remove the vanilla bean and put to one side.

Dry roast the pine nuts in a hot skillet. As soon as they have browned, crush them with one strawberry.

Lemon Verbena Ice Cream

To make the red berry compôte, wash and hull the raspberries, strawberries, blackberries, and redcurrants. Melt the honey and butter in a saucepan and cook until a caramel forms.

Cut the strawberries in half, then toss them in the caramel with the other fruit.

Deglaze the fruit with the maraschino and sugar syrup, then heat the fruit on low heat for 5 minutes. To serve, place a scoop of the ice cream on a bed of crushed pine nuts, and garnish it with a sprig of mint. Spoon the red berry compôte onto the plate around the ice cream.

Baked Apples with

Preparation time: 20 minutes
Raisin soaking
  time: 30 minutes
Cooking time: 30 minutes
Difficulty: ★

Serves 4

4	Golden Delicious apples
scant ¼ cup/ 50 g	raisins
3½ tbsp/50 ml	Calvados (or apple brandy)
½ stick/55 g	butter

generous ⅔ cup/ 150 g	superfine sugar
¼ cup/50 g	pine nuts
generous ¾ cup/ 200 ml	milk
1	vanilla bean
3½ tbsp/50 ml	light cream
1 generous cup/ 50 g	yellow cornmeal
4 scoops	vanilla ice cream

For the sweetened whipped cream:

generous ¾ cup/ 200 ml	heavy cream
⅛ cup/15 g	confectioner's sugar

Baked apples with vanilla polenta is an elegant dessert for gourmets. Our chef's creation combines ingredients from the Mediterranean coast and the Normandy hills.

There's no doubt that apples are found almost everywhere throughout the world, and they are sold all year round. Our chef has chosen the variety Golden Delicious for this dessert. It is golden yellow, and has a smooth skin, and juicy, crisp, yellow flesh. Lovers of this variety particularly like the delicate, sweet flavor with a hint of acidity.

Many apple recipes are prepared with Calvados. As far as Daniel Ettlinger is concerned, apple brandy from Normandy is an integral part of his recipe. The raisins are soaked in the Calvados for an exceptional flavor.

In fact it's the raisins that form the link between the Mediterranean coast and the north of France. Our chef

prefers using them to golden raisins, because small, dark, seedless raisins have a characteristic taste.

The cornmeal harks back to Provençal roots. Although this cornmeal, mainly used in hearty dishes, originally came from northern Italy, it is very common in dishes from the Nice area. You could also make this dessert using wheatmeal. The spicy, resinous flavor of pine nuts is similar to that of almonds, which can be used instead.

You need sweetened whipped cream, also known as Chantilly cream, for this recipe. Using a hand blender or balloon whisk, beat the cream until very stiff, then fold in the confectioner's sugar just before serving.

Peel the apples. Cut them in half and remove the cores. Soak the raisins in the Calvados for 30 minutes.

Grease a deep baking dish with butter and sprinkle over a little sugar. Place the apples in the dish, core side up.

Sprinkle 3 heaped tbsp/50 g sugar over the apples and bake them in the oven for 30 minutes at 470 °F/250 °C. Toast the pine nuts in a saucepan over low heat with 2 tbsp sugar. Stir until the pine nuts have browned.

Vanilla Polenta

To make the cornmeal, put the milk, vanilla bean, cream, and remaining sugar in a saucepan and bring to the boil. Beat in the cornmeal, and cook for 20 minutes on low heat, stirring continuously.

Drain the raisins. Deglaze the baked apples with the Calvados and put them to one side. Beat the cream.

Chop the raisins and add to the cornmeal. Use a ring mold to make a circle of cornmeal on a plate. Place half an apple on top, core side down. Add a spoon of sweetened whipped cream. Garnish with toasted pine nuts and raisins. Serve with ice cream and the Calvados sauce.

Fennel Sorbet with

Preparation time: 1 hour 30 minutes
Resting time for
    the tuile batter: 1 hour
Time for syrup
    to infuse: 1 hour
Cooking time: 25 minutes
Difficulty: ★

Serves 4

For the syrup:
5 tsp/25 g   glucose
1 tsp   honey
1 cup + 1 tbsp/
240 g   superfine sugar
¾ cup/125 g   fennel seeds

For the tuiles:
scant ¼ stick/25 g   butter
scant 2 tbsp/25 g   superfine sugar

1 tbsp/25 g   raw cane sugar
scant ¼ cup/
25 g   all-purpose flour
⅓ cup + 1½ tbsp/
100 ml   orange juice
2 tsp/10 g   fennel seeds
For the saffron custard:
1 cup/250 ml   milk
3   egg yolks
3 heaped tbsp/
50 g   superfine sugar
1 pinch   saffron
For the garnish:
                saffron threads
                fresh fennel leaves

Fennel sorbet with saffron custard is chef Christian Étienne's own creation. One day he decided to create a dessert using fennel, and then looked around for a sauce that would provide a suitable accompaniment. His imagination immediately led this connoisseur of *haute cuisine* to a custard with saffron, and a dessert with a truly amazing taste was born.

Fennel is usually used with fish in France. This bulbous vegetable with its tightly packed leaves is generally eaten as a vegetable, and as such should be firm, with an unblemished white color.

Crush the fennel seeds with a rolling pin. You could also used chopped filberts or almonds for the *tuiles*. To save time, our chef prepares the syrup a day in advance. If you would like to emphasize the delicate aniseed flavor of fennel further, you could add a dash of lemon juice before

transferring the syrup to the ice cream maker. And if you don't like the rather bitter flavor of saffron, our chef suggests you try a vanilla custard.

Tuiles are easier to make if the butter is at room temperature. If you don't have any baking parchment or silicon-coated baking paper, you could always bake them direct on a well-greased and floured baking sheet.

The *tuiles* get their characteristic shape from being rolled around a rolling pin while still warm, but take care, because they are very brittle and break easily!

Our chef arranges the *tuiles* on scoops of sorbet sitting on a pool of saffron custard.

Make the syrup using 1 cup/250 ml water, the glucose, and honey. Add the sugar and bring to the boil.

Add the fennel seeds and 1 cup/250 ml water. Leave the syrup to infuse for 1 hour or more.

Saffron custard: Boil the milk. Beat the egg yolks and sugar until frothy, then stir in the hot milk. Pour the custard back into the saucepan and gently cook until it thickens. As soon as it comes to the boil, take the pan off the burner. Add the saffron into the custard, beating well.

Saffron Custard

Strain the syrup through a sieve and adjust to taste. Pour the syrup into an ice cream maker to make a sorbet. Scoop out balls of sorbet, and store these in the freezer.

In a bowl beat together the softened butter and sugar. Add the raw cane sugar, and then the flour and orange juice, stirring all the time. Beat the batter until smooth, then leave it to rest for 1 hour.

Spread circles of batter on the baking parchment and sprinkle over crushed fennel seeds. Bake for 5 minutes at 350 °F/180 °C. Curve the tuiles with a rolling pin. Pour some custard onto a plate, and place three scoops of sorbet on top. Garnish with tuiles, saffron, and fennel.

Pine Nut Tart with

Preparation time: 25 minutes
Resting time: 1 hour
Cooking time: 20 minutes
Difficulty: ★

Serves 4

1 scant stick/100 g	butter
scant ½ cup/100 g	sugar
2 level tbsp/60 g	lavender honey
1¾ cups/400 g	pine nuts
¾ cup/175 ml	light cream

For the plain pastry:

generous ½ cup/ 125 g	superfine sugar
scant 1⅛ sticks/ 125 g	butter
1 pinch	salt
2 cups/250 g	all-purpose flour
1	egg

In Provence, a day when this pine nut tart with lavender honey is on the menu is no ordinary day ... It's a special day for children who love to eat this delicious dessert when they come home from school. This typical, southern French dessert is best served after a light main course.

Pine nuts are rich in carbohydrates and lipids and are therefore a good source of energy. Their spicy, resinous flavor is reminiscent of almonds, which can be used instead. These little, elongated nuts come from the cones of the stone pine, a tree from the Abietacea family, which grows in the Mediterranean area. They are surrounded by a hard casing and lie between the pine cone's scales.

Here's a tip from Christian Étienne to ensure perfect plain pastry every time: Bake the pastry case for ten minutes, covering it with baking parchment weighted with dried peas, lentils, or navy beans, so that the pastry doesn't rise.

Then add the caramelized pine nut filling, and bake the tart for another 15 minutes.

In ancient times, honey was regarded as the food of the gods. It symbolized wealth and good fortune, being a food and a sacrificial offering. This pine nut tart is a wonderful way to make the most of its flavor. Honey is produced by bees from the nectar in flowers, and is stored in the honeycomb cells. Honey provides far more energy than sugar. Lavender honey comes from Provence, where the whole countryside is drenched in the scent of these lilac-colored flowers. You could use another type of honey if you prefer.

Usually, in France, just a cup of tea or a hot chocolate is served with this dessert.

Pastry: Mix the sugar and butter by hand. Sift the flour and salt onto a work surface. Put the egg and also the butter mixture in the middle. Knead the ingredients together with the fingertips to form dough. Shape it into a ball, dredge it in flour, and leave to rest for 1 hour.

Grease the tart pan. Roll out the pastry and line a springform pan with it. Place the pan on a baking sheet.

Melt the butter in a copper saucepan. Add the sugar and honey, and cook until a pale caramel forms.

Lavender Honey

Add the pine nuts. Stir them well until they are caramelized.

Add the cream to the pan and stir very well.

Pour the pine nut mixture into the pastry case and bake it for 15 minutes at 350 °F/180 °C. Remove the tart from the springform pan while it is still warm.

Melon Tartlet

Preparation time:	*45 minutes*
Resting time:	*1 hour*
Cooking time:	*20 minutes*
Difficulty:	★★

Serves 4

2	honeydew melons
3 tbsp	grenadine syrup
scant	
⅛ stick/10 g	butter
⅓ cup + 1½ tbsp/	
100 ml	Muscatel wine

For the plain pastry:

scant	
½ cup/50 g	ground almonds
2 generous	
cups/250 ml	all-purpose flour
⅓ cup/75 g	superfine sugar
1¾ sticks/190 g	diced butter
	zest of 1 unwaxed
	lemon
3	eggs
3 tsp	dark rum
1 pinch	salt

For the confectioner's custard with Muscatel:

2 cups/500 ml	full fat milk
1	vanilla bean
6	eggs
½ cup + 1 tbsp/	
125 g	superfine sugar
4 tsp/20 g	cornstarch
generous ⅜ cup/	
50 g	all-purpose flour
2 envelopes	gelatin
3½ tbsp/50 ml	Muscatel wine
½ cup/120 ml	cream

For the sugar syrup:

⅔ cup/150 g	superfine sugar

For the garnish:

⅛ cup/15 g	confectioner's sugar
few sprigs	fresh mint

This refreshing dessert is the perfect way to round off a summer meal, as melon, with which the delicate pastry is filled, is at its best in summer. The dessert's name is a homage to Bel Air, one of the suburbs of the town of Salon-de-Provence.

A good melon must feel heavy, but give a little if you press with your thumb at the stalk end. The stalk should be easy to remove and the melon should be perfumed. If the melon smell is very strong, then the fruit is probably overripe. Skin colors vary from light green, through striped dark green and bright yellow, to reddish-green, with a smooth or rough skin. Melons will keep for 5–6 days in a cool, well-ventilated place. It's best not to store them in the refrigerator, because their perfume can transfer to other foods. If stored at room temperature, melons continue to ripen a little.

For this recipe we recommend a smooth-skinned honeydew melon, with its sweet, juicy, firm flesh. Use a melon baller to get even-sized balls. Instead of making a stock syrup yourself, you can always use sugar cane or sugar beet syrup to cook the melon balls.

Don't knead the pastry for too long, otherwise it will become tough. To rest it, shape it into a long roll, about the size of a rolling pin. Then it's easy to roll out slices of pastry ready for cutting. You can always use ready-made rich plain pastry, from the supermarket. You will need a 14 ounce/400 gram package.

To make the plain pastry, combine the ground almonds, flour, sugar, grated zest of ½ lemon, and a pinch of salt. Add the diced, softened butter, 2 egg yolks, 1 egg, and the rum.

Cut the roll of pastry into 1 in/3 cm-thick slices. Roll out each slice of pastry and cut out circles 3 in/8 cm in diameter. Bake the pastry circles in the oven for 10 minutes at 400 °F/200 °C. Soften the gelatin in water.

Confectioner's custard: Boil the milk with the vanilla bean. Beat together 4 egg yolks, 2 eggs, the sugar, and the cornstarch. Add the flour in a steady trickle, beating all the time. Stir in half the milk. Pour the custard into the milk in the pan. Simmer for 5 minutes, stirring all the time.

"Bel Air"

Take the pan off the heat. Drain the gelatin and beat it into the custard. Add the Muscatel wine, mix well, then leave the custard to cool. Beat the cream until stiff, fold it carefully into the custard, then put it aside.

In a saucepan combine 1 cup/250 ml water and 3 heaped tbsp/150 g sugar. Boil the solution for 2–3 minutes until a colorless syrup forms. Put aside. Scoop out 32 melon balls. Make a sauce from the melon flesh by puréeing it with the grenadine syrup and 2 tbsp sugar syrup.

Sweat the melon balls in the butter. Add 7 tbsp sugar syrup and the Muscatel wine. Drain. Spread 2 pastry rounds with confectioner's custard, then sandwich the melon balls between them. Dust with sifted confectioner's sugar. Garnish with mint sprigs and the melon sauce.

Fiadone

Preparation time: 15 minutes
Cooking time: 25 minutes
Difficulty: ★

Serves 4

1 lb/500 g	*brocciu* (Corsican soft cheese)
1	lemon
1⅓ cups/300 g	superfine sugar
6	eggs
2 tsp/10 ml	eau-de-vie
1 tbsp/10 g	butter

A favorite cake on Corsica, *fiadone* has an ancient history. Made of *brocciu* and eggs, it is often made for the festivities associated with religious ceremonies such as baptism, a young person's first communion, and marriage. Despite the small number of ingredients, this typically Corsican specialty is truly delicious.

Fiadone is very easy to make. The main thing to remember is that the mixture should fill the baking pan to a depth of 1⅝ inches/4 cm. Perhaps the most famous of Corsican cheeses, *brocciu* has been awarded a coveted *appellation d'origine contrôlée*, guaranteeing its authenticity and quality. Made since time immemorial from the whey milk of ewes or goats, whole milk, and salt, it has a very mild flavor. An indispensable ingredient in many local dishes, it is a proud reminder of the island's pastoral traditions.

A reference to the farming of animals on Corsica is found as early as the 2nd century BC in the *Rise of the Roman Re-public* by the Greek historian Polybius: "The impression that all the animals on the island are wild arises from the following cause. The island is thickly wooded and the countryside so rocky and precipitous that it is impossible for the shepherds to follow their flocks and herds about as they graze. So whenever they wish to collect them they take up position in some convenient place; from there they summon them by horn, and all the animals respond without fail to the instrument which they recognize." (Book XII, p. 430 in the translation by Ian Scott-Kilvert, Penguin Classics, 1979.)

The *fiadone* is flavored with a little local eau-de-vie (clear fruit brandy) and grated lemon peel. Known as a good source of vitamin C, lemons are grown in large numbers on the island. Choose unwaxed lemons if possible; otherwise, scrub the peel thoroughly in hot water. Firm, unblemished lemons will keep in the salad compartment of the refrigerator for at least two weeks.

Place the brocciu *in a bowl and mash it with a whisk or fork.*

Wash the lemon thoroughly, then grate the peel.

Pour the sugar into the bowl of brocciu. *Add the eggs. Mix together until smooth and evenly textured.*

Add the lemon peel, then the eau-de-vie. Mix thoroughly.

Using a brush, lightly grease the baking pan with softened butter.

Pour the brocciu mixture into the pan. Cook in a medium oven (350 °F/180 °C) for about 25 minutes. When baked, turn the cake out of the pan and serve warm or cold.

Oreillettes Filled with

Preparation time: 1 hour
Cooking time: 15 minutes
Refrigeration time for dough: 1 hour
Proving time: 40 minutes
Difficulty: ★

Serves 4

⅞ cup/100 g   flour
4 cups/1 liter   olive oil for frying
⅖ cup/100 g   superfine sugar

For the dough:
4⅖ cups/500 g   flour
2 envelopes/10 g   dried yeast

3   eggs
1 stick/100 g   shortening
7 oz/200 g   condensed milk
   grated peel of
     ½ lemon
2 tbsp/30 ml   pastis
   salt

For the filling:
5 oz/150 g   brocciu (Corsican
     cheese)
   grated zest of
     ½ orange
⅜ cup/50 g   confectioners' sugar
2 tbsp/30 ml   grape eau-de-vie
1   egg

Oreillettes (meaning "little ears") are synonymous on Corsica with special occasions. They are made for marriages, baptisms, and first communions. Fried and sugared, they are very popular, and a big pile is always placed on the table for family and friends. They can be soft or crispy, according to taste.

The dough for *oreillettes* is simple to prepare, and can be made the day before it is needed. Made from flour, yeast, lemon, salt, and eggs, it also includes a little pastis. This aniseed and herb flavored aperitif originates from Marseilles in south-eastern France, and is drunk diluted with water, when its gold color turns a pale, opaque eau-de-nil.

Traditionally, these Corsican doughnuts were served without filling. Vincent Tabarani, who learned the recipe from his mother, suggests adding a sweetened cheese filling made with *brocciu*, to make them even more special.

Brocciu is a traditional Corsican cheese made by shepherds since ancient times. To prepare it, the whey of ewe's or goat's milk is heated over a wood fire in a large metal pot. The mixture is cooled, and the whole milk and salt are added. The shepherds then skim off the solidifying cheese that forms on the surface of the milk, and pack it into small round baskets woven from reeds.

The resulting cheese is very fresh and very mild. It is used in cooking for both sweet and savory dishes. Ricotta, very similar in taste, can be used in its place.

The cheese filling is flavored with *aquavita*, an eau-de-vie (clear brandy) made from grapes. This is one of many liqueurs of this type made on Corsica, from a variety of different fruits including blueberries, grapes, oranges, and arbutus berries. A small glass of *aquavita* is offered to guests throughout the island, as a mark of hospitality.

For the dough, heap the flour and yeast on a work surface. Make a well in the center. Into this put the egg yolks, melted shortening, condensed milk, grated lemon peel, stiffly beaten egg whites, pastis, and salt. Incorporate the ingredients and knead to make dough. Refrigerate for 1 hour.

For the filling, put the brocciu into a bowl with the orange zests, confectioners' sugar, and eau-de-vie. Mash these together, then add the egg, mixing thoroughly with a whisk.

Cut the ball of dough into two pieces. Flour the work surface and roll out the dough balls to a thickness of ⅛ inch/2 mm.

Aquavita-Flavored Brocciu

Cut out circles of dough using a 4½ inch/10–12 cm cutter.

Place a little filling on each circle of dough. Slightly dampen the edges of the dough with a brush dipped in water.

Fold the dough circles to make semicircular parcels. Place these on a cloth for about 40 minutes to prove, then fry them in hot olive oil and drain on paper towels. Roll them in sugar and serve.

Cantucci

Preparation time: 30 minutes
Cooking time: 40 minutes
Difficulty: ★

Serves 4–6

⅞ stick/100 g	butter
1¾ cups/ 200 g	confectioner's sugar
1 cup/200 g	sugar
1 tbsp	grated lemon peel
3	eggs

7 tbsp	blossom honey
3 cups/500 g	strong bread flour
1½ cups/ 200 g	almonds
½ tbsp/8 g	yeast
	salt

These *cantucci* are typical of the town of Prato, not far from Florence. The Italians love eating them as the perfect ending to a meal—especially if they are served with a glass of *vin santo*.

Every baker in Tuscany sells *cantucci*, which are also known as *biscotti di Prato*. Nowadays, however, they are also available throughout Italy, and even abroad. Some people like eating *cantucci* at breakfast, while others prefer them in the afternoon with a cup of hot chocolate.

The basic dough for the *cantucci* is rolled out into small baguettes, baked, and then cut into slices diagonally. These are then dried again in the oven, hence the name *biscotti*, which means "cooked twice." Since they are dried so thoroughly in the oven, they keep for a long time; earlier, when methods of preserving food were still very limited, this was especially important.

Although *cantucci* have a long tradition, they have not changed fundamentally in terms of their shape or ingredients. The almonds can be blanched and roasted or just chopped. Many fans of *cantucci* also like a subtle flavor of aniseed. Paolo Luni recommends making the dough using half ordinary sugar and half confectioner's sugar, to make the *cantucci* really crunchy.

Honey is also added to the dough as an extra refinement. In Italy, about 85,000 beekeepers offer many different kinds of honey—choose between acacia, citrus, chestnut, heather, eucalyptus, thyme, lime, and many others.

Using a balloon whisk, beat the butter in a bowl until it is light and foamy. Then add the sugar mixed with the grated lemon peel.

Break the eggs and add to the butter mixture. Mix thoroughly.

Add the honey, the flour, almonds and yeast, and a pinch of salt.

Mix thoroughly until all the flour has been incorporated and you have made a smooth dough.

Form the dough into several long, thin rolls. Place on a baking sheet and bake for 10 minutes at 430° F/220° C.

Lay the baked rolls on a chopping board. Using a knife, cut diagonally into slices about ½ in/1 cm thick. Return to the oven and dry for about 30 minutes at 265° F/130° C.

Almond

Preparation time: 20 minutes
Cooking time: 15 minutes
Difficulty: ★★

Serves 4

1 tbsp	olive oil
3½ cups/ 500 g	blanched almonds
1 cup/220 g	sugar
1	lemon

For the garnish:
bay leaves

Bridal couples in Abruzzi were traditionally served almond cracknel in the shape of a house—symbolizing the future home of the newlyweds—as the sweetmeat was supposed to bring them good luck. With the passage of time, the almond confection became known all over the Italian peninsula. In the south it is prepared mostly on Christmas Eve, but it is found at funfairs everywhere: For children, a ride on a roundabout is incomplete without it.

Back in ancient times, the Romans used to produce sweetmeats by coating almonds in honey. The oval nuts, which came from Asia, were called "Greek nuts." Many Eastern sweetmeats are made with almonds.

For this recipe you should remove the brown skin from the almonds, by blanching them for a minute in boiling water. Once they have cooled, it is easy to remove the skins by pressing between the thumb and forefinger.

To make cracknel successfully, it is essential to stir the almond and sugar mixture vigorously all the time it is on the stove, preferably with a wooden spatula. It is also advisable to cut the cracknel on a marble slab, or at least on a very smooth surface that will not be damaged by the knife. Both the work surface and the blade of the knife should be oiled to make it easier to cut the cracknel. The lemon is responsible for the lovely caramel color.

In Abruzzi, almond cracknel is always garnished with bay leaves. Natives of Abruzzi, who are great lovers of tradition, revere the bay tree: As an ancient symbol of imperial power, it is supposed to bring wealth to the household.

Using a cloth, wipe a little olive oil over the work surface and the blade of a large sharp knife.

Halve the blanched almonds and place in a pan with the sugar.

Heat the pan, stirring the contents vigorously with a wooden spatula so that the almonds and sugar bind together well. When the almonds are browned, remove the pan from the heat.

Cracknel

Carefully transfer the almond mixture to the oiled work surface.

Squeeze the lemon over the top. Using the oiled blade of the knife, form the mixture into a rectangular shape.

Cut the cracknel into even-sized pieces. Arrange on a plate and garnish with the bay leaves.

Venetian

Preparation time: 20 minutes
Soaking time: 1 hour
Cooking time: 10 minutes
Difficulty: ★

Serves 4

⅓ cup/50 g	golden raisins
4 tbsp	grappa
1¼ cups/300 ml	milk
½ stick/60 g	butter
1 pinch	salt

1½ cups/240 g	strong bread flour
½	unwaxed lemon
3	eggs
2	egg whites
4 tsp/20 g	pine nuts
	vegetable oil for deep frying
1 scant cup/100 g	confectioner's sugar

The Venetians have always had a reputation for being particularly fond of celebrations and the sweetmeats served on such occasions. Carnival time in Venice used to last several months and was always the excuse for feasts. Men and women wearing the *bauta*, a folk costume consisting of a three-cornered hat, black veil, and white face mask, bought a wide variety of sweetmeats, for example fritters made from choux pastry, called *fritelle* or *fritole*, or other fried tidbits. Now these delicacies are available all year round.

In the 18th century, fritter sellers were an integral part of the landscape of the city of Venice. In his play *Il Campiello*, the Venetian playwright Carlo Goldoni, who reformed the Italian theater, actually gave the main role to a woman selling fritters.

A classic choux pastry, enhanced with raisins and pine kernels and fried in olive oil, forms the basis for this recipe.

It does not contain any sugar, since this could caramelize and the fritters would then be too dark in color. As soon as the butter, flour, and milk mixture comes away from the bottom of the saucepan, remove the pan from the heat. Transfer the dough to a work surface and leave it to cool. The eggs must not be beaten into the mixture while it is hot, because they would curdle and ruin the dough. As an added refinement, pour in a little grappa or aniseed liqueur.

In order to determine whether the oil has reached the right temperature, sprinkle in a little flour or a few drops of water. If bubbles rise to the surface, the temperature is perfect. Use your finger to push the dough off the spoon into the oil. It will soon be transformed into small, golden-yellow balls. Drain them on paper towels, coat in sugar, and eat cold.

Immerse the raisins in the grappa. Mix the milk and butter with a pinch of salt in a saucepan. Bring to the boil.

As soon as the milk boils, add the flour and the grated lemon peel. Stir until the dough comes away from the bottom of the saucepan. Place the dough on a heatproof work surface and leave to cool.

Transfer the dough to a bowl. Add the 3 eggs and the egg whites. Stir vigorously to bind the eggs fully into the dough.

Fritters

Add the soaked raisins and the pine nuts. Give the mixture a final stir.

Heat the oil in a skillet. Using a soup spoon, place small portions of dough in the oil. As soon as the fritters begin to rise, turn them so they become golden yellow all over.

Drain the fritters on paper towels. Dust with confectioner's sugar and serve cold.

Mirabelle

Preparation time: 40 minutes
Cooking time: 30 minutes
Difficulty: ★★

Serves 4

1½ lb/600 g	potatoes
10 oz/250 g	flour
1	egg
	salt
1¾ sticks/200 g	butter

2 cups/100 g	fresh breadcrumbs
2 pinches	ground cinnamon
3 tbsp	confectioner's sugar
10	red mirabelle plums
	salt

The popularity of mirabelle gnocchi as a dessert extends from Trentino to Friuli, and even to Slovenia. All these regions have belonged at some time in their history to the Austro-Hungarian Empire, and Bohemian chefs often cooked for the nobility when they were staying in their castles in Trieste. These chefs brought with them their own culinary specialties, which as a result became well known in Italy too.

Gnocchi normally consist of potatoes and wheat flour or maize flour, or a mixture of flour and ricotta cheese. Floury varieties of potato, such as bintje, are particularly suitable for making gnocchi, which are now famous far beyond Italy's borders. They are usually cooked briefly in salted water and then served with butter, cheese, or a tomato sauce. A fruit filling is therefore rather exotic.

Excellent mirabelles grow in the countryside around Trieste, and are eaten raw or made into schnapps. The variety called *Violine* is very popular for cooking, while the yellow and orange-colored fruit are eaten raw. The gnocchi will keep their shape better if you use fresh fruit, as frozen fruit produces too much juice. Damsons, dried apricots, or cherries can be used instead of mirabelles in this recipe.

The hot gnocchi are sprinkled with sugar and cinnamon and a sauce, made from breadcrumbs and melted butter, is then poured over them. The hot butter melts the sugar, so that the gnocchi look as though they have been caramelized. In Friuli, hot mirabelle gnocchi are often served with a goulash, but are also eaten as a dessert.

Boil the unpeeled potatoes for 20 minutes. Leave to cool and remove the skins. Cut into large cubes and press firmly through a sieve to form a purée.

Spoon a third of the flour onto a work surface. Transfer the potato purée onto the floured surface and make a hollow in the middle. Break an egg into the hollow and sprinkle a little salt on top. Knead with the hands, gradually working in the flour until you have a smooth dough.

Melt ⅞ stick/100 g butter in a pan, sprinkle in 1½ cups/80 g breadcrumbs, and mix with a wooden spatula. Stir in a pinch of cinnamon and 2 tsp confectioner's sugar.

Gnocchi

Cut open the mirabelles and remove the pits. Using a spoon, fill the fruit with the breadcrumb mixture and squeeze the plums so they close.

Divide the dough into portions the size of an egg and form into circles with your hands. Place a mirabelle in the middle of each circle and enclose it in the dough. Roll the dough into a ball.

Cook the gnocchi for 5 minutes in boiling water, then remove with a slotted spoon. Brown the remaining breadcrumbs in ⅞ stick/100 g butter in a skillet. Arrange the gnocchi on plates, dust with confectioner's sugar and cinnamon, and top with the hot breadcrumbs.

Tiramisù

Preparation time: 45 minutes
Difficulty: ★★

Serves 4

2	eggs
	salt
8 tsp/40 g	sugar
½ tsp	vanilla essence
10 oz/250 g	mascarpone

2 shots	double espresso
2 tbsp	brandy
4	ladyfingers
2 tsp/10 g	cocoa powder

For the garnish:

bitter chocolate

Tiramisù is the best-known Italian dessert of all. A veritable cult has grown up around it on the Italian peninsula, and every region, from north to south, claims to have invented this famous dish, whose name literally means "pull me up."

For the natives of Piedmont, there is no doubt: The ladyfinger cookies, called *savoiardi*, prove that the dessert was invented in their part of the country. This is disputed in Lombardy, where the natives remind everyone that mascarpone is a specialty of their region. The Romans, meanwhile, regard the dish as typical of their city. And our chef? She proudly maintains that *tiramisù* originated in the Veneto region, in the city of Vicenza.

This nutritious classic of Italian cookery is prepared in different ways in different regions. In many families, the cream is not sprinkled with cocoa powder, but is covered with fruit: for instance, peaches, bananas, or pineapple. Other variants feature different kinds of alcohol: Although in most cases Sicilian Marsala is the preferred choice for soaking the cookies, brandy, cognac, and rum are the popular alternatives.

By contrast, *tiramisù* without mascarpone is unthinkable. This delicate cream cheese is made from the cream of cow's milk, and sometimes also from buffalo milk. The milk is heated to 75–90 degrees Fahrenheit/25–32 degrees Celsius and lemon juice or white wine vinegar is added to accelerate the coagulation process. It has a fat content of 50 percent.

The espresso gives the *tiramisù* a slightly bitter tang. Espresso has been drunk in Italy since the 16th century and is sold as *caffè* on virtually every street corner.

Put 2 egg whites in a bowl with a pinch of salt. Set the yolks aside in another bowl. Beat the egg whites until frothy with a balloon whisk.

Beat the egg yolks thoroughly with the sugar and vanilla.

Fold the mascarpone into the egg yolk mixture and combine well.

Gently fold in the beaten egg whites. Spoon some of the mascarpone cream into each of 4 glasses.

Mix the espresso and brandy together in a shallow bowl. Briefly dip the ladyfingers in the coffee and brandy, break them, and divide between the glasses.

Top up the glasses with the mascarpone cream. Sprinkle with cocoa powder and garnish with chocolate.

Panna

Preparation time:	20 minutes
Cooling time:	5 hours
Cooking time:	20 minutes
Difficulty:	★

Serves 4

6 leaves	gelatin
2 cups/500 ml	milk
6 oz/150 g	sugar
1 cup/250 ml	heavy cream

For the coffee sauce:

½ cup/125 g	sugar
scant ½ cup/ 100 ml	espresso
1 scant cup/ 200 ml	light cream

For the chocolate sauce:

⅜ stick/40 g	butter
10 oz/250 g	dark chocolate
1 scant cup/ 200 ml	light cream

For the garnish:

mint leaves

The world-famous dessert *panna cotta* comes from the Aosta valley and is extremely popular in the northern regions of Italy. It is easy to prepare, but its success depends heavily on the quality of the ingredients used.

It is best to use Italian cream, as this has a very high fat content and is the crucial ingredient in this dish. Until the end of the 19th century, this was prepared by cooling milk for 24 hours and then skimming off the cream. Today it is produced in dairies with the aid of milk centrifuges. If you cannot obtain Italian cream, replace the milk with cream and use an extra leaf of gelatin.

Gelatin is also important for a good *panna cotta*. This colorless, odorless substance is extracted from the bones and cartilage of animals and certain algae, and can be bought in the form of powder or transparent leaves. The leaves must first be soaked in lukewarm water and then dissolved in hot liquid.

Sergio Pais serves *panna cotta* with coffee and chocolate sauce, but you can also serve it with a sauce made from a variety of fruits.

In the Orient, coffee has been known since the Middle Ages, but it was not introduced into Italy until the 15th century. The merchants of northern Italy had huge consignments of coffee brought to Trieste. The popularity of this new drink soon escalated, to a point at which the city fathers decided to restrict the number of establishments where the beverage could be served. In Italy today practically no other drink is as ubiquitous as espresso. It has a strong, slightly bitter flavor and is always topped by a delicate, light-brown layer of foam.

Place the gelatin leaves in a small bowl with lukewarm water. Bring the milk and sugar to the boil in a saucepan.

Squeeze the gelatin leaves, stir into the milk with a balloon whisk, and cook for about 3 minutes.

Pour in the cream. Bring to the boil and cook for 1 minute, stirring constantly. Pour the mixture into 4 molds and chill for 5 hours.

Cotta

For the chocolate sauce, melt the butter and chocolate in a bain-marie or double boiler, stirring constantly. Pour in the cream. Stir and set aside.

For the coffee sauce, dissolve the sugar in the espresso in a saucepan and cook for 4 minutes.

Stir the cream into the coffee sauce. Turn the panna cotta out of the molds and place each one in the middle of a plate. Pour the chocolate sauce and coffee sauce around the panna cotta and garnish with mint leaves.

Frozen Zabaglione

Preparation time: 40 minutes
Freezing time: 12 hours
Cooking time: 1 minute
Difficulty: ★★

Serves 4

⅔ cup/150 g	sugar
6	egg yolks
3 scant cups/ 700 ml	almond milk
3¼ cups/ 800 ml	Marsala

1 cup/250 ml	cream
1 scant cup/ 100 g	crushed almonds
	knob of butter

For the garnish:

	strawberries
	chocolate curls
	almonds
	mint leaves

Frozen *zabaglione* with Marsala is a typically Italian delicacy. It is an extremely sophisticated ice cream that has become famous all over the world. People have been enjoying it since the 16th century and it used to be served to bridal couples for breakfast after their wedding night, in order to revive them!

Zabaglione is highly nutritious and is normally eaten lukewarm. The natives of Turin claim to have invented this foaming dish; in any event, they are certainly responsible for the addition of Marsala. In Piedmont, the origins of *zabaglione* are disputed. Many people maintain it was invented by the Renaissance chef Bartolomeo Scappi, while others claim it was actually the brainchild of St. Pasquale Bayon, who was chosen by the inhabitants of Turin in 1722 as the patron saint of chefs. Supporters of this theory argue that his name in the Piedmont dialect, pronounced "sanba-jun," then became *zabagliun*.

Zabaglione is easy to prepare, but true success depends on the Marsala. This Sicilian wine became widespread thanks to the Englishman John Woodhouse, who was shipwrecked off Marsala on the Sicilian coast in 1770. When he tasted the local wine after his rescue, he decided to start making it to compete with Spanish sherry and Madeira. Each year, Admiral Nelson ordered 500 barrels for the English fleet in the Mediterranean and, with their victory over the French and Spanish at Trafalgar, Woodhouse rebranded the wine as "Marsala Victory Wine"—thus significantly contributing to its success.

You can garnish the frozen *zabaglione* with almonds or hazelnuts. The strawberries can be substituted with other fruit, according to the season.

Put the sugar and egg yolks in a dish suitable for a bain-marie or double boiler and heat a saucepan of water.

Stir the egg yolks and sugar with a wooden spatula until foaming.

Add the almond milk, stirring constantly.

with Marsala

Place the bowl containing the egg mixture over the saucepan of boiling water. Stir in the Marsala. Leave for 1 minute and continue stirring gently, then remove from the saucepan.

Pour the cream into a bowl and beat vigorously with a balloon whisk.

Add the cream to the egg mixture. Gradually add the crushed almonds. Pour the mixture into a buttered mold and place in the freezer for 12 hours. Slice the zabaglione and decorate with the strawberries, chocolate curls, almonds, and mint leaves.

Carrot

Preparation time: 25 minutes
Cooking time: 30 minutes
Difficulty: ★

Serves 4–6

8 oz/200 g	carrots
2¼ sticks/ 270 g	butter
1⅛ cup/ 250 g	sugar
3	eggs
2 tsp/10 g	dried yeast
1¾ cups/ 300 g	strong bread flour

2 tbsp	Strega (or another herb liqueur)
1¾ cups/ 200 g	ground almonds
½	unwaxed lemon
1 tsp/5 g	salt
1¾ cup/ 250 g	whole, blanched almonds

This carrot cake is typical of South Tyrol. In the mountainous region near the Austrian border, which during the course of history has changed ownership with successive invasions and has belonged first to one country, then another, eating habits have remained staunchly resistant to change. Skiers relaxing on the slopes of the Dolomites love to restore their energy with these rich cakes and pastries, which are full of butter and almonds.

It may seem unusual to bake a cake using carrot, but its flavor is not dominant, it simply adds decorative touches of orange to the mixture. You can either grate the carrot by hand or shred it coarsely in a blender.

The almonds make the cake soft and moist. Paolo Luni claims that Apulia produces the best almonds in Italy. His personal preference is for Bari almonds, because of their mild taste.

Strega liqueur enhances the flavor of the cake and has been a popular drink in Italy for 150 years. It is dark yellow in color and is now made by only one company, based in the province of Benevent. The recipe for this exclusive drink, the manufacture of which involves various wild herbs, is kept a strict secret. *Strega* is drunk as bitters or is used to enhance desserts.

Decorate the cake while it is in the pan, arranging a circle of blanched almonds around the edge. Using your finger, draw a spiral in the cake mixture and arrange more almonds along the line. You can then serve the cake with cream for afternoon tea or coffee.

Cut off the ends of the carrots, peel them, then grate coarsely.

Beat together 2⅛ sticks/250 g soft butter and the sugar in a bowl, using a balloon whisk. Add the eggs.

Mix the yeast with the flour and stir into the butter and sugar mixture.

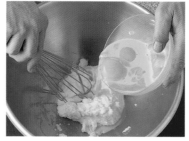

Cake

Mix in the carrot thoroughly.

Stir in the Strega liqueur, ground almonds, the grated lemon peel, and a pinch of salt.

Butter the baking pan and dust with flour. Scrape the cake mixture out of the bowl into the pan and spread evenly over the base. Decorate with blanched almonds. Bake for 30 minutes at 375° F/190° C.

Nonna Narcisa's

Preparation time:	10 minutes
Cooking time:	5 minutes
Difficulty:	★

Serves 4

3	oranges
5 tbsp/75 g	superfine sugar
1 lb/500 g	ricotta
1 tsp/5 g	powdered coffee
1 tbsp/30 g	good honey

For the garnish:

mint leaves
orange peel

As a son of Sardinia, Amerigo Murgia has chosen this very simple but delicious dessert featuring ricotta. He spent his childhood in Osini, a mountainous region of the island, and remembers that pastoral life with great fondness. His father was a shepherd, making his own cheese. His mother, Narcisa, prepared this homemade cheese in various and delicious ways.

Today, this dessert based on ricotta is a favorite with Amerigo Murcia's children. Their grandmother, *Nonna* (Grandma) Narcisa, still makes this specialty at home for them. Easy to prepare, it can be served with banana and honey.

The small town of Macomer is a celebrated center for cheese-making on Sardinia. Situated on the edge of the Campeda plateau below the Marghine chain of mountains, this beautiful town has been famous since 1907 (when its first cheese cooperative was set up) for the excellence and variety of its products. Among the local cheeses produced are ricotta, *pecorino sardo*, and the delicately flavored *dolce di Macomer*.

Made using the whey of cow's, sheep's, or ewe's milk, ricotta is frequently used in cooking, for both sweet and savory dishes. Its slightly acidic taste goes wonderfully well with the oranges used in this recipe. Ricotta, meaning "recooked," is a vital ingredient here, and can be found in most good supermarkets and food stores.

Oranges were brought originally from the Far East, and thrive in the sunny Sardinian climate. They are rich in vitamins A and C. The different varieties vary in sweetness, acidity, and flavor. For this recipe, navel oranges, with their particularly juicy flesh, would be ideal.

This delicious dessert is a tribute not only to *Nonna* Narcisa, but also to all Sardinian grandmothers.

Cut 2 of the oranges in half widthwise.

Squeeze the juice from orange halves and remove the pits.

Carefully wash the peel of the third orange. Pare off the peel and cut into fine strips. Cook these in a little water with 4 tbsp of sugar until they are caramelized. Put to one side for the garnish.

Orange Ricotta

Place the ricotta in a bowl and add 1 tbsp of sugar.

Pour the orange juice over the ricotta and mix well.

Place a metal circle on the plate. Fill it with the ricotta mixture. Lift off the circle. Sprinkle the dessert with powdered coffee. Pour over some honey. Garnish with mint leaves and the caramelized orange peel.

Blancmange with

Preparation time: 40 minutes
Cooking time: 40 minutes
Refrigerating time for
  the blancmange: 6 hours
Difficulty: ★

Serves 4

2	lemons
⅔ cup/75 g	ground almonds
⅓ cup/70 g	superfine sugar
½ cup/45 g	cornstarch

For the lemon sauce:

3	lemons
4½ oz/120 g	lump sugar
3	eggs
⅝ stick/70 g	butter

For the garnish:

sprigs of mint
orange peel
ground cinnamon

The recipe for blancmange is very ancient. Made of almonds, it is particularly popular in the Modica region of Sicily where it is traditionally eaten for breakfast or in the afternoon during the long, hot summer.

The origins of this dish can be traced back to the Middle Ages. On Sicily, it was customary to prepare a nourishing, salted dish of the same name for the sick, and for young mothers. This consisted of almond milk to which ground chicken and spices were added. In the course of time, this *biancomangiare* (meaning literally "white" and "eat") evolved into a dessert.

This delicious recipe is very easy to make. The combination of lemons, oranges, and almonds is typically Sicilian. Almonds are used in the preparation of many local sweet specialties including marzipan, *torrone* (a kind of nougat), and *pasta reale* (a kind of cake). In early spring, the Agri-

gento plain and the area around Siracusa are a mass of almond blossom.

The blancmange is traditionally poured into molds in the shape of characters from folklore. In Sicilian homes, the dessert is often served in a lemon leaf, inspiring Giuseppe Barone to add a lemon sauce to his recipe.

Famous throughout the world, many different varieties of lemons are grown on Sicily, such as *verdello*, *monachello*, and *femminello*. Lemons probably originated in India, and were introduced to Sicily by the Arabs in the early Middle Ages, where they quickly adapted to their new home thanks to an ingenious system of irrigation. For the sauce used here, the lemon skins should first be thoroughly washed in warm water.

This refreshing, refined dessert is guaranteed to please.

Wash 2 lemons. Using a sharp knife, cut away the zest in pieces, leaving the pith intact. Blanch the pieces of zest in 2 cups/500 ml water for about 2 minutes. Remove the zest and reserve the water.

Place the ground almonds in a piece of fine muslin and make into a bag. Immerse it in the reserved water used to cook the lemon zest and squeeze the bag to press out the almond "milk." Strain and reserve the resulting liquid.

Add the sugar and cornstarch to the almond milk. Warm very gently over a low heat, stirring the mixture with a whisk until it thickens into a cream.

Lemon Sauce

Ladle the mixture into molds that have first been slightly wetted. Refrigerate the blancmanges for 6 hours.

To make the sauce, carefully wash the 3 remaining lemons, remove the zest using the sugar lumps (or a special lemon zester, if you have one), and extract their juice.

Break the eggs into a saucepan and add the sugar, butter, and lemon juice. Cook the sauce in a bain-marie, beating constantly. Turn the blancmanges out of their molds. Pour some lemon sauce around each one. Garnish with mint, fine strips of orange peel, and cinnamon.

Amygdalota

Preparation time	20 minutes
Cooking time:	20 minutes
Difficulty:	★

Serves 6

5 cups/480 g	ground almonds
4 cups/450 g	confectioners' sugar
1 tsp	vanilla extract
3	egg whites

½ cup/60 g	fine semolina
½ cup/100 g	candied cherries
2 tbsp	orange flower water

Many of the islands in the Aegean Sea have their own recipes for the mouth-watering little cakes with almonds, or *amygdalota* in Greek. The recipes all differ slightly according to whether you're on Andros, Hydra, Skyros, Skopelos, Mykonos, Patmos, or even Siphnos. In olden days, the islanders on Andros used to give *amygdalota* to people who were getting married, the symbolism of the almond tree having both mythological links (the promise of virility and fecundity) and Christian links because the casing around the kernel was likened to the Virgin protecting the infant Jesus. These days, Greeks like nothing better than to nibble on them as they sip the local, strong, black, and very sweet coffee.

All recipes for *amygdalota* have one thing in common—they use almonds, or roughly crushed almonds known as *amygdale*. The almond tree is a member of the rose family and its magnificent white flowers blossom very early in the

year, followed by the leaves, and finally the fruit, which is picked between the end of August and the beginning of September. Encased in a downy, soft pale green husk, they are shelled and dried before they are sold.

Some recipes use crumbled cookies or breadcrumbs instead of the semolina to make the dough. Others suggest the addition of grated lemon, orange, or mandarin rind.

To give your *amygdalota* a pretty shape, our chef suggests you use an ice-cream scoop to mold them into little domes. You could also shape them into little "sausages" or use a pastry bag to pipe them into spirals on nonstick baking parchment. That way, they won't burn on the bottom.

When you take them out of the oven, sprinkle the *amygdalota* with a few drops of orange flower water or rose water. They'll disappear before your eyes!

Put the almonds into a bowl. Add 2½ cups/270 g confectioners' sugar and the vanilla extract.

Whisk 3 egg whites into a soft foam and fold them into the almonds and sugar.

Add the semolina. Stir briskly until it forms into a dough.

Line a baking pan with nonstick baking parchment. Use an ice-cream scoop to shape small domes of dough and arrange them on the baking sheet.

Decorate each one with half a candied cherry. Cook in an oven preheated to 340° F/170° C for about 20 minutes.

Sprinkle the cakes with the orange flower water as soon as you take them out of the oven. Sift the remaining confectioners' sugar over the top. Serve cold.

Bougatsa

Preparation time:	25 minutes
Cooking time:	20 minutes
Difficulty:	★

Serves 4

6	cardamom seeds
1¾ cups/400 ml	milk
4 tbsp/50 g	sugar
½ cup/85 g	coarse semolina
1	egg

2 tbsp	butter
8 sheets	phyllo (filo) pastry

For the garnish:

	confectioners' sugar
	ground cinnamon

In Ancient Greece the cooking skills of a young girl of marriageable age were judged by the people of her village. The future bride would have to demonstrate her abilities in particular by making *bougatsa*, a traditional cake made with tissue-thin sheets of phyllo (filo) pastry and milk, a combination loved by Greeks everywhere. This is still a popular dish with families and can be enjoyed on any occasion.

These days Greeks often eat *bougatsa* for breakfast. It's full of calories for energy and is also known as *galactopita*.

It has a very rich filling made from milk, sugar, egg, and butter flavored with cardamom. This aromatic herb originated from the Malabar coast of India. The cardamom seeds are encased in a bean and when dried are used as an oriental spice. Slightly piquant, cardamom adds a wonderful perfume to rice and sweet pastries. Our chef says you could use orange, mandarin, or even lemon instead.

Nothing can take the place of the phyllo. Typically Greek, these tissue-thin sheets of pastry are normally circular in shape and were originally made by the *karagounides*, herdsmen, of rural Thessalia. If left uncovered, the phyllo tends to dry out very quickly and starts to crumble, so leave the pile of sheets wrapped in a damp cloth. You can also buy it ready made from supermarkets and from specialist delicatessens.

According to Greek tradition, the *bougatsa* is often served at the table cut into small squares. In some families it is served with a small glass of wine.

Grind the tiny black cardamom seeds with a mortar and pestle and scrape them into a pan. Heat for 1 minute then add the milk and sugar, whisking continuously.

When it reaches boiling point, add the sifted semolina. Continue stirring until it forms into a smooth creamy texture.

Remove from the heat, wait until it is lukewarm then whisk in the egg and 1 tbsp butter. Melt the remaining butter and set aside.

Lay one sheet of phyllo pastry on one half of a baking pan, then use another sheet to line the other half. Use the remaining sheets of pastry to completely line the dish, making sure you leave a good over–hang all the way around. Use a pastry brush to baste it with some melted butter.

Tip the cardamom-flavored cream filling into the phyllo-lined pan.

Bring up the folds of the overhanging pastry and lay them on top of each other so that the filling is totally encased. Baste the top with the remaining butter. Bake in an oven at 400° F/200° C for 10–15 min–utes. Turn out, and cut into squares. Dust with confectioners' sugar and cinnamon.

Brioche Flavored with

Preparation time:	1 hour
Cooking time:	45 minutes
Resting/rising time (dough):	2 hours
	15 minutes
Difficulty:	★★

Serves 4

2½ oz/70 g	fresh yeast
	(or 5 tsp dried)
1¾ cups/400 ml	milk
3 lb 5 oz/1.5 kg	white bread flour
1¾ cups/400 g	sugar

6	eggs
1 tsp	ground mastic
9 oz/250 g	butter
½ cup/50 g	slivered almonds

In Greek families that observe the Orthodox religion, Easter symbolizes both joy and abundance. After the long weeks of simple Lenten fare, during which the consumption of certain foodstuffs is prohibited, cooks can again concoct delicious recipes with unrivaled flavors.

On the beautiful island of Chios, the locals make a delicious brioche flavored with mastic. Decorated with eggs that are painted red, a symbol of the blood of Christ and of the Life Eternal, this traditional specialty is eaten everywhere. When it comes out of the oven, the guests carefully examine the surface of the brioche for cracks, which are rumored to be harbingers of luck and happiness in the home!

This specialty can be enjoyed at any time of the year. Our chef recommends that you cover the dough, which is made from yeast, flour, sugar, and milk, with a cloth before it is left to rise. Do not open the oven door while it is cooking!

This delicately perfumed brioche gives off the characteristic aroma of mastic. Extracted from the trunk and branches of the lentisc or mastic tree, a bush that has grown for thousands of years on the island of Chios, the resin is extracted by making incisions with a sharp tool. Mastic is widely used in Greek, Turkish, and Moroccan cookery and can be found in resin or crystal form in specialty stores. It is usually pounded in a pestle and mortar.

Lentisc trees also grow in the eastern Mediterranean, South America, and North Africa. The ones from the island of Chios are said to ooze mastic "tears." The locals will tell you that this phenomenon dates back to the very beginnings of Christianity. When St Isidore begged them to do so, the bushes would start to weep!

Designed to be shared, *Paska* brioche is traditionally broken into pieces by hand and generously shared with guests.

Put the yeast and 1 cup/250 ml warm milk into a bowl (if using dried yeast, follow maker's instructions). Mix with the fingers. Add 2 cups/250 g flour and ¾ cup/200 g sugar. Mix and knead. Leave to rest for 30 minutes.

Put 5 eggs and the remaining sugar into a food processor and blend until the mixture is very pale.

Add the egg and sugar mix to the yeast preparation. Mix again with the fingers. Mix in the remaining flour, remaining warm milk, ground mastic, and melted butter. After a final mix leave to rise for 1 hour.

Ground Mastic

Sprinkle some flour onto the work surface. Shape the dough into balls, then roll out into long rope shapes.

Overlap three ropes of dough then plait them. Put them on a sheet of nonstick paper and leave to rest for 45 minutes.

Beat the remaining egg and use it to glaze the brioche. Sprinkle on the slivered almonds and bake in an oven preheated to 350° F/180° C for about 45 minutes.

Greek

Preparation time:	30 minutes
Cooking time:	35 minutes
Soaking time (tomatoes):	12 hours
Soaking time (carrots):	2 hours
Difficulty:	★

Serves 4

10	baby Santorini or
	cherry tomatoes
10	baby carrots
2 tbsp	lime juice
4 tbsp	sugar

1	vanilla bean
1 stick	cinnamon
	zest from ½ orange
1 tsp	ground alum
½	lemon
3–4 tbsp	thyme honey

For the garnish:

| ¼ cup/30 g | almonds |
| 2 sprigs | mint |

A symbol of hospitality, Greek sweetmeats are traditionally served to afternoon visitors. Made in generous quantities by every family, these pieces of tender vegetables or fruit are cooked in syrup then arranged in a large dish. Everybody has their own spoon and helps themselves from the platter, which is usually accompanied by a glass of water.

These elegant little sweetmeats, known as *glyca tou koutaliou* in Greece, were a favorite as far back as the Byzantine Age. In the 1920s, Greeks born in Asia Minor helped to spread the word about these specialties, particularly in the Cyclades. The original recipe has been handed down from generation to generation ever since.

They come in an infinite variety of forms as they are usually made with regional produce. On the island of Chios, for instance, bergamot is used, in Andros lemon blossom, in Serifos cherries, in Larissa watermelon, and in Aigion baby

eggplant. Sotiris Evangelou has chosen small tomatoes and baby carrots for his version.

Easy to make, these sweetmeats are full of Eastern flavors. After blanching the vegetables or fruit, they need to be soaked for a few hours in the lime juice or, if preferred, in lemon. This vital part of the operation helps them to keep their shape. And don't forget to wash them well before you cook them in the sugar syrup.

Cleverly flavored with cinnamon, vanilla, and orange zest, the syrup needs to be sufficiently thick. To achieve this our chef adds some ground alum, specific to the Essaouira region of Morocco's Atlantic coast. But you can get the same result by replacing it with the juice of a lemon.

In Greece, these little sweetmeats are stored in glass preserve jars where they will keep for several months.

Make a cross-shaped slit in the skins of the tomatoes, cover with boiling water for about 1 minute, refresh in ice water, and peel. Discard the leaves from the carrots, blanch for 3 minutes in boiling water, and refresh.

Fill a small bowl with water and 1 tbsp lime juice. Add the tomatoes and leave to soak for 12 hours. In another small bowl filled with water and the remaining lime juice leave the carrots to soak for 2 hours. Rinse thoroughly.

For the syrup: Heat a pan of water with the sugar, vanilla bean, cinnamon stick, and orange zest and cook for about 15 minutes.

Sweetmeats

Sprinkle the alum onto the syrup. Add slices of lemon and the carrots and cook for about 3 minutes.

Now add the tomatoes and cook for 12 minutes. Remove the carrots and tomatoes from the syrup.

Take the pan off the heat and pour the honey into the syrup. Add the tomatoes and carrots. Serve the Greek sweetmeats on a platter decorated with almonds, mint, and the vanilla pod.

Fanouropita

Preparation time:	20 minutes
Cooking time:	30-40 minutes
Difficulty:	★

Serves 4

2 cups/500 ml	fresh orange juice
1 cup/250 ml	virgin olive oil
1½ cups/350 g	superfine sugar
½ cup/125 g	black treacle (or molasses)
4⅓ cups/500 g	all-purpose flour
1 tsp	bicarbonate of soda

½ tbsp	ground cloves
½ tbsp	ground cinnamon
	nutmeg
1½ cups/175 g	raisins
¾ cup/85 g	crushed walnuts

Many Greeks call upon St Fanourios to help them find missing people or animals, even things they have lost. His saint's day is celebrated on August 27. Any woman seeking his help will bake one of these cakes and take it to the church for it to be blessed. There is therefore real competition between cooks as to who produces the best and most appetizing *fanouropita*. After Mass, the cakes are shared out and enjoyed either at the church, or exchanged between neighbors and eaten later with the family.

Fanouropita is a soft textured sort of Greek gingerbread, characterized by the lingering taste of cinnamon and nutmeg, the crunchy nuts, soft raisins and an after-taste of caramel. It uses neither eggs nor milk, which means it can be eaten during the fasting periods dictated by the Orthodox Church.

Our cake is enriched with black treacle and raisins. However, if you prefer, instead of the treacle, use a good, well-flavored Greek honey.

Raisins have been exported from the port of Patras in the Peloponnese since the 14th century. Three varieties of grape in particular are dried: sultana, very sweet small white grapes; Corinthian, small black ones; Muscat raisins from Alexandria, which are also white. After harvesting, they are left to dry in the sun for 8–12 days.

Don't be surprised if the top of this *fanouropita* quickly turns a dark brown in the heat of the oven. This is due to the presence of olive oil, nuts, black treacle, cinnamon, and ground cloves. You can remedy this by covering the pan with baking foil towards the end of the cooking time.

Put the orange juice, olive oil, and sugar into a bowl and whisk rapidly.

Add the black treacle and stir again.

Next add the sifted flour and bicarbonate of soda. Keep whisking until all of the flour has been incorporated.

Sprinkle on the ground cloves, cinnamon, a few scapings of nutmeg, and continue whisking.

Finally add the raisins and the roughly crushed walnuts to the cake batter. Whisk for one last time.

Tip the mixture into a round non-stick cake pan. Cook in an oven preheated to 340° F/170° C for 30–40 minutes. Turn out and serve cold.

Mastic Ice Cream on a Nest of

Preparation time:	25 minutes
Cooking time:	25 minutes
Difficulty:	★

Serves 4

scant ¾ cup/150 g	sugar
10 oz/300 g	morello cherries, pitted
7 oz/200 g	kadaifi (Greek angelhair noodles)

For the mastic ice cream:

1 cup/250 ml	whole milk
1 cup/250 ml	heavy cream
generous ½ cup/ 125 g	sugar
5	egg yolks
½ tsp	ground mastic (see below)

For the garnish:

| | mint leaves |

This succulent, easy to make Greek dessert is a wonderful marriage of textures and flavors. This much-loved dish is famous for its sweetness offset by the characteristic taste of the mastic and the crunchiness of the *kadaifi*.

Kadaifi are made from flour, salt, and water and come in long strands of "angel hair." To give them their characteristic shape the dough is put through a round metal disk perforated with tiny holes. Also available in good delicatessens, these "angel hair" noodles are used in the making of a variety of cakes and pastries. In this recipe the *kadaifi* must first be plaited before being shaped into a round loop and the ends loosely tied. Our chef then uses a pair of scissors to trim the ends and pops the trimmings in the middle of the nest.

Greeks have a very sweet tooth and often eat cake served with mastic ice cream. Mastic comes from the long-living mastic or lentisc tree that flourishes on the island of Chios. Its small beads of yellow resin are always used very sparingly. Widely found in both Greek and Turkish cookery, mastic is the ancestor of chewing-gum. At the time of the Ottoman empire the ladies of the sultan's harem would chew it to sweeten their breath! Usually found in resin or crystal form in Greek, Middle Eastern, or North African specialty stores, it has to be ground in a pestle and mortar or wrapped in paper and smashed with a hammer.

This elegant dessert is enhanced with morello cherries in syrup. Originally from Asia Minor, these little cherries with their slightly sour taste were already a favorite with Ancient Greeks. The traditional way of preparing them is to stone them before dipping them in water with some sugar. The syrup is then sharpened with the juice of a lemon. Some cooks occasionally add some *moshos* leaves, a Greek aromatic plant.

For the ice cream: Bring the milk, heavy cream, and half of the sugar just up to boiling point in a heavy-bottomed pan.

In a bowl, beat the egg yolks with the remaining sugar and slowly add the hot cream beating continuously. Return to the pan and stir over low heat until it thickens, add the ground mastic. Churn the cooled mixture in an ice-cream maker.

Make a syrup by heating a scant ¾ cup/ 150 g sugar in ⅔ cup/150 ml water. Add the cherries.

Kadaifi and Morello Cherries

Spread out the kadaifi and separate the strands into 12 portions. Smooth them into 12 long ribbons, twist each ribbon loosely, and trim the ends.

Lay out 3 ribbons of kadaifi and plait them tightly. Make another 3 plaits.

Shape the plait into a round "nest" and bake in an oven preheated to 320° F/ 160° C for 10–15 minutes. Arrange each nest on a plate, put a scoop of ice cream in the center, surround with cherries, and coat with syrup. Garnish with mint.

Mbourekakia

Preparation time:	40 minutes
Cooking time:	30 minutes
Refrigeration time (filling):	2 hours
Resting time (dough):	15 minutes
Difficulty	★

Serves 4

4 cups\1 l	corn oil for frying

For the dough:

2 cups/250 g	all-purpose flour
4 tbsp	olive oil

For the filling:

½ cup/100 g	pudding rice
1¼ cups/300 ml	milk
4 tbsp	sugar
1	vanilla bean
½ tsp	cornstarch

For the garnish:

	confectioners' sugar
	ground cinnamon

Mbourekakia are delicious little "pasties" from the island of Chios and depending on the filling they can be sweet, as in our recipe, or savory. They are popular during the carnival period when every village organizes a huge banquet and they are given to children in fancy dress costumes.

Easy to make, *mbourekakia* can be enjoyed on any occasion. The rice is the uncontested star of the filling. Now eaten the world over, this cereal was being produced in China thousands of years ago. It was imported into Turkistan and Mesopotamia by the Persians. Alexander the Great later introduced it to the Ancient Greeks, having brought it back with him from his expedition to India.

In this recipe the rice is cooked in milk and it must be left to rest for two hours. The delicious filling gives off the unmistakable aroma of vanilla. Vanilla beans, the only edible fruit of the orchid family, were introduced to Spain by the Conquistadors in the 16th century. Legend has it that Spanish soldiers discovered vanilla for the first time when tasting Aztec cocoa beans. Seduced by the unusual taste of the vanilla, Iberians gave it the name *vaynilla*, which means "little seeds." The fame of these beans quickly exceeded the frontiers of the Peninsula and spread all over Europe.

For that finishing touch, the *mbourekakia* are lightly dusted with ground cinnamon. This spice is also very widely used in Moroccan cookery, and is available either ground or in sticks. Appreciated for its penetrating aroma, its warm and piquant flavor adds a lift to many sweet and savory dishes.

These little carnival "pasties" are always a great favorite with children.

For the filling: Put the rice into a pan with 1¼ cups/300 ml water. Cook for 15 minutes or until the water has been absorbed.

Add the milk to the pan and stir with a wooden spatula. Add sugar to taste.

Split the vanilla bean lengthwise and add to the pan. Add the cornstarch, mixed to a paste with a little water, and cook until thick. Refrigerate for 2 hours, then remove the vanilla bean.

Sift the flour into a bowl, add the olive oil and mix by hand, gradually adding sufficient cold water to make a pastry dough. Leave to rest for 15 minutes.

Roll out the pastry thinly into a rectangle on a floured surface. Add 1 tsp of the filling at regular intervals.

Fold the pastry once over the filling along its longest edge, then fold over on itself once more. Cut along the second folded edge, then cut the flattened roll into sections. Repeat until the pastry is finished. Fry in very hot corn oil. Drain, and serve dusted with the sugar and cinnamon.

Apples Stuffed with

Preparation time: 30 minutes
Cooking time: 45 minutes
Difficulty: ★

Serves 6

6	large red apples
1 cup/100 g	walnut kernels
1¼ cups/250 g	superfine sugar
2 tsp	ground cinnamon
½ cup/55 g	raisins

scant ½ cup/ 120 ml	Metaxa brandy
3 tbsp	butter
4 tbsp	extra-virgin olive oil

Simple to make and delicious to eat, apples stuffed with dried fruit are popular throughout Greece. In summer Greeks eat this dessert warm with vanilla ice cream or *kaymak*, a thick cream specific to Greek and Turkish cookery.

Miltos Karoubas recommends that you choose red dessert apples for this recipe. In Greece the great majority of apples come from mountainous areas with a cool climate, such as western Macedonia (Florina, Kastoria, and Rodochori). The poet Homer was already praising the virtues of apples. When the nymph Thetis married the mortal Peleus, Eris, goddess of discord, tossed a golden apple bearing the inscription "to the most beautiful one." Athena, goddess of wisdom, the sciences and arts, quarreled with Hera (goddess of love) over the fruit. Zeus refused to nominate "the most beautiful one," so Paris, son of the King of Troy was asked to decide. Seduced by her beauty, he gave the fruit to Aphrodite.

In a new departure, our chef suggests you core the apples from the bottom using a small curved knife or an apple corer, but not all the way through. This gives the apple a wider base to sit on and the filling stays inside rather than spilling out onto the cooking pan.

This filling is made from chopped walnuts (or you can use a mixture of walnuts and almonds if you prefer). The raisins won't need to be soaked in advance as the Metaxa brandy added to the filling allows them to swell inside the apples. Ordinary three-star Metaxa is used for cooking, but older types can have up to seven stars and are for sipping!

Each guest is served with a stuffed apple lightly sprinkled with cinnamon.

Wash and dry the apples. Using an apple corer remove the core and seeds, working from the base, but do not bore right through.

For the stuffing: Mix the chopped nuts, ¾ cup/200 g of the sugar, the cinnamon and raisins in a bowl.

Add the Metaxa and stir well.

Dried Fruit

Use a small teaspoon to fill the cavity of each apple with the nut stuffing.

Arrange the apples, open end upward, in an ovenproof dish.

Melt the butter and oil in a pan and spoon over the apples. Scatter over some sugar. Bake in an oven at 350° F/180° C for about 45 minutes. Serve warm, surrounded by the cooking liquid and sprinkled with cinnamon.

Sperna

Preparation time:	20 minutes
Cooking time:	10 minutes
Drying time (wheat):	6–8 hours
Difficulty:	★

Serves 4

1½ cups/250 g	durum wheat
	salt
¾ cup/100 g	chopped almonds
¾ cup/85 g	walnut pieces
¾ cup/100g	sesame seeds
1¾ cups/200 g	black raisins
1 cup/100 g	white raisins

½ cup/100 g	multicolored dragees
1	pomegranate
1 scant tsp	ground cinnamon
1 tsp	grated cardamom
1 tsp	ground coriander
1 tsp	ground cumin
1 tbsp	fine breadcrumbs

To serve:

	superfine sugar or honey

In some parts of Greece, when a family wants to celebrate a member's saint's day they use a recipe for cooked wheat, dried fruits, and spices known as *sperna*. This dish is blessed in the church and then shared by the guest of honor and the family. Arranged in a big shallow dish, it is decorated with brightly colored dragees. The guests help themselves then add sugar to taste. Throughout Greece *sperna* is also made to symbolize the eternal rest of the deceased, when it is called *kolyva*. On certain days, Greeks honor the memory of the dead by making an offering of *kolyva*. Shaped into a dome, it is covered with dried breadcrumbs and confectioners' sugar—tiny, silver-ball cake decorations are used to pick out the name of the deceased.

All of these customs date back to Ancient Greece, when a similar recipe was known as *panspermia*, an offering to the gods (in particular Demeter, goddess of the harvest) and to the Greeks' ancestors.

The durum wheat that forms the basic ingredient of the *sperna* is still sacred to the Greeks, being the symbol of the earth and the basis of all foods. When cooking wheat, nobody ever pours away the juice. Instead it is reduced down a little before dried apricots, grapes, spices etc. are added and then mashed. Others mix it with honey and drink it. In our recipe, sugar or honey is added just before the dish is served so that the grains of wheat don't harden.

According to popular Greek belief, all the other ingredients in the *sperna* play their own symbolic role—the grapes evoke the words of Christ, the sesame seeds represent life and fecundity, and the almonds symbolise the blanched bones of humans when they're dead and of the vanity of life. The pomegranate is also associated with the world of the dead. In mythology, Hades, god of the underworld, sent one as a gift to Persephone, daughter of Demeter, so that she would remain in his kingdom and become his wife.

Rinse the grains of durum wheat. Tip them into a large pan filled with cold salted water. Bring to the boil and cook for 5–10 minutes until the wheat has become soft.

Rinse the cooked wheat in a strainer under cold running water.

Lay a thick dish towel on your work surface, tip the drained wheat onto it and spread out to a thin layer with your fingers. Leave to dry out for 6–8 hours.

Put the wheat into a bowl, and stir in the chopped almonds, walnut pieces, sesame seeds, both types of raisin, the dragees, and pomegranate seeds (keep back a few of each for decoration).

Sprinkle the cinnamon, cardamom, coriander, cumin, and breadcrumbs on top and stir well again.

Arrange the mixture in a shallow dish. Decorate with the reserved almonds, dragees, and pomegranate seeds. Serve cold, handing round the sugar and honey separately.

Medley of

Preparation time: 1 hour
Cooking time: 40 minutes
Difficulty: ★★★

Serves 4

about 18 sheets	phyllo (filo) pastry
9 oz/250 g	unsalted butter, melted

Filling for the baklava and saragli:

1½ cups/200 g	chopped almonds
1½ cups/200 g	chopped walnuts
4 tsp	grated nutmeg
4 tsp	ground cinnamon

Filling for the petalaki:

¾ cup/100 g	sesame seeds

Filling for the mandilaki:

1 lb/450 g	pine nuts
¾ cup/100 g	dried prunes

For the syrup:

2¼ lb/1 kg	sugar
½	orange
½	lemon
1 stick	cinnamon

If you had to come up with a quick list of Greek dishes known all over the world, it would include the famous moussaka, of course; the classic Greek Salad made with feta, olives, cucumber and tomatoes; *souvlakia*, delicious chunks of lamb cooked on a skewer; not forgetting, of course, a whole range of refreshing *meze*. This list, nowhere near exhaustive, would not be complete without *baklava* and other sweet pastries.

Extremely popular, these delights use dried fruit and syrup and were first made in the magnificent city of Thessalonike (Salonika) in Macedonia. They have different names depending on the shape of the pastry and the filling, and are usually eaten in the afternoon with friends over a cup of strong Greek coffee, accompanied by a glass of water.

They require patience to make and attention to detail, but these deliciously crunchy little confections epitomize the elegance of Greek cuisine. The sheets of phyllo (filo) are usually rectangular in shape and need careful handling because they are very fragile. They tend to dry out when left uncovered, so cover them with a damp cloth. Made from sifted flour, salt, yeast, water, and sometimes olive oil, phyllo pastry is often still home made. For this recipe, you will need three packs of phyllo, each containing six sheets.

The fillings are a rich source of energy and use dried fruit to great effect. Loved since the days of Ancient Greece, the combination of walnuts, almonds, and prunes make a very happy marriage of flavors and textures. Sotiris Evangelou suggests you try this recipe with some pistachios as well, which grow in abundance on the island of Aegina.

In Greek tradition, the little pastry bundles are arranged in a round shallow aluminum dish known as a *tapsi* before they are baked, taken to the table and served immediately.

Mix the filling ingredients for the baklava and saragli. Butter a phyllo sheet, put another on top and butter, then spread with a quarter of the filling. Fold in the outer edges and form into a roll.

Repeat the previous operation to make a second roll. Butter a fifth sheet, put another on top and butter. Place on top the 2 filled rolls alongside each other, then roll up. Cut the baklava pinwheels into small round slices.

For the saragli: Butter a sheet of phyllo. Place another sheet on top and butter it. Add the remaining filling, top with another butter sheet and roll up tightly around a narrow stick to keep the roll thin. Press between your fingers and carefully remove the stick.

Salonikan Delights

For the petalaki: *Butter 1 sheet of phyllo. Scatter over sesame seeds, and fold in half. Butter another sheet of phyllo and fold in half. Lay the 2 sheets on top of each other and roll. Butter a third sheet and roll it around the roll. Cut into sections and form horseshoe shapes.*

For the mandilaki: *Butter the remaining sheets of phyllo and layer them. Cut into rectangles. Put pine nuts in some, prunes in others, and fold into a pouch shape.*

Butter the tapsi dish and arrange the delights as shown. Butter again. Bake in an oven preheated to 350° F/180° C for about 40 minutes. Make a syrup with the ingredients and pour over the delights.

Portocalopita

Preparation time: 30 minutes
Cooking time: 40 minutes
Difficulty: ★★

Serves 6–8

For the cake:
1 cup/250 ml	virgin olive oil
7/8 cup/200 g	superfine sugar
3	eggs
1	orange
1	lemon
1 tsp/5 g	baking soda
37/8 cups/440 g	flour

For the syrup:
4/5 cup/200 ml	orange juice
4/5 cup/200 ml	mandarin juice
13/4 cups/200 g	confectioners' sugar

Portocalopita, or "orange cake," is a good example of the type of cakes sold in towns on Crete. As in many Mediterranean cakes and pastries, olive oil is used together with the eggs, citrus fruit juice and zest, and sugar. When cooked, this cake is light and not too sweet. It is generally cut into lozenges and finished with a delicious syrup of orange and mandarin juice.

The use of olive oil is so widespread on Crete that it finds its way into most dishes, even cakes. The island has been known for centuries for its many varieties of olive oil. To make *portocalopita*, the oil is beaten together with the sugar. A good-quality oil will blend with the sugar very quickly. If this does not happen, use an electric beater.

Portocalopita owes its fresh, tangy taste to the citrus fruits used in the recipe. For city-dwelling Cretans, this is a reminder of the countryside in springtime, when the scent of orange blossom perfumes the air. Crete's celebrated Maleme oranges, the island's most famous variety, are grown in the area around Khania. Round and thin-skinned, they are particularly sweet and juicy. They are used as table fruit or for juicing.

Orange trees are relative newcomers to Europe. Unknown to the Greeks and Romans of Antiquity, they were introduced from China in the 15th century by Portuguese explorers. This explains the Greek word for oranges, *portokali*, a corruption of the word for "Portugal."

When they have been cut and soaked in syrup, the pieces of cake can be decorated with slices of citrus fruit and mint leaves. They make an ideal accompaniment to a cup of tea or coffee.

For the cake, begin by pouring most of the olive oil (leaving enough to oil the baking pan) into a bowl. Add the sugar and beat for about 10 minutes until it has dissolved in the oil.

In another bowl, beat the eggs until they are pale yellow and frothy. Add the orange and lemon zest.

Stir the eggs into the oil and sugar mixture and continue beating until all the ingredients are well mixed.

Add the juice of the orange and lemon, together with the baking soda and the flour (leaving a little to flour the baking pan). Mix well. Pour the mixture into the oiled and floured baking pan. Cook in the oven for 35 minutes at 320 °F/160 °C.

To make the syrup, heat the orange and mandarin juice in a pan. Add the confectioners' sugar and mix until it has dissolved.

Take the cake out of the oven and cut it into slices without removing it from the pan. Pour the citrus syrup over the cake and wait until it has been absorbed before turning out the cake. Eat cold.

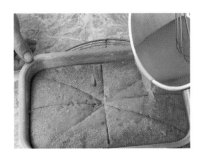

Preparation time:	30 minutes
Cooking time for custard:	25 minutes
Baking time for cookies:	15 minutes
Preparation of ice cream:	20 minutes
Difficulty:	★★

Serves 4

For the parmesan ice cream:

2 cups/500 ml	milk
1 stick	cinnamon
	zest of 1 orange
	zest of 1 lemon
1	vanilla pod
³/₈ cup/80 g	sugar
3 tbsp/100 g	honey
2 oz/50 g	grated parmesan
6	eggs
7 tbsp/100 ml	light cream

For the "village" cookies:

4	eggs
1 cup/250 g	sugar
1 tbsp/15 g	aniseed seeds
	grated zest of 1 orange
1	vanilla pod
6 cups/550 g	cake flour (self-raising)

For the garnish (optional):

	candied orange peel
	ground cinnamon

Gelat bil-gobon is said to have been invented in the mid-18th century by a Maltese chef called Michele Marceca. This curious recipe combines a spiced custard, or *crème anglaise*, with fresh cream and parmesan cheese. Iced desserts were very popular in the 18th century, when the Knights of St John still governed the island. The Knights had blocks of ice brought from the slopes of Mount Etna on nearby Sicily. The blocks were stored in cool caves or ice-houses, wrapped in straw.

The parmesan cheese incorporated into the mixture in the final stages is still made only in Parma, on the Italian mainland. Malta produces only small goat's-milk cheeses, and a kind of ricotta.

To accompany the ice cream, Michael Cauchi suggests the traditional *biskuttini tar-rahal* ("village" cookies). This simple recipe is often prepared for celebrations and ceremonies. The cookies can be flavored with a variety of in-gredients, according to preference, for example: grated or-ange or lemon peel, vanilla seeds, ground cinnamon, cloves, aniseed, or anisette.

The shape of the cookie is left to the imagination of the cook: long sticks, small round balls, small domes shaped with an icing bag, or sausage-shaped cookies made using two spoons. For the latter, dip two spoons into hot water, take a spoonful of cookie mixture and shape it by rolling from one spoon to the other. To cook, place the shaped mixture on a baking sheet covered with waxed or silicone paper and bake in a hot oven.

The cookies can be eaten as a side accompaniment or, for special occasions, chopped and then crumbled into the base of individual ice cream dishes. Spoon the ice cream over them, and press down well. To garnish, sprinkle with ground cinnamon, and decorate with strips of candied orange peel.

Begin by making the ice cream. For this, heat the milk in a saucepan. Add the cinnamon, a few strips of orange and lemon peel, and the vanilla seeds. Let these infuse for 10 minutes over a low heat.

Add the sugar and honey to the spiced milk. Mix and then strain the mixture into another saucepan. Add the grated parmesan, stirring for about 5 minutes over the heat until it has dissolved.

Beat 6 egg yolks in a bowl. Dilute them with some of the spiced milk, then add the contents of the bowl to the saucepan. Cook the mixture gently for about 10 minutes until a smooth custard has been obtained.

Bil-Gobon

When the custard is ready, pour in the fresh cream. Allow the mixture to cool, then place it in an ice-cream maker. When the ice-cream is ready, transfer it from the ice-cream maker to a container, and place it in the freezer until required.

For the cookies, beat the egg whites with the sugar until stiff peaks form. Add the aniseed, grated orange peel, and vanilla pods, together with the beaten egg yolks and most of the flour (reserving a little to flour the work surface). Mix gently until a smooth paste is obtained.

Flour the work surface. Using two spoons, shape the mixture into cookies and arrange them on a baking sheet. Cook for 15 minutes in a hot oven (400 °F/200 °C). Arrange the ice cream and cookies in glasses to serve.

Maltese

Preparation time: 40 minutes
Cooking time: 40 minutes
Marinating time for dates: overnight
Pastry resting time: 1 hour
Difficulty: ★★

Serves 4

For the pastry:

²/₃ cup/150 ml	orange juice
½ cup/100 g	sugar
7 tbsp/100 ml	olive oil
4²/₅ cups/500 g	flour

For the date filling:

2 lb/1 kg	soft dates
4 tbsp/60 ml	Maltese anisette
1 tsp/5 g	ground cinnamon
1 tsp/5 g	ground cloves
2 tbsp/30 ml	orange flower (or rose) water
1	orange
1	lemon
	oil for frying

In the summer on Malta, anyone walking by the sea at Msida, to the south-west of Valletta, will not fail to notice a wonderful scent of hot oil and aniseed. It is a sure sign that a stall has been set up nearby, selling *mqaret*, delicious Maltese fried cakes filled with a paste of dates flavored with spices and aniseed. The same tempting delicacy is sold by street sellers near the City Gate, the main entrance to Valletta, the capital of Malta. Known for centuries, this delicacy appears today not only at village festivals in the wintertime, but also on the menu in some of the best restaurants on Malta.

As can be seen from their name, *mqaret* are similar to the Algerian and Tunisian *makroud*. Date palms do not grow on Malta, so the dates used are imported from Tunisia.

Depending on the recipe, the pastry is made with oil, shortening, or butter. Butter gives a firmer texture, making the

pastry easier to roll out. The pastry needs to rest for one hour before being rolled out very thinly with a rolling pin or, preferably, in a pasta maker.

Michael Cauchi suggests flavoring the date filling with Maltese anisette. This aniseed and herb-flavored liquor is generally drunk well chilled with a mixer (water, lemonade, or orange or pineapple juice).

Citrus fruits are cultivated on Malta, including one of the most delicious oranges in the world, the celebrated "Maltese" or "blood" orange. It comes as no surprise, therefore, that orange juice is used here for the pastry, and orange flower water for the filling.

Mqaret are cut into lozenges and fried or baked. Eaten hot, they melt deliciously in the mouth, but they may also be eaten warm or cold.

Blend the pitted dates in a food processor, then cook them for 30 minutes in the water and anisette. Leave to marinate overnight. To make the pastry, put the orange juice and sugar in a bowl. Mix them together, then add the oil.

Add the flour to the mixture, kneading well until a smooth dough is obtained. Form this into a ball, cover with plastic wrap, and leave to rest for 1 hour.

Now prepare the filling. Mix together the marinated dates, cinnamon, ground cloves, orange flower water, one tbsp of chopped orange peel, and one tbsp of chopped lemon peel.

Mqaret

Roll out the pastry and cut it into large rectangles of approximately 8 inches/20 cm by 4 inches/8–10 cm. Place a line of filling down one side of each rectangle. Using a brush, make the other edge of the pastry slightly wet.

Roll the pastry around the filling. Flatten the long roll and cut it obliquely at intervals of about 1 inch/3 cm to obtain the typical lozenge-shaped mqaret.

Deep-fry the mqaret in oil heated to 350 °F/180 °C until golden. Drain on a paper towel. Eat while still hot.

Quince Stuffed

Preparation time: 25 minutes
Standing time: 6 hours
Cooking time: 45 minutes
Difficulty: ★

Serves 4

2	quinces
⅔ cup/150 g	sugar
2	apples
4	cloves
	juice of 1 lemon
1 scant cup/ 200 ml	light whipping cream
2 tbsp/30 g	confectioner's sugar

Quince stuffed with apples is a typical Istanbul dessert, and is usually served after fish. This fall dessert is often accompanied by a firm cream cheese called *kaymak*. Aybek Şurdum prefers sweetened whipped cream.

The simple dessert really makes the most of the quince. The quince tree came originally from the Caucasus and Iran. Its yellow fruits are apple- or pear-shaped, and the hard, somewhat bitter flesh cannot be eaten raw. Cooked, however, it develops a wonderfully sweet, piquant aroma.

Aybek Şurdum advises you to sprinkle sugar over the quinces—with their cores—and to chill them in the refrigerator for six hours. This helps to color the flesh. If you do not have enough time for this, you can add a little yellow food coloring to help.

This dessert is a clever combination of the aroma of the quince and the sweetness of the apple. There are numerous apple varieties on offer today, and one of their main advantages is that they are available all year round. We recommend you use a variety that is suitable for cooking and baking, such as a russet. The thick, slightly rough skin conceals a juicy, slightly tart fruit that retains its full aroma even when cooked.

Aybek Şurdum also says you can candy the apple peel for a particularly clever garnish, and arrange it on top of the sweetened whipped cream.

Garnish each quince with a few cloves before serving. Cloves are the seeds of the clove tree, picked and dried before they flower. They add a spicy aroma to this dessert.

Cut the quinces in half with a sharp serrated knife.

Cut out the cores. Remove the seeds, and place inside the halved quinces. Sprinkle 1 tsp sugar over the quinces, and place them in the refrigerator for 6 hours.

Peel and core the apples. Grate the flesh.

with Apples

Remove the seeds from the quince halves, and reserve them. Fill each half with grated apples.

Put the quinces in an ovenproof dish. Add the quince seeds, cloves, the remainder of the sugar, and the lemon juice, and pour over 1⅔ cups/400 ml water. Bake in a preheated oven at 375 °F/190 °C for 45 minutes.

Add the confectioner's sugar to the cream, and whip until stiff. Arrange the quince in dessert bowls, pour over the cooking liquid, and garnish with cloves and quince seeds. Serve the sweetened whipped cream separately.

Sweet

Preparation time:	40 minutes
Marinating time:	30 minutes
Soaking time:	15 minutes
Cooking time:	40 minutes
Difficulty:	★

Serves 4

For the pumpkin treats:

2¼ lb/1 kg	pumpkin
1⅔ cups/400 g	sugar
4	cloves

For the stuffed apricots:

20	dried apricots
scant ½ cup/ 100 g	sugar
2 cups/200 g	confectioner's sugar
1 lb/400 g	kaymak or mascarpone

For the garnish:

	halved walnuts
	peppermint leaves (optional)
	ground pistachios (optional)

Little appetizers, *meze*, have a long history in Turkish culture. They are served to guests before a meal and between courses with *rakı* (the country's famous aniseed alcoholic drink) or wine.

In the Turkish metropolis of Istanbul this ritual has become part of everyday life, and a wide range of *meze* is served in the *meyhane*, the country's *rakı* bars.

These social evenings, which are adored by the Turkish, begin with cold then hot *meze* dishes, and the sessions usually continue long into the night. It is "the done thing" to serve a few sweet treats at the end of such an evening. Fruit-based desserts are particularly popular. The pumpkin treats presented in this dish are very common and are available in every *meyhane*.

Pumpkins are grown predominantly around Bolu, and have a thick, orange, orange-green, or all-green skin. The flesh is very high in vitamin A, and extremely versatile. If you do not want to buy a whole pumpkin, choose a piece with smooth, juicy flesh, and keep it in the refrigerator. Ayşecan Tüfekçioğlu sprinkles sugar over the pumpkin and leaves it for a while, making it cook more quickly.

Stuffed apricots are eaten on any occasion in Turkey. This aromatic stone fruit comes from the Malatya region in the southeast of the country. Dried apricots should be soaked in warm water for a little while before using.

Fill the apricots with *kaymak*, a firm cream cheese with a high fat content that is made from cow's or buffalo's milk. Its consistency is similar to that of mascarpone.

Cut the pumpkin into thick slices, remove the seeds, and peel.

Put the sliced pumpkin in a pot, and sprinkle over the sugar. Add the cloves. Cover with a lid, and leave to stand for about 30 minutes.

Pour ⅔ cup/150 ml water over the pumpkin. Cover with a lid, and simmer over medium heat for 15 minutes. Lower the heat, and simmer for a further 15 minutes. Remove the lid, and cook for a further 10 minutes. Remove the pumpkin and leave to cool. Reserve the syrup.

Meze

Cut into the apricots and place in a bowl of warm water with the sugar; soak for 15 minutes. Then transfer the apricots with the soaking water in a pot, and cook for about 10 minutes.

To make the cream, put the confectioner's sugar and kaymak (or mascarpone) in a bowl and stir until smooth.

Spoon the cream into a forcing bag and fill the drained apricots. Arrange on a serving dish. Sprinkle the reserved syrup over the pumpkin, and garnish with walnuts, peppermint leaves, and the cream. Garnish the apricots with chopped pistachios.

Flour Halva with

Preparation time: 20 minutes
Cooling time: 45 minutes to 1 hour
Cooking time: 40 minutes
Difficulty: ★

Serves 4

2¼ sticks/250 g butter
4 cups/400 g flour

For the syrup:
2¼ cups/500 g sugar

For the garnish:
ground pistachios

Helva (halva) has delighted the sweet-toothed of Turkey for centuries. The delicacy of this treat, which is made of melted butter, flour or semolina, and sugar and water or milk, is the result of long stirring and kneading with a wooden spoon. The best known of the numerous variants is the sesame version (*tahın helva*), which is sometimes also enhanced with pistachios or cocoa. Mehmet Kaya's recipe uses only butter, flour, and syrup.

Country people like to get together in the long winter evenings to indulge in "halva talk." This involves exchanging the latest news while preparing the halva mix. Halva is also always served at religious festivals, weddings, and funerals. Whenever there is a death in a family, the bereaved family's neighbors cook for them for three days. As a token of their gratitude, the bereaved family presents them with a gift of halva. A friend of the family takes over the stirring and kneading of the dough and shares fond memories of

pleasant times spent with the deceased. The spoon is then passed to the next person, who does the same—and so on, until everyone has said a few words, and the pastry is ready.

Making halva requires time and patience—and a strong arm, because the pastry must not burn. Keep scraping the pastry off the sides of the pot and use a wide wooden spoon for the stirring. This will make the pastry soft and crumbly. It should be the color of milk caramel, and smell a little of toast. Then the syrup is stirred in. To further enhance the flavor, Mehmet Kaya uses a little cinnamon or pomegranate juice.

Pretty patterns can be drawn in the halva with a fork or pastry comb. It can also be cut into lozenges or other imaginative shapes.

To make the syrup, bring 2 cups/500 ml water with the sugar to the boil. Remove from the heat as soon as it bubbles.

Cut the butter into slices, and melt in a large pot.

Pour the flour onto the melted butter.

Syrup and Pistachios

Over a medium heat, stir and knead the mix for a long time until it is the color of milk caramel.

Pour the hot syrup over the halva mixture. Stir until it is thick and homogenous. It should be the color of filberts.

Spoon the halva into a rectangular pan, and smooth. Leave to cool at room temperature about for 45–60 minutes. Cut diagonally into lozenges, and sprinkle over the ground pistachios.

Künefe

Preparation time: 30 minutes
Cooling time: 15 minutes
Cooking time: 25 minutes
Difficulty: ★

Serves 4

10 oz/250 g   *tel kadayıf*
2½ sticks/300 g   butter
4 oz/100 g   *dil peyniri* or ricotta

For the syrup:
1⅓ cups/300 g   sugar
  juice of ¼ of a lemon

For the sweetened whipped cream:
1 scant cup/
200 ml   light whipping cream
2 tbsp/30 g   confectioner's sugar

For the garnish:
  morello cherries
  peppermint leaves
  ground pistachios
  (optional)

This dessert, originally from the Near East, is very popular in Turkey and is mainly served at the *kebapçı*—a hostelry specializing in kebabs. This easy to prepare dessert is eaten warm and is also a favorite in Greece.

The main ingredient is *tel kadayıf*—long, thin noodles that are made of flour, salt, and water. The noodles are placed in small molds with a perforated base to shape them into circles. Use a metal mold, 8 inches/20 centimeters in diameter and about 1 inch/3 centimeters high for the *künefe*. *Tel kadayıf* is essential for this dish, and is available in Turkish stores.

Dil peyniri is also a main ingredient. This is a fibrous, unsalted, fresh cheese that is made from cow's and sheep's milk, and plaited. According to Bayram Dönmez, neutral-flavored ricotta can be used instead.

Kaymak is usually served with *künefe* in Turkey. This is a firm cream cheese with a very high fat content and is similar to Italy's mascarpone. Bayram Dönmez adds a certain something to this dish in the form of whipped cream that has been sweetened.

The wonderful, pleasantly tart flesh of the morello cherries goes perfectly with *künefe*. Potassium-rich cherries are usually steamed, and their gently acidic aroma makes them ideal for preserves, cakes, baked dishes, and liqueurs. The cherry came originally from this area, Asia Minor, and has been cultivated in Europe ever since the Middle Ages.

Place the tel kadayıf on a worktop, separate it slightly with your hands, and put in a bowl.

Melt 2 sticks/230 g of the butter, and gently pour over the tel kadayıf. Cut the cheese into thin slices.

Lightly oil a metallic mold, and press the tel kadayıf into it. Cover with the sliced cheese.

Top the cheese with a second layer of tel kadayıf, and press down lightly with your fingers. Place in the refrigerator for about 15 minutes. Dice the remainder of the butter, and sprinkle over the künefe. Fry on top of the hob for about 15 minutes until crispy, turning once.

To make the syrup, bring 1 cup/250 ml water with the sugar to the boil, and simmer for 10 minutes. Add the lemon juice. Whip the cream and confectioner's sugar until stiff.

Pour the syrup over the künefe with a spoon. Leave to stand for 2 minutes, then lift out of the mold onto a serving dish and garnish with cherries, mint, and the sweetened whipped cream. Sprinkle with ground pistachios, if desired.

Sultan's

Preparation time: 30 minutes
Cooking time: 15 minutes
Difficulty: ★★

Serves 4

8	eggs
scant ½ cup/ 100 g	sugar
3½ tbsp/50 g	fine semolina
1½ cups/150 g	flour
2 tsp/10 g	baking powder
12 oz/300 g	stewed apple

For the syrup:

2 cups/400 g	sugar
1	lemon

Mehmet Kaya presents a delicious apple roulade, developed by pastry chefs on the Sea of Marmara, the small sea between the Mediterranean and the Black Sea. They named it *Fatih sarması*, in honor of one of the great Turkish heroes: Mehmed II, known as "the conqueror," *Fatih* in Turkish, who conquered Constantinople in 1453 and thus ended the rule of the Byzantine emperors.

The sponge mix is beaten in the kitchen mixer, but can also be made using an electric hand mixer. Gradually add the sugar to the beaten egg whites when they are firm, but not entirely stiff. Then continue beating until the mixture is very stiff, shiny, and light. Now gradually fold the semolina, flour, and baking powder into the mixture and combine well, be careful, however, to ensure that the mixture still remains light and airy.

The depth of the baking pan is unimportant; it just needs to be big enough. Whether you use a normal oven tray, the skillet pan, or a special roulade pan, the base should be covered with baking parchment so the sponge does not stick and is easy to remove from the pan.

Mehmet Kaya uses homemade stewed apples for the filling. He cooks 2¼ pounds/1 kilogram red apples with 2¼ pounds/ 1 kilogram sugar until the mixture takes on a red color and has caramelized slightly. If preferred, ready-made stewed apples or apricot jelly can be used as a substitute.

The roulade is garnished with sweetened whipped cream and ground pistachios. The Turks also like *kaymak*, a firm cream cheese with a high fat content that is quite similar to mascarpone.

Separate the eggs. Put the egg whites in the mixer bowl and whisk. When they are firm, gradually add the sugar and beat until the mixture is very stiff.

Fold in the lightly beaten egg yolks, semolina, flour, and baking powder.

Line a baking pan with baking parchment. Pour the mixture into the pan, and smooth with a knife. Bake in a preheated oven at 350 °F/180 °C for 15 minutes.

Roulade

Meanwhile, for the syrup, bring 1¼ cups/ 300 ml water to the boil with the sugar and the sliced lemon. Remove the cake from the pan and place on a clean cloth. Place the cake, with cloth underneath, back in the pan and pour over the warm syrup.

Reserve a little of the stewed apple (see above for how to make it) and spread the remainder evenly over the cake.

Use the cloth to roll up the cake and brush with the reserved stewed apple. Garnish the roulade with sweetened whipped cream and ground pistachios and slice diagonally.

Lokma

Preparation time: 20 minutes
Standing time for syrup: 24 hours
Standing time for dough: 15 minutes
Cooking time: 20 minutes
Difficulty: ✶

Serves 4

2⅛ cups/250 g   flour
1   egg

2 tsp/10 g   fresh yeast
2 tsp/10 g   sugar

For the syrup:
3⅛ cups/700 g   sugar
1   lemon

12 cups/3 l   oil for deep-frying

Lokma and other sweet treats are special favorites at celebrations and religious festivals in Anatolia. The small donuts are soaked in syrup after frying. There are numerous different recipes for them, most with flowery names such as "Beauty's lips," "The vizier's fingers," "Lady's navel" … Mehmet Kaya's recipe comes from the Aegean coast, and is a specialty of Izmir.

Before commencing the preparations for the actual *lokma*, the syrup has to be made a day in advance. It is covered with plastic wrap and left overnight at room temperature. This enables the lemon slices to impart their full flavor to the syrup.

The water used to thin the dough must be hand warm; this encourages the rising action of the yeast. Once the dough is homogenous it should be left to stand for at least 15 minutes. To check whether it has risen sufficiently, push an index finger into the dough: There should be bubbles on the inside. You can also speed up the rising process by covering the bowl with a cloth and putting it somewhere warm, such as in front of a warm oven.

Mehmet Kaya makes the *lokma* as follows: He takes a little of the dough into the palm of his hand, and makes a fist around it. This forces a little of the dough out between his thumb and index finger. He scrapes off these plum-sized pieces with a teaspoon, and drops them in the hot oil. The *lokma* rise again in the oil, and become nice and round.

The oil for deep-frying (ideally olive oil) should be very hot, but the syrup should have cooled down completely as otherwise the donuts will go soft.

Prepare the syrup a day in advance. Heat 2 cups/500 ml water. Add the sugar and sliced lemon, and bring to the boil. Remove the pot from the hob, cover the syrup, and leave to cool.

Sieve the flour into a bowl. Add the egg, crumbled yeast, and sugar.

Work the ingredients into a dough, gradually adding 1¼ cups/300 ml hand warm water, until you have a smooth dough. Leave to stand for 15 minutes.

Heat the oil until just smoking. Carefully slide teaspoon-sized donuts into the oil.

Fry the lokma until they have expanded, and are nice and round and golden in color. Remove with a spatula.

Quickly dip the lokma in the syrup, and drain. Serve cold.

Deep-Fried Pastries

Preparation time: 45 minutes
Standing time: 3 hours
Cooking time: 15 minutes
Difficulty: ★★

Serves 4

1	quince
2 tbsp/30 g	confectioner's sugar
2	egg whites

2 large sheets	yufka pastry (phyllo)
2 cups/500 ml	oil for deep-frying

For the syrup:

1⅓ cups/300 g	sugar
	juice of ¼ lemon

For the garnish (optional):

	ground pistachios

In Turkey, it is believed that people need special protection at certain stages of life. Thus, for instance, a new baby is given a small eye made of turquoise glass to ward off the evil eye. The *imam* (prayer leader) gives believers a *muska* for the same reason. Inside this amulet, a small, folded triangle, are verses from the Koran. The folding of the Holy Scriptures has made its way into the culinary world, and is now used to describe this triangular dish.

These small, triangular pastries with quince stuffing are originally from Central Anatolia, but today they are found all over the country. They are served mainly during Ramadan, after sunset.

The quince is a typical fruit of the fall, and is from the Caucasus. It was already much prized in antiquity, especially the variety from the Cretan town of Cydon. The quince is knob-like in appearance, the yellow skin of the ripe fruit often being covered in a brown down. The flesh is hard and bitter and cannot be eaten raw. Once cooked, however, the quince is pleasantly sweet-and-sour. Like apples and pears, it is a member of the rose family. You can use a slightly tart apple instead of the quince.

Yufka is a very thinly rolled Turkish puff pastry. Making it used to be a communal winter activity in the villages, with the whole community working together on the fine sheets. The pastry sheets were then dried and stacked. They were moistened a little before being used. Phyllo (filo) is the same as *yufka*; if you cannot find these, use very thinly rolled out puff pastry instead.

The pastry pockets can be garnished, if required, with ground pistachios.

To make the syrup, bring 1¼ cups/300 ml water to the boil with the sugar and the lemon juice, and boil for about 2 minutes. Remove the pot from the heat, and leave to stand for 3 hours.

Peel the quince, and cut into quarters. Remove the core, and grate the flesh.

Gently combine the grated quince with the confectioner's sugar and 1 egg white.

with Quince Stuffing

Place one sheet of yufka on top of the other, cut in half, and then repeat. Cut the pastry sheets into 1½ in/4 cm wide strips.

Spoon a little of the quince mixture onto the ends of the strips and shape into triangles. Alternate between folding the strips to the left and to the right. Seal the ends with lightly beaten egg white.

Fry the triangles (muska) in hot oil for 3–4 minutes, then dip quickly in the syrup. Drain and garnish with ground pistachios (if using) before serving.

Rose

Preparation time:	40 minutes
Preparation time:	8–10 hours
Cooking time:	15 minutes
Difficulty:	★★

Serves 4

| 2 sheets | *yufka* pastry (phyllo) |
| ⅛ stick/15 g | butter |

For the syrup:

1⅓ cups/300 g	sugar
2 tbsp	rose water
	juice of ½ lemon

For the filling:

14	May roses
4 tbsp	confectioner's sugar
1 cup/100 g	shelled walnuts
2	egg whites

This Eastern-inspired rose dessert is a very clever specialty from Izmir. It requires a little patience and great care, and is almost always made by the women.

According to chef Gökçen Adar, they even compete to create the loveliest "roses." The ladies of Izmir like to meet up once a week and enjoy this pastry over a cup of Turkish coffee.

This fine dessert is an exceptional delight. The rose petals combine the scents and aromas of the East, and must be macerated in sugar for at least 12 hours.

Gökçen Adar recommends the variety "Rose de damas" (*Rose x damascena*), or May roses (*Rosa majalis*), which are available from delicatessens. In their powdered form, these flowers—which play an important part in the cuisine of both North Africa and the Near East—are used to add aroma to sweet and savory dishes. The tiny buds are picked in May, and mostly distilled in Isparta in Central Anatolia and made into rose water.

The walnut kernels add a little "bite" to the filling. They contain plenty of carbohydrates, potassium, and copper. The Romans brought the walnut from Asia to Europe. Walnuts are best stored in a cool place in an air-tight container out of direct sunlight. A tip from Gökçen Adar: Soak the walnut kernels in warm milk for a few hours; this will make even older ones fresh and crunchy again!

This delicate rose dessert is a veritable invitation to dream … and to travel.

To make the filling, pluck the petals off the roses, and macerate in confectioner's sugar for 8–10 hours. Crush the walnut kernels in a mortar, and add to the macerated petals.

To make the syrup, put the sugar in a pot and pour over 1⅔ cups/400 ml water. Add the rose water. Bring to the boil, add the lemon juice, then remove from the heat and leave to cool slightly.

Lightly whisk the egg whites with a fork and pour over the rose petal mixture.

Dessert

Halve the pastry sheets, and spread the filling along the straight edge. Fold the pastry over the filling three times.

Cut a fan shape into the edge of the pastry sheets. Oil an ovenproof pan.

Roll the stuffed pastry sheets into circles and create rose shapes with the cut edges. Place on the pan. Cover with aluminum foil, and bake at 400 °F/200 °C for 10 minutes. Remove the foil, and bake for 3 minutes. Pour the syrup onto dessert plates, and arrange the roses on top.

Şekerpare

Preparation time: 30 minutes
Standing time: 20 minutes
Cooking time: 20 minutes
Difficulty: ★

Serves 4

2½ cups/250 g   flour
⅔ cup/75 g   confectioner's sugar
1¼ sticks/150 g butter
2 tsp/10 g   baking powder

3½ tbsp/50 g   fine semolina
3   eggs
1 pinch/2 g   vanilla sugar

For the syrup:
1   lemon
2¼ cups/500 g   sugar

For the garnish:
                 pistachios

Şekerpare are like small, golden turbans crowned with green pistachios, and are perfect for anyone with a sweet tooth. The creators of this dish from Central Anatolia gave the syrup-soaked semolina pastry the right name, which is made up of the words for "sugar" (*şeker*) and "piece" (*pare*).

So that the flour and semolina combine better when kneading the dough, Mehmet Kaya sprinkles the semolina on top of the circle of flour. Superfine sugar can be used as a substitute for confectioner's sugar if you whisk it with the eggs first.

Mehmet Kaya rolls the dough into balls, but you can also make it a rounded diamond shape. Grease the pan well before putting the pastries on it so they do not stick. Sometimes Mehmet Kaya decorates the pastries with a fork. He also likes to brush the şekerpare with beaten egg before baking and put a filbert, pistachio, or an almond in the center—or sometimes he coats them in poppy seeds.

The best results are achieved if the following is observed when baking: The şekerpare should be left to rise in a preheated oven with the door left open; then they are finished with the door closed. When ready, the şekerpare should be dry and golden. They are soaked in syrup directly after baking, and covered with aluminum foil or a second baking tin. This way, the syrup-soaked pastries will continue to rise, and the consistency will be firm but soft. Finally, the şekerpare are garnished with pistachios.

Sieve the flour onto a worktop, make a large well in the middle, and put the confectioner's sugar, 1 stick/125 g sliced butter, and the baking powder into it.

Sprinkle the semolina over the edge of the flour. Put the eggs and vanilla sugar in the middle. Knead the ingredients until you have a smooth dough. Shape the dough into a ball, and leave to stand for 20 minutes.

Break the ball into several smaller balls, then cut these into even-sized pieces and roll them into plum-sized balls between your hands.

Oil the pan well, and place the pastry balls inside. Make small circles in the middle with a round glazing-bag nozzle. Bake in a preheated oven at 350 °F/ 180 °C for 20 minutes.

Meanwhile, cut the lemon into slices. To make the syrup, bring 2 cups/500 ml water to the boil with the sugar and sliced lemon. Remove the pot from the heat when it starts to boil.

Remove the pastries from the oven, and pour over the syrup to halfway up the baking pan. Cover the pan with aluminum foil, and leave the şekerpare to cool. Garnish with pistachios.

Assida

Preparation time:	30 minutes
Cooking time:	30 minutes
To soak the pine nuts:	12 hours
Difficulty:	★

Serves 6

For the pine nut cream:

5 cups/550 g	small pine nuts (from black pines)
4¹/₂ cups/500 g	all-purpose flour
2¹/₂ cups/500 g	sugar

For the white cream:

4 cups/1 liter	milk
1¹/₈ cup/125 g	sugar
4 tbsp/55 g	cornstarch
4	eggs
1 trickle	geranium water

For the decoration:

¹/₃ cup/30 g	filberts (hazelnuts)
¹/₃ cup/30 g	shelled pistachios
¹/₃ cup/30 g	almonds (optional)

In the past, *assida* cream desserts were served on feast days, in particular on the *Mouled* (birthday of the Prophet) or for the *Aïd*. The basic ingredient of the *assida* is always the same: a kind of "milk" made from pine nuts, filberts, almonds, or nuts that have been ground and soaked in water, and then filtered. Thickened with all-purpose flour or cornstarch, the "milk" is blended to a white cream and flavored with geranium-flower water or orange-flower water. The term *assida* can also be used to refer to another thicker mixture, which is similar to a choux pastry and eaten in the morning.

To make the *assida zgougou*, Mohamed Boussabeh uses very small black pine nuts. There are two types available to Tunisian cooks: the large, white, slightly oily ones, called *bondok*, that come from the pine cones of the umbrella pine; and the minuscule black ones or *zgougou*, that come from the Aleppo pine.

Our chef has chosen to dry-roast his pine nuts in a pan, which makes it easy to see how fast they are cooking. Alternatively, you can brown them in the oven. The method you use for dry-roasting has no bearing on the final flavor of the cream. Next, the pine nuts should be soaked for a long time in water, to release all their flavor and color. It is best to carry out these first two stages the day before.

When you filter the pine nut "milk," grind the mixture with the end of a whisk to get all the flavor out of it. If the cream sticks too much to the bottom of the saucepan during cooking, add a little cold water and continue beating until it is thick and consistent.

Pour this brownish cream into your goblets until they are three-quarters full; cover it with white cream, and then decorate with ground pistachios, white pine nuts, filberts, or almonds, arranged as the mood takes you.

First prepare the pine nut cream: the day before, put the pine nuts in a frying pan and dry-roast them to dry them out and improve their flavor.

Pour the pine nuts into the food processor. Add 8 cups/2 liters water in several stages, mixing as you go along, until you have a very thin purée. Transfer to a bowl and leave to soak for 8–12 hours in a cool place.

After soaking the pine nut purée, use a small ladle to pour it into a conical strainer and filter into a large bowl.

Zgougou

Sieve the all-purpose flour and add it gradually to the liquid, beating vigorously. Add the sugar, and beat in the same way. Heat the mixture in a saucepan until it is thick like a confectioners' custard. Pour into the goblets and leave to cool.

To make the white cream, bring 3 cups/ 750 ml of milk to the boil. Mix 1 cup/ 250 ml of cold milk with the cornstarch, eggs, sugar, and geranium water in a bowl.

Pour the mixture into the hot milk, while beating vigorously. Cook until you obtain a custard. Spoon some white cream into the goblets of pine nut cream. Leave to cool. Decorate with filberts, pistachios, and almonds, if using.

Bey's

Preparation time:	20 minutes
Cooking time:	10 minutes
Difficulty:	★

Serves 4

2/3 cup/150 g	superfine sugar
1 sachet	vanilla sugar (or bury a vanilla bean in a container of sugar for a few weeks)
4 tsp/20 ml	rosewater

3 cups/350 g	ground almonds
1/2 tsp	green colorant
1/2 tsp	pink colorant

Bey's *baklawa* is a typical Tunisian sweetmeat. Although the name harks back to the Ottoman presence in this country, it bears absolutely no resemblance to the traditional Turkish *baklava*.

Going back to the 19th century when the beys ruled over Tunisia, this tri-colored confection has been brought up to date over the course of the years. Originally made from marzipan, pistachios, and filberts, bey's *baklawa* are typically diamond shaped.

Easy to make, this specialty is usually made nowadays using just almonds. Originating from Asia, and known by the Romans as "Greek nuts," these oval nuts have a thick, green shell, velvety to the touch, containing one or two seeds. The seeds are eaten fresh or broiled. Marzipan is made from ground almonds and sugar, and is a popular ingredient of cakes and candies.

With the passage of time, pistachios and filberts have been dropped from the recipe, but to maintain the principle of the three colors, Tunisians use vegetable-based food colorants. The use of additives to change the color of a product or dish goes back to ancient times. Even then, people used saffron in their dishes.

To give the syrup its particular flavor, our chef has added rosewater to the mixture. Extracted from a variety of miniature roses, originating from Damascus, the petals are distilled and bring their delicate perfume to many oriental dishes.

Generally served with a selection of other sweetmeats, these delicious candies are mainly served at marriage celebrations. However, it's not uncommon to find them in patisseries. If you want to enjoy bey's *baklawa*, as the Tunisians do, prepare a mint and pine nut tea to go with it.

Prepare the syrup by cooking the superfine sugar, vanilla sugar, and rosewater in 7 tbsp/100 ml water for 10 minutes.

Sieve the ground almonds. Transfer to a container and pour in the syrup. Mix well with a spatula, and then knead the mixture by hand until you obtain a paste-like consistency.

Split the marzipan into 3 equal portions. Add the green colorant to one portion and knead with your hands to get the colour through. Add the pink colorant to the other portion and knead in the same way. Leave the third portion of the marzipan natural.

Baklawa

Mold the 3 marzipan portions into tubes. Flatten them separately with a rolling pin. Cut them into large, very regular squares.

Place the three marzipan squares on top of each other in this order: lay the pink marzipan square at the bottom, the white on top of the pink, and finally the green on top of the white.

Cut up the baklawa into 1¼ in/3 cm-wide strips. Cut into very regular diamond shapes. Arrange the bey's baklawa on a dish.

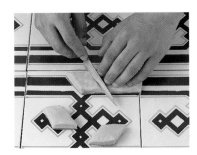

Bouza

Preparation time: 10 minutes
Cooking time: 10 minutes
Difficulty: ★

Serves 4

1¼ cups/150 g   blanched pistachios
1 can   condensed milk
3 tbsp   cornstarch

For the decoration:
pine nuts
ground almonds
filberts (hazelnuts)

This delicious pistachio beverage is typically Tunisian. It's often served at *iftar*, the breaking of the Fast of Ramadan at sunset. Easy to digest, it's a very nutritious drink, which fortifies the people during these meager days. Tunisians also drink *bouza* on other occasions, and traditionally it's served while marriage arrangements are being finalized, when the men from the two families meet each other. After they've agreed on the practical details, the hostess offers the famous beverage to celebrate the match. It is a dish that honors the person who drinks it; it shows great respect.

The pistachio is considered to be one of the most refined dried nuts, and is also found in many oriental pastries, in *baklawas*, or in tasty, honey-coated cigar-shaped delicacies. This nut is the seed of the pistachio tree. It originates from Syria, but is also grown in Iraq, Iran, and of course in Tunisia.

Condensed milk is regularly consumed in hot countries. This milk is easy to store and presents no health risk. Moreover, in the past, in countries where the refrigeration procedure was not very well established, such as in Africa, and where fresh milk could not be adequately kept in stock, or simply because there were insufficient dairy cows, this type of milk naturally became the ideal compromise if people wanted a dairy product.

The dried nuts that decorate the top of this delightful drink are as delicate in flavor as the pistachio. Almonds and pine nuts, as well as pistachios, are to be found in many of the pastries in confectioners' shops. Sometimes, filberts take the lion's share, because they are often used to replace the pistachio in making this cream. This filbert cream, which is just as delicious, is called *bellouza*. Tunisians serve it on the same occasions as the *bouza* with pistachios.

Cook the blanched pistachios under your oven broiler for 3–5 minutes. They must stay green. Process them until the nuts form a paste.

Add the condensed milk and add three times its volume in water.

Stir the cornstarch into the mixture. Mix again, stirring vigorously.

with Pistachios

Put the mixture on the heat and cook the bouza, *stirring constantly until the beverage thickens.*

Pour the bouza into four pretty glasses, sharing equally between each glass.

Decorate the bouza *with ground pistachios, pine nuts, and ground almonds. Serve the beverage hot.*

Debla

Preparation time:	40 minutes
Cooking time:	20 minutes
Leave dough to stand:	30 minutes
Difficulty:	★★

Serves 4

1	egg
⁷/₈ cup/100 g	all-purpose flour
2 tsp	cornstarch
	cooking oil

For the liquid honey syrup:

¹/₂	lemon
3¹/₂ tbsp/50 g	liquid honey

1¹/₄ cups/250 g	superfine sugar
2 tsp/10 ml	orange-flower water
1 tsp	cornstarch

For the decoration:

	sesame seeds
	ground pistachios

It's a well-known fact that the best recipes are often invented when a cook has to produce an improvised meal with whatever ingredients are in the cupboard. They have to be bold and innovative.

On that day, did Madame Boccara guess that the recipe she was preparing would be passed into Tunisian culinary heritage? At the time, the question simply didn't arise. This Italian Jewish grandmother, living in Leghorn, Tuscany, was more concerned about making a sweetmeat for some unexpected guests. All she had in the cupboard were a few eggs and some flour. With these basic ingredients, she made a dough, rolling it into an original shape. Then she plunged these "donuts" into boiling oil. Thinking that these "donuts" were a little dry and tasteless, in a moment of inspiration she coated them with liquid honey. It was the beginning of the 19th century and the *manicotti* had just been created.

Many years later, Madame Boccara's four daughters went to live in Tunisia, like many Italian Jews. They continued to make this pastry, carrying on their mother's creation. The family recipe became more sophisticated and flavors were added—notably orange-flower water was mixed with the liquid honey. They also decorated the *manicotti* with sesame seeds or ground pistachios.

Adopted by the whole of the Jewish community in Tunis, these excellent pastries then passed into Tunisian culinary heritage. Called *debla* in Arabic, they are also known as *wednin el kadhi*, which means "judge's ear."

A great favorite of the Tunisians, *debla* are usually served at family gatherings. Madame Boccara would certainly have been proud to learn that her improvised sweetmeat would be remembered two centuries later.

Prepare the debla *dough by mixing an egg into the all-purpose flour in a bowl. Mix well.*

Knead the mixture with your hands until you obtain a consistent dough. If the dough sticks, add a little more all-purpose flour. Leave the dough to stand wrapped in a dry piece of linen for 30 minutes.

Sprinkle 1 tsp cornstarch over the work area. Knead the dough. Reshape it into a ball, and continue to knead while sprinkling with cornstarch. Spread it out with a rolling pin, turning it over several times. Put it through the dough machine to make a thin layer.

Cut up the dough into long ribbons. Prepare the syrup by squeezing the ½ lemon. Cook it with the liquid honey, superfine sugar, orange-flower water, cornstarch, and 1¼ cups/300 ml water. Cook until the sugar dissolves.

Wedge a ribbon of dough between your forefinger and middle finger, then wind it up between your fingers. Repeat with the remaining dough ribbons.

Gently immerse a debla in the hot cooking oil. When cooked, drain the excess oil on a paper towel. Soak each cooked debla in the liquid honey syrup. Create variety by decorating some with sesame seeds and some with ground pistachios, and leave others plain.

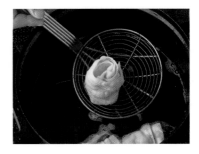

Jaouia

Preparation time:	50 minutes
Cooking time:	50 minutes
Difficulty:	★

Serves 4

1/2 cup/50 g	filberts (hazelnuts)
1 1/4 cups/150 g	blanched almonds
1/2 cup/50 g	walnuts
1/4 cup/20 g	pistachios
1/4 cup/25 g	pine nuts
1 tbsp/15 ml	vegetable oil

For the syrup:

3/4 cup/150 g	superfine sugar
1 sachet	vanilla sugar (bury a vanilla bean in a container of sugar for a few weeks)
1/2	lemon (juice of)

For the decoration:

ground pistachios
pine nuts

In Tunisia, the *jaouia* enjoys a special status. Considered to be a luxury dish, according to legend this pastry made from dried nuts was the bey's favorite sweetmeat. A symbol of wealth, today it is mainly served at marriage celebrations.

Dried nuts were already a great favorite of the Egyptians, Greeks, and Romans. Thanks to the nutritional value and high-calorie content concentrated in a very small nut, dried nuts are saturated with sunshine. Deliciously and naturally sweetened, they're rich in carbohydrates, vitamins, mineral salts, lipids, and even proteins.

Although walnuts are generally used to decorate oriental pastries, they are included in the ingredients for *jaouia*. These nuts, encased in a hard shell, contain a kernel with two halves, covered with a thin, relatively dark yellow film. To restore their youthful appearance, you can soak

dried nuts for a few hours in a container of hot milk. The film will come off by itself, restoring the attractive appearance of the flesh. For this recipe, the nuts must be ground. Don't be tempted to grind them in the blender, as the speed of the blade has the effect of removing the flavor of the oil.

Filberts, another ingredient in this pastry, are distinguished by their delicate flavor. These nuts from the hazel tree have a hard shell, containing an egg-shaped or round seed. Once they're shelled, filberts must be kept in a dark, dry place so that they don't go rancid. Both whole and ground filberts are used.

When the sugar has been cooked and mixed with the dried nuts, the *jaouia* resembles a nougatine. This Tunisian pastry, which is very high in calories, will appeal to children, giving them the energy they require.

Prepare the dried nuts separately by cooking them in the oven at 275 °F/ 140 °C: the filberts for approximately 20 minutes; the almonds for 15 minutes; then the walnuts for 5 minutes. Remove the skin of the broiled filberts.

With a rolling pin, roughly grind the almonds, walnuts, filberts, pistachios, and pine nuts.

For the syrup, heat the sugars with 7 tbsp/ 100 ml water. Bring to the boil, and add the lemon juice. To check whether the syrup's cooked, dip the blade of a knife in cold water, then in the syrup, then back in the cold water. The syrup should form a soft ball between your fingers.

Pour the syrup over the dried, ground nuts and stir well with a wooden spatula.

Lightly grease the work area and rolling pin with vegetable oil. Lay the jaouia out and flatten it. Repeat the procedure on a tray.

Cut out generous strips of jaouia on the tray and then cut them into squares. Decorate by gently dipping the surface of the jaouia squares into the ground pistachios. Top with a pine nut. Arrange the jaouia on a dish.

Kâber

Preparation time:	20 minutes
Cooking time:	10 minutes
Difficulty:	★

Serves 4

2¹/₂ cups/300 g	ground almonds
³/₄ cup/150 g	superfine sugar
1 sachet	vanilla sugar (bury a vanilla bean in a container of sugar for a few weeks)
4 tsp/20 ml	rosewater
¹/₂ tsp	green colorant
¹/₂ tsp	pink colorant

For the decoration:

superfine sugar
pine nuts (optional)

Kâber ellouz means "almond ball" in Arabic. Very easy to make, the history of this sweetmeat is worthy of being included in the *Tales from 1,001 Arabian Nights*.

Legend has it that a very long time ago, an evil spirit deprived Tunisia of its dates. The sultan who reigned at that time was a cruel man. Only date pastries had the power to soften his nature. As the days passed, date reserves continued to diminish. One of the desperate palace cooks thought she could deceive the sultan's taste buds, so she prepared some small balls made of marzipan, pistachios, and filberts. Discovering her trickery, the king beheaded her. Appalled at the thought of suffering the same fate, another cook threw the remaining balls into a sack of sugar. The *kâber ellouz* were born…

In Tunisia, these delightful treats are mainly served on important feast days, such as engagements, marriages, or circumcisions. As is the case with many of these recipes, marzipan is the star ingredient. Essentially grown in the Sfax region, the almond tree blossoms in the spring, and is recognizable by its magnificent white flowers. The first, sweet, fresh almonds have a subtle flavor. On the other hand, dried almonds, which you find whole, split, ground, in the form of a paste, or even a cream, are an ingredient of many cakes, cookies, candies, and confectionery.

Well, according to the legend, the sugar saved the second cook's head. This sweet-flavored substance forms naturally in the leaves of many plants and is concentrated in their roots or stems. In North Africa, sugar is extracted from the date palm. But the most commonly used is cane sugar. Thousands of years ago, Asians were already using sugar in the form of cane syrup, while Europeans were eating honey.

Prepare the paste by sieving the ground almonds.

Make the syrup by cooking the superfine sugar, and the vanilla sugar in 7 tbsp (100 ml) water for 10 minutes. Stir in the rosewater. Pour the syrup into the ground almonds and blend with a spatula.

Using your fingers, knead the paste on the work area.

Ellouz

Split the marzipan into 3 equal portions. Add the green colorant to one part and knead to mix the color through. Color the second part with the pink colorant in the same way. Leave the third part natural.

Roll each colored batch onto a work area to thin it out. Make 3 sausage-shapes measuring ³/₄ in/2 cm in diameter. Create a tri-colored braid from the parts.

Cut the braid into approximately 1 oz/ 20 g pieces. Roll them between the palms of your hands to form consistent, smooth balls. Coat the kâber ellouz with superfine sugar to finish. Serve in a pile on a plate, decorated with pine nuts, if using.

Leïla's

Preparation time:	30 minutes
Cooking time:	30 minutes
Difficulty:	★★

Serves 4

1¼ cups/150 g	almonds
1¼ cups/150 g	filberts (hazelnuts)
½ cup/50 g	pine nuts
2½ cups/500 g	sugar
1	lemon

1 trickle	geranium water
½ cup/100 g	unsalted butter
12	*malsouka* sheets
½ cup/50 g	ground pistachios

Our chef's mother, Leïla, inspired Ali to create this recipe, which is crunchy and yet melts in the mouth, and is highly flavored. The *ourta* is one of the great family of Tunisian pastries, a tasty combination of Turkish, Greek, and Andalucian influences.

Most of these delights are hidden in a *malsouka* sheet. Prepared with semolina and thickened with a very small amount of egg and water, the batter is stirred until smooth, and then a large copper dish is heated on a charcoal stove. The slightly runny batter is very slowly poured onto the very hot plate, until a large, extremely thin sheet of batter is obtained. The batter must be cooked until it is crispy and crumbly.

Factory-made *malsouka* sheets are a very practical solution if you want to make the *ourta* quickly. But the chef prefers to make his own. Actually, he feels that the commercially produced batter, made from flour and eggs, is not fine enough and is a little hard. He also takes the precaution of laying two sheets at the bottom of the mold to stiffen the cake, and it also enables him to remove one of the layers, should the bottom layer burn.

Ali Matri grinds the almonds and filberts only roughly, to keep a slightly crunchy texture. When preparing the *ourta*, he sprinkles just a few pine nuts over the almonds and filberts, and keeps the rest for decoration.

In the northeast of Tunisia, the Cap Bon peninsula abounds in bitter orange trees and geraniums, which are destined for the production of flower water. Actually, this country produces numerous extracts—rose, thyme, orange-flower, and geranium among others. Our *ourta* is enhanced with wild geranium-flower water, which gives this dessert a completely unexpected flavor.

Broil the almonds, filberts, and pine nuts separately on a tray under the oven broiler. Grind the almonds and filberts roughly in the food processor bowl. Place whole pine nuts to one side.

Pour the sugar and a glass of water into a heavy-duty saucepan. Squeeze a piece of lemon into it. Cook over quite a high heat, until the sugar dissolves and you obtain a syrup. Take the pan off the heat and mix in the geranium water. Stir well.

Using a brush, coat the inside of a round cake mold with melted butter. Place a malsouka sheet on the base. Brush this with the melted butter. Place another sheet on top, and coat this with butter, too.

Ourta

Sprinkle some of the chopped dried nuts over the malsouka sheets. Sprinkle with a few pine nuts. Place another malsouka sheet on top, brush with melted butter, sprinkle with dried nuts ... until you've used up all the ingredients. Finish with a malsouka sheet coated in butter.

Bake the cake for approximately 10 minutes in the oven, until the surface is golden brown and crispy. As soon as it's cooked, take it out of the oven and drizzle it with geranium syrup.

When the cake has thoroughly absorbed all the syrup, turn it out carefully onto a serving plate. Sprinkle it with ground pistachios and the rest of the broiled pine nuts.

Chamia Parfait

Preparation time: 30 minutes
Cooking time: 10 minutes
To chill: 24 hours
Difficulty: ★★

Serves 4

1⅛ cup/250 ml	light whipping cream
4	eggs
¼ cup/50 g	sugar
5 tbsp/70 g	*chamia* (or *halva*)
1	lemon
6 tsp/30 g	sesame seeds

For the orange sauce:

7	Tunisian blood oranges
1 tsp	cornstarch
3 tbsp/45 g	superfine sugar

For the garnish:

	mint for decoration

Chamia parfait is a recent Tunisian creation and can be distinguished from classic French parfaits. It is the sesame paste called *chamia*, or *halva*, that gives the dish its typically eastern flavor. As ice cream doesn't feature very much in the traditional culinary customs of Tunisia, this creation of our chef is very welcome.

Readily available in the whole of the Mediterranean region, *chamia* is a factory-made mixture produced from sesame seeds, sugar, and various other products. Sometimes, dried nuts such as almonds, pistachios, and filberts are added to the mixture. To break it up before adding it to the ice cream, place in a sieve above a bowl, and crush it through with the back of a spoon.

As when making sponge cake, the blended eggs and sugar must be beaten in a basin placed over a saucepan of hot water to produce a thick cream; then continue to beat it off

the heat, until the mixture cools down. The well-chilled whipped cream is added to the mixture after the *chamia*, so that it doesn't lose its thick consistency.

When the mixture has been freezing for 3 hours, remember to stir the parfait with a fork. If you prefer, instead of pouring the parfait into individual molds, you can place it in a cake mold, lined with plastic wrap. When it's very cold, turn out the parfait and cut it into slices.

The citrus fruit sauce is prepared with one of the best oranges in the world: the Tunisian blood orange is a semi-blood orange harvested from January to April in the Cap Bon peninsula, from Tunis to Bizerte, and in the Kairouan region. Juicy and fragrant, it has an oval or round shape, and its delicately colored, smooth skin is easy to peel when it ripens. Generally, there are no pits in these oranges. Thompson oranges are a suitable alternative.

First make the parfait. Beat the well-chilled light whipping cream until thick.

Break 2 whole eggs and 2 yolks in a basin. Stir in the sugar. Place over a saucepan of simmering hot water, and beat until the mixture turns pale and thickens.

Take off the heat, and crumble the chamia *into the egg cream. Add a few lemon shavings. Blend gently so that the mixture doesn't lose volume. Cool.*

and Orange Sauce

When the chamia cream is very cold, incorporate the whipped cream, gently folding it in to form the parfait mixture.

Place a piece of plastic wrap in individual small molds. With a tablespoon, fill each mold with parfait. Freeze for 24 hours. For the sauce, squeeze 5 of the oranges and mix the juice and the cornstarch in a saucepan.

Stir in the sugar, and mix. Bring gently to the boil until the sauce thickens. Allow to cool down. Turn out the parfaits onto plates. Decorate with peeled orange quarters, sesame seeds, and mint. Surround the parfait with the orange sauce.

Palm Grove

Preparation time: 40 minutes
Difficulty: ★

Serves 4

2½ cups/400 g	*alig* dates
3 slices	sandwich bread
3½ tbsp/50 ml	olive oil
¼ cup/50 g	salted butter
½ cup/100 g	superfine sugar

Renowned for its magnificent palm grove, the oasis of Tozeur extends over more than 2,470 acres/1,000 hectares. In this southwest region of Tunisia, many people still earn their living from the date harvest. This providential fruit is therefore found in many recipes.

Palm grove *rfiss* is a great favorite of nomads. When they're on the move, shepherds, camel drivers, and goatherds carry this candy in their *mokhla*, a small, woven, woollen bag, and they enjoy it with a glass of milk.

Easy to make, palm grove *rfiss* is essentially made of chopped dates, sugar, salted butter, olive oil, and breadcrumbs. It's very high in calories, and this dessert has the advantage of keeping for several days.

Tozeur oasis is renowned for the quality of its dates. Only the female palm trees bear the fruit. Our chef has chosen the *alig* variety for this recipe. They're mahogany in color, and quite large with a smooth, semi-dry skin, and an exceptionally sweet flavor. If you don't use fresh dates, the chef advises you to blanch the dates for 1–2 minutes in boiling water.

To make a success of this recipe, the salted butter must be at room temperature. In Tunisian cuisine, salted butter is mainly served as a condiment and brings its slightly sharp flavor to dishes and pastries.

For the breadcrumbs, you can use roasted, fine semolina instead of sandwich bread.

In the past, when feminine curves were a measure of beauty, the women of Tozeur ate the palm grove *rfiss* without restraint. Nowadays, this very oriental delight is still enjoyed, but with a lot more moderation!

Pit the dates and chop them finely in a grinder.

Break the slices of bread into small pieces and make breadcrumbs. Add to the chopped dates and mix with your fingers.

Add the olive oil and mix well with your fingers.

Rfiss

Add the salted butter and mix to form a paste.

Add ¹/₄ cup/50 of the superfine sugar. Mix again.

Make the small balls into equal sizes and roll them between the palms of your hands. Sprinkle the rest of the sugar over the rfiss and roll them between your palms. Arrange the rfiss in a large dish.

Takoua with

Preparation time: 25 minutes
Cooking time: 5 minutes
Difficulty: ★

Serves 4

2¹/₂ cups/500 g	sesame seeds
3	oranges
7 tbsp/100 ml	orange-flower water
¹/₂ cup/100 g	superfine sugar
⁷/₈ cup/100 g	confectioners' sugar

For the decoration:
mint leaves

The *takoua* with orange-flower water is a traditional dessert from the Bizerte region. This easy-to-make specialty was originally prepared in Jewish families to celebrate Shabbat (the Jewish Sabbath).

These small balls made from sesame seeds are a real delight. For this preparation, the sesame seeds must be sorted by hand to remove impurities The sesame is an oleaginous plant and its minuscule oval seeds are often used to garnish oriental pastries, such as the *halva*, along with honey and almonds. In addition, sesame oil is much enjoyed in the Mediterranean region, and particularly in the Middle East.

The orange flavor is optional in this recipe. Orange-flower water is blended with sesame seeds, and brings its mellow flavors to the dish. To make orange-flower water the flowers are gathered from the bitter orange tree, and then distilled. This delicately flavored water is used to flavor many Tunisian dishes. In some families from Bizerte, the *takoua* are made with geranium water or rosewater instead.

For his part, our chef opted to base this recipe on the orange by making juice and decorating the plates with orange segments. In Tunisia, orange groves stretch as far as the eye can see. These winter fruits are renowned for their vitamin A and C content. According to the variety, their flavor is relatively sweet, slightly acidic, or fragrant. Preferably choose bright, heavy fruits. As they're quite hardy, they keep for several days at room temperature.

This dessert is particularly rich. However, you can add a little unsalted butter, so that it melts in the mouth even more. Serve *takoua* with orange-flower water at any time with the traditional glass of mint tea.

Arrange the sesame seeds over the work area and sort them with your hands to remove impurities. Rinse in water and drain. Allow them to dry for approximately 10 minutes.

Brown the sesame seeds in a frying pan, while stirring with a wooden spatula. Squeeze 2 of the oranges and keep the juice to one side for the decoration. Thoroughly peel the remaining orange and remove the segments for the decoration.

Put the sesame seeds into the food processor and pour in the orange-flower water. Blend at a high speed.

Orange-Flower Water

Add the confectioners' sugar to the mixture. Blend until a paste is formed.

Spread out the paste on a dish and let it stand for a few moments.

Pour the confectioners' sugar over the work area and roll up the sesame paste with your hands to make balls. Arrange the mint leaves on the plates and place the takoua on top of them. Pour a little orange juice onto the plates and decorate with the reserved orange segments.

Chabakia

Preparation time: 30 minutes
Resting time: 15 minutes
Cooking time: 10 minutes
Difficulty: ★★

Serves 6

5 oz/150 g	sesame seeds
1	egg
2 tbsp	white vinegar
1½ cups/200 g	almonds
1 tsp	ground cinnamon

1 tbsp	aniseed
½ stick/50 g	butter
7 tbsp/100 ml	olive oil
7 tbsp/100 ml	orange flower water
3½ tbsp	baking powder
1 pinch	saffron threads
1 pinch	mastic
4⅓ cups/500 g	flour
	oil for frying
2¼ lbs/1 kg	honey

During Ramadan, Moroccans generally break their fast after sunset with *harira* soup, served with dates and pastries, such as crisp *chabakia* with honey. In Fez, *chabakia* are known as *griwach*, and in central Morocco as *m'kharka*. These sweet ribbons are among the various pastries offered with coffee after a wedding feast. There is another kind of *chabakia*, made from orange-colored dough and rolled up into a turban shape. They are then dipped in syrup.

Normally, *chabakia* are made without almonds, and with sesame seeds as the foundation of the dough. Sesame seeds are called *janjlan* in Moroccan. For this recipe, some of the sesame seeds are ground and worked into the dough, while the rest are used for garnish. It is best to roast the sesame seeds without fat to allow them to develop their nutty aroma to the full.

Fatima Mouzoun flavors her dough with saffron threads, orange flower water, aniseed, and mastic, a resin from a type of acacia that grows in Egypt and the Sudan. In Morocco, it is available as pale yellow crystals, while in other countries it is usually available as a white powder. The chef crushes it in a mortar with a pinch of sugar. Also crush the saffron threads with a mortar and pestle.

The chef works the dough by kneading it repeatedly between the fingers and with the palm of the hand. During kneading, she makes the dough firmer by adding flour and chopped almonds. She tastes the mix from time to time, thus checking the quantity of water and orange flower water. The vinegar serves to keep the dough elastic.

Before serving, you could sprinkle the *chabakia* with sesame seeds, chopped pistachios, or almonds.

Dry-roast the sesame seeds in a frying pan. Put the egg, vinegar, blanched and chopped almonds, cinnamon, crushed aniseed, 3½ oz/100 g of the sesame seeds crushed in a food processor, melted butter, olive oil, and orange flower water into a bowl.

Beat the mixture with a whisk. Add baking powder, saffron threads, and mastic and then the flour. Knead firmly by hand until you have a firm, smooth dough. Roll into several large balls and allow to rest for 15 minutes.

On a floured work surface, roll the dough out thinly with a rolling pin. With a pastry cutter, cut the dough into a large rectangle, then into 6 smaller rectangles.

Taking one of the small rectangles, use the pastry cutter to make 6 parallel cuts, but not quite to the edges, Separate the strips with your fingers, press two of the corners together, and then the other two corners, allowing the strips in the middle to protrude.

Prepare the other chabakia in the same way. Put into hot oil and deep-fry until the chabakia are almost dark brown. Then scoop them out of the oil with a spatula.

Immediately place the chabakia into a deep plate with honey and turn in the honey with a spatula. Then drain them in a sieve. Sprinkle with the remaining sesame seeds.

Fakkas

Preparation time: 20 minutes
Cooking time: 30 minutes
Difficulty: ★

Serves 4

1½ cups/200 g almonds
1⅛ cups/250 g sugar
8 eggs
1¾ sticks/200 g butter
1 tbsp /15 ml oil

1¼ cups/200 g raisins
¼ tsp vanilla extract
1 splash orange flower water
3½ tbsp baking powder
8⅔ cups/1 kg flour

In Moroccan families, tea is served up to three times a day. It is traditional to offer a little bowl of *fakkas* with it, together with almonds, peanuts, dates, dried figs, and raisins. In the interior of the country, people make very small *fakkas* and serve them to guests at the New Year Festival, *Ashura*.

Like many Moroccan pastries, *fakkas* are distinguished by the generous quantity of almonds they contain. Almond trees, which belong to the rose family, bear fruit from June to the end of September. The almonds are harvested by being shaken or struck out of the tree, the gray-green fuzzy fruit flesh around the shell, which is inedible, is removed. The almonds are then dried. Dried almonds are available all the year round in many different forms: in their hard shells, as a kernel only with their brown skins, peeled, or even ready chopped.

The chef sometimes uses crushed aniseed, sesame seeds, or walnuts instead of almonds. If neither almonds nor walnuts are available, she kneads sesame seeds into the dough. The raisins, which make the dough sweet and juicy, are produced in the north-west of Morocco, in the region around Khmissat and T'ifelt. In the markets, you can buy reddish, golden, or dark raisins.

Fatima Mouzoun forms the dough into *fakkas* in the shape of little baguettes, baked golden-brown in the oven and then cut into thin slices, barely one-fifth of an inch thick. These slices must be cut to regular sizes if they are to look good. The chef recommends brushing the rolls of dough with egg yolk to produce an appetizing golden-brown color in the oven. As soon as they are cooked, they are allowed to harden overnight (they can also be put in the freezer). Then the long rolls can be cut diagonally into slices easily.

Crush the almonds in a mortar and pestle, but coarsely enough for some largish pieces to remain.

Place the sugar and 7 eggs in a bowl. Beat with a whisk until the mixture is pale yellow and foaming.

Add the softened butter, oil, crushed almonds, raisins, vanilla extract, and orange flower water. Beat lightly and place on a large plate.

Work in the baking powder and the sieved flour with your hands. Continue to knead until you have a firm, smooth dough. Divide this into several balls.

Shape each ball into a roll, about 8 inches/20 cm long and 1 inch/3 cm thick. Brush with beaten egg yolk. Place the rolls on an oiled baking sheet and bake for 15 minutes in the oven until golden-brown. Allow the fakkas to cool.

Place the fakkas on a chopping board. Cut diagonally into slices about $^{1}/_{5}$ inch/5 mm thick. Bake in the oven for another 15 minutes until the slices are golden-yellow.

Figs with

Preparation time: 15 minutes
Cooking time: 15 minutes
Difficulty: ★

Serves 4

2¼ lbs/1 kg	fresh figs
½ stick/50 g	butter
3½ oz/100 g	thyme honey
5 oz/150 g	fresh goat's cheese

For the garnish (optional):
mint leaves

Although there are many lovely Moroccan desserts consisting of small pastries with dried fruit, there are no traditional sweet dishes with fresh fruit. Various kinds of fruit are offered in a basket or served in sweet salads with cinnamon and orange flower water. M'hamed Chahid has proved his creativity once again and proposes lightly frying quartered figs in butter, pouring a syrup of thyme honey over them and serving with goat's cheese.

M'hamed Chahid comes from Tangier: northern Morocco is equally famous for its figs and for its goat's cheese and honey. The chef uses thyme honey that is as dark as chocolate. If you can't get thyme honey, simply use ordinary honey and warm it in a pan with a sprig of thyme.

For this dessert, the chef likes to use white figs, which are ideal because of the combination of colors. However, purple-skinned figs are also suitable. Two kinds of figs are on offer in Moroccan markets. The *bakour*, which ripen in a single week, are the source of the proverb "The seven days of figs soon pass." All those who boast of their successes and forget that inevitably other times will follow get to hear this proverb. The other variety of fig is very sweet and has a much longer season.

Choose a good quality fresh goat's cheese. It is still made by hand in the Rif Mountains, with the milk churned by being shaken in a goatskin. The cheese is then allowed to drain for three or four days wrapped in a cloth. Little cubes of fresh goat's cheese taste wonderful with the fruit covered with honey syrup.

Rinse and wash the figs. Remove the stalks. Cut the fruits, starting from the top, into regular thirds or quarters.

Cut the butter into pieces. Melt in a pan until it foams.

Put the quartered figs into the hot butter. Shake the pan in order to coat the figs well with the butter, and brown them evenly.

Thyme Honey

Remove the figs and set aside. Instead of the figs, now add the honey to the melted butter. Stir with a wooden spatula. Reduce the sauce over a medium heat, stirring continuously.

Cut the goat's cheese into little cubes.

Pour the honey syrup onto a plate. Place the cubes of cheese in the middle, then arrange the figs in a ring around them. Garnish with leaves of mint.

Date Bites

Preparation time: 40 minutes
Resting time
for dough: 15 minutes
Cooling time: 15 minutes
Cooking time: 25 minutes
Difficulty: ★

Serves 6–8

For the dough:
1¼ sticks/150 g butter
2 oz/50 g margarine
¼ tsp vanilla extract

2⅛ cups/250 g flour
8 eggs
1 pinch instant coffee

For the date filling:
11¾ cups/2 kg dates
1 pinch ground cinnamon
⅓ oz/10 g mastic
1 pinch grated nutmeg
7 tbsp/100 ml orange flower water

The guests of the "Beach Club" hotel in Agadir hold Abdelmalek el-Meraoui's date bites in high regard. The little rhomboid pieces are both simple and sophisticated: two thin layers of sweet dough surrounding a delicious date filling. In Morocco, such little pastries are very popular, and there are many recipes with dates. The date paste produced by the chef is also suitable for filling *yufka* dough "cigars," *rziza*, and *m'semmen* (crepes).

It is the mixture of butter and margarine that prevents the sweet dough from tearing when you make it. The chef mixes butter and margarine by hand and squeezes the shortening firmly through his fingers to eliminate even the smallest lump. If the dough becomes too soft, he adds a little flour and continues to work it. The finished dough is shaped into a ball and then needs to rest in the fridge. In this way, it keeps its shape.

The date filling makes the bites marvelously soft and sweet. Abdelmalek el-Meraoui generally uses *tmar* dates with very soft flesh. During Ramadan, Moroccans often eat these dates either fresh or dried. On festive occasions, they like to offer their guests milk and *tmar* dates as soon as they arrive.

Orange flower water serves to refine many desserts. It is most often made from the flowers of bitter orange trees. Sometimes bitter oranges are also puréed with the dates to make a filling.

To garnish the pastries, the chef takes a brush and coats them with a mixture of beaten egg and instant coffee (or caramel). With a fork, he then draws lines on the surface and this gives them an attractive golden-yellow pattern after baking.

Put the butter and the margarine into a bowl. Knead together well with your hands. Add vanilla extract, flour and 7 eggs. Beat all together well at first, then knead to make a good smooth dough. Roll into a ball and allow to rest for 15 minutes in the fridge.

For the filling, bring water to the boil in the lower part of a couscous steamer. Remove pits from the dates and place them in the strainer part of the couscous steamer. Cover and steam for 10 minutes, then skin the dates.

Place the dates in a bowl. Sprinkle with cinnamon, mastic, and nutmeg. Purée in a food processor. Add orange flower water and mix again.

à la el-Meraoui

Roll out the dough with a rolling pin. Cut a large rectangle, corresponding to the size of the baking pan, out of the dough. Roll the rest of the dough out again and cut another rectangle of the same size.

Line a rectangular baking pan with baking parchment. Cover with one rectangle of dough. Spread the date paste on top of it and smooth down with a spatula or the back of a spoon. Cover with the second rectangle of dough.

Beat 1 egg with a little instant coffee. Spread onto the dough with a brush. Place in the chill compartment for 15 minutes. Cut the cake into rhomboids. Place on a baking sheet and bake in the oven for 15 minutes at 430 °F/220 °C.

Haloua

Preparation time: 30 minutes
Cooking time: 20 minutes
Difficulty: ★

Serves 4

For the dough:
2²/₃ cups/300 g   flour
2¹/₄ sticks/250 g   butter
4 tbsp   orange flower water

For the filling:
1¹/₂ cups/250 g   dates
²/₃ cup/100 g   almonds
                  oil for frying
¹/₂ cup/50 g   shelled walnuts
¹/₂ tsp   ground cinnamon
4 tbsp   orange flower water

For the garnish:
2¹/₄ cups/250 g   powdered sugar

The term *haloua* covers all kinds of sweet foods and pastries, and among them are the 20 or so different types of sweet cookies and pastries that are served on festive occasions. Here, Fatima Mouzoun introduces us to little pastries, shaped like small ships, that melt in the mouth. They are made from little circles of dough with a small amount of filling. The dough is folded over the filling and the ends pinched together with the fingers. Sometimes Fatima Mouzoun also shapes the dough into balls and decorates them with a fork. You can let your imagination run free and cut the *haloua* into all kinds of shapes.

There are many different varieties of date growing in the Moroccan palm groves. The chef recommends using only best quality dates: she prefers the large *majhoul* dates, which are rather dark but creamy, sweet, and juicy. If you wish, you can replace the dates with prunes or dried figs.

Almonds, known as *louz*, are an essential ingredient in all Moroccan cookies and pastries. Almond trees grow mainly in the south of the country, in the regions of Agadir and Rachidia—that is to say, in the Sous area.

For pastries, Fatima Mouzoun only uses almonds that have been stored with the brown skins on. Blanched almonds dry out very quickly, and if they are used for baking the result is often too firm and dry. To blanch almonds, put them into boiling water and wait until the skin begins to loosen. Then put them onto a work surface, take each one between two fingers and squeeze one end. The almonds will then slip out of their skins.

For the filling, put the dates onto a serving platter and remove the stones.

Put the almonds into a pot of boiling water. When the skins bubble, scoop out the almonds with a slotted spatula and then remove the skins.

Heat the oil in a pan. When it is very hot, put in the blanched almonds and fry for 5 minutes on a high heat until golden-brown. Take out of the oil with a slotted spatula and drain. Chop in a food processor and put aside in a bowl.

with Dates

Chop the dates and shelled walnuts in the food processor. Add chopped almonds, cinnamon, and orange flower water. Continue to use the food processor until a smooth paste is formed. Use your hands to make small "date" shapes out of the paste.

For the dough, put the flour onto a plate and make a well in the center. Put the softened pieces of butter into the well. Knead by hand. Work in the orange flower water. Knead well together and roll the dough into a ball.

Take a small ball of dough in your hand and squeeze flat. Place one of the "dates" on it and fold the dough over the top. Pinch the ends together. Form the other haloua in the same way. Bake for 15 minutes in the oven. Allow to cool and sprinkle with powdered sugar.

Millefeuille with

Preparation time: 35 minutes
Cooking time: 25 minutes
Difficulty: ★

Serves 4

4 leaves	gelatin
8 sheets	*yufka* pastry (phyllo)
	oil for frying
6 tbsp	honey
¼ glass	orange flower water
2	plums

2	peaches
1	apple (Golden Delicious)
22	large strawberries
2 slices	pineapple
2	kiwi fruit
2 cups/500 ml	milk
½ cup/100 g	sugar
2–3 sticks	cinnamon
2	egg whites
8	mint leaves
4	walnuts

Bouchaïb Kama has here created a very decorative and colorful dessert, with a tempting crisp consistency. Various small pieces of fruit have a syrup of honey and orange flower water poured over them and are then arranged on fried triangles of *yufka* pastry. This forms several alternating layers of fruit and fried pastry. To serve, the millefeuilles are topped with a small meringue, slices of strawberry, and mint leaves. Finally, a splash of strawberry sauce rounds off this sophisticated delicacy.

The peaches, plums, apples, strawberries, and kiwi fruit in this dessert all grow in Morocco. The Midelt region, to the west of the beautiful High Atlas, is famed for its peaches, plums, and apples. Golden Delicious, Mackintosh, and an elongated variety with a pale skin on one side and pinkish colored on the other are the apples mainly used for cooking in Morocco.

Strawberries are also cultivated on a large scale in Morocco. The big plantations are in the neighborhood of Asilah and Moulay Bousselham (between Rabat and Tangier), where the fields stretch to the horizon. The chef recommends using large fruit that can be easily sliced.

The fruits will stay on the sheets of pastry without difficulty, as the honey and gelatin stick them down. A great deal of honey is eaten in Morocco and there are many varieties. For this recipe, any blossom honey will do.

If you poach the beaten egg white, make sure the milk is not too hot, or the egg white will collapse. As soon as the meringues are cooked, drain them on kitchen paper. When stacking the millefeuilles, brush honey and gelatin over the triangles of pastry before placing the pieces of fruit onto them.

Soak the gelatin in cold water. Cut the yufka pastry into large triangles. Fry on a slotted spatula dipped in very hot oil until they are golden-brown. Drain on kitchen paper.

Put the honey, mixed with a little water, in a saucepan together with the orange flower water and the soaked gelatin. Beat with a whisk until a smooth syrup is formed.

Wash the plums, peaches, apples, and strawberries. Peel the apple, pineapple, and kiwi fruit. Slice all fruit thinly (reserve 10 strawberries). Put all fruit, except for the kiwi fruit, into a bowl and pour over the syrup. Allow to harden in the fridge.

Honeyed Fruits

Place a triangle of fried pastry onto a dessert plate. On it, place alternating layers of fruit and pastry.

Finish with a final piece of pastry. Form the other millefeuilles in the same manner. Keeping two for the garnish, purée the reserved strawberries and strain to make a sauce. Heat the milk with a pinch of sugar and the cinnamon sticks.

Beat the egg whites with the remaining sugar until stiff. Poach portions of the beaten egg white in hot milk. Garnish each millefeuille with a meringue of egg white, slices of strawberry, leaves of mint, and crushed nuts. Pour on a little strawberry sauce and serve.

Sfouf

Preparation time:	30 minutes
Cooking time:	20 minutes
Difficulty:	★

Serves 6

4⅓ cups/500 g	flour
3½ cups/500 g	almonds
	oil for frying
3⅓ lbs/1.5 kg	sesame seeds
2 tbsp	ground cinnamon

1 pinch	nutmeg
1 pinch	mastic
2¼ sticks/250 g	butter
1 pinch	green aniseed
1⅛ lb/500 g	honey
7 tbsp/100 ml	orange flower water

Sfouf is eaten frequently in Morocco and is known by several different names: it is also called *selou* or *zameta*. Culinary customs connected with birth are of particular importance in Morocco, and new mothers are therefore often given a plate of *sfouf* to strengthen them.

Usually, *sfouf* has no honey in it and the sesame seeds are worked directly into the mixture. Fatima Mouzoun, however, shapes the *sfouf* mixture into a dome on a plate and dusts it with powdered sugar. She then decorates the dome with fried almonds. The chef has been inspired to create another form of presentation—she has spread the paste on a bed of roasted sesame seeds and sprinkled the top with a layer of more sesame seeds. The mixture is then cut into little squares and allowed to harden.

In this recipe, the *sfouf* is not baked. It is therefore necessary to brown the flour in the oven, to fry the almonds, and to roast the sesame seeds. Dry-roasting without adding fat or oil imparts an additional nutty flavor to the sesame seeds.

Orange flower water and mastic gum also add their own particular touches. Moroccans prefer hand-made orange flower water, distilled in a container that looks rather like a couscous steamer. At weddings, the guests are sprinkled with orange flower water, and it is offered to the bridal couple to drink, together with milk, sugar, and dates.

Mastic gum is available in Morocco as yellowish crystals, which are crushed with a mortar and pestle together with a little powdered sugar. It comes from two types of acacias that grow in Egypt and in the Sudan.

Put the flour onto a baking tray and brown in the oven for 10 minutes. Then sieve it onto a large plate.

Peel the almonds and then fry them for 5 minutes in a frying pan with the oil. Allow to drain. In another pan, dry-roast the sesame seeds without adding fat, for 5 minutes.

Put 1⅛ lb/500 g roasted sesame seeds into the food processor and put the rest aside. Add the fried almonds and chop.

Put the sesame seed and almond mixture on the plate with the browned flour. Add the cinnamon, nutmeg, mastic, melted butter, crushed aniseed, honey, and orange flower water. Knead well to make a good smooth mixture.

Distribute 1 1/8 lb/500 g roasted sesame seeds evenly over the bottom of a baking pan. Cover with the mixture you have just made. Sprinkle the remaining sesame seeds on top.

Press the sfouf down flat with the palm of your hand, then cut it lengthways and across to make regular squares. Leave until the sfouf has hardened.

Dried Fruit Tarte

Preparation time: 50 minutes
Soaking time: 15 minutes
Cooling time: 15 minutes
Cooking time: 20 minutes
Difficulty: ★★

Serves 4

For the pastry:

³⁄₄ stick/80 g	butter
1²⁄₃ cups/200 g	flour
2	egg yolks
1 pinch	salt
¹⁄₄ cup/50 g	sugar
2 tbsp/30 ml	rose water
1 tbsp/15 g	butter for greasing

For the cream:

4	eggs
¹⁄₂ cup/100 g	sugar
1 tsp	ground cinnamon
2 tbsp/30 ml	cream
2 tbsp/30 ml	rose water

For the filling:

¹⁄₂ cup/100 g	sugar
4 oz/120 g	dried figs
²⁄₃ cup/100 g	dates
²⁄₃ cup/100 g each	prunes, raisins
¹⁄₂ cup/80 g	preserved apricots
2 tbsp	rose water
1 tsp	sugar
3 tbsp	clear tart glaze

This dried fruit tart is the chef's own creation. It consists exclusively of products on offer in the Ouarzazate and Zagora regions. This very rich dessert is a temptation both for children and for adults.

To make this dish, you have to prepare a very firm, plain pastry. This pastry, usually reserved for especially fine baking, is then covered with dried fruit. Reserve part of the fruit and use it for decoration.

The apricots cultivated in Morocco are famed not only for their delicious flavor, but also because they contain many vitamins, especially vitamin A. These round, yellow to orange colored fruits with their fuzzy skins owe their name to the Catalan word *abercoc*. This in turn is based on the Latin *praecox*, meaning "early, premature."

The figs that Mohamed Tastift uses for this pastry are widely distributed all over the Mediterranean region. These fruits, originating in the Middle East, are eaten fresh or dried. They are very nourishing, rich in many vitamins, minerals and sugar, and mostly come from Turkey. They are dried in the sun, washed in seawater, and then sometimes treated with sulfur. They are eaten either on their own or filled with almonds or walnuts.

Just like the chef, most of the people living in Ouarzazate like rose water. The flavor goes wonderfully well with Mohamed Tastift's pastry. Every year, in the village of el-Kelaa, the capital of damask roses, 4,000 tons of buds of the little flowers are gathered. Rose water, especially widespread in Turkish cuisine, is also often offered to guests as a refreshment before the meal.

First make a syrup: bring 1 cup/250 ml of water to the boil with the sugar. Take the pot off the heat and add the dried figs. Soak for 15 minutes.

To prepare the filling, remove the pits from the dates. Dice small, and do the same to the prunes, apricots, and figs. Mix the rose water with the sugar. Soak the chopped fruit and the raisins in this mixture.

For the pastry, dice the butter into small cubes. Put the flour onto the work surface, add the cubes of butter, and rub between your hands. Add the egg yolks, 1 pinch of salt, sugar, and rose water. Shape the dough into a ball. Roll in plastic wrap. Put into the fridge for 15 minutes.

Ouarzazia

For the cream, beat eggs and sugar with a whisk. Add and beat in the ground cinnamon, cream, and rose water.

Grease a springform pan with butter. Roll out the pastry with a rolling pin, and then lay it in the springform pan. Press the pastry into the join of base and side of the tin with your fingers. Cut off any excess pastry around the top.

Place the soaked fruit onto the base of the tart. Pour on the cream. Bake in the oven at 350 °F/180 °C for 20 minutes. Mix the glaze with a little water, and brush over the tart.

The Chefs &

Achiai, Abdellah
Morocco

Adar, Gökçen
Turkey

Aïtali, Mohammed
Morocco

Anastassakis, George
Greece

Arroum, Mimoun
Tunisia

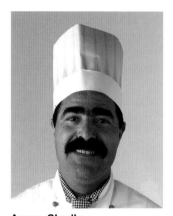

Azzaz, Chedly
Tunisia

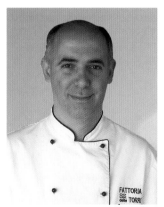

Barone, Giuseppe
Italy

Beccaceci, Maddalena
Italy

Bel Moufid, Lahoussine
Morocco

Pastry Cooks

Bensdira, Khadija
Morocco

Berdugo, Victoria
Morocco

Bouagga, Mohamed
Tunisia

Boujelben, Mohamed
Tunisia

Boussabeh, Mohamed
Tunisia

Broussier, Laurent
France

Brunicardi, Sauro
Italy

Caputo, Alfonso
Italy

Carro, Alain
France

Cauchi, Michael
Malta

Chahid, M'hamed
Morocco

Chetcuti, Johann
Malta

Chtéoui, Chokri
Tunisia

de Giovannini, Francesca
Italy

Delvenakiotis, Panagiotis
Greece

Dönmez, Bayram
Turkey

el-Meraoui, Abdelmalek
Morocco

Étienne, Christian
France

Ettlinger, Daniel
France

Evangelou, Sotiris
Greece

Fazzini, Serge
France

**Fernández-Estevez,
María Lourdes**
Spain

Fischetti, Michelina
Italy

Folicaldi, Marco und Rossella
Italy

Garrault, Joël
France

González Soto, Emilio
Spain

Herráiz, Alberto
Spain

Herráiz, José-Ignacio
Spain

Kama, Bouchaïb
Morocco

Karoubas, Miltos
Greece

Katsanis, Nicolaos
Greece

Kaya, Mehmet
Turkey

Khayar, Amina
Morocco

Korbi, Mohamed
Tunisia

Kouki, Sabri
Tunisia

Kovas, Stefanos
Greece

Ksouda, Moez
Tunisia

La Spina, Angelo
Italy

Lappas, Ioannis
Greece

Luni, Paolo
Italy

Manjarrès, Rufino
Spain

Markakis, Michalis
Greece

Marquiegui, Cesar
Spain

Martínez Plaza, Oscar
Spain

Masiques, Pep
Spain

Matri, Ali
Tunisia

Melagrana, Alberto
Italy

Minguella, Jean-Michel
France

Mouzoun, Fatima
Morocco

Murgia, Amerigo
Italy

Özçelik, Göksal
Turkey

Özkan, Sedat
Turkey

Özkiliç, Savaş
Turkey

Özoğuz, Hüseyin
Turkey

Pais, Sergio
Italy

Pasparakis, Aristedes
Greece

Pérez García, Santiago
Spain

Plouzennec, Jean
France

Reoyo, Julio
Spain

Robin, Francis
France

Rousset, Georges
France

Şurdum, Aybek
Turkey

Sarandos, Nikos
Greece

**Stamkopoulos,
Konstantinos and Chrysanthi**
Greece

Tabarani, Vincent
France

Tarín Fernández, José Luis
Spain

Tastift, Mohamed
Morocco

Tlatli, Rafik
Tunisia

Tolis, Anastasios
Greece

Torrijos, Oscar
Spain

Tounsi, Fethi
Tunisia

Trias Luis, Bartolomé-Jaime
Spain

Tüfekçioğlu, Ayşecan
Turkey

Ügümü, Feridun
Turkey

Ünsal, Ayfer T.
Turkey

Valero, Javier
Spain

Vila, Jean-Claude
France

Voutsina, Évie
Greece

Yagues, Angel
France

Zecchin, Biancarosa
Italy

Zoppolatti, Paolo
Italy

G

Ganaria Salad 70
Garbanzo Bean Dumplings, Fried 124
Garbanzo Bean Pilaf, Turkish 330
Gelat Bil-Gobon 724
Giouvetsi 564
Gnocchi, Mirabelle 688
Gnocchi, Potato, "Mora" 288
Goat Cutlets, Young, from Villena 500
Goat Milk Cheese with Honey 662
Gratin of Mussels with Tomatoes 134
Greek Meatballs with Tomato Sauce 560
Greek Salad 46
Greek Sweetmeats 708
Greek-Style Stuffed Chicken 576
Green Cabbage Rösti with Bacon Sails 122
Grilled Essaouira Fish Skewers 484
Grouper Fish, Malthout with 480
Guinea Fowl with Garlic 528

H

Hake with Filbert Sauce 374
Haloua with Dates 774
Halva, Flour, with Syrup and Pistachios 732
Harira with Rice and Figs 268
Haunch of Kid on Chichoumay 522
Hazelnut Jaouia 754
Hen Pheasant in Escabeche 510
Herb Orzotto with Shrimp 298
Hlalem with Artichokes 256
Holiday Pilaf 334
Hsou from the Oases 258

I

Icaria Octopus Cooked the Karoubas Way 44
Isabella Salad with Bottarga 40

J

Jaouia 754
Jban Briouates with Cilantro 180

Jewish-Style Fish 494
John Dory with Saffron Sauce 470

K

Kâber Ellouz 756
Kakavia 226
Kalkani with Fennel 446
Karaburun-Style Sea Perch 466
Kebab, Shish 164
Kemia Salad, Earth and Sea 82
Kid, Haunch of, on Chichoumay 522
Kid with Askolibri in Avgolemono Sauce 580
Knuckle of Pork with Garbanzo Beans
    Cretan Style 582
Künefe 734
Kusksu 244

L

La Mancha Sponge Cake 638
Lachanosarmades 568
Lahmacun 154
Lamb Abruzzi Style 536
Lamb Aknef 600
Lamb, Anatolian 592
Lamb and Potato Casserole with Yogurt 598
Lamb, Bil Meslene Couscous 344
Lamb Cutlets Steamed with Rosemary 604
Lamb, Eggplant and, Tagine 262
Lamb Goulash, Paccheri with 292
Lamb, Loin of, with a Herb Crust 516
Lamb, Loin of, with White
    Kastoria Beans 562
Lamb M'Chalouat 606
Lamb M'rouzia from Fez 624
Lamb, Oven-Baked Arni 558
Lamb Pie Canea 146
Lamb, Rack of, with Honey
    and Rosemary 498
Lamb Ragout with Lemon 610
Lamb, Shoulder of, with Apricots 618
Lamb, Steamed Chorba with 340
Lamb Stew with Fresh Fava Beans 554

Lamb Tagine with Prunes 280
Langoustine Carpaccio with Asparagus 20
Langoustines, Tomato Surprise with 28
Lasagne "Rucola" 290
Leïla's Ourta 758
Lentils and Scallops 112
Liver Guazzetto with Porcini Mushrooms 132
Lobster Couscous with Watercress Cream 358
Lobsters, May-Time 448
Lobster with Thin Noodles 370
Loin of Lamb with a Herb Crust 516
Loin of Lamb with White Kastoria Beans 562
Lokma 738

M

M'Chalouat 606
M'rouzia from Fez 624
Macaroni au Gratin 350
Macaroni Chiropoiita with Tomato Sauce 320
Mallorcan Snails 644
Malloreddus 310
Maltese Mqaret 726
Malthout with Grouper Fish 480
Mani-Style Fish Soup 234
Masfouf with Sunshine Fruits 354
Mastic Ice Cream on a Nest of Kadaifi
   and Morello Cherries 712
May-Time Lobsters 448
Mbourekakia 714
Meatballs, Greek, with Tomato Sauce 560
Meatballs, Sabbath 614
Meatballs with Sepia 502
Mediterranean Fish Soup 264
Mediterranean Meze 2
Medley of Salonikan Delights 720
Melon Tartlet "Bel Air" 676
Menorcan Crawfish Soup 200
Meze, Mediterranean 2
Meze, Sweet 730
Meze, Yogurt 60
Millefeuille with Honeyed Fruits 776
Minestrone "Nice" with Squid 206
Mirabelle Gnocchi 688
Mizyal's Börek 156

Monkfish on Bell Pepper Sauce 406
Monkfish with a Herb Crust 398
Mosaic Salad from Sfax 72
Moussaka 566
Mullet, Bouri from the Old Port 472
Mussels in Cream of Rock Fish Soup 208
Mussels, Gratin of, with Tomatoes 134
Mussels in Marjoram Sauce 428
Mussels with Saffron Rice and
   Baby Vegetables 454
Mytilene Sfougato 144

N

Navy Bean Soup with Boukovo 232
Nonna Narcisa's Orange Ricotta 698
Ntomatosoupa 228

O

Octopus Icaria, Cooked the Karoubas Way 44
Octopus Salad, Tunisian 68
Octopus with Small Pasta Shapes 452
Ojja with Shrimp from Nabeul 178
Okra Pilaf 324
Olive and Onion Salad 58
Olives, Tunisian Stuffed 608
One-Pot Stew with Baby Squid and Bacon 390
Orange Cake, Portocalopita 722
Orange Rictotta, Nonna Narcisa's 698
Oreillettes Filled with Aquavita-Flavored Brocciu 680
Orzotto, Herb, with Shrimp 298
Oscar's Ravioli 654
Ossobuco alla Milanese 546
Oven-Baked Arni 558
Oxtail with Raisins 632
Oysters Bouzigues with Swiss Chard 118
Oyster Fritters with Noilly Prat 116

P

Paccheri with Lamb Goulash 292
Paella 512

Paella with Crayfish 382

Paella, Vegetable 286

Palm Grove Rfiss 762

Palm Sunday Soup 190

Pandora R'bati 492

Pane Fratau 312

Panna Cotta 692

Partridge in Albariño Wine 508

Partridge with Polenta 548

Pasta Alla Scarpara 314

Pasta from the Seraglio, Stuffed 158

Pastilla with Pigeon 626

Patatas a la Importancia 102

Pear Pancakes 666

Pheasant, Hen, in Escabeche 510

Pigeon and Chanterelle Risotto 523

Pigeon M'fenede 628

Pigeon on Seasonal Vegetables 526

Pigeon, Pastilla with 626

Pigeon Supreme "Melagrana" 550

Pilaf, Aegean 336

Pilaf, Bulgur, with Lentils 332

Pilaf, Chicken, in Pastry 326

Pilaf, Garbanzo Bean, Turkish 330

Pilaf, Holiday 334

Pilaf, Okra 324

Pine Nut Assida Zgougou 746

Pine Nut Tart with Lavender Honey 674

Pistachios, Bouza with 750

Pisto a la Bilbaina 104

Pizza Napoli 294

Polenta, Shrimp Soup with 210

Polenta, Turbot Fillet with 424

Porcini Mushroom Risotto
    with Creamed Pumpkin 302

Porgy, Baked, with Vegetables 392

Pork Fillet with a Herb Crust 542

Pork, Knuckle of, with Grabanzo
    Beans Cretan Style 582

Pork Yiaourtlou 574

Portocalopita 722

Potato and Lamb Casserole
    with Yogurt 598

Potato Gnocchi "Mora" 288

Pot-au-feu with Sea Bass 408

Prasopita Kozanis 142

Q

Quail Tagine, Atlas-Style 282

Quails with Almond Stuffing 616

Quince Ragout 586

Quince Stuffed with Apples 728

Quince Stuffing, Deep-Fried Pastries with 740

R

R'bati Pandora 492

R'jla Salad with Lemons and Olives 86

Rabbit Angelino 552

Rabbit, Basine with, from Redjiche 602

Rabbit, Sautéed in Garlic and White Wine 584

Rabbit, Stuffed Shoulder of 520

Rabbit Stifado 572

Rabbit Thighs, Stuffed 518

Rabbit with Creamed Onions and Sóller Shrimp 514

Rabbit with Green Olives 570

Rabbit with Saffron 544

Rabbit with Swiss Chard Stems 622

Rabbit with Thyme 524

Rack of Lamb with Honey
    and Rosemary 498

Radhkha from Tozeur 64

Rafik Tlati's Couseïla 352

Ravioli, Oscar's 654

Red Barbel from Alicante 384

Red Berry Compôte with
    Lemon Verbena Ice Cream 668

Red Mullet Fillet with Nut Pesto 422

Red Mullet Fillets "Castellaras" 396

Red Mullet on a Bed of
    Pan-Fried Tomatoes 400

Rice on Green Beans 328

Rice Potatoes with Mussels 296

Rice, Saffron, with Mussels and
    Baby Vegetables 454

Risotto, Black 300

Risotto, Pigeon and Chanterelle 523

Risotto, Porcini Mushroom,
    with Creamed Pumpkin 302

Rize Beans in Batter 152

Rock Lobster Rice Santa Pola 380

Rose Dessert 742

S

Şekerpare 744
Sabbath Meatballs 614
Sabbath Soup with Garbanzo Beans 276
Saffron Rice with Mussels and
   Baby Vegetables 454
Salad, Bulgur, Antep Style 52
Salad, Chicken, with Porcini Mushrooms 36
Salad, Çoban 56
Salad "Côte d'Azur" with
   Balsamic Vinegar Dressing 26
Salad, Cucumber, with Atlas Thyme 84
Salad, Fava Bean, with Cumin and Harissa 66
Salad, Fennel, with Oranges 24
Salad, Fethi, Tounsi's Renga 74
Salad, Friulian 32
Salad, Ganaria 70
Salad, Greek 46
Salad, Isabella, with Bottarga 40
Salad, Kemia, Earth and Sea 82
Salad, Mosaic, from Sfax 72
Salad, Octopus, Tunisian 68
Salad, Olive and Onion 58
Salad, R'jla, with Lemons and Olives 86
Salad of Sweet Tomatoes 80
Salad, Tomato, Radhkha from Tozeur 64
Salad, Tuna Bottarga, with Orange and Fennel 38
Salmon Trout with Orange Sauce 432
Salmorejo de Córdoba 16
Sardine Skewers 98
Sardines in Saor 430
Sardines, Stuffed, Sousse-Style 482
Sardines, Stuffed, with Brocciu 412
Scallops with Mixed Salad Leaves 410
Sea Bass on Fennel 402
Sea Bass Fillet on Aniseed Zabaglione 394
Sea Bass Fillet with Olives and Pickled Lemon 476
Sea Bass Pot-au-feu 408
Sea Bass, Stuffed 490
Sea Bass, Tians of, with Brocciu and Tomato Coulis 414
Sea Bass with Majhoul Dates 488
Sea Bream, Stuffed, from the Tunis Region 474
Sea Bream with Celery and Avgolemono Sauce 444
Sea Bream with Pardu Dry 456
Sea Perch, Broiled, with Blood Orange Sauce 450
Sea Perch Karaburun-Style 466

Sea Perch with Rak› 462
Sea Perch with Vegetables – Apollo Style 436
Seafood and Chicken M'hancha 182
Seafood with Chermoula 76
Seafood, Deep-Fried 130
Sesame Takoua with Orange-Flower Water 764
Sfouf 778
Sfougato Mytilene 144
Shish Kebab 164
Shoulder of Lamb with Apricots 618
Shrimp Soup with Polenta 210
Small Passover Parmentiers 184
Snails, Chakchouka with 174
Snails, Mallorcan 644
Snails, Two Cretan Dishes using 148
Snails and Squid, Braised 114
Soup, Barley, Cimbri Style 220
Soup, Basque Fish, 192
Soup, Bastia Fish, 214
Soup, Bouillabaisse "Miramar" 204
Soup, Casbah Vegetable 274
Soup, Catalan Mushroom, 188
Soup, Chicken and Tomato 246
Soup, Chicken, with Avgolemono 230
Soup, Chorba with Mediterranean Fish 252
Soup, Cold Almond from Málaga, 196
Soup, Cold Cream of Almonds with Trampó 198
Soup, Cold Strawberry 194
Soup, Cream of Pumpkin, with Chives 202
Soup, Ezo Gelin Lentil 248
Soup, Fez Ramadan 270
Soup, Fisherman's 216
Soup, Ftir el Euch 254
Soup, Harira with Rice and Figs 268
Soup, Hlalem with Artichokes 256
Soup, Hsou from the Oases 258
Sooup, Kusksu 244
Soup, Mani-Style Fish 234
Soup, Mediterranean Fish 264
Soup, Menorcan Crawfish 200
Soup, Minestrone "Nice" with Squid 206
Soup, Moroccan Bissara 272
Soup, Mussels in Cream of Rock Fish 208
Soup, Navy Bean, with Boukovo 232
Soup, Palm Sunday 190
Soup, Sabbath, with Garbanzo Beans 276

Soup, Shrimp, with Polenta 210

Soup, Spring 218

Soup, St Lucy's Wheat 224

Soup, Tal-Grottli Bisque 242

Soup, Trachano 238

Soup, Vegetable, with Pistou 212

Soup with Sea Bass and Fennel 266

Soup, Turkish Yogurt 250

Soup, Xinochondro 240

Soup, Yalitiki 236

Soup, Zuppa Picena 222

Spaghetti with Langoustines 304

Sperna 718

Spinach Salad with Argan Oil 78

Spinosini with Black Truffles 306

Sponge Cake La Mancha 638

Spring Soup 218

Squid, Minestrone "Nice" with 206

Squid, One-Pot Stew with
   Baby Squid and Bacon 390

Squid Plaki 440

Squid Stuffed with Vegetables
   and Kefalotyri 442

Squid Stuffed with Vegetables
   and Shrimp 388

St Lucy's Wheat Soup 224

Steamed Chorba with Lamb 340

Stockfish "Casa Fischetti" 426

Stockfish Frecole with Nuts 416

Stockfish with Garbanzo Beans 366

Storzapretti with Corsican Cheeses 126

Stuffed Bream from the Tunis Region 474

Stuffed Cabbage 588

Stuffed Cuttlefish 420

Stuffed Pasta from the Seraglio 158

Stuffed Sardines with Brocciu 412

Stuffed Sardines Sousse-Style 482

Stuffed Sea Bass 490

Stuffed Shoulder of Rabbit 520

Stuffed Small Vegetables, Tunis-Style 168

Stuffed Squid with Vegetables and Shrimp 388

Stuffed Tomatoes and Peppers from Samos 322

Stuffed Vine Leaves in Olive Oil 54

Suckling Pig, Loin of, with Herbs 540

Sultan's Roulade 736

Sweet Meze 730

Swiss Chard Dumpling, Storzapretti
   with Corsican Cheeses 126

Swiss Chard Nests 160

Swordfish Alla Ghiotta 434

T

T'Bikha with Gourd 170

Tagine, Atlas-Style Quail 282

Tagine, Bey's 260

Tagine, Eggplant and Lamb 262

Tagine, Lamb, with Prunes 280

Tagine with Monkfish and Argan Oil 278

Tagine with Tub Gurnard 278

Takoua with Orange-Flower Water 764

Tal-Grottli Bisque 242

Tangier-Style Stuffed Calamaries 486

Tapas "Don Quixote" 94

Tapas from Alicante 92

Tapas from Andalusia 90

Tapas from Málaga 10

Tarta de Santiago 648

Tians of Sea Bass with Brocciu
   and Tomato Coulis 414

Tiramisù 690

Tiznao 386

Tocinillos de Cielo 650

Tomato Salad Radhkha from Tozeur 64

Tomato Surprise with Langoustines 28

Tortilla, Vegetable and Shrimp 106

Trachanas, Onion, and Mint Pie made
   with Phyllo Pastry 318

Trachanosoupa 238

Tride with Chicken 634

Trio of Tunisian Mini-Fritters 172

Tuna Bottarga Salad with Orange and Fennel 38

Tuna Fillet in Escabeche 376

Tuna with Zucchini Cream 22

Tuna Tonn Immellah with Garbanzo Purée 48

Tunisian Octopus Salad 68

Tunisian Ragout with Merguez 612

Tunisian Stuffed Olives 608

Turbot Fillet with Polenta 424

Turkish Garbanzo Bean Pilaf 330

Turkish Yogurt Soup 250

Turrón Parfait 640
Turtera 316
Two Cretan Dishes Using Snails 148

V

Veal Cheeks in Rioja 506
Veal Cutlets with Sage 538
Veal Escalope Alla Barbaricina 556
Veal Ragout with Pistachios 596
Vegetable and Shrimp Tortilla 106
Vegetable Antipasti 30
Vegetable Paella 286
Vegetable Soup with Pistou 212
Vegetable Stew with Ham 100
Vegetables, Broiled, Konstantinos Style 42
Vegetables, Stuffed Small, Tunis-Style 168
Venetian Fritters 686
Vine Leaves, Stuffed, in Olive Oil 54

X

Xatonada 18
Xinochondro Soup 240

Y

Yalitiki Soup 236
Yemas de Léon 652
Yiaourtlou Pork 574
Yogurt Meze 60
Young Goat Cutlets from Villena 500

Z

Zabaglione, Frozen,
  with Marsala 694
Zucchini Cream with Tuna 22
Zuppa Picena 222

British Cookery Terms

US	UK	US	UK
arugula	rocket (rocket salad)	kiwi	kiwi fruit
bacon slices	streaky bacon, streaky rashers	ladyfingers	sponge fingers
baking soda	bicarbonate of soda	molasses	treacle
beet	beetroot	offal	variety meats
Belgian endive	chicory	papaya	papaw
blood sausage	black pudding	parsley root	Hamburg parsley
bok choy	Chinese leaves	peanut, peanut oil	groundnut,
bouillon cube	stock cube		groundnut oil
broil, broiler	grill, oven grill	phyllo dough	filo dough
chicory	endive	pit	stone (of fruits)
chili pepper; chile	chilli pepper	porcini mushrooms	ceps, boletus, or penny bun
cilantro	fresh coriander leaves	powdered sugar	icing sugar
coconut, shredded or grated	desiccated coconut	rise	prove
cookie	biscuit (sweet)	rutabaga	Swede
corn	maize, sweetcorn	salad shrimp	shrimp
corned beef	salt beef	scallop	escalope (thin slice of meat)
cornstarch	cornflour	seed	pip
eggplant	aubergine	semi-sweet chocolate	plain chocolate
extract	essence	shrimp	prawn
flounder	plaice	slivered almonds	flaked almonds
flour, all-purpose	plain flour	snow peas, sugar peas	mangetout
flour, bread	strong flour	streusel	crumble
flour, cake	superfine flour	sugar, very fine granulated	caster sugar
flour, whole wheat	wholemeal flour	Swiss chard	chard
French fries	chips	tart	flan
gelatin	gelatine	tofu	beancurd
golden raisins	sultanas	tomato paste	tomato puree
grill	barbecue	vanilla bean	vanilla pod
ground beef or pork	minced meat or mince	vanilla seeds or mark	vanilla pulp
ham (cured)	gammon	whole milk	full-cream milk
heavy (whipping) cream	double cream	whole wheat	wholemeal
jelly	jam	zucchini	courgette